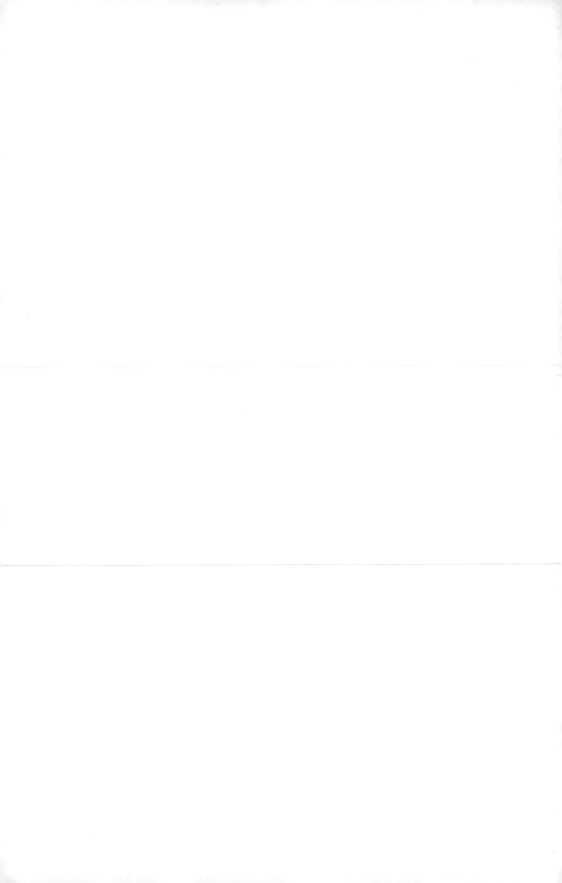

Anne Boleyn

Anne Boleyn

Adultery, Heresy, Desire

Amy Licence

AMBERLEY

For Tom, Rufus and Robin

First published 2017

Amberley Publishing
The Hill, Stroud
Gloucestershire, GL5 4EP

www.amberley-books.com

British Library Cataloguing in Publication Data.
A catalogue record for this book is available from the British Library.

ISBN 978 1 4456 4345 8 (hardback)
ISBN 978 1 4456 4353 3 (ebook)

Typeset in 10.5pt on 14pt Sabon.
Typesetting and Origination by Amberley Publishing.
Printed in the UK.

Contents

Part Four: Anne's Ascendancy

Part Five: The King's Great Matter

Part Six: Anne Triumphant

Part Seven: Thunder around the Throne

Introduction

Anne Boleyn was one of my first heroines. At the age of thirteen I consumed Eric Ives' biography and everything else about her that I could lay my hands on, clearing the shelves of my local library and staggering home with armfuls of books, to relive her story again and again. Why? Since then, I've been trying to answer the question of why Anne fascinates readers so much, why her fairytale-that-went-wrong resonates so deeply in the modern world and why she is so passionately defended. No doubt it is the injustice of her death, the love triangle between her, Henry and Catherine, the dichotomic swing from love to hate, and the essential spark of Anne's character, at a moment of immense historical change. But more subtle questions have continued to imbue the debate, about degrees of influence, shifts in power and the nature of human relationships. We wonder whether Anne was reluctant or enthusiastic when it came to Henry's wooing, who really had the upper hand in their relationship and who instigated her fall. With so many of these questions relating to personality, and the nature of personal rule, they have a timeless, unanswerable quality. It still feels like something of a mystery.

Anne Boleyn's story touches on familiar themes of love, desire, duty, adultery, heartbreak, which transcend her status and time. Hers is essentially a universal love story, which takes the reader through the classic narrative of attraction, passion, obstacles to overcome, fulfilment and then agonising descent to a tragic ending. It is a plot of Shakespearean dimensions. Yet it is also uniquely specific, arising from, and possibly failing due to, the immense changes that were taking place in her world. She lived at a time when the old and new were in collision, nowhere more sharply than in England in the later 1520s and early 1530s, when the clergy had been reared on medieval hagiographies like the *Golden Legend* and *Gesta Romanorum*, where people still crept on their knees to venerate icons, but Thomas More was writing *Utopia*, William Tyndale translated the Bible into English and Humanism was reforming the education system. In 1500, the England of Anne's birth was that 'merry' England of popular idealisation, punctuated by ritual, festival, even pseudo-pagan magic but as she grew, her eyes were increasingly opened to new ways of seeing the world, of defining the present moment in relation to the past, of new personal identities, new ways of worship and concepts of state and rule. Medieval bastions were crumbling before ideological castles in the air.

Anne's is very much a Tudor story, a narrative that balances on the cusp of old and new, equally informed by both. It has been told many times before, but what this version aims to offer afresh is a sense of continuity with earlier Boleyn generations. She was born into an ambitious dynasty, with each generation taking a step forward in terms of career and marital advancements. Anne's 'career' was the culmination of four generations of men, who had come to London from rural Norfolk and worked their way up through civic and court circles to the ultimate prize of monarchy. That she was the most successful Boleyn cannot be disentangled from her gender and class. By the definitions of her time, Anne was an overreacher in more than one sense. She was a woman, born to be a wife, but not that of the king. She was an aristocrat, descended from the influential Howards, observing but not trained in the demands of queenship. She transcended boundaries of expected behaviour on both counts, which was both her most remarkable achievement and created her two areas of greatest vulnerability. This account of Anne's life prioritises her relationship with the defining issues of gender and class, tracing their role in her rise and fall.

And yet there is so much more to Anne. Her story develops in tandem with that of the English Reformation, and the nature of her personal faith. This work accepts her well-known reformist stance but questions whether her humanist focus on charity and education may have caused her to step back from Henry's more radical, blanket monastic reforms. Anne is also a fascinating study in terms of renaissance culture, patronage and queenship, as her European experiences led her to develop a wider perspective than the insular island vision of her husband. Her connections with some of the leading figures of the day led her to develop different tastes, different standards of behaviour and expectation, than those of her home-grown peers. She was a woman who refused to be constrained by culturally imposed boundaries, embracing opportunity, following her own path and meeting both queenship and death with great bravery. This is why she so captivated Henry, and generations since. She had something like a genius for self-creation, the ultimate renaissance self-made woman who flew too close to the sun. And at the heliocentric Tudor court, that sun was the volatile, mercurial Henry VIII. For all its other qualities, hers was a love affair that went wrong. Her husband was a man who loved and hated with equal passion, but when Anne challenged his masculinity, he withdrew the support he had used to raise her, Pygmalion-like, to his side. She died because he required her death. It was a compulsive, heart-rending conclusion to a passion that the roles of monarchy were too limited to contain. Defiant, defining and brave, Anne's unique qualities speak to us across the centuries.

PART ONE

AMBITIOUS AND CAPABLE MEN

ONE

The Boleyn Origins
1420–1463

The young man paused on the north road, gazed into the distance in awe. Ahead he could make out walls, steeples, towers, roofs and the masts of ships, as he caught his first glimpse of the bustling city of London. It was 1420, or thereabouts. He was fourteen or fifteen, fresh from the country and well-dressed, but weary from the last week of travelling. While his arrival in the capital marked the end of one long journey for Geoffrey Boleyn, it was the beginning of another. He had passed through the sweeping green countryside of Norfolk, Suffolk and Essex; counties that were dotted with sheep whose wool was making the country wealthy in exports across Europe. Ahead of him lay the largest, richest city in England, home to around 40,000 residents, over six times the size of Norwich, and 400 times bigger than the Norfolk village of Salle, where Geoffrey had been born and raised. This was the metropolis of London, the heart of England's trade, government and economy, whose current mayor was the legendary Richard 'Dick' Whittington. To Geoffrey, the son of a village gentleman, keen to make his fortune, the streets of the capital would indeed prove to be paved with gold.

Geoffrey would have approached the city from the north-east, through the fields and pastures attached to the walled estates belonging to the Priory of the Holy Trinity, the Abbey of St Clare and the Hospital of St Mary Bethlehem. Perhaps he heard their bells chiming or the inhabitants chanting their devotions. Crossing the Hound's Ditch, the stench of the city would have crept into his nostrils, perhaps prompting him to raise a handkerchief to cover his face against the foul odours and the dangerous infections they might carry. Liable to flooding and choked with sewage and rubbish, the ditch stretched around the outside of the walls, running all the way from the Tower in the east to Blackfriars in the west, encircling the city with its own waste. Crossing the bridge, Geoffrey passed through the walls at Aldgate or Bishopsgate, both large, sturdy edifices of stone, castle-like with drawbridge and portcullis, for they were as defensive as they were ornamental. And London lay stretched before him, full of promise, suffused with royalty, its name part-legend through the most far-flung corners of England – and indeed, Europe. Geoffrey was plunged into the wide, open thoroughfares of Fenchurch Street and Cornhill, where markets bustled with activity, and down narrow lanes, made darker by the overhanging timber-framed buildings, some so close that you could reach out of the upper storeys and shake your neighbour by the hand. Dirty hovels stood just around the corner from the estates of wealthy merchants and courtiers, with lamps and flowering boughs hung at their gates, and their walled gardens full of fruit trees. The city was alive with noise, movement, colour, life and danger.

It must have been a breathtakng sight to the boy from Salle. Having been raised just fifteen miles from Norwich, Geoffrey had experienced the throng of those city streets, with merchants and drapers, weavers and dyers working in the shadow of the Cathedral of the Holy and Undivided Trinity. But he had seen nothing to compare with St Paul's with its 500-foot spire, standing on the highest point of Ludgate Hill, or the gothic Guildhall, on which work had begun nine years earlier, and certainly nothing like London Bridge, top-heavy with its tall buildings. Yet the city in 1420 was not as big as it once had been. Had he arrived a few generations earlier, Geoffrey would have found London almost twice its present size, with a population bordering on 80,000 and rising, cramming its narrow streets fit to burst. In a few short months, the terrible plague of 1349–50 had wiped out half of all Londoners, who lay buried in huge pits under Geoffrey's feet as he explored the streets and corners of his new home. Such a dramatic cull had left buildings and businesses empty and in need of repair. The city was rebuilding itself very slowly, as expensive labour and materials and reduced incomes left London languishing in economic decline. Another way to look at the situation was to see it as a time of great opportunity, of social mobility and the laying of foundations of future wealth. Geoffrey Boleyn may have been young but he was ambitious.

It has been suggested that the Boleyns originated from Boulogne, a short distance west around the coast from Calais, in northern France. Their surname was often spelt this way on official documentation, even into the mid-sixteenth century, interchangeable with the fishing port whose count, Eustace II, had fought alongside William the Conqueror at Hastings in 1066. Members of Geoffrey's family could well have been among them, receiving grants of English land to reward their loyalty after the victory had been secured. However, another location further south has traditionally been cited as the source of Geoffrey's family. Forty kilometres south of Paris, Brie, or Briis-sous-Forges, still claims a connection to Anne Boleyn, who appears to have stayed at the castle with Philippe de Moulin Signeur de Brie, the husband of a Marie Boleyn.[1] The grey, fairy-tale donjon of the castle remains, now bearing Anne's name, as does a nearby road, seeming to confirm local legend. This version of the family's roots has prevailed from the seventeenth century, in the work of antiquarian Julien Brodeau, through the Victorian era and to the present day. In a lecture delivered to the Kent Archaeological Society on 28 July 1865, the Reverend W. Wilberforce Battye, Rector of Hever, also affirmed that the Boleyns came from the village of Brie. Recent historians have questioned the story's provenance, though, speculating that Brodeau may have misinterpreted the Elizabethan chronicler Nicholas Sander, a source hostile to Anne, and confused her with her sister Mary, who may have gone to Brie. Even if that was the case, it still places the family in the village. Whether Brie or Boulogne, Anne or Mary, it was no coincidence that the Francophile Boleyns had French descent.

The Boleyns had made their way to Norfolk by the early twelfth century; Simon I De Boleyn, Baron Boleyn of Salle, was born in 1099, plausibly as the grandson of a man who fought at Hastings. It was the opinion in the 1930s of Reverend Walter Parsons, Rector of Salle, that Simon was an illegitimate descendant of Eustace II of Boulogne, which is as plausible a beginning to the story as the line his fellow clergyman suggested of Brie. Simon's son William, and his grandson Simon, inherited the title of Baron of Salle, along with the family crest of a white shield with a red chevron and the heads of three black bulls, making an audible connection to the 'bull' of Boleyn. Simon expanded the family property by purchasing more land in Salle in 1252, while another descendant, John, appeared in the register of Walsingham Abbey in 1283. The Boleyns remained Norfolk country gentry through the next six generations, until Geoffrey, listed as a 'gentleman', sent his teenaged son, also named Geoffrey, to London as an apprentice in around 1420. This move seems an unusual break with the family's precedent but it was consistent with young Geoffrey's status as a younger son. The heir would inherit the main estate, leaving any other brothers in need of an alternative source of income. However, Geoffrey's elder brother, Thomas, decided not to follow the expected route, being ordained as a priest in 1421 and becoming Master of Gonville Hall, Cambridge. He fathered no legitimate children, leaving the Boleyn line to pass through Geoffrey.

Geoffrey's move to London can be explained by the patronage of Sir John Fastolf,[2] a Norfolk man originally from Caister, thirty miles east of Salle, who rose to power by becoming Master of the Household to John, Duke of Bedford, brother of King Henry V, and serving in France during the Hundred Years' War. Young Geoffrey was a particular favourite or protégé of the powerful knight, who is best known today for inspiring Shakespeare's character Falstaff. It was from this patron that Geoffrey would later acquire the magnificent estate of Blickling Hall, where his great-granddaughter Anne Boleyn would arrive half a century later. Another Norfolk family, the Pastons, achieved a similar move to London at this time, when the wealthy brother-in-law of Clement Paston paid for the education of his son, William, at the Inns of Court, an education which led William to become an attorney, a Justice of the Peace and, by 1420, counsel for the Duchy of Lancaster. Cultivating influential relations and neighbours was important because the support of a powerful figure could improve the prospects of the next generation. Meteoric rises from humble origins to positions of urban power were to feature in many of the biographies of the fifteenth century's most influential men.

Geoffrey's start in London was humbler than William Paston's. He was apprenticed to a hatter, signing an indenture that would tie him to a master for seven years or more before he could be admitted to a guild and climb the civic ladder. Mayor Whittington had followed a similar route, as the son of a Gloucestershire landowner who had left home for London and served an apprenticeship to a Mercer, or general cloth merchant. Outside the aristocracy and church, London's infrastructure was dominated by the wealthy guildsmen, who filled the positions of sheriffs, aldermen and mayor, also as unofficial bankers, giving loans to royalty and financially backing foreign ventures in war and trade. Men signed up as an apprentice in their mid-teens, worked their way up through the ranks, makings connections, serving as sheriffs and aldermen and taking apprentices themselves: like the royal court, it was as much about building the network, who you knew, as what you did. Geoffrey is unlikely to have been born with a burning desire to make hats, but he did need to find the first rung of the ladder to begin a civic career. After that, it was up to him.

The hatters were one of the smaller guilds, and would be incorporated into the larger haberdashers in 1502. It was a sound trade, as hats were in continual demand, being worn by both genders and all classes, from the simple, straw wide-brims in the Duke of Berri's *Tres Riches Heures* to the elaborate chaperons that wealthy men wore wrapped about their heads or draped loose, almost turban-like at times. Hoods were also popular, as were bonnets, coifs and simple rimless caps. In the mid-fifteenth century, hats suitable for a member of the gentry could be purchased for 10 pence or 1 shilling and 2 pence.[3] The job of the guild, under the protection of the hatters' patron, St James the Lesser, was to regulate the quality of workmanship and protect the rights of its members. It was a duty they took very seriously. Back in 1311, the discovery of 40 grey and white hats, and 15 black hats 'of false workmanship', in a mixture of wool and flock, led to the confiscation of the merchandise, which was then burned in the street. Guild regulations of 1347 stated that only freemen of the city could make and sell hats, meaning those who had served an apprenticeship and been a journeyman, or employee, before gaining the status of master. Each guild appointed six wardens who had the power to examine finished hats to see that they were 'fitting' to avoid the previous 'great scandal, shame and loss' arising for the 'good folks of the said trade'. The first two offences would incur a fine, the third would see a hatter stripped of his freeman status.[4] The name of the hatter who took Geoffrey on as an apprentice is unknown, but the regulations tell us he must have been a freeman of the city, and while some young men did change masters, it was unusual, so Geoffrey probably lodged and worked with him for the next seven years. He was admitted as a freeman of London with the Hatter's Company on 23 June, 1428, by Mayor John Gedney.[5]

After eight years as a hatter, Geoffrey's career changed direction. In February 1436, he abandoned his guild and switched to the Mercers, paying £5 3s 4d for his livery.[6] He came before the Mayor, Henry Frowik, and Aldermen, at the Guildhall

> ...and showed that whereas he had been admitted into the freedom of the City in the Art of Hatter... he had long used, and was now using, the art of Mercery and not the art of Hatter. He therefore prayed that he might be admitted into the freedom of the City in the Art of Mercery. His prayer [was] granted at the instance of the Masters and good men of the said Art... Robert Large, John Dawtre, William Olyver, John Sturgeon, Richard Riche, Thomas Bataille, and others [not named].[7]

The Worshipful Company of Mercers was the leading guild of the top twelve London guilds, certainly the most powerful and influential, which may have been Geoffrey's reason for joining. Essentially traders in cloth, but also in general items, they held their meetings in the hospital of St Thomas of Acon (Thomas Becket) off Cheapside, with a chapel in the south-west side of the adjoining church. Geoffrey Boleyn knew this church, later serving as a guild warden, so he would have been familiar with the stained-glass depictions of the life of St Thomas and sat among the marble slab tombs of former Mercers, whilst listening to their obits read aloud to the congregation. Henry Frowik, the mayor who admitted Geoffrey, was laid to rest in a chapel on the south side in 1460.

Now an established man, Geoffrey was in a position to take on a number of apprentices, first William Gresham who paid his entry fee in 1443–4, then John Elys and Roger Bonefaunt in 1449–50, Edmond Josse in 1451–2, Hugh Joye and John Synte, who joined him the following year and Geoffrey Meleman, formerly hatter apprenticed to Adam Booke, then to Geoffrey in 1453. He also took on William Wells 1456–7 and a youth who was perhaps his younger brother or cousin, Geoffrey Wells in 1463–4, as well as Richard Sutton, Robert Hastynges and William Brampton, whose dates of service are unknown.[8] Just as Geoffrey's own period of apprenticeship had established ties with the mercantile and civic community, his role as a master, steering the next generation of Mercers, created ties of loyalty for the future. As he worked hard at his trade, Geoffrey built up considerable wealth. Exploring the history of the Mercers, Anne F. Sutton speculates about the development of his career based on the known activities of his contemporaries, whose everyday income was supplemented by investments, loans, shipping and other ventures, or the taking up of debts, as Geoffrey did with the debts of the London Genoese, earning him an interest rate of 14%. In 1447, he was also a creditor for over £16 of cloth at the Whitsun fair in Antwerp.[9] This indicates that he was seen as a solid financial backer, with international connections; the kind of man on whom the foundations of the city were built.

Geoffrey was also playing a trusted role within his new guild, serving as one of the four wardens in 1442–3. He ended his tenure at a supper held at the nativity of St John the Baptist at the house of John Olney in Mill Street, when each warden selected their replacement. Geoffrey chose William Olyver who had previously supported his entry to the guild. The four retiring wardens submitted their report of the Mercers' Mistery (Mystery play) for the year of 1442–3, which was essentially their accounts. They had inherited £85 17s 6d from the previous year and had received revenue in apprenticeship fees and fines but had incurred expenses for things like repairs and labour, wax for candles, bargemen messengers, fabric for clothing and altars, that left a total of £75 4s 5d.[10] Along with each guild, the Mercers were responsible for staging a play or pageant at the feast of Corpus Christi, which could be an elaborate outdoor affair with scenery, special effects and costumes. The Mercers had chosen the play of the Last Judgement, traditionally performed as the finale to all the guilds' efforts, and certainly the most lavish. Among their props were a gold mask and sunbeams of gold for the man acting the role of God, four gilded angels and a backdrop of red damask. In 1449-50, when Geoffrey would have played a significant role in the pageant, the angels were repaired at a cost of 20 shillings.[11] Geoffrey was also moving up the civic ladder, serving as sheriff in 1446–7. He must have been popular, as the other Sheriff, Robert Horne, was elected by the Mayor, while Geoffrey was chosen 'by the Commonalty'.[12] Two years later he became a Member of Parliament for London but in 1451 he narrowly missed being elected as an Alderman, coming second with rival William Dere receiving ten votes to his four. Geoffrey was, however, elected to the position in 1452.

At some point early in his career, Geoffrey married Denise, or Dionise, probably in London. Little is known about her and she died young, possibly childless, as Geoffrey later requested masses for her in his will. The inclusion of a Dionysius Boleyn along with Geoffrey in the list of patrons of Queen's College, Cambridge, suggests that Dionise bore a son, as the name is so unusual, but no more is known of this individual. Geoffrey made a significant second marriage to an heiress, Anne Hoo, the eldest daughter of Thomas Hoo, Baron Hoo and Hastings, whose many properties included the estate of Mulbarton in Norfolk. It may have been this Norfolk connection, perhaps fostered by Fastolf, that brought this second match about at some point in the late 1430s. The couple had seven surviving children: two sons, Thomas and William, and five daughters, Isabella, Alice, Anne, Cecily and Elizabeth. As Geoffrey's brother, Thomas, the priest, fathered no legitimate children, the Boleyn inheritance would pass to Geoffrey's sons.

In 1452, Geoffrey bought the Norfolk manor of Blickling from Sir John Fastolf, a former country palace of the Bishops of Norwich, situated just seven miles from Salle. Margaret Paston wrote to her husband, John, that 'My lady Hastyngs told me that Heydon hath spoken to Jeffrey (sic) Boleyn of London, and is agreed with him that he should bargain with Sir John Fastolf to buy the manor of Blickling'.[13] The sale was completed that year, giving Geoffrey's own family an even more impressive country retreat than his parents' home. It must have been a satisfying purchase for the man who had left Norfolk as a teenaged soon-to-be apprentice, a demonstration of just how far he had advanced since then. He also made his mark locally by building the chapel of St Thomas at the east side of the north aisle of Blickling church and paid for the stained-glass windows there, featuring the arms of himself and his wife.

The choice of St Thomas no doubt referenced the Mercers' connection, perhaps as a gesture of thanks to the saint for the success Geoffrey was experiencing. He held a range of properties in London and references in 1453 indicate that he owned a house in the parish of St Lawrence Jewry,[14] property in Soper Lane, a shop in St Pancras, and was paying a rent of £6 13s 4d on a tenement in Hosier Lane. That year he was admitted as Master of the Mercer's company, at the same time as the future printer, William Caxton, ten years Geoffrey's junior, was given his Mercer's livery.

In 1457, thirty-seven years after arriving in London, Geoffrey Boleyn reached the pinnacle of his career when he was elected Lord Mayor of the city. No doubt his shrewd switch to the Mercers helped, as that company had provided the largest number of successful mayoral candidates since 1400, while the hatters guild had put forward none. In the fifty-seven years preceding Geoffrey's tenure, there had been 18 mercers, 13 drapers, 13 grocers, 6 fishmongers, 3 skinners, 3 ironmongers and 2 goldsmiths in the role.[15] The Mercers' record book records the costs of his ceremonial presentation at Westminster, which required 12½ yards of murrey cloth for hoods for sixteen trumpeters, including 'Thomas with the big trumpet' at 2s 4d per yard, making a total cost of 29s 2d.[16] It would have been a splendid occasion, with all the city turning out to watch, boats crowding the Thames, flags flying and music drifting across the water. There were also Mercers' banners sewn with fringes, made from three yards of fine red tartarin at a cost of 7s, with the same amount again being spent on ribbons and laces.[17] Geoffrey would have travelled down the river on his ceremonial barge, to be welcomed at the palace, conducted into the great hall, perhaps even the king's painted chamber, to be invested and feasted. On this day in particular, Geoffrey Boleyn was a living symbol of the city; of its history and its legal, mercantile and civic practices; he was the guest of honour, the focus amid its pageantry, the figurehead of justice and peace, the man trusted with its safety, with its future security and growth. Yet at this culmination of his career, he cannot have begun to imagine that, seventy six year later, his great-granddaughter, Anne, would follow a similar path to Westminster, to receive a crown.

Through the following twelve months, Geoffrey conducted the usual mayoral business, with the help of his sheriffs William Edward and Thomas Reyner. He presided over a dinner held for the Staples of Calais, at a cost of 33s 4d, to promote peace and trade, and the Mercers' Company paid out 40s salary for his musicians.[18] Records show that Geoffrey was overseeing elections and business standards, relieving the poor and infirm from their duties and maintaining law and order. However, it was also a time of mounting tension within the city, which required a strong guiding hand. Rivalry between the houses of Lancaster and York had come to a head two years earlier, when the two sides clashed at the first Battle of St Albans and, although an uneasy truce had settled, there were still sporadic attacks among the followers of those involved. A number of Mercers' apprentices had been involved in an anti-Lombard riot that took place in June 1457, just three months before Geoffrey was elected, causing damage to property and creating a climate of fear on its streets. The Mercers investigated the event, and the involvement of their members, as their account book lists that 13d was spent on wine for those charged to look into the matter.[19] As Mayor, Geoffrey would have been involved in the 'Love Day' of 24 March, 1458, orchestrated by King Henry VI as an attempt to secure amity and peace in the city. The presence of so many Lords created an influx of retainers brought into the city and Geoffrey responded by organising a watch of around 500 citizens to patrol the streets.[20] It took a man of strength, authority and ability to keep the peace during such an unstable period. Then in his early fifties, Geoffrey had the trust of his fellow Mercers and the other guilds, of the king and his council, the lords and clerics, and the necessary experience to do the job. Just as he had risen as high as he might have hoped, he was elevated to the minor nobility, when he was knighted by King Henry VI.

One of Geoffrey's sisters, Cecily, was living at Blickling and died during his tenure as Mayor. Never married, she was fifty when she passed away on 26 June 1458, placing her birth date in 1407 or 1408, making her two or three years younger than her brother. Geoffrey may have returned to St Andrews, Blickling, in order to attend her burial in the chancel there and to commission the plaque that now records her resting place:

> Here lyth Cecilie Boleyn, sustre to Geffrey (sic) Boleyn, Lorde of the Manor of Blickling, whiche Cecilie deceased in her Maydenhode, of the age of L Yeeres the xxvi Day of Juyn The Yer of our Lord Mcccclviii whose Soule God pardoune Amen.[21]

After his spell as Mayor ended, and he approached his late fifties, Geoffrey's life became quieter. It may be that the death of his sister, close to him in age, gave him pause to reflect on his mortality. However, he had one last important mission, which involved him directly in the turbulent political events of the day.

With the struggles between the houses of York and Lancaster coming to a head, Parliament had recognised the royal claim of Richard, Duke of York, by passing the Act of Accord naming him as heir to the ruling king, Henry VI. This bypassed Henry's son and was rejected by the Lancastrians, but York was popular in London, where he had helped to maintain stability during Henry's bouts of illness. In the wake of the Act, when emotions were running high, Geoffrey was part of a delegation sent by the city to Henry VI late in 1460, in an attempt to persuade him not to raise an army against York. As it happened, Henry did not raise an army. He had no need to, as Queen Margaret and her allies already had; York was ambushed and killed at Wakefield that December. Geoffrey's loyalty and efforts stood him in good stead the following spring, when York's son, Edward of March, deposed Henry VI and was crowned as Edward IV. It was Edward who issued Geoffrey with an exemption from his former duties, 'for his good service to the king's father', in July 1461. This document gives a full sense of the extensive nature of Geoffrey's legal duties up until that point: 'from being put on assizes, juries, inquisitions, attaints or recognises and from being made trier of them, taxer, collector of customs axes, talleges, fifteenths, tenths or other subsidies, knight, mayor, sheriff, escheator, commissioner, constable, bailiff or other officer and minister of the king.'[22]

Geoffrey may have retired from some of his civic duties, but he was still keen to pursue his various claims to land and property and to expand his holdings. On 5 December 1460, he wrote to John Paston, who was the executor of Sir John Fastolf's will, asking that they may meet in order to resolve a promise Fastolf had made, that Boleyn should have his manor of Guton, in Brandiston. The letter reveals that Boleyn had been present at Fastolf's house, known as Fastolf Place, in Southwark, where his host had made the promise by swearing upon his primer, or book of hours. However, the Archbishop of Canterbury, Thomas Bourchier, also had his eye on the land[23] so Boleyn may not have been successful. Yet he did not give up and soon had another lucrative manor in his sights.

In 1462, Geoffrey Boleyn purchased Hever Castle in Kent, from Sir Thomas Cobham, beginning his family's long association with the place. Set amid the countryside beside the village church, it was a thirteenth-century castle comprising a three-storey bailey surrounded by a moat, with gatehouse and drawbridge. It may be that Geoffrey's health was failing, or that his thoughts were turning towards his own mortality, as on 14 June 1463 he composed a lengthy will. Describing himself as a 'Citizen, Mercer and Alderman of London', he requested that his body be buried not in the guild's church of St Thomas of Acol, but 'in the chapel of St John, in the church of St Laurence in the Jewry, London, on the south side of the chancel', which stood next to the Guildhall. If he were to die in Norfolk, he specified that he wished to be buried in the chapel at Blickling. His coffin was to be surrounded by black candlesticks and 13 poor men, each to be dressed in a russet cloak with black hood and a string of wooden beads, and each to carry a lit torch and receive 12d in payment. He requested no hearse or gilt candlesticks but left funds for a dinner to be hosted for his wife, brother and other executors of the will. His lands were bequeathed to his two sons, Thomas and William and to three of his daughters, Isabel, Anne and Alice; Elizabeth had possibly already married but Cecily had died by this point and was buried at Blickling. He also made a bequest to a cousin by marriage, Ann Hoo, who was a nun at Barking.[24] He left 10 marks to the vicar of St Laurence to pay for forgotten offerings and for masses to be said for his soul, £100 to pay for a new rood loft in St Laurence's, £20 for work on the body of Blickling church or to ornament it, as his brother Thomas saw fit, and 200 marks for 'good people to sing and say divine service and pray for his soul and for the soul of Dionise sometime my wife'.[25] He also left £1,000 to the city of London.

It is sometimes stated that Geoffrey Boleyn died in 1471.[26] However his will and a few pieces of evidence in the Calendar of Letter Books[27] confirm that his death occurred sooner than this. His will was proved on 2 July 1463, just over two weeks after its composition,[28] a process by which the document was judged to be valid in a church court in order for the executors to conclude the individual's affairs. The Close Rolls record that a Thomas Hoo, his wife's uncle, instructed ten men to 'perform the will of Geoffrey Boleyn, citizen and alderman of London' in 1464. On 15 May that year, Anne was referred to as the widow of Geoffrey Boleyn and provision was made in the London Letter Books for the future marriages of the children of 'Geoffrey Boleyn, late Alderman'; Alice in 1464, William and Thomas in 1466.[29] When their father died, Alice was an adult under the age of twenty-five, but the two boys were still below the age of maturity.

The fortunes of the Boleyn family really began with Geoffrey. Having remained in the countryside for generations, he made the remarkable ascent from apprentice to Mayor, accruing wealth, position, respect and a knighthood through determination, shrewd judgements and taking the opportunities on offer in his guild. It was a remarkable career arc, showing vision and bravery, and it elevated his children socially, giving them a greater range of opportunities than their Boleyn ancestors. From this point, each Boleyn would build on the success of their forerunners, up the social ladder. Geoffrey laid the foundations for the steps that his son, grandson and great-granddaughter would take, beyond the prizes the city had to offer, into the royal court, onto the international stage, and finally, to the throne itself.

TWO

From Commerce to Court
1463–1505

Geoffrey's two sons were still young when he died. Thomas Boleyn was probably born in the late 1440s, making him in his mid-teens by 1463 and William was only twelve, having arrived in 1451. Their first home was a windswept corner of north Norfolk, at the red brick manor house of Blickling, miles of open fields from their father's life in the busy, demanding city of London. Geoffrey's second wife, Anne Hoo, had retreated there to deliver her children in seclusion and comfort, but her husband may well have been absent when the boys arrived, pursuing his civic duties. Little is known about their education, but it would have followed the typical curriculum of a child of the gentry. They probably shared a tutor with whom they read the classics, some Latin, maybe French and studied a spread of mathematics, grammar, logic, rhetoric and other skills, which would equip them to follow a similar path to their father. We can catch a glimpse of Thomas when he was presented to the Norfolk church of St.Mary's, Stiffkey, eighteen miles north of Blickling, in 1461 and 1463, first as the eldest son of their lord, and their new lord, following Geoffrey's death.

Given Geoffrey's position, though, it is likely that the sons of the Mayor of London had opportunities to learn about, or even take part in, civic affairs and events. The elder, Thomas, was acting as a clerk in London by his early teens, as his name features alongside that of his father in legal documents of 1459, 1460 and 1461.[1] This was a socially higher entrance point into the London world than the humble apprenticeship Geoffrey had taken up four decades earlier and suggests that Thomas's head start could have propelled him to similar heights. He had come of age by 1466, when he was included in legal proceedings for the collecting of a fine relating to Hedenham manor and, in November 1467 was mentioned in the Patent Rolls, when another clerk, John Stones of Kent, failed to appear in order to answer him for a debt of 40s.[2]

However, Thomas's London career, and any personal promise he had shown, was unexpectedly cut short. He can only have been in his mid-twenties in January 1472[3] when he drew up his will, aware of his impending demise. No cause of death is mentioned, so it is likely that he was suffering from an illness that may also account for the lack of professional activity recorded in his final years. He does not appear to have married, either. Naming his mother as his executor, he requested that his body was buried beside that of his father in St Laurence Jewry and that money from the sale of the manor at Ingham be used by Anne 'for the health of (his) soul'.[4] Anne would have commissioned a priest to say masses for her son's soul and perhaps given alms or paid for some repairs or embellishment to one of their favoured churches in order to speed Thomas through purgatory and into heaven. The will was proved on 26 January. To complicate matters a little, from the historian's point of view, Thomas's uncle of the same name died shortly after him that year. This was Geoffrey's elder brother, who was by then around seventy or more, and the timing has led to some confusion between them in biographical accounts. Occasionally they are treated as the same person. Geoffrey's will leaves no room for doubt that he was survived by a brother named Thomas and it would have been this Thomas who was named in the accounts of the Dean and Chapter of Wells, soon after Michaelmas 1472, as dying and leaving his prebendary vacant.[5]

At the age of twenty, William became head of the Boleyn family. Perhaps inevitably, in comparison with his father's very public position, the paper trail he left was quieter, but William's life marked a steady advancement of the family. It was in 1465, when he was fourteen, that he made his most significant contribution to the dynasty by way of a very advantageous marriage. His bride was an Irish noblewoman, Margaret Butler of Kilkenny Castle, the eldest daughter and co-heiress of the seventh Earl of Ormond, who could trace their bloodline back to Edward I. Thomas Butler was to become very wealthy due to the income he acquired through wool, and as the owner of over seventy English manors, in addition to his Irish properties. There was also a guild connection, as Butler would later choose to be buried in the Mercer's chapel at the Hospital of St Thomas of Acre, the very church that Geoffrey Boleyn would have known so well. In addition, Geoffrey Boleyn's wealthy widow, Anne, financially assisted Thomas Butler in the 1480s, as he granted her 60s annually from his manor of Swavesey, until his debt of £200 was repaid.[6] Margaret was three years younger than her husband, ten or eleven, so the pair would not have lived together at first; the agreement would have been reached, and the vows exchanged, but given that Margaret's first surviving child was born in November 1475, the marriage is unlikely to have been consummated until the bride reached her late teens. Over the coming years, the Boleyns would produce at least ten children. Thomas was the eldest, arriving in 1477, followed by John and Anthony, both of whom died young and are commemorated in Blickling Church, in the years 1484 and 1493 respectively. One son named William would go on to become Archdeacon of Winchester, being buried at Blickling in 1571, while his brother James would marry Elizabeth Wood and would later settle with his family in the Norfolk manor, surviving the fall of his family and dying in 1561. A sixth son, Edward, born possibly as many as twenty years after Thomas, would go on to wed Anne Tempest. Their four sisters made good marriages: Anne to Sir John Shelton, whose daughters would enter the household of their queen and cousin in the 1530s; Jane to Sir Philip Calthorpe; Alice to Sir Robert Clere and Margaret to John Sackville, whom she bore six children.

William Boleyn was clearly a man whom the Yorkist kings trusted; as Edward IV had formerly acknowledged when it came to Geoffrey, the ties went back at least three generations. In 1482, William was the third man named in a commission from Edward IV, along with the king's brother-in-law, Anthony Woodville, to summon and examine a Norfolk couple on suspicion of murder.[7] However, that April, King Edward died unexpectedly and, after a period of turmoil, during which Edward's young sons disappeared in the Tower, the king's brother, Richard III, ascended the throne. William Boleyn was personally known to the new ruler, perhaps an advisor or even a friend, as he was chosen for the honour of becoming a Knight of the Bath on the occasion of Richard's coronation, on 6 July 1483. Such knights were selected for their loyalty and chivalric abilities. This involved an elevation in status from the knighthood that Geoffrey had received, as well as a degree of personal contact with the king, implying absolute trust. Perhaps it was also significant that William was close in age to Richard, who had been born in October 1452, and may have been one of the young knights, or 'henchmen', around him at court in his young adulthood. The ceremony took place in the Tower of London the night before Richard was crowned, during which the knights took a ritual bath, signifying cleansing and rebirth, and swore an oath of allegiance, promising that they would 'above all other earthly things love the king thy sovereign Lord, him, and his right defend unto thy power, and before all worldly things put him in worship'. Richard himself would have wielded the sword that dubbed William as a Knight of the Bath. The following day, Boleyn would have taken part in the procession through the London streets from the Tower to Westminster Abbey, in an echo of his father's important role, and probably a familiar face for those in the crowd who recalled Geoffrey's career.

From the start, security and defence were critical aspects of Richard's reign, and William was one of his trusted men. In September 1483, he was appointed to supervise the two guards who were charged to investigate the security of the Suffolk and Norfolk coastline and its fishermen[8] and he was also named in a commission of array for the defence of the land on 1 May 1484, under the direction of the Dukes of Norfolk and Suffolk, both loyal Yorkists.[9] Yet through that year it became apparent that the threat posed to Richard by the exiled Henry Tudor was a real one. By the time that Tudor landed on the south coast of Wales in August 1485, Richard had already directed his leading lords to raise their supporters and vassals in defence of the realm. His Blickling ties would have placed William under the command of John Howard, Duke of Norfolk, then a veteran of sixty, who would have issued the order for Boleyn and the men of his estate to arm themselves and march the 130 miles directly east to Ambion Hill, in Leicestershire. As the days passed, in the knowledge that Tudor and his army were approaching from the west, it is impossible to know William's true position. There is no record that places him with certainty at the Battle of Bosworth, which took place on 22 August, but given his ties to the king and Norfolk, it would have been a significant act, even an act of treason, had he failed to attend. In which case, he would have witnessed the death of the Duke, slain by an arrow to the head as he stood beside the king, and the death of Richard III, which followed soon afterwards. Perhaps he was also on the spot to see the moment that Lord Stanley, having switched his loyalty, scooped up the crown and placed it upon Henry's head, marking the start of the Tudor era (though the story is almost certainly apochryphal), the making of the man whose son would marry William's granddaughter. If he was left bloodied on Bosworth Field, or had somehow escaped the conflict, Boleyn now had to make peace with a new dynasty.

Many of the English nobility took a pragmatic decision in 1485 to accept the defeat at Bosworth and pledge allegiance to a new king. Some paid lip service but retained their old loyalties, and would join the failed uprising of 1487, under Richard's nephew John de la Pole. Others had already deserted the Yorkists, in mind or body, long before the decisive battle, joining Henry in exile or working silently for him behind the scenes. For many landowners, the switch of loyalty was a method of preserving their hard-won estates and positions, and it seems that William Boleyn was among those who made a smooth transition in the service of the crown. It was to prove a shrewd move. Swiftly demonstrating his abilities, he gained sufficient trust from Henry VII to become High Sheriff of Kent in 1489, and High Sheriff of Norfolk and Suffolk in 1500,[10] as well as having responsibility in 1490 for maintaining the coastal beacons and, in 1491, for arming the men of Norfolk against the threat of invasion from Charles VIII of France.[11]

Along with his role in the defence of the realm, William was also fulfilling the more urbane role of a courtier. In 1494, he was listed among those present at festivities to honour two of the royal children. Henry VII's eldest son, Prince Arthur, had his own establishment at Ludlow, and in November 1494, his daughter Margaret Tudor was approaching her fifth birthday, while the second son, Prince Henry, was invested as Duke of York. William would at least have witnessed, if not taken part in, the great tournament at which Margaret handed out the prizes; he was certainly among those at the feast afterwards.[12] This connection, and the experiences it would give his son, endowed Boleyn with a new social veneer, a patina of the most fashionable manners and courtly connections that represented a different set of skills to the mercantile and civic success of Geoffrey. William's success, and his marriages, allowed the family to step above a life in commerce, into the upper classes and the sphere of royalty. It was William who took the first step closer to the throne and his son Thomas who would fully embrace the opportunity.

Thomas Boleyn's early career was spent in supporting the Tudor dynasty. He would have known Prince Arthur, as far as it was possible to know a young royal whose formal establishment kept many at a distance. Nine years older than the prince, Thomas would have been the right age to enter Arthur's household as a page, or even a young companion, as was frequently the custom among the nobility. Had William Boleyn been looking to push his advantage, he would have seen the establishment of Arthur's independent household at Ludlow, from around 1491, as an excellent opportunity to establish ties between his heir and their future monarch. While there is no surviving evidence that Thomas ever went to Ludlow, it is plausible that his court career began with some connection to the households of the Tudor children, when they attended their parents in London, or at Prince Henry's home at Eltham. As a young man of twenty, Thomas was summoned to assist the king when a threat arose in the shape of the pretender Perkin Warbeck. Claiming to be a son of Edward IV, Warbeck had been agitating around the English borders and coastline before he landed in Cornwall in the autumn of 1497. Thomas was among the king's men who marched west, dissolving the Cornish rebels and capturing Warbeck, who was conveyed to London.

When it came to finding a wife for his son, William did not forget his roots, nor the experiences he had shared with a family that were so closely connected to his own. As his star rose under the Tudors, that of the Norfolk Howards had plummeted, casting the family into disgrace. It was this reversal of fortune that enabled William to secure a bride for his eldest son who, in previous generations, would likely have been out of his league. Thomas Boleyn, born in 1477 at Hever, was around twenty when he married Elizabeth Howard, eldest daughter of the second Duke of Norfolk, as the fifteenth century approached its end. Her father had been wounded and captured after fighting alongside her grandfather at Bosworth. His life had been spared, but he had been attainted and stripped of his lands by Henry VII's first parliament and spent the following four years in the Tower. During this time, he was offered the opportunity to escape and join the Yorkist rebellion of 1487, but his decision not to do so stood him in good stead with Henry. He was restored to his earldom in 1489, albeit with limited powers, and sent into the north as the King's Lieutenant.

Howard's eldest daughter Elizabeth was born in 1480. After Bosworth, at the age of five or six, she was sent to live in the household of Queen Elizabeth of York, but by her teens was spending at least some of her time under her mother's roof. She was still unwed at the age of fourteen or fifteen, according to the poem dedicated to her by court poet John Skelton, in praise of her beauty. Although not published until 1523, Skelton's *The Garland of Laurel*, was composed in the winter of 1494–5, on the occasion of Skelton's visit to the family property of Sheriff Hutton, in Yorkshire. A former Yorkist stronghold, it had been used just a decade before by Richard III as a base for his council in the north and an occasional home for his son, nephew, niece and other children in his care. The poem follows the structure of a typical Chaucerian dream vision, with the narrator walking in the woods outside the castle. Accused of indolence by the allegorical figure of the Queen of Fame, Skelton is given the opportunity to defend his poetic output and is led into the presence of Elizabeth's mother, the Countess of Surrey, her daughters and ladies. He compares the young Elizabeth to Chaucer's heroine Criseyde for her beauty, which was an unusual choice, since Chaucer's version of her story depicted her as a false lover, and to Aryna, perhaps Irene, daughter of Cratinus:

> To my Lady ELIZABETH HOWARD
> To be your remembrancer, madam, I am bound,
> Like to Aryna, maidenly of port,
> Of virtue and conning the well and perfect ground;
> Whom dame Nature, as well I may report,
> Hath freshly embeautied with many a goodly sort
> Of womanly features, whose flourishing tender age

Is lusty to look on, pleasant, demure, and sage.
Good Creisseid, fairer than Polexene,
For to envive Pandarus' appetite;
Troilus, I trow, if that he had you seen,
In you he would have set his whole delight:
Of all your beauty I suffice not to write;
But, as I said, your flourishing tender age
Is lusty to look on, pleasant, demure, and sage.[13]

After a long period of mistrust, during which he continually worked to prove his loyalty, Thomas Howard was permitted to return to court in around 1499. This is the most likely date for Elizabeth's marriage, which would have taken place with the blessing of the king, perhaps even at his instigation, as a reward for the service of William and Thomas Boleyn. It may have been that by the 1490s, when Thomas was a young courtier, he saw Elizabeth at court and a degree of mutual affection arose between them; perhaps her 'flourishing tender age', and face 'pleasant, demure and sage' prompted Boleyn's wooing. Equally, the pair may not have known each other before the ceremony, as purely dynastic matches were often arranged without any consideration of personal inclination, a type of union the Boleyns would later attempt to arrange for Anne. It seeks likely that Howard was finally summoned from the north in order to finalise the arrangements for, and attend, his daughter's wedding. Elizabeth's jointure was settled in 1501, confirming her marital settlement, a process which was usually conducted within a year or two after the ceremony. The marriage raised Thomas Boleyn from the minor gentry into the higher ranks of the nobility, as part of one of the country's premier families.

After Anne's death, her family became the predictable targets for salacious rumours and character attacks. One of the more bizarre was that Elizabeth had been the mistress of Henry VIII, either in his youth, or as a very young king, placing this in the early years of the Boleyn marriage. Elizabeth was significantly older than him, but in his early days, Henry does appear to have favoured other older women, so this is not necessarily a barrier to them having had a relationship. However, it is very unlikely, as the heir to the throne had been carefully guarded and his father had taken precautions regarding his physical health and activities at a young age. It would also make for a very precocious young Henry, who would have been in his early to mid-teens at the time the encounter was supposed to have taken place. The story was first concocted in the 1530s by those who were seeking to blacken Anne's name in support of Catherine of Aragon, and it must be seen in this context. The Catholic

Friar William Peto made the claim in 1532, followed by a letter by George Throckmorton that describes Henry being accused of meddling 'both with the mother and sister', to which Henry blushingly replied, 'Never with the mother.' It was repeated by a woman named Elizabeth Amadas, the unstable wife of Henry's goldsmith, who implicated a number of men and women of the court as part of her defence against charges of treason and witchcraft fifty years later.

The most damage to Elizabeth Howard Boleyn's posthumous reputation was done by the hostile Jesuit priest, Nicholas Sander, who would go as far as to suggest that Anne Boleyn was the daughter of Henry VIII. Writing a biography of Anne during the reign of her daughter, whilst exiled from England for his beliefs, Sander boldly claimed, 'Anne Boleyn was the daughter of Sir Thomas Boleyn's wife; I say of his wife, because she could not have been the daughter of Sir Thomas, for she was born during his absence of two years in France on the King's affairs.' Sander explained that Henry had sent Sir Thomas abroad to 'conceal his own criminal conduct' and followed this with an order to the returning Boleyn to 'refrain from prosecuting his wife, to forgive her and be reconciled to her'. The problems with this theory are manifold, not least given the purported birth dates of Anne and the fact that Henry felt no need to address the paternity rumour when removing impediments to their match. The absence of Sir Thomas for a continuous duration of two years around the possible time that Anne arrived cannot be confirmed and the birth of other siblings, who did not survive, might indicate he was not absent for such a length of time.

In 1501, William and Thomas attended the wedding of Prince Arthur to the Spanish Princess, Catherine of Aragon, in 1501. Again, as so often with Boleyn history, it was to be a London-based event, with William summoned to wait in St George's Fields outside the city to intercept the newcomers riding up from the west. He was among the group led by Prince Henry, charged to conduct them through London Bridge past the many pageants and decorations, along familiar streets that had changed little since his father's mayorality, and into St Paul's Cathedral. Catherine was due to arrive from Lambeth on 12 November and, perhaps as he waited in the fields, early on that autumn morning, William Boleyn, or 'Bolloigne' as he appears here,[14] had a chance to observe the sturdy golden-haired, ten-year-old Prince who would grow up to become Henry VIII, and choose William's granddaughter as his wife. The Mayor on that occasion was Sir John Shaa, and William would have ridden behind him in the procession, paired two-by-two with one of the Spanish visitors, among the Aldermen and Guildsmen, dressed in their finery. Shaa's uncle, Edmund, had also been Mayor of London in 1482, following a similar rise from obscurity to Geoffrey Boleyn, beginning as the son of a Cheshire Mercer, becoming apprentice to a goldsmith and ending his days as a knight.

William would have attended the wedding of the century, which took place in St Paul's Cathedral the following day, crammed with people watching the couple walk along the dais in dazzling, matching white. He would have attended the elaborate feast held in the palace, after which his son Thomas was one of the young 'bucks' of Arthur's retinue who played a role in the bedding ceremony at Baynard's Castle.[15] It was a memorable occasion, from the pageants through the London streets, to the crowds thronging the route, the ceremony itself and the weeks of feasting and tournaments that followed. Five months later, both would have grieved along with the court when news arrived from Ludlow of Arthur's unexpected death. No doubt William and Thomas donned the black of official mourning, and looked to the pre-adolescent Prince Henry as their future king. It was the end of the path they had imagined and the beginning of one they could not have anticipated.

When it came to official court business, the focus may have shifted from William to Thomas by 1503. After a year of delay, the thirteen-year-old Margaret Tudor was preparing to leave England for her future kingdom, having undergone a ceremony of marriage to James IV of Scotland. Addressed as 'Maister Bolen, son and eyre of Sir William Bolen', Thomas received a letter dated 6 May, instructing him to put off any sorrowful or mourning clothes and wear his 'best array'.[16] The party gathered at Richmond, under the leadership of Thomas's father-in-law, Thomas Howard, Earl of Surrey, which represented an important investment of trust on the part of Henry VII. On 27 June, in the company of the king, they headed north, processing through the countryside with the carts piled high with Margaret's trousseau. After three days of travel, they had reached the manor of Collyweston, in Northamptonshire, home of Henry's mother, Margaret Beaufort, where they enjoyed an extended stay. Departing on 8 July, they headed north, staying at Grantham, York, Durham, Newcastle and the border town of Berwick, before arriving in Scotland on 1 August. Thomas was a guest at the wedding a week later at Holyrood Palace in Edinburgh.

It may be that such a long journey north was ruled out for William Boleyn on grounds of health and age. He composed his will on 7 October 1505, at the age of fifty-four, desiring to be buried in Norwich Cathedral, 'near the sepulchre of Dame Ann(e) Boleyn, my mother', who had died in 1484. He willed that his son, 'Thomas Boleyn, according to the will of Geoffrey Boleyn, my father, have the manors of Blickling, Calthorp, Wykmere, Mikelbarton, to him and his heirs male... my manors of Hoo, Offley, Cokenhoo, Fylby, West Lexham, Stiffleby and Betingham in

Norfolk and Hever and Seale in Kent'.[17] When he died at Hever just three days later, on 10 October, he left his son a rich man. William was buried in a plain tomb in the first arch on the south side of the choir, between the apse and central tower. He had capitalised upon the wealth and position his father had attained in order to step out of the mercantile world and into that of the court, because of his connection to Richard III, and maintained his position through his pragmatism upon the advent of the Tudors. His was a different kind of service, a more complex, dangerous position than the economic fluctuations and rivalries of the city. William had opened the door upon a glittering but deadly world where the lives of the players were made or lost upon the whim of the king. It was for his son to step into that world under the watchful eye of perhaps one of the most despotic monarchs in English history.

THREE

Anne's World 1501–6

Anne was born at the start of a new century, a moment when everything was poised to change. The first ripples of dissent were being felt across Europe, whisperings against the old medieval certainties of faith and the church, of the stars and heavens, the limits of the known world, personal and national identity. The Catholic Church still stood proudly as a curlicued beacon in English minds, a winged angel offering salvation through the rituals of its sacraments, its calendar, red-letter saints days, fasts and the unquestioned authority of a distant pope in Rome. Eternal bliss could still be achieved by the purchase of a piece of paper with a wax seal or the building of an ornate chantry chapel. Within living memory, the old inviolability of the monarchy had been shaken. In the last fifty years, four kings had been removed from office by violent means[1] and numerous uprisings or challenges had reinforced the notion that the country was ruled by the strongest or most fortunate; the victor rather than the anointed. Lords and their vassals had been forced to play a pragmatic game, switching allegiance to individuals whilst maintaining their devotion to the crown.

The world population was somewhere between 425 and 500 million, and should probably be estimated on the lower side, around a sixteenth of that recorded five centuries later, in the count of 2001. In England, there were slightly under 3 million, with 60–70,000 of those living in London[2] but a Venetian visitor of 1500 still felt that the country was sparsely populated in relation to its 'fertility and riches'.[3] What it lacked in people, it made up for in livestock. 'They have an enormous number of sheep,' he added, 'which yield them quantities of wool of the best quality',[4] but outside that industry, with its controversial enclosures, it was clear who held the reins. 'There is not a foot of land in all England,' the Venetian noted, 'which is not held either under the king or the church and many monasteries also pay acknowledgements to the king for their possessions'.[5] The new century marked a shift into greater urbanisation and mercantilism, laying the foundations of capitalism based on the accumulation of wealth by men like Geoffrey Boleyn, Edmund and John Shaa, and their successful peers, such as the famous Cely wool family. Mercantile bankers and opportunists like the German Fuggers were to increase their capital ten times over between around 1510 and 1527. There were fortunes to be made for those ready to ride the new economic wave.

Culturally, it was a time of rapid advance. A generation since Caxton's printing press had been established in the precincts of Westminster, books were being produced in England at such a rate that they would soon become commonplace in most middle-class homes. Even the heavens seemed closer, as Amerigo Vespucci mapped the stars and Portuguese navigators landed in North America. In 1501, the estimated year of Anne's birth, Michelangelo was working on his *David*, Da Vinci completed his *Madonna of the Yardwinder* and Giovanni Bellini painted a portrait of Leonardo Loredan, the newly created Doge of Venice. It was also the year named as the date of the alleged Banquet of Chestnuts, when Cesare Borgia was supposed to have hosted a feast that descended into an orgy, with fifty prostitutes crawling across the floor to collect chestnuts. Whether or not this actually took place, the image was indicative of the corruption and excess of Renaissance Italy, of the luxury which could be bought and the absolute power of rulers over subjects, and men over women. The values and practices of the Medieval world were overlapping with those of Renaissance learning and redefinition, spreading across Europe in books and essays, disputes and sermons. It was this rub of the old against the new that would define the world where Anne's rise to power was possible. In fact, her path was part of the reshaping of England and she would be the catalyst for its change.

When Anne was born, her parents would have never suspected that she would one day become queen. Queens were usually born, not made. Birth dates among the gentry and aristocracy were rarely recorded, perhaps jotted down in the front of a family Bible, or approximately remembered for the purposes of later inheritance and 'coming of age'. They were recalled vaguely, often in relation to particular calendar days, or disputed among witnesses who might date an arrival to 'after the Michaelmas fair' or 'before the feast of St John'. Birthdays were not so specific, nor were they celebrated, in the same way as they are today. It would not be until after Anne's death that parish registers across the land began to list the exact day a baptism, marriage or burial took place, leaving the historian to estimate the day of a child's arrival to be a few days beforehand. Just like her mother and grandmother, Anne's future would have been predicated upon a suitable husband and the bearing of children. Far more important for that than a birth date, were her pedigree, her ancestry and her blood line, especially that coming from the Howard side. As a result, we do not know Anne's exact birth date, nor the place where she arrived, but the various circumstances of her life allow for some logical deductions.

Two dates are usually suggested for Anne's birth: 1501 and 1507. But where exactly do these dates comes from? Perhaps a year or two's inaccuracy might be understandable, in calculating or recalling age, but it seems unusual for there to be six years of leeway, and the relationship between the two dates is unclear, so how did this come about? While many historians have taken these literally, exploring the events of her life in order to justify one date or the other, the answer may be visual rather than factual. It may boil down to something as simple as the similarity between the digits 1 and 7. While this may sound unlikely, almost too obvious, it is worth remembering that the debate surrounding the two dates stems from a single source. And that source may have been wrong.

The first record of Anne's birth was made by the Elizabethan antiquarian, William Camden, who wrote the year 1507, in Roman numerals, in his *Annales rerum Anglicarum et Hibernicarum Elizabetha*. Camden wasn't born until 1551, but he had access to the personal records and papers of William Cecil, Lord Burleigh, who had been born in 1520, and was therefore in his early to mid-teens during Anne's reign and death. In fact, Camden was writing at Cecil's instigation, and Cecil is less likely to have been incorrect about Anne's birthdate. However, Cecil died only a year after Camden started writing, in 1598, and Camden's first volume wasn't finally published until 1615, so his information is suggestive, but not water-tight: his date cannot be relied upon. For most of the time, Camden was writing with Cecil's blessing but not his guidance; he had to make the best he could out of the statesman's surviving papers. It may have been that, years later, Cecil had recalled Anne's age incorrectly or it is entirely possible that Camden misread an earlier written date. Camden may have written his date, in numerals, after Cecil's death, after he had mistaken a 1 for a 7.

Tudor handwriting varies. The neat, tight secretary hand common to that era can include idiosyncratic loops and abbreviations, especially in personal letters. This might be more likely to happen if someone was writing at speed, or in youth, or in old age. In at least three surviving letters written by William Cecil, his handwritten number 1 could be confused for a 7. He wrote in March 1584, to the Sheriff of Staffordshire, and the formation of his number 1 has a long lead-in stroke, potentially looking like a 7, which may have caused confusion if it were not for its position at the beginning of the date, making it obviously 1584, not 7584.[6] However, had the letter been written in 1581, with this stroke used in the final number 1, a later reader may not be able to identify the potential for error. 1581 would simply have been read as 1587. Likewise, on a letter dated by Cecil on 30 June 1594, auctioned by Christie's in 2012, the upright stroke of the 1 is hooked at top and bottom, connecting to the 'e' of 'June' immediately before it, and linking to the 5 that follows.[7] The digits of the date are 'joined-up'. This effect makes it look like the number 2 but, again, logic tells us it must have been the year 1594, not 2594. A third letter, a warrant for a payment by Cecil from February 1592, contains a double hooked 1, top and bottom, looking like a 2 or 7, and was sold at auction in 2016.[8] Was it really the case that Anne was considered to be six years younger than other evidence suggests? Why six years and not four, or eight? Could it possibly be that Camden read a handwritten note by Cecil, where '1501' had been written by the elderly man in such a way that it looked like '1507?' Given Cecil's death in 1598, Camden could hardly have asked him for clarification, even if the date had looked suspect, so Camden accepted a birth year of 1507 and recorded this, in roman numerals, as a note in his book. The fact that it was added in the margin suggests that he found, or included, the information late in the process of writing, long after Cecil's death. After this, subsequent writers accepted Camden's misreading and used it to calculate Anne's age incorrectly.

One of these was chaplain Henry Clifford who produced a biography of the Catholic lady-in-waiting, Jane Dormer. Writing in 1610, he may have drawn on Jane's memoirs to calculate that Anne had been 28 at the time of her execution. Or rather, 'not twenty-nine years of age' (p80),[9] which has led to some speculation that her birthday was at the end of May or early in June. However, Jane was not born until 1538, after Anne's death. It is possible that Jane asked her mistress, Mary I, about Anne's birth date, but Clifford clearly had access to Camden's account and refers to it throughout. He was aware of the problematic nature of the text, marvelling at its omissions, such as 'Mr Camden conceals the time of the marriage of Anne Bullen, for that the Lady Elizabeth's birth was in four months after' (p76). Yet Clifford was incorrect about the timing of Anne's marriage, and was hostile to her cause, describing her as being 'brought to reckoning' for her 'corporal delights' and 'carnal pleasures' (p78). Clifford also gets the date of Anne's execution wrong, moving it forward five days, so by the time he states that she was 'not twenty-nine years of age', the credibility of his account has already been stretched.[10] Feasibly, Clifford took his date from Camden's error, and used it to calculate Anne's age incorrectly. Subsequent historians relied upon these sources, repeating the mistake through decades, even centuries, until it was generally accepted that Anne had been born in 1507. She is likely not to have been.

Firstly, there is the matter of Thomas Boleyn's own statement about his poverty as a young parent. In a letter to Thomas Cromwell, dated July 1536, he recalled that his wife, Elizabeth, brought him a child every year, stretching their annual allowance of £50 to the limit. However, this circumstance was only true for the period before 1505, when William Boleyn's death left his son a wealthy man. This would suggest that Elizabeth's childbearing years lay predominantly, if not wholly, before 1505 and with one baby arriving each year since the wedding, that she bore five children. With Anne having two surviving siblings, Mary and George, and two who died in infancy, Thomas and Henry, this would fit their father's comment, with Elizabeth's pregnancies taking place annually between 1499 and 1505. Had Anne been born in 1507, the family's financial circumstances would have been quite different, as would their location. Also, it would imply the existence of a couple more pregnancies, miscarriages, stillbirths or infant mortalities, of which no records or memorials survive.

Where Anne was born can help decide the question. Thomas and Elizabeth lived at Blickling Hall until early in 1506, after which they relocated to Hever. Had Anne been born in 1507, she would have arrived in Kent, but Matthew Parker, Archbishop of Canterbury, who was born at Norwich in 1504, knew Anne well in his position as her chaplain, and claimed her as a fellow countrywoman, from Norfolk. It is unlikely that he would have been mistaken in this. Thus, Anne was born before the move to Hever, so before February 1506.

Next, there is the question of Anne's education. It was customary to send children away from home at the age of twelve or thirteen, either to begin an apprenticeship like Norfolk gentleman Geoffrey Boleyn or, among the nobility, to join another high-ranking household. True to this, Anne was sent to join the court of Margaret of Austria in 1513. That year, Thomas Boleyn referred to his daughter in a letter to Margaret as 'la petite Boulaine', in response to which historian Retha Warnick[11] has argued that he would have used such a term to refer to a younger child, of seven rather than fourteen, but this is not a guarantee. Anne may have been 'the little Boleyn' in the family, especially if this was being used to indicate her comparative youth beside her elder sister. It may even be intended literally, referring to Anne's pre-adolescent height. Margaret commented that Anne was advanced for her 'young age', but again, this is not definitely evidence in favour of the earlier date. Anne's abilities may have been pronounced for her age, especially considering that she was being raised at court alongside Eleanor of Castile, who was born in 1498. Anne was certainly younger, but the intention of Margaret's comment may have been to indicate that Anne was bright enough to hold her own in the school room alongside Eleanor and other pupils. It is unlikely that Anne would have been sent abroad at the age of seven, when the usual age that Margaret accepted girls into her household was thirteen. Furthermore, as was identified in the twentieth century by art historian Hugh Paget, a letter Anne wrote to her father has the voice, sentiments and handwriting of a girl of thirteen rather than a child of seven.[12] Other historians of Anne's life such as Professor Eric Ives, have concurred that the handwriting is formed in a way that suggests Anne was older.[13]

It is unusual that Anne was sent to the Netherlands and not her sister Mary. Usually considered to be the elder of the two, born in 1499, Mary's education should have been arranged before that of her younger siblings, and she would have been fourteen when Anne departed in the spring of 1513. A lack of evidence, and a swathe of assumptions, have often been applied to this circumstance. We know very little about Mary's early years, even less so than Anne's. She is a blank slate until 1514. Perhaps Thomas Boleyn had already made arrangements for his eldest daughter by then, meaning that she was not available when he negotiated for Margaret to take Anne into her household. Maybe Mary had already been placed with a noble family in England, or Boleyn had earmarked her for an English court career, while he hoped that Anne would marry a foreign magnate, or serve a foreign queen. Equally, it might have been felt that Anne's talents were better suited to the opportunity, or that she was more independent, or that Mary's mother wished to keep her at her side, in anticipation of an opening in the household of Henry VIII's first queen, Catherine of Aragon. Perhaps Boleyn was hoping to arrange Mary's marriage as early as 1513, only to find his plans derailed on various counts. There may have been many reasons why Anne was sent abroad instead of Mary, but the absence of confirmation cannot be used to pinpoint her age.

The debate over Anne's birth date is inseparable from the details of her early biography. It is not merely a diverting puzzle but a critical question, defining her experiences and changing the biographer's perspective considerably, depending upon whether one opts for greater maturity or comparative youth and naivety. It concerns the difference between a girl and a woman. It may even dictate some readers' sympathies. One source that pre-dates Camden is a hostile account of Anne's life given by the Elizabethan Catholic, Nicholas Sander, in his 1585 *Rise and Growth of the Anglican Schism.* The source of many anti-Anne legends, it includes details such as her legendary six fingers, her alleged early sexual scandals and the claim that Anne was Henry VIII's daughter, conceived in adultery with Elizabeth Howard. Even when Sander relies on the birth date of 1507 to justify that astonishing assertion, this fails to make the slander remotely plausible, suggesting as it does that Henry fathered her when he was fifteen, or just sixteen. The king later denied any former relationship with Elizabeth, whilst admitting to having had relations with Anne's sister, Mary. By the Victorian era, though, perceptions on Anne's birth and character where shifting and these early texts were being reassessed, along with an increase in sympathy towards her. The editor of the 1877 edition of Sander's book, David Lewis, commented that 'the common account is that Anne was born in 1507, but for that account there is no other authority... than the herald and antiquary Camden, who also seems to have had no authority for his assertion'. Lewis adds that 'it is hardly credible that Anne Boleyn, supposing her to have been born, as Camden says, in 1507, was one of the ladies in attendance on Queen Mary of France' at the age of seven.[14]

One seventeenth-century advocate of the later birth date was the antiquarian and poet, John Weever, author of the 1631 *Ancient Funeral Monuments*. When it comes to Anne, his entry has an air of precision, correctly giving the exact number of days that she was married, and the date of her final miscarriage, before he calculates a gap of sixteen years between Henry and Anne, claiming they fell in love when he was thirty-eight and she was twenty-two, putting her birth closer to 1507 than 1501. Weever is not error-free, giving Geoffrey Boleyn the alternative name of Godfrey, and stating that he was Anne's grandfather, rather than her great-grandfather. Weever was followed by Lord Herbert of Cherbury, who wrote an account of Henry VIII's reign in 1649. However, Herbert's arguments were based on his confusion of Anne with her sister Mary. He wrote that 'if Mistress Anne Boleyn went to France with Mary the French Queen... it must follow that she was born about or before 1498'.[15] It is now known that it was Mary Boleyn who accompanied Mary Tudor to France in 1514, and that Anne joined them there from the Netherlands. Herbert also believed that Anne was around twenty when she entered the household of Catherine of Aragon. Anne returned to England from France in December 1521 and made her debut at court the following March, when a birth date of summer 1501 would have made her twenty, although the exact nature of her employment, and her employer, are less certain.[16]

Next, there is the question of Anne's fertility and her age at the time of her first attracting Henry, and her marriage, which took place in late

1532 or early 1533. Had she been born in 1507, she would have been just nineteen when she caught Henry's eye; hardly mature enough to have become the sophisticated, cultured, educated woman whose style, manners and independence surely enthralled him. Henry was certainly not averse to falling for a pretty young woman, but there was so much more to Anne's appeal. His later infatuation with the teenaged Catherine Howard was different in essence, and came about under different circumstances. Henry's obsession with Catherine in the 1540s was more physical, an old man's folly, an escape from the trap he had found himself in with wife number four, Anne of Cleves, and an attempt to feel young again. His obsession with Anne was inspired by her intelligence, her cultivation, her elegance and grace. He was attracted to her mind, as much as he could allow her to be his equal, or at least worthy of debate and pursuit. In her he saw a potential queen, a woman worthy of the crown, with international experience, a European figure known to his two main rivals, Francis I and Holy Roman Emperor Charles V. Delightful as Catherine Howard may have been, she and Anne were in different leagues. The Anne of nineteen was not the fully formed woman that she was at the age of twenty-five, nor would she have been sufficiently old enough to appreciate and absorb the culture on offer in Austria, or during her early years in France. The image of Anne as accomplished, independent and confident rings true for the older birth date.

According to the later date, Anne would have been twenty-five when she married, twenty-six when she bore Elizabeth. It also meant that she still had a number of childbearing years ahead of her at the time of her death. For Henry, these would have been years of potential, of opportunity, wasted years of fertility, as he was entering his late forties. Yet, we know that during their courtship, in 1529, Anne berated Henry for making her spend the best of her fertile years waiting to be married. This makes far more sense had she been born in 1501, and was therefore thirty-one at the time of her marriage. Had she arrived in 1507, she would have been only twenty-one or twenty-two in 1529, hardly old enough to be concerned about her waning fertility. Given that Catherine of Aragon underwent her last pregnancy at the age of thirty-three and experienced her menopause at forty – and that both Henry's sisters had completed their childbearing by the age of twenty-six or seven – Anne would indeed have had something worth complaining about, had she been twenty-eight in 1529. It would also be easier for Henry to wash his hands of a wife in 1536 whom he believed to be approaching the end of her fertility. The question of Anne's age and her potential for childbearing were not raised during his courtship of her, just as the reproductive health of her replacement, Jane Seymour, was not, in 1536. Jane was born in 1508, so she was not significantly younger than Anne, had Anne arrived in 1507. However, if Anne's birth date was 1501, Henry could have had more cause for optimism about fathering a son with a 'younger model'.

From the mid-nineteenth century onwards, scholarly support has been building in favour of a birth date for Anne of 1501. This was advocated by the biographer Agnes Strickland in 1842 and accepted by Antonia Fraser,[17] Eric Ives,[18] David Loades,[19] Alison Weir[20] and Hugh Paget, in his definitive essay of 1981. However, the matter has been far from settled, since John Lingard's 1800 *History of England*[21] and the late Victorian historian James Gairdner, both favoured 1507 for Anne's arrival, influencing historians like J. S. Brewer,[22] James Anthony Froude,[23] and Retha Warnicke.[24]

From the scant evidence, and the possibilities for error, it would seem most likely that Mary was the eldest Boleyn child, born between 1498 and 1500, probably in 1499. She was the first to be married out of the two sisters and further confirmation comes from her grandson's claim to the Irish Butler/Ormonde title, made during the reign of Anne's daughter, Elizabeth I. To follow their father's suggested timescale of a child a year, Anne would have been the third child, arriving in 1501 after Thomas, followed by Henry in 1502, and by George, in 1503 or 1504. A small brass cross surviving in St Peter's Church, Hever, is thought to commemorate Henry Boleyn, who died in infancy and another son named Thomas, who lies at St John the Baptist Church at Penshurst. These brasses are dated to the 1520s, but this only indicates the time when the memorial was erected, not the date of decease. Elizabeth may have had other pregnancies, or children, that went unrecorded, but only three of her babies reached adulthood: Mary, Anne and George.

FOUR

Change 1501–9

Assuming that Anne did arrive in 1501 at Blickling, the first home she knew would have been a late medieval manor, typically built around a courtyard, with great hall and accommodation block, ringed about by a moat and gardens. Built from red brick or grey stone, it would have been more residential than defensive, perhaps with boundary walls and a gatehouse. The days of defending individual property were essentially in the past but, as the lives of the nearby Pastons testifies, there were still sometimes assaults upon home and hearth. Just three years before Geoffrey purchased Blickling from Fastolf, the Paston's home of Gresham, ten miles to the north, was laid under siege from a rival claimant, forcing Margaret Paston out of the property. The original manor house at Blickling was probably not too dissimilar to Ightham Mote in Kent, which dates to 1340–60, or even the slightly later Caister Castle, near to the Norfolk coast, developed by Fastolf in the 1440s. It may also have been like Gresham Manor, crenelated in 1318, rectangular with round corner towers, with a curtain wall, drawbridge and moat. Anne's home was demolished in the early Jacobean period and replaced by the present building, which was completed in 1616. The church of St Andrew, where Anne was probably baptised and worshipped, still stands on the edge of the estate, proudly displaying its Boleyn connections, although it was largely remodelled by the Victorians.

Blickling was a small village but had important royal connections. One estate had been given to the Bishops of Norwich by the crown in the eleventh century. Situated thirteen miles north of the city, it was a convenient retreat, and they built a palace or country seat there, set in a large park. The area Anne would have known was purchased in 1362 by the MP, ambassador and soldier Sir Nicholas Dagworth, who had served under the Black Prince and Edward III. Dagworth rebuilt the manor house at Blickling and retired there, dying in 1402. He was buried under a marble slab bearing a brass memorial and arms at the east end of the south side of St Andrew's Church. He left the estate to his wife Eleanor, who sold it to Sir Thomas Erpingham but he relinquished it to Nicholas's nephew by marriage, Thomas Neville, Lord Furnival, who, in turn, sold it to Sir John Fastolf in 1445. From Fastolf, it passed to Geoffrey Boleyn, but it is likely that the building he knew was the one built by Dagworth. Geoffrey Boleyn may well have developed the house he found on the site, but he certainly built the chapel to St Thomas in the church next door. As a small girl, Anne would have prayed there, overlooked by the colourful stained glass her great-grandfather commissioned, showing his arms impaling those of his wife, giving her a sense of dynastic history and the importance of her successful ancestors.

Anne's early life would have been quiet, set in a far-flung corner of rural Norfolk. She would have been taught her lessons and prayers, played with her sister and brother, roamed the gardens and joined in the celebrations when her father returned home from London or Hever. Thomas must have been frequently at court, first as a Yeoman of the Crown, which was really just a glorified attendant at court, then as an Esquire of the Body. This was more of an honour, giving Boleyn personal access to the king, which brought him a salary of around £30 a year and the 'bouge of court', or right to be fed at the king's table.[1] The job's description had been drawn up in 1471, in Edward IV's *Liber Niger*, or 'Black Book of the Household', specifying that the Esquire was to be ready to help the king at all times, because 'no man else (is) to set hands' upon him. There were probably occasions when Boleyn slept in the king's chamber, on a truckle bed, or outside in an antechamber or corridor, ready for the summons 'to array and unray him, and to watch day and night' and generally be 'attendant upon the king's person'.[2] The king upon whom Boleyn attended was Henry VII, then approaching his fiftieth birthday, and frequently infirm with a poor throat and chest. Thomas is likely to have witnessed him suffering from the debilitating effects of the tuberculosis that would kill him in 1509. His court was frequently at Westminster but also, increasingly, at the king's favourite, Richmond Palace, a beautiful, innovative and enchanting place on the river, with fine ornamentation, courtyards, gardens and grounds, where there was much sport and pleasure to be had. But it was not a young man's court. Approaching thirty, Boleyn was a little too old to join the circle of youths around the teenaged heir, Henry, Prince of Wales.

Then, in October 1505, when Anne was four years old, news of her grandfather William's death changed the atmosphere in the house. Her parents would have gone into mourning; perhaps the children also were dressed in black, or in plain, dark clothes, but Anne may have sensed that this was a period of transition, of transformation for her family, that it would soon pass and the drab mood would be replaced by the colourful fabrics and jewellery that their new money could afford. Perhaps she understood some of the conversations her parents had about their future, and witnessed her mother overseeing the servants arranging and packing their belongings. The legal process took a little while but, finally, in February 1506, Thomas was granted a licence to take possession of his estates and the Boleyns left Blickling for their new home of Hever. It would have been a long journey for the children, over 150 miles, and spread over several days. When the carts and wagons finally rolled into the green vale of north-west Kent, through the 'garden of England', the young Anne would have set eyes on a small, hidden 'castle', nestling in a dip, close by the river Eden.

The land on which Hever Castle stands had been given by William the Conqueror to one of his knights. The Norman nobleman Walter de Hevere erected a simple farmhouse there, but it was his descendant, William, who obtained a licence from Edward III to turn it into a fortified manor, adding a huge fortified entrance, with a bridge and drawbridge. Anne would still recognise that frontage today, although she would spot a few new windows added during the later Tudor period.[3] Inside, the old medieval hall with its minstrels gallery and carved fireplace, would soon be remodelled by Thomas to create a larger space, running at right angles to the old hall, and a new entrance within the enclosed red-brick courtyard.[4] It was also Thomas who constructed the Long Gallery on the first floor, where his family could sit, or take exercise, along the length of the house.[5] Before the castle was transformed by the Astor family in the early twentieth century, to create a pseudo-medieval village, the house stood alone, although an account from 1870 reports that another building existed. Joseph Nash described the stable block opposite, which stood between the two moats, with apartments for sleeping on the first floor above the horses, and a 'gallery in front looking towards the mansion'.[6] It was a timber structure, built before the end of the fifteenth century,[7] so quite possibly the addition of Geoffrey or William Boleyn. Although he had relocated his family closer to London, Thomas Boleyn retained connections with his home county, being created a yeoman of the crown at Lynn on the north coast of Norfolk in 1507. He may have travelled back and forth, or appointed a deputy, but from this point his focus was increasingly on the south-east, shuttling between the various properties of the king. He was only twenty-five miles south of Eltham Palace and thirty-five from Richmond Palace. As an Esquire of the Body, he is likely to have been at Richmond early in 1509, when it became clear that the health of the old king was failing. Boleyn may even have been present when the announcement was made of Henry VII's death, a few days after his actual demise, on 21 April. A 'T Bolan' was among the Squires issued with mourning clothes in time for the funeral in May.[8]

Anne Boleyn was seven or eight years old upon the accession of England's new king. The seventeen-year-old Henry VIII was the epitome of the early Renaissance ideal; tall, athletic, handsome, with his red-gold hair cut into a bell around his head, broad-shouldered, with a muscular neck and, according to one of the ambassadors, the face of an angel. The contrast with his shrewd, austere father could not have been more pronounced and, after years in the old man's shadow, Henry was ready to burst forth in a riot of spending and splendour, colour and pleasure. With the royal coffers at his disposal, full to bursting from his father's unpopular fiscal policies, the power was dizzying for the new king. He had his serious side too, being interested in the new learning, in theology and debate, the classics and mathematics, poetry and music, science and astrology. But more than that, he had a passion for sport, for riding and hunting, jousting and hawking, playing and dancing. Above all, the new king wanted to enjoy himself. In fact, he had been wanting to enjoy himself for years, and now the restraints had been removed.

If the poets are to be believed, something like a national euphoria greeted the youth's accession. Thomas More, composing verses for the coronation pageantry, promised that Henry would free the people from the slavery and tyranny of his father's taxes and harsh policies; he would 'wipe the tears from every eye and put joy in the place of our long distress'. The Spanish Ambassador, Gutierre Gomez de Fuensalida, agreed that the people were 'very happy' and that 'few tears' had been shed for the old king, as his subjects were 'as joyful as if they had been released from prison'.[9] William Blount, Baron Mountjoy, who was the same age as Thomas Boleyn, wrote to the Dutch Humanist scholar Erasmus that 'everything is full of milk and honey and nectar' and that Heaven and Earth were rejoicing at the new king's devotion to 'virtue, glory, immortality'.[10] The Venetian Ambassador considered him to be 'much more handsome than any other sovereign in Christendom' and to 'excel all who ever wore a crown... so worthy and eminent a sovereign'.[11] Tudor chronicler Edward Hall, although born in 1497 and so twelve at the time of the coronation, later described Henry's perfections: 'The features of his body, his goodly personage, his amiable visage, his princely countenance, with the novel qualities of his royall estate, to every man needeth no rehearsal.'[12]

Thomas Boleyn would have known the young king almost his entire life. Henry was the second surviving son of Henry VII and Elizabeth of York, born at Greenwich Palace on 28 Jun, 1491. His birth was added, somewhat desultorily, by his grandmother into her book of hours, and he was sent off to Eltham Palace to be raised with his sisters, while all the resources for training the next king were focused upon Prince Arthur, five years his senior. Henry had seemed to be an exuberant, boisterous and happy child, taking after his maternal grandfather, Edward IV, and drawing attention to himself when he threw off his jacket to dance at his brother's wedding. A bust of a laughing boy made in terracotta by the Italian Guido Mazzoni, dating to around 1498, has been identified as representing Henry at around the age of seven. His golden cap, collar and clothing made from fired green glaze over tinfoil suggest royalty, but his face, with its narrowed eyes, chubby cheeks and open mouth are indicative of humour and fun. This all changed as the result of two deaths: that of Arthur in 1501 and Elizabeth of York in 1503, his brother and mother. Henry's adolescence had been a period of mourning, caution and waiting, with his father keeping him close, as the only surviving Tudor heir. The Boleyn men, William and Thomas, would have seen him grow from a child into a long-limbed athletic youth, straining at the leash, eager to escape from his father's restrictions and enjoy dancing, jousting, and to taste freedom.

Henry also wished to reward those who had done his family good service and advance the men he believed would prove useful during his reign. He was clearly appreciative of Thomas Boleyn's qualities, including him in the list of twenty-six 'honourable persons' (men) summoned by the king to the Tower of London on 22 June, 1509, for the special ceremony of investiture as Knights of the Bath.[13] Thomas may have known what to expect from accounts his father had related, having undergone the process half a century earlier. Thomas's role was to serve the king at dinner, to bear dishes 'in token that they shall never bear none after that day' and then to undergo the process of ritual bathing. Thomas was in good company. Among the up-and-coming men who would become his colleagues at court, and the stars of the new reign, were his contemporary William Blount, Lord Mountjoy, soon to be appointed chamberlain to the queen; court poet John Skelton; Robert Ratcliffe, husband of Lady Elizabeth Stafford, a lady-in-waiting; George Hastings, who would marry her sister Anne; young Henry Clifford and Henry Daubeney, both aged only sixteen; the famed jouster Thomas Knyvett, married to Elizabeth's sister Muriel since 1500, who would become Henry's Master of the Horse in 1510; Thomas Parr, soon to become the father of Henry's sixth and final wife; and Henry Wyatt of Allington in Kent, near Hever, father of the future poet Thomas.[14]

The Tower would have been cleaned, swept, decorated and guarded in advance of the occasion. Henry arrived on horseback from Greenwich, riding into the city across London Bridge and into Gracechurch Street, where he was met by the Duke of Buckingham, dressed in a golden gown, 'and other worthy gentlemen'. Thomas Boleyn may have been among the company who conducted the king to the Tower, or else he made his own way there from Hever, in time for the ceremony. Thomas and the other knights would have briefly taken the office of their social inferiors, bearing the plates to Henry's table, carving his meat and pouring his wine: yet this inversion of the hierarchy was the epitome of honour. Once the meal was over, they would have ritually bathed and sworn the oath of allegiance to their sovereign, which is unlikely to have changed since William Boleyn took it in 1483, promising to obey Richard III. Following that, they would have spent the night in prayer.

Thomas's wife Elizabeth was also in the Tower that night, but separate from her husband, in the retinue of the new queen. Just two weeks before his coronation, Henry had married his brother Arthur's widow, the Spanish Princess Catherine, a resolute, pious and proud daughter of Ferdinand and Isabella, joint monarchs of Castile and Aragon. After years spent in waiting and penury, unsure of her future, Catherine had finally become the wife of the English king in a secret ceremony at Greenwich, in time for the pair to be crowned side by side. Five-and-a-half years older than Henry, she was more mature than the young king, and represented an important international alliance for England. Although the betrothal had been off and on for years, Henry had married her willingly, claiming to be following his own inclination as well as obeying his dying father's wishes, and the pair were genuinely happy with each other, enjoying a honeymoon period of which the coronation would be the pinnacle. Catherine's presence as queen necessitated the creation of another household, and Elizabeth Boleyn was issued with cloth of scarlet in order to be suitably attired for the occasion.[15] She would have remained with Catherine, lodged in the Tower, ready to assist her preparations for the morning. This also marked a return to public life for Elizabeth, at the age of twenty-nine, indicating that her childbearing years were probably over. Her young family; Mary, Anne and George, would have been left under the watchful eye of their governesses and servants at Hever. Having both been honoured in such a way, Thomas and Elizabeth had every reason to be optimistic about their children's future in the new reign.

Around 4pm on the afternoon of Saturday 23 June 1509, the royal procession left the Tower. This late start was probably indicative of the amount of preparation required and the number of people involved. Thomas may have helped dress Henry in his crimson red velvet robe edged in ermine, a placard studded with gems, jacket of raised gold and ruby necklace. He may also have helped the king mount the horse draped in damask gold or prepared the gold canopy that would be carried above him, before the parade assembled in the Tower precincts. The knights and esquires of the king's body were also dressed in crimson velvet.[16] Elsewhere Elizabeth may have brushed out the queen's long red-gold hair, which she was to wear loose down her back as tradition demanded. She would have participated in the process by which the tiny Spaniard was dressed in a gown of white, embroidered satin, her skirts shaken out behind her, before a mantle of cloth of tissue was placed about her. Finally, the ladies placed on her head a coronet set with 'rich orient stones' before they joined the procession. Thomas was riding with the newly created Knights, dressed in their fur-lined robes, while Elizabeth took her place with the ladies, to travel behind the queen in her litter drawn by two white palfreys. The ladies rode in 'several covered chariots... each one after their degrees in cloth of gold, cloth of silver, tinsels and velvets, with embroideries'.[17] The procession passed along Tower Street, into Eastcheap and Gracechurch Street, viewing the colourful decorations and pageants that lined the route. Apart from a brief shower of rain, which forced them to seek shelter, the figures passed into Cheapside, where the Mayor, Aldermen and representatives of the Guilds had gathered, reminding Thomas of his father's transition from city to court. From there, they continued west, past St Paul's, through Ludgate, into Fleet Street and the Strand, before arriving at Westminster.

The following morning, on Sunday 25 June, Thomas and Elizabeth were among those assembled in Westminster Abbey who watched as Henry and Catherine were crowned. Dressed in crimson robes, they were anointed and swore their oath to serve the country, receiving the orb, sceptre and ring of state. Both would take this promise extremely seriously, although they would fulfil it in very different ways. Afterwards the Boleyns were among the party who retired to the palace for a three-course feast. But the festivities were not yet over: the next few days were filled with jousts, tournaments, pageants and more feasting. From Hall's account, it does not appear that Thomas took part in the chivalric events on this occasion, although his brother-in-law Sir Thomas Knyvett did.[18] Elizabeth may have sat alongside her sister, Muriel Knyvett, in the galleries, unless Muriel was heavily pregnant or actually in confinement, as she appears to have delivered five children between 1508 and her death in 1512. It must have been an unforgettable experience for the onlookers, with £1,749 8s 4d spent on preparations for the king and a further £1,536 16s 2d for the queen. No doubt the Boleyns would have had lots to tell the children waiting back at home. By the time they returned to Hever, they had other good news to impart. That July, Thomas Boleyn was promoted to Keeper of the Exchange of Calais and of the Foreign Exchange in England.[19]

FIVE

A Courtier's Daughter
1510–13

On the cold morning of 18 January, 1510, Thomas Boleyn was awake early at the command of the king. The court had recently arrived at Westminster, having come from the onion-domed palace of Richmond, where they had spent an elaborate Christmas, feasting, dancing and jousting in the park. Westminster, with its painted chamber, great hall and riverside gardens, was to be the location of Henry's first parliament, due to open in three days' time. But the young king was reluctant to end the festivities just yet. He summoned twelve of his closest men, for whom costumes had been prepared from 'Kentish Kendal', a kind of coarse woollen cloth, or baize, which was green in colour, a sort of early form of Lincoln Green. This was apt, because the men were indeed dressing up 'like oute laws or Robyn Hodes men', which was one of the young king's favourite games.[1]

Thomas and his brother-in-law, Edward Howard, were among Henry's chosen playmates, pulling on short coats, hoods and matching hose, with a sword and buckler, bow and arrows. With as much secrecy as they could muster for a crowded Tudor Palace, they crept along the corridor to the queen's chambers. Catherine of Aragon and her ladies, which probably included Elizabeth Boleyn, were 'much abashed' at 'the straunge sight' and their 'sodain commynge', accepting invitations to dance with the 'strangers' and enjoy other 'pastimes'.[2] The 'Account of the Revels' describes the incident as having been intended as 'a gladness to the Queen's grace'[3] who was seven months pregnant at the time. Such masques were common, especially with the nobility dressing as rough, wild men, albeit in their clean, newly-made costumes, and it is likely that the women had at least some warning of the arrival and identities of their guests, so as not to cause genuine alarm. Their 'abashment' was as much part of the performance as the costumes. Yet Sir Thomas may have taken note of his new king's penchant for disguise and thrown himself into the role as Henry expected. It was an apt metaphor, as the Tudor court was a dangerous place where masks concealed true feelings, roles were adopted, ignorance feigned. Boleyn's career, and those of his children, were to be an extension of this 'play', a game of costumes, where characters were handed out by the king for his entertainment and an individual's actions and speech, often indirectly scripted for them, were observed by a knowledgeable audience.

Thomas Boleyn was summoned to take part in another of Henry's courtly celebrations a year later. Queen Catherine had lost her first child, but had successfully delivered a prince at Richmond Palace on 1 January, 1511. The tournament the king planned at Westminster was to be, second only to his coronation, the most expensive event of his entire reign. Thomas jousted on the second day, along with the king's favourite Charles Brandon, Elizabeth's brother Edmund, who was to become the father of Henry's fifth wife, Catherine Howard, and Richard Tempest, a fellow Esquire of the Body, and a distant relation, following the marriage of Thomas's brother Edward to Anne Tempest.[4] Held on 12 and 13 February, the joust was headed by Henry, in his role as Sir Loyal Heart, with three other challengers, whose names were hung on a tablet in the tilt yard. Catherine and her ladies watched from a specially erected stage hung with cloth of gold and rich cloth of Arras, while the knights demonstrated their chivalric abilities. Hall's account of the second day relates how the noblemen appeared at the sound of trumpets, 'richly apparelled'[5] in cloth of gold and russet velvet but, once again, Boleyn was required to take a particular role. Along with Thomas Grey, Marquis of Dorset, he played the part of a pilgrim, as if he had come from the shrine of St James at Santiago de Compostela, in Spain, wearing a tabard and hat of black velvet, carrying a staff, all decorated with the gold scallop shell common to that route. The jousts were 'valiantly achieved' by the king until such time as every opponent withdrew.[6] After supper in the white hall, an interlude was performed by the gentlemen of the Chapel. Henry took it as another opportunity for a disguise, appearing in a company of chosen men and women to dance covered in gold spangles. Thomas Boleyn is not directly named by Hall as being present, only Thomas Knyvett was; but many of the knights' pseudonyms were listed, and as it was intended to conclude the day's festivities, he probably took part.

There was a clear correlation between Thomas's involvement in such events and his advancement at court, as he was granted, that February, the keepership of the park of Beskwode, Nottinghamshire, for life.[7] The same year he was also given the annual appointment of Sheriff of Kent, a post he would hold again in 1517. The Boleyn connection with Norfolk was still strong and in 1512 Thomas was appointed Governor of Norwich Castle and gaol, paying 3s 6d every 30 weeks for castle guards. He held this position in conjunction with his Kent neighbour Sir Henry Wyatt, who was now Master of the Jewels.[8] With Wyatt's home of Allington Castle just twenty-five miles to the east of Hever, it is likely that a friendship existed between the two families, or at least a relationship based on mutual respect and need. By 1512, it is likely that the eleven-year-old Anne knew the nine-year old son of the family, possibly as a play fellow for her younger brother, George.

Very little is known about the early education Anne received. Like other girls of her age and class, she would have been taught the traditional female accomplishments such as music, sewing and dancing, and it is likely that her mother taught her to read and write. Yet, considering the talents and interests Anne displayed in later life, she probably benefitted from a far richer curriculum. The impact of Renaissance learning and the wave of pre-Reformation literature in Europe provoked a change in the way young women were being educated and, given the time Thomas would spend at Margaret's court, it appears that the Boleyns were progressive thinkers when it came to the education of women. The two girls may even have shared a tutor with their brother. George Boleyn could speak Latin, Italian and French, so perhaps Anne had also read some of the Roman classics, even the Greeks. It was a return to these original texts, a connection with the voices of the past, that inspired scholars to desire a more direct relationship with the Scriptures, to read them in the original and rediscover, or 'rebirth' them, that created a cross-over between the Renaissance and the emerging Reformation. It was inevitable that giving the scriptures a new life necessitated change in the relationship between man, church and God.

Thomas Boleyn was only a few months younger than his namesake Sir Thomas More, a well-known advocate of the new Humanist approach of giving his daughters a classical education. The More daughters, born between 1505 and 1511, as well as his step-daughter and adopted children, were taught Latin and Greek; in fact, it was Margaret More who once diagnosed her father's illness using her copy of Galen, when a male doctor failed to recognise the symptoms. The young Catherine of Aragon and her sisters had also benefited from the teaching of some of the leading scholars of the day, drawn from universities, by parents who patronised female educators in the 1490s. Anne certainly had an aesthetic eye, appreciative of illuminated manuscripts, and an understanding of theology, which came to the fore in the years preceding her marriage. She had not received the early education of a future queen, as Catherine did, but she had a good grounding in the areas that were relevant to her father's career, probably at his instigation. It was the education and opportunities she would experience during her teenaged years that would define Anne and give her the air of royalty.

Boleyn's own ability to speak French and Latin was to determine the next stage in his career. In the spring of 1512, he was chosen to be an ambassador to the court of Margaret of Austria in the Netherlands, to negotiate the expansion of the anti-French Holy League in preparation for Henry's planned invasion of France. The daughter of Holy Roman Emperor Maximilian, Margaret was an educated, cultured woman, who had formerly been married to the elder brother of Catherine of Aragon. Having lived at the Spanish court of Ferdinand and Isabella for over three years, between 1497 and 1500, Margaret was well-known to the English queen, who would have shared her grief at the loss of her young husband, followed by her miscarriage of his posthumous child. After another brief marriage, and the early death of her brother, Margaret became the first female Governor of the Low Countries and guardian of her nephew, the future Charles V. Although Boleyn was probably well aware of the role Margaret had played in establishing commercial ties between the Netherlands and England, and the formation of the League of Cambrai, intended to keep the peace in Europe, it would seem plausible that Catherine of Aragon briefed Boleyn with her personal knowledge about Margaret before his departure. He appears to have left by 16 May 1512, in the company of Dr John Young, or Yonge, and Sir Richard Wingfield, as Henry VIII directed in a letter to Margaret dispatched from Greenwich Palace.[9]

As the eldest member of the party, at almost fifty, Dr Yonge was the senior diplomat among them. Born in 1465, he was the son of a former Mayor of London, a member of the Grocer's Guild, who was also named John Yonge, and was in office nine years after Geoffrey Boleyn. Additionally, his half-brother, Thomas Canynges, had been London's Mayor the year before Geoffrey, so the families were known to each other. Ordained in 1500, Dr Yonge was a good man to accompany Thomas on his first ambassadorial mission, having already completed two visits to the Netherlands in 1504 and 1506. Sir Richard Wingfield was also an experienced political figure, married to Catherine Woodville, the younger sister of Elizabeth, Queen of Edward IV, and Henry VIII's maternal grandmother. Catherine was the widow of Jasper Tudor, so Wingfield was the king's great-uncle by marriage twice over. In one letter, he refers to Boleyn as his 'cousin', a link that existed because his sister Katherine and Boleyn's mother-in-law, Elizabeth (née Tilney) had both been married to Sir John Bourchier. Wingfield was appointed Lord Deputy of Calais in 1511, which would have conveniently smoothed the early part of the group's passage.

Boleyn's journey to the Netherlands began in Kent. Passing through the country from London to Dover would have afforded him the opportunity to stop at Hever and bid farewell to his son and daughters, who were no longer small children. Mary, aged thirteen, was on the verge of adulthood and would soon be requiring a husband; Anne came soon after her at eleven and George at nine, still focusing on his lessons. Thomas may already have been thinking about Mary's future, as just a week earlier the king had granted him the wardship, lands and marriage of John Hastings, son and heir of Sir George, twelfth Baron Hastings, who had died that year.[10] Born in 1498, John was the right age for Mary, and would soon come into his majority but, if this was Boleyn's intention, the marriage would never go ahead due to the premature death of the young man in 1514.

Travel in Tudor times was slow and fraught with dangers. Tempestuous seas lay ahead and miles of foreign terrain to cross, so there was no way of knowing how long Thomas would be away, when his family would hear from him, or even that his return was guaranteed. It would have been a relief when his first letters arrived home. Having safely crossed the Channel, he travelled the 125 miles east from Calais to Brussels, arriving there by 28 May, when the group wrote a joint letter to Henry VIII containing the information that Boleyn had already met with Margaret, and that she had been pleased to hear from them. 'We have enclosed in this letter such answer as we [have] devised and sent unto her in writing the next morning, wh[erewith], as the said Thomas reported unto us, she was right well contented and pleased.'[11] Meeting Margaret for the first time, Boleyn would have found an imposing woman in her early thirties, famous for her pale complexion, aged just three years younger than him. An anonymous diptych painted between 1500 and 1510, depicting her at prayer before the Virgin, shows the not-unpleasant face of a woman with large eyes and the heavy nose and mouth of the Hapsburgs. Her portrait as a widow by Bernard van Orley contains full red lips in a slight smile, small dark eyes and the hint of wavy golden hair at her temples.

The ambassadors were still present in Brussels on 4 June and 7 June but, according to letters written by Wingfield two weeks later, Boleyn had departed for England on 14 June leaving Brussels at 3 in the morning and arriving in Calais the following morning at 9.[12] He was clearly carrying letters for Henry and returning with further instructions from the king, so it was merely a flying visit, lasting twelve days. The location of Hever made it likely that he was able to find time to drop in, even briefly, before he arrived back in Brussels at 2pm on the afternoon of 26 June.[13] The same day, Thomas had an audience with Margaret to present her with the king's letters and the next day the three ambassadors were invited to Margaret's court, where they heard evensong and watched her nephew, the twelve-year-old Prince Charles, shooting at the butts. On the suggestion of their hostess, Boleyn left again to meet Charles' grandfather, the Emperor Maximilian, to advance the negotiations, but he had returned to Brussels to prove to Margaret that the money for 2,000 German (Almain) troops was forthcoming from England. Boleyn's role and activities show that he was considered to be an energetic, trusted, capable and reliable diplomat. He also appears to have established a rapport with Margaret as, on 12 August, when the deal was being concluded, she asked him to make a wager upon it. 'He answered that if her Grace would give him leave, he would gladly hold that wager, and more gladly lose it; then promised she to give him a courser of Spain in case it came not to the conclusion by us desired within the space above rehearsed. If she win, to have of Sir Thomas a hobby (a horse). They shook hands in confirmation of the same.'[14]

That summer, the ambassadors followed Margaret between her various properties, writing from Mechelen, Antwerp and Barowe in late August, before returning to Antwerp on September 9 and on to Mechelen again on 25 September 1512. By mid-October, back in Brussels, Boleyn's translation skills were in use when he rendered Henry VIII's letter into French for Margaret and, believing the deal to be imminently concluded, wrote, 'I hope now that we shall go home.'[15] By 10 November, though, they were still waiting, frustrated at the lack of progress, writing that they had 'hoped to have been able to send (Henry) something more substantial than fair promises and sweet words', conscious that they were 'spending the King's money and doing him no service'.[16] Then, that December, their commission was renewed and extended, requiring them to treat with the pope, the emperor and Ferdinand, King of Aragon, along with Margaret.[17] Finally, on 5 April, 1513, Boleyn concluded an agreement with Margaret and Maximilian to enlarge the anti-French Holy League. He was free to leave, his mission completed, but he would not be returning home to Hever just yet.

Within weeks, Boleyn and Young were at Calais, waiting to join the king's forces for the invasion of France. He may also have been watching the horizon for a ship carrying Sir Claude Bouton, Captain of the Guard to the Prince of Castile, who was accompanying a very special traveller from England. For Thomas had achieved one other personal success whilst in the Netherlands. In May 1513, his departure from Margaret's court coincided with the arrival of his daughter. This is Anne Boleyn's first appearance in the historical records.

PART TWO

EUROPEAN POLISH

SIX

Burgundian Splendour
1513–14

At twelve years old, Anne Boleyn left her home at Hever, travelled to Dover and embarked for Calais. It was to be the start of the education that gave her the air of sophistication and poise that would attract Henry, a unique edge, and the cultural polish and confidence to hold her own in the courts of Burgundy, France and, eventually, England. In fairy-tale castles that outstripped any buildings she knew from home, hung with the most exquisite Flemish tapestries, in libraries housing the best illuminated manuscripts, where leading artists worked and musicians played, Anne absorbed the latest and best of the northern European Renaissance. Her exposure to its religious and cultural thinking made her something of a 'new' woman, part of a generation who would question the old ways and faiths, emboldened to reject centuries of Catholic ritual, the efficacy of saints and the pope, a dfferent world to the England in which she spent her early years.

Anne probably had a small entourage with her, perhaps a woman as chaperone and trusted servants from the Boleyn household, but they were all under the charge of Claude Bouton, Seigneur de Corbaron, a man then aged around forty with a long record of service to the Hapsburgs. Bouton was a second cousin of the influential Burgundian courtier, Olivier de la Marche, whose position as Master of the Household to Mary of Burgundy in the 1470s had influenced the restructuring of Edward IV's English court. Born amid this process, in 1473, Bouton had become Captain of the Guard and Master of the Household to Margaret's brother Philip but, after the Hapsburg's death in 1506, had transferred to the service of Philip's son, Prince Charles. Thomas Boleyn may have crossed to England to meet his daughter, but it was Bouton who accompanied her back to Margaret's court, probably as part of an exchange. This can also help date Anne's arrival. That April, Margaret had dispatched a young Burgundian of similar age to join the household of Princess Mary Tudor, to help cement her intended marital alliance with Prince Charles. It seems likely that Bouton delivered his charge to the English court and returned home with Anne. He was clearly a trusted member of the Burgundian household who may have placed his own daughter among Margaret's eighteen *Demoiselles d'Honneur.* According to Pierre Palliot, who wrote a history of the Bouton family in 1671, he also had three sons.

It has been suggested[1] that to entrust a girl of twelve to Bouton's care would have been inappropriate, because Anne was of an age to be considered a woman. Therefore, the argument goes, such a girl would have required a female chaperone. Although this could be construed as a plausible point in favour of an earlier birth date for Anne, who may have been safer in his hands as a six-year-old than a twelve-year-old, it overlooks what is known about Bouton's character and career, as well as the lack of information surrounding her journey. Firstly, it is not known who else did accompany Anne, and it would have been very unusual, if not unheard of, for a girl of her rank not to travel with at least one female servant. A woman would have attended to Anne's personal needs, and served as a companion and safeguard of her virtue, while the Captain of the Guard ensured their safety and ease of conduct. Secondly, Bouton's years of service and status at the Burgundian court guaranteed his chivalric conduct: such a man would not have been entrusted with the task if there were any doubts about his character, nor could he hope to escape any consequences had he acted inappropriately. Anne's reputation would also have been well guarded by Bouton's fame as a poet, author of *Éloge des Femmes,* in praise of women, and his citing as the possible author of the moral work *Miroir des Dames et de Mademoiselles.* Margaret selected Bouton for the task because he was above reproach.

A more serious challenge to the argument for the earlier date of birth for Anne is the presence of another English child at the Burgundian court later that year. The eldest daughter of Henry VIII's closest friend, Charles Brandon, the young Anne Brandon, was definitely born in 1506 or 1507, making her only six or seven years old, far too young to have been accepted into Margaret's household as a *demoiselle d'honneur.* It may simply be that Anne Brandon was not present in that capacity, but as a guest, the daughter of a friend, rather than an official appointee. Charles Brandon would visit the court that summer, where he appears to have indulged in a flirtation with Margaret, jokingly making a proposal of marriage by taking a ring of hers as part of a courtly game; prompting one source to refer to the couple being 'entangled in a compromising affair'.[2] Margaret viewed the badinage more seriously. Apparently Henry encouraged his friend to propose, but Margaret objected to the removal of her ring, calling Brandon a thief and issuing statements confirming her famous intention never to wed.[3] Anne Brandon's mother was dead, and the child may have been travelling with her father while he was on diplomatic business, remaining in the safety of Margaret's protection while Brandon and the king lay siege to Thérouanne and Tournai. Brandon may have been hoping to forge closer personal links with Margaret by entrusting her with his daughter but after this failed, and he remarried, Anne Brandon was summoned home.

In the early summer of 1513, Anne found herself heading towards a court whose relationship with England in the last fifty years had been close. Leading the way in material culture, in elaborate costumes, architecture and pageantry, the Burgundian courts of Philip the Good and Charles the Bold in the 1460s and 1470s had influenced that of Edward IV. Having hosted Burgundian-style jousts and married his sister to Charles in 1468, in what was described by eye-witnesses as 'the wedding of the century', Edward had sought shelter there during exile from his kingdom in 1470–71. Successfully reclaiming his throne, he restructured his household along lines drawn up by Bouton's cousin, Oliver de la Marr, and adopted more elaborate Burgundian rituals. Likewise, fashions in architecture had influenced the construction of Henry VII's Richmond Palace, which Thomas Boleyn knew well, but Anne did not at this stage. However, she may have already developed a taste for the latest developments in music and manuscript illumination being created in Flemish centres such as those under Margaret's patronage. The special relationship had foundered when Charles' widow, Margaret of York, supported pretenders to the English throne against the Tudors in the 1490s but, following her death and that of Duke Philip, ties had once again been strengthened. Henry VII had tried, and failed, to woo Margaret to become his second wife, but she had been happy to negotiate the Treaty of Calais with him in 1507, and to betroth his daughter Mary to her nephew Charles. As the grandson of Edward IV and husband of Margaret's former sister-in-law, Henry VIII was keen to resurrect the connection and form an alliance against France.

By the second decade of the sixteenth century, Margaret of Austria, Princess of Asturias and Duchess of Savoy, had become one of the most powerful and influential women in Europe. According to Jean Lamaire, her court historian, Margaret was skilled in 'vocal and instrumental music' having been taught by the organist Govard Nepotis, 'in painting and in rhetoric' and 'in the French as well as Spanish language'. A contemporary visitor described Margaret herself as 'not unpleasant looking and her appearance is truly imperial and her smile full of charm'[4] and Castiglione referred to her as one of the 'noblest' examples of contemporary womanhood, who governed her state 'with the greatest wisdom and justice'.[5] Jean Molinet, her almoner and librarian, praised using the typical symbol of the Marguerite, or daisy, a floral metaphor for most influential women of the time who bore the name. Molinet then proceeds to cite her splendour, virtue, honour, goodness and renown, her stoicism after having lost three husbands and the universal love in which she was held. Her home was the city of Mechelen (Malines in French) in the Netherlands, around 150 miles east of Calais and 18 miles south of Antwerp. Perhaps Anne smiled when she noted the existence of a small village called Hever, lying five miles to the south-east of the city on the River Dijle. Antonio Beatis, a papal secretary who visited Mechelen in 1517, three years after Anne's residence, described it as 'a superb city, very large and well-fortified. Nowhere have we seen streets so spacious and elegant… a number of canals whose waters follow the movement of the oceans traverse the city.'[6] As Anne arrived, she would have seen well-ordered streets and squares, dotted with churches, bisected with canals, and found an overall air of prosperity. The cathedral dedicated to St Rumbold dominated the main square, with its gothic tower still under construction. Anne may have worshipped there with her hosts. The tower was never completed, its top left flat for want of money.

Margaret's initial residence was at La Cour de Cambray, the Palace where Margaret of York had lived, but this was not large enough so she persuaded her father, Maximilian, to purchase the building opposite, owned by a man named Jérôme Lauwrin, of which she took possession in July 1507.[7] Margaret developed her new residence, known as the Hof van Savoye, situated on the corner of Keizerstraat and Korte Maagdenstraat, with new wings added between 1507 and 1526, designed by Rombaut Keldermans of Malines and Guyot de Beauregard of Savoy. Its inner courtyard was a dazzling mix of patterned red brick, tall, narrow stepped gable-ends, long windows and shorter dormer ones topped with gables, archways and sloping roofs, colonnaded walks and flower beds. Anne would have known this garden and the southern wing, which have changed little since her stay.[8]

Anne's safe arrival, and the good impression she swiftly made, were confirmed in a letter from Margaret to Thomas Boleyn. Anne had been presented to her by Esquire Bouton. She wrote the girl was 'very welcome to me'. Margaret hoped

> …to treat her in such a fashion that you will have reason to be content with it; at least be sure that until your return there need be no other intermediary between you and me than she; and I find her of such good address and so pleasing in her youthful age that I am more beholden to you for having sent her to me than you are to me.[9]

It was an excellent start for the intelligent, personable young girl, who found herself admitted to a court of the highest standards. The place, along with Margaret's character and accomplishments, were to provide Anne with a standard that would shape her character and set her aspirations high.

Anne's origins and her later rise to power has been the subject of much debate amongst historians. The ascent of the Boleyn family from city to court, and then into the king's confidence and his bed, has seen them labelled as social climbers, or opportunists, parvenus or nouveau riches, but their rapid rise through the social ranks was typical of the time, it was facilitated by the fluctuations arising from the post-plague economic context. The times were right for self-made men, and there were many of them, perhaps just less prominent in the history books. Henry's chief ministers, Thomas Wolsey and Thomas Cromwell, both attracted similar criticism for having been advanced on the basis of merit, rather than rank, and in this, Henry VIII was breaking with tradition, rewarding servants with ability, but also with whom he developed a strong personal relationship. His intimate circle was based on personality; his own, and that of those he chose to have about him. It would also underpin his choice of Anne, whom he chose for her worth rather than her family's pedigree. Yet Anne's origins were certainly not humble, as some historians have claimed; her Hoo, Butler and Howard descent and her placement in Margaret's household show this. Her intelligence and desire to improve certainly came from the example she witnessed from her father, and her knowledge of his recent ancestors, but as a young woman at the Mechelen court, her sense of her own intrinsic worth, her value as a marital commodity, was clarified by Margaret's influence. She may not have been born royal but, by the time she attracted Henry's attention, her demeanour, intelligence and her culture were queenly.

With eighteen demoiselles in her household and having access to some of the most significant artists of the day, Margaret offered the most desirable finishing school for the girls of well-connected families. It was a coup for Boleyn to have secured a place there for his daughter, and must have put him in expectations of her making an impressive European match. Anne is listed in the correspondence of the Emperor among the 'maids of honour and other women ordered by Madame to eat with them that are XVIII, to know: Mesdames de Verneul, Waldich, Reynenebourg, Bréderode, d'Aultroy, Hallewyn, Rosimbos, Longueval, Bullan, the two girls Neufville, Saillant, Middelbourg, Deer, Barbe Lallemand and the mother'.[10] She could anticipate being given the kind of European 'polish' that was usually reserved for princesses, marking a further rise in the status and expectations of the Boleyns, as she entered the household along with the young Hapsburgs, Prince Charles, grandson of the Emperor, and his three sisters, Eleanor, Isabel and Mary, all future queens.

English ambassador Sir Richard Wingfield had described the four siblings earlier that year in a letter to Henry VII, in which he emphasised their Hapsburg characteristic of being very tall and thin: 'The sight of whom (as I deem) was neither much pleasant or comfortable... for, blessed be God, they be all right and fair and tall, and go right up upon their joints and limbs.'[11] Wingfield described an occasion when he was summoned to the great hall of the palace to converse with Margaret, and observed the prince and his sisters dancing.[12] Again, assuming Anne's birth to have taken place in 1501, she was of an age with these young members of European royalty, with Eleanor aged fifteen, Charles thirteen, Mary nine and Isabella twelve, the same age as Anne in 1513. What they made of the young English girl, and what she made of them, is unknown. Fifteen years later, when pushed to make a decision regarding Henry VIII's efforts to divorce his wife and marry Anne, Charles would follow family and come down on the side of his aunt Catherine.

The maids of honour and women under Margaret's roof were under the charge of Elisabeth, Countess of Hochstrate[13] (née van Culemborg) the last sovereign lady of the fiefdom of Culemborg. An honoured, cultured and respected figure, she was thirty-eight in the year of Anne's arrival, and known as a devout Catholic. Later in life she would suppress heretical books, including the works of Erasmus, also present at Margaret's court in 1513. Whatever the young Anne may have thought of her formidable *dame d'honneur* as a girl, her religious sympathies would later fall more in line with the reformists.

Anne would have known Anna de Beaumont, who was in charge of the girls' chamber, herself the child of an illegitimate daughter of the king of Aragon, and married to Juan de Mendoza, from a line of Spanish noblemen. There was also the learned Marguerite de Poitiers, engaged as a tutor to the younger Mary Hapsburg and Margaret's own apothecary, the Countess de Horne, who supplied her with preserves considered good for her health.[14]

Despite the involvement of so many influential women, Margaret was unquestionably head of her household and set the tone by which she wished her young charges to live. She advised them in particular to avoid gossiping and foolish conversations and led them in sensible, enriching pursuits, exciting rides through the forests of Boisfort, Scheplaken and Groenendael[15] and in quieter pursuits, spinning flax, sewing shirts or playing chess with the ivory or red and green painted pieces listed in Margaret's inventory. Anne's role was to be a general attendant upon the household, to run errands, dance and join in with the entertainments provided for visitors, to do well at her lessons, learn good manners and be a general companion to Margaret and the other girls. It is clear from one of Anne's letters that she was taught French by an individual referred to as 'Semmonet', who appears in the household records as Symonet, but she would have received instruction from, or failing that, felt the influence of, a number of exceptional figures who were also gathered under Margaret's roof. The physician Cornelius Agrippa was employed by the Archduchess as her counsellor, having formerly been sent by her to lecture at the University of Dole, where he wrote *De nobilitate et praecellentia foeminae sexus*, an attempt to prove that women were the superior sex. There was also Hendrik Bredemers, court organist and music teacher, who gave the Hapsburg children daily lessons on the clavichord and composer Josquin des Prez, the first master of the high Renaissance polyphonic style in singing. The year before Anne's arrival, Adrian of Utrecht, the future pope, had been appointed as full-time tutor to Prince Charles and, in 1514, as mentioned, Utrecht's protégé, the Dutch Renaissance scholar Desiderius Erasmus, an influence upon Martin Luther, was appointed as Margaret's advisor.

It is likely that Anne had supervised access to Margaret's extensive library. An incomplete list of its contents compiled in 1516 includes 184 books, although a second version dating from 1523 lists 355 works.[16] It contained a mixture of religious, historical, classical, literary, genealogical and political texts from the past and some of the latest books written and published during Margaret's lifetime. The languages of these texts were probably largely French and Latin, although others had been translated into English, but their use may not have been confined to individual reading; accounts of the lives of great ladies around the turn of the century record that improving texts formed a regular part of the daily timetable, being read aloud at meal times, or in the evening, so Anne may well have heard extracts of some of them or seen the illuminations of the famous *Très Riches Heures du Duc de Berry*. Margaret also owned a number of Bibles; St Augustine's *City of God*, originally written in Latin; *Lives of the Saints* and *The Golden Legend* by Jacobus de Varagine, which was the most popular hagiographical text of the middle ages, being printed in every European language. There were four volumes of Froissart's chronicle, written at the end of the fourteenth century, editions of the lives of the Evangelists, lives of Titus Livius, Julius Caesar, Seneca's Letters, Aristotle, Ovid, Boethius, Ptolemy and Alexander the Great. The library contained a text described as *The Nature of Birds*, probably Hugh of Fouilloy's *Avarium,* and Gaston Fébus' *Book of Hunting*, composed between 1387 and 1389, and dedicated to the then Duke of Burgundy.

Margaret had copies of an anonymous Breton lai called 'Le Doon' or 'Doon', in which a knight laboured to win a lady; various Arthurian legends (although Thomas Malory is not specifically named in the list); several books by Giovanni Boccaccio, probably *The Decameron*; the story of Jason and the Golden Fleece, perhaps Raoul Lefèvre's French version of 1464, written when he was chaplain to Philip, Duke of Burgundy, or Caxton's translation from the mid-1470s; and *The Chronicles of Troy*, perhaps Lydgate's version, completed around 1420.[17] Margaret also owned *The Mirror of the World*, an early encyclopaedia published by Caxton in 1481, *The Art of Chivalry*, which may have been the Catalan Ramon Llull's 'The Book of the Order of Chivalry', and the *Dictes and Sayings of the Poets*; either the French version by Guillaume de Thionville, based on an Arabic text, or the English version, translated by Anthony Woodville and the first book printed by Caxton in English. The library also included *The Fortress of Faith*, a Christian tract against Islam, written in fifteenth-century Spain, and a copy of Niccolò Machiavelli's *The Prince*, which was in circulation from the year of Anne's arrival in Mechelen. One surprising item found among Margaret's shelves, which Anne and the other girls are likely to have been shielded from, is described in the inventory as 'Sidrak'. *The Book of Sydrac*, also known as *Sidrak and Bokkus*, written in thirteenth-century French, but widely read and translated by the sixteenth century, contains explicit material about sexual relations between men and women.[18]

Margaret was also a considerable patron of the visual arts. Her inventories list the kinds of works that Anne may have seen hanging on the walls of her palaces, giving the young girl a sophisticated taste far beyond that she would have yet developed at Hever. Margaret owned Van Eyck's Arnolfini portrait, Juan de Flanders' 'The Marriage Feast at Cana' and at least one work by Hieronymous Bosch. Among the artists actively working at her court were the Romanist Jan Gossaert, also known as Jan Mabuse, who imported techniques from the southern Renaissance, predominantly Italian, into northern Europe; the Venetian Jacopo de Barbari, making maps, engravings and trompe l'oeil still lifes; and Bernard van Orley, painter of tryptichs and designer of carpets.[19] The year after Anne's departure, Margaret would employ the miniaturist Gerard Horenbout, who would later move to England with his artist children, Lucas and Susanna, and paint the members of Henry VIII's court. These works captured a sense of playfulness and intelligence in art, where techniques established a relationship between artist and viewer demanding that questions be posed and answered, rather than a simpler function as decoration, status symbol or focus for devotion.

Walking through the rooms of the Palace, Anne is likely to have seen the portraits of Margaret's family that were listed in the inventory. There was one of her father, the Emperor Maximilian, dressed in cloth of gold and holding flowers in his hand, while another 'most exquisite' one of Margaret herself had been painted by 'Master Jacques'. One picture portrayed the Archduchess with her short-lived husband, Juan, Prince of Asturias, brother of Catherine of Aragon, whose coronation as queen of England Anne would have heard about from her parents. They were featured alongside their saintly namesakes, St Margaret and St John the Evangelist. There was also a 'little old double tableau' portraying Margaret and her brother Philip the handsome, wearing cloth of gold, painted in the time of their minority. His name would have been familiar to Anne, who could now put a face to that name for the first time. Thomas Boleyn had been Esquire of the Body at the time of Philip's visit to England in 1505, involved in the reception and celebration of the prince whose appearance and chivalric manner had left such an impression upon the future Henry VIII, then aged fourteen, that the youth hung a picture of his role model in his chamber. So Anne was exposed to a formidable dynasty, whose long-established influence stretched across Europe with far more impact than the young Tudor family, who had only occupied the throne so far for thirty years. Living among the Hapsburgs on a daily basis gave her an almost paradoxical intimacy with, and respect for, royalty.

There were exotic items in Margaret's household too; portraits of men and women in Spanish, Italian and Portuguese dress and, among Margaret's possessions, a tunic and pearls from India, a dead bird of paradise wrapped in taffeta, branches of coloured coral and tapestries from Turkey and Morocco. These influences, stemming from a formidable mentor, placed Anne at the heart of the European humanist Renaissance, at a stage of her life when her opinions and tastes were being formed. They gave her a perspective beyond the narrow focus of an island nation: while abroad, Anne developed a European picture, even a world picture, so far as the world was then known. Perhaps in a quiet moment she pored over Margaret's *mappa mundi*.

Anne had only been away from home a few months before the arrival of the English king in Europe. After Thomas Boleyn has secured Margaret's support, Henry VIII had gone ahead with his plan to invade France, winning the Battle of the Spurs on August 16 and capturing the town of Thérouanne. Margaret sent Lord Ravestein to convey to Henry her desire to entertain him, for his 'pastime' and 'repose' after his 'long travail', inviting him to the city of Lille, to 'see his brother the Prince and the ladies of the court of Burgundy'. In response, as chronicler Hall tells us, Henry mounted his horse, dressed in cloth of silver slashed with gold and a border of red roses, and put on fresh armour set with jewels. The city of Lille was a convenient middle point between Henry and Margaret but it was still just over forty miles from Thérouanne and eighty miles from Mechelen. Margaret would not have taken her entire household on the journey, but given that she invited Henry specifically to see the ladies of her court, the chances are that her eighteen demoiselles did travel with her, including the twelve-year-old Anne. It is known that Anne was among the party when Margaret travelled to Brussels in the summer of 1514, increasing the chances that she was included in this party too. Henry appointed the Duke of Buckingham, Marquis of Dorset, Earl of Essex and Lord Lisle to attend him 'and diverse others'.[20] Given his previous relationship with Margaret, it is also more than likely that Thomas Boleyn was among these 'others' when Henry arrived at Lille on 10 September. Another indication is that his expenses were paid by the king's almoner, Thomas Wolsey, in Lille on 16 October.

September 1513 may well have been the first time that Anne Boleyn saw Henry VIII. She could hardly fail to see him, although understandably the victorious king may have paid little or no attention to a twelve-year-old girl among his hostess's retinue. At twenty-two, he was tall, handsome, athletic, dazzling in his jewels, silver and gold fabrics, the epitome of chivalry and majesty. Henry was granted the keys to the town and rode through the streets of Lille like a young God, displaying the fleur-de-lys symbol of France and with swords and maces borne before him. Flaming torches lit his way and 'goodly pageants' welcomed the English all the way through the medieval streets to the Palace Rihour, where he was 'humbly saluted' by Maximilian, Margaret and Charles.

The Palace had been completed in 1477 by the Emperor's father-in-law, Charles the Bold, a huge quadrangle of a building, of which only a section remains. Still standing though, is a fifteenth-century staircase, giving a flavour of the palace where Margaret of Savoy went to meet Henry, expressing 'deep reverence'. He was lodged in four rooms hung with Margaret's tapestries, worked with gold, and containing a bed of gold, decorated with the arms of Spain. Although they began eating in their separate chambers, Margaret rose from the banquet in her quarter, took her plate with her and went to sup with the king, accompanied by some of her principal damsels, which would have afforded a good view of the king for the young Anne. There was dancing that night, during which Henry stripped down to his shirt and kicked off his shoes, before presenting the ladies with a 'beautiful diamond in a setting of great value'.[21]

While Henry was in Lille, the city of Tournai fell, and news arrived that Scotland had invaded. The city submitted to the English besiegers on 13 September, while Henry's brother-in-law, James IV of Scotland, had taken the opportunity to cross the border during Henry's absence. Henry dashed off to Tournai, taking his leave of his three hosts 'and all the ladies (for) all his high cheer and solace'.[22] There, on 25 September, he received the King of Scots' gauntlets as a sign of his death at the battle of Flodden Field, defeated by an English army led by the Earl of Surrey and Anne's grandfather, Thomas Howard. Henry set up a tent of gold to celebrate and invited Margaret and Charles to visit him, arranging a joust and a tilting competition in their honour. On 11 October, he rode out of the city to meet his guests 'and diverse other nobles of their countries and them brought into Tournai with great triumph'. This was the occasion when Charles Brandon 'made request of marriage' to Margaret and removed her ring. Margaret's party stayed with Henry for ten days, with Henry attended by knights dressed in purple velvet and gold, repelling all challengers before taking a 'lap of honour' riding about the yard and doing 'great reverence' to the ladies.[23] That night Henry hosted a banquet of a hundred dishes, after which there was a masked ball, which Anne would have attended, witnessing the king's golden mask being 'cast off' by the ladies.[24] Watching this tall, beautiful, lusty young man at play, this epitome of early Renaissance manhood, Anne cannot have foreseen the role he would play in her future.

The principal purpose of Margaret's 'finishing school' was for the young women to make good marriages. Despite the wave of humanist thought that led to young aristocratic women studying Latin and Greek, theology and law, marriage was still the ultimate goal. Margaret took an active interest in negotiating and arranging these events, providing a trousseau and requesting a position in the Imperial household for their husbands.[25] By the time of Anne's arrival, arrangements were already being made for the matches of the three Hapsburg princesses: eventually, Eleanor would become Queen of Portugal, Isabel, would be Queen of Denmark and Mary became Queen of Hungary. In the summer of 1514, Mary left the Burgundian court to pay a visit to her future husband and that July Isabel was betrothed by proxy in a ceremony held near Brussels. In a letter to her father, Margaret described the occasion, which she organised at short notice, taking place in front of the great hall on the morning of Trinity Sunday. The promises were made, with great solemnity, before all those concerned went to hear high mass. Later that day, there was a great supper, dances and tournaments, before the formal 'bedding' ceremony of the bride and the groom's stand-ins. Prince Charles danced so much that he made himself ill, performing his role with such diligence that he came down with a fever the following day. Anne was among the ladies feasting and dancing, absorbing an understanding of court ritual and the nature of royal weddings, perhaps even wondering when her time would come.

Margaret's letter was dated 12 June, from Brussels, but she was probably at the Palace of Tervuren, or Veure, located just seven miles from the city centre. Her court resided there from 1 June until 31 August, 1514[26] and Anne was definitely with her. Veure was a royal palace with a 700-acre park and hunting grounds, commonly used as a Hapsburg family retreat during the warm weather. It had been established in the thirteenth century by Henry I, Duke of Brabant, and developed into a royal palace over the following centuries, before being demolished in 1782. A print surviving from 1726 shows it dominated by a large central building with gabled roof, rising high above the three- or four-storey range with its long windows and turreted towers. There is a drawbridge across the wide moat, and an artificial square island is laid out in formal gardens.

It was while the court was at Veure that summer that the political situation changed, necessitating Anne's removal from Margaret's court. Having pushed Thomas Boleyn to ensure Burgundian support for him against the French, Henry now broke the long-standing engagement between Prince Charles and Princess Mary Tudor, and swiftly arranged a new match for his sister to the ageing Louis XII of France. They were betrothed by proxy at Greenwich Palace on 13 August 1514, with the beautiful eighteen-year-old writing to her fifty-two-year-old bridegroom that she would 'love him as cordially as she can' and claimed to have heard the vows repeated on his behalf 'with great pleasure'.[27] A formal consummation took place, with Mary taking to her bed in a state of undress 'in the presence of many witnesses'. The Duke de Longueville acted as proxy for Louis: dressed in a doublet and red hose, 'but with one leg naked from the middle of the thigh downward, he went into bed and touched the Princess with his naked leg. The marriage was then declared consummated.'[28]

Thomas Boleyn may have felt distressed at this embarrassing volte face, but he was first and foremost the king's servant. His position was a difficult one but, with the shrewdness of a politician, he knew what he needed to do. The very day after witnessing the proxy wedding, he wrote to Margaret from Greenwich, requesting Anne's departure, as Henry required attendants who could speak French to serve his sister in her new role as Queen of France. It seems that Mary had asked directly for Anne:

'the sister of the King my maiden Mary Reyne fyancee of France has asked me to have with her my daughter the little Boulain, whom my lady is now with you in your court.'[29] Something of the ambassador's feelings, and his tactful tone, can be glimpsed in his comment that he 'neither could nor knew how to refuse' the king's request.[30] It may well be that Boleyn had always intended Anne to enter Mary Tudor's household and that Anne's dispatch to the Netherlands had been a reflection of Henry's earlier foreign policy. Now that the bridegroom had changed, so had the location; requiring Anne to reject Burgundy for France. Margaret's reaction was probably a combination of surprise and disappointment, perhaps annoyance: the move represented an insult to her and her family and she may have not been willing to relinquish Anne easily. The girl had made good progress, as several of her contemporaries later recalled. Lancelot de Carles, Bishop of Riez, born in 1508, who would witness Anne's end and record it in verse, related that 'la Boullant... at an early age had come to court, listened carefully to honourable ladies, setting herself to bend all her endeavour to imitate them to perfection... made such good use of her wits that in no time at all she had command of the language'.[31]

Given that Margaret left Tervuren on 21 August, it must have been in the week following that Anne wrote to her father in French, in the first surviving letter by her hand, not all of which is decipherable:

Sir, I understand by your letter that you desire that I shall be a worthy woman when I come to the court and you inform me that the queen will take the trouble to converse with me, which rejoices me much to think of talking with a person so wise and worthy. This will make me have greater desire to continue to speak French well and also spell especially because you have so enjoined it on me, and with my own hand I inform you that I will observe it the best I can. Sir, I beg you to excuse me if my letter is badly written, for I assure you that the orthography is from my own understanding alone, while the others were only written by my hand, and Semmonet tells me the letter but wants so that I may do it myself, for fear that it shall not be known unless I acquaint you, and I pray you that the light of [?] may not be allowed to drive away the will which you say you have to help me, for it seems that you are sure ? you can, if you please, make me a declaration of your word, and concerning me be certain that there shall be neither ?nor ingratitude which might check or efface my affection, which is determined to ? as much unless it shall please you to order me, and I promise you that my love is based on so great strength that it will never grow less, and I will make an end to my [?] after having commended myself right humbly to your good grace. Written at Veure by your very humble and very obedient daughter Anna de Boullan.[32]

She expressed the conventional wishes to make her father proud and bring honour upon her family, also to reassure him of her gratitude and loyalty, in spite of difficult circumstances. In this context, the queen whom she mentioned must have been Mary Tudor, who was being referred to at the English court as the Queen of France, since 13 August that year. No doubt Anne experienced some disappointment to be leaving a court where she had done so well, which had provided her with such a contrast to the quiet Kentish countryside, placing her at the heart of a vibrant, colourful centre of culture. Perhaps she would also miss the impressive mentor who had been so impressed by the young girl's abilities and had offered her such an opportunity.

The court of France was not as sophisticated as the Burgundian one, but Anne knew that greater adventures lay ahead, and the chance to serve an anointed queen. Her reaction to the situation also helps confirm her age, showing a sensitivity, understanding and sense of duty way beyond that of a seven-year-old. She had witnessed, first hand, that the marriage market could be subject to sudden change and that the English king was a man to act upon his whims, even if it meant sacrificing his beautiful young sister to a man old enough to be her grandfather.

SEVEN

Among the Valois 1514–15

On October 9, 1514, at Abbeville, the beautiful eighteen-year-old Mary Tudor was married to the prematurely aged Louis XII, King of France. In her lavish apartments in the Hotel de Gruthuse, overlooking the pleasure gardens, Mary's ladies had brushed out her red-gold hair, placed a coronet of gems on top of her head and dressed her in gold brocade, decorated with diamond clasps and edged with ermine. The ceremony was held in a room hung with gold, where the royal couple spoke their vows and the young Tudor princess became Queen of France. Following the ceremony, she retired to dine in secluded splendour, before it was time for her ladies in waiting to prepare her for bed, for the consummation of the marriage, which was required to seal its legitimacy. Their practised fingers would have unlaced her elaborate clothes, removed her jewels and helped her into the perfumed sheets, to await the arrival of her husband. Their job done, the women melted away, the chosen few gentlewomen who could anticipate a life in service at the French court, with all the sophistication it may bring and, for some, the possibility of finding a husband among the French nobility.

There was certainly a 'Madamoyselle Boleyne' listed among the nine women 'appointed to have abidden in France with the French Queen'[1] but it was not Anne. Anne's elder sister Mary accompanied her namesake from Calais and was by her side on her wedding day. When the majority of the new queen's women were dismissed, much to her consternation, Mary Boleyn was among those who remained, perhaps because the task had been executed by her grandfather, Thomas Howard. Despite Thomas Boleyn's letter of summons to the Netherlands, Anne does not appear to have arrived at the French court yet, or else she was present in a different capacity to that which he had intended. She was not included in the list of servants retained two days after the wedding when most of Mary's women were dismissed, or the payments made by royal almoner Thomas Wolsey for service during October and November that year. Anne's name is conspicuous by its absence. If she arrived in France in the winter of

1514, we would expect to see her named on the next quarterly payments roll, but such a document does not exist, because Louis XII died on 1 January and the queen's household was disbanded. The period from mid-1514 until her return to England early in 1522 is something of a mystery, undocumented, but a few details leave the ghost of a trail and the circumstances of her life are not entirely unrecoverable.

Firstly, it is unclear exactly when Anne left Margaret's court, and whether she went directly from there to France. Margaret's household departed from Tervuren on 21 August, just days after Anne received her father's letter, which was not necessarily sufficient time to release the girl from her duties or to tie up the loose ends of her stay. Anne may have needed to return to Mechelen to say her goodbyes, or collect possessions, rather than leaving straight from Brussels for France. Had she left at once, the most likely, and closest, location was Calais, 150 miles due west, where she may have waited for the arrival of the English party in September 1514. Some historians have suggested she returned home to Hever, or even travelled to Greenwich to meet her father, but the timings suggest it is unlikely that she crossed the Channel again in the interval before the wedding. It was hardly worth her while to return to Greenwich only to leave again immediately; given the dates, it would have been too close a schedule, dependent upon the weather and tides, raising the possibility that she would have missed Mary's party. Only seven weeks elapsed between the letter and the wedding, barely long enough to make adequate arrangements. It would seem far more practical that she would have waited for her father and the court at Calais, but there is no record of this.

One alternative is that Margaret did not release Anne at once. This may have been for practical reasons, but perhaps the Archduchess was unwilling to dance to Henry's tune after the snub he had given her nephew. It would have been in keeping with her character and position, and contemporary codes of behaviour, for her to have retained Anne in order to reassert her authority, to remind Henry of his former appreciation, not quite out of pique, but more from wounded dignity. It may even have been that she suspected Henry had rearranged his sister's marriage on a whim, and might still be won back to the Burgundian alliance. She may also have been waiting for confirmation that the French union was definitely going ahead, doubting the veracity of the initial reports.

Regardless of the powerplay between rulers, court life had to go on. On 21 August, Margaret left Tervuren to visit the Zeeland Islands[2] and Anne may have gone too. There is always a chance that, if it was only written on August 14, and given the rate of travel and dependence upon sea-crossing, Boleyn's letter did not reach Tervuren before Margaret's party left. If this was the case, Anne's letter was not composed in reply to it, but in response to an earlier suggestion, in reference to a different queen, perhaps even the possibility of entering the service of Catherine of England once Anne returned home.

The Zeeland islands lay to the extreme west of Margaret's domain, comprising a number of peninsulas, islands and a strip of land bordering modern Belgium. Its capital was Middelburg, on the western end of the central portion of the area, Midden-Zeeland, around eighty miles north-west of Turveuren. Margaret would either have travelled via Ghent in the west, up to the coast and making the short river crossing from Ternuezen or Breskens, or travelled north through Brussels and Antwerp, allowing the journey to take place entirely by road. Middleburg was an important trading centre with England and, if she stayed there, Anne would have heard English being spoken at the docks and squares, flanked by red-brick stepped-gable buildings, or even in the eleventh-century cathedral. She would have seen a very different kind of landscape to that with which she was accustomed, dotted with windmills, islets in rivers, deltas, mudflats and beaches. Margaret is likely to have stayed at the gothic Abbey dedicated to Our Lady, which had been founded by monks from Antwerp. Yet Margaret's movements are unclear, as are Anne's. No evidence places Anne at the Archduchess's side during the late summer of 1514, although her presence there would explain her absence from France and fit with the little that is known. Her departure was definitely prompted by Mary's wedding, as Lancelot de Carles, Bishop of Riez, confirmed during his visit to England in 1536, stating that 'Anne Boullant first came from this country when Mary left to go to join the King in France to bring about the alliance of the two sovereigns'.[3] All that can be stated for certain is that at some point in late 1514 or early 1515, Anne arrived at the French court.

The death of Louis XII after just seventy-nine days of marriage left Queen Mary and her ladies in a difficult situation. He had suffered from a severe case of gout over the Christmas season and was given the last rites early in the morning of 1 January 1515, dying the same day at the age of fifty-two. His heir was the elder of his two daughters, Claude of France, who had been married to her cousin Francis, Duke of Valois, the previous May. As explained by the chronicler Holinshed, Francis was 'preferred to succession of the kingdom before the daughters of the dead king by virtue and disposition of the Salic Law, a law very ancient in the realm of France, which excluded from the royal dignity all women'.[4] Thus Francis was poised to become Francis I, but only in the eventuality that Louis had not fathered an heir in his final weeks. To ascertain whether or not the widowed Mary was pregnant, she was closeted away in her chambers at the Hôtel de Cluny with her ladies, a *reine blanche*, dressed head to toe in white gauze robes. The walls were draped in black and she was denied visitors. Mary Boleyn would have remained with her during this difficult time, and perhaps Anne too, although this is probably the moment when it was being decided that Anne would remain in France as a member of Claude's household. Either Mary's period must have arrived within a short time of her husband's death, or Francis acted impatiently, as his coronation took place on 25 January. It was not until 10 February that Henry VIII was informed that, despite rumours to the contrary, there was no chance that his sister was pregnant. Henry responded by dispatching a group, headed by his close friend, Charles Brandon, to establish Francis's intentions towards England, inventory Mary's valuables and bring her home. As it transpired, Brandon would exceed his mandate!

According to Mary herself, Francis's intentions towards England, specifically her person, may have been quite unexpected. It was during the period of seclusion that Mary Boleyn. and perhaps Anne, would have witnessed an uncomfortable development between Francis and the young widow. Aged twenty, Francis of Valois was tall and good-looking, characterised by his long nose and sexual appetite, but was described as great not on account of his 'tall stature and presence or his very regal majesty', as the chronicler Pierre de Brantôme explained, but 'on account of his virtues, valour, great deeds and high merits'.[5] Mary's account of his advances towards her as the *reine blanche* must be taken in the context of her later efforts to justify the secret marriage she made to Charles Brandon, before returning to England. She claimed that Francis had confessed himself in love with her and offered to put aside his wife, Claude, in order to marry her. The interest Francis showed in Mary was genuine and personal, pre-dating her widowhood, an embarrassing emotional development for which his mother had chastised him in December, just before the death of Louis.[6] Francis was prepared to overlook the fact that Claude was carrying her first child, a daughter born on 19 August that year, in his determination to switch wives. As Mary told it, Francis believed it a straightforward question of removing one wife for another for political and personal advantage, as Louis XII had done when putting aside his first wife in order to marry Anne of Brittany. Mary also suggested that Francis attempted to force himself upon her;[7] but this fits the narrative she told her angry brother that it was in self-defence, to preserve her virtue, that she chose marriage. Although Francis was certainly capable of making advances to Mary, had he actually impregnated her, his own position as heir would have been in jeopardy, as it would have been unclear whether the child had been fathered by he or Louis. Mary became increasingly upset, writing frantic letters from her confinement and Mary Boleyn was a witness to these exchanges, gaining a rapid lesson in royal male desire at the age of fifteen. Anne, at fourteen, was probably there too.[8]

Francis was well-known for his licentiousness, with commentators saying of his court that 'both maids and wives do oft-times trip, indeed do so customarily' and describing him in thinly veiled sexual metaphors as 'drinking' from many fountains and 'clothed' in women.[9] Reputed to have created spyholes in his palaces in order to watch women undressing and engaged in intimate acts, Francis would have been very aware of not just Mary's charms, but also those of the young women in her entourage. Later rumours that Mary Boleyn was seduced by Francis relate to this period, although their veracity cannot now be established. Mary was fifteen, the age at which the king himself had lost his virginity,[10] old enough to have been considered a target. It is entirely in keeping with what is known about Francis that he may have tried to seduce one of his wife's young, attractive maids, but his degree of success must have depended upon Mary's character and willingness to be seduced. After Anne's rise to power, Francis referred to her sister as 'a very great whore and infamous above all', his 'English mare', and described the dowager queen as 'more dirty than Queenly'.[11] However, some of this may relate to what Francis knew about Mary's later relationship with Henry VIII.

The extent of any relationship that took place between Francis and Mary is undocumented and recent historians have disputed whether it was of any significant duration, or even whether it happened at all. There is no evidence that Mary was seduced, or that she was of the flighty character that some historians have attributed to her. It may well be that she rejected or avoided the French king's advances, had they been forthcoming. Equally, it may have been a single encounter, or a connection of a few months' duration, entered into willingly by both partners. Francis' comments derive from 1536, long after Mary had been Henry's mistress, and the French king's standards for queenly comparison were the regal dignity of Catherine of Aragon and his memories of the long-suffering diligence of his first wife, Claude. In addition, they formed part of the anti-Boleyn feeling that accompanied Anne's fall and were reported in a letter written by the Papal Nuncio in Paris. It is not clear whether the author heard these words uttered by Francis in person, or whether he was repeating court gossip. The latter seems more likely, as Francis could have a sharp tongue, but he did insist on women being treated with respect and honour, placing this at the heart of his court's culture. Another reference to the affair comes from a letter penned by the Bishop of Faenza, Rodolfo Pio, who described Mary as Anne's sister 'whom the French King knew here in France', adding that she was 'a great prostitute and infamous above all'.[12] But this was written in January 1536 and other facts in the letter are incorrect, such as Mary's presence at court, when in fact, she had then been banished to the country. The case for Mary's liaison with the French king thus appears to stand on less solid ground. Similar salacious accusations were made about Anne in the period after her fall. The Catholic Nicholas Sander, publishing his account in 1585, related how Anne reputedly 'sinned first with her father's butler, and then with his chaplain' at the age of fifteen, giving this as the reason for her dispatch to France. He then related how 'soon afterwards she appeared at the French court, where she was called the English mare, because of her shameless behaviour, and then the royal mule, when she became acquainted with the king of France'.[13] Sander's confusion of facts and timing indicate that blackening Anne's name as a means of attacking her daughter, the Protestant Elizabeth I, was his purpose, rather than objective history.

Mary did not contract syphilis, which Francis was known to have, given all the mercury cures prescribed by his doctors. It is impossible to know which fateful encounter infected him, but any relationship with Mary would date from the very earliest days of his reign, so the chances are he was still clear of the disease. Based on a single sexual encounter with an infected king, the likelihood of Mary contracting syphilis herself were between three and ten per cent.[14] Had she done so, she would have displayed symptoms of sores, rashes and swellings that would have been remarked upon at the time. No such reports exist, and there is no evidence that Mary or, by extension, her children, were sufferers. It is possible that she and Francis had some short-term fling, or even a single encounter, from which Mary emerged physically unscathed, but it is equally likely that these rumours were politically motivated. The surviving evidence is insufficient to allow for a decisive conclusion to be drawn. The affair has been given as reason for Mary's recall to England in early 1515, but this can be equally explained by her continuing employment in the household of the dowager queen, who then left France, whilst Anne remained behind with Claude.

When Francis left Paris for Reims on 18 January, 1515, Queen Claude did not accompany him because of her pregnancy, which may well have exacerbated the range of existing physical problems that afflicted her. Despite her pedigree as the daughter of Louis, the marriage had not been a popular one. Pierre de Rohan, Marshal of Gié, told Francis' mother that he would rather see her son 'married to a simple shepherdess of this kingdom than to Madame Claude because the misfortune is such that Madame Claude is deformed in body and unable to bear children'.[15] However, Claude swiftly proved her critics wrong, by conceiving six months after the wedding. There was some truth to Rohan's claim about her appearance but this did not impede her primary dynastic purpose. And when the entire court expected her to die in childbirth at the age of fifteen, she proved herself a fighter and went on to bear seven more children.

Born in 1499, Claude was five years younger than her extrovert husband, and quite his opposite in appearance and character. Exuding a quiet dignity, she suffered from scoliosis, with the distinctive curved spine that gave her a hunched appearance and contributed to the regular pain she experienced in her legs; she was also very small and was afflicted by strabismus. In the *Commémoration* book dedicated to her in 1514, she is pictured as a tiny figure seated in a large throne, with her feet resting on a cushion of black and gold. While her contemporaries praised her virtues, sweet disposition and charity, some also remarked upon her ugliness. A posthumous illustration in the Book of Hours of her daughter-in-law, Catherine de Medici, shows Claude with a devout expression, her dark hair pulled back under a plain white hood, hands together in prayer, surrounded by her female relatives. Hers was a dynastic marriage but the tall, athletic Francis, her physical opposite, usually treated her with the dignity and respect due to a queen. It was even stated by one contemporary that he honoured her so highly that he spent every night in her bed whilst she was in Paris, only resorting to his mistresses during her absence. Whether or not he had genuinely intended to put her aside, Claude would remain his wife until her death.

The widowed queen Mary did not attend the coronation either, but she left the seclusion of the Hôtel de Cluny and was in central Paris to watch as Francis entered the capital as king on 13 February 1515. She also attended the celebratory banquet that followed, so Mary would have too, as well as Anne, in either the service of the widow or the new queen, Claude. Perhaps the Boleyn girls were also among the ten witnesses at the secret marriage of Mary Tudor to Charles Brandon on 3 March, which was an act of treason, against her brother's will, and for which the couple would have to beg forgiveness. When the newly-wed Brandons left Paris for England on 15 April, Mary Boleyn went with them, leaving Anne behind.

For the next six-and-a-half years, as far as can be ascertained, Anne was in the service of Queen Claude, but it would be a mistake to consider her to be consistently a member of the polished, hedonistic court of Francis I. The sybaritic new king has become something of a byword for licentiousness, his reputation as a seducer has cast a long shadow across his biography, sometimes eclipsing other aspects of his character and achievements. Francis was described by Brantôme as 'a goodly prince, stately of countenance, merry of cheer, brown coloured, great eyes, high nosed, big-lipped, fair breasted and shoulders, small legs and long feet'.[16] Over six feet tall, he had brown hair and a thick neck, a short beard and cleft chin, 'his eyes hazel and bloodshot, and his complexion the colour of watery milk... an agreeable voice and, in conversation, an animated expression'.[17] He loved fine clothes and was eloquent and charming in manner if, paradoxically, sometimes shy. He was energetic and active, loving to ride, hunt or perform in court entertainments, but was also a man of learning and letters, well-read and a composer of poetry.

Although the royal couple's lives frequently overlapped, Claude's court was not Francis's court, it was a separate establishment, far more quiet, withdrawn, moral and simple. Claude was devout and often unwell. She favoured the seclusion and peace of the countryside to her husband's colourful, peripatetic, energetic way of life. Brantôme described her as 'very good, very charitable and very gentle to all, never doing any unkindness or harm to anyone, either at her court or in the kingdom'. Over the course of her service, Anne would have had ample opportunities to observe and interact with the king but he was not her primary influence; more often she saw him through the filter of Claude, through the eyes of the young wife, frequently pregnant and ill, who played a limited role in Francis's life. Yet Claude and her circle were always a satellite of the king, as a miniature of the queen as a child illustrates. A French copy of Petrarch's *Remedies for Fortune Fair and Foul* depicts a four-year-old sitting on her mother's lap, surrounded by women of the court as seemingly an independent unit, worthy of veneration,[18] in an almost quasi-Madonna image. However, the artist cannot permit them to stand alone, reinforcing their relation to the king by giving over the lower left portion of the image to a depiction of masculine authority and need, in the figures of Reason and of King Louis himself, portrayed among his male advisors. The interaction with Reason also echoes a section of the text relating to Louis's concerns about his lack of a son, undermining the all-female central image, which had proved insufficient as an instrument of dynastic security. When it came to Claude's queenship, her position was even more marginalised by the presence of two other very powerful women at Francis's court.

Behind the new figure of the king, the Valois court was presided over by strong female presences, or what contemporaries referred to as the 'holy trinity' of Francis, his mother and sister. It would have been impossible for Anne Boleyn to avoid Louise of Savoy, Francis's formidable mother, made Duchess of Angoulême after his accession, and who would serve as regent in 1515 while he campaigned against Italy. Louise was forty at the time of her son's accession, and had been the main rival to Claude's mother, Anne of Brittany, during her lifetime. Widowed at nineteen, she was passionately interested in the southern Renaissance, in the Italian influence upon politics, the arts and sciences, giving her two children a humanist education, commissioning books for them and teaching Francis Spanish and Italian herself.

Then there was Francis's elder sister, Marguerite d'Alençon, later Queen of Navarre. Most famous as the author of the *Heptameron*, a collection of stories about illicit love, Marguerite has been described by one historian as the outstanding female figure of the Renaissance, in which Italian teachings and reformed thinking united. Another powerful, educated and cultured woman, her *Mirror of the Sinful Soul*, written in 1531, was a first-person narrative of a woman engaging in direct communication with God, and was read at the English court during Anne's ascendancy. In 1545, Anne's daughter, Princess Elizabeth, translated the work and presented it to her stepmother, Catherine Parr. As queen, Anne expressed affection for Marguerite and the desire to see her again, although the pair did not meet after Anne had returned to England. According to historian Will Durant,

> ...every free spirit looked upon her as protectoress and ideal... Marguerite was the embodiment of charity. She would walk unescorted in the streets of Navarre, allowing any one to approach her and would listen at first hand to the sorrows of the people. She called herself 'The Prime Minister of the Poor'.[19]

But there was also another powerful lesson that Anne could learn from Marguerite's life. In 1509, Marguerite had been married to Charles d'Alençon, second in line to the throne and the last line of his house. By the time of Anne's employment in Claude's court in 1515, and for the next six years, Marguerite and her husband repeatedly prayed and undertook pilgrimages in the hopes of conceiving a child. In seventeen years of marriage, which ended with Alençon's death in 1525, Marguerite did not conceive and his lands and title reverted to the crown, reinforcing for Anne the importance of producing a male heir.

The French court was essentially a peripatetic establishment, shifting between Paris and various favourite chateaux. While Francis's main residence was at Amboise, Claude's primary residence was at her childhood home, the Chateau of Blois, twenty miles to the north-east of her husband, where the wall carvings featured her devices of the ermine, knotted rope, full moon and the swan pierced by an arrow. When Anne arrived there for the first time, probably early in 1515, she would have been greeted by a fairy-tale castle of a style and scale she would not previously have seen. While Margaret of Austria's Burgundian court had echoed aspects of the northern Renaissance, it was still very much Low Countries in style, while the influence of Italian architecture had made its way into the commissions of the French kings of the late fifteenth and early sixteenth century.

EIGHT

French Renaissance 1515–19

A palace had been begun at Blois as early as the ninth century, overlooking the town and the river Loire, mid-way between the towns of Tours and Orléans, about eleven miles south-west of Paris. The area was subject to raids from the Vikings and in order to house and better protect their holy relics the monks built a chapel, which was soon joined by a tower and additional buildings, all enclosed by a grey stone gatehouse and walls. The large Estates General room, which still survives, was built in 1214, serving as the main hall, for feasting, meeting and dispensing justice, in a space of over 500 metres square, its roof supported by a row of six central pillars, painted bright blue and dotted with fleur-de-lys. Blois was developed by the poet Charles d'Orleans, who spent his final days there upon his release from England, where he had spent no fewer than twenty-five years in captivity after the Battle of Agincourt. It was the splendid venue where he entertained Margaret of Anjou in 1445, on the way to England and her wedding to Henry VI. Louis XII inherited the palace in 1498 and after redesigning the courtyard and palace in the Renaissance style, it became his favourite residence. In 1501 it was the venue when the king welcomed Philip of Burgundy, brother-in-law of Catherine of Aragon and Henry VIII. After his accession, Francis I would redesign it again, introducing a grand central staircase inspired by the architecture of the Vatican and laying out ornamental gardens. He brought Pacello da Mercogliano to France from Italy to design the terraced parterres at both Amboise and Blois.

Anne found a cultured world at Blois, comparable to that she had experienced under Margaret of Austria but far quieter and on a smaller, more introspective scale. The chateau contained the impressive library of Anne of Brittany's manuscripts, which later became the core of the

Bibliothèque Nationale de France and included the splendid primer that Anne of Brittany commissioned for Claude when she was five years old, which featured the alphabet, prayers and the story of salvation, as well as the *Grande Heures* of Anne of Brittany, perhaps one of the best examples of such manuscripts ever made. Created between 1505 and 1510, the book contains forty-seven full illuminations by Jean Bourdichon, a native of nearby Tours and creator of exquisite works. There are heraldic paintings, a diptych with portrait, twelve images for the calendar months and numerous floral borders. Anne of Brittany appears kneeling in prayer, with her hair scraped back and her large eyes gazing upwards; but what is of interest is the style of her clothing and headdress, the square-necked golden gown with wide, turned-back sleeves and French hood, with a pleated white coif or crepine underneath, golden paste and billament, set with jewels and black bag veil. Painted around a decade before Anne Boleyn arrived at the court of Anne's daughter, this was the exact fashion that the young Englishwoman would take home with her to the court of Henry VIII, and wear with such grace. One image shows Anne seated in an enclosed garden, a familiar medieval motif, with raised flower bed made from bricks around her, perhaps intended as a seat, topped by a lattice fence behind which white and purple flowers luxuriate. She is served by two little girls, perhaps Claude and her sister, Renée, one of whom picks the blooms while the other offers Anne a basket of flowers. Their style of dress is a simpler version of hers, the younger girl bareheaded, the elder wearing a partial hood without the veil. So little time elapsed between its creation and Anne Boleyn's arrival that it may serve as an illustration for Claude and her ladies, with the young Boleyn girl, in the gardens at Blois.

Given Anne's later love of illuminations, it is likely that her love of art and manuscripts was awakened in the libraries at Mechelen and flourished under the influence of the French royal collection at Blois. She may well have witnessed the delivery, in 1517, of the tiny prayer book commissioned by Claude, full of dazzling miniatures, so small it can be held in the palm of the hand, and a companion volume, a book of hours. Less than three inches tall and 2½ inches wide, the prayer book's diminutive size was a mark of its value; perhaps Anne had the opportunity to glimpse its jewel-like colours, depicting the Passion of Christ or read the story of St Christopher, and those of St Nicholas and St René, who were responsible for restoring dead children to life. Also of particular interest to Claude was the prayer to the Virgin Mary, in Latin and in the first person, allowing for a direct, personal connection between Queen and Saint, at a time when such methods of devotion were just starting to be adopted. In addition, the illustration of Mary and the infant Jesus contains the image of a kneeling young John the Baptist, whose position and gestures echo those found in the Madonna of the Rocks, a work by Leonardo Da Vinci, then in the collection of Francis I. An interesting reference to Claude's position in the royal family might be inferred from the illustration of the Holy Trinity, which is encircled by a loosely knotted girdle, a symbol of the house of Savoy, a tacit acknowledgement that the real 'trinity' of power was Francis, Louise and Marguerite.

The Italian Renaissance had reached the interior of Blois too. As Anne walked through the exquisite Queen's chamber on the first floor or the richly painted gallery nearby, or passed under the archways of the hall or the red brick gothic entrance, woven and painted images presented the anatomical, realistic and balanced ideal of the Renaissance, with their dark backgrounds, often set inside with glimpses of outdoors through open doors and windows. Yet Claude's was a specific, female, maternal, representation of the Renaissance. One such typical image was Sebastiano del Piombo's 'Visitation' depicting St Elizabeth and a pregnant Mary. Painted in 1518, it hung in Claude's chamber but it is not a romantic image: the weary set of Mary's features bears a realism that would have been familiar to Claude through her personal experiences. The symbolic long road behind her, in the top left portion of the screen, served as a reminder of the journeys she had endured through three pregnancies so far, still aged only nineteen, while the comfort offered by St Elizabeth combined the queen's spiritual purpose with the maternal figure she missed. Also in 1518, Pope Leo X commissioned Raphael to paint 'The Holy Family of Francis I', depicting Joseph, Mary, the infant Jesus, St Elizabeth, John the Baptist as a child and two angels. This may have been to mark the safe arrival of the couple's third child, their first son, Francis, who was born on 28 February that year. Claude had travelled the short distance to Amboise for his birth and Anne would have been in attendance.

The walls at Blois were also hung with tapestries depicting scenes from Christine de Pisan's *City of Ladies*. The famous tapestries were made in the sixteenth century, based on the century-old book celebrating 200 admirable women. Now lost, and the subject of a search and book by Susan Groag Bell, Claude's tapestries had been made by the Flemish tapestry makers the Greniers by 1491 and were still listed among the French royal assets in 1542 and 1551. In a coincidence that links to Anne Boleyn, the same firm had made another eight-panel set for Margaret of Austria in 1513. The likelihood that Anne had seen both sets seems even more certain given the existence in her daughter's garderobe accounts of 1547 of a third set of tapestries. Although it cannot be stated for certain, it seems likely that Anne commissioned her own copy of the *City of Ladies* after having appreciated them at the two European courts where she lived as a girl.

Along with Anne Boleyn, Claude's twelve ladies in waiting included the writer Anne de Granville, who commissioned a portrait of herself presenting Claude with one of her works. There was also Diane de Poitiers, a noblewoman from Drôme in the south-east of France, who was almost an exact contemporary of Claude, and just two years older than Anne. Like Claude, Diane had just been married at a young age to Louis de Brézé, seigneur d'Anet, who was almost forty years her senior and a grandson of Charles VII. Her marriage to a prince of the blood meant that Diane had seniority over Anne and she was appointed a matron of honour. An intelligent and beautiful woman, Diane had been given an education along humanist lines, could read Latin and Greek, speak modern languages, dance, play music, converse and hunt, making her the personification of the perfect female courtier. Diane would bear her husband two children, in 1518 and 1521, but would become famous for adopting black and white mourning upon her widowhood in 1531 for life – and becoming the much older mistress of Claude and Francis's second son, Henri II. It was rumoured that she may also have been one of Francis's many mistresses. The poet Clément Marot was part of Marguerite's household from 1519, and composed a series of poems to a 'Diane', who was probably Diane de Poitiers. The artist François Clouet, son of Francis's court painter Jean Clouet, would also immortalise Diane, creating the most famous image of her bathing.

As well as life at the beautiful Blois, Anne would also have become familiar with the even more splendid Chateau d'Amboise, where Louise of Savoy had raised her two children, and where Francis now made his main home. The beautiful palace was easily reachable along the Loire, allowing Claude and her party to embark from directly outside Blois and travel gently along the river, almost in a straight line to the point where the flamboyant turrets of Amboise were glimpsed above the trees, and as they drew closer, reflected in the water. Amboise had been rebuilt by Charles VIII in the 1490s, in the late gothic style with Italian Renaissance touches, to make it the first Italianate palace in France. There would have been many echoes of Blois in its architecture and gardens. Although it was also a place of sorrow tinged with bathos, as Anne of Brittany's first husband, Charles VIII, had died there in 1498, after hitting his head on a door lintel.

There was another very important Renaissance figure at Amboise, and it is almost impossible that Anne Boleyn did not encounter him on at least one occasion. Claude was certainly at Amboise for her first four deliveries, in August 1515, October 1516, February 1518 and March 1519, but her residence there would have been for extended periods, including her retirement and lying-in, as well as her postpartum recovery. She is also likely to have been a frequent visitor on other occasions, at Christmases,

Easters, other feasts and festivals, allowing for regular exchange between the two royal households. And where Claude went, Anne went. Perhaps it was at the dinner table, or in Francis' grand reception rooms, or maybe on a specific visit to the little red brick Chateau de Cloux (later the Chateau de Clos Lucé), just five hundred metres from the main chateau, that Anne first saw an old man in his sixties, with long white flowing beard and pronounced brows and nose.

Francis had invited Leonardo Da Vinci into his service in 1515, after the French king was impressed by a walking mechanical lion the artist made for him, which could open its chest to expose a bunch of lilies inside. That December, Da Vinci was appointed 'the King's first painter, engineer and architect', arriving at Amboise with his favourite students and three paintings, the 'Mona Lisa', 'Saint Jean Baptiste' and 'Sainte Anne', attending the French court via an underground tunnel that linked the properties. Da Vinci also had ideas for a new chateau for Francis at Romorantin, drawing up plans featuring a series of canals and gardens with fountains, and although this was never built, some features were incorporated into the later redesigning of Amboise and Blois. One surviving sketch he made of the king's home in 1517 shows the array of little roofs and walls in faded sepia. Anne Boleyn may well have been resident in one of those rooms while the artist sat and drew, maybe sitting behind one of the windows traced by the master's pen. In Claude's company, ushered through his secret passage by Francis, Anne is likely to have seen these works, and heard them spoken of by their creator. A decade later, when she caught the eye of a king who considered himself to be a connoisseur of the Renaissance, she cannot have failed to impress if she mentioned her connection to Da Vinci.

Another location Anne may have come to know was the Chateau of Fontainebleau, thirty miles south of Paris, where Francis loved to stay when he went hunting in the area. Although Claude was not always with her husband, she would occasionally have visited the castle, bringing Anne in her entourage to enjoy the sports in the area and the springs in the gardens and forests around it. The medieval structure remained intact until after Claude's death, when Francis began a large-scale redevelopment, so Claude and Anne would have known the place in its fourteenth-century style, with some improvements by Isabeau of Bavaria, around a hundred years earlier. They would have known the original St Saturnin's chapel, before it was destroyed and replaced, perhaps prayed there for a safe journey, but little else of today's palace would have been recognisable to them.

One of the first major events of Anne's residence in the queen's household was the Battle of Marignano, in the middle of September

1515, in which Francis defeated a Swiss army on Italian soil. The king struck a medal to commemorate his victory with the legend, 'I have vanquished those whom only Caesar vanquished' and went on to claim more territories in Lombardy. During his absence, it was his mother, Louise of Savoy, who acted as regent, which was essential given Claude's youth, and the delivery of her first child that August, from which she was still recovering. That October, though, Claude accompanied Louise south to Lyons and Marseille, to welcome Francis on his return home; Anne was probably with them, witnessing the triumphant king returning from victory. Whilst there, Claude and Louise paid a visit to the basilica of Saint-Maximin-la-Sainte-Baume, the reputed tomb of St Mary Magdalene, over which a fourteenth-century church had been constructed. Set in the south-east of France, in the foot of the mountains between Aix-en-Provence and Cannes, a hundred miles from the Italian border, it was probably the furthest south Anne ever travelled.

Anne had been in Claude's service for at least two years by May 1517, when her mistress was eventually crowned Queen of France. The ceremony had been delayed due to Claude's pregnancies and ill-health, which was not unusual for queens of the era, but the occasion was most certainly not an after-thought, as has sometimes been supposed. Genuinely fond of his wife, Francis organised an ostentatious display in her honour, at which Anne experienced the process that she would go through in London sixteen years later. The day before her coronation, Claude remembered her parents at the Church of St Denis, praying 'in great devotion and contemplation over the tomb and statue of her father and mother, and not without tears and lamentations'.[1] Anne would have been one of the ladies appointed to help her into her overgarment and bodice trimmed with the Breton symbol of the ermine, which featured on her arms, as a reminder that she was simultaneously queen and Duchess, uniting two formerly rival areas. Before her death, Claude's mother had given her a cape to wear for the occasion, 'sewn with little leaves of gold onto silver cloth, filled with beautifully fashioned ermines in the form of raised animals, all completely covered with raised pearls' and with a huge ruby set into the clasp.[2]

Seven sites of pageantry had been created in Paris, along Claude's route. Francis had hired Pierre Gringore, the most famous Parisian poet, actor and playwright of his day, who had recently composed a Mystery play about Louis XII but was also known for his satires on the papacy.[3] The first display was staged at the Châtelet, the Parisian seat of justice, featuring the genealogy of Brittany, as designed and related by Pierre Gringore:

The aforementioned lady arrived at the Châtelet of Paris, where she found a tree with many branches, like a tree of Jesse, on a large scaffolding. In the upper branches were a crowned king and queen... and on each side of these branches were several princes, princesses, kings and dukes of Brittany, demonstrating the line and genealogy from which the aforementioned lady arose.[4]

At St·Denis, an actor playing the queen stood surrounded by six biblical women, each symbolising one of the desirable qualities of a French queen: fertility (Leah), modesty (Esther), loyalty (Sarah), prudence (Rebecca), amiability (Rachel) and education (Deborah). As she moved on to the Ponceau fountain, Claude found a crowned queen and two young women, representing Claude's two small daughters, Louise and Charlotte, sitting in a field of lilies surrounded by verses about the promulgation of fruit. At the site of Saint Innocents, three large, open hearts contained female figures representing Divine Love, Conjugal Love and Natural Love. Each of these was attached to a royal coat of arms, of Claude, Francis or his mother, Louise of Savoy, expressing the triumvirate of power at the top, but unusually substituting Claude for Marguerite. The final spectacle featured a dialogue between St Louis and his mother, Blanche of Castile, another coded reference to the relationship between Francis and Louise, as if Claude required an additional reminder of who was the real female influence upon the throne.

Claude was carried into Notre Dame Cathedral on a litter draped in cloth of silver, head to toe in jewels. With Francis observing from behind the customary grille so as not to upstage her, the Duke of Alençon held the heavy crown of Charlemagne above her head, the Constable of Bourbon knelt to hold her train, the Comte de Guise held the hand of justice and the Prince de la Roche-sur-Yon held the sceptre. Under Notre Dame's gothic vaulting and great rose window, Claude was anointed and made her promises. Anne then accompanied her to the banquet held afterwards in her honour at the Palais du Justice. The food was served on gold and silver plates, set on cloth of gold covering marble tables. The following day a tournament was held, at which the Knights of the Day, dressed in white and led by Francis, competed against the Comte de St Pol and his black-clad Knights of the Night. One of the messages that Anne would have absorbed from the day's proceedings was that blood mattered. Claude may have possessed the desirable qualities of being virtuous, chaste and good, but she was no match for Francis physically, culturally and intellectually. Yet none of this mattered in the face of her pedigree, as the pageantry and symbolism was designed to state. Her personal qualities, even her very identity, was far less important than the fact that she was unifying France. The women that Francis entertained in private may have been beautiful and witty, but that did not qualify them for queenship. It would be a long journey, beginning a decade later, for Anne and Henry to overturn this status quo.

Following the Parisian festivities, the French royal family set off on progress. At Claude's side, Anne Boleyn was one of around ten thousand people accompanying the king and queen to ensure their comfort, safety and amusement.[5] They followed the route of the Seine through Picardy, almost ninety miles to Rouen, where Francis made an official entry into the city on 2 August, dressed in cloth of gold, atop a horse decked out in the same material. The following day, Claude made her entry, second to her husband according to protocol, but ensuring she was not eclipsed by him. They were welcomed by Louis de Brézé, husband of Diane de Poitiers, who conducted them to his chateau de Mauny, where Francis and his host indulged in a summer of hunting.

Anne witnessed other ceremonial occasions, such as Claude's entry to Nantes in 1518, when the town presented her with a heart made of gold, which she politely returned to them. The same year, she was likely to have been among the queen's attendants at the wedding of Lorenzo di Pietro de Medici and Madeleine de la Tour d'Auvergne, which was held at Amboise on 19 June 1518, and was planned by Da Vinci. The newly wed pair were to become the parents of Catherine de Medici, future wife of Claude's son Henri and another queen of France. Anne would have been in attendance on Queen Claude at a banquet held at the Bastille in Paris on 22 December 1518 to celebrate the negotiations for the marriage of the Dauphin Francis to Princess Mary, daughter of Henry VIII and Catherine of Aragon. If Claude was at Amboise the following spring, Anne may also have attended the funeral, or the mourning rituals, when Da Vinci died in May 1519, and sixty beggars followed his casket into the Chapel of Saint Hubert at the Chateau d'Amboise.

What effect did the culture, ceremony and experience of the French court have upon Anne Boleyn? There is no doubt that it did have an effect. The francophilia she displayed during the 1520s, permeating her style, air, conversation and polish, leave little doubt that this was a defining period in her life. As the epitome of everything French and fashionable, her exposure to Renaissance art and familiarity with the Valois court gave her an exotic edge in the English court, and her wider perspective, drawn from the Burgundian world and connections like those of the Medici and Da Vinci, developed her sense of the European stage. England was not exactly a backwater, but it all put the country into perspective. While her future husband would always take an Anglo-centric view, even a Henry-centric one, Anne's formative experiences were broader. If nothing else, her experiences accustomed her to the company of royalty, to their formalities, methods and the private people behind the royal façade. Living in proximity to Claude, and sometimes Francis, she came to understand the dynamic of a royal marriage that was based upon mutual respect despite its inequality. She saw behind the scenes in the queen's bedroom, in terms of sexuality, illness, pregnancy and childbirth.

During these years in France, another important influence was taking hold in Europe, creeping into the court in the form of educated men with reformed ideas, preachers in the pulpit and the spread of books. Anne would not have been able to avoid the latest controversies in religious thought, even coming into contact with the basic tenets of Lutheranism and the controversy surrounding it. Individuals like the reformer Guillaume Briçonnet, Bishop of Meaux, visiting his diocese in 1518, was shocked at the way the people were being 'poisoned' by the 'superstitious claptrap' of the local friars. Formerly chaplain to Anne of Brittany, and officiating at the coronation of Louis XII, he would also become Marguerite of Navarre's spiritual advisor and Abbot of the Benedictine Saint-Germain des Près. There was also Jacques Lefèvre d'Etaples, a humanist and theologian who had studied Greek and Latin and travelled extensively in Italy. He entered the Abbey under Briçonnet in 1507, publishing books of biblical studies which were condemned as heresy, although the favouritism of Francis protected him. Anne would later own copies of his works, translated by her brother from the French. Lefèvre's thinking was much in line with that of Erasmus, whom Anne encountered at Archduchess Margaret's court in 1514. It was just two years later that Erasmus published his translation of the New Testament based on Greek manuscripts, stimulating a new wave of translations that were key to the progress of the Reformation. Another important figure involved was Guillaume Budé, a scholar of Greek, who would encourage the king to found the Collège de France in 1530.

Along with Briçonnet and Budé, Lefévre founded a convocation of preachers known as the *Cercle de Meaux*, with the intention of translating the New Testament into everyday French, reforming the abuses of the church and encouraging a direct relationship with God through personal reading of the scriptures. Opposed by the Sorbonnne, the *Cercle* would become vulnerable during the incarceration of Francis after the battle of Pavia in 1525. Without the king to protect them, the leading figures were imprisoned or fled into exile. That came later: at the time of Anne's residence in France, these ideas were taking hold, under royal patronage, no doubt discussed and shared at court. The criticisms of religion made by the Meaux circle would be the same ones that Anne would hear voiced in England, encouraging Henry to reform ecclesiastical abuses and read the scriptures in English, even though he had been opposed to such things not long before. She would also intervene to secure clemency or freedom for those who questioned long-standing religious practice.

True to his purpose, the hostile Catholic Nicholas Sander would describe how Anne 'embraced the heresy of Luther to make her life and opinions consistent, for that was wrung from her by the custom of the king and the necessities of her own ambition'.[6] Others considered her 'more Lutheran than Luther' but Anne's presence in a court where discourse about new religious ideas was tolerated, does not make a Lutheran. Listening to the discussion at the chambers at Blois and Amboise, hearing the preachers promoted by the royal family and with access to their books, new and old, Anne's intellectual horizons were expanded, allowing for the questioning of established traditions. Perhaps the greatest impact of the Reformation upon Anne was her realisation that the existing order could be challenged: religious practices and beliefs, such as definition of the afterlife and the nature of Holy Communion, could be swept away – and queens who had failed to produce children, such as Louis XII's first wife, Joan of France, could be put aside. After all, as she had seen, kings and queens were human beings, liable to physical weakness, imperfections and desires, even though they may have been anointed with holy oil. The revelation was both religious and secular.

It was early in 1519 that the ideas of the German monk Martin Luther were recorded as first having an impact in France. He had nailed his now famous 95 theses to the door of All Saints' Church in Wittenburg on 31 October 1517. It is easy to overstate this moment, to see it as a line in the sand, or the first step, when in fact, it was part of a continuing dialogue. The Basle printer, John Froben, wrote to Luther in February 1519, telling him he had sent 600 fresh copies of his works to Spain and France: 'They are sold in Paris and are being read even at the Sorbonne... they meet with everyone's approval.'[7] A Swiss student in Paris, named Pierre Tschudi, described them as being received with 'open arms', especially the criticism of papal indulgences, pardons that could be purchased to relieve a sinner from punishment.[8] By September 1520, the text of a debate Luther had at Leipzig with the German theologian Johann, or John, Eck, was being debated at the Sorbonne, without resolution. Having initially believed their views to be compatible, Eck accused Luther of promoting anarchy within the Catholic church and of favouring the 'heresy of the Bohemian brethren'. This was a fifteenth-century sect, who had presaged the Reformation by standing against indulgences, the papacy, the transformation of the mass and the exclusivity of the Bible in Latin. They were also connected to the much older Waldensians, on the French/Italian border, heavily persecuted by the early sixteenth century, and who would later influence the thinking of Calvin and Zwingli.

In the summer of 1521, Luther became the Catholic church's official enemy, when the pope pronounced a sentence of excommunication against him for burning the papal bull issued against his Wittenburg theses. Marguerite d'Alençon, who corresponded with Briçonnet, had shown great interest in Luther, even sharing some of his ideas but rejecting others. She particularly retained her belief in the transformation of the host into the body and blood of Christ, rather than the symbolic change he favoured. Now there was a clear choice; one could not support the monk and the papacy at the same time. In April 1521, Luther had been summoned to appear before the Diet of Worms, a general assembly of the estates that comprised the Empire, and questioned about his beliefs. On 25 May, Charles had pronounced him a heretic, and ordered the destruction of his works and his immediate arrest, but with help from his supporters, Luther escaped to Wartburg Castle, where he immediately commenced a translation of the New Testament from Greek into German. The pope then followed the Emperor's lead, establishing a pattern which would alter the course of Anne's life.

As well as the Bohemian Bretheren and the Waldensians, another important sect championed the new calls for religious reform, achieving particular influence at the Valois court. Marguerite's faith was shaped by a group named the Brethren of the Common Life, who originated from the Netherlands, initially with papal blessing. The group, who were founded in the fourteenth century by the preacher Gerard Groote, advocated a simple relationship with God, overseeing mostly lay members, who did good works in the community and denounced the corrupt lives of clergymen who did not follow their vows. They established a number of schools and numbered among their pupils Thomas à Kempis, author of the highly influential *The Imitation of Christ*, Pope Adrian VI, the physician Andreas Vesalius, and Erasmus. By 1500, the school at Deventer alone had 2,000 students enrolled. Their ideology, the *Devotio Moderna*, was the root of Marguerite's belief in a simpler faith and direct prayer, her focus on the Bible, meditation and the desire to imitate Christ in individuals' private lives.

While the question of religion and a potential spectrum of reforms were still was being debated, the emerging mindset of the French court was one of tolerance towards new learning and a reluctance to make blanket accusations of heresy. For such a nuanced debate, with sincere intent, the label was often too simplistic. The patronage of Francis and Marguerite reveals that they recognised this as a period of transition, in the arts as well as in religion, with similar ideological tenets underpinning the changes in each. As part of their world, Anne cannot have escaped hearing theological opinions expressed, or news about key figures like

Luther, perhaps reading some of the new literature and translations. Anne's spiritual influence upon Henry indicates a long-established interest in, and a receptiveness and tolerance for, religious debate, which she developed during her years in France. In contrast, her future husband's response to these immense changes was one of intolerance and punishment. His response was one of simplistic denial and destruction. On 12 May 1521, at Henry's command, John Fisher, Bishop of Rochester, had preached a sermon against Luther and his books were publicly burned in the churchyard of St Paul's Cathedral.[9] The king then set about preparing his arguments on paper, as outlined by John Clerk, whose job it was to present the finished work to the church council:

> Many wonder how a prince so much occupied was led to attempt a work that demanded all the energies of a veteran man of letters; but having already defended the Church with his sword, Henry felt it needful to do so with his pen, now that she is in much greater danger. Not that he thought it glorious to contend with one so despicable as Luther, but he wished to show the world what he thought of that horrible portent, and to induce the learned to follow his example, by which Luther might be compelled himself to retract his heresies.[10]

While Henry was composing this book in defence of the seven sacraments, prompting the pope to award him the title *Fidei Defensor*, or Defender of the Faith, his future wife was resident in a court where royal support was being given to heretics. Where Anne was intellectually flexible, Henry was rigid and certain of his position, until such time as it benefitted him personally to raise questions – after which he never found a spiritual equilibrium to compare with Catholicism.

When Marguerite d'Alençon (by then Marguerite of Navarre) published her *Mirror of a Sinful Soul* in 1531, the work was immediately condemned by the Sorbonne, who ordered its destruction and proclaimed the unknown author a heretic. The University was forced to retract its position on discovering the identity of the writer, proving the latitude that royalty enjoyed when it came to breaking even canonical rules. Anne's future position would give her a degree of licence, a place of safety from which to voice controversial doubts, for as long as Henry permitted it. A king, queen, or their close relations might espouse a personal faith, a rejection of traditional ideals, that could mean death or disgrace for their subjects. It was a position that Henry would later exploit to the full. However, once he withdrew his support for Anne, when that permission and tolerance were retracted, he left her vulnerable to accusations of heresy, even witchcraft.

NINE

An Anglo-French Woman
1519–20

Across the Channel, Henry VIII had undergone a gradual transition from the enthusiastic young king who had invaded France in 1513 and danced at the court of Margaret of Austria into a man in whom the seeds of disappointment and disillusionment had started to grow. His Spanish bride, Catherine of Aragon, whom he wed despite her former marriage to his elder brother, had produced six children, of whom only one survived. Princess Mary arrived on 18 February 1516 and Thomas Boleyn was present at Greenwich Palace for her christening two days later. The ceremony took place in the Church of the Greyfriars, hung with 'cloth of needlework garnished with precious stones and pearls', with the baby carried in the arms of Anne's aunt, Elizabeth Howard, Countess of Surrey, under a canopy held in the four corners by Thomas Boleyn, Thomas Parr, David Owen and Nicholas Vaux.[1] If Anne's mother was not present, it was because she was tending to the queen, who remained sequestered in her chambers, according to the traditional period of confinement. Elizabeth Boleyn did take part in the banquet held for the Spanish envoys on 7 July 1517, seated between the Bishop of Spain and the Provost of Cassel[2] and, ten days after that, she acted as deputy for Queen Catherine at the christening of Mary Tudor and Charles Brandon's first child, Frances, at Bishop's Hatfield, in Hertfordshire.[3] Still in his late twenties, while Catherine approached her mid-thirties, King Henry was wondering what he had done to displease God so much that he had been denied a legitimate son. The birth of a boy to Henry's mistress, Elizabeth Blount, in the summer of 1519, seemed to confirm to the king that his fertility was not at fault.

Thomas Boleyn's career during this period was solid but not dazzling. He was still an important figure at court, a member of Council, a Knight of the Body, featuring in land transactions, recognizances and commissions for the peace, as well as the usual ceremonial occasions and festivities. Yet these years have the dragging feel of duty, dull management, even treading water. His initial trajectory slowed and there was to be no repeat of the success he had achieved at the Burgundian court, even though Henry was conducting important foreign business. It was Richard Pace, Wolsey's secretary, to whom Henry turned in 1515–16, when attempting to negotiate an alliance with the Swiss, who had been resoundingly defeated by Francis at the Battle of Marignano. Boleyn might have seemed the natural choice, given that the negotiations took place with the Emperor Maximilian, father of Margaret of Austria, although it may have been considered that his relationship with the Imperial family had been compromised by the slight offered to Margaret upon Anne's removal from her household. Swiftly promoted to secretary of state, Pace was very clearly the cardinal's man, corresponding with him in detail on official matters and on those of espionage. His preferment over Thomas Boleyn may have been a function of Wolsey's own meteoric rise at this time, providing one reason why there may have been a coolness on the part of the Boleyns towards the Chancellor.

There were questions of family and property to be resolved. The death of Sir Thomas Butler, Thomas Boleyn's father-in-law, on 3 August 1515, triggered disputes between his two surviving daughters and their distant cousin, Sir Piers Butler, over the family inheritance. Butler was claiming sole rights as male heir, prompting the two sisters to launch a suit against him that December. They were granted livery of the lands, but Butler had taken on the title of Earl of Ormond with the backing of the Irish Parliament. The dispute was to rumble on for a good few years yet. Boleyn was called upon to conduct an important visitor south from Scotland, a task for which he received £10 for forty days' service, in May 1517. Henry's elder sister, Margaret Tudor, had been ousted by a coup in favour of her infant son and Thomas was one of a relay of courtiers employed to ensure her safety as she fled home to England and to her brother's court.

In 1515, the Boleyns had acquired Rochford Hall in Essex, a turreted manor house built in the early thirteenth century on the banks of the river Roach. In October 1517, Thomas was granted a licence to export from his Rochford mill wood, billet and similar made 'within the said lordship', in a vessel of his own named the *Rosendell*.[4] Yet the family's main residence was still Hever as, the following month, Boleyn was named as a Sheriff of Kent.[5] Boleyn was also in the possession of a house called New Hall at Boreham, in Essex, which had been part of his mother's Irish Butler legacy, after it was awarded to the family by Henry VII in 1491. Once owned by Waltham Abbey, it was already an important building, conveniently located not too far from London, with good hunting and close to the River Blackwater that flowed to the North Sea. Either by choice, or by royal suggestion, Thomas sold this property to Henry in 1516 for the considerable sum of £1,000 and the king set about transforming it into Beaulieu Palace, his first major building project. The total amount spent on the project would reach £17,000, and the Boleyns would return in the summer of 1527, once the work was complete, in a very different position to that they had enjoyed eleven years before.

The international scene was changing, swinging back towards the Anglo-French alliance that would require Thomas Boleyn's special knowledge and abilities. The death of Henry's father-in-law, Ferdinand of Aragon, in 1516, changed the face of Europe, meaning that the Emperor's grandson, the 16-year-old Charles, inherited a vast legacy combining the Spanish Empire with that of the Low Countries, making him a far more significant player than either Henry or Francis. This served to unite them. In 1518, Boleyn took part in the king's negotiations for cross-Channel peace, as one of thirty-four leading clerics and councillors who signed the Treaty of Universal Peace with France on 2 October, along with his father-in-law Thomas Howard, Charles Brandon, Duke of Suffolk and the rising privy councillor Thomas More. The papal ambassador, Sebastian Giustinian, witnessed the proclamation of the peace at St Paul's, which was sworn 'in a tone audible only to the parties concerned' after a 'solemn mass' celebrated by the newly appointed cardinal and Lord Chancellor, Thomas Wolsey. After this, Wolsey led his guests back to his London residence of Durham House, where they enjoyed 'a most sumptuous supper' the like of which, Giustinian was certain, had never been given 'either by Cleopatra or Caligula', in a banqueting hall decorated with huge vases of gold and silver, which he likened to that of King Croesus. It was followed by a mummery of twelve female and twelve male actors, masked and sumptuously dressed, led by Mary and Charles Brandon, after which followed 'countless dishes of confections and other delicacies' and the affair ended with ducats, dice and dancing.[6]

Two days later, Boleyn's name also appears on a second treaty, arranging the future marriage of Princess Mary with Dauphin Francis, and he was probably in the Queen's Great Chamber at Greenwich on 5 October to witness the formal betrothal, as the Admiral of France took the hand of the Princess and espoused her in the name of the Dauphin,[7] giving her a small ring set with a large diamond. Giustinian observed that the Princess was dressed in cloth of gold, with a black velvet cap and many jewels, and that the church where they went to hear mass was also hung with cloth of gold, in 'such rich array' that the ambassador 'never saw the like, either here or elsewhere'.[8] Boleyn would have taken part in the dinner that followed but was among those who withdrew for the night, before the final meeting between the French ambassadors, Henry and Wolsey, which took place in a separate room. Henry also made generous gifts to the French, impressing Francis with a suit of horse harnesses, made out of gold filigree and rich embroidery, and offering a rich robe of 'cloth of gold, line with cloth of silver, made for the king's use', to Bonivet.[9]

The peace treaty referred to a planned meeting between the two monarchs in the coming year and, to help bring this about, Thomas Boleyn embarked for France in late December 1518 or early January 1519. Also named in the commission were Richard Weston, Nicholas West, John Peachy and a Master Fitzwilliam, and West had certainly reached Paris by 7 January, from where he wrote to Thomas Wolsey that he would 'do his best to induce the French council to condescend to the King of England's desires'.[10] The ambassadors were plunged into talks with Francis at once, who offered to send hostages to Henry's court as a guarantee of peace, which was an old diplomatic method common to Anglo-French negotiations. Yet Henry was not satisfied with the individuals Francis had identified, because they were not people of his chamber, or any whom the king particularly favoured, so the discussions continued. The situation was complicated further when news arrived in both courts of the death of Emperor Maximilian on 12 January, leaving a vacancy at the heart of European politics that both Henry and Francis were keen to fill.

No doubt Boleyn was eager to see Anne again, after a separation of at least four years, but when exactly this happened depended upon the whereabouts of Queen Claude. She would give birth on 31 March that year, at the Chateau de Saint-Germain-en-Lye, twelve miles to the west of Paris. Given her former reluctance to travel during pregnancy, or the advice of her doctors not to, it is likely that entering her final trimester she was at St Germain already when the English embassy arrived. It would not have been too difficult for Anne to make a short trip, by river or road, into Paris, or for Thomas Boleyn to ride to visit his daughter. It is possible that the last time he had seen her was before her departure for Burgundy in 1513, although they may have met during her early days in Paris in late 1514. Boleyn had last seen his daughter as a twelve- or thirteen-year-old, still a child, on the cusp of adolescence. By 1519 she was definitely a woman, at a marriageable age. They might have been reunited in the gardens at Saint-Germain, or in the gothic chapel, or in one of the reception rooms, as the ambassadors paid their respects to Queen Claude. Anne may even have been called upon to act as interpreter between the queen and her father. Four years in France had changed his daughter, giving her the polish of a courtier and the linguistic skills of a diplomat, as well as an increased maturity and a beauty that was not typical of its time, but more individual, making her an ornament to the French court. Thomas Boleyn would have been swift to notice that Anne had fulfilled the promise she had displayed in her 1513 letter from Tervuren: she was a new, and valuable, asset to the family.

Thomas Boleyn wrote to Henry from Paris in February 1519, describing a discussion he had had with Francis regarding the election of a new Emperor. Boleyn waited to intercept the French king as he came from mass in his chamber, intending to deliver to him two letters sent by Henry, one to Francis, and one to Louise of Savoy. Francis then took Boleyn aside to the window and told him he had 'heard of Henry's satisfaction at the entertainment of his ambassadors' but that Henry had set their example, and he could do no more than half that himself. Flattery aside, Francis then added his hopes that England and France would 'act in perfect unity… prudently and harmoniously' regarding the coming election, as the role was vested with the monarchy of Christendom. Realising that Francis wanted the position for himself, Boleyn followed the king's lead as he leaned out of the window to avoid being overheard, to tell the ambassador that several of the Electors had 'expressed themselves favourable' to him, 'because of the greater service he might do against the infidels'.[11] After receiving instruction from England, Boleyn offered Francis 'the great desire Henry had for the increase of his honour, and the service he intended to do in advancing him to the preferment of his imperial dignity'.[12] In response, Francis removed his bonnet and gave his 'hearty' thanks. Henry of course nurtured a secret desire to take the prize for himself and, to this effect, dispatched Richard Pace to visit the Electors, to 'explain to (them) the king's mind touching the election'.[13] Both would be disappointed when the Hapsburg Charles of Austria was appointed that June.

This latest court news would have reached Anne, as she helped Claude to undress, or made the preparations for her coming confinement. She knew better than to communicate any private thoughts she had on the matter, but the issue raises the interesting question of where her sympathies lay, and perhaps, the key to her identity. She had spent her teenaged years in France, important years of transition and self-definition, in loyal companionship to Claude, an observer of her marriage to Francis and her constant physical struggles, most of all in childbirth. Her early years at Blicking and Hever, and even her family, may have faded in comparison. By her later behaviour, adopting French styles and customs, Anne clearly identified with the culture of France, perhaps even the wider culture of northern Europe, which was less clearly defined than the English island mentality, given the fluidity of European boundaries, the relative ease of travel and the complex inheritances of thrones and duchies. But if Anne was in part defined by European culture in her youth, her earlier and later actions prove that she never forgot her origins and loyalties to her family. She may have listened as Claude told her of Francis's plans to be elected, then listened again as her father spoke of Henry's secret wish to take the role for himself – but her loyalties lay with the Boleyns. She was a true woman of her times, in that she gave her obedience to her father, and she was fortunate at this point, that Thomas Boleyn's service to King Henry meant that to serve him meant to serve England. This would not always be the case.

On March 14, Boleyn wrote to Wolsey regarding the impending delivery of Queen Claude. Although Anne is not specifically named, as Claude's waiting woman she would have been included in these movements, and privy to the general concern regarding the queen's health:

> The Queen and my Lady left Paris the same day [11 March] for St Germain, where the former was to be confined, but was taken ill by the way, and was obliged to rest at the village of La Porte de Neuilly, and that night she was in great danger. False reports were spread, first of her death, afterwards of her delivery; which kept Boleyn away from court on Saturday, when he had appointed to meet the Great Master. He was sent for, however, yesterday, and saw the lodgings of the King and Queen, my Lady the king's mother, the duchess of Alençon... If the Queen is strong enough, she is to be conveyed by water to St Germain's in 'close barges with chambers made in them'; if not, she must remain.[14]

On 25 March, Boleyn was at Saint-Germain, where Anne would have been too, probably receiving first-hand information from her about Claude's situation. The child was expected imminently, as he wrote to Wolsey, stating that she 'looketh her time every hour'.[15] Two days later Boleyn saw the queen, who was 'accompanied with 14 or 15 lords and gentlewomen, in a nightgown, and nothing [upon her] head but only a kerchief, looking always her hour when she shall be brought in bed'.[16] One of those gentlewomen was Anne Boleyn. Her duties would have been to help satisfy the expectant mother's needs, fetching and carrying for her, making her comfortable and keeping up her spirits, with music, singing and playing games such as cards, chess and dice.

On the last day of the month, Queen Claude safely delivered a son, whom she named Henri, the future Henri II. Francis was back at Saint Germain by 5 April at the latest, to greet his new son, and writing to

Wolsey to enquire whether the boy's godfather, Henry VIII, might be prepared to loan him 100,000 crowns![17] Separately from this request, Henry sent £100 to Boleyn to be distributed amongst Claude's midwife and the women in the nursery.[18] Boleyn wrote to Thomas Wolsey describing the solemn procession of thanks that took place at court, attended by Francis and his mother, 'in honour of the holy cord with which our Lord was bound to the pillar'. Considered to have healing powers, this and other relics had been sent to Claude 'on her delivery' from the Abbey of the Holy Cross at Poitiers. The papal legate and eleven bishops went to Claude's chamber, inside which Anne was in attendance, carrying out the relics on little cushions and then placing them on the high altar.[19] Given her later beliefs, what did Anne make of this process? Voices of criticism, including that of Erasmus and Luther, had already been spreading dissent across Europe about the use of relics, religious images and appeals to the saints. Did Anne see this as a necessary part of the proceedings? Did she simply accept it as Claude's will? Did she believe the relics had been beneficial? She would have been a lone voice at the French court, had she raised any doubts: after all, Henri's safe arrival had validated their use. The presence of Francis, Louise and her sister Philiberta, Duchess of Nemours, suggests that their use was not in question. 'The King attended the procession all the time, bareheaded, with one usher only before him,' continued Boleyn, 'then came the queen mother an old gentleman bearing her train; a little behind her the duchesse, her sister, having her train like[wise].'[20]

The christening of Prince Henri was delayed 'because the child hath a disease in his eyes, as he saith all his children have shortly after they be born, saying 'also it was my lady his mother's mind that the child should be clean whole of this disease afore the christening, whose advice he said he would follow therein'.[21] When it went ahead, in early April, Thomas Boleyn also took the important role of deputising for Henry at the child's christening, after the king accepted Francis's offer to stand as his godfather as a sign of the new friendship between them. It is likely that Anne attended too. Gifts were sent from England, including a gold cup and salt cellar, and £100 in gold coins, to be distributed amongst the nurse, four rockers and gentlewomen of the Queen's chamber.[22] Henri was Claude's fourth child, but the first to live well into adulthood. Not yet twenty, the queen had passed through a dangerous ordeal, reminding Anne of the perils of birth, but also that the odds could be defied to produce a royal son. If the frail, deformed Claude could produce a son, surely the healthy Anne Boleyn would be capable of it?

Thomas Boleyn kept in touch with Henry through the month of May, after the French court had moved to Poissy to escape the outbreak of plague in Paris. His letters speak of the dissatisfaction of Francis at the refusal of the Swiss to support his imperial bid, of the suits of English merchants, piracy and the wearing of beards, as he conveyed to Francis that Henry had refused to shave until he met his French counterpart. In the middle of the month, a letter Boleyn wrote to Wolsey reveals the dissatisfaction he was feeling about his lack of advancement at court. Having learned that Sir Thomas Lovell was intending to resign the treasurership of the king's household, Boleyn believed that he should be awarded the position, because he had been petitioning Henry for the job for four years. However, now 'nothwithstanding his promises to Boleyn', the king was on the verge of appointing Sir Edward Poynings to the role, due to the 'laudable' service he had given. Wolsey, though, had advised Boleyn that the king would soon appoint Poynings a baron and would then make Boleyn treasurer. In recollection of Henry's 'faithful' promise and when, 'at Boleyn's last departing from him, he bade him undoubtedly trust thereto', Thomas was now concerned that 'the king will appoint someone else to the controllership' in which he had been living in hope.[23] He requests Wolsey

> ...to assist him in obtaining the fulfilment of the King's promise. Asks him to consider what a discouragement it would be to him and his friends, to whom he has disclosed his hopes, to be thus disappointed. If the fruit of his service is the prolonging of the King's promise, and if his absence is to be accounted a hindrance because he may not occupy the office without being there, he had better have stayed at home. [He] supposes Wolsey has perceived some fault in him, and therefore will promote a worthier man. If he will favour him this time, will take care that neither the King nor he repent themselves of it.[24]

As it transpired, the position of Treasurer of the King's Household was granted to Sir Edward Poynings in 1519, which he held until his death in October 1521, after which it was given to Boleyn. However, what is interesting at the end of Thomas's letter, is the suggestion that he believes, or 'supposes' Wolsey to have 'perceived some fault in him'. This supports the notion that Wolsey and Boleyn were not close, that Anne's father felt that the cardinal was an obstacle to the advancement of his career, and that he did not feel sure of the man's support. The Tudor court worked on the system of patronage, with juniors seeking to enter service in established households or ride on the coat tails of more successful men. The right connections could open doors. It was also a world in which the opposite was true, and powerful enemies, once made, might act to advance their candidate over yours, or block particular appointments.

Boleyn's choice of words is clever. He specifies that any fault Wolsey finds in him is 'perceived'; thus, as merely an apprehension rather than a fact, it is a mistake that might be easily cleared up.

Boleyn was shrewd enough to understand that a man like Wolsey was won over by mutual advantage. He dangled in front of the cardinal the very thing that he wanted most: the papal see, drawing on his access to Francis to prove what an influential friend he might prove. 'If Wolsey would aspire to the popedom,' Thomas wrote, 'Francis would secure it for him on the first opportunity. He commanded, he said, the voices of fourteen cardinals, and of the whole Orsini faction at Rome. Let but the king of England and himself remain at one, and they would make popes and emperors at their pleasure.'[25] This sweetener may have swung the deal, as Wolsey did lend his support to Boleyn's cause that September, for which he expressed his gratitude in a letter written to the cardinal from the ambassador at Blois.[26] When Leo X died in December, 1521, though, it was not Wolsey who was awarded the prize, as the international scene had changed again. Even more powerful than Boleyn's influence, or that of Francis over his fourteen cardinals, was that of the new Holy Roman Emperor, Charles V, who gave the position to his former tutor, Adriaan Boeyens, who became Adrian VI.

Yet there may be something in Wolsey's 'perceived' criticism of Boleyn. For some reason, Boleyn was recalled to England on 21 February 1520 and Sir Richard Wingfield was appointed to succeed him at the French court, receiving 'instructions to make himself agreeable to all parties'. He was considered a contrast to his predecessor, as 'Sir Thomas was uncourtly, plodding, business-like, and niggardly; Sir Richard, free, open and liberal'.[27] Arriving at Francis's court, Wingfield declared Henry was sensible 'of the services rendered him by Sir Thomas Boleyn', yet, so Wingfield was instructed to say, in consideration of their ancient amity, his love could not be satisfied without sending 'one of his trusty and near familiars, to the intent that by renovelling of ambassadors new testimonies might be found, as well of the perseverance of fraternal love on both parts, as also by such means to further the augmentation thereof from time to time';[28] a diplomatic mouthful that damned Thomas with faint praise. It was not in question that Thomas Boleyn was talented, but that his manner was more driven, perhaps more persistent and given to detail (business-like and niggardly) than might be desirable in the suave atmosphere of Francis's court. This suggests a potential cause for any slump in his career in the later 1510s; although the commission he received at the end of the decade would become his crowning achievement to date.

Anne's life in the second half of 1519 was dominated by the question of health; preserving her own and caring for others. In September, as

Boleyn relates, the king was injured during a day's hunting at Blois, riding 'under a tree with a bough' and striking his head, causing him to remain in his chamber the next day.[29] The plague was still raging in Paris, and it had been forbidden for 'anyone coming from Paris, Tours, Amboise or Vendôme' to enter the town. Six months after the birth of Prince Henri, it was rumoured that the queen was pregnant again.[30] That December, Boleyn was able to confirm that she was expected to deliver the child at the end of the following July.[31] (Princess Madeleine would actually arrive on 10 August 1520.) As part of Claude's retinue, Anne was with the king, queen and Louise of Savoy at Blois in mid-October, when a day's hunting was planned 'in a forest two leagues hence'. Anne might have attended Claude on the hunt, given her later proclivity for riding and hunting, and especially given the queen's condition, or she may have remained behind at Blois. The decision was to prove a significant one. During their absence, the Bishop of Limoges arrived at Blois, only to fall ill and die 'of the common sickness'. The royal family removed at once to Amboise and a proclamation was made that 'no townsman enter the castle where the King's children are'.[32] Anne would have either been sequestered with the family at Amboise, or would have had to wait at Blois with her father until their safe return on 31 October. By mid-December the court was at the Chateau de Cognac, where Francis had been born, where it passed Christmas.[33] The stone castle, with a new façade added by Francis in 1517, formed a grey rectangle along the bank of the Charente. Here, Anne passed the festive season of 1519–20 with the pregnant Claude, the king, Louise of Savoy, and her father.

That Christmas, Anne could not have avoided another significant figure in the king's life, Françoise de Foix, Comtesse de Châteaubriant. Born around 1495, Françoise had appeared at court with her husband in 1516, swiftly attracting the king's attention, who began to shower her family with gifts and titles. She was certainly his mistress by early 1519, at which point she was ranked at official occasions alongside the royal princesses. That December, when her husband was sent on a diplomatic mission to Brittany, Françoise was appointed a lady in waiting to Queen Claude, entering the same household as Anne, probably joining them at Cognac. Anne had ample opportunity to observe the advantages the de Foix family received – and the disgruntlement of Louise of Savoy, who had never liked the family. Anne could see how uncomfortable factions might develop as the result of royal affections, and how a woman might be brought right into the bosom of the royal family, under the queen's nose, as an open, acknowledged mistress. But this was France: such a move would not prove so easy in England.

Sir Richard Wingfield arrived in France early in February 1520, and was briefed by Boleyn about current affairs at court and introduced to Francis. The king and queen were still at Cognac when Anne's father was recalled to England on 21 February 1520. The Boleyns said their farewells, in anticipation of being reunited soon, at the planned meeting between Francis and Henry. In a letter to his fellow king on March 8, Francis complimented Boleyn on his years of service[34] and Claude added her own letter, indicating that she had entrusted Boleyn with her opinion of the new ambassador, which he was to convey to Henry:[35]

> Has received his letters by Sir Richard Wyngfilde, his councillor and ambassador, declaring the great affection he bears to the King her lord and her, and his desire to hear from them and the Dauphin. Assures him she entertains a like disposition towards him, as Henry's ambassador, le sieur Boulan (Sir Thomas Boleyn) will show; to whom she refers Henry for news.[36]

At Claude's court, Anne would have heard much talk of the English king and perhaps even assisted the queen in composing her comments in her native tongue. She would have recalled the young man she saw as a guest of Archduchess Margaret seven years before. With the plans proceeding for the Field of Cloth of Gold that summer, she was soon to see him again.

TEN

Gold 1520–21

In the spring of 1520, Anne was a witness to the preparations in France for the long-awaited meeting of Francis and Henry. Just three years apart in age, the two kings were very similar in their aspirations in championing the new Renaissance style; and in character, being educated men who loved nothing more than spending the day in the saddle and dancing away the night dressed in cloth of gold and jewels. Their personal rivalry, masked behind diplomatic friendship, was real for them, and each saw the other as the standard which they had to outdo. When Thomas Boleyn was recalled to England, it may well have been to provide Henry with insights into the character and nature of the French court, especially what the king might expect from Francis. The proposed meeting gave Boleyn's career a new impetus and, on 26 March he was appointed to be one of the few who were 'to ride with the king at the embracing of the two kings'.[1] Anne was to be present as one of the ladies waiting upon the heavily pregnant Claude but she was also to prove more valuable, on this occasion, as a translator.

Thomas Wolsey, Henry VIII's exceptionally able Lord Chancellor and Cardinal, was co-ordinating the arrangements across the Channel. As early as 12 March, he laid out the details for the two kings: Henry, Catherine of Aragon and Mary Tudor, former Queen of France, were to stay at Guines Castle, while Francis, Claude and Louise of Savoy were based at the castle of Ardres, on the border of that portion of northern France that still remained an English territory. This presented enormous difficulties for Francis, as Guines Castle was practically in ruins and Ardres had been sacked during Henry's campaign of 1513. Neither was in a fit state to receive or host royalty. It was tantamount to issuing a challenge to Francis to defy the odds and maintain his regal splendour, almost putting him on the back foot, to see whether he could outstrip the English who were planning a dazzling construction of brick, wood and glass, to be a temporary palace. Unconcerned about the practical difficulties, Wolsey pressed on to organise the meeting of the monarchs at a mid-point between the two castles, where they would be on horseback, in an open place, with gentlemen present to ensure they were not interrupted. Each king would also dine with the foreign queen, and 'fair feats of arms' were to be performed, with deference given to the monarch on whose land they were.[2] Careful advanced planning specified which king should run first in the tournament, how the honours should be reversed in the interests of fairness, how the horsemen should be armed, how many there should be and which colours would be worn. It was all to proceed according to protocol, which was delineated precisely so that each king might demonstrate his generosity in showing deference to the other.

At court, a frantic burst of activity took hold as costumes, tents, banners, canopies and horse trappings were prepared, in Francis's colours of white, yellow and black, and the seven knights to appear with him at the tournament were summoned to appear in all their finery.[3] Francis kept busy, as Richard Wingfield reported, constantly on the move, and enjoying his favourite pursuits of women, hunting and dancing until three in the morning.[4] The royal family spent Easter at Blois, perhaps with Anne plying her needle along with the other ladies to sew the embroidery on cuffs or collars, or the lavish motifs upon back cloths. She may also have been pondering her role, and that of the women in the household she had come to know, such as Diane de Poitiers and Françoise de Foix; as Wingfield wrote to Wolsey, a 'great search is made to bring to the meeting the fairest ladies that may be found'.[5] Francis consented to the delay Wolsey requested, to fix the kings' meeting for 31 May, but explained that he could not extend it further, due to Claude's condition.[6] He confirmed that 'the time when the Queen may be present has been carefully calculated, and cannot be put off for a month' and in the event 'of her being delivered upon the confines, and the king and queen of England being present to christen the child, it would not be commodious for them to tarry all that time'.[7]

Soon, the French were able to confirm that Claude's household for the event would comprise 1,175 people and 778 horses, alongside Francis's 3,997 people and 2,087 horses. Anne Boleyn featured fairly low down the list, after the duchess, countesses, baronesses and knights' ladies, as either one of fourteen ladies entitled to a woman, a servant and three horses each, or one of the six ladies of the chamber, with a single servant and two horses:

For the Queen: 1 duchess, with 4 women, 6 servants and 12 horses; 10 countesses, with 3 women and 4 servants, and 8 horses each; 12 baronesses, with 2 women, 3 servants and 6 horses each. 20 knights' ladies, with 1 woman, 2 servants and 4 horses each; 14 ladies, with 1 woman, 2 servants and 3 horses each; 6 ladies of the chamber, with 1 servant and 2 horses each; 1 earl, with 42 servants, 3 to be chaplains and 9 gentlemen; horses 20. 3 bishops, to have 44 servants, 4 to be chaplains and 6 gentlemen; horses 60. 4 barons, with 22 servants, 2 to be chaplains and 2 gentlemen; horses 48. 30 knights, with 12 servants, 1 to be a chaplain; horses 240; 6 chaplains with 3 servants and 2 horses each. Grooms 50, officers of the King's chamber, with 20 servants and 30 horses; officers of the King's stable 60, with 70 horses. Sum total of the Queen's company, 1,175 persons and 778 horses.[8]

There was some uneasiness at the French court about the impending visit of Emperor Charles to England, re-establishing a connection that could prove a threat to Anglo-French peace, but the preparations went on. On April 18, the queen and ladies of the French court left Blois and began their journey to Paris. Travelling with them, Anne could anticipate her reunion with the mother and sister she had not seen for seven years. Francis, following them to the capital, wished to know 'if the King his brother will forbear making rich tents and pavilions, and looketh daily to receive from him as well his measure for the making of the cuirass as also to receive the vauntbrasse and gauntlet'.[9] The queen's entourage arrived in Paris on 5 May, where they rested for a few days, before heading on to Abbeville,[10] sixty miles south of Ardres, with 'great diligence' and a determination not to stop on the way.[11] To prove how keen he was to meet Henry, Francis said that 'Wingfield should be a witness for him that his desire for it was no less strong, considering the continual travel he caused the Queen here to take, being in the case that she is in... I assure your grace you would have no little compassion if ye saw the poor creature with the charge she beareth.'[12]

On 25 May, Wingfield wrote from Montreuil, where the French had arrived just over thirty miles from Ardres. After dinner, Francis 'assembled all the great personages of the realm in his bedchamber (and) informed the audience that he had been advertised of Henry's departure from his manor at Greenwich, and his voyage towards Dover, and he trusted the meeting would take place shortly. He intended to entertain Henry as 'the prince of the world whom he esteemed, loved and trusted most'. He urged his nobles to receive the English in a friendly manner, and avoid bringing any 'evil advised persons to the meeting'.[13] They spent Whitsun there, where they were joined by more dignitaries, before heading north on the final leg of the journey. The anticipation must have been mounting among Claude's ladies, excited for the coming festivities and the opportunity to see the English king and queen, as well as to compare the splendours of the two courts.

As she approached Ardres, a town on the very edge of French rule, Anne could see the workmen and suppliers heading up and down the road as the place was prepared for the unprecedented events that lay ahead. Two temporary cities had sprung up in the Vale Doré, a dazzling, colourful sight, with the sun rising and setting on fields of shimmering cloth of gold. The French had pitched three or four hundred tents in a meadow by a river outside Ardres, covered with velvet, cloth of gold, embroidered with coats of arms and topped with pennants. The tallest was Francis's tent, 'as high as the highest tower, and three of a middle size, as high as the walls of a town, of wonderful breadth, covered with cloth of gold outside, and inside cloth of gold frieze. The great one was covered at the top with cloth of gold frieze, and below with velvet *cramoisy* violet, powdered with gold fleurs de lis'[14] and 'the orbs of the heavens by the craft of colours in the roof were curiously wrought in manner like the sky or firmament' and a crescent sundial covered in yew knots.[15] It was supported by two ships' masts tied together, made from cloth of gold, culminating in a life sized statue of St Michael, carved out of walnut, 'gilt with fine gold, as large as a man, having a mantle *en escharpe*, painted with fine azure, and powdered with fleurs de lis, and holding a dart in his right hand, and in the left a shield with the arms of France very brilliant'. Anne would have been lodged in, or nearby, 'the pavilions of the Queen, Madame, Mons. d'Alençon, the Constable, Messieurs de Lorraine, de Vendosme, de Guise, St. Pol', which were 'all very fine'. However, the splendour was not to last long, as the weather conspired against the tents, or perhaps Francis had overreached himself: 'The large pavilion of the King was afterwards blown down and the mast broken.'[16]

Word reached them that the English crossed the Channel on 31 May and that they had arrived at Guines on 5 June. On the following day, Henry ratified the former treaty for the marriage of Princess Mary and the Dauphin Francis, but it was not until the day after, 7 June, that the long-awaited meeting between the two kings took place. Claude and her ladies watched as Francis rode away, 'mounted on a beautiful charger, and clothed with a cassock of cloth of gold frieze, a mantle of cloth of gold, richly jewelled, the front and sleeves set with diamonds, rubies, emeralds and large pearls, hanging loose; his *barette* and bonnet of velvet, set with plumes, and resplendent with jewelry'.[17] His Swiss soldiers marched ahead of him, dressed in royal livery with white feathers, trumpets and heralds playing and banners displayed,[18] on towards the encounter 'with all the rufflers and galliants of the French court'.[19]

Anne was not present at the meeting, nor was Claude, nor any of the English women, but Thomas Boleyn was there, as a translator and a familiar face for the French. According to another eye-witness, the camps were about two leagues, or six miles, apart, so a deputation headed by the Cardinal of York arrived at the French court to announce Henry was on his way. Boleyn may have been among the 'number of princes and nobles' that led the way, or been one of the 'fifty gentlemen' of Henry's household, 'bareheaded and bonnet in hand, mounted on good horses and clothed in crimson velvet, each with a great gold chain... their horses richly caparisoned'.[20] Then followed another fifty, the king's ushers, bareheaded and bearing gold maces, along with the bearer of Henry's 'double cross of fine gold' topped with a crucifix of precious jewels, four lackeys in doublets made of cloth of gold, two guards of the Legate, two young men carrying poles, the Papal Legate himself, in red velvet and tasselled hat, riding a mule, then five or six bishops and 100 of the king's archers in white and green velvet, well-mounted, with their bows at their side. Then the king: Henry was dressed in cloth of silver, richly jewelled, with white plumes.[21] The meeting of these two dazzling figures, well-matched in every respect, was guarded but cordial.

> Then the two companies approached, the Kings descended the valley, gently, with their constables bearing naked swords. On coming near, they gave their horses the spur like two combatants about to engage, but instead of putting their hands to their swords, each put his hand to his bonnet. They then embraced bareheaded, dismounted and embraced again, and took each other by the arm to a fine pavilion all like cloth of gold, which the king of England had prepared. After a dispute which should go last, the two Kings entered together.[22]

Anne and Claude would have heard the detail afterwards, when the French returned to camp. On the following day, it was for the ladies to wait again, whilst the Admiral of France, Archbishop of Sens and a few others were entertained at the English camp at Guines. They returned to report that 'the King received them very honourably, amid great noise of artillery and music' and had been feasted 'marvellously, from the greatest to the least'.[23] This group would have brought back the first descriptions of the opulent village Henry had built, whetting Anne's appetite, and when she finally did venture into the English camp, she would have been astonished by what she saw. Preserved in the famous painting of the event, now hanging at Hampton Court Palace, Henry's workmen had been labouring to create 'a banqueting house, the most sumptuous that has long been seen... the foundations are of stone, the walls brick, and the rest wood; surrounded by cloth painted like brick; the covering painted *à l'antique*. Inside was tapestry of cloth of gold and silver, interlaced with white and green silk, the colours of the king of England. It contained four great *corps de maison*, eight saloons, chambers and wardrobes.'[24] Painted in around 1545, the work, which was formerly thought to have been by Hans Holbein but is now considered unattributed, shows Henry processing in the direction of this building, with red brick foundations and pillars, cloth sides and large entrance arch, set before fountains flowing with wine. Its dimensions were huge, with the great chamber being 'six score and four (124) foot in length, 42 foot in breadth, and 30 foot high, which is longer and wider than the White Hall; the second chamber to dine in to be in length four score foot, in wideness 34, and in high 27 foot, which is larger than the greatest chamber in Bridewell; and the third chamber to withdraw his highness in shall be in length 60 foot, in wideness 34, and in height 27 foot'. Just visible in the painting is the entrance to the Great court yard, which was 'garnished with roses, which were 'large and stately' and casts of the king's arms and heraldic beasts'.[25] Queen Catherine, Mary, dowager Queen of France and Cardinal Wolsey were also lodged within and there was a chapel painted blue and gold, with hangings of gold and silver, and rich cupboards of plate.[26] Anne had to wait.

It was another four days before Henry came to visit Queen Claude at Ardres. There is no question that Anne saw him on this occasion, perhaps even being used as a translator between the two parties. Back in 1513, in Burgundy, he had been in his early twenties, tall, golden-haired, chivalrous and optimistic. Now, he was a year off thirty, touched by the disappointment of failing to father a legitimate son, but still an impressive figure. Anne waited inside the Queen's lodgings, perhaps among of the women specially selected there to greet him, 'the most beautiful that could be, dressed in cloth of gold',[27] or perhaps with the queen herself. The man she saw enter was smooth-faced, his hair cut fashionably short, tall, broad and athletic, dressed 'in a double mantle of cloth of gold made like a cloak, embroidered with jewels and goldsmith's work... a beautiful head-dress of fine gold cloth (*toile d'or*), a beautiful collar *en escharpe* made of jewels, three of which were very conspicuous'.[28]

It is tempting to imagine this occasion, with hindsight, to picture a moment between the two, perhaps the meeting of eyes, or of some feeling stirring inside Anne, but to do so would be misleading. Henry certainly had an eye for a pretty face, but there is no reason to assume he even saw Anne; she was one of many women around the queen. She may have found him an impressive figure, physically and in terms of his presence and manners: it was a daunting thing to meet a king, especially one capable of making such an impression, but Anne's years spent among the royalty of the Burgundian and French courts equipped her to meet a king with poise, and not be overawed.

And yet there is a chance that Anne looked at Henry with particular interest, as a man, rather than as a king. It all depended upon what she knew, and whether there was anything to know, at this point. On 4 February 1520, her elder sister Mary had been married to William Carey, a gentleman of the Privy Chamber, close to the king. He was a direct descendant of John of Gaunt, albeit through the female line, making him a distant royal cousin on the Lancastrian side. In fact, Henry had attended their wedding at the royal chapel at Greenwich and made an altar offering of 6 shillings and 8 pence, indicating that he certainly approved of it, perhaps even had a hand in organising it. Anne would have been aware that Mary and her new husband were somewhere in the English camp that summer, but she may have known even more about her sister, had information been imparted to her by other family members. At some point around this time, Mary Boleyn became Henry's lover. Very little is known about the duration of the relationship, but most historians date it to the early 1520s. They appear to have been involved by March 1522, so it is plausible that during June 1520, the king had at least noticed the elder Boleyn girl, or may have been actively pursuing her. His liaison with Elizabeth Blount had ended with the birth of their son in 1519, and no other mistress is recorded for Henry at this point. Yet it is impossible to know whether Mary had yet begun sharing the king's bed, or whether Anne knew about it when she saw him enter the queen's tent that day at Ardres.

It was Louise of Savoy who welcomed Henry at the entrance to Francis's apartments, and conducted him along the alley to where the queen waited. Anne helped Claude into her dress of cloth of gold frieze, heavily embroidered, gold kirtle, sleeves covered with diamonds and other stones, diamond brooch and headset with rubies, emeralds and more diamonds.[29] As Anne watched, Claude rose from her chair and came forward to meet Henry. He knelt before her and removed his bonnet, before Claude took him by the hand and made him sit beside her. One eye-witness to the event described him as 'a very handsome prince, in manner gentle and gracious, rather fat, and with a red beard, large enough and very becoming'.[30] They dined together, served by men in gold gowns, with instruments played to mark the arrival of courses, comprising a vast number of 'viands, plates, vessels etc'. Afterwards, the tables were removed and Claude led Henry into 'a high room richly adorned with tapestry of cloth of gold and carpeted with crimson velvet, where they talked at leisure'. Afterwards, as Henry took his leave, he impressed the company by mounting his horse and spurring it to 'bound and curvet as valiantly as a man could do'. Rounds of artillery sounded as he rode away.[31] Was Anne impressed?

At the jousting on 11 June, Anne had the opportunity to see her mother and sister for the first time in many years, serving in the household of the English queen. It was probably also the first time she had ever seen Catherine of Aragon, as the queens 'saluted each other right honourably'[32] and took their places on the galleries alongside the lists. Catherine was then thirty-four, small, with red-gold hair, regular features and the decisive character of the Hapsburgs. Having endured six pregnancies to produce one living daughter, her losses had taken their toll on her tired body. Always more serious in nature than her much younger husband, her household had become a far quieter, moral and studious place than in former years, far more like that which Anne had experienced with Claude, and Anne probably saw the English queen in a similar light. But there was also something formidable about Catherine, something absorbed from her Spanish heritage, that gave her a fierce determination to see her duty through, to play the role of the Catholic queen to its fullest and to put everything she had into her queenship. If the young Anne did not detect this at the Field of Cloth of Gold, she would soon come to experience it first-hand.

Each king had twenty men with him in the lists, where two triumphal arches had been built and the shields of the monarchs were hung. The two queens and their ladies were all present, 'richly dressed in jewels', seated in a glazed gallery hung with tapestries. The eye-witness observed that Claude and Catherine 'talked together about the tourney' (tournament) but that 'many persons present could not understand each other and were obliged to have interpreters'.[33] No doubt Anne was invaluable at such a time, being bilingual, perhaps even being the one called upon to translate for the queens themselves. After such a long time spent at the French court, through such a formative period of her life, her English may have taken on a slight accent. There would have been much to observe and discuss. The horses were colourfully trapped in purple satin edged with gold, embroidered with raven's feathers on the French side, and the English in tissue of gold, cut 'in waves of water work', loose over russet velvet.[34] Each of the colourful riders rode past and did 'reverence' to the two queens before many lances were broken 'right valiantly'.[35]

Anne's next opportunities to observe the English king came in the following days, with 'course after course' being run on 12 June, before more 'dancing, wrestling and other pastimes' on 13 June, where 'the two kings surmounted all the rest in prowess and valiantness'.[36] On this occasion, Anne could hardly have failed to observe two men whom she would later come to know, her cousin, the privy councillor and 'hell-raiser' Francis Bryan, and the privy chamber member Henry Norris, who was soon to marry Mary Fiennes, also a relation of Anne's. Francis, Mary and Anne shared the same grandmother, Elizabeth Tilney, Countess of Surrey. Half the English were dressed in blue velvet, embroidered with the device of a man's heart burning in a woman's hand, while the others wore white satin embroidered with gold lettering.[37] Anne's maternal uncle Edmund Howard took his place in the lists, riding close to pay his respects to the queen, dressed in crimson satin covered with flames of gold. The following day saw more feats of chivalry and more finery. Both kings were keen to show off their abilities, without appearing to be trying too hard, so their efforts at foot combat, thrusting lances and fighting with swords were conducted with an edge of underlying tension.

Henry dined with Queen Claude at least once more, being received 'with much honour' and displayed his love of disguise, absenting himself and his company after the feasting in order to return, masked and dressed in green and gold, 'to glad the queen and the said ladies'.[38] And when the queen had seen them, 'these revellers took ladies and danced, in passing the time right honourably'. Then, at Claude's insistence, they removed their masks, before a banquet of spices, fruits and jellies was brought. They then concealed their identities again and rode out into the night.[39] Did Anne dance with Henry that night? Or with Bryan, or Norris? As chronicler Hall stated, 'to tell you the apparel of the ladies, their rich attires, their sumptuous jewels, and the goodly behaviour from day to day since the first meeting, I assure you, ten men's wits could scarcely declare it.'[40]

More tournaments followed, but when the lists were finally declared closed, both sides met at a temporary chapel which had been erected a fathom and a half high. It contained an altar and reliquaries, with two canopies of cloth of gold and chairs for the royal parties, their legates and bishops.[41] The kings and queens knelt on a platform to hear the high mass and kiss the Gospels. The crowd were awe-struck by the appearance of a strange creature in the sky. A 'great artificial salamander or dragon, four fathoms long and full of fire, appeared in the air from Ardres'.[42] Many people were afraid, thinking that it was some monster or comet, as they could see no strings attached to it. But the nature of the creature was a clue, as the salamander was one of Francis's best-known emblems, pointing to him as the instigator of the device. It passed overhead, 'as fast as a footman can go and as high as a bolt shot from a crossbow' before the royal party resumed the mass 'with great honour, reverence and devotion'.[43]

It is interesting that Francis was prepared to interrupt the holy ceremony and outshine all with a dramatic device representing himself, an action that some present might have considered irreverent in context, one which indicates a different tone to the French and English courts of 1520. Henry may have been famed for his love of masques and disguise, his high-spirited games and surprises, such as bursting into Catherine's chambers in costume, but matters of religion were still very serious to him and especially to his wife. His relationship with God at this stage was a devout, complex one; his faith was very powerful, self-defining, but he was also confused as to why God would deny him a legitimate son. His many pilgrimages and prayers had not borne fruit, so he was anxious not to displease God any further, as he was starting to believe that his choices had already caused a rift between himself and his maker. Francis, on the other hand, open to the disputations of heretics and those seeking to challenge and redefine Catholic practices, had a nursery full of children and, seemingly, God's blessing. He had achieved a great victory at Marignano and had yet to suffer the terrible defeat of Pavia. Under the surface, the two king's religious attitudes were quite different, and only Francis would have dared perform such a feat at such a time. In the years to come, all this would change, as Henry's love for Anne prompted him to become the greater iconoclast of the two.

On the final day of the camp, Henry again dined with Claude, before the farewells were made. Presents of horses, litters and necklaces were exchanged, as were promises and regrets at the imminent departure. Then, on Sunday 24 June, the two sides parted. Thomas Boleyn, Elizabeth and Mary went back to England with Henry, Catherine and their entourage, while Anne returned to Claude's court.

At the age of nineteen, she must have wondered what the future held for her, whether she was expected to marry and in which country her life would lie. It may be that Thomas had already spoken to his daughter about this question, because soon after his return, the idea of Anne's marriage had been proposed to the king. Anne may well have known that her time in France was limited, expecting the summons to bring her home, in order to settle down and become a wife and mother; it was an ambitious match that was proposed for her, with the prospect of advancing her family a step further, resolving a key inheritance dispute and making her a countess. It is impossible to know whether she welcomed the idea of exchanging Claude's court for her own household but, as ever, she was a dutiful daughter and knew that her family's fortunes must always override her personal feelings.

The husband being proposed for Anne was her distant cousin James Butler, son of Sir Piers Butler, from the Polestown line of Irish Butlers from which her mother derived. The dispute over Margaret and her sister's inheritance had not been settled since the death of their father in 1515, as even though the court had ruled in their favour, Piers was physically in possession of their lands in Ireland, and an important figure in his own right, whom few were willing to attempt to dislodge. A suitable solution would be the marriage of Piers' son to Margaret's daughter, which Boleyn raised at some point during the summer of 1520. This may have been prompted by James Butler's arrival in London, to serve in the household of Thomas Wolsey, who considered him to be 'both wise and discreet'.

It would have been a good match for Anne, a step up the social ladder, bringing wealth and influence, and there were no personal objections to the young man, who was a few years her elder. Born around 1496, James Butler had been raised in Ireland, had fought with Henry in France at the age of around seventeen and was seriously wounded in the leg, causing him to limp for the rest of his life. Henry initially supported the idea, writing in September 1520 to Anne's uncle, Thomas Howard, 2nd Earl of Surrey, who had been appointed Lord Deputy in Ireland that March, offering 'to advance the matter' if Piers was 'minded' to the match.[44] On 6 October, Surrey replied that it 'would be advantageous if a marriage were solemnized between the earl of Ormond's son, now in England, and Sir Thomas Boleyn's daughter,'[45] as it would cause 'a final end to be made between them, for the title of lands depending in variance... we see not but as he is well minded thereunto, and as ready to give his good advice and counsel'.[46]

At first, it looked as if the auspicious union would be beneficial to all parties and receive the king's blessing, and a very different future appeared to unfold before Anne.

In the meantime, Anne went back to serving in Claude's household. The queen's impending delivery was not far off and, in early July, she was at Abbeville, where Francis was hunting, before departing with him by water to Picquigny, and then on to Saint-Germain-en-Laye, arriving by 12 July.[47] On 10 August, the queen gave birth to Princess Madeleine, her fifth child. She would go on to have two more children, but this was the last lying-in of hers that Anne would attend. In early August 1520, ambassador Sir Richard Wingfield had 'leave to return home on private affairs' and was replaced by Sir Richard Jerningham. Louise of Savoy wrote to Wolsey from Saint-Germain, saying that Wingfield was 'leaving all here satisfied with his good offices' and that he had 'conducted everything to the honour and exaltation of the king'.[48] After the Field of Cloth of Gold, the English were still in high favour, and Jerningham was able to report to Henry on 21 September that Francis was being 'so good' to him, that he was invited 'into his privy chamber early or late, while the other ambassadors are standing outside'.[49] That autumn, the royal family returned to Blois, where they remained through the winter, celebrating Christmas there.

The culture of Anglophilia under Francis in late 1520 must have been particularly gratifying for Anne, seeing her countrymen praised and elevated, perhaps even benefiting herself from the long golden shadow cast by that summer's meeting. In February 1521, Claude was ill with a 'rheum in her cheek' but still found time to write to Henry in person, thanking him for his letters, and expressing her gladness to hear of the good health of the English royal family.[50] Yet as Anne entered her final year at the French court, increasing rivalry between Francis and Emperor Charles threatened to damage the fragile European peace. Francis was not ignorant of the fact that, immediately before and after their meeting, Henry VIII had met with his wife's nephew, and that Anglo-Imperial relations were once again cordial. Yet even with Henry increasingly trying to assume the role of mediator, disputes over territories along the French-Spanish border became violent, and both sides looked to the English king to take sides.

That spring, Claude and her household were at Romorantin, before travelling to Troyes, where they arrived on 23 April. Jerningham left them on 11 May, having been unable to see Claude and Louise in person, because they were about to make their ceremonial entry into Dijon, which he was forced to witness at a distance, and then, on Whitsunday, the king was occupied 'with ceremonies and healing sick folk'.[51] But the special relationship was still intact, with the Admiral of France, Bonnivet, writing to Wolsey on 25 May because Francis had heard Henry was suffering from a fever, and 'will not be at ease till he is told of his recovery'.[52] Richard Wingfield had been dispatched to the court of the Emperor Charles and the letters between himself, Jerningham and others, illuminate the nature of the growing dispute over the realm of Navarre: 'I see that the French king will not desist from war, as you have requested him,' Wingfield wrote. 'As for the Emperor, notwithstanding the ruffling which the French king has made in Navarre, he still wishes Henry to be mediator, although the variances are greater than before the invasion of Navarre, for which he trusts to have redress according to the treaty.'[53] The Emperor believed that Francis was

...the breaker of the peace. Whatever the French king say, it cannot be shown that his dominions have been invaded by the Emperor; and if he had had just cause of war he would not have delayed his answer. He may be sure the saying of Wolsey to his ambassadors, which he finds strange, was not said without sure ground. Francis will find the Emperor does not sleep, if he compel him to war.[54]

By mid-June, Charles had 'determined to invade France, even if England should refuse him aid, which he cannot believe'.[55] Fighting broke out in Navarre, Italy and north-eastern France's border with the Low Countries.

It cannot have been an easy situation for Anne, with her personal connections to both courts, anticipating war between the French and the Burgundians. Louise of Savoy confided to the Ambassador that she did not want war, and it may have been pressure from the women closest to him that made Francis draw back on 1 July. The king issued letters under his great seal, 'consenting to an abstinence from war between himself and the king of Castile, and to an arbitration of their differences by the mediation of Henry VIII'.[56] In private, it was a different matter: he thought it 'strange that the King wished him to submit to his arbitration, for no king of France had ever bound himself in such fashion, but he would yield to the King's request as much as he could with honour'.[57]

Henry issued Wolsey with a commission to settle the peace between Francis and Charles but that August, Sir Thomas Fitzwilliam wrote to him in cipher: 'I advertise your grace plainly what I see and hear. I think verily the French king will give battle to the Emperor's folks shortly.'[58] On 3 September, Wolsey confided to Henry that he had 'this day [received] writings, both from the ambassador at... [and from] the Emperor's court, of the news of Italy, and from Fitzwilliam... that the French king intends to give battle to the Emperor within 14 days. If so, and he lose the battle, the King will see his advantage; if he win, it will not be without marvellous and irreparable loss on his side. In either case, Henry will find small resistance at his entry, and may wait his opportunity in peace.'[59] Thomas Boleyn was also drawn into the diplomatic process, no doubt on account of his former connection with both courts. The Emperor thanked Wolsey for letting his ambassadors in England see letters from France, 'which the sieur de Boulan (Boleyn) showed them'[60] and by October Wolsey was writing back to request 'credence' for Boleyn and others, who were to be dispatched to Burgundy to 'dissuade the Emperor from war'.[61] Likewise, the Earl of Worcester and Bishop of Ely in France were to 'acquaint the lord St.

John's, Sir Thos. Boleyn and Sir Ric. Wingfield what towardness they find in the French king, as the others will give them like information of the Emperor; and, if the case require, may personally resort to the Emperor to remove ambiguities.'[62] On 25 October, Boleyn arrived at the Imperial court, which was then based at Courtray, or Kortrijk, sixteen miles north-east of Lille. He presented Wolsey's letters and remained with Charles, attempting to smooth over the impending crisis. He moved with the court on 2 November, when they relocated 13 miles east to the city of Oudenaarde, but soon Wolsey was warning that if Charles and Francis could not agree to a truce, then all the English ambassadors in both countries would be recalled. Boleyn was ordered to return 'forthwith'[63] leaving at 11 a.m. on 17 November. Two days later he wrote to Wolsey from Bruges, to confirm his departure, the letter sealed with a bull's head, for Boleyn; his arms were a red chevron with three black bulls' heads.

At the end of November Wolsey presided over a meeting known as the Calais Conference, along with the Chancellors of France and the Empire, and a Papal nuncio, to try to broker a peace.[64] Although the conference met for ten sittings, with a truce declared for its duration, neither Francis nor Charles were prepared to cease their hostilities, each blaming the other for initiating the conflict. It was clear that England would have to choose a side, as earlier treaties signed with each party promised that they would defend France, or the Empire, against their enemies. Wolsey's negotiations in Burgundy had committed Henry to war with France, and the perpetual peace of 1518 was now broken, along with the betrothal of Princess Mary to the Dauphin Francis. Instead, she was to be married to her cousin, the Emperor. Mary was only five years old at this point so although her future marriage was a good bargaining chip, the reality of it was distant. It must have been an awkward moment at court for Anne, when Francis realised that Henry had chosen to back the Emperor. She was recalled home at some point between the end of the Calais conference and the New Year, saying her goodbyes to Claude, Louise, Marguerite and her French friends after seven years of service – knowing that her country may soon to be at war with them. Given Marguerite and Louise's desire for peace, there must have been a sense of female wisdom being forced to bow to the men's desire for conflict. On 26 January 1521, Louise wrote to Wolsey, 'God knows what I myself have done for the love of the two princes, and to prevent the shedding of blood.'[65] The following February, she 'sent 50 carts of good wine as a present to Madame Margaret, requesting her to reconcile the Emperor to her son, and offering to do the like on her own part, but they have effected nothing whatever'.[66]

The same day, Francis wrote that 'the English scholars at Paris have returned home, and also the daughter of Mr Boullan'.[67] Anne's departure made him suspicious, and quite rightly so, as ships were being readied at Dover and musters being taken, in preparation for an invasion of France. At the end of January, Henry wrote to Margaret of Austria, to inform her that she might rely upon an English army of '16,000 English foot, 2,000 English mounted archers, 4,000 foreign foot and 3,000 foreign horse'.[68] The imperial ambassadors recorded a different reason for Anne's return home, reputedly from Wolsey himself: 'The Cardinal said that he himself was responsible for her recall, because he intended, by her marriage, to pacify certain quarrels and litigation between Boleyn and other English nobles.' There was truth in both explanations.

PART THREE

LADY IN WAITING

ELEVEN

Perseverance 1522

Late in 1521 or early in 1522, Anne Boleyn set foot back in England for the first time in seven years. The most likely route she took was from Calais to Dover, and it is possible that her father attended the Calais Conference, and that she arranged to meet him there so they might return together. Her age and gender dictated that she would have required a chaperone, and there was no Esquire Bouton provided on this occasion, especially as her recall to England was sudden – and even something of an embarrassment, as an indicator of deteriorating relations across the Channel. The presence of Sir Thomas in Calais suggests an ideal opportunity for her return under her father's supervision, perhaps even travelling with Cardinal Wolsey. As she stood on deck, watching the white cliffs looming, topped by the great grey fortress of Dover Castle, she would have understood that she was at a turning point in her life. At twenty, she was already quite old in a marriage market that commonly saw aristocratic girls partnered off in their mid-teens. The Boleyns' precedent of marital advancement, typified by the matches of Geoffrey, William and Thomas, indicate that her parents were waiting for an alliance with the right family, the Butlers, who could push the dynasty to the next level. As she sailed towards home, did Anne picture herself as an Irish countess?

Anne's progress back through Kent would have been slow, but her father could have taken advantage of the usual castles, manors and abbeys offering hospitality to royal servants, or the houses of friends, from Dover to Canterbury, on to Faversham and Ospringe, Sittingbourne, Rochester and Dartford. The green fields, orchards, churches and Kentish towns would have changed little in the intervening years, but it was not a route Anne would have travelled often during her childhood. Soon their surroundings became more recognisable as they neared home. From Dartford or Rochester, they would have dropped off the main road and headed through the winding lanes down towards Hever, but who Anne met there would have depended upon which of her family members were currently on duty at court. Elizabeth was serving in Queen Catherine's household, as was the married Mary, and Anne's younger brother George, now aged around eighteen, was possibly there too, showing up in official records for the first time in a royal grant that April. The terms of court officials were rotated, allowing them time to visit home between stretches of service, so Anne may well have enjoyed a warm family welcome, or else she had to wait a little longer for it, until she reached court.

By the start of March, Anne was in London. It was, plausibly, her first experience of the capital, but certainly her first visit as an adult, entering a world which had been integral to the rise of her family. Riding through the streets, she would have seeing the Boleyns' history written in its buildings, with the guildhall and Mercers' Company hall and church associated with her great-grandfather Geoffrey's term as mayor; the palaces of Westminster and the Tower, along with the Abbey and Cathedral of St Paul, integral to the rise of her grandfather William and father, Thomas. As the fourth-generation Boleyn in the city, Anne's perceptions of the place, and her hopes for the future, would have been shaped by her knowledge of the past and her sensitivity to her inheritance.

Yet the path by which she might attain glory was different from that of her male forebears. The Tudor gender dynamic dictated that women conform to certain roles, occupations, forms of expression and behaviour, rights and responsibilities. It prohibited actions that were commonplace for men. Biologically, spiritually, legally and culturally, women were considered inferior to their male relatives, who had the final say over their lives in all but the most exceptional cases. Anne could not simply follow her father's lead, no matter how skilled or able she was. Gender came first, merit second.

Ambition, activity, vision and leadership were considered to be male characteristics. Women might demonstrate shadows of these qualities in their work as supporting figures, by helping their husband, or serving the queen, by doing what they might within the female sphere to further the careers of their fathers and husbands, but the specific traits of innovation and drive were not considered appropriate when displayed by women. It would have been unfeminine and therefore a social disgrace for Anne to attempt to emulate her masculine forebears. She might enter a guild under certain circumstances, she may run a successful business in the event of her husband's death, even taking on apprentices, but she could not aspire to becoming a sheriff, alderman or mayor. Women were subordinate, although paradoxically they were supposed to be capable managers, organisers and hostesses, demonstrating sophisticated levels of ability, so long as they knew their place after the man of the house. They were to be contained within the patriarchal household at all times, rather than living independently, even within aristocratic circles, with that household a microcosm for the king's rule, making insubordination a kind of treason. They should not aspire to become better than their male peers or relatives, let alone attain a position of authority over them. Anne had the examples of her mother and sister to follow: to produce a large family, to enter the household of the queen and, in Mary's case, to bring social cachet and financial reward by becoming the king's mistress.

Stereotypes about women who did not fit the mould were a Tudor commonplace, the most obvious being the criticism and even downright disgust that deconstructed the gender of Anne's daughter, Elizabeth I, to present a perverted form of masculinity. Her resilience, strength and unwillingness to marry could not be comprehended by a percentage of society used to defining women as the opposite, as meddlesome and weak, easily tempted and lascivious; in short, as Eve. In opposition to this, the exemplars of Tudor womanhood were the idealised virgin mother of the Marian cult and the secular version of a docile, fertile queen. Even though common sense dictates that perfect examples of this type must have been scarce, if in existence at all, the symbol persisted in popular culture, in sayings and songs, medical advice and the visual arts. The lingering medieval tradition of rhyme and song depicted the expectation of women to fall prey to sin, or to fail, and expressed a relieved outrage when they did, and surprise when they did not. Such images were manipulated by those with an axe to grind, who sought to bring about a specific woman's downfall due to a difference in religion, or as part of the realpolitik of the Tudor court. Accusations of lewdness, fickleness, manipulation, scheming and witchcraft played particularly well to contemporary male fears, creating an undercurrent to gender relations that frequently surfaced, as attested in court depositions, gaol records and court gossip.

Yet in her years abroad, Anne had encountered other role models, who broke those gender rules to offer real female leadership in political, religious and cultural spheres. The examples of Margaret of Austria, Louise of Savoy and Marguerite d'Alençon showed Anne that women could play as significant a role within their families as men, not in denial of their gender, but in addition to it, as a function of it. It was a delicate path to negotiate, and their femininity made them vulnerable to the abuses of power that existed within every family and state. Although exceptional, high-born women could take leading positions on the international stage, the ceiling to their powers remained, with Margaret guided by her father Maximilian and brother Charles, while Louise and Marguerite were unable to prevent Francis embarking upon a war they regretted. Still, Anne had learned that women might wield influence and play an active part in shaping the courses of their own lives. Anne's story cannot be told in isolation from the gender politics of her day, of the way she overreached the expectations of her sex – with masculine permission – and how she became the scapegoat for male fears and weaknesses once that permission was withdrawn.

Beginning a new phase of her life in England, Anne was perhaps more aware than many young women her age of the need to seek out opportunities that may present themselves for her family's advancement. This quality has been subject to harsh criticisms by later historians, defined through the male gaze as an unattractive ruthlessness unbecoming to a woman, but such assessments are as anachronistic as they are simplistic and miss the essence of Anne's brilliance. They are, in fact, hangovers from the Tudor era. As Henry's attraction to Anne would prove, there was nothing less feminine or appealing about her for her ability to understand the operations of the court, ride the waves of Tudor patronage and enter negotiations at the appropriate moment. It was shrewdness, a kind of intelligence, part innate, part developed from her experiences and observations abroad. Her French style and manners, her very different background and European polish made her desirable in a world where everyone, regardless of gender, wanted to be desirable in the eyes of the king. The Tudor court was a giant wheel of fortune, a game of chance, and Anne was adept at the game. She had the acumen of a politician and a foreign charm in the body of an elegant young woman. This made her an unusual figure at the English court, exotic, different and challenging to men who were used to taking wives from their neighbourhood circle or the small, known aristocratic gene pool.

Anne had arrived in court by the start of March, as ambassadors from Emperor Charles broke their journey in London, on their way to Spain. Her time spent at Mechelen made her one of the few women besides Queen Catherine who had personally met Charles' aunt Margaret, and who had known Charles in his youth. Some of the visitors arriving from Burgundy may well have been familiar to Anne from her year at the Imperial court, and her skills as a translator would have established her as a useful addition to the party. When Henry ordered a joust to be held in their honour, Anne would have been among those watching in the galleries as the men rode out into the field to display their chivalric abilities. The king wore the colours silver and gold, bearing the same emblem he had displayed once in France, of the man's heart in a woman's hand, this time accompanied by the legend 'she hath wounded my heart'.[1] Was this a mere convention of the game of courtly love, or did Anne wonder to whom this referred? Did she suspect it may have been directed towards her sister?

As she watched, the leading gentlemen of the court rode out in turn in their finery, giving Anne a good introduction to the king's inner circle. The theme of the tournament was unrequited love, and the costumes with their symbolism followed the king's example. Anne would have recognised Sir Nicholas Carew, who came next, wearing white damask and cloth of gold, as he had recently been sent on an embassy to France, being received by Francis in January 1521. With a reputation as something of a rake, Carew was one of the young men whom Wolsey currently felt was exerting a bad influence upon the king, but his jousting abilities had impressed Henry sufficiently for him to retain his position, and the king had created a tiltyard especially for him at Greenwich. After him came the Earl of Devonshire and Lord Roos, both dressed in white velvet embroidered with gold and the images of a heart in chains and hands holding spears and feathers. Then followed two young gentlemen, Anthony Kingston and Anthony Knyvett, in crimson satin, on which was depicted a heart bound in blue lace and the motto 'my heart is bound', before Nicholas Darrell in black satin and Anthony Browne in silver and gold, both bearing more images and mottoes of heartbreak. Finally came Henry's brother-in-law, Charles Brandon, Duke of Suffolk wearing russet and silver, whose path had crossed Anne's in Mechelen, Paris and Guines,. Many lances were broken during the combat and the performance of the Burgundian visitors was 'much commended'.[2]

It was the influential Thomas Wolsey who played host to the ambassadors during much of their visit, capitalising on his international profile after the Field of Cloth of Gold and the recent Conference of Calais. Wolsey was one of the first servants Henry had selected on merit rather than pedigree. He had risen from humble origins in Suffolk, reputedly the son of a butcher or cattle dealer who had benefited from a good education at two local schools before proceeding to Oxford to study theology. By his late forties, Wolsey was approaching the height of his career, moving from the position of Henry's almoner and privy councillor to that of chancellor. He had been made a cardinal in 1515, but had recently missed out on his dream of occupying the papal see when Adrian VI had been appointed to replace Leo X in January 1522. In spite of his standing, he was still an outsider in aristocratic court circles, a man whose abilities had enabled him to transcend his class and rise higher than those who perceived themselves to be his masters. This created an uneasy balance of power, which would make his position uncomfortable and earn him enemies who would be all too swift to rejoice at his fall. His career underlines another truth about the nature of the Tudor court, that favour and advancement were dependent upon the king's pleasure. Henry's will was absolute and, with his support, a man might rise as far as he might fall, if that precarious support was withdrawn. As the recent execution of the Duke of Buckingham illustrated, the king could prove a fickle friend and the lives of even those closest to him were dependent upon his approval.

The eminently able Wolsey had quickly learned that Henry preferred pleasure to business. Wherever possible, the minister took over the tedious tasks of administration and organisation, and used the rewards he reaped to offer the king opportunities to relax and indulge. On the night of 3 March 1522, he invited Henry, his party and the ambassadors, to a 'great and costly banquet', followed by a play and a masque, enacted by players in parti-coloured clothes, half in russet satin, half in yellow.[3] The following day, 4 March 1522, was Shrove Tuesday. Wolsey had again devised a splendid entertainment, a symbolic masque featuring many of the leading figures of Henry's court, and offering a role to Anne, the newly arrived daughter of the diplomat, Sir Thomas Boleyn.

As far as is known, this was the first such entertainment in which Anne Boleyn was involved. Along with her sister Mary, the French dowager Mary, Duchess of Suffolk, and the rest of the players, Anne was conducted to York Place (later Whitehall Palace) to which Wolsey had made significant repairs in 1514–16 and again in 1519, making it a palace in miniature. It had a great gatehouse, chapel and garden, wardrobe, scullery, counting-house, fish-house, bake-house, wine cellar, buttery and steps to the river, by which the party are likely to have arrived. Anne was led to the great hall, hung with tapestries, set up in readiness for the guests. The place was dazzlingly lit with 'many branches', on each of which were fixed thirty-two 'torchettes' of wax.[4] Their flickering light revealed an elaborate castle at the far end of the hall, painted green and decorated with leaves, where banners hung from three towers, decorated with a thinly veiled declaration of love. The first banner bore the image of three hearts, torn in half; the second showed a lady's hand gripping a man's heart and the third showed another female hand 'turning' a man's heart.[5] The pageant was entitled the *Chateau Vert*, or *The Assault on the Castle of Virtue*.

Eight ladies waited inside the castle, dressed in Milanese bonnets and gowns of white satin, each named after abstract virtues, which were embroidered across them in gold. They were led out by Mary, Duchess of Suffolk, who played the role of beauty, followed by Gertrude Blount as honour. Anne and Mary Boleyn came next, as Perseverance and

Kindness, and the other roles of Constance, Bounty, Mercy and Pity were played by the Countess of Devonshire, Lord Morley's daughter, Jane Parker, Mistress Browne and Mistress Dannett, all of whom were locked inside the castle. From underneath them, more figures appeared, but these were a grotesque parody of the courtly women trapped within. Played by choristers of the Chapel Royal, attired 'like to women of Inde' (India), they represented the negative qualities of lovers: Danger, Disdain, Jealousy, Unkindness, Scorn, Strangeness and Malbouche, or bad (harsh) tongue. Then, eight Lords entered the hall, dressed in blue capes and golden caps, yet not so dazzling as their leader, who took the role of Ardent Desire in a costume of crimson satin adorned with burning flames of gold.[6] For once, Henry did not take this lead role, leaving it to William Cornish, who was nearing the end of a long career as actor, musician and master of the Children of the Chapel Royal. Accompanying him were Love, Nobleness, Youth, Devotion, Loyalty, Pleasure, Gentleness and Liberty. A mock battle followed, an allegory for the overcoming of a lover's scruples, in which the ladies wished to yield to Ardent Desire but were dissuaded by scorn and disdain. In their defence, the women threw rose water and comfits, whilst the men replied with dates and oranges and suggestive 'other fruits made for pleasure'. The firing of a cannon marked the end of the drama, after which the guests partook of another 'costly banquet'.[7]

The Boleyns were certainly high in Henry's favour at this point, which was partly the result of his relationship with Mary. A month before the *Chateau Vert* pageant, on 5 February, her husband William Carey was appointed keeper of the manor of Beaulieu or New Hall, the property in Essex which Boleyn had sold to the king in 1516, and bailiff of several nearby manors. That April, Thomas was given the position of treasurer of the king's household that he had long coveted, and the manor of Fobbing, in Essex. Five days after that, Henry granted him and his son George various offices in the manor, honour and town of Tonbridge in Kent, close to Hever, and the manors of Brasted and Penshurst, also in Kent, along with the parks of Penshurst, Northleigh and Northands.[8] No doubt Anne benefitted from Mary's intimacy too. Her presence at court was not necessarily a natural appointment; positions in Queen Catherine's household were highly sought after and by no means guaranteed, even to those with existing court connections. It is difficult to locate references that place Anne in the queen's employment, although her contemporary, George Cavendish, the biographer of Thomas Wolsey, states she was employed there soon after her arrival from France. There is a chance that Anne was actually a member of the household of Mary, Duchess of Suffolk, who had requested her presence in 1514 and whom she may have served in France. It was certainly Mary, not Catherine, with whom she was connected at York Place in 1522. However, since Cavendish entered Wolsey's employment in 1522, his observation is likely to have been accurate. Perhaps Catherine lent her sister-in-law some of the best dancers in her household for the occasion. And perhaps Anne was happy to oblige.

The French ambassador's assistant, Lancelot de Carle, or Carles, painted a rather sombre picture of Catherine's household, as a place of strict regulation and duties, with ladies sitting at their sewing or tapestries, where song, dancing and reading were forbidden. Catherine was deeply devout but her life did accommodate pleasure, especially in her younger years. She was thirty-six when Anne returned to England, with a six-year-old daughter whose dancing was much praised, and although Catherine had not conceived for three years, she had not yet reached her menopause, or given up hope of bearing another child. Catherine's household was not too different from that of Claude of France. There was time for fun, for poetry and music, and sometimes it was serious-minded, but its moral and religious tone could not prevent the flourishing of courtly love or prohibit visiting gentlemen flirting with the ladies, or their participation in dances and masques. What did set the English queen's life apart from Claude's was the French queen's string of pregnancies and deliveries. Claude had been heavily pregnant when Anne left France, and news may have reached her of the arrival of another son, Charles, that January. By September 1522, Claude would embark upon her final pregnancy, while Catherine's hopes in that department receded.

The king and queen spent that Easter at Greenwich, away from the bustle of the city, surrounded by the Kent fields. The palace was a favourite of Henry's and it stood just twenty-five miles north of Hever, so whether Anne was resident in Catherine's household, or a regular visitor, she would have had ample opportunity to observe the royal couple and the workings of their court. Catherine's establishment was a large one, catering for as many as 200,[9] containing many of the original Spanish staff who accompanied her to England in 1501, as well as long-standing English servants. A list of the women who were included in her train at the Field of Cloth of Gold two years earlier includes faces Anne would have recognised upon her return. Some were stalwarts of the Tudor court, while others were members of the Boleyn's wider family circle. They were also the women who were to witness Anne's rise to power over the coming years, through her period of service, to the moment she captured the king's attention and beyond. The ties of loyalty, family and patronage which they had already established would help determine their reactions to Anne when she became queen, but these years were also important in the degree of influence Anne could exert upon this circle, and the seeds of later alliances and enmities that were sown in the early 1520s. The circle of nobility in the early sixteenth century was small; many were related by blood, marriage or feud, each conscious of the deference due to them, and the pecking order. Anne was entering a closed world of allegiances and she quickly had to learn the ropes.

In Catherine's rooms, as the women sat sewing, or in the galleries overlooking the jousts, feasting in the hall or walking in Greenwich Park, Anne would have come to recognise Gertrude Blount, Countess of Devon, the daughter of Catherine's chamberlain, who was a similar age to her, and had married Henry Courtenay, a close childhood friend of the king. Her father, William, had taken as his third wife Alice Keeble, who was listed among the queen's retinue in 1520 but died the following year. Having grown up in the queen's household, Gertrude would remain loyal to Catherine, despite Anne's later efforts to befriend her. Her father would be charged by the king to relate the terrible news to the queen that she was being replaced by Anne in 1533. There was also Anne Hastings, Countess of Derby, whose mother was a Woodville and whose step-father had been Jasper Tudor. Anne was now approaching forty and the mother of eight children, but the king may have had an affair with her in his youth. Her sister Elizabeth Stafford, Lady Fitzwalter, was present, having a close friendship with the queen, which had prompted her to warn Catherine about her sister's relations with the king back in 1510. Another face from that time was Anne Hastings's friend Elizabeth Carew, a first cousin of the Boleyns, and sister to Sir Francis Bryan, who had also reputedly been a mistress of Henry in the past. Perhaps one of the most stalwart of the queen's supporters was her close Spanish friend, Maria de Salinas, now Countess Willoughby d'Eresby, once a member of the royal household of Castile. The king admired her so much that the same year Anne Boleyn returned to England, in 1522, he named a ship in his fleet the HMS *Mary Willoughby*.

As well as Anne's own mother, there was Elizabeth Boleyn's half-sister Anne, Countess of Oxford, since her marriage to the fourteenth Earl, John de Vere, who was Henry's Lord Great Chamberlain, but his excessive lifestyle and extravagant spending was earning him reprimands from the king. The countess's aunt by marriage, Margaret Scrope, the widow of the thirteenth Earl, was also sometimes included in Catherine's household. Anne may have also met cousins at court, the two daughters of her mother's younger sister, Muriel Howard, who had married Sir John Grey and died in 1511. Elizabeth and Anne Grey were a year or two younger than Anne, but she may have been introduced to them before in France in 1520. Anne may also have met her namesakes, her aunt Anne Tempest, who was married to her father's brother Edward Boleyn and her father's sister, Anne, the wife of John Shelton. The Shelton daughters, Mary and Margaret, would also appear at court in the coming years, to play key roles during their cousin's queenship.

Others with whom Anne would have become acquainted were Mary Stafford, Lady Bergavenny, Lady Scrope, Lady Morley, Lady Montague, Lady St Leger, Lady Parr, mother of Henry VIII's sixth wife, Lady Daubeney, Mary Fiennes, newly married to Sir Henry Norris, the widowed Lady Willougby de Broke, who would marry Lord Mountjoy in 1523, Lady Guildford and Elizabeth Hart, Lady Cobham, who was the third wife of Thomas Brooke, whose first wife had been a granddaughter of Geoffrey Boleyn. Thomas's daughter, who was Geoffrey's great-granddaughter, had married the poet Thomas Wyatt, a Kent neighbour of the Boleyns, whom Anne would also meet again at court. There was Margaret Bryan, Lady Guildford, wife of Henry's close friend Sir Henry Guildford, Master of the Horse, granted custody of Leeds Castle in Kent, in 1521, also close to Hever. Another close associate of Henry's, Sir William Compton, was a familiar figure at court, and although Anne may have seen his first wife, Walburga, at the Field of Cloth of Gold, Lady Compton had died in 1521, and William would soon marry Elizabeth Stonor. There was also Jane Parker, daughter of Lord Morley, with whom Anne had danced in the *Chateau Vert* pageant that March, who was to become her sister-in-law three years later.

One figure Anne may not have seen, but would have been aware of, was Eleanor Percy, Duchess of Buckingham. Her husband, Edward Stafford, the third Duke, had been one of the king's closest relations, being a nephew by marriage of Henry's grandfather, Edward IV. His consciousness of this proximity had led Stafford into some grandiose behaviour that irritated the king, who ordered his arrest on charges of prophecying and planning Henry's death. Buckingham had been condemned and executed for treason in May 1521, just nine months before Anne's return, although the news of it had certainly spread to France. Buckingham had been a colourful, highly visible character at the Field of Cloth of Gold whom it would have been impossible for Anne to miss, and his death was a shocking reminder of the power of the king and the dangerous line that a subject might overstep, no matter how wealthy or high-born. Close in age to Anne was Eleanor's daughter-in-law, Ursula Pole, granddaughter of George, Duke of Clarence, who was one of the last surviving members of the York family, and thus had her own claim to the throne. Ursula was eighteen and married to Henry Stafford; she had attended the Field of Cloth of Gold, having been four months pregnant at the time, but her father-in-law's disgrace had cast a long shadow over his children. Ursula had royal blood in her own right, which would later cause the Pole dynasty to be targeted by the king, but her husband's family would slowly regain their position, receiving the baronetcy after Henry VIII's death.

Anne was adept at court life. She probably took all these new faces and complex relationships in her stride. Her time in Mechelen and France gave her a familiarity, even an ease, with the manners and methods required to succeed, and it is likely that she settled quickly in the queen's household and made friends. She was unquestionably an asset to the court and, when the Emperor visited England that summer, it was natural that Anne was included in the festivities. Thomas Boleyn, along with Anne's Howard grandfather and uncle, were among those named by Henry to present themselves at Canterbury on 27 May 1522 in order to welcome Charles.[10] Wolsey met him on the sands at Dover and accompanied him on the short ride to the castle and thence north to the city, where the full reception committee was waiting. Kent's aristocrats and noblemen turned out in their finery to line the route. The ambassadors accompanying Charles described him entering Canterbury at sunset, where he was 'met by all the clergy' and 'placed under the canopy on the king's right hand' for the procession to St Augustine's Abbey.[11] He was then led to his lodgings in the Archbishop's Palace, where he had stayed in 1520, and only then, 'after many loving compliments exchanged mutually', the two kings parted. Boleyn and the Howards were present as part of the king's retinue, but it is likely that their wives and daughters remained at Greenwich to prepare the second welcome. One ambassador's account placed Catherine at Eltham[12] waiting to greet her nephew along the route, although other accounts state that the queen met him at Greenwich[13] and the route the kings took through Kent does not include Eltham. Anne can't be located on this occasion; she may have remained behind with the other women at Greenwich, rehearsing dances and helping the queen prepare, but her linguistic skills and former connection to Charles would have equipped her to be among those who travelled to Canterbury. On this, and other occasions, her abilities mean that she defies obvious categorisation, fitted to two potential roles. Did Anne's gender place her at Greenwich in the early summer of 1522, or did her talents take her to Canterbury?

The following morning, 31 May, Henry and Charles attended mass together, then set out to London via Sittingbourne, Rochester and Gravesend. From there, on 2 June, they took a barge on the Thames, arriving at Greenwich around 6pm. At the entrance to the Great Hall, the Emperor was reunited with his aunt Catherine and his young cousin Princess Mary, 'and all the ladies', expressing 'great joy' to see the pair of them. If Anne was seeing him again for the first time since 1514, she would have recognised the thick lips and oversized jaw of the boy she had known, despite his increased height, status and fashionable clothing. How he greeted her, and whether he recalled her fondly, or not at all, has gone unrecorded. Perhaps, at the English court, she was merely another face in the crowd. Charles was lodged in the Henry's apartments by the river, which were so richly hung with tapestries that the visitors marvelled at them.

No doubt Thomas Boleyn took part in the joust held at Greenwich on 4 and 5 June, in the Emperor's honour, with his wife and children watching from the galleries as Henry rode into the lists, dressed in gold and silver, with plumes on his head. This was the first occasion that Anne had seen the English court mount a major celebration with an international dimension, although she had seen much to surpass it in Europe. Copious amounts of cloth of gold and silver were made into hearts and mountains, yards of russet velvet were cut and shaped, fringed with Venice gold and silk points, yellow satin was cut into coats, black buckram used to embroider the tents and boards were covered with powdered clouds, made with Venice gold and silver.[14] The revels were designed by the master of the early Tudor court entertainment, William Cornish, and performed first at Greenwich, and on 15 June at Windsor. The dancers include Burgundian counts, the Prince of Orange, Charles Brandon, Duke of Suffolk and the Earl of Devon, resplendent in black bonnets with bright yellow bands, crimson satin mantles with gold knots, blue satin cloaks, Milanese bonnets and Portingale hoods.[15] Anne's sister Mary and her husband William Carey were also among the performers on June 5, along with Henry Norris and Mary, dowager Queen of France. There was a familiar theme to the action, which long-standing members of Henry's court recognised in the use of green foresters' coats and hoods, and the creation of costumes for 'Wodwos', which were 'wodwose', or wildmen.[16] The tension between chivalrous ideals and the unruliness of outlaws and wild figures had been a favourite motif of the king's since at least January 1510, when Thomas Boleyn had participated in an entertainment dressed as an outlaw in green. A 'stuffed body' was also part of the festivities in the summer of 1522, and a great number of tents and pavilions were erected at Greenwich, while the king's shoemaker was charged with the task of making twenty pairs of dancing shoes.[17] Whether or not she was dancing, Anne would have been a useful presence, on hand to welcome former friends, make introductions and translate.

After the Greenwich festivities, the king and Emperor made their official entrance to London, as recorded by eye-witness Gasparo Contarini. The streets were hung with tapestries and eight triumphal arches had been erected, representing messages relevant to the Burgundians, such as the order of knighthood, the genealogy of the families and the start of the western empire. No doubt Thomas Boleyn was among the procession, following the 400 'English gentlemen and Imperialists... but the majority English', who were dressed in black velvet, with expensive gold chains around their necks, preceding Henry's councillors. They paused in the Cathedral of St Paul's before retiring to their lodgings in the newly finished Bridewell Palace.[18] Over the coming days, the Emperor's party played tennis, attended more masses, dined with the Duke of Suffolk in Southwark and hunted in his park. On 7 June, Cardinal Wolsey hosted a dinner, at which he displayed just how far English foreign policy had swung away from the French and back towards the Empire when, in the middle of the meal, he began 'vituperating the French'. As Contarini reported, 'he said that if peace was to exist in Christendom they must be exterminated, as they were always fomenting strife and discord among the Christian powers' and that the 'King of England was better entitled to the crown of France' than Francis 'and meant to possess himself of it'.[19] This was the sentiment behind the Treaty of Windsor that was concluded on 16 June, attacking Francis for creating war in Christendom at a time when it was under attack from the Turks.[20] That evening, Henry hosted a banquet followed by a play. 'It was a farce, and in it the King of France and his alliances were ridiculed,' as one eye witness described. Two figures, of Friendship and Prudence, united to 'perform very great deeds' together, assisted by Might. When a man brought a wild and ferocious horse onto the stage, they joined forces to tame its unruliness, causing it to follow them with its head lowered. 'The meaning of it is clear. The horse is the King of France. Whether they have bridled and tame him he is unable to say.'[21]

The mask was acted by young gentlemen, but afterwards 'ladies came into the room in fancy dresses and danced the Pabana' with the gentlemen whom they chose as partners. The Spanish witness claims there were eight ladies[22] while chronicler Hall places the number at twelve, and dresses them in gold and silver lace over red satin.[23] With Anne and Mary Boleyn chosen to dance key parts in the *Chateau Vert* a few months before, they were surely called upon again to perform for the Emperor. If Anne was involved, her participation would have made her complicit in this criticism of France. The allegory of the horse would not have been lost on her, either. Such a role may have made her uneasy; or else she embraced it as a pragmatist, accepting the change in direction of the king's foreign policy and aligning herself with England and the Empire in their drive against France. Yet Anne's identity, her style and upbringing, her process of definition as an adult, was European, specifically French. The part she played on this occasion must remain another of the many mysteries of her life, but raises interesting questions about the interplay of her emerging identity and the mood of the court.

The cleverest members of the English court appeared able to take a pragmatic approach and bend to the change in mood according to the king's whim, some compromising their own principles or beliefs. Or that is the way the realpolitik of Tudor service was sometimes perceived by external observers. At the end of July, after the Emperor had departed, Contarini, who had witnessed the whole visit, gave his private thoughts about Thomas Wolsey in a letter home to Venice:

> With regard to Cardinal Wolsey, the Chancellor said he was a man of little religion, and that during the negotiations between the Emperor and England, Wolsey rejected a clause which had been inserted respecting the defence of Hungary against the Turk, saying, 'Let us first expel these Turks here at hand,' meaning the French. The Chancellor also accused him of avarice, and stated that Wolsey was not ashamed to demand of the Emperor, for himself and some other personages of the English Court, an annual pension of twenty-two thousand ducats, saying that such was the amount received by them from France; to which terms the Emperor was compelled to agree, and he accordingly promised them this sum.[24]

Contarini's account also mentioned that Wolsey had 'meddled' between the Emperor and Venice, 'for the sole purpose of gaining a considerable amount of ducats from the Republic'.[25] Despite his vows, Wolsey had no qualms about accruing wealth, titles and lands, or living an extravagant lifestyle, building himself a palace on the Thames at Hampton Court suitable for a Renaissance cardinal, modelled on those he had seen abroad. He was not alone in this, nor in the way he lived in a 'non-canonical' marriage and produced two children. His status meant he may have been the most visible clergyman committing these sins, although as Henry's later investigation into the monasteries revealed, his choices were fairly representative of the time. But the tide was turning. Voices of criticism in Europe were being raised against such abuses, with the formation of pockets of resistence, which tried to capture a simpler way of worship. Key texts engaging in the questioning of Catholicism were Sebastian

Brandt's *Ship of Fools* in 1494 and Erasmus's *In Praise of Folly*, written in 1509, through to Luther's pamphlets of the 1520s. It was in 1522 that Luther published his translation of the New Testament in German from Hebrew and Ancient Greek, as well as a book entitled *Against Henry, King of the English*, in which he called the king a 'disgrace of God', a fool, liar and damnable, rotten worm, for Henry's defence of the pope the previous year. For the time being, Henry had no intention of questioning the centuries-old models of religion in England or the means his god-fearing servants used to advance their careers. Later, it would suit his purposes to do so.

TWELVE

First Love 1522–4

Anne is difficult to locate during the second half of 1522. The war with France continued, as the feet of English soldiers trampled down the grass in the valley of Gold where just two years before there had been oaths of brotherhood and friendship. It is likely that she remained in the queen's household, or as one of the women her mother was entitled to keep at court, although it is equally possible that she spent some time at the family home in Hever when she was off duty. The king and queen kept that Christmas at nearby Eltham Palace in Kent, and if Elizabeth Boleyn and Mary Carey were present in their official capacities, then surely Anne was too.

It is also highly likely that at some point Anne met the young man her parents intended her to marry. James Butler was in the household of Thomas Wolsey, along with George Cavendish, who wrote a life of the cardinal, in which more information about Anne's early life surfaces. Like Cavendish, Butler was probably a gentleman usher, attendant upon Wolsey, a witness to the many occasions when he hosted entertainments for the king and sometimes accompanying him to court. He and Anne may have been introduced as the candles flickered low at York Place, in the gardens at Eltham, or in the courtyard at the cardinal's new palace of Hampton Court. Given Wolsey's stated commitment to the Butler-Boleyn match, a meeting between the intended pair would have taken place at one of the royal palaces, at Wolsey's main residence of York Place or even at Hampton Court, which he had begun building in 1515.

The young man Anne met in 1522 was known by his contemporaries as 'Butler the lame' on account of the injury he had sustained to his leg whilst fighting on the king's French campaign as a youth in 1513. A portrait by Hans Holbein the younger, in the Royal Collection, once thought to depict Thomas Boleyn on account of the label 'Ormond', has recently been re-identified as James Butler in later life.[1] Painted around 1533, it depicts a man in a red cap, with dark brown hair trimmed in a smooth line around his head, dark hooded eyes and a red moustache and beard. His features are regular and not unpleasant, the nose a little long, but well-shaped, the mouth resolute. There is nothing obvious to object to in his appearance, and although the extent of his lameness cannot be measured, he proved himself perfectly capable of marrying and fathering seven sons.

The Butler match would have been a perfect solution to the question of the Boleyn family's stake in Ireland, and all was moving in its favour in 1521–2, but then, for some reason, the notion was dropped. Anne had not yet caught the king's attention, and Henry had backed Wolsey's proposals for the match. It must have been that there was some personal objection raised on the part of the families, or that the young people themselves were not keen. Personal inclinations were not often taken into account, and families might even insist upon politic alliances between individuals who actively disliked each other; but it may have been that Butler was aware Anne's affections were engaged elsewhere. It was another young man, living under Wolsey's roof, who stole her heart away from her intended fiancé.

Cavendish describes in detail the nature of Wolsey's household, second only to that of the king, or even considered by some to surpass it. The little satirical poem penned by court poet John Skelton, 'why come ye not to court? To the King's court, or to Hampton Court', exposes just how close to a royal lifestyle Wolsey was then living. He had 'a great number daily attending upon him, both of noblemen and worthy gentlemen, of great estimation and possessions, with no small number of the tallest yeoman he could get within all this realm', particularly choosing the most 'comely' yeomen.[2] Two yeoman ushers and two grooms always sat on his second table at dinner, and he looked after his servants well, with even his cook being dressed in damask satin with a gold chain around his neck.

A board was continually kept in his chamber to feed the 'young gentlemen', among whom were Cavendish, Butler and their contemporary, Henry Percy, as part of a total community of around five hundred.[3] Along with the other gentlemen in his service, they were dressed in his livery of 'crimson velvet of the most purest colour that might be invented, with chains of gold about their necks'.[4] Their role was to join him in his privy chambers after mass in the morning, to help him into his robes and accompany him into his presence chamber, carrying before him the great seal, or his cardinal's hat, calling those present to make way for him. Often they would accompany him to Westminster by horse, where he would sit in the Chancery court, hearing cases, and then into the court of Star Chamber. Every Sunday, he attended the king's court, most often at Greenwich, travelling by barge 'with all gentlemen within with him',[5] visiting Henry's chambers and staying to dine before returning home. Henry might return the visit, 'at which time there wanted no preparations... with viands of the finest sort... such pleasures were derived for the king's comfort and consolation,' including banquets of two hundred dishes or more, followed by 'masks and mummeries in so gorgeous a sort and so costly a manner, that it was heaven to behold'. It was on such occasions that Wolsey's servitor, Henry Percy, first saw Anne, who 'for her excellent gesture and behaviour did excel all other'.[6] In the words of Cavendish, who was an eye-witness:

> My Lord Percy, the son and heir of the Earl of Northumberland, who then attended upon my Lord Cardinal, and was also his servitor... when it chanced the Lord Cardinal at any time to repair to the court, the Lord Percy would then resort for his pastime unto the Queen's chamber, and there would fall in dalliance among the queen's maidens, being at the last most conversant with Mistress Anne Boleyn than with any other, so that there grew such a secret love between them that, at length, they were ensured together, intending to marry.[7]

The duration of Anne and Percy's romance cannot be ascertained. The young man may well have witnessed Anne's performance in the *Chateau Vert*, in fact, it seems very likely that he did, along with a number of other of Wolsey's gentlemen ushers, given that it took place at the cardinal's residence of York Place. There is even a chance that he performed in it too, as one of the unnamed eight gentlemen. Cavendish's report suggests that their relationship evolved over a period of time, dictated by natural inclination, until the feeling between them deepened into love.

Henry Percy is thought to have been born around 1502, making him a few months younger than Anne, and aged around twenty at the time of their meeting. He was a first cousin of Anne's brother-in-law, William Carey, and had been raised in the north before being sent to join Wolsey's household, where he did well, being knighted in 1519. A marriage had been planned for him with the heiress Mary Talbot, daughter of the Earl of Shrewsbury, in 1516, but the pair had reputedly disliked each other on sight. No image survives of him in his youth, but a later medallion shows him in middle age, in profile, with a prominent nose and full beard. The romance progressed through the end of 1522, into 1523. It was probably that spring or early summer that the pair reached an understanding that they would like to be married. Anne would have been aware that it was not the match her father had intended for her, and it did nothing to settle the Irish question, but it was at least an equal match in terms of status. With Percy being the heir to his father's Northumberland title and estates, Anne would have become a countess in due course. The fourth earl was then in his mid-forties and would die in 1527 after a long career at court, making Henry the fifth earl. If Boleyn could set aside his Ormond ambitions, or settle them in another way, Anne had every reason to hope her father might grant her choice, especially if vows had been exchanged, making the liaison semi-official.

Yet, Thomas Boleyn knew nothing about his daughter's hopes. As the romance blossomed, he was out of the country on the king's business, unable to keep an eye on what was happening. Perhaps it was due to his absence that it reached such a point, although Anne's mother, and her mistress, whether the queen or Mary Tudor, should have been aware of what was developing.

Boleyn and Richard Sampson, dean of the chapel, were issued with instructions for an embassy to the Emperor in Spain, in August 1522. They were to inform Charles that Henry would be ready for a joint enterprise against France and that the English Admiral had already landed at Calais.[8] In addition, they were given further, secret, guidelines about their mission, to flatter the Emperor and discover the real state of affairs in Europe:

First, they are to dwell much on the King's great affection for the Emperor, with as pleasant words as they can devise, marking his gesture and countenance, and how he receives it; and to discover in what sort of esteem he is held by his subjects, and whether they are likely to provide him with money. 2ndly, what is really the state of the enterprise against France. 3rdly, how he is stored. 4thly, on what terms the Burgundians stand with the Spaniards. 5thly, what means were used with the Pope for an abstinence of war between France and the Emperor, what is the Emperor's inclination, and what secret messages pass. 6thly, what drifts are practised between the Emperor and the king of Portugal. 7thly, to urge him to invade Guienne.[9]

While Anne was dallying with Henry Percy that autumn, Boleyn was at Plymouth, having been delayed by bad weather; some ships were driven back to shore and others were lost. By 16 October he had landed at Laredo, near Santander, on the northern Spanish coast, and wrote indignantly to describe how they had been attacked by six ships from Brittany, who came along the windward side 'and pressed them hard', firing arrows, against which the English defended themselves with straw mattresses and anything else to hand. He reached Valladolid on 31 October and was granted an audience with Charles on 5 November. In January 1523, Boleyn's expenses of £60 were paid 'by warrant of the Cardinal'[10] who wrote to Thomas to 'hasten the Emperor's answer as much as possible'. Wolsey wanted to know how many men and ships Charles was prepared to commit to guarding the seas, hoping for four or five, along with two 'zabres' of thirty or forty tonnes, so they could attack the French coast.[11] Boleyn replied giving assurances that he had spoken with the Papal ambassador, who assured them that England would always be included in any European peace[12] and contradicting a rumour they had heard, suggesting that Wolsey was unfavourable to the Imperial alliance.[13] In the third week of March, Thomas received his letters of recall to England but before he departed, he remembered the terrible voyage out and undertook a pilgrimage to the cathedral of St James at Compostella, to give thanks for his safe arrival and, no doubt, to ask for protection on his return journey.[14] It was during his absence that he was invested as a knight of the Garter at Windsor in April 1523, raising the Boleyns higher than ever before. He had departed Spain by 10 June, although his colleague Dr Sampson remained behind and was back in England by 3 July.[15]

Thomas Boleyn may have arrived back in England in time for the visit of King Christian of Denmark, Norway and Sweden, and his Queen Isabella. Anne knew the queen from her time in Mechelen, as Isabella was the younger sister of the Emperor Charles, and had been in the schoolroom of Margaret of Austria. Anne had attended Isabella's wedding in July 1514, before being summoned from the Netherlands for France. In the intervening seven years, Isabella had born three surviving children out of six pregnancies, become queen and been deposed by the Swedish nobility. Anne and her mother would have been at Greenwich when Catherine stood under the cloth of estate in the Great Hall, to receive the royal guests. Accompanying the royal couple were their three children, including a two-year-old daughter Christina, who would feature fifteen years later in Henry's marital plans, famously rejecting the king with the promise that if she had two heads, she would happily give him one of them. After feasting every day at Greenwich 'for a season', the family were lodged in Bath Place in London, before being accompanied to Dover with many gifts from Henry and Catherine. The king was clearly pleased with Boleyn's service, as in September, he was granted the office of Keeper of Bekeswood Park in Nottinghamshire.[16] But it would have been around this time, or soon after, that the behaviour of his daughter during his absence came to light. According to Cavendish, it was not only Boleyn and the cardinal who were displeased, but the king was angered by Anne's illicit betrothal too.

Somehow, the couple's secret was exposed. It may have been that they naively took the step of formally requesting permission to marry, or that their preference was observed, or their confidences betrayed. Cavendish's account states that they had exchanged promises in front of witnesses, suggesting the likely source of the leak.[17] With Wolsey responsible for the morality of the young men in his house, the threat posed to an established dynastic negotiation by a love match could not be tolerated. It was not so much that any sexual impropriety had taken place, but that they had offended by the way they went about it, taking matters into their own hands instead of following the usual diplomatic channels. Aristocrtic marriages were not simply family matters, they had to be politically and practically viable, and receive royal support. The cardinal intervened, calling Percy before him and berating him in front of the servants of his chamber. Cavendish reports the rebuke:

I marvel not a little of thy peevish folly that thou wouldst tangle and ensure thye self with a foolish girl yonder in the court. I mean Anne Boleyn. Dost thou not consider the estate that God hathe called thee unto in this world for after the death thy noble father thou art most like to inherit and possess one of the most worthiest Earldoms of this realm and therefore it had been most meet and convenient for thee to have sued for the consent of thy father in that behalf.[18]

Percy had been already matched

...according to your estate and honour, whereby you might have grown so by your wisdom and honourable behaviour in to the King's high estimation that it should have been much to your increase of honour. But now behold what you have done through your wilfulness, you have not only offended your natural father but also your most gracious sovereign.[19]

George Wyatt also confirmed this report during the reign of Elizabeth, but what is interesting about Cavendish's version is that he believed Henry was 'offended' by the engagement, 'wherefore he could hide no longer his secret affection but revealed his secret intention unto my Lord Cardinal in that behalf'.[20]

This comment is often dismissed as incorrect, as Anne Boleyn's relationship with Henry did not begin for at least a couple more years, around 1525 or 1526, but we should be careful not to reject this entirely. A pre-existing admiration on the part of the king is not precluded, even though the match was rejected on dynastic grounds. It is plausible that Henry had noticed Anne already and hoped to add her to his list of conquests, perhaps after her marriage to Butler. Had he already appreciated her charms, it would have been quite in character for the king to be piqued that she had wilfully bestowed her affections elsewhere, and to feel she needed to be taught a lesson to pull her back into line. After all, Cavendish was present in Wolsey's household at the time, an eye-witness to the development of the king's affairs and privy to the couple's developing feelings. If Percy was going to confide his secret in anyone, the most likely candidates would be found among the other young gentlemen of Wolsey's household. Although it is true that Cavendish records Anne's history with hindsight, the notion that Henry had already been drawn to the woman with whom he would soon fall passionately in love is not at all difficult to believe. Yet Henry was not committed at this stage. The timing was not right. His wife had not yet reached her menopause and he had not considered Anne as a potential wife, only a mistress, if at all. If he did intervene in the Percy-Boleyn betrothal, it would have been primarily to restore the Butler match for its political usefulness and preserve the Percy-Talbot connection. Those marriages, and the land settlements they provided, were infinitely more important to the country than the inclinations of two young people. In 1522–3, not even the king was allowed to disregard the commonweal in order to follow his heart. Not yet anyway.

Yet Percy was initially prepared to fight for his love. He seems to have genuinely wanted Anne for his wife, according to Cavendish, as he attempted to stand up to the cardinal and argue in her favour, even though he was 'weeping' as he did so. He stated that he 'knew nothing of the king's pleasure' and was very sorry for any displeasure he had caused, but 'thought (him)self sufficient to provide me of a convenient wife where as my fancy served me best but that my lord my father would have been right well persuaded and though she be a simple maid and having but a knight to her father, yet she is descended of right noble parentage as by her mother she is nigh of the Norfolk blood and of her father's side lineally descended of the Earl of Ormond.'[21] As Percy explained, the understanding had become common knowledge amongst the couple's acquaintances, having 'gone so far before so many witnesses that I know not how to avoid myself not to discharge my conscience'.[22]

Such a process of formal betrothal was sometimes finalised by the consummation of the match and Percy specifically refers to it, in Cavendish's words, as a 'precontract'. It has been suggested by some writers that Anne and Percy might have slept together, as their vows would have entitled them, but it is unlikely that the king would have later pursued Anne for seven chaste years in the knowledge that she had slept with another man, or that Anne would have taken such a step to compromise the Boleyn name without her father's blessing. Cavendish's account makes it sound like a genuine love match, which both parties believed would have a good chance of taking place.

Percy remained adamant until Wolsey summoned his father, the fifth earl. Henry Percy senior 'made quick speed to court' on hearing of the matter, and went at once to the cardinal, meeting him 'in secret communication' in his gallery.[23] Then, he called for wine and sat down upon a bench for the waiters, before summoning his son. The harsh character assassination ascribed to him by Cavendish gives a one-sided impression of the young man to whom Anne had contracted herself: 'Thou hast always been a proud, presumptuous, disdainful and a very unthrifty waster...' The young Percy had now 'misused' himself, with 'no manner of regard to' his father or king by 'ensuring' himself to Anne. Warning his son, 'use thyself more witter hereafter', the Earl assured him that if he did not 'amend his prodigality' he would be the last Earl of their house, due to his natural inclination to be a wasteful prodigal. Thankfully, the father had 'more choice of boys' to choose from, who he trusted would 'prove themselves much better and use them(selves) more like unto nobility'.[24]

With this diatribe and threat, he obtained Percy's promise that he would be married to Mary Talbot, daughter of the Earl of Shrewsbury, according to the terms of the betrothal. Cavendish related that the 'former contract was clearly undone, wherewith Anne Boleyn was greatly offended saying that if it ever lay in her power, she would work the Cardinal as much displeasure'. Percy was 'commanded to avoid her company and Anne was 'commanded to avoid the court and... sent home again to her father for a season whereat she smoked for all this while she knewe nothing of the King's intended purpose'.[25]

Cavendish's account can be read as fairly trustworthy, but it can be questioned where he puts words into the mouths of the key players. It is unlikely, even if he had witnessed these events in person, that he would be able to recall their speech with any degree of precision; but considering his position in Wolsey's household, his version of events must contain more than an element of truth. The basic facts are sound regarding the betrothal. Percy and Anne clearly fell in love at court, as he sought her out in the queen's apartments, perhaps dancing together, playing cards, reading or taking part in court entertainments. Catherine's court in the 1520s has been presented by some historians as being dour and solemn, with women sitting in silence and reading, devoid of books, dance and song. This is almost certainly misleading, given the references to Catherine's role in the court entertainments and masques in the chronicles of Hall. While the queen may have withdrawn more from public life, she had not taken up the life of a vowess. Catherine was becoming increasingly religious and her court may not have been as colourful as it once was, but this image of an overly austere queen belongs more to the coming years: the poetry of Thomas Wyatt attests to the tone of her court at this time and if her ladies were busy sewing, they would have been working on the costumes and elaborate disguises that Henry still loved. Catherine might set the tone of her household, but Henry set the tone of the court.

The implications for Anne were considerable. With the Butler and Talbot matches both still viable in 1523, the young couple took quite a daring step in 'ensuring' themselves to each other, to borrow Cavendish's word. Conscious of her family's ambition, she had attempted to take her future into her own hands, even if the results might have concurred with the wider Boleyn vision.

Evolving out of Percy's attentions to her at court, and purely of their own choosing, it would seem this is the first occasion that Anne experienced romantic love. No records survive of any liaisons or preferences during her years abroad, as the close supervision of Margaret's and Claude's households ensured. Although Anne's feelings on the matter were not recorded elsewhere, the wrath they evoked, and her apparent removal from court, support Cavendish's suggestion that she took 'great offence'. And there is the comment previously quoted: 'If it lay ever in her power, she would work the cardinal as much displeasure.'[26]

Percy was 'commanded to avoid her company' and she was 'commanded to avoid the court, and sent home again to her father for a season'.[27] It had been a brutal lesson for her about the boundaries of love at Henry's court and the dangers of letting emotion take precedence over dynastic might. She had broken the rules when it came to courtship and marriage: only the king was allowed to do that.

The question of the Ormond/Butler inheritance was finally settled in February 1528, which was probably after Anne had accepted the king's proposal of marriage. An indenture was made between Henry and the heirs of Sir Thomas Butler, Earl of Ormond and Sir Thomas Boleyn, Viscount Rochford, for which Wolsey was to act as mediator. From that point forward, the title of Earl of Ormond was to revert to the grant of the king.[28] He would give the title to Anne's father in 1529 and after the death of Sir Thomas, it passed briefly to Piers Butler and then to his son, James, and his heirs. Given the dating of this indenture, it might seem that the Boleyn-Butler match was eventually abandoned because of Henry's interest in Anne, although in reality, it had lost its impetus five years before:

Indenture tripartite between Henry VIII. on the one part; dame Ann Seyntleger, widow, and dame Marg. Boleyn, widow, daughters and heirs of Sir Thos. Butler, earl of Ormond, and Thos. Viscount Rochford, son and heir apparent of dame Margaret, and Sir Geo. Seyntleger, son and heir apparent of dame Anne, on the second part; and Sir Pierce Butler, cousin and heir male of the said Earl, and Jas. Butler, his son and heir apparent, on the third part; witnessing an agreement between the parties through the mediation of Wolsey;— that the title of the earl of Ormond, with the annuity of 10*l.* out of the fee farm of Waterford, shall be henceforth at the King's disposal; that Sir Pierce shall be allowed peaceable possession of the manors of Cloncurry and Turvy in Ireland, and the said dame Ann and dame Margaret of the castles and manors of Carrykmakgryffen, Roskre, Kilkenny, and a number of others; that dame Ann and dame Margaret grant to farm, to the said Sir Pierce and James his son, the castle of Kilkenny, and other lands on the west side of the river Barowe, in the counties of Kilkenny, Tipperary, and Ormond, for the term of 30 years, at a rent of 40*l.*; that if Sir Pierce Butler, and James, or any of their heirs, do within that time recover possession from the wild Irish of other lands west of the Barowe which should belong to dame Ann and dame Margaret, the said Viscount and Sir George, they shall enjoy them to the end of that term without paying any more rent; that dame Anne, dame Margaret, the said Viscount and Sir George, and their heirs for ever, shall enjoy the castle of Carrykmakgryffen, and other lands east of the Barowe, without let or hindrance, except the manors of Cloncurry and Turvy, but that they will grant Sir Pierce and James reasonable leases, a year after the feast of the Annunciation of Our Lady next.[29]

The Percy-Boleyn precontract would raise its head once more. By 1532, when Anne was poised to become queen, and Percy's unhappy marriage to Mary Talbot had broken down, his disgruntled wife sought a divorce, citing the previous arrangement with Anne as grounds for annulment. However, when the allegation was investigated, Percy was questioned about his love affair and the nature of the understanding between them. Under oath, with the potential to derail the king's imminent marriage, he wisely denied that there had ever been a formal engagement ten years earlier. Or rather, he neatly circumvented it, to the peril of his mortal soul, writing on 28 May, that it 'may be to my damnation, if ever there were any contracte (sic) or promise of marriage between her and me'.[30] These sound very much like the wise words of a courtier who had already been stung by the king once.

THIRTEEN

Hever 1524–5

Fortunately for Anne, her entanglement with Henry Percy appears not to have damaged the favour that the king showed to the Boleyn family. In November 1523, Thomas was named in the commission to collect the subsidy in Kent, which was the unpopular tax levied by the king in order to subsidise his coming war with France. Along with other local dignitaries in the county, who owned more than £40 in goods or lands, he was charged to pay up himself and to support the levy.[1] It was not a pleasant duty, and the subsidy would continue to cause trouble, but it demonstrated that Boleyn still had the king's trust. The following April he was granted the position of parker at Thundersley in Essex, with revenue deriving from the manor and honour of Rayleigh and that June and December, he was named in commissions of the peace for Kent and Sussex. In July 1524, Anne's brother George was granted the manor of Grymston in Norfolk, formerly held by Sir Thomas Lovell, the wealthy Chancellor of the Exchequer and Secretary to the Treasurer, who had died that May.[2] In November, Thomas was granted the collation and disposal of the next prebend in the collegiate chapel of St Stephen's inside Westminster Palace, which gave him the opportunity to appoint someone sympathetic to that influential position.[3] As it happened though, the existing incumbent, Dr John Chambers, who had been appointed in 1515, would be the last Dean, remaining in position until the dissolution of the 1530s. The following April, in 1525, Boleyn was granted the stewardship of Swaffham in Norfolk and from the crown lands, a 'parcel of the honour of Richemond' in the same county.[4]

Anne had no choice but to leave court. It is possible that the king's reaction to her behaviour may have been influenced by his relationship with her sister, or that her family feared the episode might have an impact upon Mary. At this point, the family fortunes were riding on the elder Boleyn sister, and the career of George, with Anne bringing their name into disrepute through her wilful actions. Perhaps Henry was more lenient with Anne because of the connection, or perhaps the opposite was true. Equally it is not possible to know whether Anne's sentence of banishment originated from the top, being ordered by the king himself, or whether it was suggested by Wolsey, in order to allow the Percy-Talbot match to be completed, an event which was accomplished in late 1524 or in 1525. If not a court directive, it might have been at the instigation of Thomas Boleyn that Anne remained in the countryside until late 1525 or early 1526, as a punishment for her efforts to secure her own husband. It is usually assumed that she spent this time at Hever Castle, but she may also have socialised with neighbours and friends, or stayed with her sister in Essex, using the experience she had gathered at the court of Claude of France to help Mary through the ordeal of childbirth.

The paternity of Mary's children has led to speculation among historians, some of whom considering that one or both were fathered by the king. The timing would fit with a long affair, conducted through the first half of the 1520s, although lack of evidence means that no specific perimeters can be placed on the relationship. Her first child was a daughter named Catherine, possibly after the queen, and her arrival may have taken place any time between 1522 and 1526, although the date preferred by most historians is 1524. Mary's son, Henry, was probably conceived that year and arrived in March 1525, or else she fell pregnant in 1525 and delivered him in 1526. Her intimacy with the king does not guarantee Henry's paternity, though, especially if she was still sleeping with her husband; Mary herself was probably not certain about the identity of her children's father, which helps explain the fact that Henry did not acknowledge these offspring. There are also the possibilities that Henry did know Catherine was his, but did not feel the need to acknowledge her as such owing to her gender, or that he knew for certain that she and her brother were not his, as the affair had already ended or the dates of their encounters were decisively against it. Then there was the legal question. Mary's situation was quite different from that in which Henry found himself in 1519, when the unmarried Elizabeth Blount bore the illegitimate Henry Fitzroy. It was one thing to acknowledge a love child born to an unwedded mother, but quite another to admit to sleeping with a married woman. The king could not tolerate such a public stain on his character. In Mary's case, as with any married woman, the paternity of any children she bore was automatically ascribed to her husband and it would require lengthy legal wranglings and a degree of scandal for Henry to own them as his. The only exceptions to this rule were in very unusual circumstances, such as if the husband was seeking a divorce or one partner had absconded. Henry already had one illegitimate son and had little to gain in the 1520s by acknowledging the pair.

According to the date inscribed on his tomb in Westminster Abbey, Mary's son was born on 4 March 1525, although other sources place the event later. This dates his conception to late May or early June 1524, requiring his sister's birth date to adjust around it. If Mary had conceived again quickly after delivering Catherine, it would push the little girl's conception interval back even earlier, into 1523, which creates a time span of around a year between the *Chateau Vert* and the moment of conception. According to chronicler Edward Hall, Henry was staying at Mary's residence of Beaulieu in Essex in March 1525, and was either still there, or had returned by St George's Day, almost a month later.[5] With the ceremony of the Knight of the Garter traditionally held at Windsor on 23 April, Henry's prolonged stay during this time was an interesting choice. Perhaps his presence there offers a significant piece of evidence that has hitherto been overlooked, as he waited to be on hand, in order to hear news of Mary's delivery and to see the child.

The boy was named Henry, which linked him with the king and with Henry Fitzroy, his potential half-brother. Yet it was fairly standard at the time to name a child after a monarch. Only one contemporary source attributed the child's paternity to the king. The vicar John Hale claimed that Henry Carey had been pointed out to him as a royal bastard but this dates from 1535, when the author was using his best efforts to discredit the king as 'mired in vice' and enjoying 'foul pleasures... defiling himself in any filthy place... fully given to his foul pleasure of the flesh and other voluptuousness'.[6] Hale also made the unlikely claim that Henry kept his own brothel at Farnham Castle in Surrey, the property of Richard Fox, Bishop of Winchester through the 1520s, so he was keen to besmirch the king's name. In every respect, William Carey treated Catherine and Henry as his own children. Their resemblance to Anne's daughter, Elizabeth I, was to be expected, as even if they were not her half-siblings, they were cousins through the Boleyn line. Both Carey children made good marriages and established careers at Elizabeth's court, with Catherine serving her cousin as chief Lady of the Bedchamber and Henry becoming Baron Hunsdon and Knight of the Garter. It is also possible that Mary's affair with the king ended when she became pregnant, as it had with Bessie Blount, which would have made Catherine his daughter and Henry the son of William Carey. The likelihood is that Mary herself was not completely certain. Any challenge Henry might make to the legal presumption of Carey's paternity would have required an act of Parliament and that was a scandal the king was not prepared to weather.

Henry may have loved Mary Boleyn but not in the way he had loved Catherine of Aragon, nor in the way he would love Anne. He did not decide to replace his queen with her, with all the consequences that would entail, nor woo her for years without certainty of success or, as far as we know, barrage her with persuasive love letters. He may have loved her for what she represented to him; a pliant, pretty diversion who had provided an easy chase and conquest, in the same manner as Bessie Blount. One often quoted fact about Mary is that Henry owned a ship named after her, but when he purchased this from Thomas Boleyn in 1523, it already bore that name. However, this might be an indication of the shifting royal attachment, as he would also later purchase its partner, which was named after Anne. There is some evidence from the 1530s that he did retain some affection for Mary, writing to intervene when Sir Thomas Boleyn refused to help his daughter in her hour of need, but she was never the king's *grand amour*.

It is impossible to know how Mary felt about him. As her affair with Henry ran its course, she would have seen his interest in her younger sister deepen into love. Perhaps she would welcome this with relief or perhaps it was difficult for her to see herself replaced. Maybe she later advised Anne about how to handle her former lover, or counselled her to be cautious, or avoid his advances if she could: it is impossible now to know. Anne was absent from court during most of the period traditionally considered to have marked the intimacy between Mary and Henry, so she did not witness their relationship first-hand.

While the careers of her sister, father and brother were advancing, Anne was sent back to her family's home of Hever in the Kent countryside. The length of her rustication is unclear, and although Cavendish comments that she was banished 'for a season',[7] this term is unspecific and merely designates a period of time rather than the duration of a season of the year. In contrast with her experiences abroad, and at the English court, life at Hever represented a considerable change of pace for Anne. She would have had plenty of time to enjoy riding and hunting, reading and playing music, but the exciting interactions of the court, the international visitors and grand entertainments, were all denied to her. There was none of the glamour and culture of Mechelen, Paris or Greenwich. For any member of the aristocracy with ambition, the king's court was the centre of the world, and Anne's removal from it sidelined her, and threatened to jeopardise any future marriage arrangements. She was intelligent enough to recognise that passion had led her down a path that had caused her career to atrophy. Although her initial response may have been one of anger and frustration, her banishment may have restored a sense of humility, or at least reminded her of the need to play by the rules. No doubt as time passed her personal pain gave way to pragmatism.

At Hever, she was within striking distance of several other great Kentish houses with which her family had connections. Outside court circles, it was the country homes of other magnates that provided the essential company and connections for the landed gentry, dictated by class and proximity. Twenty-five miles to the east lay Allington Castle, home to the Wyatt family, with whom Boleyn shared joint custody of Norwich castle. Even closer to home, just five miles distant, was Penshurst Place and twenty miles east was Tonbridge Castle. The Boleyns had control of both, with Thomas paying £100 in March 1525 for repairs on the manors of Penshurst and Tonbridge, and the stone bridge at the latter, over the river Medway.[8] Anne may have been forbidden from attending the queen when she visited Greenwich Palace nearby, but she surely visited these other places during this period, especially given that memorials survive in the church at Penshurst to two of her brothers who died in infancy. It was a particularly grand residence, technically owned by the crown, but overseen by Boleyn as a result of its former owner's fall. In 1521, Thomas Boleyn had been given no choice but to obey the king's summons to sit on the jury that had convicted the Duke of Buckingham of treason, but whatever his conscience had dictated, he had benefited from the Duke's execution by gaining access to the house when it became a royal hunting lodge.

At Hever, Anne may have relied upon the society and distractions of her near neighbours, and the Wyatts of Allington were the most likely comparable family, in social, political and cultural terms. Henry Wyatt had been a key figure in the life of the king in his youth, becoming a Privy Councillor and Knight of the Garter, and with Sir Henry and Sir Thomas being appointed joint guardians of Norwich Castle in 1511, it is likely that their children met at some point in the following decade. His eldest son, Thomas, had been born at Allingham in around 1503 and, at the age of eighteen, had married Elizabeth Brooke, a Boleyn cousin, as her paternal grandmother was a Howard. However, after the birth of their son, this match quickly turned sour. By the time Anne had arrived at court in 1522, the handsome poet had already been in the king's service for several years and in 1524 he became clerk of the king's jewels.[9] That Christmas he took part in a great masque danced in the Queen's chamber at Greenwich, along with William Carey and others, where a castle with four silver turrets had been built, called the *Chateau Blanche*. Anne may have received letters from her mother, sister, brother-in-law or friends, telling her the details of the masque, the banquets and jousting that were devised to amuse the Scottish ambassadors at the palace just a short ride north from her Kent home. Perhaps she reflected on the difference in her circumstances, on the interval of time between the creation of the *Chateau Vert* and the *Chateau Blanche*, realising that the glittering machinery of the court continued to turn in her absence. If she wanted to return to it, she would need to accept its rules.

Another of Anne's Kent friends was Thomas Wyatt's sister, Margaret, born around 1506, whom Anne would later take into her inner circle as a lady-in-waiting, suggesting an existing connection between the two women. There was also Bridget Wiltshire, daughter of Sir John Wiltshire, who had been born at Stone Castle, in Dartford, around twenty-five miles directly to the north of Hever. Slightly older than Anne, Bridget had married the ambassador and diplomat Sir Richard Wingfield in 1513, whom Anne would have known in France. Bridget would bear him ten children before his death in 1525. Again, Anne may have travelled to be with her friends during any of her confinements that coincided with her period of exile, perhaps recalling the years she and Richard had shared at the French court. It was during this period that Anne would have heard of the death of her former mistress, Queen Claude, on 20 July 1524, at Blois, at the age of twenty-four. Contemporary rumours ascribed her premature death to syphilis contracted from her husband, or to childbirth, but no evidence survives of a final pregnancy or that she was being treated for the disease, which Francis may not have contracted yet. Plausibly, she died as the result of the strain on her already weakened body by years of relentless pregnancies, exacerbating some underlying condition, or because she was not strong enough to fight off some final complication. The suggestion that she suffered from bone tuberculosis like her mother complies with the physical symptoms Anne would have recalled afflicting her. There is no reason to doubt that Anne sincerely mourned her former mistress and remembered her in her prayers.

Anne would also have learned of the death of her Howard grandfather, Thomas, second Duke of Norfolk, in May 1524. Having lived to the incredible age of eighty, or eighty-one, he had been active until the end, leading the army that defeated the Scots at Flodden in 1513, escorting Mary Tudor to France in 1514 and negotiating her return, suppressing rioters in the streets of London on May Day 1517 and weeping whilst he pronounced the death sentence on the Duke of Buckingham in 1521. It is unlikely that Anne had seen him since she left court, as he had retired to his country home of Framlingham Castle in Suffolk in April 1523, after resigning his positions due to ill health.

It is possible, but undocumented, that Anne travelled with her family to attend his funeral at Thetford Priory in Norfolk, where he was laid to rest in spectacular style, on a bier topped with 700 candles and 100 wax effigies, amid a procession of 400 hooded men bearing torches. A sermon was delivered on the text from the Book of Revelations, 'Behold the lion of the tribe of Judah triumphs', which reputedly so terrified the congregation that the mourners fled the church.[10] After the dissolution of Thetford Priory, his tomb was relocated to Framlingham church. His eldest son, Thomas Howard, Anne's uncle, inherited his dukedom and became head of the family.

The following February, more news came from France. While Claude's loss prompted a mood of mourning in the household of Queen Catherine, the king was galvanised by what followed. The Emperor and Francis had met in battle at Pavia, after the French had attempted to recapture Lombardy, a territory they had previously been forced to concede to the Empire. Following a confusing battle, which had dragged through the morning of 24 February, the French were utterly defeated, suffering an estimated 15,000 casualties and Francis I had been captured by Charles' troops and taken to Madrid, where he would remain for the following year. To Henry, this was the perfect opportunity to invade France during his rival's absence and he urged the speedy collection of the subsidies he had levied, with Boleyn as treasurer responsible for their collection. However, this was to cause unrest in Anne's home county, with many men unwilling or unable to pay. Groups began to resist, refusing to contribute, prompting the Archbishop of Canterbury, William Warham, to write to Thomas and the other collectors. Their duty was to convince the rebels to pay, especially those living in Kent, as the king trusted 'in them specially… forasmuch as his Grace was born in Kent' (at Greenwich). He wrote that 'if the King lost the opportunity now offered him in France, through their backwardness, his displeasure would fall heavily upon them'.[11] Yet Warham was not unsympathetic. He had spoken with some of the petitioners, who 'declared how they were decayed, with weeping tears', and confided his belief to Boleyn that 'there is great poverty in Kent, and lack of money'. Writing from Canterbury in May, he described having witnessed fairs where wares and cattle went unsold, as the locals lacked the means to purchase them.[12] However, he had his orders and asked Thomas, in the greatest secrecy, to look out for any 'dangerous assemblies' being held, especially during holidays and in the hot weather, and to suppress them.[13]

Henry's intentions towards France were resolved by the Treaty of the More, which was signed at Wolsey's Hertfordshire home. It was made on 30 August 1525, between the cardinal and the interim French government, headed by Louise of Savoy, who was keen to restore peace between them, so that she might secure her son's release.[14] Henry agreed to relinquish his claims to French lands that had formerly been part of England's Plantagenet heritage, and received in return a pension of £20,000, with some of his chief ministers also in receipt of smaller amounts. There was additional grievance on the English side over the dowry of Mary Tudor, which had not been returned since the end of her short lived marriage in 1515. That was now agreed and, in return, Henry vowed to assist Louise in her efforts to negotiate with the Emperor to return Francis I.[15] In reality, Henry did little on this front, as the French king's captivity suited him well, and he also gained a promise from Louise to assist him in his dealings with the Scots, who were once again threatening his northern borders. In all, it was a highly successful treaty, the terms of which were created out of necessity, and it was highly unlikely that Wolsey could have achieved such a coup under different circumstances. Francis I was finally released in March 1526, but only after having agreed to send his two eldest sons as hostages in his place.

The summer of 1525 saw Thomas Boleyn ennobled further. On 18 June, he was present at Henry's magnificent new Bridewell Palace on the bank where the river Fleet ran down to the Thames, with its two brick courtyards and a long gallery connecting it with Blackfriars. There, he was conducted along a gallery that flanked the privy garden to the king's apartments on the second floor of the inner courtyard. Senior members of the court had gathered to witness the process by which Henry's illegitimate son was to be ennobled; Wolsey was present, along with the other two Dukes of the realm, Norfolk and Suffolk, the Earls of Worcester, Northumberland, Shrewsbury and representatives of the church. The six-year-old Henry Fitzroy was dressed in the robes of an Earl and accompanied by the Earls of Oxford and Arundel as he knelt before his father. Henry placed a girdle around his neck and Thomas More read aloud the patent that conferred the Earldom of Nottingham upon the boy, with an annuity of £20.[16] After this, Fitzroy retired from the chamber and returned in the robes of a Duke, with a procession of nobles carrying his train, sword, cap of estate and rod of gold. The same process was repeated, only this time Fitzroy was granted the Dukedoms of Richmond and Somerset.[17] From that point forward, he would be referred to in official documentation as the 'right high and noble prince Henry, Duke of Richmond and Somerset'. At the same time, Thomas Boleyn was created Viscount Rochford. The message to the assembled men was clear. The king was attempting to create ties of loyalty to his son, currently his only surviving acknowledged son. It may not have been public knowledge at the time that Queen Catherine had reached her menopause and would not bear any more children, but the ceremony offered a stark choice. If his courtiers had to choose between backing their queen and backing their king and Fitzroy, Henry was pointing the way: he was establishing connections that indicated a division between himself and his wife. In the coming year, this division would take on momentous proportions for the Boleyn family.

At some point in late 1524 or early 1525, Anne's brother George was married to Jane Parker, the daughter of Henry Parker, tenth Baron Morley and Alice St John. The families had long-standing connections with Norfolk and Essex, and had served in the early Tudor court, so were therefore already well known to the Boleyns. Henry was an educated humanist, translating Greek and Latin works into English and undertaking a diplomatic mission in 1523 to Germany to present the Order of the Garter to Archduke Ferdinand, brother of Emperor Charles. Jane's elder sister, Margaret, married John Shelton, the son of Anne's aunt and uncle from Norwich, Sir John Shelton and her namesake Anne Boleyn, sister of Sir Thomas. No details survive about the exact location or timing of the ceremony, but the match clearly had royal approval. Jane's father was unable to pay the 2,000 marks dowry requested by Thomas, so the king intervened to pay the difference. She was given certain manors in Buckinghamshire and Norfolk and guaranteed 100 marks per year for life, in the event that George should predecease her. The ceremony might have taken place in the church near Jane's family home at Great Hallingbury in Essex[18] around fifty miles north of Hever.

The terms of the Eltham Ordinances, drawn up by Wolsey to reform the king's household at the end of 1525 include the newly married pair: 'Yong Bolleyn to [have] xx^{li} yeerly above the... the hath gottyn to hy[m a]nd hys wyfe to lyve therapon: and also to admyt [h]ym to be one of the kupberers when Kyng dynyth [o]wt.'[19] Whilst Wolsey took the opportunity to purge the court of excess staff and expense, as well as the young men he considered to be undesirable influences upon the king, the Boleyns' position remained secure. Among those assigned lodgings in the king's house were Anne's uncle, the newly created Duke of Norfolk, Thomas Boleyn, the treasurer and his wife, 'Mr Carey, Mr Boleyn and their wives', Henry Wyatt and Francis Bryan. This may have been the time that Anne received her summons back to court, or soon after. If so, she may have been included in the accommodation arrangements for the queen's side, along with Mary Tudor, dowager Queen of France and

Anne's widowed step-grandmother, the Duchess of Norfolk, Anne being among 'the Queen's maidens'.[20]

At Christmas that year, the plague was raging in London, so the king withdrew to Eltham Palace, 'with a small number' and no man was allowed to approach 'but such as were appointed by name'.[21] but Wolsey risked disease and controversy by keeping open court at Richmond, on a grander scale than Henry. Wolsey's Ordinances were published in January 1526 and Anne's recall would have arrived at Hever soon afterwards. What mixed emotions did she experience, at the age of twenty-five, realising she had an opportunity to re-enter the court, and that with both her siblings married, her own marital future must be her parents' priority?

FOURTEEN

Return to Court 1526

So far as we know, Anne's return to court went unmarked. Unmarked, but probably not unnoticed. Those friends and admirers from her first sojourn in the queen's household would have spotted her again, following her mistress in the corridors at Bridewell, seated beside her mother in the tiltyard at Greenwich, or taking part in a dance at Eltham. Perhaps Wolsey recognised her form in the distance, or Henry Percy spotted her crossing a courtyard. Maybe she passed by Thomas Wyatt at a banquet or the king picked her out in the crowd as he played tennis, or returned from the hunt. What they saw, with differing degrees of attention to detail, was a young woman of twenty-five, slender, dark haired and elegant, dressed in clothes influenced by the recent fashions of France.

It seems to have been the consensus among her contemporaries that Anne was not a conventional beauty, as Catherine had been in her youth, but that she exerted a compelling fascination that made her irresistible to men. Her best feature, according to the Venetian diplomat Sanuto, was her 'black and beautiful' eyes, but apart from these, he described her as having a 'swarthy complexion, long neck, wide mouth, bosom not much raised'.[1] The French diplomat de Carles agreed that her eyes were 'most attractive' and that she knew how to use them to good effect, to send flirtatious messages, so that 'many a man paid his allegiance'. He found her beautiful, 'with an elegant figure... so graceful that you would never have taken her for an Englishwoman but for a Frenchwoman born'.[2] The poet Thomas Wyatt referred to Anne in poetry as 'brunet' and the following century, his grandson, George, echoed the idea of her dark colouring and confirmed rumours of her legendary sixth finger, by admitting 'there was found, indeed, upon the side of her nail, upon one of her fingers some little show of a nail, which yet was so small, by the report of thise that have seen her, as the work master seemed to leave it an occasion of great grace to her hand, which with the tip of one of her other fingers might be, and was usually by her hidden without any blemish to it.' He also stated that 'there were said to be upon some parts of her body, certain small moles incident to the clearest complexions'.[3]

The most hostile account is to be found, inevitably, in the writings of the Catholic priest Nicholas Sander, who claimed that she was 'rather tall of stature, with black hair and an oval face of sallow complexion, as if troubled with jaundice'. Having cast aspersions on the 'health' of her appearance, implying to his contemporary readers a concomitant moral degeneracy, he continued to describe various physical defects: 'a projecting tooth under the upper lip and on her right hand, six fingers'. If that was not enough, he added that she had a 'large wen under her chin', which she hid by wearing 'a high dress covering her throat', in spite of the portraits that depict her in the low-cut necklines of the day. Despite this, Sander was forced to concede that 'she was handsome to look at, with a pretty mouth'.[4]

Anne's physical attraction lay in her exotic difference from the English concept of curvaceous, blue-eyed, blonde or red-gold haired beauty typified by Catherine of Aragon. Where the queen had introduced a new style in 1501, when she wore the first hooped farthingale skirt in England, Anne was also a trend-setter, but with a different influence. According to French chronicler Brantôme, she set a new fashion with her French style, devising new clothes that were copied by other ladies at court, and was 'the fairest and most bewitching of all the lovely dames'.[5] The admiring George Wyatt:

In this noble imp, the graces of nature graced by gracious education... a beauty not so whitely as clear and fresh above all we may esteem, which appeared much more excellent by her favour passing sweet and cheerful... her noble presence of shape and fashion representing both mildness and majesty.[6]

George Wyatt's account must be read with caution, as he was born after Anne's death and never saw Anne in the flesh. The surviving portraits of Anne are not to be trusted either, as the identifications cannot be verified and many do not date from her lifetime. It is almost inconceivable in a court where the master portraitist Hans Holbein was employed that Anne did not sit for him as queen. In fact, the survival of a chalk sketch identified by Dr John Cheke, who served Anne, which depicts her in a bonnet and state of undress, may well have been in preparation for a larger work. Holbein is known to have designed jewellery for Anne and designs for the pageantry accompanying her coronation, so it seems likely that a portrait would have been commissioned from him at some point during Henry's courtship of her, or their marriage: a most likely date would be to celebrate the coronation itself. The image is inscribed 'Ann Bollein, Queen', but includes an unflattering double chin, which it is unlikely that Holbein would have included, or Anne would have approved. Perhaps this is the reason why the sketch never became a full portrait, although the lack of official surviving pictures of Anne as queen points to a concerted campaign of destruction after her fall. Just as Henry would order the destruction of religious statues at whose feet he had previously worshipped, it appears that he would also ensure that the image of Anne was eradicated from his palaces.

Two other significant portraits, held at Hever Castle and in the National Portrait gallery, depict a woman with clear facial similarities; a long face, with small pert mouth, dark eyes and high cheekbones, whilst the clothing and French gable hood are so close as to suggest one was a copy of another. In the Hever one, the sitter holds a red flower between finger and thumb on their right hand, while the National Portrait image is the most famous image of the queen. These two pictures bear close resemblance to the Chequers ring, a possession of Anne's daughter, Elizabeth, which contained the portraits of mother and daughter. Although the images are very small, worked on enamel, the features echo the two other portraits sufficiently to indicate this is probably the truest likeness in existence. An unidentified picture of a woman from 1526–7 by miniaturist Lucas Horenbault has been named as Anne, but it does not look like the image of Anne in the ring and has been cited alternatively as a possible portrait of Mary Boleyn.[7] Likewise, a recently discovered painting from Nidd Hall shows completely different facial dimensions, and variants based on it contain different details, including the essential AB brooch that prompted the identification.

A literary portrait of Anne and her world can be found in the poetry of her Kent neighbour and friend, Thomas Wyatt. His words shed light on the nature of courtly love and the flirtations that were conducted in and around the queen's apartments: hardly the dour, joyless places they were supposed to have become. Written to entertain an elite circle, the poems were riddles and games, literary exercises designed to tease and titillate, amuse and suggest, intended for performance in the chamber, tucked into a lover's pocket or read at a pageant, rather than for publication.[8] Wyatt was described by one hostile observer as one of an inner coterie who 'spend their time in vainful vanity, making ballades of fervent amitie'.[9] Yet this was only one aspect of the man. His private life was desperately unhappy and his work indicates that he fell deeply in love with Anne. We don't know when. It may have been in the early 1520s and, therefore, concurrent with her relationship with Henry Percy, but the traditional notion that Wyatt was supplanted in Anne's affections by the king must date their flirtation to her second term at court, after her return from exile.

In 1526, Thomas Wyatt was twenty-five, and a sketch by Hans Holbein the Younger shows a young, bearded man with passionate and resolute features. His poems reflect the intimate courtly culture, the 'in-jokes' of the time with references to love affairs and affections that would have immediately been understood by the inner circle. With some poems referring to 'Brunet', that 'did set our country in a roar', 'falcon', Anne's badge and 'Anna', Wyatt describes a world where the need for secrecy in love is essential, particularly when the participants are married, like Henry or Wyatt, or engaged to another, like Anne and Percy.

> Take heed betime lest ye be spied
> Your loving eyes you cannot hide
> At last the truth will sure be tried
> Therefore take heed!
>
> For some there be of crafty kind,
> Though you show no part of your mind,
> Surely their eyes ye cannot blind.
> Therefore take heed.

Percy's courtship of Anne would have been apparent to those observant members of the queen's household, as they danced or sang together, or engaged in conversation and whispered secrets; rejected by her himself, Wyatt may have observed her, sitting demurely sewing, pretending not to notice her lover, or even awaiting his arrival:

> She sat and sewed that hath done me the wrong
> Whereof I (com)plain and have done many a day,
> And whilst she heard my plaint in piteous song
> Wished my heart the sampler as it lay.
>
> The blind master whom I have served so long
> Grudging to hear that he did hear her say.
> Made her own weapon do her finger bleed
> To feel if pricking were so good indeed.

The internal evidence of his poems suggests that the married Wyatt's attentions did not find favour with Anne, either during 1522–3, due to her affection for Henry Percy, or afterwards, because of his married status. By the time she returned to court, Wyatt's marital unhappiness was widely known, as he created a scandal at court by repudiating his wife as an adulteress. Anne was wise enough not to get involved in that, but it is likely that her friendship with Wyatt was renewed at this point and may have developed into an emotional connection. Even if she had developed feelings for the poet, she could not risk another violation of the rules so soon after the Henry Percy disgrace.

Wyatt's grandson, George, would later suggest that a love affair had developed between Anne and Thomas shortly before she attracted Henry's attention, which must point to a date of late 1525 or 1526. Henry's love letters to Anne include the detail that he had been 'struck by the dart of love' for a year, and internal evidence would place the composition of those around 1527, moving the king's awakening interest in her to spring 1526. The hostile Jesuit Sander later went so far as to relate a scandalous account of the poet visiting Anne in her chamber and taking physical liberties with her before she fled upstairs at the summons of another lover, but it is so ridiculous as to be easily discounted.[10] A story related by George Wyatt sounds more credible, in which the king recognised a ring or jewel Thomas had taken from Anne during courtship. Recognising the item and its symbolism, Henry declared that he had been deceived, at which point Wyatt realised he must abandon his pursuit.

Wyatt's awareness of having been supplanted by a superior suitor appears to have inspired his best-known work, a Petrarchan sonnet that exposes the rivalries and darkness beneath the court's glittering exterior. In typical Tudor style, he puns on the heart and the pursuit of the hart, which he realises has been in vain, and is now only able to follow the crowd of admirers, as she has been won by Caesar, or the king:

> Whoso list to hunt, I know where is an hind,
> But as for me, hélas, I may no more.
> The vain travail hath wearied me so sore,
> I am of them that farthest cometh behind.
> Yet may I by no means my wearied mind
> Draw from the deer, but as she fleeth afore
> Fainting I follow. I leave off therefore,
> Sithens in a net I seek to hold the wind.
> Who list her hunt, I put him out of doubt,
> As well as I may spend his time in vain.
> And graven with diamonds in letters plain

> There is written, her fair neck round about:
> Noli me tangere, for Caesar's I am,
> And wild for to hold, though I seem tame.

In spite of some of Wyatt's more intimate poetry, there is no evidence that he and Anne were ever lovers, or even that she returned his affection before she was thus 'collared' by Henry. As previously noted, Sander reported that Anne had lived an active sex life before arriving at court, sinning first with her father's butler and then with his chaplain, before becoming the 'royal mule' of the king of France, but these slanders are spun out of the Jesuit's desire to blacken the name of a woman who 'embraced the heresy of Luther… but nevertheless did not cease to hear mass with the Catholics', a performance 'wrung from her by the custom of the king and the necessities of her own ambition'.[11] Sander also reported a scene where Wyatt confessed his adultery with Anne to Henry in these early days, warning the king away from entering a relationship with a fallen woman, but such a salacious anecdote denies the dynamic of the three participants. Writing during the reign of Mary I, Nicholas Harpsfield describes Wyatt dissuading Henry with the line that Anne was 'not meet to be coupled with your grace', which he claims came from a source close to Percy, implying that consummation had taken place with him, or Wyatt, or both, but that Henry did not believe him and dismissed it.[12]

The king would not have made such a scandalous woman his second wife, for whom he hoped to obtain papal blessing and with whom he wished to produce a legitimate heir. There is also Anne's awareness of her dynastic duty and her understanding of women's positions that she had developed abroad to argue against the stories. It was partly hostility to Anne's apparent faith that prompted these colourful stories; her stigmatisation as sexually voracious and deceptive helped support the later Catholic narrative of her as a catalyst for the Reformation and the driving force behind Henry's cruelty to his eldest daughter. No genuine evidence for any scandalous behaviour or sexual activity survives for Anne's early life, and had she indulged in any affairs similar to those of her sister, they would have provided rich fare for her later detractors. As a woman, she was vulnerable to such slurs upon her sexuality and modesty, as these were considered the defining characteristics of her gender. When the wolves closed in upon Thomas Wolsey, it was not for sexual misconduct, of which he was more guilty than Anne, but for his perceived greed and pride.

The evidence in Wyatt's poems suggests that his desire for Anne went unrequited, although this would not have prevented him from imagining consummation, or weaving images of it for his work. One of his most famous poems gives a glimpse of the transition from courtly love to sex, the shifting boundaries of intimate relations between ladies in waiting and their lovers:

> Thanked be fortune it hath been otherwise
> Twenty times better, but once in special
> In thin array after a pleasant guise,
> When her loose gown from her shoulders did fall
> And she me caught in her arms long and small,
> Therewithal sweetly did me kiss,
> And softly said, 'Dear heart, how like you this?'

While the poem suggests a tone of easy licentiousness at court, Anne's recent experiences, her awareness of her sister's relationship with Henry and her unmarried status caused her to tread a far more cautious path.

By the time Anne returned to court, Henry was already experiencing doubts about his marriage. He did not blame Catherine, yet he still did not have the legitimate son he needed to secure his throne. Searching outside the marriage for a reason, he questioned whether this might be God's judgement for some legal impediment, arising from Catherine's former union with his elder brother, Arthur. The shortlived marriage had taken place in November 1501 and lasted until the following April, but Catherine remained adamant that it had not been consummated. Had circumstances been different, Anne Boleyn might have simply become another one of Henry's mistresses, like her sister Mary. She may even have been his first maîtresse-en-titre, a title the king offered her inspired by the court of his rival Francis I. Perhaps she would have reigned at court for half a dozen years, borne a couple of illegitimate children and died in a comfortable old age. But the timing dictated that her life would be very different. When Henry fell in love with her in 1526, Catherine's child-bearing days were over and he was already halfway towards the decisive mental leap to reject his wife and replace her with a younger, fertile model. Anne's charms were probably the final proof he required to convince himself that Catherine was not his legal wife and that they had been living in sin for seventeen years. Perhaps Anne's will and ambition were also a driving force in this monumental shift; the hostile Richard Pole certainly thought so, claiming that the experience of her sister had taught Anne how fleeting the king's affections were, so 'she herself sent her chaplains, grave theologians, as pledges of her ill... not only to declare to (Henry) that it was lawful to put (Catherine) away but to say that (he) was sinning mortally to keep her as (his) wife even for a single moment'.[13] Yet the evidence of Henry's letters suggests that Anne actually resisted the king for as long as she could, for a whole year beginning at some point in 1526. He was the driving force in their relationship, not her.

Henry may have fallen in love with Anne in or around February that year. At the Shrovetide jousts, held at Greenwich, he dressed in embroidered gold and silver, bearing the device of a 'mannes harte in a presse, with flames about it' with the motto 'declare, I dare not'. His opponents, headed by the king's cousin, Henry Courtenay, Marquis of Exeter, were dressed in green and red velvet, decorated with the image of burning hearts, over which was a woman's hand 'commyng out of a cloud, holdyng a garden water pot, which dropped silver drops on the harte'. The symbolism revealed a new object of affection, the pain of concealed love and the remedy, within the reach of the right woman. Henry 'did service' to the queen and her ladies, which probably included Anne, to whom his cryptic message may have been directed. It is likely that by this time she was aware of it, although Catherine may not have been: it is impossible to know just how aware the queen was of flirtations taking place in her household. After all, Anne had been able to carry on her own secret relationship that led to an engagement. However, almost as if to foreshadow the coming years, the joust then took a violent and shocking turn. In an accident reminiscent of the jousting accident Henry himself had endured in 1524, when a lance splintered against his visor, Sir Francis Bryan was injured by the 'chance shivering of the spere'.[14] He lost an eye and would always wear a patch as a consequence. It was another reminder of the fragility of life. If the king was to meet an untimely end, the kingdom would be left in the hands of a ten-year-old girl.

Henry's embroidered motto may have stated that he dared not declare his love, but this was in a public arena. The queen was watching. In private, though, he soon made his feelings plain. At some point in 1526, he found an opportunity to speak to Anne alone, perhaps as she sewed costumes of silver and gold, or sat reading in a garden or alcove: the scene has been imagined many times by historical novelists. He also ordered his goldsmiths to make four gold brooches that continued the motifs of desire and hope, using the visual symbols of hearts and hands, tongues and eyes, which poets like Wyatt deployed in verse. It was part of the playful, romantic games of the age to send coded messages in gifts, in metaphor, of items that represented some virtue or desire, or the language of flowers, picking nosegays or bouquets for the significance of colour and kind: as Shakespeare reminds us, there was rosemary for remembrance, pansies for thoughts, daisies for unhappy love, violets for faithlessness. The royal wardrobe in 1532 included a range of symbols once created as messages, before having lost their context: eight separate legs made of silver, a silver hand, a tooth of silver and two silver breasts. Perhaps at some point they had been lovers' tokens.

Placed in order, the four brooches Henry commissioned suggest a promise to Anne: a brooch of Venus and Cupid, another of a lady holding a heart in her hand, a third portraying a man lying in a lady's lap and the last one, foreshadowing her future, of a lady holding a crown. Was Henry considering making Anne his wife as early as spring 1526? It is more likely at this stage that the crown was symbolic of Anne's rule over Henry's heart, rather than any specific promise, although that was only a year away.

Exactly how welcome were Henry's attentions? Anne was in her mid-twenties. She had already seen two potential husbands disappear, and had been wooed by a married man who could not promise her a respectable future. In 1525–6, she was in no position to anticipate that Henry could offer her the ultimate prize of becoming his wife and while his attentions were flattering, he was ultimately attempting to talk her into his bed, as he had done her sister. Henry was no longer the young, romantic figure who had attracted such admiration and universal praise in his youth. Yet neither had he become the obese invalid of his later years. He was older and wiser than he had been, an experienced lover who still retained some of his good looks, although tempered by maturity.

FIFTEEN

The King's Secret 1527

In 1527, Henry VIII was thirty-eight. An imposing, powerful figure, he was a man of many paradoxes, outwardly supremely confident in his person and position, but also prone to insecurity and doubt. This anomaly is surely the reason for our endless fascination with him. Henry liked to think of himself as an intellectual, a scholar of theology and classical civilisation, a musician and dancer; although in reality, there was little he enjoyed more than to spend the day in the saddle and he often disliked reading and composing letters. He was tall, strongly built in the mould of his Yorkist grandfather, but he was pushing the boundaries of middle age by 1527; and he was disappointed. The Tudor court was designed to satisfy the king's every whim: servants attended him at every occasion, meeting his physical, spiritual, practical and constitutional needs, and the wealth he had inherited from his father paid for years of extravagant pageants and escapades, for the creation of jewelled clothing and the building of magnificent palaces, the jousts to entertain ambassadors – or on foreign wars. He had inherited the throne and married just before his eighteenth birthday and, after two decades during which nobody refused his will, he was at a loss to understand why he had not been blessed with the many children he had hoped would secure his dynasty. He was a man accustomed to getting his own way, and what he perceived to be a rejection by God fuelled in him a destabilising chain of questions. In 1527, he decided that the answer to those questions was Anne Boleyn.

Christmas 1526 had been a busy and joyful affair, with entertainments held at Greenwich and hosted by Wolsey at York Place. There were 'great plentie of victuals', revels, masques, banquets and jousts, held on 30 December and again on 3 January, when Edward Hall reports there were three hundred 'spears' broken. That same night, Henry selected a small band of young gentlemen and headed to Bridewell Palace, where they donned masks and took his barge to Wolsey's residence. A 'great compaignie of lords and ladies' was dining there, after which much 'good pastime' was enjoyed, before the disguises were removed and the identities of the players revealed.[1]

If Anne was present, it would have been satisfying for her to take centre stage under Wolsey's roof, as the favourite of the king. The events of two or three years earlier, when the cardinal had broken her engagement, could not have been far from her mind as she entered his property. Henry Percy would have relinquished his former role as a gentleman usher now that he was a married man, and the chances are that he had moved on from Wolsey's service, but there would have been those present who had witnessed Anne's former disgrace, and were now forced to accept her new position.

As Anne's favour at court increased, so did Henry's willingness to return to his former friendship with France. The two events were not necessarily linked, but the close association of Catherine with Spain, in opposition to Anne's education and Valois style, cannot be completely dismissed. Anne did not commit her thoughts on the the shift in foreign policy to paper, but she knew her first loyalty lay to the English king. Back in March 1526, the Emperor had incurred Henry's displeasure by breaking his betrothal to the ten-year-old Princess Mary and uniting himself with Isabella of Portugal, strengthening the Hapsburg Empire. Apart from the political upset, Henry took this rejection personally and attempted to negotiate a marriage for his daughter with the widowed Francis I, who was then aged thirty-two, or with one of his sons. Henry dispatched the Bishop of Bath to secure a treaty, offering to renounce his claims to the French throne, but he was not prepared to meet their demand of sending Mary to be raised at the Valois court, as her youth and diminutive size meant she was 'not yet ripe' for *carnali copula*.[2] Wolsey was also keen to bring about a French marriage, although he was as yet ignorant of Henry's connection with the francophile Anne.

The return visit of the French ambassadors that May provided an opportunity for Anne to demonstrate her abilities and her new role. Henry hosted a huge joust and banquet at Greenwich where Nicholas Carew, Robert Jerningham, Anthony Browne and Robert Harries acted as challengers, their clothing embroidered with the word 'loyaltie' and the motto 'by pen, pain nor treasure, truth shall not be violated'. Opposing them, Henry Courtenay and his men responded in costumes of gold and silver, set with mountains and olive branches and ran 'fair courses' for two-and-a-half hours, in spite of the rain. A banqueting house a hundred feet long and thirty feet wide had been built on one side of the tilt yard, to Henry's specifications. It had two triumphal arches of 'antique work', decorated by two Italian painters who received 20s for a week's work, and guilders who were required day and night, along with bricklayers, plumbers and the solderers who cast the lead for numerous knots, roses, leaves, castles, lions, dolphins and greyhounds.[3] Henry, Catherine and Mary, Countess of Suffolk, sat on the top table while the ambassadors sat on the right 'each pairing with some great lady'. No doubt Anne played a key role there, as a hostess among visitors she probably knew well.[4] Two cupboards of immense dimensions formed a semi-circle, from floor to ceiling, to display the king's gold and silver plate.

After the feast, the company were ushered along a corridor into another hall, which had been decorated, with the floor covered with 'cloth of silk embroidered with gold lilies' and the ceiling painted to represent 'a map of the world... the names of the principle provinces being legible... also the signs of the zodiac and their properties... supported by lions'.[5] A pageant had been devised entitled the Father of Heaven, in which the lions, dragons and greyhounds held candlesticks. The figures of Love and Riches were forced to debate their various merits before the figure of Jupiter, as each believed themselves to be more important than the other. The writer of the dialogue 'and making in rhyme', in both English and Latin, was paid the sum of 3s 4d.[6]

The visiting Venetian, Gasparo Spinelli, described the ladies of the court, 'whose various styles of beauty and apparel, enhanced by the brilliancy of the lights, caused me to think I was contemplating the choirs of angels'. Inside the pageant that followed, the women were more beautiful still,

> ...as to be supposed goddesses rather than human beings. They were arrayed in cloth of gold, their hair gathered into a net, with a very richly jewelled garland, surmounted by a velvet cap, the hanging sleeves of their surcoats being so long that they well nigh touched the ground, and so well and richly wrought as to be no slight ornament to their beauty.[7]

This echoes the old legend that Anne instigated the fashion at court for long, trailing sleeves, perhaps even 'greensleeves', either as a French fashion or to cover the little extra nail that reputedly grew on one of her fingers. Queen Catherine sat beside Henry under the 'goodly' cloth of estate, hung with the royal motto *dieu et mon droit*, but it was Anne whom the king deliberately selected as his dance partner. 'We were in the Queen's apartments where there was dancing,' reported the ambassadors, 'and the king (danced) with Mistress Boulan who was brought up in France with the late queen'.[8]

> Dancing thus they presented themselves to the King, their dance being very delightful by reason of its variety, as they formed certain groups and figures most pleasing to the sight. Their dance being finished, they ranged themselves on one side, and in like order the eight youths, leaving their torches, came down from the cave, and after performing their dance, each of them took by the hand one of those beautiful nymphs, and having led a courant together.[9]

Anne could well have been among these women who danced around the bejewelled mountain, or who was claimed again by the king when he suddenly disappeared and returned in a gold Venetian mask.[10] Predictably, the end of the evening saw all the masks removed; soon enough, greater secrets would be made public.

A play in Latin, commanded by the king, was performed before the court on 6 May. Yet this was no mere entertainment, it was clearly a political and religious satire, featuring figures representing Religion, the Church and Truth, dressed like novices in garments of silk and lawn veils. The actors representing Heresy, False Interpretation and the Corrupt Scriptures were dressed in silk of various colours, while the figures of Luther and his wife wore costumes of red silk and russet damask. The revels also featured the two sons of Francis I, then imprisoned by the Emperor, actors in German costume and three women cast as Lady Quietness, Dame Tranquility and Lady Peace.[11] Exactly what story these figures enacted that night is unknown, but it would not be surprising if the play was penned by Thomas More's son-in-law John Heywood, who was well known for his satirical entertainments by the 1530s. One of his early plays, *Witty and Witless* takes the form of an Erasmian debate about the nature of folly, while his *Pardoner and the Friar* satirises the sale of indulgences and the veneration of relics, and was printed in 1533. Probably in circulation a little before this time, the *Pardoner and the Friar* drew comedy from the frailties and vices of women, with lines such as 'women in hell such shrews can be, and here so gentle, as far as I see', along with the the Pardoner's claim that he had known five hundred thousand women,

> Yet in all places where I have been
> Of all the women that I have seen,
> I never sawe nor knewe in my conscience
> Any one woman out of pactience.

There is little doubt that Anne was aware of Heywood's work, given the many plays he would write during her reign, and it seems most likely that this story from 1527, featuring Luther, was an early work of his. As the most popular playwright of Henry's court though, he was responsible for reflecting and perpetuating popular stereotypes about the sexes. Watching his dramas, Anne may have laughed along with the audience, or rolled her eyes at the tired clichés, but there was no escaping the mood that Heywood reinforced, which would contribute to masculine interpretations of her own character.

On 8 May, Henry finally confided in Wolsey his doubts regarding his marriage to Catherine. They probably debated the finer points of theology behind closed doors, but the king's admission to the cardinal aligned him more closely with his minister than his wife, whom Wolsey believed was still being kept in the dark. Catherine had always preserved a distant respect in her relations with Wolsey but, around this time, as he soared past her to the pinnacle of his career, his attitude towards the queen changed. This reflected a subtle shift in the mood at court, as individuals gradually became aware of the need to take sides. In Wolsey's eyes, the queen was no longer Henry's cherished spouse, the figurehead of adoration, the courtly symbol of reverence; she was a challenge, an obstacle, an inconvenience that he needed to find a way to remove. Yet Wolsey was not the driving force, he was the able servant fulfilling Henry's will. None of what ensued would have happened, had Henry not wished it to be so. And Henry did not yet wish to admit to Wolsey that he wanted to make Anne his queen. The cardinal assumed Anne was to take her place as the king's mistress, as her sister had done, while Wolsey worked to secure a new, foreign bride for Henry. The ideal candidate, he thought, would be Renée, Princess of France, sister to Queen Claude. To this end, he set aside his former distaste for the French and raced headlong into the negotiations, believing that he was serving his master's purpose. On 17 May, Thomas Boleyn and Sir Anthony Browne were issued with instructions to 'take the oath of Francis I to the treaty of closer alliance between the two crowns' at Greenwich.[12] They left at once, as the Venetian ambassador reported, after an embargo had been laid 'on all the ships in the Thames for the conveyance of Cardinal Wolsey, who is going to confer with the most Christian King'.[13]

The same day, Wolsey opened judicial proceedings at York Place to investigate the validity of the royal marriage. The reason given for this was that French had raised doubts about the legitimacy of Princess Mary during the marriage negotiations, conveniently distancing the matter from Henry, denying his instigation. According to Edward Hall, the ambassadors told Henry that Thomas Boleyn was in possession of a portrait of Renée, at which Henry should look before marrying her at Calais that summer. Hall's exact words are that 'Viscount Rochford had brought with him the picture of the said Lady',[14] which raises interesting questions. It was an act of unconscious irony, requesting that Sir Thomas help facilitate a French match, but it must be significant that the Boleyn family had the image in their possession. When, and why, was it brought from France? It may have been a fairly new arrival, from Boleyn's most recent travels, or it may have been requested, or brought, by Anne, upon her return late in 1521. Anne certainly knew Renée, who would recall Anne and speak kindly of her to the English ambassador during the reign of Anne's daughter, Elizabeth I. They may also have shared cultural ideals and reformist leanings, as Renée would later create a court at which both Rabelais and Calvin were welcome. She would also be arrested for heresy later in life and only just escape with her life. Aged only eleven when Anne left the French court, Renée is likely to have been a frequent presence in her sister's household, but she was just a little girl, growing up alongside the royal children, sharing the simpler aspects of domestic routine, education and play with the young Anne.

Like Henry, Anne may have hoped that Catherine remained in ignorance regarding Wolsey's York Place court. However, thanks to her network of loyal connections, Catherine had been aware of the cardinal's intentions for a while and was already formulating her counter-arguments. In theory, it could have been a straightforward matter to annul or invalidate the match, and allow the king to take a new wife. There were significant legal precedents. Louis XII of France had set aside his wife of twenty-two years, Anne, Duchess of Berry, in order to marry Anne of Brittany in 1499, and as recently as March 1527, the pope had granted a divorce to Henry's older sister Margaret, Queen of Scots. The king had every reason to believe that Clement VII would do for him that summer what he had done for Margaret that spring. He might have anticipated being married to Anne before the end of the year, so the trial should really have been a formality. With Henry seated beside him, Wolsey quoted a passage from Leviticus that condemns marriage to a brother's wife as unclean and destined to remain barren: 'If a man shall take his brother's wife, it is an unclean thing: he has uncovered his brother's nakedness. They shall be childless.' Although a contrary verse existed in Deuteronomy, stating that 'the wife of the deceased shall not marry to another, but his brother shall take her and raise up seed for his brother'. Henry's council advised that Leviticus took precedence over Deuteronomy in canon law. The assembled clergy and lords met at York Place on two further occasions to debate the question of Catherine's legality as the king's wife, before admitting on 31 May that they were unqualified to reach a decision.

The next day, some devastating news arrived in England. Hundreds of miles away, over thirty thousand mutinous Imperial soldiers had been left unpaid and unfed for weeks during the war Charles had been waging against Francis. Partly inspired by their condition and partly by a swell of anti-Catholic feeling, they attacked the walls of Rome and burst into the city, embarking on a campaign of destruction, murder and pillage that would last for days. Symbolically, the tomb of Julius II, the very pope who had issued the dispensation for Henry and Catherine back in 1503, had been ransacked. By the time Wolsey's secret court met, Pope Clement, on whom he was pinning his hopes, had been driven to flee to safety in the Castel Santangelo: effectively, the pope was now Charles' prisoner. This made the Emperor the most powerful man in Europe.

He was also a devoted nephew. Under different circumstances, Henry's first marriage might have been quickly swept away, but the conjunction of these events on the European stage tied a Gordian knot of diplomacy and legal wrangling that would take years to unravel.

Unaware of the full impact this event would have upon his marital plans, Henry was appalled by the assault upon the seat of Catholicism. In his capacity as Defender of the Faith, he wrote to Cardinal Innocenzo Cybo, vowing to do all he could to restore the holy city:

> No one can receive the news of the disaster at Rome without grief and indignation. What could be more nefarious among Christians than to conspire the destruction of that city, and to treat with contumely the Vicar of Christ. They have not even spared holy places, but have imprisoned the Pope, and committed all kinds of sacrilege. As a champion of the Faith, is determined to resist this storm, and leave nothing undone to restore the Pope to liberty, and vindicate the dignity of the Church. Has no doubt the Cardinal, and those of his brethren who have been spared this degrading bondage, burn with the same zeal. Has accordingly despatched the cardinal of York to the French king, to consult upon this matter. Hopes Cibo will meet him, and take measures for the Pope's liberation.[15]

At this point, Henry was not just a committed Catholic still, but a 'champion' of the faith, a figure who was prepared to defend it on an international platform, either by the pen or by the sword. He continued to persecute those guilty of heresy in England, such as the Dutchman Abraham Water, then living in Colchester, who was interrogated that June for stating that all those upholding the sacraments were heretics and deserved to be punished, and for preaching in public that 'he could make of a piece of bread the body of Almighty God, as well as the best priest of them all'.[16] Yet the spoliation of Rome had a greater significance. It was not simply a stage in the war between the Emperor, France and the papacy. Its symbolism went much deeper. Until that point, the Vatican had seemed inviolable. Once it had fallen, or rather, once Henry perceived that God had permitted it to fall, its tenets, its authority, even its existence could be questioned. Only five years would pass before he decisively broke with Rome and titled himself 'Supreme Head on earth of the Church of England'.

Meanwhile, rumours about the royal marriage ran rife through the English court. On 25 May 1527, the hesitant French ambassadors looked to take their cue from the king, when it came to sharing sensitive political information in front of his wife. This suggests they were already aware of Henry's desire for a divorce and Wolsey's intention to secure Princess Renée as the next royal bride. Superficially, the incident appears to show Henry being solicitous for Catherine's feelings, but it shows that significant secrets were being kept from her. It was Henry himself who sent the ambassadors up to the queen's chamber after dinner, where 'they talked about the King's prosperity and the friendship of the two monarchs' (Henry and Francis) but then Catherine started asking questions, requiring the Bishop to tell her whether they intended 'to treat for a universal peace'. He answered cryptically, saying that 'the object for which they had come must precede, but did not state what it was, as he did not know whether it ought to be mentioned to the Queen'. That was when Henry stepped in, 'smiling, to her, that he was speaking of the marriage of the Princess'.[17] Catherine would not have been fooled by the show of harmony, knowing how her husband was working against her behind the scenes, seeking French support to divorce her and remarry. Did she yet guess at his intention to replace her with Anne?

Soon after the failure of the York Place court, Wolsey embarked for France, hoping to negotiate terms for Henry's marriage with Renée. He lodged the first night on his way down through Kent at the home of Sir John Wiltshire, Stone Castle, where he also met Warham and discussed 'the king's secret matter', how 'displeasantly the Queen takes it' and 'what the king has done to pacify her'. Warham, who had counselled Henry against his marriage in 1509, was 'astonished' to hear that Catherine was aware of the situation, but believed 'truth and the law must prevail' and promised to comply.[18] With Wiltshire's daughter, Bridget, being a friend and neighbour of Anne, and also employed in Catherine's household, the details of this meeting might have reached her at Hever, where she had retired for the duration of the hearing. On 5 July, Wolsey wrote again, en route after having stayed at Rochester, concerned that rumours had reached Henry of his opposition to the divorce. He assured the king of his continuing support and was relieved to find, when he arrived down in Dover on 10 July, that Henry had dispatched 'a fat hart' for him to dine on.[19] He embarked for Calais the next day. Whilst away, Wolsey was 'daily and hourly musing' about Henry's 'great and secret affair' and how it 'may come to good effect and desired end', to deliver the king out of the 'thrall, pensive and dolorous life' and 'for the continuance of (his) health'.[20] He came to the conclusion that 'the Pope's consent must be gained in case the Queen should decline (Wolsey's) jurisdiction', which could only happen once the pope had been restored to liberty. This could only happen once peace was settled between Charles and Francis, which was 'not likely', but Wolsey would 'endeavour to see what could be done on this matter'. He was certain that Clement VII 'would be easily induced to do everything' to Henry's satisfaction, once he had been released.[21] However, Wolsey was unaware that word of Catherine's treatment had already reached the ears of the Emperor and that Charles was preparing to enter the lists on his aunt's behalf. Nor did he know in which direction Henry's satisfaction lay.

If Henry had thought the sack of Rome posed difficulties for his plans, the objections of the Emperor were to reveal what a complicated political move his divorce might become. Catherine had dispatched a messenger with a letter to her nephew and, despite Henry's best efforts to intercept the man, her words got through. Charles considered Henry's intentions to be a scandal, scarcely believable, which would cause concern among a number of European heads of state. He wrote to Catherine, Henry and to the pope, requesting that he revoke Wolsey's powers, considering the cardinal to be instrumental in the case. On 29 July, he wrote at length to Don Inigo de Mendoza, his ambassador in England, who had been detained for four months by the French during his journey:

We have duly received your despatches of the 13 July, and at the same time the letter of the Queen our aunt, of which Francis Phillips was the bearer. He, in virtue of his credence, has told me in substance what we already knew by your letters, respecting the affairs of the said Queen. You may well imagine how sorry we were to hear of so scandalous a proceeding as the one in contemplation, one of such bad consequences, and from which so many evils are sure to originate, besides occurring at such a time and in so unfavorable a conjuncture. It is, however, our intention not to be in fault with the Queen our aunt, but, on the contrary, to do everything in our power on her behalf.

To this end, it seems to us, as a commencement of remedy to the impending evil, that the affair ought to be treated at first with all possible moderation, and by means of kind remonstrances. We have, accordingly, written a letter to the King in our own hand, begging that he will place full credit and reliance in whatever you may have to communicate to him on this affair; and we also send you a copy of the said letter of credence, that you may judge yourself of its contents.

You will inform the King how, through yourself, or in any other way you may deem more fitting and appropriate for the occasion, we have had cognizance of the actual state of things between his serenity the King and the Queen, his wife and our aunt. How, immediately after the receipt of such intelligence, we took up pen, and wrote to him the inclosed letter in our own hand, without communicating its import to any member of our Privy Council and others, or asking their advice upon it, as the matter is of such nature and importance.

You will further tell the King that, in order better to keep secret the contents of our letter to him, we have abstained from sending to him one of the gentlemen of our chamber, as we at first thought of doing; and that, foreseeing that this dispatch, as well as our private letter to him, must needs go by land, we have, with infinite trouble to ourselves, put the same in cipher, difficult and intricate as you know it to be.

That, knowing her great virtues, his good and righteous intentions, and the perfect love he has always borne towards us and our affairs, we cannot in any manner be persuaded to believe in so strange a determination on the part of his Serenity, and one which is calculated to astonish the whole world, were it to be carried into effect. In fact, we do not believe it possible, considering the good qualities of his Serenity and of the Queen his wife, the honorable peace in which they have lived together for such a number of years, as is notorious throughout the Christian world; the Queen herself being so good and virtuous, loving the King as she does, having always conducted herself towards him in the most irreproachable manner, and being of such high royal blood. To which we may add that, having so genteel a Princess for their daughter, it is not to be presumed that his Serenity the King would consent to have her and her mother dishonored, a thing in itself so unreasonable that there is no example of it in ancient or modern history.

For even if it were right and allowable to say or think – which is by no means so – that the Pope could not dispense in this marriage, and even supposing the existence on that occasion of the motives alleged, or other causes and reasons still stronger of any kind whatsoever, of which there is none, to procure such a scandalous dissolution of the match, it would be a far better and more honorable proceeding to keep the matter secret, and work out its remedy, if necessary, though we again say that such motives and reasons do not and cannot exist.

Nor is it likely that such innovations proceed from his Serenity, but from persons who bear ill-will towards the Queen and ourselves, and who care not what evils and disasters may spring therefrom. For, as we have no doubt that you will be able to show and prove to the King, the present affair is one in which several princes of Christendom are deeply concerned, and which in future times may prove to be the cause of great troubles and dissensions among them; some maintaining that the Princess his daughter, after the King's death, is legitimate and true heir to his crown; whilst others may say that the king of Scotland, by his mother's right, ought to succeed to the throne of England; besides which, other political questions connected with the above might give rise in England to everlasting feuds and partialities.

You are, therefore, to entreat his Serenity, in our name, well to consider and ponder the whole matter, and to call his especial attention to the three following points: 1st, to take in good part what we tell him in a friendly way, and to believe that in thus addressing him we have only said what we knew to be most advantageous to himself and to us. 2nd, that he may be pleased, for the honor and service of God, to put an end and remedy to so scandalous an affair. 3rd, that he may also be pleased to treat it with such secrecy and reserve as is needed in a case of this sort, and which concerns alike him and ourselves, a precaution and warning which the King, in his great prudence and discretion, is sure to duly appreciate. And you are also to promise, in our name, that whatever measures may be required to ensure the said secrecy we are ready to take, out of perfect love for him, and for the said Queen our aunt, and for the Princess their daughter, and for the whole kingdom of England.

A duplicate of this dispatch shall be forwarded to you by sea, and at the same time Francis Phillips shall return to England. He shall, moreover, be the bearer of a letter of ours to the Queen our aunt, to whom you may, as soon as possible, communicate the contents of this dispatch in the manner that you think most proper for her tranquillity and satisfaction, giving her at the same time such advice as may console her in her present affliction.[22]

Wolsey had his answers ready. He wrote to his representative in Rome, Gregory Casale, setting out the scruples of the king's conscience.

Partly by his assiduous study and learning, and partly by conference with theologians [Henry had] found his conscience somewhat burthened with his present marriage; and out of regard to the quiet of his soul, and next to the security of his succession, and the great mischiefs likely to arise, he considers it would be offensive to God and man if he were to persist in it, and with great remorse of conscience has now for a long time felt that he is living under the offence of the Almighty, whom in all his efforts and his actions he always sets before him.[23]

Not taking such a situation lightly, Henry had sought advice and 'made diligent inquiry whether the dispensation granted for himself and the Queen as his brother's wife is valid and sufficient, and he is told that it is not'. Henry attributed to this 'the death of all his male children' and dreaded the 'heavy wrath of God if he persists'. He believed himself entitled to the annulment, being convinced that his special relationship with the pope, – 'out of consideration of his services to the Church' – meant that Clement 'will not refuse to remove this scruple out of the King's mind'. Understanding that the pope's captivity could prove critical in securing the annulment, Wolsey urged Casale to 'obtain a secret interview with the Pope' and offered to pay 10,000 ducats to Casale's Venetian bankers in order to bribe papal officials to enable it to take place.[24] Yet there were voices in Europe already being raised against the pope's authority. English ambassador to the Netherlands, John Hackett, wrote to Wolsey from Ghent on 30 July, 1527:

> Some here say they are [not] sorry for the Pope's misfortune, and think that God has punished him for defying the Emperor in a rightful quarrel and taking the French king's part in a wrong one, and also for dispensing the French king to perjure himself, when he might as well have induced him to keep his promise. Every man here has his tongue at liberty.[25]

Wolsey was adamant that the royal marriage could no longer continue, but in his private letter to Casale, he went much further, stating that sexual relations were now impossible between Henry and Catherine, as 'certain diseases in the queen defying all remedy, for which, as well as for other causes, the king will never again live with her as a wife'.[26] Some intimate illness, Wolsey suggested, meant that Henry was 'utterly resolved and determined never to use' her again and that 'danger... may ensue to the king's person by continuing in the queen's chamber'.[27] This was quite a dramatic claim. It implied that Catherine had some infection, illness or condition that affected her sexual organs and that this might be transmitted to her husband, or that the queen was capable of doing violence to Henry. Was this really true, or were Henry and Wolsey prepared to use whatever weapon they thought might prove successful in separating the king from his wife? Considering that Wolsey also lied to the pope that the blood-stained sheets from Catherine's 1501 wedding night to Arthur had been sent to Spain, and defamed the queen as frenzied with desire for sex, his argument about her disease appears incredible.

At Windsor on 22 June, Henry informed Catherine that their marriage was over. Outlining the questions of conscience that had been troubling him, he told the queen that they had been living in mortal sin since 1509 and that she must retire to a convent. Catherine replied that she had never consummated her marriage to Arthur and that she was Henry's lawfully wedded wife. Henry asked her to choose a place where she would like to retire. Although this interview convinced her that he was serious, Catherine was going nowhere. Henry asked her to keep the matter, the worst kept secret in Europe, between themselves. This suggested to the queen that any separation was still merely theoretical at this stage. She still had time; she might be able to change his mind. The situation in 1527 was volatile, a dream, a theoretic solution for Henry that had seemed plausible, then suddenly became unlikely. Winning over Anne had not been an easy matter but, to make her his wife, Henry now had to face the formidable opponents of Catherine of Aragon, her nephew the Emperor Charles V and his puppet, Pope Clement VII. He was taking England to war with the most powerful family in Europe, the Hapsburgs, and the bastion of the Catholic faith.

PART FOUR

ANNE'S ASCENDANCY

SIXTEEN

Love Letters 1527

During the early summer of 1527, while Wolsey's court was in session at York Place, Anne made a tactical retreat to Hever. There, in the peace and quiet of the Kent countryside, she waited to hear the result of the hearing, although she may not yet have been fully aware of the implications of the event. Equally, it could have been a tactical withdrawal, while she considered her position, unsure of the king's intentions. A total of seventeen love letters survive to her from Henry, six of which were sent during the June and July of this year. From their evidence, it appears that at the time of her departure from court, Anne had not yet decided whether she returned the king's affections, nor whether she was willing to enter into a relationship with him. She may well have believed that Henry intended to take Renée of France as his second wife, just as Wolsey did. This may even have been Henry's intention before the force of his desire for Anne, and her reluctance to succumb to it, demanded a different solution. It was not until halfway through the sequence of letters that summer, that Henry refers to the possibility of their marriage and Anne first glimpsed the possibility of becoming queen of England. Suddenly the greatest prize of the Tudor age, the pinnacle of a woman's worldly achievement, was offered to her. It was not just about power, riches and status. To be anointed as queen with holy oil, by an Archbishop in Westminster Abbey, was to accept the will of God. If Anne truly believed that Henry's marriage with Catherine was invalid, in the way that Tudor people believed the will of God underpinned everything, then it made her the instrument by which the dynasty was to be restored.

The survival of Henry's letters is probably the result of their theft from Hever in 1529.[1] They were taken in an attempt to provide evidence about Henry's relationship with Anne. The identity of the thief, and the exact date of their removal, is unknown, but they ended up in the Vatican archives. The order of their composition has been disputed[2] and no replies from Anne survive, so it is only possible to estimate her emotions by using the limited evidence of Henry's responses and his references to things she has written. Thus, the letters must be treated with caution, as they only provide a one-sided snippet of a developing picture. Even amid continuing editorial debate, though, they provide a valuable snapshot of the techniques Henry used to woo Anne: they offer a direct, intimate connection with the voice of the king as lover, whispering his secret desires through a language of rhetorical devices, conventions and promises.

Much of Henry's prose is romantic and tender, decorated by his drawings of hearts and coded initials, but this style belies the true dynamic of their relationship. Professing himself her 'loyal servant and friend', the king's bombardment of Anne by passionate letters actually tells a more sinister story. It raises the question of whether she ultimately had a choice when it came to her relationship with the king, and her difficult position as a woman, a subject and a Boleyn. By the letters' internal evidence, she resisted him for over a year, being frequently absent from court and his presence, sometimes as a deliberate move to avoid him. Henry's presentation of the trope of courtly love, of the pursuit of the unattainable woman, is belied by his offering her the unprecedented position of his official mistress. She may have been the object of his affection but he was also her king. In places, the letters read like the record of a developing love affair, in others, the gradual wearing down of a woman's resistance. Henry loved the idea of being in love and, for the time being, he was content to place Anne on a pedestal in anticipation of her future surrender. Together, the seventeen letters make a compelling case for coercion. Henry's language and tone illustrate just how little real choice Anne had.

The first letter was written after Anne had left court in the second half of May 1527:

In turning over in my mind the contents of your last letters, I have put myself into great agony, not knowing how to interpret them, whether to my disadvantage, as you show in some places, or to my advantage, as I understand them in some others, beseeching you earnestly to let me know expressly your whole mind as to the love between us two.

It is absolutely necessary for me to obtain this answer, having been for above a whole year stricken with the dart of love, and not yet sure whether I shall fail of finding a place in your heart and affection, which last point has prevented me for some time past from calling you my mistress; because, if you only love me with an ordinary love, that name is not suitable for you, because it denotes a singular love, which is far from common. But if you please to do the office of a true loyal mistress and friend, and to give up yourself body and heart to me, who will be, and have been, your most loyal servant, (if your rigour does not forbid me) I promise you that not only the name shall be given you, but also that I will take you for my only mistress, casting off all others besides you out of my thoughts and affections, and serve you only. I beseech you to give an entire answer to this my rude letter, that I may know on what and how far I may depend. And if it does not please you to answer me in writing, appoint some place where I may have it by word of mouth, and I will go thither with all my heart. No more, for fear of tiring you. Written by the hand of him who would willingly remain yours, H. R.[3]

Henry begins from a position of uncertainty, the traditional 'great agony' of the lover, as he has been unable to interpret her words. Anne appears to have sent the king mixed messages, instead of a conclusive acceptance of his love, as well she might, being unwilling to encourage the man, but desperate not to offend the king. He commands her to be clearer, stating it is 'absolutely necessary' for him to 'obtain' her answer, revealing the intent to extract the information, regardless of her will. He is determined to pin her down and presents the duration of his infatuation as reason for his entitlement. Under the guise of inviting her to commit to him, he compels her compliance, by inverting their roles, and calling himself her servant when, in fact, he remains in control, dictating the terms of their relations. The position he offers her, of his 'only mistress' appears to offer her power, status and exclusivity, but it is a power based on his permission, given, and presumably, withdrawn, at his pleasure.

The second letter, written soon afterwards, still attempts to define their relationship. From his first sentence, it sounds as if Anne has responded to remind him that she is his servant, rather than the other way around. She was not comfortable at that point with his suggestion of becoming his official mistress but had tipped the power balance back to that which their comparative status dictated. Yet why exactly did Anne resist the king for so long? In terms of ambition, she could hardly have aimed higher. George Wyatt suggests this was from loyalty to Catherine of Aragon, giving Anne two speeches which are not her recorded words, but capture the emotional truth of her answers, resonating with the direction of the letters:

I think your Majesty speaks these words in mirth to prove me, but without any intent of degrading your princely self. To ease you of the labour of asking me any such question hereafter, I beseech your Highness most earnestly to desist, and to take this my answer in good part. I would rather lose my life than my honesty, which will be the greatest and best part of the dowry I shall have to bring my husband.

Your wife I cannot be, both in respect of mine own unworthiness, and also because you have a queen already. Your mistress I will not be.[4]

Later historians point to a mixture of reserve, predatory design or belief that Anne had learned from the example of her sister, Mary. Having served, and presumably admired, great female rulers who were the relatives or friends of Catherine, it may be that Anne did not aspire to the role of the woman who briefly shared their husbands' beds. It may also have been that she feared the consequences, given the way that Henry's mind was working and the upheaval that would result, at court and in Europe. She knew that the stakes would be high. It is in the speculation surrounding such questions of Anne's true feelings and motivations that historians and biographers have defined their Annes. According to their interpretations of Anne's resistance to Henry, and then her capitulation, she has been painted as mercenary, grasping and cold-hearted, or as Henry's quarry, his plaything, his obsession, perhaps even his victim. Much depends upon the reading of the letters, as to whether biographers see her as cleverly planning her every move to ensnare him, or whether she was reacting to his pursuit, unsure, even confused, about where her duty lay and how to handle this unsought onslaught of passion. There is also the possibility that she had genuine feelings for the king as a man, or genuine admiration for him as a king, and felt that as his subject she was not in a position to deny his request forever. Perhaps she was playing for time, hoping his interest would fade in her absence, or else she was navigating between the conflicting extremes of love and duty. Her situation was almost absurdly complex and is likely to have shifted several times as the relationship unfolded.

Though it is not fitting for a gentleman to take his lady in the place of a servant, yet, complying with your desire, I willingly grant it you, if thereby you can find yourself less uncomfortable in the place chosen by yourself, than you have been in that which I gave you, thanking you cordially that you are pleased still to have some remembrance of me.[5]

By the time Henry composed what is considered to be his third letter, he was referring to Anne as his mistress, but chiding her for not being in touch. It seems from his opening lines that she had not replied to him at all, choosing silence rather than the difficult task of disappointing the king. Henry uses the excuse that he is performing the office of a 'true servant' by enquiring about her health, but it is actually an intrusive act, with a selfish motive, rather than the act of service he pretends. Having had no encouragement, he pursues her again under the guise of concern. To encourage her response, and to create a debt of gratitude, he sent her the gift of a deer carcase, with the obvious parallel of pursuit and capture; a reminder that Henry was a master hunter and no prey was safe. Anne could be left in little doubt that he was fixed upon her as his next target, and that he did not intend to let her escape.

> Although, my Mistress, it has not pleased you to remember the promise you made me when I was last with you, that is, to hear good news from you, and to have an answer to my last letter; yet it seems to me that it belongs to a true servant (seeing that otherwise he can know nothing) to inquire the health of his mistress, and to acquit myself of the duty of a true servant, I send you this letter, beseeching you to apprise me of your welfare, which I pray to God may continue as long as I desire mine own. And to cause you yet oftener to remember me, I send you, by the bearer of this, a buck killed late last night by my own hand, hoping that when you eat of it you may think of the hunter; and thus, for want of room, I must end my letter, written by the hand of your servant, who very often wishes for you instead of your brother. H. R.[6]

Henry's fourth letter, written that June or July, refers to his surrender, but it is not clear whether this is a gesture that Anne has invited, or whether the king was offering this unsolicited. Her absence only served to inflame his passion, to which he refers in a typical astrological metaphor of the times, but this device could equally be representative of him basking in her rays, or the sun representing his burning ardour, growing hotter despite her distance. His only comfort in her absence is 'the firm hope I have of your unchangeable affection for me', but his comfort is in the hope, rather than any confirmed declaration or promise on Anne's part. Again, he tries to pin down her affection and make real something that may not have been offered, securing this with another expensive gift, this time a bracelet bearing his face, so that she cannot avoid his gaze.

> My mistress and friend, my heart and I surrender ourselves into your hands, beseeching you to hold us commended to your favour, and that by absence your affection to us may not be lessened: for it were a great

pity to increase our pain, of which absence produces enough and more than I could ever have thought could be felt, reminding us of a point in astronomy which is this: the longer the days are, the more distant is the sun, and nevertheless the hotter; so is it with our love, for by absence we are kept a distance from one another, and yet it retains its fervour, at least on my side; I hope the like on yours, assuring you that on my part the pain of absence is already too great for me; and when I think of the increase of that which I am forced to suffer, it would be almost intolerable, but for the firm hope I have of your unchangeable affection for me: and to remind you of this sometimes, and seeing that I cannot be personally present with you, I now send you the nearest thing I can to that, namely, my picture set in a bracelet, with the whole of the device, which you already know, wishing myself in their place, if it should please you. This is from the hand of your loyal servant and friend, H.R [7]

This is the point when Anne appears to have given the king a definite response, either voluntarily, or as a result of his pressure – or perhaps the encouragement of her family. Yet her reaction still implies uncertainty. True to the use of imagery, symbolism and metaphor in courtly play, Anne sent the king a gift with a coded message. The details of it only survive in Henry's next letter, along with his 'cordial' thanks for 'a present so beautiful nothing could be more so'. The present he referred to was a jewel in the form of a solitary damsel tossed inside a ship, indicative of Anne's internal struggle. It came accompanied by a diamond and a letter, including 'demonstrations of your affection' and 'beautiful mottoes… so cordially expressed' that they obliged Henry 'for ever to honour, love and serve you sincerely'. Anne had given some of the reassurance the king had been seeking, but without the evidence of her letters, it is impossible to know whether she did so willingly. She was being asked to distinguish between her feelings for him as her monarch and as a man, which might have been a straightforward question for Anne, or it may have been fraught with difficulty. The length of his courtship before her capitulation suggests the latter.

In response to her gift, Henry promised that 'henceforward my heart shall be dedicated to you alone. I wish my person was too.' Some kind of understanding has been reached, as the king then first raises the possibility of being Anne's husband. He hoped to be hers in person, assuring her that 'God can do it, if He pleases, to whom I pray every day for that end'. From this point, Anne could be in no doubt that Henry hoped to make her his wife, and that the proceedings at York Place were intended to achieve that purpose.

In this exchange of letters we see how the rules of courtly love allow the usual gender codes to be subverted – apparently. With the king offering to be Anne's servant, he makes himself subordinate to her, albeit in a kind of play, just as he enjoyed putting on a mask and acting a role. He gave her mastery over his heart but it was a complex, conditional mastery, so long as it continued within certain rules. He might move heaven and earth for her, put aside his queen and ultimately, break with Rome, but he still retained ultimate control as a king and a man. By laying himself at her feet, Henry gave Anne permission to 'rule' him according to an intricate code of behaviour, yet if he perceived that she had broken these rules at any point, been disrespectful, insincere or untrue, that permission would be revoked. This was an unprecedented situation. Henry and Anne were rewriting all former rules of the game, and the delicate balance of mastery and subordination, the dynamics of gender and royalty, would be difficult to get right.

For a present so beautiful that nothing could be more so (considering the whole of it), I thank you most cordially, not only on account of the fine diamond and the ship in which the solitary damsel is tossed about, but chiefly for the fine interpretation and the too humble submission which your goodness hath used towards me in this case; for I think it would be very difficult for me to find an occasion to deserve it, if I were not assisted by your great humanity and favour, which I have always sought to seek, and will seek to preserve by all the kindness in my power, in which my hope has placed its unchangeable intention, which says, *Aut illic, aut nullibi.* [Either there, or nowhere.] The demonstrations of your affection are such, the beautiful mottoes of the letter so cordially expressed, that they oblige me for ever to honour, love, and serve you sincerely, beseeching you to continue in the same firm and constant purpose, assuring you that, on my part, I will surpass it rather than make it reciprocal, if loyalty of heart and a desire to please you can accomplish this. I beg, also, if at any time before this I have in anyway offended you, that you would give me the same absolution that you ask, assuring you, that henceforward my heart shall be de dicated to you alone. I wish my person was so too. God can do it, if He pleases, to whom I pray every day for that end, hoping that at length my prayers will be heard. I wish the time may be short, but I shall think it long till we see one another.

Written by the hand of that secretary, who in heart, body, and will, is, Your loyal and most assured Servant, H. aultre A.B. ne cherche R

The 'A.B.' at the bottom of the letter was in a heart. By the time Henry wrote his sixth letter that July, he had seen Anne again, perhaps having ridden to visit her at Hever, and an understanding had passed between them. Yet, just at the point where he believed he had achieved some kind of security, further doubts arose, as Anne appeared to have changed her mind. She was refusing to return to court, either alone or with her mother, at which Henry could only 'marvel' and consider it a 'very poor return for the great love which I bear you'. Here, the voice of the king overrules that of the man. Even though Henry plays the lover, the tone of his 'marvel' subtly stresses Anne's obligation and his failure to recall what he may have done to 'offend' her implies that he has, in his opinion, done all he could to be of service and to please. Henry is using the literary technique of litotes, the employment of negatives and ironic understatement, to highlight the tension between what he might ask of Anne, and what he might command. Her aloofness 'seems a very poor return for the great love which I bear you' and he hopes she loves him 'with as much affection as I hope you do... though this does not belong so much to the mistress as to the servant'. It was a clear reminder to her that he deserved better treatment, as if he had been mistaken, he would then mourn his 'ill-fortune' and 'great folly'. Although Henry had not yet become the figure notorious for removing his former favourites swiftly after minor, or non-existent, transgressions, his will was absolute and he did not flinch from executing his wrath, as in the case of Buckingham. Anne may have intended, quite simply, to avoid him while committing to nothing further. If so, the sixth letter was a subtle warning that she needed to commit fully to the role he had assigned to her:

To my Mistress. Because the time seems very long since I heard concerning your health and you, the great affection I have for you has induced me to send you this bearer, to be better informed of your health and pleasure, and because, since my parting from you, I have been told that the opinion in which I left you is totally changed, and that you would not come to court either with your mother, if you could, or in any other manner; which report, if true, I cannot sufficiently marvel at, because I am sure that I have since never done any thing to offend you, and it seems a very poor return for the great love which I bear you to keep me at a distance both from the speech and the person of the woman that I esteem most in the world: and if you love me with as much affection as I hope you do, I am sure that the distance of our two persons would be a little irksome to you, though this does not belong so much to the mistress as to the servant. Consider well, my mistress, that absence from you grieves me sorely, hoping that it is not your will that it should be so; but if I knew for certain that you voluntarily desired it, I could do no other than mourn my ill-fortune, and by degrees abate my great folly. And so, for lack of time, I make an end of this rude letter, beseeching you to give credence to this bearer in all that he will tell you from me.

Written by the hand of your entire Servant, H.R.[8]

Henry juxtaposes the roles of sovereign and subject uncomfortably with that of man and woman. His words confuse the expectations of gender and politics. Had she received such a missive from Percy or Wyatt, Anne's responses would have been more her own: but it is from the king, and it raises the question of just how much autonomy she really had in the relationship. With Henry switching between roles, as lover and king, Anne had to work out just how much licence he was prepared to give her to 'rule' him, and when she needed to submit to his authority, in the interests of herself and her family. The lack of response and coolness Henry complains of may well have been less the calculation of the hard-headed manipulator that Anne's critic Nicholas Sander suggests, playing the long game to hook the king, than a confused young woman unsure how she should respond, backed into a corner. Perhaps Anne stayed away from court, and from Henry, because this was too dangerous a game, which, initially, she did not want to play. Her king though, was not going to allow her that option.

This situation persisted for at least a year, with Henry's reference to the 'dart of love' in his first letter indicating that Anne put up considerable resistance to his advances. To Henry's mind, her reluctance made her an even greater prize, a challenge of the kind he had previously not encountered, raising Anne's value in his eyes. There was nothing the king liked better than the chase, and the opportunity of playing a role which had a courtly or chivalric element to it. Anne's changes of mind, her absences and her unwillingness to commit to him, all played to his notions of romance and offered yet another contrast with his wife. In one sense, during her long widowhood of 1502–9, Catherine had been forced to wait and Henry was the prize to be won, against all odds. He never had to pursue her, or wear down her resistance, and it is unlikely that this was ever the case with Elizabeth Blount or Mary Boleyn. This certainly served to increase Henry's desire for Anne, but it may also have created an element of doubt. Given her reluctance, he may have entertained misgivings about her sincerity, then and in the future. He knew that his ardour for her was stronger than her feelings for him. She had never chosen him. When she finally capitulated and accepted him, did he ever wonder whether she had done so out of desire for him as a man, or whether she was obeying her king? If Henry retained the slightest shred of doubt about her motivation, justifiably or not, he would have found it easier to believe that she was untrue to him at a later date.

At the end of July 1527, Henry was at the Palace of Beaulieu, where William and Mary Carey lived, entertaining on a grand scale. His guests included Anne's uncle, the new Duke of Norfolk and his wife, Charles Brandon, Duke of Suffolk and Anne's father, Viscount Rochford, 'and others'. The three men were 'privy to' the letters the king was sending to Wolsey[9] and, probably, the fact that Henry was misleading his servant, by not being honest about his intentions for Anne. It is plausible, amid such a family gathering at her sister's home, that Anne was also present, but she is not mentioned by name. Henry's plans for the coming month were to visit 'Hennyngham' (Helmingham or Heveningham in Suffolk), then head to Greenwich at the end of August to await Wolsey's return from the continent, whilst also fitting in some hunting in Waltham Forest.[10] However, news of 'the sickness' changed his mind and his route, although his final destination remained the same. It is likely that he travelled to Hever at some point after he finally arrived at Greenwich, or that Anne was summoned to join him there. When Wolsey arrived that September, bringing news of the Treaty of Amiens he had agreed with the French, he found Anne at Henry's side, and was unable to secure an interview with the king without her presence. Suddenly, he realised that the negotiations he had been making on behalf of Princess Renée had been meaningless – and that his own position was under threat from a very powerful new player at court. The summer of 1527 changed Anne's focus, and her life. She had gone from entertaining doubts to being the king's accepted love and, as he hoped, his future wife and queen.

SEVENTEEN

Turning Point 1527–8

Through the late summer and autumn of 1527, Henry prepared his case for the divorce to be submitted to Pope Clement VII. Wolsey tried to dissuade him from marrying Anne, but he could not stir the king 'to the contrary' even though he went down on his knees to do so, because the king was so amorously affectionate' that 'high discretion (was) banished for a time'. George Cavendish continued, 'the long hid and secret love between the king and Mistress Anne Boleyn began to break out into every man's ears'.[1] News rapidly spread across Europe about the state of Henry's marriage, opening all eyes to his recent deceptions regarding the French negotiations for the hand of Renée. It also threatened to throw the delicate balance of European diplomacy into disarray. That October, the Grand Master of France, Anne de Montmorency, with whom Wolsey had recently been negotiating, received a letter from an acquaintance, who had been 'informed' by someone who was 'very familiar' with the

> ...vice-chancellor of Flanders, the cardinal of Liège, and De Berghes, that some persons in England who favor the Emperor are intriguing against the King and Cardinal because the King is putting away his wife, the Emperor's aunt, which, they say, will make it impossible ever to reconcile the Emperor to Henry; and if the latter were dead, they could re-marry the Queen or her daughter to some prince of England, who would make perpetual alliance with the Emperor against the king [Francis][2]

With the pope under the control of the Emperor, relations with France improved as they soured with Charles. Records from that November show that Thomas Boleyn was among those still receiving a pension from France, according to the Treaty of the More, arranged in August 1525. The 262½ crowns Boleyn received was only a fraction of the 67,218 crowns paid out by the French government, but it was symbolic of the superior English position and power at the time, and the inclusion of the family as significant players, even before Anne had caught the king's eye.[3] That October, a French embassy led by Anne de Montmorency arrived in England and Thomas Boleyn was among those sent to meet them at Blackheath to convey them to the Bishop of London's palace, where the citizens presented them with gifts of oxen, sheep, swans and other fowl, eight hogsheads of wine, loaves of sugar, comfits and other sweets. They went by barge to Greenwich for further entertainment with the king and Wolsey, culminating in Henry's decision to award Francis I the Order of the Garter. There was more jousting, banqueting and pageantry, presided over by the king and queen, but no doubt Anne was there too, to witness the 'place of pleasure' that had been constructed for the occasion, requiring 12 reams of silver and gold paper, vermilion, verdigris and sap green paint, gold foil and four dozen birds to create 'trees, bushes, branches, roses, rosemary, hawthorn, mulberries, panes of gold and stars'. It had taken a month to build, before the revels were held on 10 November.[4] Louise of Savoy wrote to Wolsey on 12 November to offer her thanks for Francis's selection, and her promise that 'he will do his best to observe the statutes'.[5]

After the failure of Wolsey's court, William Knight, archdeacon of Chester and Henry's secretary, was dispatched to Rome. In December, he received his instructions from the hands of Thomas Boleyn's chaplain,[6] which may have been the rising clergyman Thomas Cranmer, who was involved in assisting with the divorce proceedings from this point onwards. Knight promised to approach the pope as soon as possible, in secrecy, given the extraordinary nature of the king's desires. The instructions accompanying the bull to be submitted to Clement VII opened with the directive that the pope was 'bound to listen to the prayers of the faithful, especially to such a person as Henry VIII' because he had 'distinguished himself in the defence of the church' and, by his accession, had 'reconciled the dissensions of York and Lancaster'. Once again, Henry believed his actions and pedigree entitled him to a special audience, just as he had felt he deserved the affections of Anne and would not accept a rejection. He requested that the pope pronounce the marriage invalid in the light of Catherine's former marriage to Arthur, legitimising their daughter and removing all scruples as to the king's conscience, allowing him to remarry.[7]

As the King of England 18 years ago was married to Katharine at the persuasion of the councillors, and on the force of a pretended Papal dispensation; on a further examination of the ecclesiastical canons, and as the dispensation was granted on false pretences, and for this and other reasons appears to be invalid, &c. &c., we, considering these things, the anxiety of the King's conscience, and his services to the Holy See, appoint Cardinal Wolsey for his justice and his virtue, with to proceed conjointly in this cause, with a proviso that if one cannot act the other may. You are to proceed summarily *sine strepitu et figura judicii* to inquire into the said bull, and if you jointly or severally are satisfied of its invalidity, to declare the marriage between Henry and Katharine null and void, allowing the parties so separated to enter upon a new marriage *citra omnem recusationem aut appellationis interpositionem* [roughly 'on this side, or short of, the excuse for the appeal']. By authority of this present you are to override all canonical defects and objections, declaring the issue of the first marriage legitimate, if you think fit, as well as that of the second. Whatever is done in this matter by you, judicially or extrajudicially, we shall ratify in the most valid and efficacious form, and never infringe it.[8]

Wolsey wrote at length to the English ambassador to the papacy, Gregory Casale, offering his 'great grief' at the calamity which had befallen the pope and 'even at the cost of my life, to remove and repair it'. Yet he foresaw the split that would arise with England and knew where his first loyalties must lie. Stating his hope that the friendship between Clement and Henry 'will be permanent', he followed with a warning that, if pressed, he would be forced to choose his king over the pope: 'Unless some occasion should be offered for alienating the king's mind, in which event it will never be in my power to serve his holiness.' Casale was to impress upon the pope just how much the situation 'concerns the king's conscience, the prosperity of his kingdom and the security of his succession'. It was also, in Wolsey's eyes, 'agreeable to God'.[9] Wolsey understood that his career, even his life, was tied to the outcome of these proceedings, telling Casale that 'if the Pope is not compliant my life will be shortened and I dread to anticipate the consequences'. He could already foresee that Henry would break with Rome over this issue, as he was 'absolutely resolved to satisfy his conscience' and would, 'of two evils choose the least, and the disregard for the Papacy must grow daily'. Wolsey pleaded, 'not so much as an English subject, as one who has certain knowledge of what the result must be', or else he was powerless to do anything on the pope's behalf.[10]

Wolsey sent Casale clean copies of the commission, which required 'nothing more than the Pope's signature'.[11] It made the matter sound simple, just one signature, to allow the case to be opened, but the pope feared the influence of the Emperor, and the extent of his power in Europe. Having narrowly escaped once, during the sack of Rome, he even feared for his life. It was not conducive to Henry and Anne's situation, but Clement eventually granted Wolsey the commission to try the marriage. As Casale explained:

> Great labour had to be used to get the Pope to grant it; not because he does not wish to please the King and the Legate, but because he never was in greater fear of the Spaniards, who hold all the lands of the Church, 'et suo judicio Ga[lli] non videntur quicquam boni velle agere' [meaning the French were unwilling to act]. The Friar General forbade the Pope to grant this to the King. [He fears] that when the Emperor knows of it, the Imperialists will ruin and even kill him, unless the King helps him. When he was advised not to hesitate, and to put himself entirely into the hands of the King and the Legate, he replied that he did so, for he had exposed himself to death, unless the King helped him; that is, if the Emperor is allowed to possess more of Italy than the kingdom of Naples, he will be master of everything.[12]

Before signing, Casale wrote, the pope 'had many altercations about it' and wept as he said this would be his ruin, as his 'sole hope of life' lay in the Emperor. Casale encouraged him as best he could, swearing that Henry would not desert him, so that Clement granted the brief, saying he put himself in Henry's hands, ready for when he was drawn into the inevitable war with the Emperor.[13] With promises and bribes, Henry had got his way, but he would think nothing of abandoning the pope once he could no longer grant his wishes.

Back in England, Anne had to wait for permission to arrive, a situation that was becoming increasingly awkward. In 1528, Henry housed both women together under the same roof at Greenwich, and although they had separate establishments within the large complex and could have used them to maintain a degree of privacy, encounters would have been unavoidable in the public arenas. In fact, it seems that the queen went out of her way to meet Anne and Henry, singly and together, using her presence in an attempt to divide, or at least chaperone them. According to George Cavendish, Catherine employed various methods to keep the lovers apart, 'the oftener had her at cards with her, the rather that the King might have the less her company', on which occasion Catherine reputedly uttered the ironic line that Anne had 'good hap to stop at a king, but you are not like others, you will have all or none'.[14] Otherwise, chronicler George Wyatt suggests that she behaved impeccably, never showing 'any spark or kind of grudge or displeasure'. Perhaps Catherine decided it was safest to keep her enemy close and that her presence would prove restrictive to the pair, preventing them achieving greater intimacy or plotting her downfall behind her back. Also, she would have maintained that as England's anointed queen of eighteen years, it was her right and her duty to be visible at court, in the palaces she had been inhabiting for so long, accessible to the people and served at table according to her due. She may have hoped that her presence would be enough to provoke Anne to shame or drive her away. At some point in February 1528, Anne was away from court, as Henry's letter to her from this time shows, but it was a temporary departure, and he was anticipating her return. More that that, he was hopeful that the matter would soon be concluded so they might marry:

Darling, these shall be only to advertise you that this bearer and his fellow be dispatched with as many things to compass our matter, and to bring it to pass as our wits could imagine or devise; which brought to pass, as I trust, by their diligence, it shall be shortly, you and I shall have our desired end, which should be more to my heart's ease, and more quietness to my mind, than any other thing in the world ; as, with God's grace, shortly I trust shall be proved, but not so soon as I would it were; yet I will ensure you that there shall be no time lost that may be won, and further can not be done; for *ultra posse non est esse*. [repeating no more can be done, 'what is impossible cannot exist']. Keep him not too long with you, but desire him, for your sake, to make the more speed; for the sooner we shall have word from him, the sooner shall our matter come to pass. And thus upon trust of your short repair to London, I make an end of my letter, my own sweet heart.
Written with the hand of him which desireth as much to be yours as you do to have him.
H. R.[15]

Early in 1528, news arrived in London that Clement had escaped from captivity, walking out past his guards disguised under a long beard. Finally, he could act independently of the Emperor, although he could act with little real influence against Charles and his agents. It was symbolic of the state of the papacy that Clement was now sheltering in the wreckage of his former palace, still in fear of his life. As Wolsey wrote to Casale, the news filled him and Henry 'with delight', along with the hope that Casale would 'now have free access to his Holiness' and could soon gain 'the dispensation, commission and appointment of the Legate'. As they hoped, Clement agreed to the draft bill allowing Henry to remarry once he was free from Catherine, even if his choice fell on a woman forbidden to him by a former connection with a relative of hers. The dispensation permitted him 'to marry another, even if she have contracted marriage with another man, provided it be not consummated, and even if she be of the second degree of consanguinity, or of the first degree of affinity, *ex quocumque licito seu illicito coitu*; in order to prevent uncertainty in the succession, which in past times has been the occasion of war.'[16] This was clearly paving the way for his marriage to Anne. In February 1528, Wolsey applied for a commission to open a papal court in London, in order to appease Henry's 'troubled conscience'. In response, Clement issued a bull that April empowering Wolsey as his vicegerent 'to take cognisance of all matters concerning the king's divorce', in conjunction with Warham. Then, on 8 June, Clement authorised Wolsey and Cardinal Campeggio to oversee the proceedings, but these could only begin once the aged Campeggio arrived in England.

Wolsey was also anticipating the inevitable reaction from the Emperor, taking steps to prepare the country for anything from a cooling of relations to a potential Imperial invasion. He summoned the Justices of the Peace and other 'honest people' to the Star Chamber, to hear his announcement that Henry was now at war with the Emperor. Charles was described to the audience as proud, ruling over a cruel people who pulled down 'God's vicar of Rome'. Worse than that, they had persecuted the holy fathers by 'extreme tyranny, violated the Holy Sacrament and threw the host down on the altar'. They had violated virgins and matrons, despoiled holy relics and left the streets strewn with 'the privy members and genitures of the cardinals and holy prelates' in such a way that not even the Turks would countenance.[17] It was an emotive diatribe, delivered to an audience accustomed to thinking of their queen's nephew as an ally, and the reactions were mixed, although ultimately, as Hall says, 'Englishemen were content to obey their King and his Counsel.'[18] Other former friends were less pleased. Hearing of this declaration, Margaret of Savoy responded by placing restrictions upon all English merchants then in the Netherlands, and confiscating their goods. The English ambassador to the Emperor also found himself under restraints.[19] For the moment, though, Henry's actions in defence of the pope were interpreted in a spiritual context, with his remarriage a secondary matter.

At the start of 1527, Henry was still known as a defender of the Catholic faith, on account of the response he had made six years earlier to Luther's attacks. As recently as that January, Cardinal Campeggio had 'praised the King's book... highly, which, he says, is to be reprinted *in multa exemplaria millia*, to show that he can defend Christendom not less by genius and learning than by money and arms'.[20] Since Luther's notorious challenge, the persecution of his followers and the burning of their texts had been taking place across England under the leadership of Wolsey and Sir Thomas More. In March 1526, around 3,000 copies of William Tyndale's translation of the New Testament were printed in Worms by Peter Schoeffer, allowing it to be read in English by anyone literate, instead of the formal Latin for which priests acted as interpreters. Tyndale was a native of Gloucestershire, a gifted scholar and linguist, who began to question the restrictions placed on the Scriptures whilst studying for his MA in theology at Oxford. He was in the right location to do so. In 1408, the Convocations of Oxford had ruled that it was forbidden to translate the Bible into English, in response to the calls of the Lollards following the teachings of John Wycliffe. In 1523, aware of the convocation's stance, Tyndale had sought permission to make a translation from Cuthbert Tunstall, Bishop of Durham. Tunstall's connection with Erasmus, with whom he had worked on a Greek edition of the Bible, encouraged Tyndale to hope for his sympathy, but Tyndale had been rejected, with the news that there was no room for him in the Bishop's household. In 1524, he travelled to Europe, possibly visiting such centres of reform as Hamburg, Wittenberg and Worms, while he worked on his translation.

The reaction from the conservative English church was predictable. Tunstall rejected it, ordering copies to be burned in public and forbidding booksellers from stocking it, while Wolsey condemned him as a heretic. By early 1527, copies of the translation had been smuggled into England in bales of cloth and may have been read by hundreds, even thousands, based on the consigments arriving in different places.[21] Those who preached similar ideas, or concepts perceived to be similar to those of Tyndale or Luther, were immediately under suspicion. That January, the Augustinian prior Robert Barnes was arrested for preaching against the celebration of holy days and the wealth of the clergy. He recanted when faced with the prospect of burning, escaped and fled to Antwerp. In November, the Cambridge preacher Thomas Bilney was arrested and questioned by Wolsey, for doubting the nature and purpose of pilgrimage and rejecting the veneration of saints and relics, although Bilney still believed in the authority of the pope, the importance of the mass and in transubstantiation. His views were typical of the changes in religious thinking in England in the 1520s; few were completely Lutheran, rejecting all aspects of Catholic practice. Many were in two minds, critical of the abuses of the faith, desiring a more direct connection with God, but still true to the tenets of the faith and papal rule. Like Bilney, a number of Henry's subjects could be considered to be emerging reformers, or questioners, just like those Anne had encountered among the French royal family. On this occasion, Bilney swore an oath that he rejected the teachings of Luther and was released, although he was not to enjoy his liberty for long. Neither was Tyndale.

Henry was also fighting the campaign against heresy abroad, targeting the sources of the books that were infiltrating England. At the start of 1527, his ambassador to the Netherlands, Sir John Hackett, received instructions to move against printers and booksellers who produced or distributed translations of the New Testament and, in January and February, enough copies had been gathered to enable the burning of 'many hundreds' in Antwerp, Worms and other places.[22] That May, the Archbishop of Canterbury, William Warham, arranged the purchase of copies abroad in order for them to be destroyed and Hackett wrote to Wolsey to report on the production of such works in Antwerp, having found twenty-four books in the possession of one man. He had also heard of some 2,000 in circulation in Frankfurt. There was, he explained, much sympathy for Luther in that country, and a desire to 'leave all good old customs'. As was known, he reported that 'some English disciples of Luther are beginning to translate the Bible into English' and believed 'there is great danger in these Low Countries'. Worse still, he had been told 'there are many in England, but they dare not declare themselves'. Hackett had assembled the English community in Antwerp in order to read them a letter against heresy from the king and forbidden the purchase, selling and reading of such books.[23] Even before the pope started dragging his heels over the king's 'great matter' there was an undercurrent of religious reform in England, in line with some key aspects of the Reformation. Yet it would not influence Henry's personal faith at this point. Instead, it encouraged him and his servants to consider their own religious institutions and stamp out instances of corruption in the centuries-old abbeys and monasteries that covered the length of the country and held most of its wealth and lands. In November 1527, Wolsey summoned the leading clergy to Westminster and informed them that 'all the abusions of the church should be mended'.[24] In practice, much of the revenue derived from monastic closures between 1527 and 1529, went towards funding the new colleges Wolsey was establishing at Ipswich and Oxford. One of those to benefit was Thomas Boleyn, who was granted the lease to the manor of Tonbridge at an annual rent of £26 8s, from Cardinal's College, Oxford.[25]

By 1528, Henry was prepared to consider his enemy's enemy his friend. Martin Luther had been denounced by the Emperor, and now Henry was at war with the Empire. There was a neat, if heretical, symmetry to it; Henry sought to canvas Luther's opinion in case it served his cause. The relationship between the English king and the German reformer had not been a smooth one. Luther had attacked Henry for his 1521 defence of the faith, questioning his authorship, and responding to his arguments in *Against Henry, King of the English*. Four years after that, in the belief that the English king had become 'inclined towards the Gospels',[26] Luther had written to Henry, apologising for making the accusation that Wolsey had been responsible for writing the king's book. He even begged Henry for his forgiveness and friendship, praying 'that God who has begun it, will cause your Majesty to grow and increase in the attainment of the inclination towards the Gospel' and hoping that the king would ignore the 'flatterers and sweet-spoken hypocrites' that called Luther a heretic. In his defence, Luther summed up his teachings as 'charity towards one's neighbour, obedience to secular authority and mortification of the sinful flesh'. He also deplored the 'abuse and tyranny of the bishops... who chase after tithes, rents, splendour, lusts of the flesh, yea after kingdoms, empires'.[27]

Yet in 1525, Henry had not been receptive. He saw Luther as 'wretched, vile and detestable, provoking the world to mischief, encouraging the world to sin'.[28] In response he wrote criticising Luther's marriage, having taken a nun and 'openly abused her in sin' and deplored the reforms that meant nuns and monks were forced to leave their establishments, the 'good religious folk folke be dayly by your meanes expelled oute of their places in whiche they were determyned in chastity, prayer and fastynge to bestow their lyves in goddess (God's) service'.[29] The chaotic and bloody German peasants' revolt that erupted that spring seemed to confirm to the English that the spiritual turmoil of the country had led directly to civil unrest. In 1525 Henry had no intention to dispute further with Luther and wrote that he would leave him to his lewdness. Even as late as 1527, Henry wrote an open letter to Luther, commenting on the social disorder as a result of his influence, as 'always where lacked faith there reigned heresies, sensuality, voluptie, inobedience, rebellion, no recognition of superior, confusion and total ruin in the end'.[30]

By 1528, things had changed. Henry made a shocking U-turn and appealed to the Emperor's sworn enemy, Martin Luther, to support his divorce. Francis I had already played a wild card by sending out feelers for an alliance with the great enemy of Christendom, Suleiman the Magnificent, Sultan of Turkey, so Henry was not to be outdone in the question of making friends outside the usual coterie. It is a measure of the extent of redefinition that Henry was undergoing that he attempted to enlist Luther's support for the dissolution of his marriage in spite of their former history. He may have seen Luther as another pioneer who was prepared to defy the religious establishment, to break with the conventions of the church and act according to his conscience, even if Henry disagreed with his faith. This move led Henry into direct opposition with the pope but at this stage, he would still have rejected many teachings of Lutheranism completely, even been outraged at the suggestion that the two men had any theological common ground. Yet it suited him to explore aspects of Luther's outsider status when support for his case was thin on the ground at home.

It was the king's former enemy, the exiled heretic Robert Barnes, who was approached to undertake the task of winning Luther over to Henry's cause. But the king was not to find the support he had hoped for. When it came to marriage, Luther took a far more traditional stance, only considering divorce to be permissible in cases of adultery, desertion or incapacity. In Luther's eyes, Catherine would always remain Henry's wife and queen, as the existence of Princess Mary proved, and Henry's attempts to prove otherwise were a violation of God's work. If Henry put Catherine aside, he would make 'the mother as well as the daughter into incestuous women'.[31] It was not what Henry wanted to hear.

The factors influencing Henry's shifting position in 1527–8 are not in question. He had genuine doubts about the legality of his marriage, he wished to make Anne his wife, and the pope and emperor were complicating a situation he hoped would be swiftly resolved. What is unclear is the weight of influence that these differing factors exerted upon the king. The question of Anne's role in this is two-fold. On one level, the purely personal question dictated that Henry was keen to marry her and father sons, and her refusal to become his mistress inflamed this desire further. But the king was not so simplistic a figure, to be swept away by lust and dynastic need alone. It was typical of Henry that his motives were woven into a tortuous knot, where the personal fed on the theological, and vice versa, then unpicked and rewoven by international and political developments. It is impossible to identify the driving force behind Henry's actions at this time, and perhaps it is to afford Anne too much influence at this point to consider her a significant factor. Henry had made up his mind that his marriage was invalid and he wanted to take another wife. Until the point in 1527 when Anne refused to become his mistress, he may have been hoping to bed her, like her sister, and to make a diplomatic match with someone like Renée of France. Anne's refusal may have been the trigger. Equally, it may have been Henry's own choice, and Anne's refusal could have been a calculated move to keep the king at bay, in the wake of her realisation of the enormity of the situation.

Until mid-1527, the thought that Henry might marry Anne may not have occurred to either of them, or to his court. Perhaps, in an attempt to resist his advances, as the letters suggest, she took the gamble of saying she was saving herself for a husband. If she hoped this would make him desist, it had the opposite effect. If it galvanised Henry to propose to her and dissolve his marriage, it offered Anne an unprecedented prize. No matter what her personal feelings were, she was no different from any other aristocratic Tudor woman in that she had been raised in the expectation of making the best marriage she could. There was no better than the king. This was not an opportunity that many women would, or could, have refused. This does not make Anne ambitious, scheming, cold-hearted or deceptive, as some historians have claimed. By a strange confluence of circumstances, the greatest prize of all in the Tudor world had fallen into her lap, and she would have been incapable of refusing what would have seemed to her to be her duty to her family. Yet it is an inescapable fact that Anne's rise to power was bound up in the English Reformation, being both a driving force for, and a result of, change. Perhaps less so than her beliefs, her life, her very existence, was integral to the process of reform. It was not so much what Anne believed that made the difference to England in the late 1520s, it was what she represented to Henry. His love for her lit the fire that had been building in recent years. She was the catalyst, not the cause.

EIGHTEEN
Anne and Wolsey 1528

The fractious history between Anne and Thomas Wolsey might have been overcome under other circumstances, had their paths not crossed so intimately again. The cardinal had been at the height of his power around the time Anne returned to court, and she was shrewd enough to follow her father's lead and cultivate smooth relations with such an important patron, who had the king's ear. However, in 1527, Anne overtook Wolsey in terms of influence over Henry and this subtle power shift meant she was less obliged to display deference to the Lord Chancellor, a fact he had noticed at once upon his return from France. While Anne had previously been his subordinate, a diplomat's daughter whom he had rejected for Henry Percy, Wolsey now found that service to the king was synonymous with service to Mistress Boleyn. No matter how diligently Wolsey ministered to Henry, and no matter his ability, he could not attain the special position reserved for the woman with whom Henry was in love. In this once instance, Anne's gender provided her with a trump card. She might exert that womanly influence that consisted of promises, caresses, looks and smiles that go unmeasured and unrecorded in the history of royal women but yet accumulate to comprise real power.

By February 1528, Wolsey's eyes had been opened to the true nature of Henry's intentions for Anne. So had those of Clement VII. The cardinal immediately perceived the threat to his position and wrote to Stephen Gardiner, Bishop of Winchester and Edward Foxe, Bishop of Hereford, to tell them that the pope 'had been labouring under some misapprehension, as if the king had 'set on foot this cause, not from fear of his succession, but out of a vain affection or undue love to a gentlewoman of not so excellent qualities as she is here esteemed'.[1] Wolsey feared that his negotiations for the divorce had been compromised, that the pope might believe he had been working on Anne's behalf and protested that 'not for any earthly affection to his prince, or desire of reward' would he have transgressed from the truth or 'swerve(d) from the right path'. It had been his genuine conviction that Henry's marriage to Catherine was inadequate and he maintained that the king's desire was 'grounded upon justice and not from any grudge or displeasure to the Queen', whom Henry honoured and loved and would 'treat as his sister, with all manner of kindness'.[2] However, Wolsey continued, the marriage was 'contrary to God's law' and, as a result, the king's conscience was 'grievously offended'.[3] No doubt aware that he might be talking about his future queen, Wolsey then offered a glowing testimony of Anne's character and suitability to reign:

> On the other side the approved, excellent virtuous qualities of the said gentlewoman [Anne], the purity of her life, her constant virginity, her maidenly and womanly pudicity [from the French, modesty, chastity], her soberness, chasteness, meekness, humility, wisdom, descent of right noble and high through regal blood, education in all good and laudable qualities and manners, apparent aptness to procreation of children, with her other infinite good qualities, more to be regarded and esteemed than the only progeny... [These are] the grounds on which the King's desire is founded, which Wolsey regards as honest and necessary.[4]

In March 1528, Henry's Groom of the Stool, Sir Thomas Heneage, reported an interesting exchange between himself and Anne that took place at Windsor, which Heneage duly related to Wolsey. As the king was on his way to dinner, Thomas reported, Anne took the groom aside and remarked that 'she was afraid Wolsey had forgotten her, as he sent her no token' by his visiting messenger, Forest. Heneage assured her this was not the case, but that Forest's message had been of 'such importance' that Wolsey had forgotten to add anything else. Apparently Anne's mother, Elizabeth, had requested that Forest ask Wolsey to send 'a morsel of tunny' (tuna) to her daughter. That night 'the King sent him down with a dish to Mistress Anne for her supper. She caused Hennege to sup with her, and wished she had some good meat from Wolsey, as carps, shrimps or other.'[5] Was Anne genuinely feeling overlooked or neglected by Wolsey? It seems she may have been testing the water, to see what kind of reaction she received and hoping the cardinal would defer to her wishes. Alternatively, she might genuinely have perceived his actions as a slight and wished to remind him of her position. Perhaps these comments to Heneage were barbed, intended as a reprimand for Wolsey. It is interesting that in relating this to the cardinal, Heneage interpreted the *primum mobile* of Anne's comments as her womanhood. Deference might be due to Anne because of the status she had been granted by the king, and Heneage's behaviour towards her would have contained all the necessary signs of respect; but when it came to his private communication with Wolsey, man to man, he was dismissive of Anne's actions, apologising for the necessity of mentioning them and explaining them in terms of gender stereotype: 'I beseech your Grace, pardon me that I am so bold to write unto your Grace hereof; it is the conceit and mind of a woman.'[6] The patriarchal culture of the Tudor court permitted such comments between men, even about a king's mistress, perhaps even because she was the king's mistress, as she owed her status entirely to her gender, not her birth. It was considered a legitimate comment, that women were capricious. The only circumstances in which this kind of behaviour was expected were during the months of pregnancy, or upon the sickbed, when the whims of a woman were indulged. Henry's elective subordination to Anne, the subordination of kingship and masculinity, to a female 'master' who was not born to be a queen, went against the long-established order of the Tudor world. Seeing their king submit to a symbolic form of emasculation must have been challenging for some men who served him, giving rise to an undercurrent of disapproval, even hostility. A man ruled by a woman was a Tudor nightmare (or joke) and when that man was a king, responsible for the welfare of his country, it set tongues wagging. Heneage's comment was mild in comparison with others over the coming years and, at some point, the king himself would absorb some of this dialogue and employ it when he felt the need to remind Anne who was in charge. Heneage's words prompted Wolsey to send word to Anne at Windsor, upon which Anne thanked him for his 'kind and favourable writing unto her'.[7] Yet she also used the occasion, and her feminine influence, to intercede on behalf of Sir Thomas Cheney, as she was 'marvellously sorry that he should be in your Grace's displeasure'.[8]

Early in May 1528, Edward Foxe's letter to Stephen Gardiner captures another sighting of Anne at court with Henry. Arriving at Greenwich after his mission to Rome, Foxe was instructed by Henry to 'go to Mrs Anne's chamber', only to find her housed in the gallery of the tiltyard because the 'princess and others of the Queen's maidens were sick of the smallpox'.[9] There, Foxe conveyed to Anne Gardiner's 'singular diligence and dexterity in obtaining such expeditions, and in hastening the coming of the Legate with (his) hearty recommendations'. In response, 'she seemed to be most grateful' and made 'promise of large recompense for your good acquittal'.[10] When Foxe related his news to the king, Henry was 'marvellously well pleased' and summoned Anne, requiring him to repeat the information again to her. Between them, Henry and Anne questioned him 'at great length' about the pope's attitude towards them and 'how much his Holiness pondered the dangers of the realm if the King's purpose should not take effect'. Clement had informed Foxe that he believed Henry only wanted this because Anne was pregnant and unworthy: 'He had been told, long before our coming, that the King wanted this only for private reasons and that she was with child, and of no such qualities as should be worthy that Majesty.'[11] Foxe was able to reassure Henry and Anne that 'Wolsey's letters proved the contrary'.[12]

Anne wrote to Wolsey that June, insisting that Henry added his own words to the bottom of the letter, reinforcing the message of their unity to the cardinal:

My Lord, in my most humble wise I desire you to pardon me that I am so bold to trouble you with my simple and rude writing, proceeding from one who is much desirous to know that your Grace does well, as I perceive by this bearer. The great pains you take for me, both day and night, are never likely to be recompensed, 'but alonely in loving you, next unto the King's grace, above all creatures living', as my deeds shall manifest. I long to hear from you news of the Legate, and hope they will be very good.

[Added by the king] The writer of this would not cease till she had called me likewise to set to my hand. Both of us desire to see you, and are glad to hear you have escaped the plague so well, trusting the fury of it is abated, especially with those that keep good diet, as I trust you do. The not hearing of the Legate's arrival in France causeth us somewhat to muse; but we trust by your diligence shortly to be eased of that trouble.[13]

Anne's relationship with Wolsey may not have been an easy one, but both were able to assess the standing of the other in the king's eyes and play the diplomatic game. Wolsey was swift to recognise his own volatile situation, refusing to be torn between allegiances to king and church, putting Henry's desires first, but aware that the king had not been completely open with him. No woman, neither Henry's mistress nor his wife Catherine, had ever come between the king and the cardinal. Their close compact had been mutually beneficial for years and Wolsey now saw himself threatened by a woman who had the potential to undermine his influence, even his career. For Anne, Wolsey still held formidable powers as the negotiator of the divorce, and Clement's nomination of him as the joint overseer of the impending papal court in England meant that the cardinal was still of use to her. If Wolsey could only achieve a settlement to facilitate the marriage, necessitating Catherine's withdrawal, the uneasy triangle might remain intact despite whatever the European powers threw at it.

Then Anne became ill. On June 18, French Ambassador Jean du Bellay wrote to Montmorency, having left Hampton Court five days earlier. He had spent quite some time walking in the gardens with a 'wonderfully grave' Wolsey, discussing the international reaction to the divorce and the danger to the realm if Henry died without male issue. 'On Tuesday,' du Bellay recounted, 'one of the ladies of the chamber, Mademoiselle de Boulan, was infected with the sweat.'[14] Henry was terrified of illness, particularly the one that might have accounted for the demise of his elder brother twenty-six years earlier, and left Hampton Court 'in great haste' to another property twelve miles away. Anne was sent home to Kent and the ambassador speculated whether this might be the end of the affair: 'As yet the love has not abated. I know not if absence, and the difficulties of Rome, may effect anything.'[15]

Du Bellay also gave a description of the illness that Anne was suffering from:

> This sweat, which has made its appearance within these four days, is a most perilous disease. One has a little pain in the head and heart; suddenly a sweat begins; and a physician is useless, for whether you wrap yourself up much or little, in four hours, sometimes in two or three, you are despatched without languishing, as in those troublesome fevers. However, only about 2,000 have caught it in London. Yesterday, going to swear the truce, we saw them as thick as flies, rushing from the streets and shops into their houses to take the sweat whenever they felt ill.[16]

Henry may have fled but he dispatched one of his own physicians, William Butts to Hever to care for Anne, although he was not necessarily the king's first choice. His eighth letter dates from this time, in early June:

> There came to me suddenly in the night the most afflicting news that could have arrived. The first, to hear of the sickness of my mistress, whom I esteem more than all the world, and whose health I desire as I do my own, so that I would gladly bear half your illness to make you well. The second, from the fear that I have of being still longer harassed by my enemy. Absence, much longer, who has hitherto given me all possible uneasiness, and as far as I can judge is determined to spite me more because I pray God to rid me of this troublesome tormentor. The third, because the physician in whom I have most confidence, is absent at the very time when he might do me the

greatest pleasure; for I should hope, by him and his means, to obtain one of my chief joys on earth, that is the care of my mistress, yet for want of him I send you my second, and hope that he will soon make you well. I shall then love him more than ever. I beseech you to be guided by his advice in your illness. In so doing I hope soon to see you again, which will be to me a greater comfort than all the precious jewels in the world.
Written by that secretary, who is, and for ever will be, your loyal and most assured Servant,
H. (A B) R.[17]

Wolsey's secretary, Brian Tuke, related to his master a conversation he had recently had with the king, in which he passed on Wolsey's advice to Henry for avoiding infection. Knowing the king so intimately for so long, the cardinal understood his Achilles' heel; his almost paranoiac terror of ill-health and the compulsion to do anything to avoid it. He saw that Henry needed reassurance, telling him what he had observed about the manner of the infections, 'how folks were taken, how little danger there was if good order be observed, how few were dead of it'. Wolsey begged the king to 'keep out of infection, and that you will use small suppers, drink little wine... and once in the week use the pills of Rasis; and if it come, to sweat moderately, and at the full time, without suffering it to run in'.[18] Tuke said that Henry was pleased with letters that had arrived from the Bishop of Bath and ones written by Francis I to the pope, and was planning to 'send copies of them to Mistress Anne for her consolation'.[19]

Henry's ninth letter to Anne has been dated to 20 June 1528, and recounts his relief at the fact she had not suffered much so far:

The uneasiness my doubts about your health gave me, disturbed and alarmed me exceedingly, and I should not have had any quiet without hearing certain tidings. But now, since you have as yet felt nothing, I hope, and am assured that it will spare you, as I hope it is doing with us. For when we were at Waltham, two ushers, two valets de chambres and your brother, master-treasurer, fell ill, but are now quite well and since we have returned to our house at Hunsdon, we have been perfedlly well, and have not, at present, one sick person, God be praised; and I think, if you would retire from Surrey, as we did, you would escape all danger. There is another thing that may comfort you, which is that, in truth in this distemper few or no women have been taken ill, and what is more, no person of our court, and few elsewhere, have died of it. For which reason I beg you, my entirely beloved, not to frighten yourself

nor be too uneasy at our absence; for wherever I am, I am yours, and yet we must sometimes submit to our misfortunes, for whoever will struggle against fate is generally but so much the farther from gaining his end: wherefore comfort yourself, and take courage and avoid the pestilence as much as you can, for I hope shortly to make you sing, *la renvoyé*. No more at present, from lack of time, but that I wish you in my arms, that I might a little dispel your unreasonable thoughts.
Written by the hand of him who is and alway will be yours,
Im-H. R-mutable.[20]

His final comment, about dispelling her 'unreasonable thoughts' suggests that Anne may have written to Henry, or that her feelings were reported to him by a third party. Perhaps they were fears about his commitment to her, given that he had deserted her during her time of suffering. Two days later, he wrote again:

The cause of my writing at this time, good sweetheart, is only to understand of your good health and prosperity; whereof to know I would be as glad as in manner mine own, praying God that (an it be His pleasure) to send us shortly together, for I promise you I long for it. How be it, I trust it shall not be long to; and seeing my darling is absent, I can do no less than to send her some flesh, representing my name, which is hart flesh for Henry, prognosticating that hereafter, God willing, you may enjoy some of mine, which He pleased, I would were now. As touching your sister's matter, I have caused Walter Welze to write to my lord my mind therein, whereby I trust that Eve shall not have power to deceive Adam; for surely, whatso ever is said, it cannot so stand with his honour but that he must needs take her, his natural daughter, now in her extreme necessity. No more to you at this time, mine own darling, but that with a wish I would we were together an evening.
With the hand of yours,
H.R.[21]

The day after this, 23 June, it was reported that Anne and her brother George were both recovering. As Brian Tuke related, 'Mistress Anne (Boleyn) and my lord Rochford both have had it; what jeopardy they have been in by the turning in of the sweat before the time; of the endeavor of Mr. Buttes, who hath been with them in his return; and finally of their perfect recovery.'[22] Henry had been at Hunsdon House but moved to Tittenhanger around this time, an estate and house near

St Albans, owned by the Abbey located there, but currently being used by Wolsey. Sir John Russell, Knight of the Body, wrote to the cardinal on 28 June:

> Since the King's coming to Tittenhanger he has been very well, and merrier than he was since his departure from Greenwich. He likes your house very well; and where he was to fore in great fear and trouble for this plague, and that he left some of his chamber in every place where he went, and as this night, thanked be God, there was none sick, whereof his Majesty is very well recomforted. I would not for all the good in England but that he had come to your Grace's house; and this day he has received the good Lord, and so has the more part that be about him, and he rejoices much that he has done so, and says that he is armed towards God and the world. He has eaten more meat today than he did three days before. When he heard you were coming hither, he was sorry that you should come in the 'efexseon' [infection], especially as there is no lodging for you.[23]

Thomas Heneage added that Henry was 'merry' and recommended himself to Wolsey. He had also sent him a Manus Christi, a religious token believed to preserve life. The cardinal might be forgiven for having thought that in Anne's absence, his old closeness with the king had been restored, and that Henry's faith in the old Catholic symbols was intact.[24] He did report, though, the number of people who had fallen ill, including Thomas Cheney, Brian Tuke and many others at court. On 30 June, Wolsey was at Hampton Court, where he heard of the death of the king's old friend and partner in crime, Sir William Compton. He was 'sorry to be so far away from the King, but (would) at any time attend him with one servant and a page to do service in the King's chamber'.[25] Anne remained at Hever, as Du Bellay reported: 'The young lady is still with her father.'[26] Of the 40,000 cases of the illness in London, the ambassador believed, 2,000 were dead, 'but if a man only put his hand out of bed during twenty-four hours, it becomes as stiff as a pane of glass'.[27]

Henry and Wolsey remained in isolation as members of the court died, including Mary Boleyn's husband, William Carey, who succumbed on 22 June at his house of Plashey in Essex. Anne was granted the 'custody of the lands of William Carye, deceased, during the minority of Henry Carye, his son and heir, with the wardship and marriage of the said heir'[28] but not of his sister Catherine, then aged fourteen. Carey's death left Mary in considerable debt and Henry's old fondness for her prompted him to request, in a later letter to Anne, that their father might help her, as 'it cannot stand with his honour, but that he must needs take her his natural daughter now in her extreme necessity'.[29]

Three weeks later, on 21 July, Du Bellay reported:

The danger in this country begins to diminish hereabouts, and to increase elsewhere. In Kent it is very great. Mademoiselle de Boulan (Boleyn) and her father have sweated, but have got over it. The day I sweated at my lord of Canterbury's there died 18 persons in four hours, and hardly anybody escaped but myself, who am not yet quite strong again. The King has gone further off than he was, uses great precautions, confesses himself every day, and receives Our Lord at every Feast. So also the Queen, who is with him, and Wolsey for his part. The notaries have had a fine time of it. I think 100,000 wills have been made off-hand, for those who were dying became quite foolish the moment they fell ill. The astrologers say this will not turn into a plague, but I think they dream.[30]

It cannot have been easy for Anne, knowing that Catherine and Henry were together during this difficult time. While Henry had left her alone in her illness, he had carried his queen away with him to the seclusion of the countryside, where they were living with a reduced household. If Anne had any doubts about Henry's devotion, or fears about Catherine's influence, they must have surfaced during these weeks. Yet she had survived a terrible ordeal, which had taken many lives of those close to her at court. In an era keen to read divine will into every occurrence, Anne may have considered that she had been spared for a reason.

While Anne was recovering, a question arose that would prove decisive for Wolsey's career. It had begun that April, when he had received notification from a Thomas Benet about the death of Cecily Willoughby, Abbess of Wilton:

The abbess of Wilton died today, and Prioress and Convent will shortly write to Wolsey for their *congé d'élire*. Most of the convent favor dame Isabell Jordayn, the prioress, sister to the abbess of Syon, who is ancient, wise and discreet. There will also be great labor made for dame Eleanor Carye, sister to Mr. Carye of the Court.[31]

Unsurprisingly, Anne backed Eleanor Carey, Mary's sister-in-law, who was already a nun at the establishment, but when her reputation was investigated, Eleanor was discovered to have borne at least two illegitimate children 'by two sundry priests' and was currently involved in a third relationship. Anne then offered Eleanor's sister, Anne Carey, as a replacement, while Wolsey proffered his own candidate, Isabella Jordan. Henry's next letter to Anne was written on 20 July 1528, and referred to the delicate situation:

Since your last letters, mine own darling, Walter Welshe, Master Browne, Thos. Care, Grion of Brearton, and John Coke, the apothecary, be fallen of the sweat in this house, and, thanked be God, all well recovered, so that as yet the plague is not fully ceased here, but I trust shortly it shall. By the mercy of God, the rest of us yet be well, and I trust shall pass it, either not to have it, or, at the least, as easily as the rest have done. As touching the matter of Wilton, my lord cardinal hath had the nuns before him, and examined them, Mr. Bell being present: which hath certified me that, for a truth, she had confessed herself (which we would have had abbess) to have had two children by two sundry priests; and, further, since hath been kept by a servant of the Lord Broke that was, and that not long ago. Wherefore I would not, for all the gold in the world, clog your conscience nor mine to make her ruler of a house which is of so ungodly demeanour; nor, I trust, you would not that neither for brother nor sister, I should so destain mine honour or conscience. And, as touching the prioress, or Dame Eleanor's eldest sister, though there is not any evident case proved against them, and that the prioress is so old that for many years she could not be as she was named; yet notwithstanding, to do you pleasure, I have done that neither of them shall have it, but that some other good and well-disposed woman shall have it, whereby the house shall be the better reformed (whereof I ensure you it had much need), and God much the better served.

As touching your abode at Hever, do therein as best shall like you, for you best know what air doth best with you; but I would it were come there-to (if it pleased God), that neither of us need care for that, for I ensure you I think it long. Suche is fallen sick of the sweat, and therefore I send you this bearer, because I think you long to hear tidings from us, as we do likewise from you.

Written with the hand *de votre seul*,

H.R.[32]

As it transpired, Wolsey would go ahead and give the position to his candidate, Isabella Jordan, in the election of 24 November, against Henry's express wishes. This would prompt a serious breach between the cardinal and the king, as well as displeasing Anne. It was to be the beginning of the end of their attempts at friendship.

NINETEEN

The Ideal Woman 1528

In 1528, as Henry and Anne had reached their romantic agreement and were buoyed by hopes of imminent matrimony, one of the most significant Renaissance texts appeared in print for the first time. The Italian diplomat and soldier, Baldassare Castiglione had been working on *The Book of the Courtier* for two decades, framed in the popular convention of a dialogue, to expound the essential qualities of the perfect courtier, and the perfect lady. The original Italian text, printed in Venice, would not be translated into English until 1561, when Thomas Hoby's edition would define concepts of the English gentleman for the Elizabethans and for subsequent eras. Anne's education at the Valois court, with its many cultural debts to Italy, placed her amid that very European dialogue about what constituted ideal conduct, at the time when Castiglione was reflecting upon the topic. Although Francis' court was a sensual, erotic environment, it also preserved a formal code of manners and etiquette that the French king had borrowed directly from the Italian example. Anne's impact in England was partly the result of her difference in manners and conduct, which *The Book of the Courtier* represented more closely than contemporary English concepts of the Renaissance woman, still becoming defined, and to which Anne's example contributed.

Castiglione's summary of masculine ideals identifies that the main objective for a courtier was to achieve perfect 'grace'. This is a state of ease, naturalness or effortlessness, resulting from the use of the voice, expression and movement, in which the arts of rhetoric and oratory combine to make the speaker a 'beautiful spectacle'. At the end of the second book, the Duchess of Urbino requests a definition of the paragon of womanhood, 'such a woman that these adversaries of ours shall be ashamed to say she is not equal in worth to the Courtier'. The dialogue highlights the mixture of misogyny and worship to which a high-born woman was frequently exposed, with some commentators believing they should follow the same codes as men, so 'far as her stupidity permits', and others being 'afraid' of the ideal lady, discussion of whom was 'irrelevant'.[1] Yet the text exposes these masculine rejections of women, only to refute them, because 'no court, however great it be, can have in it adornment or splendour or gaiety, without ladies, nor can any courtier be graceful or pleasing or brave, or perform any gallant feat of chivalry, unless moved by the society and by the love and pleasure of ladies'.[2] Yet this still casts a woman's position as that of adornment, the cultural icing on the proverbial cake, the unattainable spur to achievement, which validates an external view of women, defined through the male gaze, rather than a female-centred attempt to define perfection. Even this praise is ridiculed by other men, who laugh at the speaker, saying he must have had 'a taste of that bait which makes men fools',[3] casting women in the role of seductresses, able to interfere with masculine objectivity. This was the reaction that many of Henry's court, both male and female, would have to the king's feelings for Anne, and to explain her influence over him. The character in the text called the 'Magnifico' considers such a potential woman to be a creature of his own definition and possession, much as Henry would see himself creating, elevating and owning Anne: 'I will speak of this excellent lady as I would have her and when I have fashioned her to my liking, not being able then to have another such, like Pygmalion I will take her for my own.'[4]

The text allows women to share some of the qualities desirable in an ideal male courtier, especially the desire to 'adorn herself with admirable accomplishments'. Yet she was essentially present by his sided in a supporting role. Like Anne, she should be able to hold a conversation, but also to entertain and accommodate male company with a 'certain pleasant affability' so she might engage 'politely (with) every sort of man with agreeable and seemly conversation, suited to the time and place and rank of the person... with calm and modest manners, and with that seemliness which should dispose all her actions, a quick vivacity of spirit whereby she might show herself alien to all indelicacy'. Like a more friendly, accessible version of the traditional object of courtly love from medieval poetry, she should possess 'such a kindly manner as shall make us think her no less chaste, prudent and benign, than agreeable, witty and discreet,' but she must also preserve distance, 'a certain mean (difficult and composed almost of contraries) and must barely touch certain limits but not pass them'.[5] Sometimes Anne's conversation, her courtly wit and confidences, would overstep this mark.

It was considered essential that, like Anne, such an ideal woman should be of gentle birth, 'to avoid affectation, to be naturally graceful in all her doings, to be mannerly, clever, prudent, not arrogant, not envious, not slanderous, not vain, not quarrelsome, not silly, to know how to win and keep the favour of her mistress'.[6] These attributes, by their negative examples, indicate the awareness of other types of femininity, the worst of female stereotyped behaviour. They also indicate the ubiquitous awareness of class, almost synonymous here with gender. A woman of good birth was presumed to have been raised to behave better than her peers, but her femininity in the text is presented as a function of her class. To behave badly, breaking these rules, would have been considered a social transgression, a betrayal of her birth. In *The Book of the Courtier*, such a woman is clearly distinguished as below the queen, who set the standard of female behaviour but had different, royal attributes. The role of the female courtier, drawn from the upper classes, was to serve the queen, not seek to replace her. Such a transgression would have been considered as being unwomanly by the characters in Castiglione's book, both male and female. With the two identities being so closely bound, it is easy to see why the attribute of ambition in an aristocratic woman posed challenges of definition to the men of the late 1520s. The concept of the ideal Renaissance woman forced able and attractive individuals like Anne to balance on a knife's edge. They might display the extent of their minds within certain contexts but the lowest common denominator, the fall-back position in times of threat or distress, was the stereotype of female beauty, weakness and dependence:

> While some qualities are common to both and as necessary to man as to woman, there are nevertheless some others that befit woman more than man... in her ways, manners, words, gestures and bearing, a woman ought to be very unlike a man, for just as it befits him to show a certain stout and sturdy manliness, so it is becoming in a woman to have a soft and dainty tenderness with an air of womanly sweetness in her every movement... beauty is more necessary to her than the courtier, for in truth that woman lacks much who lacks beauty.[7]

Castiglione included words of caution about female conduct which are pertinent to Anne's situation, both in aspiring to become queen and during her reign. The female courtier should not 'utter unseemly words or practise a certain wild and unbridled familiarity and ways likely to make that believed of her which perhaps is not true'. Those who were most offended by such behaviour, according to the Book, were other women, who especially deplored the immodesty of one woman attacking another. Those who listened to the 'unseemly ways' of other women lost men's respect and projected an invitation that perhaps they had not intended. Such women were often accused of sexual laxity. By the definitions of 1528, Anne's position as a female courtier of gentle, but not royal birth, who anticipated replacing the mistress she was serving, left her beholden to a swathe of intricate rules about gender and class, behaviour and reputation, which she would struggle to master. Perhaps she stayed away from court that summer, recovering her health, playing for time as she considered her next move on this treacherous stage.

It was considered essential by Castiglione that a noble woman should look the part and it was a reflection of her new status as the king's fiancée that Anne was equipped with fashionable riding items in the French style, including a saddle with a down pillow, covered in black velvet fringed with silk and gold, the head of which was made of copper and gilt, engraved in 'antique' style. This came with a matching footstool, saddle hose, bits with gilt bosses and a harness with pear shaped buttons, tassels, buckles and pendants of copper and gilt.[8]

There also came the timely reminder of Anne's connection with France and the potential friendship between Francis and Henry, which would be essential for England if Henry broke with Rome. Francis' sister Marguerite, for whom Anne would later express affection, was now married to the King of Navarre, and found herself pregnant at the age of thirty-six, a time when many of her contemporaries were becoming grandmothers and experiencing an early onset menopause as the result of bearing large families from their teens onwards. No doubt Marguerite's letter to Wolsey was shared with Henry and Anne, who may have imagined a future where their own child was raised in friendship with the new French generation of royals. Anne is not mentioned by name, though, perhaps due to the political delicacy of the situation, as Francis was considering taking Eleanor, a sister of Emperor Charles, and thus a niece of Catherine of Aragon, as his second wife. Marguerite wrote:

> Thinks, from his letter to her, that hers will not be unpleasant to him. Commends herself to him as the means of good to Christendom, and the bond of friendship between the two Princes. The sieur De Morette will tell him the news. Madame desires her to inform him that she is in the fourth month of her pregnancy, which she dares not believe herself. Prays to have a son. She and the king of Navarre will leave him to inherit their affection for the King and Wolsey.[9]

By the third week of July, either Anne was considering returning to court, or else Henry was urging her to return. In his twelfth surviving letter, he wrote that he could not wait to see her, communicating his ardent desire for her presence:

The approach of the time for which I have so long waited rejoices me so much, that it seems almost to have come already. However, the entire accomplishment cannot be till the two persons meet, which meeting is more desired by me than anything in this world; for what joy can be greater upon earth than to have the company of her who is dearest to me, knowing likewise that she does the same on her part, the thought of which gives me the greatest pleasure.

Judge what an effect the presence of that person must have on me, whose absence has grieved my heart more than either words or writing can express, and which nothing can cure, but that begging you, my mistress, to tell your father from me, that I desire him to hasten the time appointed by two days, that he may be at court before the old term, or, at farthest, on the day prefixed; for otherwise I shall think he will not do the lover's turn, as he said he would, nor answer my expectation. No more at present for lack of time, hoping shortly that by word of mouth I shall tell you the rest of the sufferings endured by me from your absence.

Written by the hand of the secretary, who wishes himself at this moment privately with you, and who is, and always will be.
Your loyal and most assured Servant,
H. no other A B seek R.[10]

There is no question that the whole Boleyn family were party to Henry's wooing of Anne. As a dutiful Tudor daughter, especially coming from such an ambitious line and recently stung by her experience with Henry Percy, Anne would have been sharing the contents of Henry's letters, his wishes and promises, with her parents. Such an important secret, such a potential source of influence, was not just a personal matter. Anne would have been considered remiss by the Boleyns had she kept it to herself. Courtiers struggled for years, even decades, to gain the ear of the king, but Anne had achieved it purely on personal merit. No doubt Thomas and Elizabeth had advised Mary when it came to her relationship with Henry, benefiting from the favour they received by association, and Anne's new-found power over the king offered them a second opportunity to rise higher, to move even closer to the throne and to enjoy the associated titles and advantages this might bring. Any Tudor parents worth their salt would have done the same. As the twelfth letter indicates, Henry had already extracted a promise from Thomas Boleyn to 'do the lovers' turn', or facilitate their relationship, and was attempting to bring Anne closer to him with her father's collusion. His next letter, also written that July, suggests that some problem had arisen, though, which the king sent George Boleyn back to Hever to communicate to Anne in person.

It appears that their secret had been spread through 'lack of discreet handling', perhaps suggesting one or more of their letters had been read by others; his desire to see her was better known in London than among Henry's close circle:

> Darling, I heartily recommend me to you, ascertaining you that I am not a little perplexed with such things as your brother shall on my part declare unto you, to whom I pray you give full credence, for it were too long to write. In my last letters I writ to you that I trusted shortly to see you, which is better known at London than with any that is about me, whereof I not a little marvel; but lack of discreet handling must needs be the cause thereof. No more to you at this time, but that I trust shortly our meetings shall not depend upon other men's light handlings, but upon our own.
> Written with the hand of him that longeth to be yours.
> H. R.[11]

In the end, it was Elizabeth Boleyn who planned to bring her daughter back to court in the third week of July, 1528. Thomas was to have gone, as Heneage related in a letter to Wolsey, 'but because of the sweat he remains at home'.[12] Henry, having recently returned from Ampthill and Grafton, rode back to London with the intention of greeting Anne, but whether she actually made the rendezvous on this occasion is unclear. Her whereabouts are unknown until 20 August. If she made a temporary visit to court, or met the king at some other place, the reunion was brief. This may have been due to the continuance of illness in the family, or difficulties of travel, or else it was a conscious policy adopted by the Boleyns in order to keep Anne from the king. Such a move could be the result of a genuine desire to prevent the affair from advancing, owing to Henry's existing marital state, given that Elizabeth Boleyn had served Catherine of Aragon for decades and, perhaps, feared the consequences of attempting to set the queen aside to replace her with her own daughter. It may have been a method of testing the seriousness of the king's intentions, to see whether he persisted in his promises, or whether it would prove a short-term affair, as with Mary. There is also the possibility that Anne was deliberately kept away from Henry to encourage him to actively pursue his separation from Catherine, to prevent him from pressuring Anne, or attempting to seduce her before the necessary annulment had taken place and they were free to marry. If Anne had fallen pregnant before the king was legally free to remarry, her child would have been illegitimate rather than becoming the future royal heir. Previous assessments of Anne, which have portrayed her as scheming to keep Henry at bay with the intention of inflaming his desire during this period, of playing a game of manipulation, ambition and temptation, must cast their nets wider. Any conscious policy regarding Anne's relations with Henry, which was enacted between 1527 and 1529, was the policy of the Boleyn family, rather than their daughter alone. The references in the king's letters and of his courtiers indicate that Thomas, Elizabeth and George Boleyn all played a part in the process by which Anne was wooed and won. There were certainly rewards for George through 1528, when he became keeper of the palace of Beaulieu, keeper of the park and a handful of other Essex manors,[13] and appointed Esquire of the Body and Master of the King's buckhounds.

Just like the letters of 1527, the evidence from 1528 suggests that Anne resisted falling in love with Henry, either for personal reasons or an awareness of the wider implications of her actions. The Spanish humanist Juan Luis Vives was commissioned by Catherine of Aragon in 1524 to write a book of advice to young women, specifically for her daughter, Princess Mary, which follows traditional gender lines. Women fancying themselves in love were advised to tread cautiously, as 'it is in your power to let love in, but once you have let it in, you no longer belong to yourself, but to it. You cannot drive it out at your pleasure, but it will be able and will take pleasure in ousting you from your own house... while this passion violently sweeps away all human hearts, it does so all the more with women's feelings, which are more tender than men's.'[14] Vives paints women as the victims in love, and if he is right he brings up the difficult question of just who was steering Anne and Henry's relationship. With the vehemence of the king's passion not in doubt, contemporary advice like that of Vives highlighted that for a woman to surrender in love was to lose personal control, to sacrifice her own identity. Yet when the alternative identity on offer was that of a queen, an ambitious woman might find the yoke inviting. Once Anne finally agreed to become Henry's wife, she was committed, and there was no turning back.

That August, Henry wrote again, missing Anne. He makes reference to physical intimacy taking place between them, hoping to kiss her 'pretty dukkys' (breasts) soon, although this does not necessarily imply that they had already been that close:

Mine own sweetheart, this shall be to advertise you of the great clengeness [loneliness] that I find here since your departing; for, I ensure you methinketh the time longer since your departing now last, than I was wont to do a whole fortnight. I think your kindness and my fervency of love causeth it; for, otherwise, I would not have thought it possible that for so little a while it should have grieved me. But now that I am coming towards you, methinketh my pains be half removed; and also I am right well comforted in so much that my book maketh substantially for my matter; in looking whereof I have spent above four hours this day, which causeth me now to write the shorter letter to you at this time, because of some pain in my head; wishing myself (especially an evening) in my sweetheart's arms, whose pretty dukkys I trust shortly to kiss.

Written by the hand of him that was, is, and shall be yours by his own will,

H.R.[15]

Henry and Anne's separation may have been a question of delicacy. The Tudor court was constructed around the establishments of members of the royal family, the king's all-male household, that of Queen Catherine and that of their daughter Mary, which was separate, and based at Ludlow after 1525. Physically placing Anne within the royal palaces was difficult, especially as Henry was still aiming at discretion, to the point that even Wolsey was unaware of his intention to marry her. Along with other members of the court, and the country, the cardinal considered Anne to be the king's latest mistress, and it would probably not have occurred to him that the King might be so immodest or inappropriate as to break convention and wed a 'commoner', instead of one of the European princess who would have forged powerful connections abroad. Yet this is exactly what Henry's maternal grandfather, Edward IV, had done, although he, too, had achieved it in a veil of secrecy. It would have been awkward for Anne to be part of Catherine's household, resulting in conflicting loyalties of service as to whose wishes she ought to obey, those of her mistress or those of her master, her king and fiancé. Prioritising Henry might have led to some awkward questions. It could also have raised the queen's suspicions when Anne was absent and evidence of Henry's superior claim upon her could not be ignored. Yet in the king's masculine household, no independent female position existed that Anne might comfortably occupy. Records of lodgings and provisions for Henry's staff indicate that women were considered appendages of male courtiers, as their wives, mothers or daughters, without a specific role or function of their own. Henry's resolution of this situation in August 1528 demonstrates that Anne had achieved a status beyond that defined by her male relatives; she had now superseded them. As such, she required the unprecedented arrangement of a separate suite of rooms, closely connected to those of the king, which could ensure intimacy and discretion. She is unlikely to have had much privacy, and would have frequently been chaperoned by family members and allies, but Henry's reference to kisses indicates that there would be windows of opportunity for them to indulge in some limited degree of sexual activity. He wrote to inform her that Wolsey had vacated his lodgings at Greenwich, ready for Anne's occupation, and again appealed to her father to be swift in his arrangements for her return:

> Darling, though I have scant leisure, yet, remembering my promise, I thought it convenient to certify you briefly in what case our affairs stand. As touching a lodging for you, we have got one by my lord cardinal's means, the like whereof could not have been found hereabouts for all causes, as this bearer shall more show you.
>
> As touching our other affairs, I assure you there can be no more done, nor more diligence used, nor all manner of dangers better both foreseen and provided for, so that I trust it shall be hereafter to both our comforts, the specialities whereof were both too long to be written, and hardly by messenger to be declared.
>
> Wherefore, till you repair hither, I keep something in store, trusting it shall not be long to; for I have caused my lord, your father, to make his provisions with speed; and thus for lack of time, darling, I make an end of my letter, written with the hand of him which I would were yours.
> H.R.[16]

In this letter, Henry also took pains to reassure Anne that his 'great matter', the investigation into the case of his first marriage, was progressing. She may have insisted upon this as a condition of her return, or else it was Henry's attempt to reassure her of the seriousness of his intention. Du Bellay was able to write to Montmorency on 20 August announcing that 'Mademoiselle Boulan has returned to court'.[17] All seemed set for Henry's tortuous domestic situation to be resolved, and for Anne to become his wife and queen.

TWENTY

Anne the Heretic 1528–9

By the autumn of 1528, Henry's old friend from childhood, Erasmus, considered that the king of England's mortal soul was in peril. He was alerted to this fact by William Warham, Archbishop of Canterbury, prompting Erasmus to send a letter to the king, whom he had first met as a child of seven or eight in the Eltham schoolroom. Henry responded in his own defence, to explain his position regarding religion and the source of his change of heart. Apparently, it was not Anne. Although it suited Anne's detractors to label her as a great heretic, more Lutheran than Luther, Henry's words clarify that his dissatisfaction with the church predates his association with Anne. 'I have myself felt for some years,' he wrote from Otford, in Kent, 'the same desire of restoring the faith and religion of Christ to its pristine dignity, and repelling the impious attacks of the heretics, that the Word of God may run on purely and freely... such is the infelicity of the times, and the prostration of good manners, that all things degenerate.'[1]

Yet the definition of heresy was a fluid one, never more so than the late 1520s, when those who reflected upon the nature of Catholic practice began to question the individual tenets of faith, rejecting centuries of tradition. Heresies would become law in a few years.

A flurry of new books across Europe heated the ongoing debate about the nature of religious reform. Their areas of focus reveal just how precise and complex were the emerging range of arguments and how subtle the distinctions. Already outlawed for his translation of the scriptures, William Tyndale published *Parable of the Wicked Mammon* in Antwerp under a pseudonym in 1528. Responding to some of the criticisms aimed at German spiritual progressiveness, he stated that Lutheranism was radical in terms of theological change but that contrary to accusations, it actually promoted social stability. That October, he published the influential *The Obedience of a Christian Man* arguing in favour of a personal relationship with God that could be created by reading the Scriptures in the vernacular. Another key element of the reforms was addressed by Martin Luther in *Confession Concerning Christ's Supper*, in which he affirmed his belief in the real presence of the body and blood of Christ during the Eucharist, a phenomenon he referred to as the sacramental union, to distinguish it from the existing notion of transubstantiation. Catholics had previously held that the wine and bread were literally transformed into the body and blood of Christ, but Luther asserted that the physical properties of wine and bread co-existed in union with flesh and blood. It was a subtle difference but it kept him from a complete rejection of the mystical nature of the Mass. Others would go further and reject the physical presence of God entirely, seeing a process of consubstantiation instead, in which the Eucharist was entirely symbolic. Predictably there was a counter-response. In 1529 Simon Fish's *Supplication of the Beggars* argued in favour of the old belief in purgatory but criticised the clergy for spending their wealth on feasting, clothing and property, instead of using it for the relief of the poor. His work was classed as heresy by the church in 1530 and he was arrested and on the verge of standing trial before his death from plague. In addition, Thomas More wrote his *Dialogue Concerning Heresies*, condemning any deviation from church teaching as a crime against God. The effect of this dialogue was to raise awareness across the country of the corruption of the church, leading the House of Commons to petition Henry to instigate reform. With her reformist views shaped by her youth in France, Anne must have welcomed, if not encouraged, this. Nor was it just her.

A flurry of individual heresy cases in 1528 reveals just how far ideas of reform were spreading among the commoners of England – bakers, fletchers, tanners, husbandmen and their wives – along with the nature of those views and the sanction they risked. The beliefs of a John Hig, of Cheshunt in London, who was questioned by Cuthbert Tunstall, are typical of the moment. He felt that 'all men, whether temporal or spiritual, might preach the Gospel' and had claimed 'Martin Luther was more learned than all the doctors in England'. He believed that men should not make financial contributions to the church, admitted that he had spoken against pilgrimage and purgatory, that he had a copy of the Bible in Dutch and was convinced that 'the church is blind and leads people the wrong way'.[2] Having confessed and promised to mend his ways, Hig was ordered to head 'the procession to St. Paul's Cathedral, bare-headed, bare-legged, shoeless, and carrying a faggot on his left shoulder' on Good Friday and Easter Sunday, and to wear a 'silken faggot embroidered on his sleeve' for the rest of his life. The faggot, or bundle of sticks used as fuel to light the heretic's pyre, had become a symbol of the ultimate sacrifice one might pay for unorthodox beliefs, of being burned alive at the stake.

The proceedings against heretics continued in earnest, with a Robert Forman forbidden to preach by Tunstall on 19 March, for 'retaining Luther's books after their condemnation', alongside seven other individuals examined, who all denied the charges.[3] A William Pykas, who refused to swear an oath of loyalty, was sent to the Lollards' Tower and put in the stocks and his brother John, a baker from Colchester, confessed to owning a New Testament in English and was accused of saying the host was only bread.[4] John Girling stated the belief that those who punished heretics had 'stony hearts' and would be punished by God, as well as agreeing that man should pray directly to Him.[5] A William Raylond and his son Henry were questioned for speaking out against pilgrimage and the worship of images, and being critical of the baptism of infants with water. Marion Mathew had the Epistles and Gospels in her house and 'knew them by heart', as well as associating with other 'known' women. Thomas Parker rejected pilgrimage and said that 'men should worship God and not saints'.[6] The list of heretical views is illuminating and complex. An individual might accept some and not others, and the extent of the wrongdoing was determined by the number and importance of the tenets that were embraced. Some of the interrogations read like a numbered list, boxes ticked for the transgressions the heretics believed in.

Neither Henry nor Anne made a comparable statement of faith in such detail. They are best described as emergent reformers, accepting the need for some reforms and not others. However, one figure very close to the king was soon to be exposed as responsible for preaching heretical views.

In 1527, a nest of heretics had been exposed in Essex, in and around Colchester, who had been influenced by the preaching of Sir Richard Foxe, a man 'as anxious for the reformation of the clergy as Simeon the Righteous for the coming of the Messiah'.[7] Foxe had been Bishop of Exeter, Bath and Wells and Durham, before becoming Bishop of Winchester. Like Wolsey, he had come from humble origins, from parents of yeoman class but he had attended Cambridge and was taken into the service of Henry VII during his exile, early in 1485. He had Henry's confidence and had baptised his son, the infant Henry VIII, at Greenwich in 1491. His humanist principles came to fruition when he founded Corpus Christi College, Oxford, to which the Spanish scholar Juan Luis Vives was brought to teach Latin. Foxe's influence in Essex had been profound, but he escaped the traditional punishment, dying of natural causes in October 1528, at the age of eighty. As a family with Essex properties, especially Beaulieu and Rochford, the case may have been of interest to the Boleyns.

Those involved were investigated by Cuthbert Tunstall, Bishop of Durham in the spring of 1528. Their depositions expose the connections and allegiances of a close-knit community, of brothers, wives and friends. John Pykas, a baker, owned the Bible in English and denied the transformation of the host, William Raylond, Thomas Bourges and Thomas Parker rejected pilgrimage and the worship of saints and their images. Many of the individuals lived in Steeple Bumstead, where Foxe had been a curate,[8] including the ploughwright William Bocher, who also rejected pilgrimage along with the notion of purchasing indulgences, or papal pardons. Husbandman Robert Hemstede, who lived in the village, stated that he had been led into heresy by the preaching of Foxe, rejecting the use of pilgrimage and the literal transformation of the Mass. In addition, his wife had taught him to recite the Credo, Ave Maria and Paternoster in English, as had the fiancée of another man, revealing the influence of the women as well as female literacy. One family stood out during the investigations: Edmund Tibauld spoke out against the worship of images. John Tibauld also rejected images, along with the transformation of the Mass, pilgrimage and purgatory, and believed in clerical marriage, and that any man might administer the sacraments. He had disputed these ideas with Foxe, who read him a copy of the fourteenth-century reformer John Wycliffe's book, *The Wicket*, and with a number of the other villagers under examination. John was clearly an intelligent, reflective and brave man, but he was not fully literate, signing his confession with a mark, and typical of the wider population who would benefit from the Bible being read aloud in the vernacular. Their mother Ellen and John's wife Alice were also found guilty of belief in the same articles as the brothers.[9] Ulitmately, John Tibauld would be the only one of the group to suffer death, being burned at the stake for his views and refusal to recant.

Another significant figure was apprehended in 1528, London draper Humphrey Monmouth, of the parish of All Saints, Barking. Monmouth was a member of the secret group the Christian Brethren, organised by city merchants to facilitate the importation and spread of reforming literature under the cover of their trade. Works by Luther and Tyndale were smuggled into England wrapped in bales of cloth. Four years earlier, Monmouth had offered William Tyndale food and lodgings before helping him escape the country. He was found to be in possession of prohibited books, which he had contributed to in translation, and the printing and distribution of works 'against the sacrament of the Altar, the Mass and other observances of the Church'.[10] He confessed to having eaten flesh in Lent, to believing that faith alone was enough, than men should pray to God, not to saints, rejected pilgrimages, fasting, pardons and images. However, he denied having received any books in the last three years and nothing was found at his house.[11] He then added that he would be forgiven 'if he had broken most of the Ten Commandments, as he had pardons granted him by the pope at Rome, when on his way to Jerusalem, and had received a similar pardon from Wolsey, when his Grace was last at St Paul's'.[12] Monmouth escaped punishment, living on to make his will in December 1537.

Cardinal Campeggio was concerned at the number of heretical works arriving in England, commenting that during Easter week, 1529, 'certain Lutheran books, in English, of an evil sort, have been circulated in the King's Court'.[13] This is likely to have been Tyndale's *Obedience of a Christian Man*, which reformist thinkers were using a starting point for a new national faith, in the hope that Henry and Francis, 'this king and the Most Christian King, will undertake to reduce the ecclesiastical state to the condition of the primitive church, taking from it all its temporalities'. Campeggio warned Henry that this was the work of 'the devil dressed in angels' clothing' and the object was to seize the property of the church, to which the king replied that the Lutherans argued that the ecclesiastical rights to hold the property had been decided by the ecclesiastics themselves. He 'insinuated' that is was now 'for the laity to interpose'. Campeggio tried to convince Henry that this would be 'directly against his interests' but the king riposted with the view that many of the clergymen 'live very wickedly' and had 'erred in many things from the Divine Law'.[14] Henry's position had changed by 1529, to the extent that he was prepared to employ Lutheran arguments. He was not simply bringing about change in order to marry Anne, he was genuine in his belief that the Catholic Church needed reform. His view had evolved into something far more open and tolerant to the new ideas, closer to the approach of the Valois family during the previous decade. It is interesting that Henry and Francis were coupled together by Campeggio as the possible joint instigators of change. Not only was Henry moving away from his old certainties and alliances with the pope and the Empire, he was more in sympathy with France, and the support that the enlightened Valois dynasty could offer him. Those threads were all entwined with his desire for a new marriage and a male heir, and found their embodiment in Anne Boleyn.

Anne's reformist sympathies led her into danger. Just as these heretics were being questioned and persecuted for the translation, importation and circulation of seditious books, a copy of Tyndale's *Obedience* fell into Boleyn hands. A text of 1579, which was found among John Foxe's papers, relates how Wolsey discovered a gentleman of the court in possession of Tyndale's book, and the trail led back to the king's fiancée. Apparently, Anne had lent it to a lady-in-waiting, Anne Gainsford, from whose hands it had been snatched by her suitor, George Zouche. Richard Sampson, Dean of the Chapel and former ambassador who had accompanied Thomas Boleyn to the Netherlands, discovered Zouche reading it and was horrified. Sampson confiscated it and informed Wolsey, who learned that it had originated with Anne but, before he could approach Henry with the information, Anne spoke to the king directly, asking for its return and even daring to suggesting that Henry read it. It was a bold move. Presumably word of its confiscation had got back to Anne and, fearful of the consequences, she decided to pre-empt the consequences.

According to John Louthe, Henry read and appreciated the work, saying 'this book is for me and all kings to read' and in Louthe's opinion, Anne had caused Henry to 'deliver his subjects out of the Egyptian darkness'.[15] Tyndale's view that there was no higher earthly authority than a king meant that rulers were not obliged to owe any allegiance to the pope. For Henry, this was a liberating idea, confirming his current frustrations with Clement's slowness and deliberate obfuscations and his increasing disillusionment with Rome. This incident has been placed by some historians in the period 1532–3, as it refers to Anne by her later title, although it has the details of that title incorrect. She was made Marquis, not Countess of Pembroke, in 1532, yet it is possible the title might be retrospectively misapplied. There is no contemporary source that echoes Louthe's account, but Anne Gainsford was well-placed to reminisce in later life about her service in Anne's household. The incident could have occurred as early as 1529. The earlier date actually makes more sense in terms of Henry's psyche, as by 1532 he needed no external prompting to consider a breach with Rome. It was a remarkable coup for Anne, dangerous considering that it involved a controversial text, but successful due to the personal appeal she held for Henry and her understanding of his character. It turned Henry's head at just the right moment and would have huge consequences for England.

Anne Gainsford, or 'Nan', as Anne Boleyn called her, had entered her mistress's service in 1528 and would remain there until her death. She married George Zouche in 1533 and served at least one of Henry's subsequent queens, with her husband being made a gentleman pensioner to the king. Anne lived into considerable old age, dying in 1590, after she had shared her memories of her former friend with Louthe, whose version of the incident George Wyatt cited in producing his own account of Anne's life. As Louthe relates:

There was a young, fair gentlewoman waiting upon the countess of Pembroke, the lady Anne Boleyn. There was also in the service of the same noble countess, one Mr George Zouche, father to Sir John Zouche. This young gentleman was a suitor in way of marriage to the said young gentlewoman, called Mrs Gainsford, and among other love tricks, Mr Zouche plucked from her a book in English called Tyndale's Obedience. At the same time the cardinal had given commandment to the prelates, but specially to Dr Sampson, dean of the King's Chapel, that they should vigilantly give eye to all men for such books, that they came not abroad, specially to the king's knowledge but it fell upon the wicked man's head that he most feared; for Mr Zouche was so ravished by the spirit of God, speaking now as well in the heart of the reader as first in heart of the maker of the books, that he was never well but when he was reading of that book. Mrs Gainsford wept because she could could not get the book off her wooer George Zouche... and he was as ready to weep as to deliver the book.

But see the hap, yea the providence of God: Mr Zouche standing in the chapel before Dr Sampson, ever reading upon this book, called the gentleman to him and snatched the book out of his hands, asked his name, whose man he was, and delivered it over to the cardinal. The countess asked Gainsford for the book. Gainsford on her knees (sic) and told all the circumstances. She was not sorry, nor angry with either of them two, perceiveing thereby that the young gentleman was caught with God's spirit... The noble woman goeth to the king; upon her knees she desired the king's help for her book. Upon the king's token the book was restored. Now bringing the book to the king, she besought his grace most tenderly to read the book. The king read and delighted in the book, for (sayeth hee) this book is for me and all kings to read.

In little time the good king and faithful servant of God, by the help of this virtuous lady by means that you here, had his eyes opened to see the truth, to advance God's religion and glory, to abhor the Pope's doctrine, his lies, his pomp and pride, to deliver his subjects out of the Egyptian darkness and Babylonian bondage that the Pope had brought him and his subjects unto. And so contempnyng the threats of this world, the power of princes, rebellions of his subjects at home, and raging of so many and mighty potentates abroad, set forward a rebellion in religion.[16]

Louthe, and other writers including George Wyatt, present Anne as being the catalyst for the Reformation, reading her possession of this book, her influence over Henry and her approval of his break from Rome as significant. However, Anne's actual degree of religious influence, and that of her faction, is difficult to determine. There is no question that the Boleyns were an educated family with an interest in reform. Erasmus wrote to Thomas Boleyn in 1527, praising him for his love of learning and sending him a copy of his Commentary on Psalm 23.[17] Additionally, Boleyn's godson Thomas Tebold, or Theobald, a Cambridge graduate, was a student at the University of Louvain in the Netherlands, acting as an agent for English prelates. He later travelled in France and Germany, supplying information to his godfather and Thomas Cranmer about the movements of the Emperor. Boleyn consciences aside, the Reformation was a European process that it would have been impossible for England to resist, even had Henry desired to do so. Far-reaching change could not have been kept at bay; it was just a question of when, rather than if. However, Henry's marital problems, and perhaps the influence of Anne, perhaps of her family, sped up the process.

Anne's influence might be traced in Henry's expression of interest in meeting the French scholar Guillaume Budé, an expert in Latin and Greek, and a favourite of Francis I. It is likely that Anne spoke of her time in France, and Budé's work, in sympathetic terms, which inspired Henry to connect with the scholar. He conveyed this wish to Wolsey, who wrote to the Bishop of Bayonne, to convey the king's desire to see Bude, 'and have a literary conversation with him, from the great esteem he has for him'.[18] Bayonne warned Henry he 'must not be surprised if Bude was some time in coming, owing to his age and illness'.[19] The meeting did not take place, and Budé remained in France, where he would convince Francis not to prohibit the printing of certain reformist texts, as had been advised by the Sorbonne.

There is no doubting Anne's sympathies with reformers. In 1528, she wrote to Wolsey on behalf of the prior of Reading, who had been arrested for the possession of Lutheran books. Foxe's *Book of Martyrs* states that Anne was in possession of not only Tyndale's *Obedience of a Christian Man*, but a copy of Simon Fish's controversial *Supplication of the Martyrs*, and that George Boleyn suggested she pass this work on to Henry. Given his positive response to the Tyndale, she may well have done so, if she judged the circumstances to be right. George's library also contained a book based on the work of the French scholar Jacques Lefèvre d'Etaples, *The Epistles and Gospels*, a collection of Bible readings for each week of the year, followed by a short homily, or commentary, by the German Evangelist Johannes Brenz, inspired by the writings of Luther. This emphasises the importance of the Bible over the traditions of the church and was translated into English by George, although the copy he gave to Anne retained the French text.[20] Out of the few books that can be stated for certain as having belonged to Anne, seven were religious in nature and six of these were reformist. She interceded on behalf of a merchant Richard Herman, imprisoned for facilitating the translation of the Bible, and sought to support those who were persecuted for their reforming tendencies, such as Nicholas Bourbon de Vandoeuvre, whose collection of poems, *Nugae*, or Bagatelles, led to his imprisonment in France. She later appointed evangelical chaplains, gave each member of her household their own copy of the *Book of Psalms*, translated into English, and intervened to secure the release of Thomas Patmore, parson of Hadham in Hertfordshire, who had been imprisoned in the Lollards' Tower for two years. In 1536, she would prompt her almoner to preach a sermon on the story of King Ahasuerus and Esther, in which the queen stepped in to correct the king's mistaken religious direction, but the context for this, just days before her arrest, was somewhat different.

Anne was clearly in favour of the reform of the church and it was during the spring and summer of 1529, in conjunction with the Boleyn influence, that this process was instigated by the king. At the end of May, Henry requested papal bulls for restructuring the monasteries, converting abbacies into bishoprics, and merging archdeaconries with parish churches, dividing their possessions and dispensing with the episcopal vestments. In addition, he desired Clement to grant him the ability to suppress any monasteries with a smaller annual yield than 6,000 ducats and divert their possessions to the colleges of Windsor and Cambridge. Any establishments with less than twelve members were to be targeted by Wolsey and Campeggio, who were to 'make one perfect out of several imperfect'. They were to prescribe what was to be given to the poor and ensure the nuns were enclosed within walls[21] This was six years in advance of the actual suppression of the monasteries, whose wealth was subsumed into the crown and much of their artwork and iconography destroyed. Again, Anne's influence is felt because, as she later expressed, her preference was for the use of the appropriated funds in educational institutions and charities. Unwilling to grant Henry the annulment he wished, Clement issued the bull with willingness, paving the way for the opening of the Reformation Parliament that October.

PART FIVE

THE KING'S GREAT MATTER

TWENTY-ONE

Campeggio and the Legatine Court 1529

Cardinal Wolsey had already been appointed by Pope Clement to investigate the legitimacy of Henry's marriage to Catherine and, that June, the second cardinal was selected. A woodcarving in Canterbury Cathedral depicts Wolsey and the Milanese Cardinal Lorenzo Campeggio flanking a miserable-looking Catherine and haranguing her. Its tone of sombre disappointment reflects the fact that the Legatine court they would hold at Blackfriars was doomed to failure even before it had begun. Furnished with instructions to frustrate the verdict and delay as long as possible, Campeggio set out for England, travelling slowly as he was riddled with gout. Both pope and cardinal were aware of the tide of feeling against the divorce among Catherine's followers, and the pressure from the emperor and his family. That July, a petition was presented to Clement by a Neapolitan nobleman, John Musettula, protesting against the suit, 'as the marriage was contracted in accordance with an apostolic ordinance and consummated by thee cohabitation of many years and the birth of children'.[1] Musettula warned that 'wars between Christian Princes will be the result' and that a ruling in Henry's favour would 'impugn' the Catholic church and 'restrain the Pope's power'. No marriages in Christendom would remain secure if Catherine's was dissolved – and the loyalties of Wolsey were suspected.[2] Clement agreed with much of this in theory but wanted above all to preserve both himself and peace in Europe.

As Campeggio travelled as slowly as possible, Henry and Anne remained hopeful, even optimistic about swiftly obtaining their desires. The king even dispatched Sir Francis Bryan to Europe, to intercept the cardinal and speed him on his journey. He received his instructions from Wolsey on 21 August and was to travel with a guard and mule for Campeggio's use:

On meeting him he is to thank him for his diligence on behalf of the King and Wolsey, to deliver the King's letters and the mule, and conduct him to Calais, accompanied by the said spears and horsemen.

If on Campeggio's coming to Paris he be in need of horses, the Master of the Rolls shall supply him with such as he has in those parts, to be sent back again with some of his own servants.[3]

Once Bryan had met with the cardinal, he informed Wolsey that Campeggio's gout in his hands and feet meant he was unable to bear the pressure of the stirrups or hold the bridle and was therefore incapable of riding. The aged Campeggio, crawling along in spite of Bryan's best efforts, had in fact reached Paris in mid-September, but his health deteriorated again and he had to be carried to Calais on a litter, necessitating even slower travel. Then, the weather was so terrible that the ships intended to carry him were driven back into harbour, causing further delays.[4] Henry wrote to Anne in anticipation of the intimacy that he hoped would soon follow. He again used the metaphor of hunting the hart:

The reasonable request of your last letter, with the pleasure also that I take to know them true, causeth me to send you these news. The legate which we most desire arrived at Paris on Sunday or Monday last past, so that I trust by the next Monday to hear of his arrival at Calais: and then I trust within a while after to enjoy that which I have so long longed for, to God's pleasure and our both comforts. No more to you at this present, mine own darling, for lack of time, but that I would you were in mine arms, or I in yours, for I think it long since I kissed you. Written after the killing of a hart, at eleven of the clock, minding, with God's grace, to-morrow, mightily timely, to kill another, by the hand which, I trust, shortly shall be yours.
Henry R.[5]

Campeggio and Bryan's crossing was successfully made on 29 September, and the party was at Canterbury on 1 October, with Bryan's clerk requesting that wine was dispatched for the cardinal ahead of his imminent arrival at Dartford (probably not the best provision in view of his crippling gout).[6] However, although the cardinal arrived in London on 8 October 1528, he took at once to his bed, in acute pain. A swift start to the proceedings seemed unlikely. Anne had not yet returned to court, with Du Bellay writing on 6 October that 'both the King and Queen are coming to Greenwich today; but I do not think Mademoiselle De Boulan will yet leave her mother in Kent'.[7] In her absence, she and Henry appeared to have reached some agreement, or compromise. At the end of the month, he wrote to her once more, to express his delight that she had set aside certain fears and questions and to have acceded to his 'reason', perhaps reassured by the final arrival of Campeggio. Yet there is something of the taming, or 'bridling' of Anne's wild thoughts in Henry's language that echoes the realities of the gender dynamic: that Henry may choose to play the role of subordinate to his mistress, but that he retained ultimate control. It echoes Wyatt's image of the hind, or lover, claimed by the king, whose message was written about her throat in diamonds: 'noli me tangere, for Caesar's I am.' For both men, the woman was wild, animal-like, requiring the taming hand of man to capture, claim and subdue her, through the restrictive collar or bridle. The king was full of joy at Anne's acquiescence, her decision to conform with 'reason', synonymous here with his wishes:

> To inform you what joy it is to me to understand of your conformableness with reason, and of the suppressing of your inutile (pointless) and vain thoughts with the bridle of reason. I assure you all the good in this world could not counterpoise for my satisfaction the knowledge and certainty thereof, wherefore, good sweetheart, continue the same, not only in this, but in all your doings hereafter; for thereby shall come, both to you and me, the greatest quietness that may be in this world. The cause why the bearer stays so long, is the business I have had to dress up gear for you; and which I trust, ere long to cause you occupy: then I trust to occupy yours, which shall be recompense enough to me for all my pains and labour. The unfeigned sickness of this well-willing legate doth somewhat retard his access to your person; but I trust verily, when God shall send him health, he will with diligence recompense his demur. For I know well where he hath said (touching the saying and bruit that he is thought imperial) that it shall be well known in this matter that he is not imperial; and thus, for lack of time, sweetheart, farewell.
> Written with the hand which fain would be yours, and so is the heart. R.H.[8]

In the meantime, Henry arranged to meet Anne midway between Hever and London, at Beddington Place, the 'fair house' or 'paradise of pleasure' [9] of her cousin and Henry's obliging courtier and friend, Sir Nicholas Carew. Having been placed in Henry's household at the age of six, Carew had been raised alongside the king, and was one of his closest companions and 'minions', at his side during the joust, and getting into trouble for his hell-raising with Sir Francis Bryan in Paris. The pair, and their friends, had been ejected from court by Wolsey as being bad influences upon the king, but made a swift return, nursing a grudge against the cardinal that tallied conveniently with Anne's. In recent years, he had been made Master of the Horse, Knight of the Garter, and undertaken further diplomatic missions. His sympathies for Anne would become stretched in the years to come but in the autumn of 1528, he was one of her staunchest supporters. Carew's wife, Elizabeth, sister of Francis, was also a Boleyn cousin, almost Anne's exact contemporary, and reputed to have been Henry's mistress before her marriage. Situated twenty miles to the north-west of Hever and twelve miles south-west of Henry's birthplace of Greenwich, Beddington Place was surrounded by a deer park and water gardens. Today, only the great hall remains, with its hammerbeam ceiling, as part of the present-day Carew Academy School. Between 10 and 14 November 1528, Henry and Anne were guests of Nicholas and Elizabeth, enjoying some rare privacy before Henry returned to London and they were parted again. There was still a long way to go before the king could call Anne his own.

The weeks passed and Henry grew more frustrated with Campeggio. 'Little has been done in the matter of the doubt depending on the King's marriage,' wrote John Casale, 'in consequence of the Legate being marvellously vexed with the gout; and though the King has repaired to a place near the Legate's lodgings, it was ten days after his arrival before he (Campeggio) was able to come into the King's presence. Even then he had to be borne in a chair, and has ever since kept his chamber. The King and the Queen have familiarly and apart visited him; so that more knowledge will be had of the validity of the marriage.'[10]. Early in December, Henry dispatched Francis Bryan and Wolsey's servant, the Italian-born Peter Vannes, to speak directly to the pope, alternating between threats, promises and hopes, and to 'put him on his guard, assuring him his safety depends on France and England, and to offer him some contributions for the support of an army'. When Clement was accused of attempting to hinder Henry's cause, he replied 'that Campeggio told him he had used his endeavors to persuade the Queen to the divorce, but found her adverse to it'.[11] This was nothing that Henry and Anne did not know.

Around the same time, Wolsey wrote to John's brother, Gregory Casale in Rome, putting forward his case for the swift conclusion of the papal court, but also his recognition of the potential catastrophe Henry's wishes could unleash. Wolsey also foresaw the danger to himself, should he be unable to procure the result the king and Anne desired:

The King feels his honor touched by this, especially considering what a benefactor he has been to the Church. I cannot reflect upon it, and close my eyes, for I see ruin, infamy, and subversion of the whole dignity and estimation of the See Apostolic if this course be persisted in. You see in what dangerous times we are.

If the Pope will consider the gravity of this cause, and how much the safety of the nation depends upon it, he will see that the course he now pursues will drive the King to adopt those remedies which are injurious to the Pope, and are frequently instilled into the King's mind. Without the Pope's compliance, I cannot bear up against the storm; and as often as I reflect on the conduct of his Holiness, I cannot but fear lest the common enemy of souls, seeing the King's determination, inspires the Pope with his present fears and reluctance, which will alienate all the faith and devotion towards the See Apostolic. The sparks of that opposition here, which have been extinguished with such care and vigilance, will blaze forth, to the utmost danger of all here and elsewhere.

It is useless for Campeggio to think of reviving the marriage. If he did, it would lead to worse consequences. Let him, therefore, proceed to sentence. Prostrate at the feet of his Holiness, I most urgently beg of him to set aside all delays. If the divorce be carried, we may expect an alliance between the kings of England and France and the Emperor, who can take no offence at the King's honorable proceedings.[12]

In the first week of December, Anne returned to court after a short absence. She was visibly on the ascendant in contrast to Catherine, and while many remained loyal to their mistress, others sought patronage from the rising star. Outside court circles, it was a different matter, with the Catholic queen and her daughter retaining popularity. The French ambassador, Jean Du Bellay, believed Henry's championing of Anne was an attempt to accustom Henry's subjects to the idea of her as queen, and that there would have been demonstrations of discontent at the scandal, if only Catherine's subjects had been stronger:

Mademoiselle de Boulan is at last come thither, and the King has lodged her in a very fine lodging, which he has prepared for her close by his own. Greater court is now paid to her every day than has been to the Queen for a long time. I see they mean to accustom the people by degrees to endure her, so that when the great blow comes it may not be thought strange. However, the people remain quite hardened, and I think they would do more if they had more power; but great order is continually taken.[13]

It made for one of the most awkward family Christmases ever, with Henry, Anne and Catherine together under one roof; but the king was still optimistic that the period of waiting would be brief. Du Bellay reported on Christmas Day that 'the whole court has retired to Greenwich, where open house is kept both by the King and Queen, as it used to be in former years. Mademoiselle de Boulan is there also, having her establishment (*son cas*) apart, as, I imagine, she does not like to meet with the Queen. I expect things will remain in this state till the return of Bryan.'[14] Effectively, there were two queens with two courts, and while Anne wisely chose to keep her distance from her former mistress, the situation forced courtiers to choose sides. The decision facing them depended on a complex combination of family ties, established loyalties, religious and cultural views and the patronage network by which success and influence were to be gained. The individuals at the head of both factions divided the court in terms of their adherence to either Catholicism or reform, and Spain or France. Under the rulership of an absolute king, politics depended upon gaining Henry's approval, and by 1528 Anne clearly had the upper hand. Courtiers who had not yet nailed their colours clearly to the mast of the Aragon faction would have seen the Boleyns as the best bet for achieving promotion. It was the same with the arrival of every new favourite: there would be new positions within Anne's household and new opportunities to serve members of her family. There were rewards for the Boleyns too, with George receiving an annuity of fifty marks payable from the profits of the chief butler of England, out of the issues of the prize of wines.[15]

Anne's new domestic proximity to Henry, coupled with the anticipation of divorce and the tone of the king's letters to Anne through the latter part of 1528, brought the pair into a new stage of intimacy. Having written of the pleasure of having Anne in his arms, or being in hers, Henry now had the opportunity to do so. Anne was not present at court as the king's mistress, but as his intended wife, even if their intention to marry was still secret. In this respect, allowing for Catherine's marriage being invalid, Anne had the same legal status as she had after having given promises to Henry Percy. Verbal agreements were considered binding by the church and gave sufficient licence to allow the couple to indulge in various acts of foreplay, or 'bundling'. It is very unlikely that Henry and Anne slept together this early, as they would have wanted to be certain of the legitimacy of any child she may conceive, but it is not impossible. Rudimentary forms of contraception did exist, and Anne may have taken the risk and yielded once, in order to make their betrothal legally binding and secure her position. However, it seems more likely that they indulged in limited intimate acts, by which Anne allowed Henry to glimpse their future sex life without fully becoming his lover.

Anne was certainly alluring, elegant, intelligent, sophisticated and different, but what also drew Henry to her most powerfully was what she represented. In these years of waiting, she became for him something akin to Castiglione's ideal, in that she offered Henry the possibility of the future he desired. Her attraction for him was bound up in the promise she symbolised, in the perfect vision he imagined, and the children she would bear. Henry constructed this ideal future, surely a gilded cage for Anne, to be the answer to his needs. It would be Anne who had to inhabit it.

While the case for divorce was being prepared, Anne understood that it was prudent to maintain good relations with the men who would pave her way to queenship. She wrote from Greenwich on 4 April to Stephen Gardiner, a doctor of canon and civil law, who was Wolsey's secretary:

Master Stephen,
I thank you for my letter, wherein I perceive the willing and faithful mind you have to do my pleasure, not doubting but as much as it is possible for man's wit to imagine, you will do. I pray God to send you well to speed in all matters, so that you will put me in a study how to reward your service. I do trust in God you shall not repent it, and that the end of this journey shall be more pleasant to me than your first, for that was but a rejoicing hope, which ceasing, the lack of it does put to the more pain, and they that are partakers with me, as you do know. Therefore I do trust that this hard beginning shall make the better ending.

Master Stephen, I send you here the cramp-rings for you, and Master Gregory, and Master Peter; pray you to distribute them both, as she, that (you may assure them) will be glad to do them any pleasure which shall be in my power. And thus I make an end, praying God send you good health.
Written at Greenwich the 4th day of April,
By your assured friend,
Anne Boleyn.[16]

Poised on the verge of success, Anne also wrote to Wolsey, to thank him for the efforts he was making on her behalf. Regardless of their past awkwardness over Anne's engagement to Henry Percy, she and the cardinal redrew their battlelines to take account of her new position. She was shrewd enough to recognise his influence and the fact that he may be of use to her; and he was shrewd enough to see her as a potential rival, who was insinuating herself between himself and the king.

My Lord,
After my most humble recommendations, this shall be to give unto your grace, as I am most bound, my humble thanks for the pain and

travail that your grace doth take in studying, by your wisdom and great diligence, how to bring pass honourably the greatest wealth that is possible to come to any creature living, and in especial remembering how wretched and unworthy I am in comparing to his highness. And for you, I do know myself never to have deserved by my deserts that you should take this great pain for me; yet daily of your goodness I do perceive by all my friends, and though that I had no knowledge of them, the daily proof of your deeds doth declare your words and writing towards me to be true.

Now good my lord, your discretion may consider as yet how little it is in my power to recompense you, but all only with my goodwill, the which I assure you, that after this matter is brought to pass you shall find me, as I am bound in the mean time, to owe you my service, and then look what thing in this world I can imagine to do pleasure in, you shall find me the gladdest woman in the world to do it. And next unto the kings grace, of one thing I make you full promise to be assured to have it, and that is my hearty love unfeignedly during my life; and being fully determined, with God's grace, never to change this purpose, I make an end of this my rude and true-meaning letter, praying our Lord to send you much increase of honour, with long life.

Written with the hand of her that beseeches your grace to accept this letter as proceeding from on the is most bound to be
Your humble and obedient servant,
Anne Boleyn.[17]

On 31 May 1529, the long-anticipated Legatine court opened. Cardinals Wolsey and Campeggio assembled in the Parliament Chambers at Blackfriars Priory, situated to the east of Henry's new Bridewell Palace. The venue had been established in the 1270s as a home to London's Dominican community, whose distinctive dark garb had given them their alternative name of the Black Friars. By the mid-fifteenth century, Blackfriars had a large church 'richly furnished with ornaments' and a number of other buildings, including a hall that was frequently being used for meetings by Parliament. The Emperor Charles had been accommodated there on his visit in 1522 and a long gallery of over seventy feet had been built on that occasion to connect the site with that of next-door Bridewell. As the players prepared themselves to enter the spotlight for what they anticipated would be a dramatic piece of political theatre, it was ironic that Henry also chose Blackfriars in 1529 as the new location for his Office of the Revels, so that costumes and props were stored there. Fifty years later, a long time after the friary had been dissolved, it became the site of one of London's early theatres. Anne and

Henry anticipated a swift resolution of the Great Matter, followed by their wedding, but neither of them could have foreseen that Catherine of Aragon was to put on the performance of her lifetime.

On the last day of May, the proceedings were opened by John Longland, Bishop of Lincoln, the confessor in whom Henry had confided his first doubts about his marriage and one of the most driven advocates of his annulment. Longland presented the papal commission to Wolsey and Campeggio, which was then read aloud by the notary Florian Montini, before a company of abbots, notaries, archdeacons and bishops. In it, the pope declared that it had 'frequently been related to him by trustworthy persons that there was a question about the validity of the marriage' between Henry and Catherine and 'because of the importance of the matter a rapid judgement was required'. He urged the court to proceed 'summarily and plainly, without judicial fanfare and form' to determine whether the marriage was valid or invalid. Then, if one of the parties were to request it, they were to 'confirm the marriage or declare it null'.[18] Thus the proceedings were cleverly framed as if they were an independent inquiry prompted by the pope rather than the king, who was equated with Catherine as one of the parties under investigation. The two cardinals then appointed Longland and John Clerk, Bishop of Bath and Wells, to summon the king and queen to appear before the court on the morning of 18 June, between the hours of nine and ten.[19] Anne would not be present to witness proceedings but she was waiting nearby, to hear accounts of the court sessions from those of her supporters who were in attendance, including Stephen Gardiner, Bishop of Winchester, whose expertise in canon law had served him well as Wolsey's assistant in securing the existence of the legatine court.

Blackfriars had been decked out in splendid detail, with Campeggio and Wolsey seated on two chairs of cloth of gold, and cushions of the same, before a table with a railing around it, covered in tapestry, like a 'solemn court'.[20] Henry's chair was to the right, made of rich tissue under a cloth of estate, while Catherine's on the left, was simply a 'rich chair'.[21] There needed little reminder that this was an ecclesiastical court, with the cardinals and their entourage arriving with crosses, pillars, axes and 'all the ceremonies belonging to their degrees'. The commission was read again and then Henry and Catherine were both summoned by name.

The queen was accompanied by four bishops and a large number of her ladies and gentlewomen. She stood before the legates and issued a formal protest, as well as submitting a written one which she had prepared, then she submitted her appeal to the pope and asked for it to be recorded. The initial challenge she offered the court was that those judges arranged before her were not qualified to hear her case because of their close association with Henry, as both Wolsey and Campeggio had been promoted by the king. Catherine's speech has become the stuff of popular legend, appealing to the hardest of hearts, sounding much like the death of Anne and Henry's hopes. Rising from her seat, she knelt before her husband, addressing him as the only other person in the court of equal rank:

> Sir, I beseech you for all the love that hath been between us, and for the love of God, let me have justice. Take of me some pity and compassion, for I am a poor woman, and a stranger born out of your dominion. I have here no assured friends, and much less impartial counsel. Alas! Sir, wherein have I offended you, or what occasion of displeasure have I deserved? I have been to you a true, humble and obedient wife, ever comfortable to your will and pleasure, that never said or did any thing to the contrary thereof, being always well pleased and contented with all things wherein you had any delight or dalliance, whether it were in little or much. I never grudged in word or countenance, or showed a visage or spark of discontent. I loved all those whom ye loved, only for your sake, whether I had cause or no, and whether they were my friends or enemies. This twenty years or more I have been your true wife and by me ye have had divers children, although it hath pleased God to call them out of this world, which hath been no default in me. And when ye had me at first, I take God to my judge, I was a true maid, without touch of man, and whether it be true or no, I put it to your conscience. If there be any just cause by the law that ye can allege against me either of dishonesty or any other impediment to banish and put me from you, I am well content to depart to my great shame and dishonour and if there be none, then here, I most lowly beseech you, let me remain in my former estate and receive justice at your hands. The King your father... and my father, Ferdinand, King of Spain... thought then the marriage between you and me good and lawful. Therefore, it is a wonder to hear what new inventions are now invented against me, that never intended by honesty... I most humbly require you, in the way of charity and for the love of God, who is the just judge, to spare me the extremity of this new court, until I may be advised what way and order my friends in Spain will advise me to take. And if ye will not extend to me so much impartial favour, your pleasure then be fulfilled, and to God I commit my cause![22]

Henry attempted to raise Catherine from her knees twice but she would not move. Finally, she rose, curtseyed, and turned to walk straight out of the court room. An official called to her to return, but she responded that 'it makes no matter, for it is no impartial court for me, therefore I will not tarry. Go on!' With her head held high, she never returned to the court room. Henry, moved by her performance, echoed that she had indeed 'been to me as true, as obedient, and as conformable a wife as I could in my fantasy wish or desire. She hath all the virtuous qualities that ought to be in a woman of her dignity... she is also a noble woman born.'[23] Anne cannot have been pleased to hear the report of these words, but perhaps Henry's next arguments encouraged her. The king outlined his suspicions: 'All such male issue as I have received of the queen died incontinent after they were born, so that I doubt (not) the punishment of God in that behalf.' He explained that he wished to 'take another wife in case that my first copulation with this gentlewoman were not lawful, which I intend not for any carnal concupiscence, ne (sic) for any displeasure or mislike of the queen's person or age, with whom I could be as well content to continue during my life, if our marriage may stand with God's laws, as with any woman alive'.[24]

A number of witnesses were called upon to make their statements regarding the marriage of Henry and Catherine. Thomas Boleyn, who had been present on the occasion of their wedding, was among them. On 15 July, at the Friars Minors, he affirmed that he was fifty-two years of age and that he had been a witness to the lawful marriage that took place at St Paul's on 14 November, 1501. Arthur, he related, was 'above fifteen years of age, which Boleyn knew from the books in which the births of the children of the kings of England are entered,' and he had 'heard from Spaniards that Catherine was more than sixteen'.[25] He related that 'after the marriage they dwelled together as man and wife, to his knowledge, at the King's court and at Ludlow'. He offered his opinion that the marriage was consummated, having heard from witnesses the famous line uttered by Arthur the following morning that 'he had been in the midst of Spain'. He concluded that he had 'not been subjected to undue influence'.[26] Boleyn had done all he could in the promotion of his daughter; no self-respecting Tudor father could have done more.

Eventually, at the end of July, after much lengthy deliberation, Campeggio prorogued the Blackfriars court on the pretext that papal business was suspended over the summer. He stated that it would reconvene on 1 October, but this was never his intention. Those involved recognised that the king had failed to secure his objective and Anne and her followers were swift to blame Wolsey, according to the Spanish ambassador, Inigo de Mendoza:

This lady, who is the cause of all the disorder, finding her marriage delayed, that she thought herself so sure of, entertains great suspicion that this Cardinal of England puts impediments in her way, from a belief that if she were Queen his power would decline. In this suspicion she is joined by her father, and the two dukes of Suffolk and Norfolk, who have combined to overthrow the Cardinal; but as yet they have made no impression on the King, except that he shows him in court not quite so good countenance as he did, and that he has said some disagreeable words to him.[27]

In contrast, the Boleyns and their followers were showered with new appointments, partly in reward for their support, partly in compensation for the court's failure. The grants made at the end of July included Anne's paternal uncle William, along with George's governorship of the hospital of St Bethelehem (later Bedlam) and Thomas's first connection with the rectory of All Hallows, London,[28] the custody of lands in Lathingdon and Hadleigh in Essex, followed by the wardship he was granted in August, of young William Strongman, his father's heir.[29] Nicholas Carew received confirmation of lands leased to him in Essex, George Zouche was granted the livery of his lands and William Brereton, a groom of the privy chamber, was made the keeper of Merseley Park, on the Welsh Marches. Their time was coming.

TWENTY-TWO

Wolsey's Fall 1529

The castles in the air that Henry had constructed for himself and Anne dissolved at the suspension of the legatine court. There would be no quick marriage, no summer honeymoon, no swiftly conceived heir, and Henry's anger needed an outlet. As they rode away from Bridewell, on the start of their first summer progress together, the writing was on the wall for Wolsey. His biographer, George Cavendish, relates how 'the king commanded the queen to be removed out of the court, and sent to another place, and his Highness rode in his progress, with Mistress Anne Boleyn in his company, all the green season'.[1] On 15 July, they visited Thomas Boleyn at Durham Place, before heading to Greenwich, from where they travelled to Waltham Abbey in Essex, almost eighteen miles directly to the north. Much larger than the present-day church, Waltham was an imposing site that stretched into an abbey and cloisters founded by Henry II on an eighth-century site. The gatehouse through which Anne made her approach on 2 August still survives, along with the early sixteenth-century porch, covered in the black and white chequer-work Henry would soon employ when converting Wolsey's old London home of York Place into Whitehall Palace.

Unless they were lodged with the prior, Henry and Anne stayed in the adjoining house called Romeland, located where the street of that name now runs parallel to the church's south wall. Whilst in residence, Henry discussed the matter of his divorce with a triumvirate of Cambridge clerics: Stephen Gardiner, Edward Foxe and the newly discovered Boleyn ally Thomas Cranmer, who suggested that the king appeal to the universities of Europe about the finer points of canon law. Like many of Henry's ablest servants, Cranmer did not come from the aristocracy, being the younger son of a Nottinghamshire family. His intelligence had taken him to Cambridge, where he had studied the Humanist writings of Erasmus and Lefèvre d'Étaples, which no doubt gained him Anne's approval. He was also a newly qualified Doctor of Divinity and had been assisting with research into the validity of Henry's first marriage. Cranmer's presence in Waltham was not planned, but it proved serendipitous for Anne. He was staying with relatives nearby in order to escape an outbreak of the plague in Cambridge, but this chance connection would ultimately prove the means by which Henry's first marriage would finally be ruled invalid.

Whilst at Waltham, Anne would have seen the tomb of Harold Godwinson and the large doom painting on the wall of the fourteenth-century Lady Chapel, depicting the salvation of the good and damnation of the bad, set either side of a pair of scales. Perhaps, with her reformist views, she disapproved of such a representation of the afterlife and mentioned this to Henry. She was probably the last queen to see the work, as imminent changes would soon sweep away notions of purgatory and prayers to intercede for the dead.

From Waltham, they travelled around twelve miles east to the Manor of Barnet (also known as Chipping, or High, Barnet), then in the possession of Thomas Wolsey, although there is no record of him ever having visited the property. Standing near the church of St John the Baptist, which is adorned with the same fashionable black and white chequer-work as Waltham Abbey, the manor was probably located near the present-day 'Manor Close', 'Manor Road' and the large recreation ground opposite where a later court house stood. Lysons' late eighteenth-century descripton of the area notes that the house was 'ancient' with some surviving wooden cloisters, suggesting that it was an appendage of a local priory, used as a summer residence by the monks.[2] Henry and Anne arrived on 11 August and remained there for three days, before departing on the morning of 14th, and riding eight miles north-west to Tyttenhanger house, which lay just to the south of St Albans. Again, this was a property which had come into Wolsey's possession, after he had acquired the local abbacy in 1522, surrounded by woods and fishponds. Henry had enjoyed the house when escaping there from the sweating sickness the previous summer, having told Wolsey that he liked it 'very well'. He was still keeping Stephen Gardiner, Bishop of Winchester, at his side to discuss the divorce, as Gardiner wrote to the cardinal on 12 August that Henry had 'bid him stay' there. Anne's uncle, Thomas Duke of Norfolk, was also present for at least part of this part of the progress, as he remained at Barnet in the days after Henry and Anne's departure; from where he wrote to Wolsey, enclosing letters regarding the king's Irish affairs. Henry and Anne stayed one step ahead of business, moving on to Olborne on 16 August, and from thence to Windsor.

On 21 August, Henry and Anne arrived at Reading, where they would have stayed in the same abbot's house that Henry would convert into a royal palace at the time of the dissolution a few years later. The solid inner gateway survives, through which Anne would have ridden, otherwise only fragments remain of the buildings and cloisters where she passed two days that summer. From there, they headed twenty-two miles north through the Chilterns to Great Haseley in Oxfordshire, arriving on 23 August. A tiny village centred around the parish church of St Peter, it contained a manor house which Edward IV had granted to the dean and canons of St George's Chapel Windsor, suggesting the most likely location in which the king and Anne would have lodged. A day or two later, they were at the royal palace at Woodstock, on the other side of Oxford, a former favourite of the Plantagenet kings. Now replaced by Blenheim Palace, the medieval Woodstock boasted an impressive two courtyards, the outer of which was huge, set with a great fountain adorned by beasts and with an entrance gateway flanked by the heraldic devices of Henry VII. There were extensive gardens, tennis courts and more than ninety rooms at Anne's disposal for the next seven days. Stephen Gardiner reached Woodstock on 24 August, which he described as their 'moving day', the day of travel between the two properties[3] and he was still there four days later when he wrote to Wolsey regarding the treaty of Madrid.[4] Brian Tuke, Treasurer of the Household, was also present, writing to the cardinal on 29 August, saying the king had gone hunting with the Dukes of Norfolk and Suffolk, and that Thomas Boleyn, Lord Rochford, was there too. During this progress, in the presence of Anne's family and friends and with Wolsey kept at a distance, the cardinal's fate was discussed.

The records place Henry at the Old Palace of Langley, or King's Langley, in Hertfordshire, fifty miles south of Woodstock, on 1 September. It is plausible that he made the trip south for purposes of business, perhaps leaving Anne and most of his court behind, to ride swiftly to deal with matters concerning his marriage. One of the State Letters, written by Gardiner to Wolsey from Woodstock, states that Gardiner had been 'with the King at Langley yesterday'. Marked as having been written on 4 August, it was identified by the State Letters and Papers' editor as incorrectly dated and amended to 24 August, when Henry was indeed at Woodstock. However, the trip to Langley took place early in September, so it is likely that the letter was misdated by month, rather than date, and that discussions regarding the divorce were still continuing. Gardiner reveals that the subject of their meeting was various letters, clauses and papal briefs concerning the pope's secret instructions to Wolsey and Campeggio.[5] Henry was back with Anne at Woodstock on 4 September. They remained there, with their inner circle, including Rochford, Norfolk, Suffolk, Gardiner, Cranmer, secretary Brian Tuke and Thomas More until 9 September. Gardiner wrote from the palace to Wolsey, telling him that Henry desired the release of the Prior of Reading, who was then in prison for 'Lutheranism'.[6]

The following week, the court moved on to spend the night at Buckingham, a market town close to the Oxfordshire border, which was home to Anne's widowed sister Mary Carey and her two children. With Anne having been granted the wardship of her young nephew Henry, it was an opportunity to visit her family in the property that the king had granted them back in 1526. This is more likely to have been the manor house in Church Street than the Norman castle located on the hill. Inside the half-timbered house, which is now divided in two, recent prebends had installed fireplaces and fashionable twisted chimneys. Next door, the local church was dedicated to the seventh-century St Rumbold of Buckingham, whose shrine and well were located nearby. Henry and Anne passed one night with the Careys before moving on to the Manor of Grafton Regis in Northamptonshire, which Henry had purchased from the Grey family in 1526, the descendants of his maternal grandmother, Elizabeth Woodville. It was a fitting association as, like his grandfather Edward IV, Henry was intending to marry for love, and keep the circumstances secret. For Wolsey though, it was to have tragic connotations, as the last place he would ever see the king.

George Cavendish was present to relate details of the meeting that took place when Wolsey and Campeggio rode north from The More to meet Henry at Grafton. Campeggio was to take his formal leave of the king and return to Rome but Cavendish reports that the court gossip suggested the Italian would be received by the king but that Wolsey would not. It was not an auspicious start, as they rode up to the manor house on a Sunday morning to discover that Wolsey had not been provided with lodgings, at which oversight or deliberate slight the cardinal was 'astonished'. Sir Henry Norris, Groom of the Stool, permitted him the use of his rooms to change his clothing and receive visitors but Wolsey would be forced to sleep that night at a property three miles away. When Henry appeared in the presence chamber, he raised the kneeling Wolsey to his feet, and drew him aside to a 'great window, where he talked with him' in some privacy. Members of the court were surprised to witness this, as Cavendish commented, 'to behold the countenances of those that had made their wagers to the contrary, it would have made you... smile'.[7] Wolsey was required to explain the contents of a letter in his own hand, but all seemed to go to the king's satisfaction and Henry promised to see him again after dinner.

Anne was not pleased at this development, though, surely having believed that Henry would snub the cardinal. That evening, she and the king dined together in her chamber where, according to Cavendish, she kept 'an estate more like a queen than a simple maid'.[8] Of course, Anne was no simple maid, she was an intelligent and driven politician, as well as a woman able to exert influence over a man who loved her. She was the king's fiancée and, accordingly, her estate was justified. Cavendish's insult implies that Anne was overstepping the mark, overreaching her position in terms of class and gender, with implicit questioning of her integrity and honour, but this is to be expected, as he considered this the point where she stuck the metaphorical knife into his master. Cavendish's comment is ironic in that, if Anne was not acting according to her 'true' position in society, nor was Wolsey, who had risen from humbler origins.

Anne was not prepared to hand the cardinal back an inch of the power she had won. Now, according to this account, she proceeded to strike Wolsey's death knell. Cavendish heard it reported 'by them that waited upon the king at dinner, that Mistress Anne Boleyn was much offended with the king, as far as she durst, that he so gently entertained my lord', commenting upon the 'debt and danger' which Wolsey had brought Henry into with his subjects. She then spoke even more explicitly of the slanders made against the king, adding ominously, that 'there is never a nobleman within this realm that if he had done but half so much as he (Wolsey) has done, but he were well worthy to lose his head'. When Henry replied that he saw Anne was 'not the Cardinal's friend', which can hardly have been news to him, she replied that she had no other cause but Henry's.[9]

The hostility of the Boleyn faction was apparent that evening when Norfolk suggested Wolsey should be sent back to his benefice, predicting an event that would soon come to pass, indicating the nature of the discussions that had been taking place behind the scenes. However, the king still had some residue of affection for his former friend. After dinner, Henry spoke to Wolsey again, and invited him into his private chambers, 'which blanked his enemies very sore and made them to stir the coals, being in doubt what this matter would grow into, having now none other refuge to trust but Mistress Anne'. Apparently, Henry then extended the invitation to Wolsey to return early the next day in order to finish their discussion.[10] The following morning, when Wolsey rose at dawn to ride the three miles to Grafton, he found that Henry had not waited for him. Depending on the two sources reporting the event, he had either gone, or was going, hunting, so commanded Wolsey to depart with Cardinal Campeggio. Cavendish was in no doubt that this change of heart was due to 'the special labour of Mistress Anne, who rode with him, only to lead him about, because he should not return until the cardinals were gone'.[11]

In total, Henry and Anne remained at Grafton for a full two weeks. On the return south, they passed the night of 24 September at Buckingham again, with Mary Carey, before moving on to Notley Abbey, an Augustinian foundation to the south of the same county. On 28 August, they arrived at Bisham Abbey in Berkshire, where the surviving manor house then stood next to the monastery, and was home to Margaret, Countess of Salisbury, the king's aunt, and one of the last survivors of the York-Plantagenet line. From there it was only ten miles south-east to Windsor, where Henry and Anne arrived the following day.[12] Henry had clearly been reflecting upon the Blackfriars proceedings and the intentions of the pope, as on the last day of September he wrote to Clement to express his incredulity at the court's failure and to offer one last attempt at reconciliation:

> On the return to your Holiness of Cardinal Campeggio, we could have wished, not less for your sake than our own, that all things had been so expedited as to have corresponded to our expectations, not rashly conceived, but owing to your promises. As it is, we are compelled to regard with grief and wonder the incredible confusion which has arisen. If the Pope can relax Divine laws at his pleasure, surely he has as much power over human laws. Complains that he has often been deceived by the Pope's promises, on which there is no dependence to be placed; and that his dignity has not been consulted in the treatment he has received. If the Pope, as his ambassadors write, will perform what he has promised, and keep the cause now advoked to Rome in his own hands, until it can be decided by impartial judges, and in an indifferent place, in a manner satisfactory to the King's scruples, he will forget what is past, and repay kindness by kindness, as Campeggio will explain.[13]

It was only a matter of days before Henry moved against Wolsey. The cardinal was stripped of all his secular titles, offices and properties, including Hampton Court, only being permitted to remain Archbishop of York. On 9 October, he was charged with a host of crimes, including praemunire, by which he had reputedly placed his service of the pope above his allegiance to Henry. Du Bellay visited Wolsey a week later, describing him as 'the greatest example of fortune that one could see', as the cardinal wept, desperately hoping to receive aid from France and was completely failed by his 'heart and tongue'. The ambassador urged Francis and his mother that if they wished to do anything to help Wolsey, they should act soon, as they could not hope to intervene before he was forced to surrender the Great Seal, the symbol of his highest secular office. The worst of 'this evil', he wrote, was that 'Mademoiselle de Boulen has made her friend (Henry) promise that he will never give him a hearing, for she thinks he could not help having pity upon him'.[14] The very same evening, on 17 October, at around 6pm, Norfolk, Suffolk, Gardiner and others arrived at York Place to confiscate the Seal. Three days later it was in Henry's hands, but he did not keep it long, already having a new Lord Chancellor in mind.

Du Bellay reported the news as it arrived, on 22 October:

While writing, I have heard that Wolsey has just been put out of his house, and all his goods taken into the King's hands. Besides the robberies of which they charge him, and the troubles occasioned by him between Christian princes, they accuse him of so many other things that he is quite undone. The duke of Norfolk is made chief of the Council, Suffolk acting in his absence, and, at the head of all, Mademoiselle Anne. It is not known yet who will have the seal. I expect the priests will never have it again; and that in this Parliament they will have terrible alarms.[15]

In the privy chamber at Greenwich on 25 October, the king formally handed the Great Seal to Thomas More, 'a good servant of the queen', who assumed Wolsey's old job, swearing the oath of office before a crowd of witnesses that included Thomas Boleyn, Norfolk, Suffolk, Bishop of Durham Cuthbert Tunstall and Anne's former love, Henry Percy, Earl of Northumberland. More was a lawyer, philosopher, statesman and humanist, who as a young man studying at the Inns of Court had witnessed Catherine's arrival in London back in 1501. Since then he had become Henry's secretary and personal advisor, working in the treasury, although he deeply disapproved of the reformist literature arriving in the country and had assisted Wolsey in suppressing it. He had produced, in 1516, the powerful political work *Utopia*, a cultural meme that has far outstripped its original story of an imagined island nation. The newly arrived Imperial ambassador, Eustace Chapuys, whose harsh condemnations of Anne would colour her reputation in the centuries after her death, commented that 'everyone is delighted at his promotion, because he is an upright and learned man'.[16]

Henry and Anne, accompanied by her mother and Henry Norris, took to the river and sailed from Greenwich to York Place, where the coals in the kitchen fires had barely had a chance to cool. Entering the newly vacated property, they found Wolsey's possessions to be 'much greater than... expected'.[17] The detailed inventories of his London effects alone give an indication of the wealth and splendour in which the cardinal had maintained his household, considered by poet laureate John Skelton as rivalling Henry's own court. The items also reflect the allegiances and tastes of an era that had now come to an end. Six large hangings were embroidered with roses, daisies and the arms of England and Spain, while those designed for use at Hampton Court featured the stories of Biblical figures like Sampson, Absalom, Hester, Suzanna, Solomon, Joseph and David, as well as St George and the dragon, a wild boar hunt, various Roman Emperors, card games, the wheel of fortune, woodcutting, harvest, and the woodwoses, or wild men, that Henry used to enjoy dressing as, or including in masques. Some hangings in red and green, yellow and violet, had been used at old Westminster Hall, in chambers, galleries and kneeling places, while an eight-piece set from the hall at Durham House, had survived for use on 'inferior' days.[18]

There was a bed of rich tissue, which had been made for Wolsey to take to Guines in 1520 for the Field of Cloth of Gold, along with pillows embroidered with fleur-de-lys, chairs of estate with gold tissue or decorated with cardinal's hats and Catherine of Aragon's symbol of the pomegranate. There was also a sequence of twenty-two hangings of velvet and cloth of gold, which Wolsey had commissioned especially for the occasion. A cushion of green and blue velvet on which Wolsey had used to rest his Bible during Mass was there, and clothing made to adorn statues of saints, including coats of crimson, damask, gold and pearls for the Virgin Mary, a blue cloth to hang before her, a kerchief for her head, a black and gold coat for the infant Jesus and a blue coat for St John. Wolsey's gold and silver plate; the bowls, cups, drinking vessels, plates and basins were engraved with flowers, figures, animals, Spanish work and the initials H and K. There were also n barrels of salmon and stockfish.[19]

It is not a pleasant image, Henry and Anne picking through Wolsey's effects, assessing the quality of his fabrics and plate with an acquisitive eye. Yet this was the realpolitik of the Tudor court; favourites rose and fell, and the symbols of status were passed amongst many hands. Even though some contained monograms or crests, they had less personal significance than we might imagine, and were used more as a backdrop to majesty. Ownership of such items was really more of a custodianship, like dwelling in a house that had previously been inhabited and would welcome new guests again soon. Even clothes were repaired and passed on. Only the very wealthy commissioned new clothes, others made their own, passed down clothing in wills, shared, patched and borrowed, or 'turned' their trousers to conceal the dirt. Two notable exceptions when it comes to the personal possessions of royalty belonged to Catherine of Aragon. In 1532, she would object strongly to relinquishing her jewels to Anne, although this was less about the connection with the items than the transference of queenship. The historic crown jewels were at the disposal of the queen, whoever she was, so to yield them would be an acceptance of Anne's queenship. The following year, in the autumn of 1533, Catherine also refused to hand over a christening gown she had used for Mary and her other live-born children. The gown had been given to her by her mother on her departure from Spain, so clearly had sentimental value beyond its intrinsic worth. Anne did get the use of the jewels, after Henry ordered it, but the Spanish christening robe remained with Catherine.

Anne was shrewd enough to see that Wolsey's fall was an essential counterweight to her own rise. She had played the cyclical game of the Tudor court, in the knowledge that servants and lovers came and went, creating absences that were opportunities to the new rising stars. Yet she must also have been painfully aware of the limitations of her position following the failure of the legatine court, and that it was still far from secure. Individual and dynastic success depended upon the favour of the king – but Anne was also cautious here, as Cavendish had observed at Grafton, saying she was as displeased with him as she 'durst' (dared) be. Just like Wolsey, she owed her influence to her abilities, but primarily to the king's preference and, with Wolsey, she witnessed the outcome of that favour being withdrawn. Her fear that Wolsey could still affect Henry and win a reprieve led her to try to keep them apart, as she understood just how unpredictable and complex Henry's heart could be. In her ascendancy, with the king desperate to make her his wife, moving heaven and earth to keep her by his side, she was shrewd enough to have glimpsed the Achilles' heel of her own power and realised that she must retain personal contact and proximity with Henry as much as possible. Whether or not this realisation was accompanied by humility, or by confidence, depends upon the bias of different commentators upon her life and reign. Anne knew she was playing a dangerous game but although she had not yet attained the crown, she held Henry's affections and believed in his intention to make her his wife.

Through the final months of 1529, the king showered his lover with gifts, making Anne increasingly look like a queen. The privy purse expenses for November and December 1529 show that 12s 8d was paid for a yard and a quarter of purple velvet for Mistress Anne, followed by £217 9s 8d to Walter Walshe for 'certain stuff by him prepared' for Anne and settling the bills of his jewellers, with over £24 going to John Crepye and a similar sum to William Hoyson.[20] On 29 November, a third jeweller named Morgan Fenwolf received £26 16s 3d for nine and three quarter ounces of Paris work for Anne and December saw a further jeweller's payment of £10 for a ruby and an emerald, while £100 went to Cornelius Hayes, Henry's goldsmith.[21] A more substantial reward was soon to follow, as on 9 December Anne's father was made the Earl of Wiltshire and Earl of Ormond. He was the first Boleyn to attain such a rank.

The mounting tension at court was proving impossible to avoid. When Henry dined with Catherine on St Andrew's Day, 30 November, her composure snapped. As related by Chapuys to Emperor Charles, the queen 'said to him that she had long been suffering the pains of Purgatory on earth, and that she was very badly treated by his refusing to dine with and visit her in her apartments'. Henry replied that she had no cause to complain, as she was 'mistress of her household' and could 'do as she pleased'; furthermore, that he had been busy recently cleaning up the mess that Wolsey had left. He added that 'as to his visiting her in her apartments and partaking of her bed, she ought to know that he was not her legitimate husband, as innumerable doctors and canonists, all men of honour and probity, and even his own almoner, Doctor Lee, who had once known her in Spain, were ready to maintain'. Catherine replied that Henry knew full well 'that the principal cause' alleged for the divorce did not really exist, 'as he himself had owned upon more than one occasion'.[22] She went on to challenge him that 'for each doctor or lawyer who might decide in your favour and against me, I shall find 1,000 to declare that the marriage is good and indissoluble'. After a 'good deal of talking and disputing', Henry abruptly left Catherine at the table and headed off to sup with Anne, 'very disconcerted and downcast'.[23] According to Chapuys, Anne reproached him with the words: 'did I not tell you that whenever you disputed with the Queen she was sure to have the upper hand? I see that some fine morning you will succumb to her reasoning, and that you will cast me off. I have been waiting long, and might in the meanwhile have contracted some advantageous marriage, out of which I might have had issue, which is the greatest consolation in this world; but alas! farewell to my time and youth.'

It is difficult to know how accurate these recorded speeches are, passed on second- or third-hand, and composed for an audience hostile to Anne, but there may be something in the sentiment expressed about her age and the passage of time. At well past the age that many women were already mothers, their 'greatest consolation', and with two broken engagements behind her, Anne must have been conscious that her 'time and youth' were passing while the Great Matter was being debated. By her age, Catherine had already undergone five pregnancies. There must have been times when, in spite of Henry's attentions and her position at his side, Anne experienced doubts about her future.

This argument may have prompted Henry to send Catherine away from court, or she may have been ill. The queen was obliged to leave Greenwich at the end of November and go to Richmond, although she would be permitted to return for the Christmas season.

The final list of charges against Wolsey was drawn up on 1 December 1529. It must have seemed to the cardinal that all the recent arduous services he had performed for Henry, at the king's personal instigation, were being used against him. He was accused of obtaining legatine authority in England to the injury of the king's prerogative, for making treaties with the French, the pope and the Duke of Ferrara against Henry's wishes and for referring, in letters, to 'the King and I' implying an inappropriate equality between them. He had made his household swear loyalty to himself before the king, against the custom, obliged ambassadors to visit him before they had an audience with Henry, and redirected foreign letters to himself first. He had operated a ring of spies, used the Great Seal to import his own grain, raised rents, appropriated the goods of spiritual men, shamefully slandering and suppressing 'good religious houses', threatening judges, violating promises and 'keeping great estate at court', among a congeries of other crimes. Most bizarrely, he had deliberately 'endangered the King's person in that he, when he knew himself to have the foul and contagious disease of the great pox broken out upon him in divers places of his body, came daily to your Grace... blowing upon your most noble Grace with his perilous and infective breath'.[24] The Lords who signed the charges, 'begging' the king to make the cardinal an example, included the familiar names who had accompanied Anne and Henry on progress that summer; her father, Norfolk, Suffolk, Thomas More and Henry Percy; but there were others, like Henry Courtenay, Marquis of Exeter and William Blount, Lord Mountjoy, who were keen to see Wolsey fall but still remained loyal to Catherine of Aragon.[25]

If Wolsey was already far from well, the news shattered his health. He wrote to his most trusted advisor, Thomas Cromwell, that his fever was 'somewhat assuaged and the black humour also' but that he was entering into 'the kalends of a more dangerous sickness, which is the dropsy' and there was little hope for him unless he was 'removed to a drier air'.[26] Soon, Wolsey was so poorly that Henry relented enough to send his own physician Dr Butts to attend him, taking leeches and 'vomitive eluctuary'.[27] Wolsey absolutely refuted that he had done anything but serve the king in good faith and was prepared to relinquish all that he had and live in a hermitage if this would solicit Henry's forgiveness. In vain, he entreated Cromwell to ask the king 'to be gracious to him, and to practise that the lady Anne may mediate for him'.[28] However, the same month, Cromwell commented that 'none dares speak to the King on his part for fear of Madame Anne's displeasure' and that Wolsey's letters had been delivered to Anne. 'There is yet no answer,' the secretary reported. 'She gave kind words, but will not promise to speak to the King for you.'[29] Chapuys, who is always a witness to be heard with a dose of scepticism, on account of his bias and the fact that he only ever saw Anne Boleyn once, had been told by a cousin of Wolsey's physician that 'the lady had sent to visit him during his sickness and represented herself as favouring him with the King'. Even Chapuys found this 'difficult to be believed, considering the hatred she has always borne him'. He considered that 'she must have thought he was dying, or shown her dissimulation and love of intrigue, of which she is an accomplished mistress'.[30]

As Wolsey fell, so the Boleyns rose even higher. Upon the return of Francis Bryan to England, George was appointed ambassador in his place, to secure a closer friendship with France, on which Henry planned to rely when he announced Anne as his queen.[31] George received his instructions that December along with his fellow-ambassador, John Stokesley, to confer with Bryan regarding the Franco-Scottish connection and press Francis on the question of a General Council, the creation of which, Henry feared, would give the pope and Emperor too much power.[32] George also became Lord Rochford upon his father's elevation to Earl of Wiltshire and Ormond,[33] the charter for which he received at York Place on 8 December. This was followed by a feast at which Anne was seated at the king's right hand, placed above Henry's sister Mary and 'occupying the very place allotted to a crowned queen, which, by the by, is a thing that was never before done'. Such dancing and 'carousing' followed that there had been nothing wanting, said Chapuys, 'except for a priest to give the nuptial ring and pronounce the benediction'.[34]

Desperate to save himself, Wolsey tried to appease his enemies, making one grant to George of an annuity of £200 from the lands and bishopric of Winchester, and the same amount again from those of St Albans.[35] The following January, Thomas became keeper of the Privy Seal, with a daily payment derived from the customs of Pool, London, Bristol and Bridgewater.[36] His next diplomatic mission would be to visit the Emperor with professions of friendship, and to convey Henry's wish 'to open to him the depth of his conscience in the weighty cause' of his marriage.[37] Tongues were already wagging across Europe when the Emperor wrote to his brother, Archduke Ferdinand, on 11 January, in advance of Thomas's arrival, with a response that indicates the ambassador was unlikely to receive a warm welcome:

> They say the king of England already holds his mistress as his wife, and maintains that, whether the Pope will or no, he will make her so. He treats the Pope as a heretic, and says he might be degraded. On one hand, the Pope would not consent, the affair being too scandalous; on the other, he does not like to incur disgrace and the loss of Henry's obedience. Suspects he will commit some folly. In any case this will be a sufficient cause of new war.[38]

It did not take long for Thomas Boleyn to assess the Emperor's attitude towards Henry and his marital dilemma. Such a reaction can hardly have come as a surprise, in spite of Boleyn's former favour at the court of Charles and his aunt, Margaret. According to the Bishop of Tarbres who witnessed the conversation, Boleyn explained himself that 'what he did was not as a father but as a subject and servant of his master'. It had been sufficient for him that Henry had expressed 'the remorse and scruple of conscience' but, as he later confided to the Bishop, 'if his daughter came to be Queen, she would be all her life your (Francis's) very humble servant'.[39] The personal was not so easy to disentangle from the political in this case, for both Boleyn and Charles. Finding himself unable, after two or three meetings, to make the Emperor concede that the question of the marriage was one of law, to be settled by theologians rather than the pope, 'the Earl took his leave'.[40] Boleyn wrote to Henry to admit defeat in April 1530:

> By the Almoner, who now goes to you, you will know how stiffly the Emperor is set against your cause. He is much guided by the Chancellor,

who affirms that the greatest number of divines is against you; and his ambassador in England is led the same way. The Pope is governed by the Emperor, and the Italian divines will support his authority.[41]

From there, Boleyn went to France, where he was able to follow this bad new, with the promise that Henry had the full support of Francis I and Louise of Savoy, writing from Angoulême that May:

> The King and my Lady will help what they can in your great matter, and speak of you with great affection. I received your letter about the salt by Wellysborn. Am lodged here in the court, and feasted daily.[42]

Erasmus also heard the news, in Freiburg in Germany, reporting with emotion that 'the great Cardinal of England has been thrown into prison, and was even in danger of his life. Oh, the slippery turns of this world!'[43]

TWENTY-THREE

Days Spent Waiting 1530

Frustrated by the failure to secure his annulment, Henry threw himself into discussions about the finer details of canon law. Thomas Boleyn's aborted mission also raised concerns about the European situation, so Henry sent out more ambassadors to watch over his interests. In August 1529, while the legatine court had occupied Henry's mind, Charles and Francis had signed the Peace of Cambrai, posing a potential threat to the former good Anglo-French relations that Henry was so keen to cultivate in support of his marriage to Anne. It also served to bring the pope even closer under Imperial control.

When the blows came from Rome, they were devastating. In response to requests from his aunt Catherine, Charles instructed Clement to issue a brief, forbidding Henry from making a second marriage before the Pope had passed sentence.[1] Then, on 21 March, Clement issued a bull 'forbidding all ecclesiastical judges, doctors, notaries, advocates etc to speak or write against the validity of the marriage between the king and queen of England on pain of excommunication'.[2] They were prohibited from 'alleging anything in the cause, or intermeddling with it, against their conscience, for bribe, entreaty, or any other unworthy motive'.[3] In response, Henry directed the Spiritual and Temporal Lords of England to sign a request to Clement, 'praying him to consent to the King's desires' and to 'point out the evils which arise from delaying the divorce'.[4] In addition, Henry petitioned the European universities for their opinion on his situation. The answers from France, Italy and Germany were mixed and, closer to home, Cambridge ruled in favour of Catherine, while Oxford concluded, on 8 April 1530, that it was 'forbidden by divine and natural law for a Christian to marry his deceased brother's wife'.[5]

There was little that Anne could do but wait. No doubt she and Henry discussed the developments regularly, sharing their joint disappointment or joy at each new setback or triumph. The king recruited theologians, debated and read widely, summoning books from his different palaces and calling for certain abbots to send him inventories of their libraries, so that he could see what resources were available to him.[6] Anne's gender excluded her from the more formal of these interactions and her position as Henry's 'mistress' made it indelicate, even inappropriate, for her to play an active role in pursuing the divorce. Yet there is no doubt that she made her feelings clear to Henry, and maintained her circle of supporters, being a powerful and imposing figure at court in her own right. Letters and dispatches of the time, both in her favour and those of her opponents, reveal the general understanding that her influence over the king was significant. He was the outwardly active force in terms of pursuing the divorce, but Anne's voice was powerful behind the scenes. Rarely separated from Henry, her life was a blend of the regular domestic routines that her gender and status dictated, as well as travel and entertainments with the king, all underscored by their constant mutual theme, their desire to become man and wife.

Anne still had her own establishment at court, separate from that of Catherine, whom she avoided as much as possible. The personal nature of Henry's monarchy, in which all decisions and power was invested in a single individual, meant that his interactions with Anne could be determined according to his own desire. His kingship and policies were inseparable from his own self. To a large extent, he could organise his time and decide who would be permitted access to his person, in his personal chambers and during times of retirement, and for how long. Henry used this as a facet of his majesty as the Sun King would at Versailles, to confer favouritism, which resulted in power and influence for those who had the king's ear and, also, as a tool to distance those rejected, to keep ambassadors waiting and to prevent Wolsey from regaining his sympathy. Thus, he might visit Anne in her rooms, invite her to dine and hunt with him, to spend their leisure time together in cards or dice, listening to music, dancing, watching performers and discussion. Sometimes the king was engaged in royal business, pursuing their case, meeting advisors, dictating his correspondence, attending sessions of the Reformation Parliament, from which Anne was excluded. Henry's overwhelming motivation was to marry her, but her presence had clarified the doubts he had already been experiencing regarding the nature of his first marriage and the need to father sons.

Had Henry never met Anne, his need for a son would have sent him down this route, probably resulting in the selection of a European Princess such as Renée of France as his next queen. But he had met Anne, and his love for her became indivisible from the dictates of his conscience, to invalidate his first marriage. In spite of the difficulties they encountered in terms of domestic, European and papal reactions, she remained the primary influence over him as a man, and thus over his policies.

While the machinery of government and Henry's pursuit of his liberty continued to tick over through 1530, a picture of Anne's life at court, at the king's side, emerges of hunting and sports by day, feasting and the playing of music and games at night, broken by meetings and travel. The Privy Purse accounts reveal some of their activities, such as the payments in March that year to the king's minstrels, and for their sport with horses, hounds and hawks.[7] The close-knit circle around Anne also emerges, with names that were to become familiar, or significant, to her during the coming years. Some were employed at court, others were servants or playmates of the king. Some who were less close sought to ingratiate themselves or their families with gifts to Henry, wherever he happened to be. Early in 1530, rewards were given to the servants of Lady Weston, either the mother or wife of Francis, for bringing Henry her gift of some baked bream, and those of Lady Anne Sidney, who brought orange pies to the king. They were known to Anne, through their residence at Penshurst. Henry Norris was recompensed for having purchased the hose for the king's boys, as was Thomas Heneage, who paid those who brought sturgeon, and Henry also paid the minstrels of Charles Brandon, Duke of Suffolk.[8]

Anne's family and allies feature among the accounts too, with a record of the payment of Thomas Boleyn's expenses, the settling of a bet won by George Boleyn on a tennis match played between the king and Francis Weston, Henry's games of dice with Norfolk. Sir Edward Boleyn, Anne's paternal uncle, was rewarded with the large sum of £10 for bringing the king a gelding. A 'Master Baynton', who is included for winning a bet against the king on a tennis match played between Thomas Knyvett and Edward Seymour, was Edward Baynton, an ardent religious reformer who would become Anne's Vice-Chancellor. In March, there was also a payment made of £5 for a sermon preached by Hugh Latimer,[9] who had gained his degree in 1524 with a disputation on the religious reforms emerging from Europe. Latimer was a member of a group meeting at the White Horse Tavern in Cambridge to promote the translation of the Bible, a group that included the well-known heretics and future martyrs, Robert Barnes and Thomas Bilney. In 1528, he had received a warning from Wolsey for his activities, but with the cardinal's fall, and Henry's changing priorities, Latimer's career was on the rise.

Wherever Henry was in 1530, the chances are that Anne was there too. That April he was at The More, where he healed the sick and summoned several pairs of virginals to be brought from Greenwich for his entertainment.[10] In May, a payment of 5 shillings was made to one in reward for bringing home Ball, the king's dog who was lost in Waltham Forest, suggesting that Henry and Anne were visiting the Abbey again.[11] Soon after this, they were at York Place and then, as one witness observed, 'the king and queen are this day at Hampton Court, with the Lady Anne'.[12] Anne is likely to have attended a wedding on 26 May, on which occasion the young page 'Master Weston' was married, with Henry making a contribution of £6 13s 4d towards the event. Having been a page at court since the age of around fifteen, Francis Weston was now nineteen and his bride was Anne Pickering, daughter of Sir Christopher of Killington in Cumberland. In 1532, he would be promoted to the role of Gentleman of the Privy Chamber. The tailor and skinner who were paid for their workmanship and 'certain stuff' for Lady Anne, may have contributed towards her clothes for the wedding.[13]

On 14 June, Catherine had an audience with her husband that lasted for some time. Her attempt to dissuade him from his current course of action was more than simply personal; she believed she was acting as a queen, with dignity and concern for her country and the soul of its king, the man she had married and still loved. For Catherine, Henry's soul was in peril and she was the instrument of his salvation. She exhorted him to 'be again to her a good prince and husband, and to quit the evil life he was leading and the bad example he was setting, and that even if he would shew no regard for her, who was, as he well knew, his true and lawful wife, that he should at least respect God and his conscience'. She added that Henry should not ignore the words of the pope in forbidding him to remarry until their case had been judged. After 'many words and much commendation of those who had written in his favour', Henry replied that the pope was simply 'compelled to act as the Emperor wished' and then 'left the room abruptly without saying another word'.[14] Anne had previously warned Henry not to allow Catherine another private interview with him, recognising that the queen's intelligence and single-mindedness meant she would always get the upper hand. Anne cannot have been pleased to hear of this encounter.

Another incident from the same month illustrates the tension under which the three were living. It is related by the ambassador Chapuys, drawn largely from rumour and court gossip, but still illustrative of the atmosphere. Chapuys described how Catherine was still making Henry's shirts, a task she had always willingly done, as her mother had for her father. It was not a necessary chore, as the king was well provided for with seamstresses, but it was a symbolic gesture, an intimate act of service, which the king was loath to strip from his wife, understanding its significance to her. When Henry sent her some cloth, 'begging her to have it made into shirts for him', Anne sent for the bearer of the cloth, one of Henry's Gentlemen of the Bedchamber, and interrogated him. 'Although the King himself confessed that the cloth had been taken to the Queen by his order,' the ambassador explained, 'she abused the bearer' in Henry's presence, threatening to have him severely punished. There was also talk at court of some of the officers of the Royal Household being dismissed to please Anne, following on from the dismissals at Anne's request of three women from Catherine's household 'in whom she (the queen) found more comfort and consolation than in any others'.[15]

In the early summer, the sports, games and gifts continued. The Privy Purse entries illuminate the different nature of the interactions these individuals had with the king, some distant and some direct, determined by class. Some were tradesmen presenting bills like the man named Scawesby paid 4s 8d for bringing bows, arrows and shooting gloves for Anne.[16] Others were employed in important households and were fulfilling errands, such as the servant of the mayor of London who was rewarded on 5 June for bringing cherries for Anne. The servant pocketed the tip for his pains but the credit and goodwill for the gift went to the mayor. Some were close associates, even friends. On 12 June, the king made a payment of £40 to William Brereton, one of four brothers from Cheshire who were employed at court.[17] William was slightly older than Henry, having been born in the late 1480s. He had married in 1529, to Elizabeth Somerset, a second cousin of the king on the Beaufort side, and had been a groom of the Privy Chamber since 1524, rising in Henry's favour. By mid-June, the court had moved to Windsor, where cakes were sent to the king from the provost of nearby Eton College, founded by Henry VI.[18] As well as the practice of gift-giving in order to help secure patronage, items were brought to the court to ensure a fresh supply for the royal table, often by the king's gardeners from other local properties. While Henry was at Woking, or Oking, on 8 July, payment was made to a servant bringing fresh herbs from the garden at York Place, as well as an individual who brought carp and bream. Also during this stay, 10s was paid to a servant of Sir Francis Bryan for bringing the king a hound and, on 19 July, a Frenchman sold the king two clocks at Woking, receiving a payment of £15.[19]

It was during this time that Henry took the decision to continue his liquidation of Wolsey's assets. Having retreated in disgrace the previous winter and relinquished his secular titles and properties, the cardinal had been left with no living save that of his appointment as Archbishop of York. In February, Henry had allowed him a generous pension, with additional funds for his food and clothing, along with furishings and plate. The condition, however, was that he was not permitted to return to

York Place, so although he had never before visited the city of York, he was now forced to head north and take up residence there. At this point, it appeared that the former favourite might still live out his final years with some dignity, in quiet contemplation. Yet Wolsey's character was such that he would never have been content with a near-monastic existence. He had lived well for too long, at the heart of the court, accustomed to all the advantages it could offer. He could not suppress the sense of entitlement that bubbled up around all his protestations of humility.

Wolsey arrived in York on 28 April 1530, but found conditions at the archbishop's palace of Southwell to be far inferior to the standard he had expected, and wrote to Henry to complain of this, 'wrapped in misery', requesting to be sent quails for his table. Yet he was to receive less, not more, and his secretary Cromwell advised him to be more cautious in his communications. On 20 July, Henry dissolved the college Wolsey had founded at Ipswich and siphoned off its funds, then ordered that all the cardinal's coats of arms at his Oxford college should be replaced with the king's own. Sir James Boleyn was responsible for overseeing the acquisition of Wolsey's goods in Norfolk, Sir Francis Bryan received his lands that were part of the priory of Raunston, while Edward Seymour and the Abbot of Waltham also profited.[20] Wolsey's own letter to Cromwell was full of pathos:

Trusts that he will show himself his friend and comfort. If he knew his increasing heaviness of mind, his gentle heart would have compassion on him. Though he has quieted his m[ind with his] assurance concerning the inquisitions of the lands app[ertaining to] his archbishoprie, such bruits and opp[inions] have sprung up in these parts that he is weary of hearing them. There is nothing here [but] lamentation and mourning, not knowyng sertenly [what will follow]. I pray God that I may be once in repose, and [regard] may be had to my poor estate and old servys.[21]

Wolsey followed this with an emotional letter to Henry, exiled and unwell, hoping to remind the king of his long years of service:

Most gracyous soverayn lorde and mercyfull prince, prostrate at your Majesty's feet, wtth weepyng tears, this shall be in moste reverente and humble maner to recomende unto your excellente charyte and goodness the poore college of Oxford, which for the great zeal and affection that your Grace beareth to good letters, vertue, and nourishing of learning, and in consideration of my painfull and long continued service, [your Grace was] contented that I should erect, found and establish. And where, notwithstandyng my convyction in the præmynere, of your most excellent nature which hathe ever been more [incli]nd and propensyd to clemency and mercy then to rigor and severyte, it hath pleasyd your Highness to your perpetuall merit, honour, and renowne to imparte your mercy, [li]berallyte, and bountifulness unto me, for the which I accept myself of all creatures living to be most obliged and bounden unto Your Majesty.[22]

Such emotional pleas would do Wolsey little good.

That June, Thomas Boleyn's efforts to woo Francis to Henry's cause finally began to pay off. The Sorbonne was in the process of considering their verdict on the divorce when the French king wrote to the President of Paris, making explicit his desired outcome:

Is much dissatisfied with the conduct of Beda and others at the assembly of divines at Paris, who met to give an opinion on the king of England's divorce. The President must order him to correct his fault, else Francis will punish him. If he say it is a matter of conscience on which he must consult the Pope, you must forbid him, as this would be against the rights and privileges of the kingdom. If hereafter he (Francis) should happen to be at war with the Pope, there is nothing in the said kingdom from which he would more vigorously defend himself, in virtue of the said privileges, than from the Gallican council and the faculty of Theology.[23]

For added weight when it came to the Sorbonne's decision, the Duke of Norfolk wrote to Anne de Montmorency, Constable of France:

Thanks him for his devotion to England, and for his entertainment, and assistance given from time to time to Sir Francis Bryan. The King had fully expected a perfect resolution, by this time, on his matter proposed to the university of Paris; but he has been informed by his agents there that the matter is strangely altered; for whereas 56 doctors had been instructed on his side, and 7 on the opposite side, at the Congregation lately held there were 36 doctors opposed to his purpose, and only 22 on his side. This looks suspicious. I trust you will use your influence with your master to obtain the desired object at Paris.[24]

In return for Francis's support, Henry assisted with the negotiations for the liberation of the Dauphin and his brother, who had taken his place as hostages of the Emperor after the French defeat at Pavia. On 8 July, hearing that the boys were finally released, Henry wrote that he had as much joy of the news as if they were his own sons.

At the start of July, the thirty-four doctors of law at the University of Padua ruled that the pope had been wrong to grant the dispensation back in 1503 for Henry to marry Catherine, and extracts of their discussion that were favourable to his cause were dispatched for his use.[25] The very next day, the sentence of the faculty of theology of the University of Paris was passed, also in favour of the king, and the Italian University at Ferrara followed suit. Yet agents of the Emperor in Paris had threatened Henry's supporters at the Sorbonne, drawing up a list of his supporters,[26] as the king's former tutor in Greek, Richard Croke, informed him from Italy. Henry's Yorkist cousin, Reginald Pole, a Catholic theologian, who had fled into exile rather than support the divorce, also wrote about subterfuge at the Sorbonne:

> The conclusion of the divines in the university of Paris in 'your great matter' was 'achieved' according to the King's (Francis's) purpose on Saturday last; but the sealing of the same has been put off, and to this day the King's agents have not been able to obtain it. The adverse party use every means to 'embecyll' the whole determination, that it may not take effect. The bearer, Mr. Fox, has used great diligence and prudence in withstanding them; whose presence he had urged at the first breaking of the matter among the faculty.[27]

As expected by by Henry and Anne, the Spanish universities of Salamanca and of Alcalá de Henares, the birthplace of Catherine of Aragon, ruled that 'marriage with a deceased brother's wife is not contrary to divine law'.[28]

The summer progress of 1530 was slow to start, with Henry and Anne initially staying close to home, perhaps awaiting further news from the European universities. On 29 July, the accounts show that a man brought a glass of rosewater from Guildford to the king at Windsor, but the court had moved to Hampton Court by the middle of August, when philiberts and damsons were presented to Henry by his gardeners from Richmond.[29] They would have been made into desserts or sauces, or else cooked with meat or fish on the huge roaring fires of the kitchens, and set before the king and Anne. Just days after this, they left Surrey and removed forty miles north to the College of Bonshommes, a thirteenth-century religious order at Ashridge, on the Hertfordshire border near Berkhamsted. With the reformation parliament heavily critical of the abuses of the church, a visit from the king may have caused some alarm. By 1530, the establishment was already being warned that the brethren needed to live more strictly and desist from moral lapses, such as eating and drinking between meals, profiting from selling items to the house and allowing women to stay there. It is unlikely that Henry witnessed any of this behaviour during his visit, when the best hospitality would have been on offer from the recently appointed rector, Thomas Waterhouse, elected in 1529. During Henry's stay, the servant of Sir Edward Donne brought him a buck, to be taken down to the monastic kitchen and prepared, and a payment was made to the keeper of Berkamsted Park nearby, where Henry and Anne may have ridden or hunted.[30]

In the final week of August, the court removed twenty miles north to Ampthill in Bedfordshire, where there was a royal lodge and hunting park. Henry and Anne put the facilities to good use, rewarding Lord Buckley's servant with 40s for bringing hawks and greyhounds to them and giving rewards to the keeper of the park, his wife and two helpers, for fishing there. Their evenings were spent in gentler pursuits, with £4 paid to Peter Tabaret and John Bolenger, the king's minstrels for their performances.[31] By 5 September, they had travelled the thirty miles south-east to Hertford Castle, which had been in royal hands for centuries. Lemons and oranges were brought to the king there on 5 September by a James Hobart and, two days later, Jasper, gardener at Beaulieu in Essex, thirty miles to the east, was rewarded for bringing artichokes, cucumbers and other herbs.[32] From Hertford, it was a short distance of thirteen miles directly south to Waltham Abbey, where the court stayed between 11 and 20 September. During their stay, £5 12s 6d was paid to George, Lord Rochford, for shooting at the nearby house of Hunsden, and a payment was made for the finding of a buck and hounds in Waltham forest where, like the king's dog Ball the previous year, they had become lost.[33]

It may have been while they were at Hertford or, more likely, after they had moved twenty-five miles east to The More on 23 September, that Henry and Anne received a letter from Gregory Casale in Rome containing a bizarre offer from the pope. Clement had taken Casale aside and secretly proposed that Henry might be allowed to have two wives, to have formal papal permission to commit bigamy if it would resolve their dispute. Casale replied that he could not accept the offer 'because I did not know whether it would satisfy your Majesty's conscience' and promised to put the question to Henry.[34] Given the king's well-known scruples about the legality of his union with Catherine, this solution was unlikely to find his favour but, by this point, his desire to marry Anne might have led him to be tempted. However, the thought of any shadow of doubt cast over the legitimacy of their future children would have been enough to make him dismiss the idea. There was another sour note struck whilst they were at The More, when compensation was paid for a cow that was killed by hounds owned by Anne and Urian Brereton, brother of Francis.[35]

A strange note made by ambassador Chapuys at the end of November gives pause for thought. He recorded that the Duchess of Norfolk, Anne's aunt by marriage, Elizabeth Howard (née Stafford), had sent a gift to Queen Catherine of 'volaille' or poultry, possibly duck, and an orange.

Chapuys believed this gift was a cover by which to conceal a letter from Gregory Casale in Rome, the contents of which the ambassador did not know. However, he could report that Catherine believed Elizabeth had done this 'out of regard for her', which is plausible, as the duchess had first come to court in her early teens in 1509, when Catherine became queen, and had served her as a lady-in-waiting. No doubt a friendship and ties of loyalty had developed over the years, leading the Duchess to sympathise with the queen's plight in spite of her family connection to Anne. Elizabeth was also the daughter of the Duke of Buckingham, executed by Henry in 1521, so she understood how it felt to be abandoned and disgraced by the king. She also had a volatile relationship with her husband, so may have been acting out a desire to oppose his loyalties. Chapuys feared the motive was less pure, believing Elizabeth had sent the gift 'with the knowledge of her husband, as a means of entering into some secret communication' with Catherine.[36] If this was the case, it would imply that Norfolk was dissatisfied with Anne, as he had become by 1535, but at this early stage, there was still all to play for in terms of the family's rise. Norfolk may have found Anne difficult, or wilful, even insulting, as Chapuys' later letters imply, but in 1530 he was still supportive of her bid to become queen. It may be that Norfolk knew nothing of his wife's gift, which was given in sympathy from one woman to another, or that it was an attempt to open a channel of communication with the queen as a double bluff, to feed information about her activites back to Anne, or Norfolk.

Thomas Wolsey was arrested on 4 November, being taken by surprise at the arrival of guests after dinner. By a twist of irony that may have been deliberate, it was Henry Percy, Earl of Northumberland, who was sent north to arrest the man who had prevented him from marrying Anne Boleyn. Percy was to bring Wolsey to London, in anticipation of imprisonment and a trial, which instilled a terrible fear into the cardinal. The intention was for him to be 'lodged in the same chamber in the Tower where the Duke of Buckingham was detained', with all the ominous connotations of the Duke's execution, but the cause of his arrest, the charges, were 'mere conjecture'.[37] Immediately after his arrest, his physician, Dr Augustine, was questioned and made some form of deposition against Wolsey, which must have contributed to the case against him. As Chapuys related, he 'remained for some days without food, hoping rather to finish his life in this way than in a more shameful one', but this did not stop Percy from setting out with his prisoner.[38] They had reached Leicester when Wolsey was taken ill.

According to Cavendish, Wolsey was in no doubt about who his real enemy was, and that he believed he would have found royal favour again, as the signs indicated early in 1530, if it had not been for Anne. Cavendish's account likens Anne to the Biblical serpent, encouraging Henry with sexual temptation, a creature of darkness. 'There was a continual serpentine enemy about the king,' he wrote, 'that would, I am well assured, if I had been found stiff-necked, (have) called continually upon the king in his ear (I mean the night crow) with such vehemency that I should (with the help of her assistance) have obtained sooner the king's indignation than his lawful favour.'[39] Chapuys also believed that Anne was behind Wolsey's end, writing that 'nothing would satisfy the Lady short of the Cardinal's arrest'.[40]

Chapuys recorded more court gossip which, if true, suggests there was a real danger that Henry would reinstate Wolsey, and that Anne did influence him heavily to bring about his arrest:

A gentleman told me that a short time ago the King was complaining to his Council of something that was not done according to his liking, and said in a rage that the Cardinal was a better man than any of them for managing matters; and repeating this twice, he left them. The Duke, the lady, and the father have not ceased since then to plot against the Cardinal; especially the lady, who does not cease to weep and regret her lost time and her honor, threatening the King that she would leave him, in such sort that the King has had much trouble to appease her; and though the King prayed her most affectionately, even with tears in his eyes, that she would not speak of leaving him, nothing would satisfy her except the arrest of the Cardinal.[41]

The pretext for the arrest is said to be that he had written to Rome asking to be reinstated in his ecclesiastical possessions, and to France also for support and credit, and that he was actually beginning to resume his former habits of pomp and splendour, and trying to corrupt the people.[42]

This may have been the case. The nature of Tudor realpolitik may have led Anne to believe that her position would only be secure once the former great influences over Henry, Wolsey and Catherine, were both eradicated. They were rivals for the king's attention and favour, at a court where everything depended upon personal relationships and, while the gender question ensured that Catherine's age counted against her as a wife, Wolsey, at the age of fifty-seven, could potentially rise again. At some future point, the pendulum could swing back and he might be able to damage Anne. Anne's desire to be rid of him was a recognition of his extraordinary abilities and the extent of the influence he had enjoyed over Henry. It would have been a prudent move, but it may not have been she who actually made it.

The theory that Anne hated Wolsey rests on the testaments of those who had reason to dislike her. It is a tragedy for Anne, and for her biographers, that the most prolific recorders of her life were also her self-confessed enemies. Cavendish's account is almost hagiographical in its desire to rehabilitate his former master's reputation and Chapuys had been given an express mission by the pope to support the saintly Catherine. Cromwell believed that none at court dared speak to the king on Wolsey's behalf after his fall, for fear of displeasing Anne, but this may have been his perception, or a reflection of the regrouping of court factions. This view may have also been designed to conceal the harsh truth from Wolsey, that he had few friends left by 1530, having alienated the nobility by successive domestic policies that complicated or diminished their legal capabilities and status.[43] He had identified and attacked aristocratic abuses of power in the Star Chamber, purged the court of Henry's young favourites and caused bad feeling, even revolt, with his unfortunately named Amicable Grant, the forced loan of 1525 that had failed to raise funds. However, the recorder of this anti-Wolsey feeling, Polydore Vergil, also had an axe to grind, having been briefly imprisoned by the cardinal for having written critically about the pope. If Anne disliked Wolsey, she was not alone; the surviving letters she wrote to him in the late 1520s are courtly and polite, in keeping with the formal tone of mutual patronage. Later, she responded to his distress with sympathy and restraint, showing herself to feel for his woe but not willing to intercede on his behalf, an act which could have been construed as overstepping a political line and opposing Henry. Chapuys reported that she had sent a servant to visit the cardinal in 1529, with an offer to intercede with Henry, but Chapuys considered this was motivated by dissimulation and intrigue on her part, rather than genuine concern. No evidence survives that indicates Anne did send such a servant. In the spring of 1530, after Wolsey had been forgiven, Anne did join Henry in sending the cardinal a token of good will in the form of a ring, which gave him a brief surge of hope. In her own words to Henry at Grafton Manor in 1529, she only had one cause, and that was the cause of the king. She adjusted her outward behaviour towards the cardinal to match that of the king. What she inwardly felt about Wolsey was never recorded.

Wolsey's most powerful political opponent may not have been Anne, but her uncle, the Duke of Norfolk. Like Anne, the ambitious Thomas Howard recognised that his enemy's exceptional skills may lead to his restoration, and that swift action was required to prevent this. Norfolk coveted Wolsey's position of influence over Henry and, in fact, did go on to become the king's chief minister after the cardinal's fall, at the apex of a triangle of which Suffolk and Thomas Boleyn formed the lower angles.

In mid-1530, when warned by an ally that there was a real chance of Wolsey's return, 'the Duke began to swear vehemently, declaring that sooner than allow the Cardinal's return to favour… he would eat him up alive'.[44] When Wolsey's doctor, Dr Augustine, was arrested in November, it was to Norfolk's London house that he was taken to be interrogated, possibly by the Duke himself, or if not, upon his explicit instructions.[45] Norfolk also invited the Papal Nuncio to his house on 29 November, to try and obtain a cardinalcy for his candidate, Girolamo Ghinucci, reputedly on Henry's instigation. Then, having heard of the pope's latest directive against Anne, he attacked:

> The Duke took the Nuncio apart, and told him that the King felt great surprise at his not having been informed of the letters received from Rome, and was still more surprised and annoyed at what His Holiness had said to his ambassadors on the subject of a last monition of excommunication and the dismissal of the Lady from Court. This (the Duke added) was a most outrageous measure on the part of His Holiness, and such as he (the King) had not deserved on any grounds, since he had always shewn himself a dutiful son of the Church, and had never offended him intentionally in any respect.[46]

Wolsey's fall may have been welcomed by Anne, who recognised him as a rival for Henry's favour, but the active political power urging the events of his downfall forward was the triumvirate of Norfolk, Suffolk and Wiltshire. There was no doubt that Anne was powerful: in many ways she was a skilled, shrewd and influential politician, but her field of influence was relegated by her gender to the informal, expressing her desires through emotions, conversation, suggestions, exchanges that occurred largely behind the scenes. When it came to toppling such a figure as Wolsey, she was the representative of a faction which embodied the very fabric of the court; class, aristocracy and patronage, and brought its considerable weight to bear against the cardinal when he was at his weakest.

Wolsey died at Leicester on 29 November, at the age of fifty-seven. He had been unwell for years and, no doubt, his disgrace and arrest were significant factors, but Chapuys reported a rumour that 'he took or was given something to hasten his end':

> On Monday the captain of the guard arrived to conduct him to London, and both supped together cheerfully enough. Soon after, however, the Cardinal was taken violently ill, so much so that it was thought he could not live through the night; yet he lingered till Wednesday.[47]

The king's most able servant was buried at Leicester, in the church that Chapuys described as 'the Tyrant's Grave' because it already contained the bones of Richard III. George Cavendish was summoned to Hampton Court to describe his master's final hours to Henry, after which the king made the comment that he would give £20,000 to have Wolsey alive again. It was an easy sum to wish away, now that the cardinal was dead.

In other areas, the event unleashed reactions that indicated how far the question of class underpinned the hatred that had been directed towards Wolsey, even by those whom he had considered to be his friends. Whilst he had enjoyed Henry's backing, few would have dared comment upon the man's humble origins, which were believed at the time to dictate character, the opposite side of the coin to Castiglone's belief that noble birth imparted admirable qualities. Birth counted for everything, yet Henry was unusual in facilitating the rise of a number of individuals from the lower and middle classes, due to their exceptional ability. Along with Wolsey, Thomas More, Thomas Cranmer, Hugh Latimer and Thomas Cromwell would all rise further than their origins indicated, a fact of which they and their contemporaries were acutely aware. Meritocracy was not an easy bedfellow with aristocracy. Francis I, whom Wolsey had hoped might come to his aid, now commented to Francis Bryan that 'so pompous and vicious a heart, sprung out of so vile a stock, would once show forth the baseness of his nature' against the king who 'hath raised him from low degree to high dignity'.[48] Thomas Boleyn commissioned actors to create and perform a play, printed and distributed upon the orders of Norfolk, entitled *Of the Descent of the Cardinal into Hell*.

Wolsey's death unleashed a torrent of abuse against him. This was typical of the vulnerability of those whom Henry raised for their merit through his personal favour. Whilst Wolsey, or others, retained royal approval, any less socially desirable qualities, such as national, cultural, class or gender differences, might be tolerated, but the withdrawal of that favour gave permission for these weaknesses to be targeted. For those who overreached their social position at court, those humble origins were their hamartia. In many cases this proved to be the gateway through which their enemies might attack.

Reputedly, the news of Wolsey's death gave Anne confidence. She became 'fiercer than a lioness', and dared to take a shot at her remaining enemy, saying that she 'wished all the Spaniards were at the bottom of the sea' and would rather see Catherine 'hanged than have to confess that she was her queen and mistress'.[49] Anne was in her ascendancy and did not see her own areas of vulnerability. With Wolsey it was class. With Anne, it would be gender.

TWENTY-FOUR

Stalemate 1531

On 23 December 1530, while the English court was gathering at Greenwich for the Christmas season, a secret meeting was taking place over a thousand miles away. Recovering after being ravaged by the Emperor's troops, the Apostolic Palace at Rome was the chosen location for a gathering of the cardinals of the Catholic Church. One by one, they trooped through its corridors in their red robes and hats, in a building that had become metonymic with the papacy. Michelangelo had recently completed its Sistine Chapel, where the story of the downfall of Adam and Eve, eagerly reaching for the apple of temptation, stretched over the heads of the cardinals assembled below. The recent disgrace and death of one of their number, the only Englishman among them, cannot have increased their sympathy when they came to consider Henry's plight.

Cardinal Innocenzo Cibo read aloud the letter that Henry had written to Clement on 7 December, complaining that he had found it impossible to 'obtain from the Pope and order that his matrimonial cause be proceeded with out of Rome' and requesting that the cause might be decided in England. The pope opened the discussion with the directive that 'this business ought to be ripely discussed, and treated with the greatest consideration'. A report was given by Paulus de Capisuccis, Dean of the Roman Rota, the highest tribunal of the church, which presented the recent appeal of Queen Catherine. She asked the pope to forbid the Archbishop of Canterbury and all other English prelates from having the power to rule on the matter, delegating it entirely to Rome. She also requested that Clement confirm all the existing inhibitions imposed upon the case, to forbid Henry to 'cohabit with any other woman, and especially a certain lady Anne, or to contract marriage, and in case that such a marriage should be contracted, to declare it null and void'. Furthermore, Catherine petitioned that the pope 'should forbid the said lady Anne, and all women in general, to contract marriage with the king of England'. After long deliberations among the cardinals, they ruled in

Catherine's favour, concluding that the 'afore-mentioned petitions were justifiable in law' and that the briefs should be granted.[1]

Oblivious to this ruling about their fate, Henry and Anne's preparations went ahead for the festive season at Greenwich. In December, Anne received a payment of 20s in silver, £5 for 'playing money' and £13 for linen cloth, for 'shirts and other necessaries', while £80 went to the skinner Adyngton, for the furring of her gowns. The Privy Purse records further expenses that might have contributed towards Anne's gifts that season, with Italian jeweller John Baptist receiving an initial 1,225 crowns, followed by 1,601 for pearls and an Alart Plymmer being paid a huge 7,437 crowns for various jewels. £100 was also given to Anne to contribute towards the purchase of gifts that she would distribute at New Year.[2]

Catherine had been unwell in November and stayed away from court, but she had recovered sufficiently to return to Greenwich in time for the festive celebrations, which lasted until Twelfth Night. Anne cannot have welcomed her presence, hearing of her rival dining with Henry and sitting beside him in estate in the great hall, 'where as were divers interludes, rich masks and disportes, and after that a great banquet'.[3] Briefly, the appearance of harmony between the royal couple was resumed, but it was only an illusion, another of Henry's performances. With the death of Wolsey and the rulings of many of the universities being returned in their favour, Henry and Anne were more determined than ever to be married; it was a question of how they might accomplish this in a legal sense, so that their union and thus their children were considered legitimate. Catherine might have been sitting in the great hall while Anne presided over her own celebrations in her chambers, but the rumour at court was that she would soon be queen, and that the marriage would 'undoubtedly be accomplished in this parliament'.[4] Perhaps Henry and Anne also believed this was the case, before they heard of the cardinals' ruling.

Bad news of a different kind arrived in England at the start of 1531, of the death of Margaret of Savoy. Seventeen years after Anne had arrived in her court at Malines, she may have considered that she had much to thank Margaret for, given the opportunities and education Anne had received, and the polish and connections she had acquired. Margaret's Mechelen household had provided Anne with her first experience of life at a royal court, in the largest European dynasty of its time, and the example of a strong, ruling woman. She never, according to the surviving records, expressed the kind of affection for Margaret as she did for Marguerite d'Alençon, and her stay in the Netherlands ended abruptly and perhaps with some awkwardness, but the news must have given Anne pause to remember her youth.

Having come to consider his former friend as an enemy to his divorce, Henry's response to her death was crass to say the least. 'The death of Madame (Margaret) is regretted by those who have intercourse with Flanders,' Chapuys wrote to console Charles, who was his aunt's sole heir. 'I am told the king of England said it was no great loss for the world. He delights in everything that is to the disadvantage of your Majesty; but these are not things to take notice of, for the blindness of his miserable *amour* makes him talk indiscreetly. One reason why he is glad of Madame's death is because she took great interest in the Queen's matter, and also because she was the real means of concluding the amity with France.'[5] The cardinals' decision was delivered to Henry in a letter dated 5 January:

At the request of the Queen, forbids Henry to remarry until the decision of the case, and declares that if he does all issue will be illegitimate. Forbids any one in England, of ecclesiastical or secular dignity, universities, parliaments, courts of law, &c., to make any decision in an affair the judgment of which is reserved for the Holy See. The whole under pain of excommunication. As Henry would not receive a former citation, this is to be affixed to the church gates of Bruges, Tournay, and other towns in the Low Countries, which will be sufficient promulgation.[6]

Clement's accompanying letter was firm in its decision. It took the opportunity to remind Henry of how far he had departed from his former position in relation to the church. Clement entreated the king 'to consult his better nature alone' and, recalling his title of Defender of the Faith, to 'peaceably arrange this cause' or else to 'acquiesce in the judgement of the Holy See'. Clement warned that 'if scandals and calamities arise, they must be laid to the charge of those who have been the authors of this evil'. The letter attempted to reach out the hand of friendship to England, with Clement's comment that 'however bitter the King's letter may be, (he) will never forget their ancient amity'. He added that:

We will speak with you as a friend, and beg of you to put away the false suspicion you have conceived of us. There are many things in your letters in which we miss your usual wisdom, and even your modesty, especially in that reiterated taunt that we are governed by the Emperor... When we have, we shall act impartially; but we must request of you not to demand in this more than duty allows us to grant. If you persist, we shall be sorry; but even if we do not give you satisfaction in the matter of law, we shall diminish nothing of our affection to you.[7]

In spite of its flashes of warmth, the letter left Henry in little doubt that this was a question for his conscience. He would be considered responsible for the ill-effects of a situation he had created. In the space of a decade, he had gone from being the author of a tract in defence of the pope, to the 'author of evil'.[8]

Henry did not react well. Chapuys reported that 'on the 11th the King received letters from Rome... which did not please him much, nor the Lady either,'[9] and even more explicitly, 'I hear the King was never in greater perplexity than since the last news from Rome, and that neither he nor the Lady sleeps at nights.'[10] In addition, as the ambassador reported, Luther had come out against the divorce, 'which has increased the King's headache and restlessness'.[11] The unwelcome news may even have led to tension and sharp words between Henry and Anne, although the source for their dispute was not one close to the court. The Imperial ambassador, Micer Miguel Mai, reported to a number of interested parties in Europe that he had been told that Henry 'has quarrelled with his Lady, Mistress Anne, because she had ill-treated a gentleman in his presence, but that they afterwards reconciled themselves with each other. According to what happens generally in such cases, their love will be greater than before.'[12] Not everyone was so generous when it came to interpreting their relationship. Another of Charles's informants, the Neapolitan Giovan Muxetula, Henry 'had been crying very much in consequence of the quarrel he had had with his mistress; and that the theologians advised him to cry for the discharge of his conscience'.[13] He had heard from the pope, who had heard from France, 'that the king of England is so passionately in love with the woman whom he wishes to marry, that, having some difference with her, he summoned certain of her relations, and implored them with tears to make peace'.[14] Muxetula, and probably his sources too, considered this to be emasculating and embarrassing; Henry had forgotten to behave in the manner his rank required: 'By this he has shown himself so forgetful of what is right, and of his dignity and authority, that everybody thinks little of him, as of a man who is acting against his truth, honor, and conscience.'[15]

Towards the end of February, Chapuys believed that Henry had been intimidated by the papal response, 'of which he has very great dread, for all his bragging'.[16] The ambassador thought that the king 'was intending, seeing that he would ultimately be compelled to it, to separate the lady from him' and had been told that Henry was 'putting in order for her a house that he gave her some time ago'. Chapuys did not expect that situation to last long, though, anticipating that the king would soon recall her, but hoping that once Anne was sent away, 'God and the Queen will guard against her return'.[17] Chapuys probably misread the signs.

There are no other indications that Henry was intending to send Anne away from court, although she may have left temporarily, or kept her distance from him, following their recent quarrel. The ambassador soon realised his mistake, commenting that 'instead of talking about sending away the Lady, she remains more openly acknowledged than ever'.[18] Now, he thought that 'if the Pope had ordered the Lady to be separated from the King, the King would never have pretended to claim sovereignty over the Church; for, as far as I can understand, she and her father have been the principal cause of it'.[19] At Shrovetide, 1531, Henry and Anne feasted the French ambassador, in such style that Chapuys thought it would guarantee Francis's support for their marriage.[20]

In response to the pope's ruling in favour of Catherine, Henry began to amass a large amount of literature on the topic of the divorce, both for and against. Among the books and documents were reports from the universities and lists of the doctors according to which side they had voted, treaties and opinions on the marriage of Catherine and Arthur, depositions of witnesses from their wedding in 1501, copies of the original brief issued by Julius II in 1503, to permit Henry to marry Catherine, and a copy of the objection Henry made to the marriage at the age of 14 in 1505.[21] Among the huge compendium of papers was a list of bachelors of divinity who might be consulted on the divorce and specific treaties by individuals such as Minorite Friar Marcus Genoa of Venice, Edward Lee, Archbishop of York, John, provincial of the Carmelite Friars, quoting Hildebert, Bishop of Le Mans, priest John Abell and a Dr Sherwood. Precedents were sought, with papers recording examples of royal divorce in recent history, questions converning the interpretation of Leviticus, extracts from the gospels and epistles and arguments drawn from the stories of Herod and Judah. There was a statement of arguments against the validity of the queen's appeal to Rome, intended to show that the judges might proceed notwithstanding the revocation of the cause, the case made by the Spanish against the divorce and objections to objections that had been raised.[22] This huge collection of sources, contemporary and ancient, the *Colectanaea Satis Copiosa*, was intended to establish that the king had spiritual supremacy over the church of England and that papal control was a comparatively new imposition.

In tandem with Henry's impasse with the pope, and his preoccupation with theological texts, came a list of grievances from the House of Commons against the clergy. It included the imposition of excessive fines, the clerical occupation of farms to the exclusion of husbandmen and the engagement of the clergy in business, buying and selling wool like merchants. It was a cause of resentment that wealth was kept within the monastic establishments and that little was given in charity to those in need, and that clergymen had their living from their flocks and 'lay in the court in lord's houses', living well, 'and spent nothing on their parishoners'. The education of the clergy was also considered to be important and worthy of reward, because benefices were perceived to not be given out on merit.[23] This was a subject close to Anne's heart, as she would later advocate a policy of redistributing monastic resources for purposes of education and charity. According to William Latimer, who was writing in the reign of Elizabeth, when Anne learned of Henry's intention to suppress any establishments of less than £200 income a year, she instructed Hugh Latimer that, in his next sermon to the king, he should attempt to dissuade him from the act.[24] If this is correct, Anne may have initially favoured a less drastic approach to reform, opening a potential area of conflict with the king. The main closures of the dissolution still lay in the future. Henry and Anne had more in common regarding their reformist ideals than in their disagreements. When Henry moved against the clergy early in 1531, appearing in the Canterbury Convocation to pressure them to paying £100,000 for a general pardon against their many sins, it also came with the condition that they must accept Henry as their 'sole protector and supreme head' of the English church. Although this would not become an act of Parliament until 1534, it moved Anne one step closer to becoming queen.

Parliament had not finished yet. Henry was angered at being forced to restate his position regarding Anne, as the result of some outspoken supporters of Catherine in the House of Commons. It had been claimed that 'the King pursued this divorce out of love for some lady, and not out of any scruple of conscience', leading Henry to respond that 'he was only moved thereto in discharge of his conscience, which, through what he had read and discovered from doctors and universities, was in bad condition by his living with the Queen'.[25] It was Norfolk who interrupted the protesters, reminding them that the king did not intend to discuss the matter, but to conduct necessary business, after which he, Suffolk and the Chancellor, John Bourchier, Lord Berners, took a petition to the Commons to sign. Several bishops swore that the king's marriage was illegal, which pleased Henry greatly.[26] Catherine believed this had happened 'on account of the shameless life he leads with the woman whom he keeps with him, and because he thought that showing them would be enough to make the kingdom consent'.[27] Once again, Anne's opinion was not recorded. That April, business was halted when Parliament was prorogued until the following year, on account of a sudden pestilence that broke out at Westminster.[28]

During the spring of 1531, Henry was still appearing alongside Catherine on feast days and ceremonial occasions, and is only recorded as dining with Anne in public once. This move was intended to prove that his motivation was not that of lust, that he still respected Catherine, that his actions were dictated by questions of conscience. This approach was not particularly successful, as the recent ruling from Rome proved. Worse still, it had caused division between Henry and Anne, who objected to the mixed messages this sent, knowing full well that it had given Catherine and her party cause to hope that the marriage might be restored if only Anne was removed from the picture. Until the summer season when Henry could depart on progress, and live a little more informally, the machinery of court life continued to turn and life for Anne was fairly formal. Catherine's presence was as important symbolically as it was physically, while Henry still permitted her the status and role of his wife and queen. Less obvious and less visible was Anne's establishment, competing with Catherine's for the attention of visiting dignitaries, ambassadors and courtiers, and for the king's time. In terms of protocol, Anne would always have to come second while the king and queen were living under the same roof.

Domestic details of court life survive from the spring of 1531, giving an insight into the life Henry and Anne shared; what they did, where, with whom, and what they ate. If Henry dined with Anne in private, either in her chambers or his, they may have enjoyed the artichokes, baked lampreys, sweet oranges and marmalade that were brought to the king at York Place on 19 March.[29] During inclement weather, they may have been entertained by Thomas the jester, little John the minstrel, John Bolenger, one of the sackbuttes, Arthur the lute player, or Clays the minstrel, and on fine days, enjoyed archery, falconry and exercising the dogs.[30] On 7 April, 44s 7d was paid to a man named Rasmus, one of the armourers, for garnishing a desk with gold 'for my Lady Anne Rochford' and for 'the stuff thereunto belonging'.[31] The names that recur as their companions are Francis Bryan, Francis Weston, and the Knyvett brothers, Edmund and Henry, Boleyn cousins on Anne's mother's side. They occupied the newly acquired York Place, which still rang with the echo of Wolsey's footsteps, and Bridewell Palace, which had been leased to the French Ambassadors, and was soon to become the setting for Holbein's famous painting. With its coded symbols and mysteries, the work depicts Francis I's envoy Jean de Dinteville and Georges de Selve, Bishop of Lavaur, standing before the optical illusion of a flattened skull. Anne's biographer Eric Ives suggests that this now-famous work was commissioned by Anne as Holbein's patron, but while this cannot be ruled out, there is little tangible evidence to support her desire to see a portrait of these two particular individuals completed.

By mid-April, the court had moved to Greenwich, where red deer were brought to the king by a servant of the Earl of Oxford and a payment of

£18 14s 9d was made to William Lylgrave, embroiderer, 'upon his bill for stuff made for lady Anne'. £20 in rent was paid to a Richard Breme for the rent of a house in Greenwich 'wherein my lorde of Rocheford lyeth for 2 years', so as to be close when the court were in residence.[32] One name that features regularly in the accounts is that of Jasper the gardener at Beaulieu Palace in Essex, who was rewarded for bringing herbs and garden produce to the king at various locations.[33] It may have been that the Beaulieu garden was larger or more productive than other royal properties, or perhaps that the estate was then in the possession of George Boleyn, suggesting that the supplies were brought as much for the benefit of Anne and her circle, than for Henry himself.

Anne appears in the records in May, as 40 shillings was paid as her gaming fund and the bill was settled of a Thomas Osborne of London for 8¾ yards of crimson cloth of gold for 'my lady Anne Rochford', at 33s 4d the yard. On 7 May, clothing was transported from Bridewell to Greenwich, where more gifts were brought to the king, of a buck and peascods, and Henry played tennis. He also paid out on some more expensive items, including £100 to Cornelius Hayes, the king's goldsmith, £24 to Anthony Boulloigne, merchant of Paris, for certain jewels that the king's grace bought from him, £173 12s to John Angell for jewels and a sum to Nicholas the astronomer for the mending of a clock.[34]

By 12 June 1531, Henry, Catherine and Anne were at Hampton Court. Wolsey's original plan for a five-quadrangle palace had not yet been completed by the time he had relinquished it to the king in 1526, and had required a further year of work before it was ready. The visiting Venetian, Mario Savorgano, saw it that August complete, recording that, 'with its furniture, it is supposed to have cost the cardinal, who built it, 200,000 crowns. Here there is space for the King to inhabit the centre-floor, the Queen the one above, and the Princess the ground floor; in addition to which there are dwellings for the rest of the Court.'[35] In the high summer of 1531, Hampton Court's imposing brickwork, twisted chimneys and gardens set with carved, painted heraldic beasts, played host to the court. Barges and carts transported the belongings and clothing of the king and queen from Greenwich, along with Anne's wardrobe and personal artifacts, and all the supplies required to sustain the hundreds of courtiers on site. It took eleven men two days to bring the king's necessities from Greenwich, with more servants required to transport his hawks and dogs. Fresh produce in the form of venison, pomegranates, strawberries, artichokes, cherries, oranges and lemons were brought the fifteen miles from Windsor to Hampton Court. A payment of £58 was made to George Boleyn, 'my lord of Rocheford, for shooting with the king's grace' at the archery butts, a sport which appears to have been a particular favourite of the family, given the expenses paid out for Anne in bows, arrows and other equipment.[36] At least a week was spent in the comfort and leisure of the Surrey countryside before Henry was required to return to London. He appears to have been at York Place on 3 July, when his hounds were brought to him, and perhaps when a linnet, a songbird, was brought there, two days earlier.[37] Savorgano recorded his visit to York Place less than a month later, when Henry was not in residence, noting the changes that the king was making to Wolsey's original building:

> I saw a palace, built by the late Cardinal, which now belongs to the King, together with other property of that prelate. The building is now being enlarged; and I saw three so-called 'galleries', which are long porticos and halls, without chambers, with windows on each side, looking on gardens and rivers, the ceiling being marvellously wrought in stone with gold, and the wainscot of carved wood representing a thousand beautiful figures; and round about there are chambers, and very large halls, all hung with tapestries.[38]

By 9 July, Henry had removed to Windsor, where he received cherries, apples, bucks, fish, dogs and hawks, and caused new shooting butts to be built.[39] He, Anne and Catherine were still at Windsor when Henry made the decision to leave the queen forever.

Towards the end of the month, he left without saying goodbye to his wife and rode away with Anne to Guildford. It was the victory Anne had been longing for: neither she nor Henry would ever see Catherine again and Anne would no longer be in direct competition with her for his time, or for precedence at court.

The physical details of Henry and Anne's life together are easy to trace through the Privy Purse accounts, sources such as the State Letters and Papers and the surviving evidence of their world, such as the palaces they inhabited and the portraits painted of the members of their court. It is far more difficult to try to capture the nature of the relationship between them; their feelings, interactions and the balance of power. Anne's role in the relationship is more tenebrous for the historian than Henry's, due to the greater body of evidence relating to him, and the posthumous eradication of material about, and images of, Anne. The king's surviving letters, and his desire to make Anne his wife, leave little doubt about the strength of his feelings for her and the fact that that he was the driving force in the relationship, pursuing her despite her initial reluctance. Some historians have deduced that, in emotional terms, Anne had the upper hand in the relationship, and this appears to be true during these years of their courtship. Much supporting evidence for this lies in the responses of their contemporaries, who felt the king was behaving in an unseemly way by allowing Anne to have control. The sight of a woman leading a man ran contrary to gender expectations, and was usually fodder for ridicule in contemporary literature. Yet Henry was always king. Although his deep passion for Anne may have led him to lose control on occasions, for instance weeping when they argued, this was in keeping with his larger-than-life character. Such deference to Anne was possible because Henry allowed himself a degree of conscious, or unconscious, licence. He indulged the passion, wallowed in it, inhabited it. The initial performance of courtly love had become a reality, but the pressures of their situation sometimes tipped the king into genuine scenes of drama and theatricality. There is no question that Henry fell madly in love with Anne, but he did so because he chose to, he allowed himself to. As king, he always retained control, even if that control temporarily appeared in abeyance. As a man, Henry never forgot who was the master.

To attempt to describe what it was like being loved by a king is not easy. Of course, it brought Anne and her family increased power, wealth and respect, and gave her access to an exciting life of privilege, far above that to which she had been born. As he would later remind her, Henry had raised her above her position, out of her class. But with Henry still married, the circumstances of their relationship were controversial, creating awkwardness and division at court, even after Henry had left Catherine. Once he rode away from her in 1531, all those under his roof were forced to consider their loyalties, although many did not have the luxury of choice, as their path was dictated by their duties. Yet the king could not see into men's hearts. At court, Anne was conscious of Catherine's remaining friends and supporters, knowing that some were hiding their true support of the queen, or seeking Anne's patronage out of necessity. The hierarchy of the Tudor court was based on patronage. It was difficult, if not impossible to operate independently without immense wealth, and class dictated whom you might genuinely consider as a friend. Strong ties did exist between members of the nobility and their servants, such as the close-knit group that remained with Catherine, several of whom had accompanied her to England from Spain in 1501, and the connections of George Cavendish and Thomas Cromwell to Wolsey, but these were formed by time and service, which bred loyalty, and the appreciation of an individual's personal qualities. Such friendships had a more formal nature, of mistress and servant, and never approached a semblance of equality between those involved. In terms of friends and allies, Anne's focus was on the small, elite group at the top, but her interactions with all members of the court, her practice of good ladyship, the feminine version of good lordship, would dictate the way others chose to bestow, or deny, their allegiance. Some members of Henry's court flocked to Anne as a patron, a figure of influence, useful while she retained power, to ride on her wave. There was nothing unique in this; it was the world Anne had been raised in, and she was shrewd enough to understand.

Then, as now, Anne's situation elicited strong reactions, but the question of whether or not she enjoyed any general popularity in the early 1530s differs, depending upon which sources are trusted. On the whole, though, the balance of evidence does seem to suggest that Anne suffered as a result of the general affection in which the English people held the queen. Catherine had been a presence in England for three decades, since her arrival as a teenager, riding through the streets of London with her unusual clothes and long red-gold hair hanging loose. Now the queen's position was being challenged in a way that did not endear women to Anne's cause, conforming to the cultural and literary trope of a husband seeking to replace his loyal wife with a younger model. In November 1531, Lodovico Falier, recently returned from spending three years in England, reported that Catherine was 'beloved by the islanders more than any queen that ever reigned'.[40] Falier considered that Catherine was so loved by the people that any attempt to replace her might result in rioting:

> This event might easily prove a source of trouble to the King, should the Queen's faction rebel; her Majesty being so loved and respected, that the people already commence murmuring; and were the faction to produce a leader, it is certain that the English nation, so naturally prone to innovation and change, would take up arms for the Queen, and by so much the more, were it arranged for the leader to marry the Princess [Mary], although by English law females are excluded from the throne.[41]

In late 1531, Anne Boleyn found herself the target of a swell of feeling in London, according to a report that reached Venice. Allegedly a huge mob of women, and men dressed as women, gathered in London and stormed the house on the river where Anne was staying. This may have been Durham House, which was being used by her father. It was rumoured that they intended to kill her and apparently Anne escaped downriver just in the nick of time.[42] The details are related in a letter from an unknown source, dated 24 November, received by the French ambassador in Venice:

> It is said that more than seven weeks ago a mob of from seven to eight thousand women of London went out of the town to seize Boleyn's

daughter, the sweetheart of the King of England, who was supping at a villa on a river, the King not being with her; and having received notice of this, she escaped by crossing the river in a boat. The women had intended to kill her; and amongst the mob were many men, disguised as women; nor has any great demonstration been made about this, because it was a thing done by women.[43]

The veracity of this event cannot be established (and the numbers surely look too high), but the very real existence of a mob of Oxfordshire women who threw stones at Henry's confessor John Longland makes it seem not totally impossible. There may have been a smaller number of rioters, possibly targeting the Boleyn residence, or perhaps she thought it prudent to move on an occasion when there was discontent in the city. What is significant, though, is that there was sufficient feeling against Anne for the report to have been repeated as credible. It is also interesting that when reports of this nature surface, it is usually women who are the perpetrators, suggesting that there was considerable support for Catherine as a wronged wife. Chronicler Edward Hall reported that 'all wise men in the realm abhorred that marriage, but women, and such as were more wilful than wise or learned, spoke against the determination'.[44] Popular sympathy for Catherine was demonstrated when people turned out onto the roads to cheer her as she travelled between residences; but it wasn't the common people who made queens, it was a matter for the king, the theologians and the church.

There are also isolated cases of individuals speaking out against Anne, many of which conform to the usual slanders, against her 'shameless' life. The case of an old man named Roger Dycker, who was imprisoned in the Marshalsea in 1531, is of interest, though, as it highlights the class and gender expectations set out in Castiglione's *The Book of the Courtier*, suggesting that the dislike of inappropriate behaviour for one's station in life underpinned public responses to Anne. Dycker found himself in trouble not for direct slander, but for refusing to believe that in the king's case like called to like, and saying that Catherine was the king's equal in birth so he would not forsake her for a prosaic 'Mrs Anne Bullen':

About the Feast of St. John the Baptist 23 Hen. VIII., Roger Dycker, Harry Bothemer, and Thos. Hetton went out to welcome home Sir Roger Page, vicar of Kyrk Holland, Derbyshire, who told them that the King was about to marry another wife, and that one Mr. Cromwell penned certain matters in the Parliament house, which no man gainsaid. He said Dycker knew the gentlewoman, and that her father's name was Sir Thos. Bullan. Dycker then said that her name was Mrs. Anne Bullan, and he was sure it was but tales, 'for so noble a lady, so high born, and so gracious, he would not forsake and marry another'. This accusation was brought against him because Sir Antony Babyngton was displeased with him. He is 69 years of age, and has been 'sore bryssyd' in the King's wars, and they do all this to undo him utterly.[45]

The Abbot of Whitby commented in 1530 that 'the King's Grace is ruled by one common stewed whore, Anne Boleyn, who makes all the spirituality to be beggared, and the temporality also'. Catherine would refer to her as the 'Scandal of Christendom'.

It is no surprise that there were strong reactions against Anne; there would have been similar responses to any woman who was in her position so, in a sense, these were not personal attacks, rather they were expressing antipathy to what she represented, whether as a Francophile, a reformer, or the 'other woman'. The methods of attack were sometimes underhand or indirect, as such feeling could not be expressed openly agaist the king; instead it is found in rumour, veiled threats and the strange story of Anne finding a book of prophecies left in her apartments, open at a page to reveal an illustration of herself with her head cut off.

There is no doubt that Anne was a threat to Catherine, so the queen's supporters would be expected to oppose her, as would anyone who felt sympathy for the queen's situation. Some spoke out, such as John Fisher, Bishop of Rochester, and Catherine's chaplain, Thomas Abell: both would pay for this with their lives. It was far easier to blame, and demonise, a figure close to Henry, upon whose shoulders could be laid the responsibility for any bad decisions he made. Until recently, the scapegoat had been Wolsey, whose unpopularity had covered a multitude of reputed errors and sins, and his humble roots provided an 'explanation' for his corruption in the popular imagination. One of the ironies of his fall, which Anne and her party applauded, was that this position was now vacant, and the blame for Henry's religious doubts was being placed firmly in her camp. As Chapuys recorded in September 1532, 'Francis has lost nothing by the death of the Cardinal of York, for besides… the lady is more mischievous and has more credit than he had.'[46] Anne took these attacks buoyantly, briefly adopting as her motto the phrase 'ainsi sera, groigne qui groigne', or 'this how it will be, no matter who grumbles'.

TWENTY-FIVE

Life with Henry 1531–2

By the summer of 1531, Anne found herself in an unprecedented situation. She had agreed to marry Henry four years earlier, but still they seemed no closer to achieving this end. At times, Anne must have considered what her future role would be if Henry's Great Matter failed. On at least one occasion, she berated the king about the years of fertility passing her by, during which she might have been married and borne children. Having taken the decisive step of becoming the king's fiancée, there was no turning back in terms of social standing, no greater accolade awaiting her if she failed. Once committed, she could not reject the king without retiring to a nunnery, or leaving the country and causing the Boleyns' status to plummet. Henry's former mistress, Elizabeth Blount, had consented to marriage as an honourable form of retirement, but she had never been a projected queen. Turning thirty in 1531, Anne must have feared the years of waiting meant that by the time they finally got married, she would be too old to conceive.

Setting aside the issue of Henry as king, Anne was also dealing with Henry the man; a complex, difficult, changeable man, whose character historians have pursued with differing degrees of sympathy for centuries, resulting in a wide range of conclusions. Some interpretations have been coloured by his treatment of his wives or his interactions with his favourites and the way in which a number of his servants fell from grace. In recent years, this has created a critical consensus, characterising him as despotic, even psychopathic, and while this trend has its roots in the nature of a personal, absolute monarchy, it is too simplistic and anachronistic to consider Henry in this way. There is no doubt that the man who fell in love with Anne was the product of his circumstances, a man of absolutes and strong passions, whose early kingship had been spent in exuberant pursuit of his military, cultural and amatory passions. He was also a man of paradoxes, of tensions between desire and restraint, extremes and subtleties, physical and intellectual, caution and spontaneity, formality and play. Literally and metaphorically, he was a man who liked to play games, to dress up and assume a character, playing out a role in disguise, or behind the scenes in the ritual of courtly love. He was conscious of what was due to him, and breaches of protocol were taken seriously, although he might choose to take a humble position when it suited him. The court was aware of his games and were compelled to play along, as Thomas and Elizabeth Boleyn had in former years, acting in role, adopting costumes, feigning surprise when the king's identity was revealed. Henry was not a king to whom anyone said no, not until he believed that God was denying him the heirs he felt should have been his due. He was a man of absolute faith, but recently that faith had been challenged, making for a mixture of anger, uncertainty and intellectual curiosity. This led the king to redefine his relationship with God. It would be anachronistic to talk about Henry having a sense of entitlement, which has different modern connotations, but instead to consider all his actions as a function of his awareness of his birth and kingship. Equally inappropriate are descriptions of Henry going through the Tudor equivalent of a mid-life crisis. In the late 1520s, he began an extensive and life-changing redefinition, and his position meant that this process dictated much of English politicial, religious and cultural life. It was a profound change, with deep and lasting ramifications for his court, the country and the church of England. All roads led back to Henry and his character shaped the nature of his relationship with Anne at all its stages.

In November 1531, Venetian Lodovico Falier left an extensive description of Henry, which provides an interesting contemporary, if foreign, insight into the man with whom Anne was now living. It captures not only his appearance, abilities and character, but also the piety and charity he continued to display:

In this eighth Henry, God combined such corporal and mental beauty, as not merely to surprise but to astound all men. Who could fail to be struck with admiration on perceiving the lofty position of so glorious a Prince to be in such accordance with his stature, giving manifest proof of that intrinsic mental superiority which is inherent to him? His face is angelic rather than handsome; his head imperial and bald, and he wears a beard, contrary to English custom. Who would not be amazed when contemplating such singular corporal beauty, coupled with such bold address, adapting itself with the greatest ease to every manly exercise. He sits his horse well, and manages him yet better; he jousts and wields his spear, throws the quoit, and draws the bow, admirably; plays at tennis most dexterously; and nature having endowed him in youth with such gifts, he was not slow to enhance, preserve, and augment them with all industry and labour. It seeming to him monstrous for a Prince not to cultivate moral and intellectual excellence, so from childhood he applied himself to grammatical studies, and then to philosophy and holy writ, thus obtaining the reputation of a lettered and excellent Prince. Besides the Latin and his native tongue, he learned Spanish, French, and Italian. He is kind and affable, full of graciousness and courtesy, and liberal; particularly so to men of science whom he is never weary of obliging.

Although always intelligent and judicious, he nevertheless allowed himself to be so allured by his pleasures, that, accustomed to ease, he for many years left the administration of the government to his ministers, well nigh until the persecution of Cardinal Wolsey; but from that time forth he took such delight in his own rule, that from liberal he became avaricious, and whereas heretofore no one departed from his Majesty without being well rewarded, so now all quit his presence dissatisfied. He appears to be religious; he usually hears two low masses and on holy days high mass likewise. He gives many alms, relieving paupers, orphans, widows, and cripples; his almoner disbursing annually ten thousand golden ducats for this purpose.[1]

Falier also left a description of Anne's uncle, the Duke of Norfolk, who was now the real power behind her family, whilst Anne remained the nominal, visible, leader:

His Excellency the Duke of Norfolk is of very noble English descent. His Majesty makes use of him in all negotiations more than any other person. Since the death of Cardinal Wolsey, his authority and supremacy have increased, and every employment devolves to him. He is prudent, liberal, affable and astute; associates with everybody, has very great experience in political government, discusses the affairs of the world admirably, aspires to greater elevation, and bears ill-will to foreigners, especially to our Venetian nation. He is 58 years old; small and spare in person, and his hair black. He has two sons.[2]

It must have been with a sense of exhilaration that Anne rode away from Windsor Castle with Henry in July 1531, leaving Catherine behind. She and Henry spent that summer together, in pursuit of pleasure, escaping from the commitments and duties that the queen represented, travelling through the castles and estates of sympathetic friends through the southern counties, anticipating a time when they might legitimately be husband and wife. From Windsor, they went south to Guildford, just twenty miles away, arriving by 29 July, when payments were made to the friars of Guildford and keepers of Guildford park.[3] It was here that Anne could finally enjoy her new, unchallenged position at Henry's side, as his acknowledged partner and future consort. The same day, they moved eastwards to Farnham, either the imposing twelfth-century castle or the red-brick bishop's palace owned by the see of Winchester. Recent improvements had been made to the gatehouse and accommodation in 1475 and 1520, but the main attraction for the king would have been hunting in the extensive grounds. Henry rewarded the keeper of the park there on 3 August, shortly before they left for Odiham Lodge in Hampshire, eight miles to the north-west. Mario Savorgano finally caught up with Henry at Odiham, which he described as 'a park some thirty miles from London', where the king was 'taking his pleasure in a small hunting-lodge, built solely for the chase, in the middle of the forest'.[4] He described the king as 'tall of stature, very well formed, and of very handsome presence, beyond measure affable, and I never saw a prince better disposed than this one. He is also learned and accomplished, and most generous and kind', and received a warm welcome, with Henry kissing his hand and embracing him 'joyously', professing himself glad to see foreigners, and especially Italians. After that, Henry went off to hunt with between 40 and 50 horsemen. Savorgano then qualified his praise, saying that Henry was kind, but 'were it not that he now seeks to repudiate his wife, after having lived with her for 22 years, he would be no less perfectly good, and equally prudent'.[5] The Italian continued, in little doubt about who had the upper hand between Henry and Anne, but doubting their union would ever become legal:

> …this thing detracts greatly from his merits, as there is now living with him a young woman of noble birth, though many say of bad character, whose will is law to him, and he is expected to marry her, should the divorce take place, which it is supposed will not be effected, as the peers of the realm, both spiritual and temporal, and the people are opposed to it; nor during the present Queen's life will they have any other Queen in the kingdom. Her Majesty is prudent and good; and during these differences with the King she has evinced constancy and resolution, never being disheartened or depressed.[6]

On 4 August, payments were made for items belonging to Henry to be brought ten miles north-east from Odiham Lodge to the Vyne in Hampshire, home to William, Lord Sandys. Large enough to rival the grandeur of Hampton Court, the Vyne was imposing and extensive enough to be described in the early 1540s as 'one of the principal houses in all Hamptonshire'.[7] It had undergone extensive repairs between 1524 and 1526, and stood in red-brick spendour around several courtyards. Their host for the visit was William, Baron Sandys, the sixty-year-old Lord Chamberlain, who was also a Knight of the Garter and had been instrumental in the organisation of the Field of Cloth of Gold. During the visit, payments were 'keeper of lord Sandys park' on 6 August, also for hounds being brought to Henry there, and to a servant of the Baron for 'bringing of a stag to the Vyne which the king had stricken before in the forest of Wolmer'.[8] This suggests that Henry enjoyed hunting in Woolmer forest, the royal forest lying to the south of the Vyne on the South Downs, as well as nearby Beaurepair Park, two miles away at Bramley, near Basingstoke, also owned by the Sandys family. On 5 August, a reward was paid by Henry to the keeper at 'Baroper' (Beaurepair) Park. Five days later, he made another payment to the keeper of Bagshot park, 20 miles east from the Vyne in the direction of London, indicating that Henry was riding over an extensive area.[9] With the surviving details about saddles being made for Anne, there is no reason to believe that she did not accompany him.

From the Vyne, Henry and Anne moved twenty miles away to the hunting lodge at Easthampstead, where gifts of oranges and lemons were brought to the king.[10] Built on three sides of a courtyard, the maintenance of the house fell under the remit of Baron Sandys, but the location placed it within Windsor Great Park, and Henry made payments to the keepers of both Easthampstead and Windsor Parks on 12 August. As had happened at Waltham, one of his dogs had become lost in the forest and was brought home to the king by a local.[11] From there, Henry and Anne travelled to the park at Barnwood, a manor near Reading, before moving north to Ewelme Manor in Oxfordshire, home of the Dukes of Suffolk, granted to the king's sister Mary and her husband, Charles Brandon, in 1525. Most of the palace dated to the 1450s, but it incorporated elements of the ancestral home of the Chaucer family, being enlarged after the marriage of his granddaughter Alice to William de la Pole. It was a pleasant house, described by Leland in 1542 as 'set within a fair moat and (being) builded richly of brick and stone';[12] but it may not have been a pleasant visit for Anne. Having known Catherine of Aragon since childhood, Mary had been close to the queen, and recalled Anne and Mary Boleyn in their capacities as ladies-in-waiting during the brief time they overlapped in France, in 1514–15. Whether or not this made for an uncomfortable visit is unknown, but other indications suggest the Suffolks' loyalties may have lain with Catherine, and that Brandon disliked, or grew to dislike, Anne. Mary had been offended at Christmas 1529 when Anne was given precedence over her and the Duke of

Norfolk, a slight which was considerable at the time. From Ewelme, they headed north-east to Woodstock, to which palace Henry's hounds were transported and a payment of 22, 4s 8d was made to a 'poor labouring man in the harvest at Woodstock by the king's command'. George, Lord Rochford was paid for shooting arrows there, the bills of the Duke of Norfolk and Robert Heneage were settled, crimson velvet and gilt bells were bought and, on 28 August, William Otener the jeweller sold 'divers jewels' to the king.[13]

While Henry and Anne were passing their days hunting, a controversial death sentence was enacted upon a young preacher from Norfolk. On 19 August, the burning of Thomas Bilney took place at the Lollards' Pit in Norwich, for preaching in favour of ecclesiastical reform after he had been forbidden to do so. In his mid-thirties, Bilney was a Cambridge graduate and friend of Hugh Latimer and Matthew Parker, both of whom were reformers associated with Anne Boleyn. Bilney and Latimer had both attended meetings of the Christian Brethren at the White Horse Tavern, which Tyndale's supporter Humphrey Monmouth had attended; Latimer preached regularly for Anne and later, Parker would become her chaplain. Bilney had been arrested and questioned by Wolsey, but was released when he agreed to not spread his views. In 1531, he was rearrested and condemned by Richard Nix, Bishop of Norwich, for preaching in the fields against pilgrimage and the veneration of saints and relics. Until the end he denied that he was a follower of Luther and upheld the Catholic doctrine of the power and influence of the pope, the authority of the church and the transformation and sacrifice of the Mass.

Bilney's views appear to have been more orthodox than otherwise, as he desired reform on a few points that would make for a closer relationship with God, rather than rejecting the pope, as the king was soon to do. When news of his burning reached the king, Henry must have been surprised, as Parliament would later threaten an inquiry into the matter on grounds that it had taken place without the proper approval of the state. Bishop Nix had his property confiscated as a result in 1534. The case was an interesting one, illustrating just how quickly the legal lines were shifting in this changing religious climate.

Through the end of July and into August, Catherine had remained at Windsor, anticipating the king's return. Henry had no desire to see her again and, hoping to return to the Castle soon, sent orders for her to leave. As Chapuys reported to the Emperor, 'the king, under pretence of hunting about Windsor, has ordered the Queen to dislodge and retire to More, a house belonging to St Albans, and the Princess to Richmond. Many think this very strange, and think it an extreme determination for the divorce.'[14] Savorgano saw Catherine after she was established at The

More, in Hertfordshire, which had come into royal possession on the death of Wolsey. Rebuilt after a fire of 1426, the house stood around three sides of a courtyard and, at its height, invited comparisons with Hampton Court. In the 1460s, vaulted cellars were added, the plumbing system was developed and the residential apartments redecorated. The most extensive changes had been made by Wolsey as recently as the 1520s, when three new wings and an outer walled courtyard were added, with corner towers and a gatehouse. He added a second moat, enclosing the original structure and the formal gardens within.[15] The Venetian recorded his arrival 'at a palace called the More, where the Queen resides'. He saw Catherine dine, with 'some 30 maids of honour standing round the table, and about 50 who performed its service. Her Court consists of about 200 persons, but she is not so much visited as heretofore, on account of the King. Her Majesty is not of tall stature, rather small. If not handsome she is not ugly; she is somewhat stout (*piuttosto grassa*) and has always a smile on her countenance.'[16]

In the first week of September, Henry and Anne were back at Grafton, where their last meeting with Wolsey had taken place. Pears were brought to the house by a local to grace their table and a poor woman saw the king in the forest and made him a gift of some nuts. Henry made his usual payment to the keeper of the place where he hunted,[17] in this case Whittle Wood, before they moved on to Ampthill, arriving on 15 September, as a stop-over on the way back to Waltham Abbey. Henry and Anne remained at Waltham for a considerable time, through September and into October, although they may have left it briefly and returned. They were there on 20 September, when a woman brought apples to the king at the abbey and a certain Walsh of Greenwich brought cucumbers and artichokes.[18] It was there that they would have heard the news in late September of the death of Louise of Savoy, mother of Francis I, whom Anne would have known from her time in France, although she had lately been more associated with Wolsey. Aged 55, Louise had reputedly caught a chill whilst watching a comet. Henry ordered that a 'solemn obsequy was made and kept' for her at the Abbey, and paid for mourning clothes for a number of the nobility to attend.[19] On 2 October, Henry dispatched a letter from Waltham and issued a warrant from there on 8 October. They were still at Waltham on 13 October, when Henry granted the parks of Le Posterne and Le Cage, in Kent, previously belonging to the Duke of Buckingham, to Thomas, Earl of Wiltshire and his heirs male, or 'in default, to his daughter Anne Boleyn'.[20] Two days later, he wrote letters to the king of Portugal. It was not until 20 October, a whole month after their arrival, that Henry paid a reward to a keeper of the forest of Waltham and the couple headed east to Havering atte Bower, then in

Essex.[21] They remained there for a few days, perhaps enjoying the end of the hawking season in the extensive grounds. Henry paid the £100 bill of his goldsmith, Cornelius Hayes, on 22 October and money was given to 'a poor woman the king healed at Havering' the following day.[22] On 23 October, Henry, Anne and others dined at the lodgings of Sir Brian Tuke, which must have been close by, with the Bishop of Bayonne:

> Yesterday (Sunday) the King came to the lodging of Brian Tuke, where the said Bayonne and John Joachin were lodged, a mile from the King's lodging, and supped there with much company. Above the table were the King, the lady, and Bayonne; below it, John Joachin, Norfolk, Wiltshire, and his wife, the secretary elect of Winchester, the treasurer Fitzwilliam, and two ladies.[23]

By 25 October, they were back at Waltham Abbey again, where a servant was rewarded for bringing quinces, oranges and pomegranates and the next day instructions to the Wardrobe were issued. By the end of the month, they had concluded their progress and returned to Greenwich in anticipation of the winter, receiving gifts of marmalade, oranges and pomegranates.[24] While travel was still possible they enjoyed hunting, an activity which appears to have taken up much of Henry's time. The Privy Purse records show which were the king's most commonly visited properties during this time, and those courtiers whose homes he felt that he and Anne would be welcome in. These places, with their parks and gardens, their halls and bedchambers, where music and cards were played and meals were eaten, form the often-overlooked physical fabric of Anne's life during these days.

Further details about Henry and Anne's movements are revealed by the Treasurer of the Chamber's Accounts, which survive from October 1528 to May 1531. These record the offerings that Henry made in church every Sunday, with the exception of a couple, and on the occasion of major religious festivals. They show that by far the king's most regular residence during this period was Greenwich, which he attended consistently through the three years. Hampton Court was the second favourite, receiving visits during 1529 and 1530 but, once Henry had acquired Wolsey's London home of York Place, he was there with far more regularity in the latter part of 1530 and into 1531. After that, Windsor was the next most visited place. Occasional stays were made at Bridewell, but Richmond, Woodstock and Durham Place only welcomed the king on a handful of Sundays.

By November 1531, Henry had not seen Catherine for four months, reassuring Anne that their split was permanent. An awkward situation

Above: The church of St Peter and St Paul, dominating the tiny village of Salle in Norfolk, where generations of the Boleyns lived and died. A pair of brasses still commemorate Geoffrey and Alice, Anne's great-great-grandparents.

Below: London's medieval Guildhall, completed in 1440, during Geoffrey Boleyn's residency in the city. Here he would have attended meetings, feasts and perhaps trials.

Above left: Blickling Hall, Aylsham, Norfolk, the most likely birthplace of Anne Boleyn in around 1501, and her home until early 1506. Most of the current house dates from the reign of James I but this western service wing may have been part of the building that Anne knew.

Above right: St Andrew's Church, Blickling, situated to the south-east of the Hall; the Boleyn family worshipped here, and are commemorated in brasses.

Below: Hever Castle, set in an idyllic location in Kent, which Geoffrey Boleyn purchased in 1462 and passed on to his son William. Sir Thomas Boleyn inherited it on William's death in 1505 and the family moved in a few months later.

Above left: St Peter's Church, Hever, just on the edge of the Castle's estate, in the centre of the village. There was no private chapel in the Boleyn family home, so they would have walked the short distance to worship here.

Above right: Sir Thomas Boleyn, by Hans Holbein. Anne's father worked his way up through the ranks of the Tudor court, as his linguistic abilities helped him to win ambassadorial positions. His marriage to Elizabeth Howard represented a significant step up the social ladder.

Below left: Henry Howard, Earl of Surrey, by Hans Holbein, Anne's cousin, the son of her maternal uncle. Some confusion has arisen as to the identity of the sitter, as the portrait has been labelled 'Thomas Howard', but the dating in relation to Holbein's arrival in England suggests it must be Thomas' son.

Below right: Duke Philibert II and Margaret of Savoy. From 1513, Anne spent a year at the court of Margaret of Savoy, who was then a widow. The intelligent and competent Margaret was a significant role model for Anne, who may have had access to her extensive library and art collection.

Above left: Charles V, the future Holy Roman Emperor, was a youth at his aunt Margaret's Mechelen court during the time of Anne's residence. Later, he would provide opposition to Henry's attempts to divorce his aunt.

Above right: In 1514, Henry VIII arranged a marriage for his young sister Mary to the aged Louis XII of France. Mary Boleyn was included in the list of women who accompanied her from England, and Anne may have met them in France, late in 1513 or early in 1514.

Right: Anne was placed in the household of Francis' young wife, Claude, Queen of France. She would have attended her mistress's coronation, which was held at the Basilica of St Denis on 10 May 1517. The event was depicted in this illumination of a contemporary tapestry, painted by Jean Coene.

Below: Louis' death on 1 January 1515 led to the succession of Francis I of France, a figure who was to become significant in Anne's life, both as the king whose wife she served, but also as her husband's foreign counterpart in years to come.

Above: Anne would have spent much time at Claude's main residence at Blois, a fairy-tale chateau on the Loire. Inside its walls, Anne would have experienced the influence of the Italian Renaissance, in its furnishings, paintings and tapestries, as well as its extensive library of illuminated manuscripts and early books.

Below left: Francis I invited the Italian artist Leonardo da Vinci to spend his final years in a chateau in the grounds at Amboise. With Anne visiting the castle often with Claude, she is likely to have met the master, or seen him at work, between his arrival in 1515 and his death in 1519. She may even have attended his funeral.

Below right: The ideas of the German reformer Martin Luther spread across Europe during Anne's time in France. The Valois court was receptive to reformed ideas and Anne probably had a better understanding of his 95 Theses than Henry did at the same time. Henry continued to reject Lutheran teaching until he decided to break with Rome, when he looked to the monk as a potential ally.

Above: While Claude's main residence was Blois, that of Francis was the glorious chateau of Amboise, a little further along the river. It had been rebuilt in the 1490s to reflect the latest in Italian architecture and garden design.

Left: The Humanist scholar Desiderius Erasmus, an early friend of Henry VIII, was critical of pilgrimage and what he saw as the more superstitious aspects of the Catholic faith.

'Anne Bullein' by Hans Holbein, an
informal sketch that depicts her in
what appears to be a nightcap, perhaps
made before she became queen.

Anne Boleyn, depicted by a later artist.

Courtier Sir Nicholas Carew, one of Henry's closest favourites, was related to Anne by marriage. Initially supportive of his cousin, he later turned against her and promoted Jane Seymour's cause.

Harry Guldeford Knight.

Sir Henry Guildford, Master of the Horse and Comptroller of Henry's household, disapproved of Henry's marriage to Anne, leading to sharp words passing between them. She threatened to ruin him, prompting his resignation, but the king told Guildford not to heed the words of women.

Above and right: Henry VIII, a manuscript illustration from the British Library's copy of 'The Penitential and other Psalms', which was reputedly given to Anne on the scaffold by one of her ladies.

Below left: Henry VIII, Rex Fidei Defensor, depicted in 1618 or 1628, in *The History and Lives of the Kings of England*.

Below right: Henry VIII's field armour, made in Italy towards the end of his life, from gold, steel, leather and other materials. The decoration includes typically renaissance designs of putti, foliage, running dogs, grotesque ornaments and candelabra.

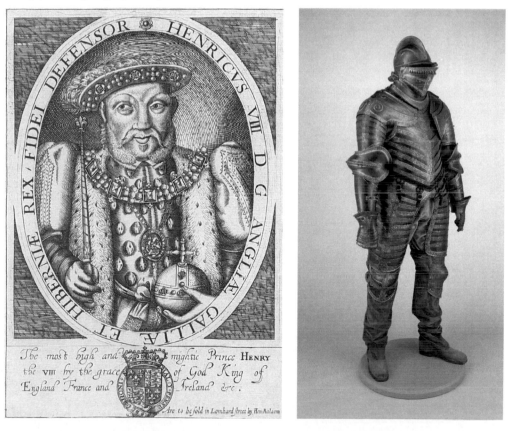

Left: Raised in another Kent household, not far from Hever, Sir Thomas Wyatt composed poems to 'Brunet' that suggest his passion for Anne. She appears to have resisted his advances, but this did not prevent his arrest as part of the investigations of May 1536. Locked in the Tower while his friends were executed, Wyatt wrote about the 'bloody days' that had broken his heart.

Below: An illustration, taken from a later painting, of Henry and Anne at Wolsey's home, York Place. The cardinal looks back over his shoulder at them as if suspicious or disapproving.

Above left: William Warham, Archbishop of Canterbury until 1532. Having initially questioned Henry's first marriage back in 1509, Warham was still dubious about the steps Henry took to dissolve it and break from Rome. Essentially a conservative, he died before his loyalties could be put to the test with the Oath of Supremacy.

Above right: John Fisher, Bishop of Rochester, incurred Henry's displeasure by being an outspoken advocate for Catherine of Aragon. Imprisoned for refusing to swear the Oath of Supremacy, he was made a cardinal by Pope Paul III, in the hope that this would preserve his life. It had the opposite effect, and he died a traitor's death in June 1535.

Below left: Sir Thomas More had no personal dislike of Anne but, like Fisher, could not find it in his conscience to swear the Oath of Supremacy, to replace the pope with Henry as Head of the Church of England. He suffered execution for his convictions in July 1535.

Below right: Thomas Cranmer, Archbishop of Canterbury from 1532. It was Cranmer who advised Henry to procure his divorce through canon law, and who pronounced Catherine of Aragon's marriage to Henry invalid. Upon Anne's arrest, he would tactfully attempt to speak up for her, certain of her good name, but had to bow to Henry's wishes.

Above: Henry acquired Hampton Court in 1528 from Thomas Wolsey, who sacrificed his new home in the hopes of renewing his favour with the king. Henry had his initials carved there together with Anne's, some of which still survive on one of the gateways.

Left: A hardly flattering silver testoon of Henry VIII in his mature years, 29 mm in diameter, from the Metropolitan Museum of Art.

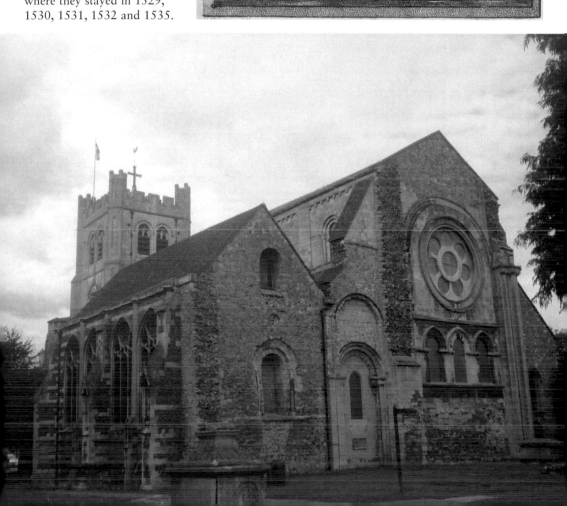

Right: William Somers, Henry's court jester, with whom Henry was once angry for speaking ill of Anne and Elizabeth. Somers escaped the king's wrath by sheltering at the home of Nicholas Carew.

Below: Waltham Abbey, a favourite location for Henry and Anne to visit on progress, where they stayed in 1529, 1530, 1531, 1532 and 1535.

Above: The doom painting at Waltham Abbey, depicting the fates of individual souls, for good or bad. Anne is likely to have seen this in the Lady Chapel on one of her visits, perhaps with some cynicism about the medieval vision of judgement and damnation.

Left: Tewkesbury Abbey, Gloucestershire, where Henry and Anne stayed in July 1535, as part of their summer progress.

Above: Thornbury Castle, Gloucestershire, home of Sir William Paulet, which Henry and Anne visited in August 1535. Ten months later, Paulet was one of the few statesmen who treated the accused queen with respect.

Right: Having been a close friend of Wolsey, Thomas Cromwell survived the cardinal's fall to replace him as the king's chief minister. He appears to have had a good working relationship with Anne until the end of 1535, perhaps even later, seeing his service to her as an extension of his service to the king. In the spring of 1536, though, those two objectives diverged and he was responsible for gathering evidence against her.

Anne arrived at the Tower of London on the eve of her coronation at the end of May 1533. New apartments had been prepared for her. She departed from here in splendour, to process through the streets towards Westminster. This aerial view gives a sense of the Tower as a castle, a sprawling complex of different buildings. When Anne returned to the Tower on 2 May 1536, it was under very different circumstances. Sir William Kingston met her again, and conducted her to the same apartments. This time she was awaiting her death, not her coronation.

Above: Anne's execution, as depicted in a Victorian volume, took place on 19 May 1536, at the Tower of London. 'I am judged to die and therefore I will speak nothing against it.'

Left: Elizabeth I, the daughter of Henry VIII and Anne Boleyn, pronounced illegitimate before her third birthday, who possessed a ring bearing portraits of herself and her mother.

arose when both king and queen were invited to dine at Ely House, in Holborn, the London residence of the Bishop of Ely. A feast for the Serjeants-at-Law was taking place across a five-day period from Friday 10 November, but when Henry arrived on the Monday to dine, he was entertained in a different room from Catherine, who was also present, and the pair did not set eyes on each other.[25] He and Anne headed to Hampton Court, where he paid the bills of his jewellers goldsmiths and skinners.[26] The Christmas season was kept at Greenwich, as Hall related, 'with great solemnity, but all men said that there was no mirth in that Christmas because the Queen and her ladies were absent'.[27] Catherine remained at The More.

In December 1531, the execution took place of Rhys ap Gruffydd, husband of Catherine Howard, sister of the present Duke of Norfolk, making Rhys Anne's uncle by marriage. He had expected to inherit his father's lands upon his death in 1524, but Henry gave them instead to Lord Ferrers. The resulting feud escalated into rioting and a full-scale confrontation in Carmarthen, after which Rhys was imprisoned and his wife's supporters attacked the castle. This led to the transfer of Rhys to prison in London, whereupon Henry claimed he was attempting to overthrow him, according to old Welsh prophecies. Rhys had spoken openly against Anne and against religious reforms. Many believed that this was the real reason for his execution, with Chapuys writing that 'it is a common report that, had it not been for the King's lady, of whom Ris and his wife had spoken, he never would have come to this miserable end'.[28]

In the list of New Year's gifts for 1532, Sir Thomas Boleyn and George, Lord Rochford, received gilt bowls, goblets and cups, and the Countess of Wiltshire, Anne's mother, along with Bessie Blount, now Lady Tailboys, and Mary Rochford, were given gifts that included gilt cruets, bottles, cups and goblets. In return, Anne's parents gave their future son-in-law a box of black velvet with a glass set in gold and a coffer of needlework containing three silver collars and three gold, while the widowed Mary Boleyn gave Henry a shirt with a black collar. In the records, a space was left by the queen's name. Henry gave Catherine no gift, for the first time, and had forbidden her to send him anything for Christmas. However, he had not mentioned anything about New Year, so Catherine sent him a gold cup. It was intercepted before the official presentation and therefore went unrecorded in the privy accounts. Henry returned it to her with the message that because they were no longer married, it was not an appropriate gift for her to have sent.[29] Anne gave Henry a set of rich and exotic boar spears or darts from the Pyrenees and 'in return, he gave her a room hung with cloth of gold and silver, and crimson satin with rich embroideries. She is lodged where the Queen used to be, and is accompanied by almost as many ladies as if she were Queen'.[30] At the end of January, the European grapevine was busy with rumours. The pope told the Cardinal of Osma, who told Charles V, that Francis I had 'advised the king of England to marry *la manceba* (the girl) because he thought this act would bind the king to him, so that he could never fail to assist him with men and money when he had need of them'.[31] If this was true, it was a cynical move on the part of Francis, but it was towards France that Henry would turn for support and recognition of his union with Anne.

For Anne, much of 1532 passed in a similar way to the previous year, with the essential difference of Catherine's absence. Through the early months there were dogs and hawks to occupy her and Henry, along with games of indoor tennis and other sports. In mid-January, 20s was paid 'to the fellow with the dancing dog' and £9 went to William 'who won of the king's grace at shovelboard'.[32] They were at York Place soon after, enjoying a gift of cranes that was bought for their table, paying a bookbinder to bring books to them and making more payments for victories over the king at shovelboard, of £45, £5 12s 6d, £40 10s and £36 to Anne's brother George. Either Anne or Henry may have been unwell during this time, as early February saw £4 being paid to a Doctor Yakisley and another, unnamed physician 'by the king's command', then a further £7 10s given to Thomas Boleyn, for a physician named Doctor Nicholas.[33] By April, the indoor games had been swapped for bowls, with Thomas and George Boleyn beating the king and Edward Baynton. The next day, Henry was beaten again by George, this time at tennis and then, again, at bowls, before George and Thomas teamed up a second time to win £30 from Henry at another bowls match. A week or two later, Thomas, Francis Bryan and Norfolk beat the king on three more occasions.[34] Lest this suggests that Anne's family were consistently the winners (and a little foolish to have done so), it should be recalled that only the king's losses are recorded in his payments book, not the occasions when he won. The Boleyn men were surely not so insensitive to their monarch's ego. The steady stream of gifts included lampreys, oranges, lemons, chickens and quince pies; Henry bought a gold brooch and an unnnamed German brought him a lion, for which he was rewarded £6 13s 4d.[35]

In April, Chapuys had asserted that Anne 'becomes more arrogant every day, using words and authority towards the King, of which he has several times complained to the duke of Norfolk, saying that she was not like the Queen, who had never in her life used ill words to him'.[36] Just as Chapuys had previously reported that her aunt, the Duchess of Norfolk had sent Catherine the gift of an orange, now he related that the Duchess reported this to the queen, 'telling her moreover that her husband was in marvellous sorrow and tribulation, and that she saw quite well she would be considered the ruin of all her family, and that if God wished that she should continue in her fantasy it would be a very good thing for the Queen'.[37] Some historians have accepted this statement, accepting the narrative that the seeds of dissent had begun to spread among Anne's family and followers, with P. Friedman describing her as becoming 'daily more overbearing',[38] while Froude has her making herself 'disliked by her haughty and arrogant manners'.[39] It is difficult to know how to read Anne's character at any point, with the absence of surviving documentation, and the lack of balance in the hostile ambassador's account. It may be that, having reached a position of pre-eminence over her father and uncle, Anne overreached herself, forgetting the men who had helped her. This would go against the letter she wrote at the age of fourteen, when she hoped always to make her father proud, but her personal circumstances had been transformed since then. Perhaps she forgot herself so far as to be rude to her elders, and to family members, contrary to the way she had been brought up, contrary to the expectations of respectful female behaviour and subordination. If she did have words with her uncle, or others, it may have been that she was not being rude, but that she was not conforming to their intentions, or wished to act independently, and her opposition was *perceived* as insulting. It is impossible now to recapture the truth of her personal interactions, even less so to hear her tone and voice across the centuries. But Anne was not one to conform, nor to keep quiet; later events would expose her willingness to speak out, along with the male reaction that she should have remained quiet, as her betters had. If she did feel secure enough in Henry's support to transcend gender expectations and challenge her male relatives, she would have been aware that these were powerful and dangerous men to alienate.

At the end of March, a payment of £10 was rewarded 'to the lady princess by commandment of the King'.[40] This was Princess Mary, Henry's only surviving daughter by Catherine, who was now aged fifteen. For the first decade of her life, Mary had been the fêted heir to her father's realm, her accomplishments celebrated, and her hand sought in marriage by various European princes. Henry's attempts to separate from her mother had affected Mary deeply, who had been brought back from her residence at Ludlow Castle, where she had been sent in the tradition of Princes of Wales, and was now living apart from her mother, not permitted to see her. She was frequently unwell with irregular menstruation, toothache and depression; March 1532 also saw the amount of £26 13s 4d paid to her physician for his services.[41] Anne had been at Greenwich in May

1528, 'lodging in the tiltyard' while Mary was ill with smallpox and in late 1529 Chapuys had been alarmed that Henry was so besotted with 'the lady' that he had agreed to her suggestion to wed Mary to Norfolk's son, but this came to nothing. Anne was not to have an easy relationship with Princess Mary, who spent most of her days in her establishment at Hunsdon House, refusing to accept that her parents had not lawfully been married. Chapuys, who always ascribed to Anne the worst feelings and motives, commented on her response to Mary in April 1532:

> The Princess has not yet quite recovered from her stomach attack, but it is not serious. She wrote lately to the King that no medicine could do her so much good as seeing him and the Queen, and desired his licence to visit them both at Greenwich. This has been refused her, to gratify the lady, who hates her as much as the Queen, or more so, chiefly because she sees the King has some affection for her. Of late when the King praised her in the lady's presence the latter was very angry, and began to vituperate the Princess very strangely.[42]

In the future, Anne would attempt reconciliation, but there was no way of avoiding Mary as a difficult obstacle, as a rival to any future child Anne may bear the king, and as a figurehead for devout Catholicism. Mary also represented the Imperial alliance over that of the French. She would continue to deny that her mother's marriage was invalid and her relations with Anne were to be fraught with difficulty.

On Easter Sunday 1532, Henry and Anne were at Greenwich, where they attended a sermon preached by Friar William Peto, a member of the Franciscan Order of Observant Friars, who had been appointed as confessor to Princess Mary. As they filed into the chapel where Henry had been christened, they did not anticipate that Peto would take the opportunity to try and change the king's mind over his Great Matter and to threaten him with the greatest danger of all, a threat tantamount to treason. Yet the friar worded his sermon carefully, referring to a potential situation, using the Biblical parallel of Ahab, who was unduly influenced by his wife Jezebel, and who reputedly had his spilt blood licked by dogs and pigs. As Peto preached, indirectly warning Henry that attempts to annul his marriage would result in his loss of the crown, the king grew increasingly angry, until he rose and walked out in silence. That September, a rumour began that the pope had sent a curse, which was coming to England and into the hands of the Observant Friars.[43] Peto would preach the same message a year later, prompting Henry to order his arrest. He only managed to save his life by fleeing abroad. Henry's mind was still firmly set on the health of his soul and in mid-May he gave money to a Master Garneys who was undertaking a pilgrimage for him to Our Lady at Walsingham.[44]

A few details emerge specifically about Anne at this point; small, domestic details that tell of the passing of her days. She was to have a few new items for her wardrobe, in gold and black, with a huge £70 13s 4d being paid to a servant of hers for 32 Flemish ells of gold arras and a more modest £4 16s going to a John Malte for 12 yards of black satin for a cloak. The cloak was to be edged in black velute, which was also to be used with black satin for the collars and to line the vents and sleeves, and buckram to line the upper sleeves. Thirteen yards of black satin were purchased for a nightgown for Lady Anne, lined with 8 yards of black taffeta and 16 yards of green damask, costing £6 12s. On 29 May, Anne was rowed down river to visit her father at Durham Place, for which the king's watermen were paid 7s 6d. By the start of June, she was with Henry at Eltham Palace in north Kent. The couple's enjoyment of bowling, which features all through the spring and summer months of 1532, hd not palled, even though they had changed residence, as £4 4s 8d was paid to a Robert Lee for making a bowling alley at Eltham. Tennis, hunting and hounds still featured, with 45s being won by Sir William Pickering when his dog won a course against Henry's on 13 June.[45]

The same month, Henry granted Anne Hanworth Manor and Park, in Middlesex, close to the heath where the king enjoyed hunting.[46] That July, they returned to Waltham, which appears to have been a favourite place, staying for around five days, before they moved on to Ampthill. Chapuys recorded a strange snippet of gossip on 11 July, which sounds like reported speech but, as always with such sources, may have suffered the fate of words passed through several mouths, Chinese Whispers. He reported Anne's influence in a particular case, along with her reputed dislike of the Catholic clergy:

> The King pardoned a French innkeeper for a similar offence, but would not listen to any intercession in his behalf, either from hatred of theology or from love of the Lady, who told her father that he did wrong to speak for a priest, as there were too many of them already.[47]

The court was at Ampthill on 21 July, remaining for at least a week, after which Henry paid rewards to the park keeper there and the one at Brombery Park. On 29 July, Chapuys reported another incident, which, again, must be treated with caution, as it contains his surmises. He wrote to the Emperor that Henry's intention had been to go 'northwards to hunt' and that 'great preparations had been made' but that he had changed his mind and turned back. 'Some say the cause,' said Chapuys, was that 'in two or three places that he passed through, the people urged him to take back the Queen, and the women insulted the Lady'. He also acknowledged that it may have been due to a raid by the Scots, but it is interesting that he singles out the women's responses, as other sources do. Just five days earlier there is a record of women rioting in Great Yarmouth, necessitating an inquiry. Henry and Anne were not near the Norfolk town, but the cause of the riot is unclear and it may not have been an isolated incident.[48] If Henry had changed his plans, it may have been the result of his anger at a further setback from Rome:

> The King, either hearing from Rome or expecting that the Pope will decree censures to cause him to take back the Queen and banish the Lady, has said publicly, and in great anger, that he would not allow the Pope to treat him as he had done, that the Pope had no power over him; he was resolved to celebrate this marriage in the most solemn manner possible, and the necessary preparations must be made. He ordered Tallebo to be sent for, as he is Great Master, and fills some other office at the Queen's coronation. No one dared say a word, and most of the Court are scandalized, fearing that the King will carry out his intention, which is incredible. Has informed the Queen, and will not fail to keep watch, and prevent it if possible.[49]

It may have been this news that prompted Henry to plan the greatest honour of Anne's life to date, for which they would need to be at Windsor for the start of September.

Other members of Anne and Henry's close circle received rewards at the end of July 1532, their promotions linked with Anne's rise. Young Francis Weston, only twenty-one, received the livery of lands inherited from his wife Anne. He would also become a gentleman of the bedchamber that year. Anne's distant cousin, Nicholas Carew, already Master of the Horse, received a grant for manors and parks in Surrey, with an annual rent of £40 and 'free warren', or permission to kill small game there, specifically hares, rabbits, pheasants and partridges. Anthony Knyvett, a twenty-five-year old gentleman usher of the Privy Chamber, who had begun his service in the household of the Duke of Norfolk, became the keeper of Horsfrith Park in Essex, with a salary from the nearby manor of Writtle. Norfolk himself was one of a few individuals to benefit from the dissolution of the monastery at Snape in Norfolk, a cell of the Benedictine St John's Abbey in Colchester, which had come to Henry from Wolsey's hands, and brought considerable lands. Also favoured by the king was the new Abbot of Waltham Abbey, Robert Fuller, who had been elected to the position 'to please the king' at the end of June, following the death of William Bolton. One more figure to receive a reward was the up-and-coming Thomas Cromwell, formerly Wolsey's servant, who had stepped into his shoes to prove himself more than capable as a Privy Councillor and, in 1532, as treasurer of the Crown Jewels. At the end of July he was appointed clerk of the Hanaper of Chancery, a supporting role to the Keeper of the Great Seal, with salary and expenses.[50]

Henry and Anne had travelled from Ampthill to Grafton by the end of July, where a reward was given to the smith who transported the king's private lock, affixing it to each door where he lodged, and removing it again for use at the next location.[51] On August 6, they revisited Buckingham, home of Mary Carey and her children and by 9 August had arrived at Woodstock, where they remained until the 16th. The following day, 40s was given to a servant of Lady Russell who brought a stag and greyhound to Lady Anne, before they arrived at the Old Palace of Langley.[52] Through the final weeks of that month, Henry and Anne's court moved to Abingdon Abbey, Ewelme, with the Duke of Suffolk and Mary, to Reading Abbey, and back to Windsor. At some point during the last stretch of this trip, they heard news of the death of William Warham, Archbishop of Canterbury, a significant event of course. The leading role among the English clergy was now vacant, and could be bestowed upon an individual who was sympathetic to reform, and to Henry's divorce. As they rode down the long avenue of trees over which the solid grey castle brooded, a change was in the air. The following events marked the end of this transitional period for Anne, the end of the waiting, the limbo, the anticipation and fears; finally, things started moving for her.

PART SIX

ANNE
TRIUMPHANT

TWENTY-SIX

The Return to France 1532

France, along with the family and court of Francis I, had played a definitive role in the early lives of both Anne and her fiancé. Henry had always seen the Valois king as his closest rival, comparable in age, reputation, learning and interests, and had been blooded in early campaigns on French soil, prior to the dazzling event of the Field of Cloth of Gold. Anne's seven years of service had shaped her cultural, religious and moral tastes, giving her the continental sophistication and manner that set her apart from her English contemporaries. By the summer of 1532, Henry's relationships with the pope and the Emperor had reached an impasse, so he looked to France again as his major European ally, and sought its support for his relationship with Anne. After discussions with the French Ambassador, Jean Du Bellay, Henry began to plan a visit to Calais that autumn, to cement the friendship and present Anne as his future consort. Yet France was more than this to the hopeful couple, it was symbolic of separate pasts coming together and their shared interests: it defined their direction in 1532 as profoundly as did Henry's rejection of Catherine and Spain.

Du Bellay was experienced in Anglo-French relations by this point and appears to have been something of a favourite with Henry, who dined with him often. Holding the bishoprics of Bayonne and Paris, he was a Privy Councillor of Francis I and had undertaken a series of diplomatic missions to England from 1527, returning as Ambassador Extraordinary in the summer of 1532. Writing to Anne de Montmorency, Grand Master of France with responsibility for overseeing the king's household, Du Bellay reported in July that Henry was 'much pleased with Montmorency for negotiating the interview between him and the king of France', which was to take place in the English territory of Calais. The ambassador was with Henry and Anne at Ampthill, privy to their thoughts, when he wrote to Francis that 'the greatest pleasure that the King can do to this King and Madame Anne is to write to Du Bellay to ask the King to bring Madame Anne with him to Calais'.[1] Henry's eagerness for Francis to validate Anne was revealed by the request he conveyed through Du Bellay to have ladies present at the event, but he wished this to only apply to himself, not the French. The ambassador stated that he was sworn not to tell where he had heard this, but that Henry did not wish Francis to bring his wife Eleanor, sister of the Emperor, 'for he hates the Spanish dress', likening it to that of the devil.[2] This was as transparent as it was ungentlemanly. The widowed French king had been married to Eleanor of Austria on 4 July 1530, a daughter of Philip the Handsome and Joanna, and Catherine of Aragon's niece. Although she had shared a schoolroom with Anne Boleyn in the household of Margaret of Savoy, Eleanor could not now accept her as her aunt's replacement and declined to meet Anne at all during the visit, even to attend. Anne suggested that Francis' sister, Marguerite, who she 'ever hath entirely loved', might take Eleanor's place, but the new Queen of Navarre was said to be ill and unable to travel.

The Duke of Norfolk advised Francis, through Du Bellay, to 'remove two classes of men' from Calais, those who supported the Emperor and 'those who have the reputation of being mockers and jesters, who are as much hated as any people by this nation'.[3] The ambassador reported that Henry treated him 'familiarly' and was sometimes 'alone with him all day hunting'. On other occasions, Henry placed 'Madame Anne and the Bishop together with their crossbows to shoot the deer as they pass, and in other places to see coursing', the chasing of hares. Anne had given Du Bellay the gifts of a hunting frock and hat, horn and greyhound, which he related to demonstrate 'how the affection of the king of England for Francis increases' but also that 'all that the Lady does is by the King's order'.[4]

Preparations for the visit stepped up apace in August. From King's Langley, Henry issued a warrant to Sir Thomas Wriothesley, his Garter King-of-Arms, to be ready at Canterbury on 26 September, and to summon the other kings-of-arms, heralds and pursuivants to do the same. All their servants were to be dressed in 'light tawny coats' bearing their device upon the sleeve, and 'red Milan bonnets'.[5] Norfolk wrote to Cromwell from the same location on 21 August, with a change to the plans. Formerly, Henry had wished that crimson velvet be provided for three countesses, but he had changed his mind so that robes of estate were to be made only for Norfolk's wife, according to the design he enclosed.[6]

A letter was dispatched by the Duke of Norfolk instructing Catherine to hand over her store of royal jewels for Anne, so that she might be suitably attired. Her collection of gems included some state pieces, gifts from her husband and inheritances from other family members, but also some that she had brought with her from Spain. They were far more than just wealth; their possession was a critical indicator of status and a connection to her past, both as queen and the legacy of her parents; they were also heirlooms for her daughter. Catherine responded with righteous passion, refusing to 'give up my jewels for such a wicked purpose as that of ornamenting a person who is the scandal of Christendom'. She would only relinquish them if Henry issued a direct order, so Henry did. It was another humiliation for Catherine in a long line of humiliations; she was permitted to keep a small gold cross that reputedly contained a shard of wood from the real cross, but the knowledge that the jewels had gone to her rival, who was about to be feasted and treated as a queen in France, must have been a bitter pill to swallow. The event was probably the most significant shift in symbolic power from one woman to the other. As Anne opened the treasures, one by one, touching the polished stones and seeing the different colours and designs, it must have seemed that her dream was finally within reach. The collection contained emeralds, rubies, diamonds, sapphires and pearls, with some items recalling Anne's predecessor directly, such as the chain in the Spanish style[7] and the gold tabernacle of St Katherine that accompanied it.[8] They were an intmate legacy, used to lying close to, even upon, the former queen's skin, but also imbued with history and status. With Anne wearing the precious stones that had adorned Catherine as queen, it was just a short step to wearing her crown and sharing her husband's bed. Many believed that Henry would marry Anne whilst they were in France, although some were still labouring under the delusion that he would take a French princess as his wife, as Chapuys noted:

> There is a little more open speaking about the marriage of the King and the eldest French princess. Some French merchants offer heavy wagers on it. If the French really have such a hope, either they will be disappointed, or the lady, who wrote a week ago to one of her principal favorites that she expects what she so long desired will be accomplished at this journey.[9]

Henry also took another significant step to elevate Anne to a position suitable for the French visit, but also to ennoble her in advance of his marital intentions. This was an implicit recognition that she was aristocratic but not born into the small pool of royal genes, that she was essentially an outsider. The distinction was subtle, but definitive. On Sunday, 1 September at Windsor Castle, Anne was created Marchioness, or Marquis, of Pembroke. This appointment broke tradition in making her the first woman to be elevated to the hereditary peerage, and it was Henry who facilitated this. Anne was conveyed by a party of noblemen and the castle's officers-at-arms into the king's presence for the honour, with the process mirroring in miniature the rituals of the coronation. Anne's cousin, Mary Howard, daughter of the Duke of Norfolk, and later to become the wife of the king's illegitimate son Henry Fitzroy, carried the coronet and a crimson furred mantle, lined with ermine. Anne wore a matching crimson surcoat with straight sleeves, also with ermine, and with her hair loose as was traditional. She knelt before Henry to receive the patent of her creation and another of £1,000 a year. Then, no doubt exhilarated by the significance of her new status, she bade the king a dignified thanks and 'returned to her chamber'.[10] Three men were issued with the commission to take possession of the lands granted to her, which included Curry Mallett in Somerset, Hundson and Eastwick in Hertfordshire, and the manors of Stansted, Roydon, Coggeshall and Westall, with others in Wales, totalling £1,023 13s 2d.[11] Afterwards, according to Chapuys, 'Dr. Foxe made a speech in praise of the alliance between England and France, of which God, not man, must have been the inventor, as it was the best means for resisting the Turk, and was inviolable and eternal.'[12] Anne celebrated by hosting a dinner for Henry at her manor of Hanworth. His love for her seemed only to have increased, as he was unable to 'leave her for an hour... he accompanies her everywhere' and 'preferred all that were of her blood'.[13] Du Bellay interpreted this as a form of madness, an imbalance resulting in the reversal of the intended order between Henry and Anne, as man and woman, king and subject. In his opinion, only God could abate Henry's insanity.

Late in September 1532, just before they were due to set out for Calais, Anne was walking in the countryside with Henry when they came across Princess Mary. Chapuys dates the incident to 23 September, when the Privy Purse expenses and records of the jewels received suggest that Henry and Anne were at Hampton Court. It is not clear where Mary's household was based at that time, but they were clearly staying nearby. The ambassador has holding Anne the upper hand in the relationship, as if she was able to intimidate Henry and prevent him from having as close a connection with Mary as he might wish. Undoubtedly, this account is coloured by Chapuys' agenda, painting Anne as the temptress who had lured the king away from his wife and daughter. Chapuys' timid, controlled Henry does not sit comfortably with what is known of the king's character. No matter how much he was in love with Anne, it seems unlikely that he would have allowed himself to be cowed by her when it came to his own daughter:

Eight days ago the King met the Princess in the fields, but did not say much to her, except to ask how she was, and assure her that in future he would see her more often. It is certain that the King dares [not] bring her where the Lady is, for she does not wish to see her or hear of her. Thinks he would have talked with the Princess longer and more familiarly, if the Lady had not sent two of her people to listen. There is no likelihood of a treaty of marriage between the duke of Orleans and the Princess, as the King did not speak of it to her. The Princess will be at Windsor during the King's absence. The arrangements for the Queen are not known. The Queen was very much afraid that the King would marry the Lady at this meeting; but the Lady has assured some person in whom she trusts, that, even if the King wished, she would not consent, for she wishes it to be done here in the place where queens are wont to be married and crowned.[14]

The trip to Calais started with a scare. Plague had broken out in Rochester so Henry and Anne travelled from Greenwich to Gravesend by barge. On 4 October they stayed at Stone Castle, the home of Anne's friend Bridget Wiltshire, although it is unclear if Bridget herself was present. Her second husband, Sir Nicholas Hervey, had died that August, and her father was already dead, but whether or not the widow returned to her family home and was there to welcome her friend and the king is unknown. From Stone, Henry and Anne passed through Mote Park, in Maidstone, which was owned by the Woodville family, descendants of Henry's maternal grandmother, and where there was a large deer park. Next, they took a route to the north-east, proximate to the present A249, towards the river Medway, where the royal barge was waiting to take them to the Isle of Sheppey. Their host for the next few days was Sir Thomas Cheney of Shurland Hall, at Eastchurch, on the north-east tip of the island, overlooking the Thames Estuary. Built between 1510 and 1518 of red brick decorated by black diaper work, with octagonal towers, battlements and a new gatehouse, it echoed the style of Hampton Court, with acres of grounds. Anne had championed Cheney's cause with Wolsey in 1528–9 and he had become Treasurer of the Household in 1530. He may have been distantly related to Anne too, through the marriage of Sir Geoffrey Boleyn's daughter Isabella, and was a cousin of Sir William Sandys of the Vyne. After their visit to Shurland Hall, Henry and Anne travelled to Canterbury, staying there the night of 10 October, before the final leg of the journey down to Dover. They embarked for Calais, aboard *The Swallow* at five the following morning, arriving the same day, at around ten.

An official account of the visit was published by Henry's private printer, Wynkyn de Worde, who had taken over William Caxton's press at Westminster. They were lodged at The Exchequer, where Henry and Catherine had stayed in 1520, and where they awaited the arrival of

Francis. It was Anne's uncle, the Duke of Norfolk, who rode out to meet Montmorency to devise a suitable place for the two monarchs to meet. Dressed in a coat with braids of gold laid loose on russet velvet and set with trefoils full of pearls and stones, Henry met the equally gorgeous French king, who had chosen a coat of crimson velvet, with the gold lining pulled through the slashes. On 21 October, the two men came face to face at Sandingfield, twelve years after they had first met at Guines: both had aged, with Francis undergoing defeat and a long imprisonment, whilst Henry was still in the midst of his Great Matter. The official account related that they felt great pleasure upon their reunion, with 'the lovingest meeting that ever was seen, for the one embraced the other five or six times on horseback' and rode hand in hand, 'with great love the space of a mile'.[15] One-hundred-and-forty gentlemen in velvet coats rode with him, and forty guards, accompanied by around six hundred horsemen; but four of the key players from 1520 were missing. Henry had sent the Duke of Buckingham to the block, arrested Wolsey and banished Catherine, while Francis had lost his first wife, Claude. If the meeting of 1532 was intended to be an occasion as splendid as the Field of Cloth of Gold, it failed to provide even an echo of it.

Etiquette dictated that Anne was unable to join the two kings, owing to the absence of a corresponding household from the French queen, so she remained behind in Calais awaiting their return with thirty of her ladies, including her sister-in-law, Jane Boleyn and her sister Mary for company. Also in attendance were Honor Greville, Lady Lisle, wife of Arthur Plantagenet, Captain of Calais, who was an uncle of Henry, although he had been born illegitimate; Anne's half-aunt Elizabeth Howard, who was Lady Fitzwalter by marriage to Henry Radcliffe; another half-aunt, Dorothy Howard, Countess of Derby; and Elizabeth Harleston, Lady Wallop.[16] In a twist of fate, Anne's former admirer Thomas Wyatt was also present, perhaps somewhat reluctantly if his poem on the occasion is to be trusted, but he would have accompanied Henry rather than remained behind with Anne. Henry's illegitimate son, Henry Fitzroy, who was aged around thirteen, was part of his father's entourage. Privy Purse records include supplies of grapes and pears that were brought to her by a servant of Montmorency, as well as others who provided her with red deer pasties, carp and porpoise for her table. The time was whiled away as they played dice, dominoes and other games.[17] Anne waited from Monday until Friday, while the kings stayed in Boulogne, preparing for their return. She would have heard as they drew near – with the guns of Calais shooting 2,000 rounds, prompting the servants in their tawny coats and the soldiers in red and blue to line the streets in welcome.[18]

Francis was lodged in the Inn of the Staple, a 'princely house', in rooms hung with tissue and velvet, embroidered with flowers, where he dined on 'all manner of flesh, fowl, spice, venison, both of fallow deer and red deer, and as for wine, they lacked none'.[19] Francis sent Anne a diamond as a gift of friendship and welcome, but they would not meet again for another forty-eight hours, attending mass and council meetings on the Saturday, before the Sunday was spent watching bull-baiting. Henry also made payments to Francis's minstrels and jester.

On Sunday 27 October, when the kings' business was concluded, Anne finally made her international debut as Henry's partner. That night, Francis came to dine with Henry, in a chamber hung alternately with panels of silver and gold tissue, with seams covered with embroidered gold, full of pearls and gems. A cupboard with seven shelves displayed plate of gold and gilt, while white silver branches bore chains from which were hung wax lights.[20] Three courses were served, a hundred and fifty dishes of 'costly and pleasant' food, with the meat dressed in the French style for Francis and in the English style for Henry. Anne entered the chamber with seven ladies including Mary Carey and Jane Boleyn, all masked, wearing crimson tinsel satin with cloth of silver 'lying lose' and caught up in gold laces.[21] A Richard Gibson was paid £11 3s 1d for 'masking gear' while much larger sums, exceeding £8,000, were spent on jewels for the occasion.[22] Every lady 'took a Lord', with Anne partnering Francis, before her mask was removed.[23] The pair had not seen each other since Anne's departure at the end of 1521 but, clearly, the French king had followed the developments of Henry's relationship and now met with her on a different footing. The account tells us that they talked 'for a space' before the French king retired for the night, without revealing the subject of their conversation.[24]

On 29 October, after exchanging gifts, Henry and Anne bade farewell to Francis and prepared to leave Calais. The weather, though, was terrible, with storms making it dangerous to cross the Channel and 'such a winde, tempest and thunder that no man could conveniently stir in the streets of Calais'.[25] Henry lost at cards to Francis Weston and to Anne, who won 15 shillings from him on 9 November, helping to pass the days.[26] Waiting for two weeks at the Exchequer in their fine rooms, linked by a connecting door, this may well have been the moment that Henry and Anne consummated their love. If they had not slept together before, this event had been eagerly anticipated for seven years. If Anne had successfully held Henry at bay all that time, protecting the virginity she now yielded to her experienced lover, it must have signified that she felt certain of their future. They finally left Calais at midnight on 12 November and after a terrible crossing sailed into Dover early in the morning of 14 November, St Erkenwald's day. According to Hall and Sander, they got married secretly the same day, probably in the chapel or their apartments at Dover Castle.

Their progress back to London was steady. They were at Sandwich on 16 November and then at Canterbury from 17 to 19 November, where the expenses of the fool were paid, as were the Canterbury waites, or musicians, and the Abbot of St Augustine's was rewarded for bringing the king a book.[27] They stayed one night at The Lion in Sittingbourne, probably the Red Lion, an old coaching inn in the High Street, reputed to have housed Henry V on his return from Agincourt. There, rewards were given to the wife of the owner, to a poor woman who brought the king pears, and to a sailor.[28] It may have been the use of the royal barge again, avoiding the plague-ridden Rochester, that allowed them to sail from Faversham's harbour to reach Stone on 20 November, moving on by road to Eltham Palace soon afterwards. Whilst at Eltham, they received a gift of falcons and hawks sent by Francis. By the end of the month they were at Greenwich, playing a new card game called Pope Julius, at which Henry lost again to Anne, Francis Bryan and Francis Weston.[29]

Henry and Anne observed that Christmas at Greenwich. Henry made a gift to Anne of plate, or tableware, that came from a variety of sources; some from the royal coffers, some of which may have belonged to Catherine, old possessions of Wolsey's from York Place and some owned by Sir Henry Guildford, who had died that May. Anne would not have been sorry to lose Guildford, who had been Henry's Master of the Horse and Comptroller of the Royal Household. He had been outspoken against her marriage, to the extent that Anne had warned him she would strip him of office once she became queen. Sir Henry had promptly resigned his post to deny Anne the opportunity, even though the king begged him to continue and told him not to heed the words of women. That December, Anne received sufficient from her old enemies to equip her as a queen:

A gilt cup with a cover, Spanish fashion, chased with 'holines leaves', with a tower on the top. A gilt cup of assay. 2 gilt cups of assay with the King's arms in the bottom. 6 plain gilt bowls with a cover. A pair of gilt pots chased with daisies. A pair of great gilt pots, plain, with the King's arms in the bussells. A pair of gilt pots, plain, without plaits in the bussels in the top of the cover. 2 gilt layers, chased, upright. 18 gilt trenchers of Flanders touch. A pair of covered gilt basons; one chased wreathen, the other upright with beasts. A cup with a cover, of Almain making, and on the pomell of the cover a man holding the King's arms. A great double cup, 'gilte arsed', of Almain making. A double cup gilt, with white leaves of silver about the borders. A pair of gilt pots with high tirrettes on the lids. 2 gilt pots. A pair of flagons with roses embossed upon the sides, with plaits in the midst, and therein the King's arms. A gilt cup with a cover, with three borders enamelled blue, with the King's arms in the bussells. 6 gilt bowls stricken with martlets. 2 pairs of gilt pots chased with damask flowers. 3 goblets chased with drops and scriptures about them. 3 goblets chased, feather fashion, having a boy bearing a shield with the King's arms. 3 gilt salts; another of antike work, with white and red roses and scallop shells. 2 gilt basons with ewers, graven with roses and flower deluces. 2 gilt standing trenchers with salts at the corners. 5 gilt chaundillers plain, parcel of the King's plate at York Place, in Sir Thos. Alvard's charge. 5 parcel-gilt bowls without a cover, with martelotes.[30]

From that specifically left by Sir Henry Guildford, she was given:

Two gilt pots with round knops behind the covers. A pair of gilt flagons or bottles with the arms of France. 6 plain gilt bowls without a cover. 3 low salts, gilt with a cover of Paris touch. 12 gilt spoons with half knops at the end. A pair of parcel-gilt pots with round knops behind the cover. Two pairs of parcel-gilt pots. 6 parcel-gilt bowls with a cover. 2 parcel-gilt basins and ewers. 11 white spoons, with roses at the ends. 4 white chaundillers with high sockets. A round bason of silver for a chamber, and a silver pot with a lid. A chafing dish, parcel-gilt.[31]

These were very generous New Years' gifts, but they were more than that. They helped establish the material culture of Anne's queenship, in the wake of her secret marriage at Dover, or in advance of the ceremony that was about to take place. This was her dowry. By Christmas, Anne was already pregnant, and with Henry so keen to ensure their child would be legitimate, he showered his new wife with the visual signifiers of rank. It was accompanied by the declaration Catherine was no longer to be referred to as queen, but instead to be called dowager princess, her title from her marriage to Arthur, and she was to be treated accordingly. On 25 January 1533, in a secret service in the king's chapel at Whitehall, Henry and Anne went through a second wedding, presided over by Rowland Lee, the newly elected Bishop of Coventry and Lichfield, and witnessed by Anne's gentlewoman Anne Savage and Henry's close companions Henry Norris and Thomas Heneage.

At the start of 1533, married to the king and pregnant with his child, Anne could not resist dropping hints at court, about her craving for apples, or the need to go on pilgrimage. Her chaplain, Thomas

Cranmer, had been recalled to England from Italy in order to become the new Archbishop of Canterbury. Henry hoped Cranmer would prove sympathetic to their cause and declare the marriage valid. On his way back to England, Cranmer wrote to Henry about an omen appearing in the skies, a sign of great change to come:

> A blazing star, called Cometa, has appeared in the East every morning since the 5th or 6th inst. for two hours before daylight. Its beam inclines upward, partly toward the south, and it is much whiter in colour than that which appeared last year. Mine host at a city called Indiburs, and many other persons, have seen a blue cross above the moon; a flaming horsehead and a flaming sword have also been seen; but I have seen nothing but the comet. What strange things these tokens do signify to come hereafter, God knoweth, for they do not lightly appear but against some great mutation. And it hath not been seen (as I suppose) that so m[any] comets have appeared in so short time.[32]

Such signs in the night sky were portents of great change; for the reformist Cranmer, for the most reactionary Catholic. As he returned to England to take up the Archbishopric, Cranmer would find the country on the verge of redefinition.

TWENTY-SEVEN

Queen at Last 1533

News about Anne's new status and condition were revealed to the court slowly, piece by piece, through the winter and spring of 1533. The marriage was still an official secret on 9 February, when Chapuys wrote that Henry 'never talked so much or so openly as he does now of carrying his marriage into execution'. The ambassador had also heard Anne using similar tactics, preparing the court to accept her as Henry's wife, whilst concealing the truth that the ceremony had already taken place. Anne had commented to a priest who wished to become her chaplain that 'he must have patience for a short time until she had actually married the King'.[1] According to Chapuys, Anne had also said, whilst dining in her apartments, that 'she was as sure as she was of her own death that she should be very soon married to the king', and on another occasion, Thomas Boleyn was convinced that 'the king was determined no longer to be so considerate as he had been... but to marry his daughter at once'. When the Duke of Rutland refused to accept Boleyn's statement, Thomas reputedly 'got into a passion as though Rutland had uttered a blasphemy and began to taunt him in very gross language'.[2] However, by 23 February, the ambassador had heard from his informer that the new Archbishop, Cranmer, had 'pledged his most solemn word to adhere entirely to the king's opinion in this matter of the divorce, so much so that he has actually married the King to the Lady in the presence only of her father, mother, brother and two intimate female friends of the Lady herself'.[3]

Towards the end of February, French visitors to the court were invited to dine with Henry, during which Anne 'occupied the same place and seat as the Queen in former times'.[4] However, when the Papal Nuncio tried to gain access to Henry, it 'happened to be on the day when the Lady had invited the King to dine in her apartments' so he was unable to get an audience and Henry deputed Norfolk to listen to him instead.[5] This may have been the feast day of St Mathias, 24 February, when Anne 'treated the King to a banquet in her apartments, beautifully ornamented with splendid tapestry hangings and the finest of buffets covered with gold plate'. Anne sat on the king's right, while her step-grandmother Agnes Howard, Dowager Duchess of Norfolk, sat on the left, but lower down. Chapuys was indignant to hear how Henry's attention had been focussed on Anne and her friends:

> During the dinner the King was so much engaged in play and conversation with the ladies that he scarcely talked to the rest of the company, or if he did no one could hear what he said, save once that he addressed the duchess of Norfolk, and asked her if she did not think that Madame, the marchioness, had a fine dowry and a rich marriage portion.[6]

By the end of March, even though rumours were rife that Henry and Anne had undergone a secret ceremony, some of those at court were still uncertain whether or not they were man and wife. Neither the king nor Anne yet took steps to dispel these doubts, almost enjoying the ambiguity of their situation, revelling in the privacy of their new arrangement, before her advancing pregnancy ensured that some formal declaration had to be made. It was also a way of taking back the control of their relationship, given the recent years of helplessness in the face of Rome. Chapuys reported the general belief that they would be wed before Easter, as a royal household was being appointed for Anne,[7] but he was afraid of what she might do once her power was official. He was concerned that Anne's influence would alienate the kingdom from the Holy Faith and turn it over to the Lutherans, an 'irreparable evil' in which she was being assisted by Cranmer. In his eyes, Anne was truly a pernicious influence, a danger to Henry's character and soul, his family and country, she had rendered him unrecognisable from the man he had been: 'Though the King is by nature kind and generously inclined, this Anne has so perverted him that he does not seem the same man.'[8]

The ambassador also had no doubt that Anne would attempt to do Catherine and Mary 'all the harm she possibly can' and 'make of the Princess a maid of honour in her Royal household, that she may perhaps give her too much dinner on some occasion, or marry her to some varlet', which is almost comical, although there was some foundation in the concern about Mary's position. Anne would indeed place her within the household of her soon-to-be-born daughter.[9] After having a conversation with Henry about his role as a parent, Chapuys recorded the following exchange:

> The King said that he wished to ensure the succession to his kingdom by having children, which he had not at present, and upon my remarking

to him that he had one daughter, the most virtuous and accomplished that could be thought of, just of suitable age to be married and get children, and that it seemed as if Nature had decided that the succession to the English throne should be through the female line, as he himself had obtained it, and therefore, that he could by marrying the Princess to some one secure the succession he was so anxious for, he replied that he knew better than that; and would marry again in order to have children himself. And upon my observing to him that he could not be sure of that he asked me three times running: 'Am I not a man like others?' and he afterwards added: 'I need not give proofs of the contrary, or let you into my secrets', no doubt implying thereby that his beloved Lady is already in the family way.[10]

Chapuys had also heard, from his 'very good source' and from 'the lips of a person who was present' that Anne had taken a piece of cloth to add to her dress, 'as ladies in a family-way are wont to do in this country, when they find their robes get too tight'.[11] Presumably this was to conceal the swelling of her belly, as her father reputedly told her she should not use it and instead to 'thank God for the state in which she found herself', upon which Anne hinted at her marriage, saying that 'she was in better plight than he would have wished her to be'.[12] Regardless of whether Chapuys' reported conversation was accurate or not, news of Anne's condition was spreading across Europe. By the approach of Easter, which fell on 13 April that year, she was four months pregnant and this was the point Henry chose to make her position public.

On 12 April, Anne attended Mass in the Queen's closet at Greenwich, in full Royal state, wearing diamonds and a dress of tissue and with the train carried by her cousin, Mary Howard, daughter of the Duke of Norfolk. A horde of female attendants followed her as she was conducted to and from the service, with 'greater ceremonies and solemnities than those used with former queens on such occasions'.[13] For the first time, prayers were said naming her as queen, instead of as marchioness, at which Chapuys reported that the people were 'astonished' and that it seemed 'like a dream' leaving them unsure whether to laugh or cry.[14] Yet among the many ladies of Anne's household who were her intimate companions in her apartments, responsible for dressing her and engaging in her bedtime rituals, who knew that the king came to her bed and that her monthly period had ceased, there cannot have been much surprise. Nor would this have been such surprising news for the inner circle of courtiers who had been anticipating this event for years. Chapuys related how the reaction angered Henry, so that the king acted to control his subjects' prattling on the topic:

...the King was so much disgusted that he sent word to the Lord Mayor of this city that unless he wished to displease him immensely he must take care that the thing did not happen again; and he gave orders that in future no one should dare speak against his marriage. In virtue of which orders the Lord Mayor caused all the crafts and guilds to assemble in their various halls, and commanded them under pain of incurring the Royal indignation not only to abstain from murmuring about the King's marriage, but to command their own journeymen and servants, and a still more difficult task their own wives, to refrain from speaking disparagingly about the new Queen.[15]

After an incident at Westminster, where public prayers were said for Catherine and Princess Mary instead of Anne, Henry also tried to ensure that no future sermons would be delivered in their support, with no one from the four Mendicant Orders permitted to preach without licence from Cranmer. It became a crime 'under pain of capital punishment' for anyone to mention Catherine by her former title.[16] Catherine, of course, continued to insist her title had not changed.

On Easter Day itself, Anne returned to Mass at Greenwich 'with all the pomp of a queen, clad in cloth of gold and loaded with the richest jewels', after which she dined in public, as a statement of her new role.[17] Easter Monday saw her publicly proclaimed in the King's Court as queen and numerous officials were sworn in as members of her household.[18] At the same time, Cromwell was appointed Chancellor of the Exchequer and George Boleyn returned home from France, to be present for Anne's impending coronation. The Venetian ambassador, Carlo Capello, was one of the first to salute Anne as England's new queen. He was invited to dine with the king at Greenwich and was received 'most graciously' by Thomas and George Boleyn, Norfolk and Cromwell, and conducted into Henry's presence, who was 'with a number of Lords and Queen Anne', to whom he was presented, and to whom he saluted.[19] The Venetian Marin Guistinian confirmed that 'Queen Anne appeared with the royal insignia and dined in public and the king appointed her officials and they believe her to be pregnant'. Norfolk and Suffolk were dispatched to inform Catherine of the situation.[20] Yet, as his reaction on Easter Eve indicated, Henry was unsure about the wider responses to Anne's elevation, sending instructions to all the city crafts not to 'dare speak otherwise than well on this new marriage and Queen Anne, and to prepare the entertainments and expenditure usually made for the Queen's coronation'.[21] It is an interesting measure of change in the Boleyn dynasty, of 'giddy Fortune's furious fickle wheel', that the city guilds, who constituted the world of Geoffrey Boleyn and among whose ranks and rituals he had risen, were now being warned to fulfil their allotted role in honouring his great-granddaughter.

Then Archbishop Cranmer did what Wolsey had been unable, or unwilling, to do. On 16 May, he opened proceedings at Dunstable Priory in Bedfordshire, to investigate the circumstances of Henry's first marriage. Just a week later, on the morning of 23 May, he pronounced that it was invalid, against the law of God, making Henry's marriage to Anne legitimate.[22] With just days to go, the final preparations were being made for Anne's coronation, which would see her riding, visibly pregnant, through the London streets where Catherine had been welcomed and cheered twenty-four years earlier. Capello recounted how jousts and entertainments were being planned, along with the king's intention to confer a number of new knighthoods.[23] Henry issued letters to the Mayor and commonality of the city of London, 'signifying to them that his pleasure was to solemnise and celebrate the coronation of his most dear and well beloved wife Queen Anne... willing them to make preparation as well to fetch her Grace from Greenwich to the Tower by water, as to see the city ordered and garnished with pageants in places accustomed, for the honour of her Grace'.[24] Henry was calling upon the resources of the city, through an infrastructure that supported the rise of Anne's great-grandfather, Geoffrey, and to the pinnacle of which she had risen.

The formal proceedings began on Thursday, 29 May 1533. That morning, Anne awoke at Greenwich and with the assistance of her ladies adorned herself in jewels for the day ahead. By one o'clock, the Mayor of London, Sir Stephen Peacock of the Haberashers' guild had assembled the civic dignitaries at St Mary's Hill, where they had taken to their barges. A flotilla of around fifty ships was filled with lords and ladies dressed in their finery and bearing minstrels, shawms, sackbuts, trumpets and other instruments, 'richly decked with arras, hung with banners and with pennons of the arms of the crafts in fine gold'.[25] Leading them was a boat filled with guns to fire salutes for Anne, decorated with a red dragon that breathed fire and also carried terrible monsters and wild men. Then, according to precedence, came the Mayor's barge and the barge of the bachelors. As the guild company of the incumbent mayor, the Haberdashers were responsible for the creation of the latter. It was full of trumpets, hung with bells and decked with flags and banners bearing the Haberdashers' devices. After them came the barges of the Mercers and Grocers, who were the largest, richest guilds, followed by the rest. Hall's account likened the occasion to the annual inauguration of the mayor at Westminster in October.[26] Another vessel, presumably the 'highly decorated little ship' prepared for Anne to travel, bore her device of a mount with a crowned white falcon standing upon it, surrounded by red and white roses. Around this symbol sat virgins singing and playing. They sailed down river to Greenwich, where Anne took her seat at about three in the afternoon. From there, she was rowed to the Tower, with the 'constant discharge of artillery' and the barges of her father, Suffolk, and other noblemen and bishops on either side.[27]

As they approached Wapping Mills, the Tower began to fire its cannon.[28] Anne was met at the landing stage by Sir Edward Walsingham, Lieutenant of the Tower and Sir William Kingston, the Constable, who conducted her to the spot where Henry was waiting, through a 'long lane' which had been made for her among the people. She thanked the Mayor and citizens, and entered the Tower to 'great melody' from the boats.[29] The dowager duchess of Norfolk, her step-grandmother, bore her train, with Anne's Vice-Chamberlain Edward Baynton bearing its weight, and she was attended by the Officers-of-Arms, before being greeted by the Lord Chamberlain, Sir William Sandys of the Vyne, the Bishops of London and Winchester, and others. Among the welcoming committee was her uncle, William Howard, Lord Hanworth, Marshal of England, who was standing in for his brother Thomas, Duke of Norfolk, who had left the country on ambassadorial work that week. Inside the Tower, Henry was waiting and 'laid his hands on both her sides, kissing her with great reverence and a joyful countenance' and led her to her chambers.[30] Henry and Anne had supper, followed by a 'sumptuous void' of wine and spices. Anne rested overnight and through Friday 30 May, while Henry created eighteen new Knights of the Garter, in the same ceremony that William and Thoms Boleyn had undergone. Among them were the brother of George Boleyn's wife, Sir Henry Parker, and Sir Francis Weston.[31]

On Saturday 31 May, Anne prepared to leave the Tower for the procession across London to Westminster. Dressed in silver tissue, with her hair loose over her shoulders and a coronet upon her head, she sat in a chair of cloth of gold, under a silver canopy, between two mules trapped in silver damask.[32] Venetian Capello described how she was accompanied by 'the greater part of the nobility of this kingdom, with the utmost order and tranquillity' through the decorated streets where the houses were 'crowded with persons of every condition, in number truly marvellous'.[33] The order of precedence had been set down well in advance, with the king's messengers first, followed by the ambassadors' servants, the trumpets, the gentlemen ushers, chaplains, Squires of the Body, pursuivants, knights, aldermen, heralds, Knights of the Bath, baronets, abbots, Knights of the Garter, the chief judges and Master of the Rolls, the lords and barons after their estate, the bishops, earls, ambassadors,

Comptroller of the Household, Treasurer, Steward and Chamberlain of the same, the Lord Privy Seal, the Lord Admiral, the Great Chamberlain, archbishops, representatives of the Dukes of Normandy and Aquitaine, Lord Mayor and Garter, the Marshal, Constable, Anne's Treasurer and Chancellor, the sergeants at arms and, finally, Anne herself.[34] After her came twenty-eight ladies of the highest estate, in crimson velvet, borne along in four gold chariots, the first containing the dowager Duchess of Norfolk, Anne's step-grandmother and the widowed Marquess of Dorset, while Anne's mother, Elizabeth, Countess of Wiltshire, sat in the second with two other countesses. The third carriage contained Anne's sister Mary, her sister-in-law Jane's mother Lady Morley, one of her aunts listed as Lady Boleyn, who must have been either Elizabeth or Anne, Mary Zouche, Lady Fitzwarren and Margery Horsman, while in the fourth sat Anne's cousin Mary or Margaret Shelton, also known as 'Madge', Katherine Ashley and others. Riding alongside on horseback were her sister-in-law Jane Boleyn, Lady Rochford, her cousin Mary Howard, daughter of the Duke of Norfolk, her aunt Dorothy Howard, the Countess of Worcester, the Countess of Sussex and two other ladies. Then came thirty gentlewomen, in velvet and silk, bearing the liveries of their ladies, followed by more women on horseback, in black velvet. After them came the Captain of the Guard and the King's Guard 'in their rich coats'.[35]

The details were recorded slightly differently by those who participated in the event, from Capello, who was riding with the ambassadors before Anne, to the herald who recorded the official account, the author of the pamphlet *The Noble Tryumphaunt Coronacyon of Quene Anne,* to those who gathered gossip about the day, like Chapuys. But the expenses for the occasion agree from one to another on many of the details, on the yards of crimson velvet and damask, and the gold silk fringe for Anne's litter; on the scarlet saddles and collars with gilt bosses and bells; on 10,000 gilt nails, black reins, gilt roses and pommels; on the yards of white, black and red satin for her gowns, the flat gold chain she would wear and the 17 pieces of goldsmith's work.[36]

Anne's coronation procession took a slightly different route from that which Catherine had followed in 1501 and in 1509. Upon leaving the Tower, she passed Tower Hill and All Hallow's Church, riding a little way along Tower Street before heading north-west, probably up Marke Lane to Fenchurch Street, instead of continuing to the main thoroughfare of Gracechurch Street. It may simply have been a practical decision, as the first pageant in her honour awaited her there, where children dressed as merchants sang verses of welcome in English and French. This was mounted by the guild of Ironmongers, one of the Great Twelve city livery companies, whose first hall had been built in Fenchurch Street back in 1457, opposite the junction with Marke Lane. The guild had incurred costs of £11 18s 10d in taking part in the flotilla to accompany Anne from Greenwich, for the barge, painted banner staves and provisions.[37]

After this, Anne headed west, past the church of St Mary's that stood in the centre of Fenchurch Street, past St Dionis and St Benet, to the junction with Gracechurch Street, which rose up from the south. At Gracechurch Corner, a mountain of white marble flowed with four streams running with Rhenish wine, where Apollo and Calliope sat on Mount Parnassus, surrounded by the nine muses, playing music and praising Anne in epigrams. Melpomene declared, 'O everyone that sees these shows, that sees Anna in her passing beauty riding through the city, do you bring incense, and pray first that the crown may sit well on her forehead.'[38] This was the 'marvellous and cunning' work of the Merchants of the Steelyard, who had commissioned Holbein to design it for them and the surviving sketches give an impression of the imposing majesty of the finished product, placed atop a triumphal arch.

Next, the procession turned right up Gracechurch Street towards the conduit that marked the crossroads with Cornhill. On the top at the right stood Leadenhall, a site that had been given to the city by Mayor Richard Whittington shortly before Geoffrey Boleyn's arrival, which had been developed in the 1440s into a two-storey quadrangle that served as a market place and public granary. Awaiting Anne was a mountain under a gold canopy, set with red and white roses, where her badge was displayed as a falcon landing on a stump, being crowned by an angel in armour. St Anne, mother of the Virgin, sat below the stump and a child 'made a goodly oration to the Queen about the fruitfulness of St Anne... trusting that like fruit should come of her'.[39] Here, Anne was addressed in verses written by antiquarian John Leland and Nicholas Udall, a protégé of Cromwell's:

> This White Falcon,
> Rare and geason,
> This bird shineth so bright;
> Of all that are,
> No bird compare
> May with this Falcon White.
>
> The virtues all,
> No man mortal,
> Of this bird can write.
> No man earthly

Enough truly
Can praise this Falcon White.

Who will express
Great gentleness
To be in any wight;
He will not miss,
But call him this
The gentle Falcon White.

This gentle bird
As white as curd
Shineth both day and night;
Nor far ne near
Is any peer
Unto this Falcon White,

Of body small.
Of power regal,
She is, and sharp of sight;
Of courage hault
No manner fault
Is in this Falcon White,

In chastity,
Excelleth she,
Most like a virgin bright:
And worthy is
To live in bliss
Always this Falcon White.

But now to take
And use her make
Is time, as troth is plight;
That she may bring
Fruit according
For such a Falcon White.

And where by wrong,
She hath fleen long,
Uncertain where to light;
Herself repose

Upon the Rose,
Now may this Falcon White.

Whereon to rest,
And build her nest;
GOD grant her, most of might!
That England may
Rejoice always
In this same Falcon White

Beyond Leadenhall lay the thoroughfare of Cornhill, past the churches of St Peter and St Michael, and the Merchant Taylor's Hall. In the centre of the street sat the main Conduit, where the three graces Juno, Pallas and Venus were waiting to greet Anne in a pageant of The Judgement of Paris. A child declamed that Anne, 'most excellent that ever was', should receive the 'crown imperial... to your joy, honour and glory immortal'.[40] The procession then took Anne through Scalding Alley, past the Stocks Market and through Le Pultrye, the heart of commercial London, into Cheapside, which was hung with banners of arms and painted images of kings and queens were displayed. She would have had a good view of the Mercer's Hall and the Hospital and Church of St Thomas of Acon, where her great-grandfather had attended meetings of the Worshipful Company of Mercers and served as a church warden. Next, they passed along Goldsmith's Row, famous for its luxury wares, and in through St Paul's Gate, where Cheapside divided in two, either side of the Church of St Michael le Querne. Above her head, wafers inscribed with welcome messages rained down upon her, chimes sounded and choirs sang. Anne 'highly commended' the singing of the boys from the newly founded St Paul's School.[41]

Just inside the precincts, at St Paul's Cross, Anne was greeted by two angels bearing a crown and was presented by Master Baker, the recorder, with a purse of gold containing a thousand marks, 'which she thankfully accepted with many goodly words'.[42] Three ladies held tablets, speaking a prophecy that Anne would one day bear a son who would bring 'a golden world unto her people'. The cross itself, a significant site for preaching and proclamations, had been newly gilded in her honour and the aldermen were gathered there to greet her. The procession passed around and beyond the cathedral along Bower Row to Ludgate, a gate that allowed them to pass out of the city walls and into Fleet Street. The last building before the gate, St Martin's Church, hosted a choir who sang ballads to Anne from the rooftops before she rode out of the city and crossed the Fleet River. A little further along, after the various inns that clustered outside the gate, stood the Fleet conduit. The final pageant of a tower with four turrets had been erected upon it, upon which the figures of different virtues were positioned, each promising that they would not desert Anne. Music was played from within on 'solemne instruments' that sounded like 'a heavenly noise'.[43] Further along, where the road split at Temple Bar, another choir greeted Anne, before she headed along the Strand, through the newly built Whitehall and down towards Westminster. The hall there was hung with cloth of arras and newly glazed, and she was conducted to a spot under a cloth of estate and given wine and spices.[44]

Predictably, negative accounts of the day survive, written for the benefit of the Emperor, the pope, or the friends and supporters of Catherine and Mary. Chapuys told Charles that it had been a 'cold, meagre, and uncomfortable thing, to the great dissatisfaction, not only of the common people, but also of the rest'.[45] Another, anonymous, manuscript asserted that even though it was 'customary to kneel, uncover and cry "God save the King, God save the Queen," whenever they appeared in public, no one in London or the suburbs, not even women and children, did so on this occasion'.[46] The source continues with as much vitriol as he (or remotely possibly she) can muster whilst remaining plausible, and some blatant errors:

One of the Queen's servants told the mayor to command the people to make the customary shouts, and was answered that he could not command people's hearts, and that even the King could not make them do so. Her fool, who has been to Jerusalem and speaks several languages, seeing the little honor they showed to her, cried out, 'I think you have all scurvy heads, and dare not uncover.' Her dress was covered with tongues pierced with nails, to show the treatment which those who spoke against her might expect. Her car was so low that the ears of the last mule appeared to those who stood behind to belong to her. The letters H. A. were painted in several places, for Henry and Anne, but were laughed at by many. The crown became her very ill, and a wart disfigured her very much. She wore a violet velvet mantle, with a high ruff of gold thread and pearls, which concealed a swelling she has, resembling goitre. She was crowned by Cranmer, who is called 'one of the judges of Susanna,' and 'le pape patriarche...' The duchess of Norfolk, daughter of the duke of Buckingham, would not appear at the ceremony, from the love she bore to the previous Queen, although she was Anne's aunt. The French ambassador and his suite were insulted by the people, who called him 'Orson queneve, France dogue' (whoreson knave, French dog).[47]

In contrast, Sir Anthony Browne, who was then in Paris, and Sir Edward Baynton, wrote to Cromwell and George Boleyn respectively to comment how glad they were to hear that the coronation had been so 'honourably' done.[48] Edward Hall's account is also to be considered reliable, as he had been appointed a Common Serjeant of London on 17 March that year and would have been present on the occasion in his official capacity. The reports of negative responses among the crowd, or the meagreness of the occasion, come from hostile sources and the latter charge at least can be easily disproved by the records of spending on jewels, clothing, ceremony and chariots.

On Sunday 1 June 1533, between eight and nine in the morning, Anne processed from Westminster Hall to the Abbey on the traditional ray cloth, surrounded by the nobility and clergymen of England. She wore a surcoat and robe of purple velvet, with the jewelled circlet on her loose hair again and her long train carried by the Duchess of Norfolk. The lords and ladies following were all clad in scarlet, with the fur collars powdered according to their degrees. When the Mass was concluded, Anne mounted a specially constructed platform and sat on an elevated seat, which was covered in tapestry, for the duration of the service. Then she was invited forward by Archbishop Cranmer and prostrated herself at the High Altar. He anointed her on the head and breast and placed the crown of St Edward briefly upon her head, before the crown was substituted for a lighter one of her own. She made an offering at the shrine of Edward the Confessor, before placing her right hand in that of her father and being led out to to the sound of trumpets. The king watched the proceedings from a little closet, accessed by the cloisters.

At the banquet that followed, Anne was attended by the leading lords of the court, most of whom were well known to her. They had witnessed her journey from being merely Thomas Boleyn's daughter to queen – her return to court from France, the disgrace with Henry Percy, the infatuation of the king, and the years of waiting. Many were to play significant roles during her reign and downfall. Charles Brandon, Duke of Suffolk, was High Steward of England, wearing a coat and jacket set with pearls and a gown of crimson velvet, carrying the white rod of office in his hand. His wife Mary, the former French queen, did not attend, more likely as the result of illness rather than disapproval, as she died twenty-four days after the coronation. Anne's uncle, William Howard, served as deputy for his absent brother the Duke of Norfolk in the role of Earl Marshal, overseeing the serving of the food. At Anne's feet sat two ladies, the widowed Countess of Oxford and Elizabeth, Duchess of Somerset, who were placed under the table to serve her secretly with what she might need; and two others near her, one on each side, often raised a great linen cloth to hide her from view, when she wished to spit or wipe her mouth. John de Vere, Earl of Oxford, Henry's High Chamberlain, had borne the crown at the coronation and now helped preside over the meal. Henry's cousin, Henry Bouchier, Earl of Essex, was Anne's carver, Henry Radcliffe, Earl of Sussex, the son of Anne's half-aunt, served as sewer, or leading server. William FitzAlan, Earl of Arundel, had carried Anne's sceptre and dove in the cathedral and was now chief butler, serving the wine. The cupbearer was Edward Stanley, Earl of Derby, a ward of the Duke of Norfolk, who had briefly been married to his daughter, Katherine Howard, Anne's cousin, before the bride's death from the plague. Arthur Plantagenet, Lord Lisle, an illegitimate son of Henry's grandfather, Edward IV, and recently appointed Captain of Calais, was the pantler. George Neville, Lord Bergavenny, had come back into royal favour after the execution of his father-in-law, the Duke of Buckingham, after supporting Henry over the divorce, and was now appointed Chief Larder. Edmund Bray was the almoner, the Mayor of Oxford kept the buttery bar and Sir Thomas Wyatt stood in as chief sewer for his father, Sir Henry.[49]

Anne sat at a long table, at a distance from those around her; although Cranmer sat on her right, he was still not close. In fact, she was surrounded by 'an enclosure, into which none entered but those deputed to serve her'.[50] Guests were seated on four main tables, according to rank, extending the entire length of the hall; conduits at the door poured with wine and food was distributed by the kitchens to all comers. The king himself watched through a little closet out of the cloister of St Stephen's, accompanied by the ambassadors of France and Venice,[51] probably Jean de Dinteville, of Holbein's 'The Ambassadors', standing in for Du Bellay, who was out of England until that November, and Carlo Capello.

The first of three courses was heralded by the Duke of Suffolk and William Howard on horseback, accompanied by the serjeants-of-arms, the sewer and Knights of the Bath. Sir Giles Allington, knighted by Henry in 1530, bore Anne the first cup. Each course that followed, comprising around thirty dishes, was announced by trumpets and proclamations. Capello estimated that there were around 800 guests, treated to a 'very grand and most sumptuous banquet'.[52] The feast lasted a long time: when the final wafers and hippocras, spices and confections arrived and Anne washed, drank from a gold cup brought to her by the Mayor of London and departed, it was six o'clock in the evening.[53] The following day, Monday, a tournament was held, eight knights against eight, each running six courses, led on one side by William Howard and on the other by Sir Nicholas Carew.[54] More banquets and balls followed.

Not everyone welcomed the recent events. On 12 June, the Mayor of Sandwich in Kent wrote to Cromwell regarding the treasonous words spoken by a local man:

> On Tuesday last, Gervase Shelbye, inhabitant of the parish of St. Peter Thanet, who was arrested on Monday at Ramsgate, was brought before us by commandment of John Crips and Edw. Monynges, King's commissioners. The said Shelbye, in the presence of Wm. Saunders and Simon Graunte, spake these words: that his conscience grieved him sore to take the oath commanded to be taken of all the King's subjects in Kent, as the King had broken the sacrament of matrimony, and that when he went over the sea he went to Rome to the Pope to have his favor to marry with queen Anne, but the Pope would give him no licence. He is now in the gaol at Sandwich till the King's pleasure be known. Sandwich, 12 June.[55]

Gervase Shelbye posed no threat to Anne, but the pope and cardinals were more formidable enemies. Four days after the Mayor of Sandwich wrote his letter, the Cardinal of Jaén, the Spanish Esteban Merino, wrote to the Emperor to report his recent conversation with the pope about the heretic king of England:

> The Pope gave me to understand that he should try to take away the hopes of the French about Italy; they should be content with a good intelligence with him and the Emperor, and could gain more, with greater ease, in other kingdoms. I understand him to mean that he wished to set them against the king of England.
>
> Subsequently he opened this more clearly, saying that the king of England deserved punishment for his sin, and proceedings might be taken against him as a heretic. As the affair was of importance, he wished no one to know of it till he had communicated with the Emperor. Replied only that the king of England had deserved this and more, and that the king of France ought to separate from him.[56]

TWENTY-EIGHT

Elizabeth 1533

Anne now had three months to wait until the arrival of her child. The mood in her Greenwich apartments was a merry one, as Sir Edward Baynton, her newly appointed Vice Chamberlain, wrote to George Boleyn: 'And as for pastime in the Queen's chamber was never more. If any of you,' he teased George, 'that be now departed have any ladies that they thought favoured you, and somewhat would mourn at parting... I can no whit perceive the same by their dancing and pastime they do use here.'[1] Baynton's letter refers to the introduction of a new hawk, a merlin, which was not yet ready to hunt larks, and passes on messages to Charles Brandon and thanks to Norfolk for a token Baynton had received from the Duke. Norfolk was still in Paris, where Anthony Browne, Henry's ambassador to France, wrote that the Duke had 'great cheer... everywhere in these parts, which could not be improved on'.[2] Norfolk himself wrote to Henry that June, passing on the good wishes of Francis's sister Marguerite, now Queen of Navarre, both to Henry and, significantly, to Anne:

> Since coming here (Paris) I have been twice with the queen of Navarre, and both times for at least five hours. She is one of the most wisest frank women, and best setter forth of her purpose, that I have spoken with, and as affectionate to your Highness as if she were your own sister, and likewise to the Queen.[3]

As queen, Anne had access to far greater resources than before and required a wardrobe and furnishings to match those of the king. It was as an important visual confirmation of her position and one which she and Henry took seriously. On 8 July, the king issued instructions to Lord

Windsor, the Keeper of the Great Wardrobe, to deliver to his yeoman, Edward Flowde, a number of items for Anne's use. These included lengths of cloth of gold tissue, fringed with silk and gold, to be used as the cloth of estate above her chair. It was described as being, in size, like Henry's own purple velvet cloth of estate, embroidered with his arms. Anne was to have two timber chairs, one covered with similar cloth of gold tissue, with gilt and enamelled pommels, fringed with silk and gold and the other covered with plain cloth of gold. She was also to receive three iron chairs, two covered in crimson silk, one in purple silk, five small Turkey carpets to drape over her cupboards, blankets, sacks and hides, white thread for the mending of sheets, six brushes, four hammers and 2,000 hooks.[4] Just as she had acquired Catherine's jewels before the Calais trip, another process of material transformation took place around the new queen although, owing to Catherine's continued presence in the countryside, Anne had to receive the trappings of her new status piece by piece.

Anne's household as queen had been established prior to her coronation. Appointed to serve her were members of her family, who were benefiting from her new position. Jane Boleyn, Viscountess Rochford, was now in her late twenties and had been married to George since late 1524 or early 1525, although the couple were childless. They divided their time between court and their main residence of Beaulieu in Essex, where they lived in almost regal splendour, sleeping in a bed draped with cloth of gold, under a canopy of white satin, surrounded by expensive furniture and plate, with hot and cold running water, tennis courts, a library and a new chapel. The nature of their marriage has divided historians, with some suggesting that it was unhappy, based on George Cavendish's reports of George Boleyn living a promiscuous life and Jane's later actions, but no surviving evidence from their life together supports this.

Evidence for animosity between Anne and Jane is only to be found after Anne's fall, as with her other gentlewoman and aunt, Anne Shelton. The elder sister of Thomas Boleyn, Anne had married a Norfolk neighbour, Sir John Shelton, before 1503 and had ten children, including Mary and Margaret, who may both have served at Anne's court. Queen Anne clearly trusted her aunt, as she placed her in charge of Princess Mary's new household at Hatfield, along with her sister Alice Boleyn, who had married Sir Robert Clere, also from Norfolk. Lady Anne Boleyn was then in her late fifties, while Alice was aged around forty six.

One more of Anne's aunts also found preferment at her new court, Lady Elizabeth Boleyn, née Wood, wife of Sir James Boleyn, a younger brother of Thomas, Anne and Alice. Elizabeth was probably a similar age to her husband. She may only have been a decade older than the new queen, perhaps even less. She does not appear to have been a favourite of Anne's as, after her arrest in 1536, the queen would comment that she had never loved her, and that it was an act of cruelty to appoint Elizabeth to wait upon her. By this point though, she was also including Anne Shelton in this description, along with Margaret Dymoke and Lady Kingston. Margaret was Anne's contemporary, being born in 1500 and, after being widowed, had made a second marriage to William Coffin, Anne's newly appointed Master of the Horse. Mary Scrope, Lady Kingston, was wife to the Lieutenant of the Tower who had welcomed Anne there before her coronation. She had served Queen Catherine since her coronation in 1509, and been married to Sir Edward Jerningham, before Anne's rise.

Also among those appointed to attend the new queen was Anne 'Nan' Gainsford, who had been involved in the incident with the Tyndale book, and who would marry George Zouche that year. Bridget Wingfield of Stone Castle may have continued to serve Anne after her coronation, although she died in 1533 or 1534, possibly in childbirth. The new queen's elevation provided an opportunity for the rise of a woman of more humble birth; Elizabeth, or Bess, Holland, who had been a member of the household of Anne's aunt by marriage, Elizabeth, Duchess of Norfolk. Bess was the daughter of Norfolk's secretary, and worked for eight years in the laundry of his house, becoming his mistress. She came to court to take her place in Anne's establishment as the result of this connection, as a maid of honour. Another member of Anne's new household was Elizabeth Stoner, wife of William Stonor, who had been knighted by Anne's grandfather after the Battle of Flodden in 1513. Elizabeth was given the title of Mother of the Maids, responsible for the behaviour and welfare of the younger women employed by Anne at court, probably including the young Shelton girls. A Mrs Marshall was Mistress of the Maids, who may have supported Elizabeth, or replaced her. A young Jane Seymour, then aged around twenty-five, would also join Anne's household, having previously served Queen Catherine.

Some of Anne's household are trickier to identify. Margery Horsman had also been a maid of honour to Catherine and worked in the wardrobe, responsible for maintaining Anne's clothing and possibly helping her to dress. Her origins are something of a mystery, but a letter from her to Cromwell surviving from November 1534[5] reveals that she was a cousin of Martin Hastings (1505–75), who was a younger son of George, 12th Baron Hastings. Margery married Sir Michael Lister of Hurstbourne in Hampshire in 1537. A sketch by Holbein in the Royal Collection, labelled as 'Lady Lister', has been identified as Margery's mother-in-law Isabel, and as her stepmother-in-law Jane Lister, although it may equally be of Margery, as it depicts a young woman. There was an Anne, or 'Nan' Cobham, also called

'Mrs Cobham', who has proved more difficult for historians to identify, who might have been part of the Kentish Brooke-Cobham family, and perhaps the queen's midwife.[6] One Anne Cobham was the mother of Thomas, Lord Burgh of Gainsborough, who was prominent at Anne's court, but she was a much older woman, having been born before 1471, and who inherited her father's baronetcy, so she is unlikely to have been referred to as 'Mrs'. Finally, there was Elizabeth Browne, Lady Worcester, a sister of Anthony Browne, who was close enough to Anne to borrow £100 from her in 1536. Later they would be joined by Henry's niece, Margaret Douglas, daughter of his sister Margaret by her second marriage, who was then aged around nineteen and reportedly got on very well with Anne.

Anne's household was run by men who were related to her, or who had proved their worth through years of service. Her uncle James Boleyn, then aged about forty, was appointed as her Chancellor. He shared her views about religious reform.[7] Thomas, Lord Burgh of Gainsborough was appointed her Lord Chamberlain, who had borne the weight of Anne's train at her coronation and demolished Catherine of Aragon's barge in an act symbolic of the transference of queenship. He had been a bodyguard to Henry before becoming a Member of Parliament and was in his mid-forties. Slightly older than the Lord Chamberlain was the Vice-Chamberlain, Sir Edward Baynton, a favourite of Henry who had formerly been close to Catherine of Aragon. However, Baynton was also an advocate of religious reform, making him in sympathy with Anne.

Another significant appointment, of a man rapidly rising through the ranks, was that of Thomas Cromwell as her High Steward. Having moved beyond his early connection with Wolsey, Cromwell and Anne's initial relationship appears to have been a harmonious one, united in their self-professed desire to serve the will of the king and their focus on reform. He had played a significant role in Anne's creation as Marquis of Pembroke and in the organisation of her coronation. Acting as Henry's unofficial secretary, before receiving the official title in 1534, Cromwell slipped quietly into the position of facilitator that the cardinal had fulfilled, quicky making himself invaluable to the king. Gregory Casale in Rome thought Cromwell sufficiently close to Anne to beg him to make overtures of friendship to her, on his behalf, in case she had 'conceived an unfavourable opinion of him'.[8] John Uvedale, or Udall, was Anne's secretary and William Coffin was her Master of the Horse. George Taylor had been in her service for a while prior to her coronation, possibly as a lawyer, who now took the role of Receiver General, while John Smith became her surveyor, or auditor.

Those promoted to serve Anne in a spiritual capacity were, without exception, sympathetic to religious change. Anne may have relied on the help of Henry's physician, Dr William Butts, to select 'the most promising reformist scholars' from Butts' old college of Gonville Hall, Cambridge, and those who excelled at other colleges.[9] Hugh Latimer was already preaching for Anne before her marriage, influenced by Thomas Bilney and the Cambridge circle who followed Tyndale. Her first chaplain was a Gonville graduate named William Betts, who had escaped investigation for possessing heretical books in 1528. Before his death in 1535, he would recommend Matthew Parker, a Norwich man around the same age as Anne, who would later become Archbishop of Canterbury. Another Gonville man was John Skip, Anne's almoner, who also preached regularly at her request.

Francis I showed his public approval of the marriage by sending Anne the gift of a fine rich litter and three mules which, Chapuys observed, Anne 'immediately used' to travel three miles from Greenwich.[10]

Others who spoke openly against the match included a Sir Thomas Gebons, a priest, and Sir Rauf Wendon, who were both examined after Wendon commented to Gebons that the queen was 'a whore and a harlot and that there was a prophecy that a many (sic) should be burned in Smithfield, and he trusted it would be the end of Queen Anne'.[11] Elizabeth Amadas, widow of Henry's former goldsmith, made a number of wild accusations suggestive of an unbalanced mind, culminating in a direct attack that Henry could not ignore: 'She rejoiced when the Tower was made white, for she said shortly after my lady Anne should be burned, for she is a harlot; that Master Norris was bawd between the King and her; that the King had kept both the mother and the daughter, and that my lord of Wiltshire was bawd both to his wife and his two daughters.'[12] A Lancashire priest, Sir Jasper Harrington, found himself in trouble for asserting that 'queen Katharine should be queen ; and as for Nan Bullen, who the devil made her queen? And as for the King, should not be king but on his bearing' and 'I will take none for queen but queen Katharine'.[13] Attempts to make Catherine submit to the title of Princess did not meet with success either, as she maintained her position and refused to imperil her soul. When informed that the 'marriage with Anne Boleyn had been adjudged lawful by the universities, the Lords and Commons', she replied that 'the King might do in his realm by his royal power what he would; that the cause was not theirs but the Pope's to judge'. Nor would she listen to any arguments that her position would compromise her daughter and servants: 'she would not damn her own soul on any consideration, or for any promises the King might make her' and 'would daily pray for the preservation' of Henry and the return of his affections to her.[14]

Predictably, Chapuys noted that 'the Lady is very much displeased, and would like much to punish the people. This may serve as an indication of her perverse and malicious nature.'[15] Displeased or not, Anne was in the ascendant; as a pregnant, anointed queen, she had never been in a stronger position. As Sir William Kingston reported on 20 July, 'the King and Queen are well and merry, and all the Court'.[16] All that remained was for her to deliver a son. In July, just weeks before she was due to enter her confinement, Anne asked Henry to demand that Catherine yield up a 'very rich triumphal cloth which she brought from Spain to wrap up her children with at baptism... which she would be glad to make use of very soon'. This was the cloth that Catherine's mother, Isabella, had packed for her when she originally came to England in 1501; Anne saw its symbolism as a validation of royalty, wishing to continue the tradition after it had been used for those children of Catherine who had survived birth. Catherine replied that 'it has not pleased God she should be so ill advised as to grant any favor in a case so horrible and abominable'.[17]

As Anne's pregnancy advanced, Henry was preparing for the inevitable clash with the pope. On 11 July, Clement issued his sentence, declaring that the divorce from Catherine and marriage to Anne were both null and that Henry had incurred the greater charge of excommunication, although this was suspended until September.[18] Chapuys believed this information was deliberately kept from Anne on account of her condition:

> The last news the King has received from Rome are not very agreeable to him. I know not the particulars, for they are kept very secret that they may not injure the Lady and endanger a miscarriage. To disguise the case, the King, on pretence of going to hunt, left her at Windsor, and went to Guildford, where he has summoned some of his Council and many doctors, who are hard at work.[19]

However, the pope took the decision not to proceed against Anne herself:

> As soon as the news came that the king of England had married Anna, it was considered whether she should be proceeded against, but it was determined not to do so, for fear of hindering the expedition of the principal cause.
>
> It is true the marriage of Anne could not be much hindrance to the expedition of the cause, as it is notoriously invalid, and so the Pope determined in Consistory, as appears by the sentence sent by Rodrigo Davalos.[20]

Instead, Clement issued a bull on 8 August, commanding Henry to restore Catherine 'and put away Anne in ten days on pain of excommunication'. In the event that Henry was disobedient, Clement called upon Charles V and 'all other Christian princes and Henry's own subjects, to assist in the execution of the bull by force of arms'.[21] It was tantamount to asking Henry's subjects to rise up against him. Norfolk advised him by letter to 'not care a button about the said sentence', for Henry would 'not fail of adherents who would defend his right by the sword'.[22] A note surviving in the hand of one of Cromwell's secretaries shows that he and Henry were already gathering their evidence and reasons 'to clear the clergy for condescending to the King's Marriage and for abolishing the Pope's supremacy' with the support of Archbishop Cranmer. The clerk, probably taking dictation from Cromwell, or summarising his thoughts, recorded:

There be, I think, in this realm that be not in their minds full pleased and contented that our Sovereign hath married as he hath done, some bearing their favor to the lady Katheryn princess dowager, some to the lady Mary, some because the Pope's authority was not therein. And for this they lay the blame alonely in some of the prelates. And albeit that the prelates have none otherwise done in this matter but as it became them, and according to the very law of God, yet many of the inconstant commons be not therewith satisfied. And though they forbear to speak at large for fear of punishment, yet they mutter together secretly, which muttering and secret grudge within this realm, I think, doth not a little embolden the King's adversaries without the realm. And as this muttering is not against the King (for every one says he is the most geutle and upright prince that ever reigned), but only against some of the prelates, especially the archbishop of Canterbury, I think he ought to show that he has done nothing but according to the very law of God. And though the suspicions and muttering against him are untrue, he should endeavour to pluck it out of their heads by loving manner. Also if the Pope be excluded out of this realm, the Archbishop must be chief of the clergy here, which will be lightly accepted in the people's hearts, because it has been so long otherwise, unless the people find themselves by the alteration in better case than they were before. I think therefore the Archbishop should make out a book, not over long, to declare that what he has done is not only according to the law of God, but for the wealth and quietness of the realm.[23]

Early in July Henry and Anne had fled into the countryside near Woking with a diminished court on account of a new outbreak of the sweating sickness.[24] When it was safe to return, they travelled to Hampton Court and then on to Windsor, where they were in the middle of August, when Henry wrote to Bishop Bonner, then his agent in Rome, stating that he intended to appeal Clement's decision.[25] It was probably in the fourth week of August that they made the journey to Greenwich for Anne's lying in. If she bore a boy, the line of Tudor succession would be unquestionably settled and the Boleyns' power inviolable. Writing to celebrate the coronation, John Leland had written: 'may heaven bless these nuptials and make her a fruitful mother of men-children. Fruitful Saint Anne bore three men, the offspring of her body... by her example, may you give us a race to maintain the Faith and the Throne.'[26] Chapuys asserted that Henry's certainty about the child's gender was based on the reports of his physicians and astrologers, so he had 'determined to hold rejoicings and solemn jousts' and 'some of the Lady's favourites had been sent to Flanders to buy horses'.[27] If it was a boy, he intended to call him Henry or Edward.[28]

An undated note in the correspondence of the Emperor, included among the State papers for August 1533, suggests that all was not well between Henry and Anne, but sounds very much as if it had been composed, or influenced, by Chapuys. It was 'said that the English nobles are ill-disposed towards Anne on account of her pride and the insolence and bad conduct of her brothers and relations. For the same reason the King's affection for her is less than it was. He now shows himself in love with another lady, and many nobles are assisting him in the affair.'[29] In a letter of 23 August, he related that 'the King's great affection and passionate love for the Lady had greatly diminished'[30] and also gave the impression of a breach between Henry and Anne in a dispatch of 3 September. He recorded that one of the 'richest and most triumphant beds' from the royal treasury, which had been used as a ransom for the Duc d'Alençon back in 1515, was awaiting Anne in her new apartments. It was a good thing for her, the ambassador said, that it had been delivered two months ago, 'for she would not have had it now', because they had argued. Reputedly Anne was 'full of jealousy, and not without cause' but had 'used some words to the King at which he was displeased'. He had replied that she must 'shut her eyes, and endure as well as more worthy persons and that she ought to know that it was in his power to humble her again in a moment more than he had exalted her'. After this, Chapuys wrote, Henry had not spoken to Anne for two or three days, but dismissed it as a 'lovers' quarrel' to which should not be attached 'too great importance', although he wished it to be of significance in alleviating Catherine's position.[31] That December, Chapuys was to return to his former position on Anne's influence, stating that 'he (Henry) is bewitched by this cursed woman in such a manner that he dares neither say nor do except as she commands him'.[32]

If the tale contains an element of truth, it would highlight a changing dynamic in the royal marriage. The majority of Chapuys' letters prior to Anne's coronation stress Henry's devotion to her, and his need to be with her every moment of the day; but during the summer of 1533, the tone changes to suggest friction between them. If it is true, this is the first recorded instance of Henry reminding the married Anne of her place, both of her social standing in relation to Catherine of Aragon, and of the obedience that was due to him as her husband. For Anne, it was a reminder of where the real power in the relationship lay. Having given her his permission to rule him as a mistress, Henry's flash of temper exposed the potential dangers to Anne when it came to her behaviour. Mistresses were expected to be provocative and challenging; they might excite and entice men by not following the rules, playing upon the affection between them, or displaying emotions such as jealousy. It was part of the pre-marital play, the courtship dance by which supposed gender qualities were exaggerated and the knight wooed his damsel. Yet this was a temporary period of role-reversal, not dissimilar to the theme of carnival that ran through many of the pre-Reformation religious and folk rituals, where masters could be ruled by slaves, men by women, or boys might become bishops. Once that damsel had been won, though, the couple were expected to revert to the normal male-female roles of mastery and submission respectively. A wife's purpose was very different from that of a mistress. She must listen, obey, show respect, act competently and discreetly, and look to her husband as the king of her little realm, culturally and legally. When that husband was the actual king, and their marriage the subject of gossip on the international stage, Anne's absolute conformity was expected by Henry. Yet it appears that Anne was not prepared to make this transition smoothly.

On 26 August 1533, Anne heard Mass and made her formal retreat into her suite of rooms at Greenwich. The huge bed must have dominated her chamber, which was hung with tapestries depicting the life of St Ursula and decorated with gold and silver plate brought up from the treasury. Between three and four o'clock on the afternoon of Thursday 7 September, she was delivered of a healthy child. Contrary to all the predictions, it was a girl. The arrival of daughter was a setback for Anne, but she hoped it would be a temporary one. At least she had survived the process and had proven to Henry that she was capable of bearing a healthy heir. Still, the mood of disappointment lingered at court. The celebratory jousts were cancelled and the paperwork announcing the birth was altered from 'Prince' to 'Princess'. Chapuys reported that the baby had arrived 'to the great regret both of him and the lady', for which there is no evidence, but he was correct that it was also 'to the great reproach of the physicians, astrologers, sorcerers, and sorceresses, who affirmed that it would be a male child'.[33]

The baby's christening was held at the Grey Friars' church at Greenwich on 10 September, three days after her birth. Anne did not attend, as was the custom, but she was still in confinement anyway, recovering from the ordeal. Arrangements were handed over to the Princess's godparents, Archbishop Cranmer, the dowager Duchess of Norfolk and the dowager Marchioness of Dorset, Margaret Wotton. This latter choice may suggest a particular closeness Anne felt for the marchioness, or else it was due to her marriage into the Grey family, headed by Henry's half-uncle. The church was hung with arras and the paths strewn with rushes; the silver font from Canterbury stood on a podium beneath a crimson canopy and Anne's relatives assisted in the ceremony. The widowed duchess carried the child in a purple mantle, with a long train that was held by Thomas Boleyn. The Dukes of Norfolk and Suffolk flanked the child and the canopy overhead was carried by George Boleyn and other Howard relatives. Norfolk's daughter Mary, soon to be married to Henry's illegitimate son, Henry Fitzroy, bore the chrisom, or christening cloth, decorated with pearls and precious stones.[34] Chapuys reported that the baby was to be called Mary, perhaps in an attempt to displace the existing Princess but, as on many other occasions, he was incorrect. She was named Elizabeth, after the mothers of both Henry and Anne. A formal procession of the mayor, aldermen and nobility watched as she was anointed with holy water and prayers were said for her future. Wine, wafers and comfits were distributed and Elizabeth was carried out, followed by her string of gifts borne by members of the court.

TWENTY-NINE

Disappointment 1534

Anne passed most of September in the traditional month of post-partum lying-in, before she was churched and made her formal return to court. This marked the resumption of her duties and, like all royal and aristocratic mothers, she was not given the supervision and care of her small daughter, which was considered to be a job for her servants. As David Starkey points out, a story suggesting that Anne wished to breastfeed Elizabeth but Henry forbade her because it would interrupt his sleep, is implausible on several levels. As a member of the nobility, Anne was well aware of the conventions of childrearing, and unlikely to have been possessed of an anachronistic sense of attachment parenting, nor would she and Henry have slept together in the same bed for the duration of the night. It was usual practice, as glimpsed in the Eltham Ordinances of 1526, for the king to visit the queen in her chamber, where sexual encounters took place, after which he was conducted back to his room by his servants. Anne is likely to have handed over her daughter, as expected, to a wet nurse, and a new household that was being established for her at Hatfield House under the watchful eye of Margaret, Lady Bryan. Then in her mid-sixties, Margaret (née Bourchier) was the half-sister of Elizabeth Boleyn, making her Anne's aunt, and the mother of Sir Francis Bryan. Also appointed was Anne's aunt, Lady Anne Shelton and her sister, Alice. Chapuys made noises of dissatisfaction about the plan to disband Princess Mary's household and install her as a 'lady's maid' to Elizabeth[1] but Henry was keen to establish Elizabeth's new precedent over her sister. Norfolk was sent to break the news.

A little later, Henry went to visit Mary, lodged with Elizabeth at Hatfield. His intention was to persuade her to renounce her title but, according to Chapuys, Anne feared that Mary would be able to influence her father and that he would be lenient to her. Reputedly, Anne sent Cromwell 'and other messengers' after Henry, 'to prevent him from seeing or speaking with Mary'. The result was that the king visited Elizabeth's chamber and sent Cromwell to deal with his elder daughter, refusing her request to come and kiss his hand. As he was departing, Henry saw Mary on a terrace at the top of the house, having 'either been told of it or by chance turned round' and bowed to her.[2] Chapuys also related that Anne, 'having heard of the prudent replies of the Princess, complained to the King that he did not keep her close enough, and that she was badly advised, as her answers could not have been made without the suggestion of others, and that he had promised that no one should speak to her without his knowing it'.[3] The ambassador claimed Anne was threatened by Mary's beauty and virtue, so refused to allow her to come to court, as 'she would win the heart of all',[4] and told Lady Shelton to 'box her ears as a cursed bastard' if she did not conform and refused to allow Mary to dine in the privacy of her own chamber.[5] Norfolk and George Boleyn had also 'reprimanded' Anne Shelton for treating Mary 'with too much respect and kindness, saying that she ought only to be treate as a bastard'.[6] Of course, Chapuys' reports are always coloured, but so little information survives about the relationship between Anne and Mary that they cannot entirely be dismissed. As far as Anne was concerned, Catherine and Mary's continuing refusal to accept a demotion in their status was not only a direct challenge to her position and that of her daughter, but provided a rallying point for supporters of the Empire and Catholicism. But it was Henry who was enraged by his daughter's refusal to submit, after she requested his blessing as Princess of Wales, prompting his comment that 'he would soon find the means of humiliating her and subduing her temper'.[7]

Anne kept Christmas 1533 with Henry at Greenwich. Edward Hall reported that this took place in 'great solemnity'[8] but John Husee wrote to Lord Lisle that 'the king has kept a great court and is as merry and lusty as ever I see'.[9] Anne's New Year's Gift to her husband was 'a goodly gilt bason, having a rail or board of gold in the midst of the brim, garnished with rubies and pearls, wherein standeth a fountain, also having a rail of gold about it garnished with diamonds; out thereof issueth water, at the teats of three naked women standing at the foot of the same fountain'.[10] The design of this gift had been commissioned by Anne from Hans Holbein, of which a partial sketch survives, showing a three-tier table fountain adorned with the women. Later, Anne would commission a second work from him, an elegant cup, now known as the Basel Cup, featuring four satyrs and Anne's device of the falcon standing upon a woodstock. The implication of this New Year's gift, with its connotations of voluptuousness and fertility, is that Anne had again conceived, within weeks of her churching. If this took place after the traditional interval of a month, placing it on 7 October, or after four weeks, making it as early as 1 October, Anne's menstrual cycle had, at most, a further two months to become re-established before conception took place.

The fulsome praise that Henry included for Anne in his instructions of 5 January to the new Ambassadors to the German princes, Nicholas Heythe and Christopher Mount, suggests he was already aware of Anne's condition:

> And, therefore, by the consent of his nobles, spiritual and temporal, and to the comfort of all his commons, and finally the judgment of the abp. of Canterbury, he has been divorced from that unlawful marriage with the princess dowager, and has espoused the lady Anne, marquess (sic) of Pembroke, 'whose approved and excellent virtues, that is to say, the purity of her life, her constant virginity, her maidenly and womanly pudicity, her soberness, her chasteness, her meekness, her wisdom, her descent of right noble and high parentage, her education in all good and laudable thewes and manners, her aptness to procreation of children, with other infinite good qualities, more to be regarded and esteemed than the only progeny, be of such approved excellency as cannot be but most acceptable unto Almighty God, and deserve His high grace and favour, to the singular weal and benefit of the King's realm and subjects.[11]

On 23 January, the Count of Cifuentes noted the arrival of a new English Ambassador to the court, who brought the information that Anne was pregnant again.[12] Historian Eric Ives postulates that this was Anne's uncle William Howard, whose departure was noted by Chapuys on 20 November, although he thought the embassy was to France.[13] It is certainly possible that a conception early in this time period, at the start of October, would allow Anne to have been aware of her condition by the time of his departure. Anne's news was known at court by 28 January, when it was reported by Chapuys that she was 'pregnant and in condition to have more children'.[14] The following day, Sir Thomas Palmer reported that 'the king and queen are merry'[15] and, at the end of February, Henry confessed his confidence to Chapuys that this time she would bear a son.[16] By this point, Anne might have been nearly five months pregnant, or as little as three months. Everything appeared to be progressing well. Perhaps it was considered one of the whims of Anne's condition that Lady Lisle was persuaded to part with her little dog, Purquoy, which 'grieved' her 'not a little'[17] to send as a gift to the queen. Anne was upset when the dog died in an accident soon afterwards, the news of which Henry broke to her himself.

In the first part of 1534, Henry finally took steps to deal with one of the most vocal critics of his marriage. Elizabeth Barton, a poor nun from Aldington, just outside Canterbury, had initially found favour with some of the high-profile anti-reformers at court when she reported that she was experiencing divine visions and revelations. Supported by the former Archbishop of Canterbury, William Warham, and by the Bishop of Rochester, John Fisher, an ally of Catherine's, her attacks upon heretics posed no threat to the king in the late 1520s, as he attempted to stamp out Lutheranism. However, Barton reacted strongly to Henry's marriage to Anne and rejection of the pope, making a number of treasonous statements, including the prediction that if the wedding went ahead, the vengeance of God would plague Henry, and having a vision of Henry, Anne and Thomas Boleyn plotting, as well as seeing a devil prompting Boleyn to action.[18] Worse still, she warned Henry that 'he shall not be king a month after he married the Queen's grace'.[19] Elizabeth was arrested late in 1533 and, the following January, an act of Parliament had made it treason to 'impugn' the marriage of the king and queen, specifically to deal with her case, and allowing for a verdict to be passed without a trial. Cromwell, Cranmer and Hugh Latimer were charged with the task of uncovering her deceptions. The usual accusations of sexual immorality and mental instability were levelled against her, just as they had been with women of previous centuries, whose unruly speech had threatened the legal or temporal order. Barton would suffer the ultimate penalty for 'impugning' the marriage, by a law brought into place after her words were spoken, being hanged at Tyburn on 20 April 1534. Anne and Henry were not opposed to prophecies in theory, as the king's earlier patronage of Elizabeth indicates. It was not the divine ability that was in doubt, rather the content of the revelation. At the same time, a William Glover approached Anne, claiming to be a messenger from God, saying that she 'should have been queen of England ten years past',[20] which was a far more acceptable divine comment than Barton's.

In February, Anne was saddened to learn of the death of Nicholas Hawkins, a priest and former Lutheran, who had recanted his more extreme views and was assisting in building the theological case for Henry's divorce. He had replaced Cranmer as the English ambassador to the Imperial court at the end of 1532 and was in the process of translating into Latin *The Glass of Truth*, a tract Henry had written outlining the legalities of the question of marriage to a brother's widow. Hawkins was at Balbase, in Aragon, when he suffered from an attack of dysentery and died in spite of medicines sent to him by the Emperor. Chapuys stated that

Henry 'regretted deeply the loss' but reported Dinteville's comment that Anne showed more grief and 'wept bitterly, saying that an apothecary must have given him some medicine which caused his death, implying that he had been poisoned'.[21] Perhaps it was the connection with the Emperor, and Hawkins' location in Aragon that caused her to be suspicious, but her comment tapped into a wider dialogue of fear on the Spanish part that Anne and her friends were seeking to poison Catherine and Mary. In 1531, their supporter, Bishop Fisher, had survived a case of poisoning in his own home, when his cook had either mixed up the herbs or made a real attempt upon Fisher's life by administering powders in a dish of gruel. Whether it occurred by accident or design, two died and many were very ill as a result, and the cook, a Richard Roose, was boiled to death at Smithfield. The case made both sides sensitive to the possibilities of such attacks by their opponents, at a time when the lives of both Catherine and Anne would have been made easier by the disappearance of the other. In the same letter, Chapuys warned, 'Anne is aware of the King's affection for the Princess, and does not cease to plot against her. A gentleman told me yesterday that the earl of Northumberland told him that he knew for certain that she had determined to poison the Princess.'[22] Such tactics would have been in keeping with the extremes of Italian Renaissance politics – Lucrezia Borgia's rumoured hollow ring, used to administer deadly concoctions – but so far as we know, they were not Anne or Henry's style. As historian S.T. Bindoff commented, 'where a Borgia used poison, a Tudor used the law'.[23]

On 7 March, Anne went to visit Elizabeth at Hatfield and attempted a rapprochement with Mary. Urging the young woman to accept the change in her circumstances and recognise Anne as queen, she offered to intercede with Henry and try and bring about a reconciliation. Mary might come to court and be 'as well or better treated than ever'.[24] Anne may have been playing a cunning game, as some supposed, trying to keep her enemies close, but this incident could represent a genuine attempt to win her step-daughter over, and return her to her father, which Anne knew would greatly please Henry. There was nothing to be gained by Anne making overtures to Catherine, but Mary's youth, and her popularity, made it a shrewd move to establish goodwill between her and the girl. Mary, though, rejected Anne's effort with cool politeness. She knew no queen in England except her mother and 'if madame Anne de Bolans would do her that favour with her father she would be much obliged'.[25] Chapuys' account makes it sound as if Anne saw Mary in person, under which circumstances her pregnancy would have been visible, writing that she 'repeated her remonstrances and offers' and 'in the end threatened her' but failed to move Mary. Following this, the ambassador assumed that Anne was 'very indignant' and reported that she 'intended to bring down the pride of this unbridled Spanish blood'.[26] The Duke of Norfolk was sent to remove Mary's 'principal jewels and ornaments... in consequence of her refusal to pay her respects to the lady'.[27] When the time came at the end of March for Elizabeth's household to move, Mary had to be carried by force into the litter with Lady Shelton. When she and Catherine persisted in challenging Anne's marriage, Norfolk's reply was that 'it was needless to discuss the case of the marriage further since the thing was done, or to impugn the validity of their statutes, which they would defend to the last drop of their blood'.[28]

In March, Parliament passed the Act of Succession, which declared Mary to be illegitimate and Princess Elizabeth to be Henry's heir. All subjects, if commanded, were obliged to swear an oath affirming that Anne's marriage was valid and the supremacy of the king over the English church. To refuse to do so was made a capital offence under the Treasons Act, which followed immediately after,[29] when it became high treason to 'maliciously wish, will or desire, by words or writing, or by craft imagine, invent, practise, or attempt any bodily harm to be done or committed to the king's most royal person, the queen's, or their heirs apparent, or to deprive them or any of them of their dignity, title, or name of their royal estates, or slanderously and maliciously publish and pronounce, by express writing or words, that the king our sovereign lord should be heretic, schismatic, tyrant, infidel or usurper of the crown'.[30] Subjects had to swear that 'all the issue had and procreate, or after to be had and procreate, between your Highness and your said most dearly and entirely beloved wife Queen Anne, shall be your lawful children, and be inheritable and inherit'.

Henry was anticipating the arrival of Anne's child, which he hoped would be a son, whose rights, along with those of any future male siblings, were to be clearly established. Anyone speaking critically of the marriage, or of Henry and Anne in person, were liable to be imprisoned, have all their goods, lands and properties confiscated, and to suffer death.[31] In addition, Anne was named regent and absolute governess of her children and the kingdom in the event of Henry's absence abroad or his death. Waiting to deliver a son, Anne's power was now at its apogee. She could scarcely rise higher, and had afforded the Boleyn family the ultimate rewards for their decades of ambition and application.

Anne's new position may be commemorated in an illustration that appears in the *Black Book of the Garter*, now held in Windsor Castle. The beautiful, colourful spread depicting Henry's court ceremonies has been attributed to Lucas Horenbout, a Ghent-born miniaturist who had arrived in England with his father Gerald and sister Susanna, both also painters. In June 1534, Lucas' position as king's painter was confirmed for life, which may have been prompted by, or occasioned, the commission of the *Black Book*. The garter ceremonies of 23 April 1534, were portrayed in all their glory, around the central images of a crowned king and a queen presiding over the tournament, reputedly Edward III and Philippa, but which are clearly modelled on Henry and Anne. The seated figure, depicted square-on to the reader, wears clothing contemporary to the time; a dress of cloth of gold with the fashionable square neckline, heavy sleeves furred with ermine and folded back to reveal red sleeves beneath, slashed with white. She wears a traditional square gable hood, like that in a portrait of Anne recently discovered at Nidd Hall in Yorkshire, and that depicted in a medal struck of Anne that year, instead of the rounded French version more familiar from other portraits, and it is topped by a crown. It would appear that in 1534, Anne adopted this style of hood on several occasions, not least ceremonial ones, or ones in which her image was being recorded. The facial features of the *Black Book* portrait are a little indistinct but, around the queen's neck, hangs a medal with the clear initials A.R., for Anne Regina. In the light of this, and the date of the work, there seems to be a convincing case that the image is a surviving contemporary portrait of Anne. The brushwork on the dress, and the inclusion of a girdle, imply the presence of a visible pregnancy, again dating the work to the time of the Garter ceremony or immediately after; late April, May or June 1534.

Assuming a conception window of early October through to the end of November 1533, Anne would have anticipated retiring into confinement in June or July and giving birth in July or August. At the end of March, precautions were taken when an outbreak of sickness spread through her household, with her two chamberlains, Lord Burgh and Edward Baynton, falling ill, along with William Lord Sandys, whose life was prematurely despaired of, and Lord Kingston, who kept to his room.[32] John Rokewood's letter to Lord Lisle, of 1 April, illustrates just how serious the illness was, and how the same doctors who were caring for Anne during her pregnancy, were sent to attend upon him:

> Excuses himself for not writing oftener by his continual sickness. Was never so sick in his life as this day. It is a sickness that many have in the head and stomach. Mr. Baynton is in great danger from it, and many a one dies. There is no news to write but what every one knows. All the King's physicians and the Queen's were with me six days together, and now they have given me over, so I trust only in the High Physician,

by whose help I still hope this summer to make good cheer with your lordship and my lady at the town of Marke.[33]

By 4 April, Sir John Husee was able to report that Edward Baynton had recovered. There is no report of Anne suffering any kind of pain or discomfort, but she was in contact with those who were ill, and it cannot be ruled out that she may have been exposed to an undiagnosed virus, which may have been of significance in her pregnancy.

The preparations began in April, with a nursery being planned, 'against the coming of the Prince', at Eltham Palace, the location where Henry had spent much of his childhood. This planning would follow Anne's experience of the quickening of a child, at around four or five months, suggesting all was on track. In mid-April, Henry was considering visiting France again and was 'very desirous of it, and in wonderful haste to go,' wishing Anne to go with him 'notwithstanding she is enceinte'.[34] This plan was still going ahead on 3 June, when he requested that the streets of Calais be cleaned and cleared of any infected individuals, in advance of his arrival.[35] Henry also ordered a cradle fit for a prince, which was made by his goldsmith Cornelius Hayes, with images painted by Hans Holbein:

A silver cradle, price 16l. For making a silver plate, altering the images, making the roses underneath the cradle, the roses about the pillars, and new burnishing, 13s. 4d. For the stones that were set in gold in the cradle, 15s.; for fringes, the gold about the cushions, tassels, white satin, cloth of gold, lining, sypars and swaddlebands, 13s. 6d. Total, 18l. 1s. 10d. The silver that went to the dressing of the Adam and Eve, the making of all the apples, the gilding of the foot and setting of the currall, 33s. 4d. To Hance, painter, for painting the same Adam and Eve, 20s. A silver and gilt dial, 16l. 4s.[36]

A medal depicting the new queen, with her motto 'The Moost Happi' and initials A.R., for Anna Regina, was commissioned in advance of the birth, of which the original survives in the British Museum. The use of these initials in a royally issued medal might also confirm the identity of the sitter in the *Black Book of the Garter*. Anne's features on the medal, which has been reconstructed and recast in bronze by Lucy Churchill,[37] are visible on the original tiny disc of soft lead, just under 4 centimetres across. Although some of the raised surfaces have been eroded, Churchill's copy allows the image greater clarity, giving the impression of a woman with a long face, prominent chin and cheek bones, like the portrait of Anne at Hever Castle, but also with the strong nose that is evident in the Nidd Hall picture.

Predictably, though, in spite of this 'moost happiness', people continued to speak against Anne, with Catherine's chaplain imprudently saying that 'it was a pity the king was not buried in his swaddling clothes' and that anyone calling Anne, not Catherine, queen, 'should be knocked to the post'. He added that he 'hoped to see Lady Anne brought full low, and we should have no merry world till we had a new change'.[38] Such reports of hostility fuelled Anne's concerns about the influence of Mary and dictated her treatment at Hunsdon House, and that of her staff who refused to swear obedience to Anne as queen:

> The King has lately been two days at the place where the Bastard is, and meanwhile the Princess has been commanded not to leave her chamber. Care has been taken of this by the Lady, who was there with the King, and a weak maid of hers who refused to swear to the statute made about the succession was during that time locked up in her chamber, and compelled to swear by a threat of being taken to prison, for which the Princess has felt much regret. But this is a small thing in comparison with what happened to the Princess herself at the same time, to whom the aunt of the said Anne Boleyn, who has her in charge, said that the King her father did not care in the least that she should renounce her title, since by statute she was declared a bastard and incapable; but that if she were in the King's place, she would kick her out of the King's house for disobedience, and moreover the King himself has said that he would make her lose her head for violating the laws of his realm.[39]

On 27 April, George Taylor wrote to Lady Lisle from Greenwich, with the news that 'the king and queen are merry and in good health' and that 'the queen hath a goodly belly, praying our Lord to send us a Prince'.[40] However, on the same day, Lord Lisle received a letter from a Francis Halle, who commented that the son-in-law of George Hastings, one of Henry's close friends, had fallen ill. Only one of Hastings' two daughters had married by this point, so the son-in-law referred to must have been Thomas Berkeley, then in his late twenties and husband of Mary Hastings. As Halle related, Berkeley had been involved in the traditional St George's Day ceremony at Windsor, bearing the sword before the king.[41] Presumably Berkelely was suffering from the same illness that had affected Anne's household and, in fact, he did die in 1534, athough the exact date is unclear. It would seem a reasonable deduction that his decease was the result of this illness, and that he had been in close proximity to Henry as the symptoms took hold.

Anne's routine continued as before, with no outward indications that anything had changed. On Sunday 5 May, she was presented with eighteen dottrels (plovers), a gift from Lady Lisle of Calais. Anne immediately allocated six of the birds for her supper that day, six for Monday's dinner and the final six for her supper following. They were taken to her by her brother George, who informed her that they were killed at Dover at 12 o'clock that day.[42] This might represent a pregnancy craving, as Anne's successor, Jane Seymour, would develop a taste for quails whilst carrying her child. A John Brown was charged with conveying Anne's thanks to Lady Lisle. He wrote from Greenwich on 12 May to report that 'the Queen was very much pleased with your present of dottrels and your linnet that hung in your chamber'.[43] Anne also intervened on behalf of a Richard Herman, an Antwerp merchant, who had lost his freedom and fellowship under Wolsey, for 'setting for the New Testament in English'. Anne asked that Cromwell intervene to 'restore him to his pristine freedom, liberty and fellowship'.[44] On 14 May, Anne and Henry dined in public to celebrate the return of George Boleyn from France, on 17 May they travelled from Greenwich to Richmond for Whitsun.[45] On 11 June, Sir Edward Ringeley visited the court at Hampton Court and reported that 'the king and queen are in good health', and that Henry had just created a new garden there.[46] Ringeley reported that Henry intended to travel, that day, to York Place, then on to Waltham Abbey and then to Hunsdon, where he would stay for a week.

In mid-June, a Joan Hammulden, wife of Walter of Watlington, was questioned by Sir Walter Stonor, for reporting a case of slander against Anne. On the verge of bearing a child, Joan had sent for a woman known as Burgyn's wife, presumably a local midwife. Burgyn's wife had reputedly said to Joan that 'for her honesty and her cunning she might be midwife unto the queen of England', a boastful but harmless comment about her own abilities, until she went on to add that this was only 'if it were Queen Catherine, and if it were Queen Anne, she was too good to be her midwife, for she was a whore and a harlot of her living'. When the authorities caught up with Burgyn's wife, she denied saying the words, but stated instead that they had been uttered by one Collins' wife, adding that it was 'never merry in England since there was three queens in it' and asserting that Joan had said there would be fewer queens shortly. Of course Joan denied this.[47] Such exchanges probably tell us most about the relationships, rivalry and gossip between villagers, but they also show that Anne Boleyn's life and marriage, unlike Catherine's, was a topic on which her subjects felt able to comment and that she was considered a viable target for criticism. There are no comparable records of private individuals attacking Catherine throughout her entire residence in England. No matter the king's position on the legality of his first marriage, Anne could not avoid comparison with the popular queen of the last two decades, however unjust. Rumours were spread even by those close to, or at, court, out of sympathy for Catherine and Mary, as Chapuys reported on 23 June:

> I am informed by a person of good faith that the King's concubine had said more than once, and with great assurance, that when the King has crossed the sea, and she remains *gouvernante*, as she will be, she will use her authority and put the said Princess to death, either by hunger or otherwise. On Rochford, her brother, telling her that this would anger the King, she said she did not care even if she were burned alive for it after.[48]

On 26 June, the king and queen were again 'merry', as reported by Ringeley from Hampton Court. Then, on 2 July, Henry left Anne behind and travelled twenty miles north to The More, where he summoned Cromwell and Norfolk to meet him three days later. It was during this time that a decision was made to dispatch George Boleyn 'with all speed' for France, with the news that the proposed visit by Henry and Anne must be delayed. The whole process was very quick, with George leaving the country on 9 July. There was no question that Anne was the cause, and the excuse given was that the timing 'would be very inconvenient to her' as she was 'so far gone with child' and therefore could not cross the Channel, but did not wish to be 'deprived of his Highness's presence' when it was most necessary:

> Rochford is to repair to the French king with all speed, and in passing by Paris to make the King's and Queen's hearty recommendations to the queen of Navarre, if she be there, and say that the Queen his mistress much rejoices in the deeply-rooted amity of the two kings, but wishes her to get the interview deferred, as the time would be very inconvenient to her, and the King is so anxious to see his good brother that he will not put it off on her account. Her reasons are, that being so far gone with child, she could not cross the sea with the King, and she would be deprived of his Highness's presence when it was most necessary, unless the interview can be deferred till April next. Rochford is to press this matter very earnestly, and say that the King having at this time appointed another personage to go to his good brother, the Queen, with much suit, got leave for Rochford to go in his place, principally on this account.[49]

The Count of Cifuentes believed that 'the chief cause was that Ana de Bolans feared that something might be done there to her detriment, and there was fear of the people rising in favor of the Queen during the King's absence',[50] but then he was not privy to the developments of Anne's pregnancy.

During Anne and Henry's separation, a Thomas Winter described to Cromwell an audience he had with Anne. When he went to pay his respects to the queen, she 'received me very kindly, saying to me, I am aware... that you are beloved by the King and have many friends who wish you well. Reckon me among the number'.[51] On July 18, John Husee reported that Henry was at Woking, but was about to travel on to Eltham Palace, Woodstock and Langley. After a month of being apart, he was due to be reunited with Anne at Guildford[52] and on 27 July, Chapuys was still able to write of Anne's 'condition',[53] indicating that there was a general anticipation of her imminent confinement. Yet no child came. There are no records of Anne entering confinement or the usual preparation of a suite, which would have been expected to be prepared at Greenwich. Nor are there any surviving reports of a miscarriage or stillbirth, although this is the most likely explanation of what happened. It may have been a spontaneous, unpredictable and natural occurrence, or else Anne's contact with the severe virus that affected her household in March and April might have affected the child. Although the illness is unidentified in the records, it was clearly serious, possibly fatal, and caused a number of individuals in close contact with Henry and Anne to despair of their lives. Exposure to a virus like rubella or chickenpox can result in miscarriage.

It would appear that Anne carried her second child almost to term, before losing it around a month before her due date. If she was anticipating giving birth in August, she would have been due to enter isolation in mid-July, but no preparations appear to have been made. The establishment of the nursery at Eltham might suggest she had intended to deliver the child there. Henry's sudden departure from Hampton Court, the meeting with Cromwell and Norfolk, and the dispatch of George to France, with excuses about Anne's absence, suggest that she lost the child after Ringeley's observation that she was merry, on 26 June, and before Henry left on 2 July. The postponement of the Calais trip may have been occasioned by pregnancy, but is likely to have been concocted to conceal the truth, that Anne had lost the child. The matter was simply not spoken of. There is not a single reference to what would have been a traumatic event, not even among Anne's enemies, who could have construed a stillbirth or miscarriage as a sign of divine disapproval. However, Chapuys' report of 26 September suggests that there was some question over whether Anne was actually pregnant in the first place, or if she had experienced a phantom pregnancy caused by an infection, a pseudocyesis, as Catherine had in 1510.

Chapuys also suggests that Henry's realisation of the facts had driven him into the arms of another woman, resulting in an argument in which the king had again reminded Anne of her roots:

> Since the King began to doubt whether his lady was *enciente* or not, he has renewed and increased the love he formerly had for a very beautiful damsel of the Court; and because the said lady wished to drive her away, the King has been very angry, telling his said lady that she had good reason to be content with what he had done for her, which he would not do now if the thing were to begin, and that she should consider from what she had come, and several other things. To which it is not well to attach too much importance, considering the changeable character of the said King and the craft of the said lady, who knows well how to manage him.[54]

Once again, Henry ominously reminded Anne of her status, and the fact that he had raised her above her origins; Pygmalionesque, he had 'made' her, elevating her to the position of queen, and he could just as easily destroy her if he chose. Worse still, he stated that if things were to begin again, he would not do the same – that he regretted having done those things on her behalf. To Henry, Anne was ignoring, or breaking, the expected order between man and wife, by which it was a woman's uxorial duty to tolerate her husband's misdemeanors, according to the sexual double standard of the day. As Anne's sympathetic biographer George Wyatt states, rather than upbraiding him for his infidelities, she should have followed 'the general liberty and custom' of overlooking it.[55] As far as Anne was concerned, Henry had made her a number of promises, including to forsake all others for her, as far back as his letter of 1527, and then in marriage. After their long struggle and defiance of the pope to be together, along with their status, she did not consider them to be a 'normal' or 'typical' couple, bound by the gender customs of the day. She was more idealistic, perhaps more ambitious about their union: they were a unique couple, the realisation of romantic love triumphing against all odds. As king and queen, they presented both the ideal and an atypical masculinity and femininity. Henry's infidelities did not fit that image. To use a prosaic metaphor, the king wanted what his status had always allowed him; to have his cake and eat it. Anne felt this as a betrayal and a threat. There was also the realisation that the profoundly expressed devotion of his early letters, which she had allowed to persuade her into a relationship with him, had either been a convention, a kind of trope, or had faded. Had those promises been merely part of the 'play' of courtly love? An absolute monarch who had rarely been told 'no' did not take kindly to having his behaviour circumscribed by his wife. Some time around this point, he silently withdrew the permission he had previously granted Anne to rule him, exercise power over him. The game was over, the mask was removed. Henry became his own man again. Anne had put herself in the hands of a man of mercurial, changeable character.

Henry was clearly displeased about Anne's failure to produce a son. The 'moost happi' medal was decommissioned. The Count of Cifuentes reported the dilemma to Charles, that the rumour in France was that Anne 'was in disfavour with the King, who had fallen in love with another lady'[56] and Chapuys later clarified that the king had 'renewed and increased the love which he formerly bore to another very handsome young lady of his court', at which, Anne had apparently 'attempted to dismiss the damsel from her service'. He also related how Jane Rochford, Anne's sister-in-law, had been banished from court because she conspired with the queen 'to procure the withdrawal from Court of the young lady whom this king has been accustomed to serve, whose influence increases daily, while that of the Concubine (Anne) diminishes'.[57] This mysterious lady, sometimes referred to as the Imperial Lady, on account of her sympathies, reputedly told Mary to be 'of good cheer, and that her troubles would sooner come to an end than she supposed, and that when the opportunity occurred she would show herself her true and devoted servant'.[58]

Whatever the truth of Anne's pregnancy, by September 1534, she had no second child and Henry's attention had strayed. Coming just sixteen months after her glorious coronation, it must have seemed that the wheel of fortune had turned decisively against her.

THIRTY

Marriage as Battle 1534–5

Historians have offered a range of narratives to help interpret Henry and Anne's marriage. At the remove of five centuries, while the passions between husband and wife still speak vividly to us, authors are keen to capture the nature of their relations and to identify the moment, or series of moments, when things started to go wrong. We are still fascinated by the strength of feeling contained within the restrictive boundaries of a royal marriage, beset by problems of legitimacy, jealousy and the struggle for power. The combination of two strong personalities, deeply in love, in the public eye and whose intimate feelings were the subject of international gossip, is fascinating. Some have seen their marriage, confined and pressured in so many ways, as too fragile a vessel to contain their passion. It is impossible to analyse their relationship without an awareness from the beginning of its terrible implosion, but people disagree as to when it all started to go wrong, and whether or not this was inevitable. Due to the lack of surviving sources, we will never know how Anne felt about her life in 1534–5; whether she was content and secure, if she was personally happy, or if she felt insecure in Henry's love or in her position at his side. Did she feel jealous, or threatened, did she become argumentative and critical of Henry, did she speak harshly to her relatives or was she grateful for their support? In all likelihood, there was a mixture of all these emotions and reactions, as she charted her way through uncertain waters at the side of a man who could be self-absorbed and volatile.

Unlike Catherine, Anne had not been trained in the art of queenship and the difference began to show. Catherine had been raised to be a future queen of England since the age of three, when her marriage contract with Prince Arthur had been signed. She had been taught by two of the most powerful, authoritarian figures of late medieval Europe, Ferdinand and Isabella, who subjugated all things beneath the preservation of their majesty. Their daughter understood how to project that image of majesty and to follow a path dedicated to her country, subsuming individual feelings behind the mask of regality. Catherine had seen her mother turn a blind eye to repeated infidelity, treating it as a bodily function, not allowing it to touch the dynastic union; she had seen her mother employ dress, wealth and spectacle to dazzle troops heading to battle or to impress foreign ambassadors; she had seen her father conceal intense grief and pain whilst continuing to rule. Anne had been raised at home at Blickling and Hever, in a rural family environment, followed by positions at the courts of Burgundy and France. The sixteenth-century aristocratic family unit was different from that of today, frequently prioritising duty over affection, and the intention was to prepare Anne for a dynastic marriage. Although she had observed foreign courts at close quarters, and lived among those who were royal, she did not experience what it was like to have to maintain the face of dignity and poise whilst constantly in the public eye, and the sacrifices and control this entailed. There is no doubt that Anne was exceptionally able in many ways, that she was skilled at commanding attention, able to fascinate with her talents and conversation, able to dance, sing and compliment the king and was a fitting individual as the object of devotion. But she was disadvantaged in comparison with Henry and Catherine, who had been learning the lessons of how to be a king or queen since infancy. Unlike them, Anne had never been destined for the throne and was thus never trained for it. She had been equipped with suitable talents for her intended, fairly exalted position in life; but no one could have predicted that she would one day become queen. The skills of Renaissance royalty couldn't simply be picked up, especially when the court was accustomed to seeing her as the daughter of Thomas Boleyn. When she was under pressure, it showed.

Broadly, historians offer three plausible interpretations of what happened, three different narratives of the speed at which all unravelled. Firstly, there is the opinion that the marriage was in difficulty early on, from the birth of Elizabeth in September 1533, or even before then. The long courtship had drawn out Henry's desire for Anne over seven years, building an expectation that could hardly be matched in reality, a desire that was quickly sated. Some have argued that he began to question her sexual experience, suspecting her of having become too worldy and sophisticated in France, which may even have included limited sexual activity. No evidence survives to support this, although some historians have asserted it as fact. As an experienced man, Henry's anticipation of relations with Anne, which grew and fuelled itself over the course of seven years, might have found the culmination of those desires to be disappointing. This may also have worked the other way, with the new bride left unsatisfied, and unable to conceal this from her husband. Anne's rapid conception, either before or soon after the secret November ceremony, would have allowed little time for the couple to evolve their sexual relationship, given that relations during pregnancy were considered harmful to the foetus. Henry would not have been prepared to take any risks with the child he hoped was the longed-for heir. The anticipated consummation had been short-lived. Anne's pregnancy was her trump card in 1533, but it may also have served to divide her from Henry in an intimate sense, just as their physical relationship was getting established. Then, the baby proved to be a girl. The theory that the marriage was in trouble from this time points to Henry's hopes that Anne would go on to bear a son in good time as keeping the union alive. It would have created an unstable and volatile dynamic between the pair, during which Anne's insecurities might be visible, although this narrative must be detached from hindsight and the events of 1536 to make sense.

Secondly, historians have argued that Henry and Anne's marriage was viable, and still might have had a chance of success, right up until the end. There is no doubt it was a passionate and tempestuous union, disturbed by power struggles and jealousy, but they continued sleeping together through affection and out of the desire for a son, until a series of events in the spring of 1536 caused Henry to snap. This narrative puts Anne in a more secure position, disapproving of Henry's affairs but perhaps developing a more pragmatic approach to them, or unwilling to see them as a threat to her position, which they did not actually become until the emergence of Jane Seymour in the spring of 1536. According to this line, Henry did not find Anne a disappointment sexually, and maintained his deep affection for her regardless of other flirtations, and had a continuing desire to be reconciled with her, until he was surprised by a realisation, or evidence, right at the end. Thus, it was a volatile but viable and loving marriage throughout much of its duration.

A third narrative lies somewhere between the two accounts, with a critical turning point occurring in the relationship punctuating a longer period of disillusionment and disappointment. Anne failed to deliver the son Henry wanted, he turned to other women, Anne refused to conform to the expected role of submissive wife and arguments followed. The crisis of summer 1534, with Anne's miscarriage or phantom pregnancy, appears to have precipitated a separation and Henry's involvement with another woman. This constituted a significant breach, yet he and Anne were reconciled afterwards and began trying again for a son. Anne's peace of mind depends upon when Henry first contemplated replacing her and whether or not he communicated this to her, or to others who passed the information to her, by way of friendly warning or through hostile malice. Anne had seen one queen put aside and knew what Henry was capable of. His assertion that 'she had good reason to be content with what he had done for her, which he would not do now if the thing were to begin',[1] coming soon after what would have been a traumatic loss, or mistaken pregnancy, must have shaken her. It is plausible that this was a significant turning point in the marriage, after which Henry became increasingly disillusioned and Anne more insecure, which tallies with several reports of her behaviour through 1535–6. There are fewer reports of the king and queen being merry together and more terse exchanges where Anne appears on edge, or cynical. This was her response to Henry switching roles. Over the coming months he set aside the character of devoted lover and became more like the king that Catherine had seen towards the end: hard, determined and focused on his goals.

As Henry set his mask aside, and Anne realised that the 'power' she had exerted over him had been entirely at his whim, she found it increasingly difficult to play the role he wished for her. If she had not yet fully appreciated just how completely and utterly her position and identity, even her existence, were dependent upon Henry's character, she must have experienced an unpleasant wake-up call by the autumn of 1534. Yet, depending upon elusive, intimate elements of Henry's character – the sexual and personal dynamic between them – there may have still been all to play for. The pair were in love, passionately so, as evidenced by their dramatic and often extreme responses to each other. The truth seems to be that a royal marriage was too constrictive and limited a vehicle to contain the tempestuous feelings between Henry and Anne. The marriage was a battle because of the situation and the characters of the two personalities involved. Henry had played the game of courtly love, moved mountains to make Anne his wife, and wished to return to his position of absolute authority with an acquiescent queen. We can see Anne as the ultimate Tudor 'career woman', having reached the pinnacle of achievement entirely on her own merits, in expectation that her self-professed servant would remain as loyal and faithful as he had promised. This third narrative, allowing for a complex and shifting relationship between the pair, alternating between disappointment and hope, love and hate, is convincing in the light of the records that survive.

Through the early autumn, the court was at Woodstock in Oxfordshire on 1 September, and ten days later, fifty miles east at the Old Palace at Langley, in Hertfordshire, where they stayed for the next few days. They may have returned to Woodstock again between 20 and 23 September, before arriving at Grafton in Northamptonshire at the end of the month.

On 2 October, they were 25 miles to the east at Ampthill, in Bedfordshire. George Boleyn was back at Hampton Court by 17 October and his father, Thomas, was at Hever on 28 October, writing to Cromwell to ask favour for his neighbour, the Abbot of Robertsbridge, who was coming to court. Another family member, though, was causing trouble for Anne. Since being widowed in 1528, Mary Boleyn had lived quietly in the countryside at Buckingham with her two children, where Henry and Anne visited her on progress. She had accompanied Anne to Calais in the autumn of 1532 and become a member of her household, with a privileged position as the sister of the new queen. She is likely to have been close by Anne's side throughout her pregnancy of 1534 and to have been travelling in Anne's entourage that September, when her own secret came to light: earlier that year, she had made a second, secret marriage, to the son of an Essex landowner, William Stafford. He was distantly related to the family of the former Duke of Buckingham, but too far to give him any status and had served the king as a soldier, also travelling to Calais in 1532, a possible catalyst for the romance with Mary. She continued in favour, attending Anne at her coronation and appearing on the list of New Year's gifts for 1534 but, by September, Mary was pregnant and unable to conceal the fact any longer, so her secret came out.[2] Anne was not sympathetic. Not only was Mary's successful pregnancy an untimely reminder of her own recent failure but she had breached protocol in a way that her ambitious family could not forgive. The Boleyns were furious that she had married without their approval and banished her from court.

Mary appealed to Cromwell for help, championing the cause of love and marital happiness over wealth and status. Perhaps, in the final line, Mary deliberately refers to Anne's volatile situation:

Desires him to be good to her poor husband and herself. He is aware that their marriage, being clandestine, displeases the King and Queen. 'But one thing, good master Secretary, consider; that he was young, and love overcame reason. And for my part I saw so much honesty in him, that I loved him as well as he did me; and was in bondage, and glad I was to be at liberty; so that for my part I saw that all the world did set so little by me, and he so much, that I thought I could take no better way but to take him and forsake all other ways, and to live a poor honest life with him; and so I do put no doubts but we should, if we might once be so happy to recover the King's gracious favor and the Queen's. For well I might a had a greater man of birth and a higher, but I ensure you I could never a had one that should a loved me so well nor a more honest man.' Begs him to put her husband 'to the King's grace that he may do his duty as all other gentlemen do;' and persuade his majesty to speak to the Queen, who is rigorous against them. 'And seeing there is no remedy, for God's sake help us; for we have been now a quarter of a year married, I thank God, and too late now to call that again. Wherefore it is the more almons to help [us]. But if I were at my liberty and might choose, I ensure you, master Secretary, for my little time. I have tried so much honesty to be in him, that I had rather beg my bread with him than to be the greatest Queen christened.[3]

Mary's appeals did her little good, as she disappeared from court records after this, retiring to the countryside and not regaining favour until 1539. It is possible that the sisters did not see each other again after this point.

The following month, William Brereton was dispatched on embassy to Ireland and in November, George Boleyn was given the task of meeting the Admiral of France, who was arriving to discuss a marriage settlement between Princess Elizabeth and the Dauphin Francis. Philippe de Chabot, Monsieur de Brion, Admiral of France and ambassador to England, arrived at Dover on 11 November, after several delays. George conducted him from there to Canterbury, Sittingbourne, Rochester, Dartford and Blackheath, where Norfolk met him on 17 November.[4] Anne had set much store on her French sophistication, her connections with the Valois family and the support of Francis, but this visit did not go as she might have hoped.

Reputedly, the ambassador did not give her the time or respect she felt she deserved, which was 'noted by several persons' and then he proposed a match for the Dauphin with Mary, who was closer to the boy in age. Henry replied by suggesting a match between Elizabeth and Francis' third son, the Duke of Angoulême, which was really no substitute for marrying the heir to the French throne. If the events occurred as Chapuys wrote in his letter, he would have been correct to surmise that these events made Anne 'very angry'.[5] It would have represented a slight to her queenship, to the validity of her marriage and the status of her daughter, and the assumption that Mary had a better claim to the English throne than Elizabeth. Such was the controversy that the Emperor even feared that as the result of these negotiations, 'perhaps Anne de Bouland might take the proposal so ill that the Princess's life might be in danger'.[6] It was true that Mary had the advantage of age, but she also had the general consensus of Rome, that any child conceived within a marriage that the parents considered to be legally binding, even if it was later annulled, was considered to have been conceived in good faith, and therefore, legitimate. The negotiations were a blow to Anne, in part occasioned by Francis' efforts to play both sides simultaneously and marry at least one of his sons to a daughter of the Emperor.

Rumours of Henry's attention straying and Anne's unpopularity persisted. On 18 October, the Count of Cifuentes wrote to Emperor Charles that 'Ana de Boulans was disliked by the lords of England on account of her pride and that of her brothers and kinsmen, and because the King did not like her as much as he did. The King was entertaining another lady, and many lords helped him with the object of separating him from Anne.'[7] Three days later, Chapuys reported that Henry's attitude towards Mary had softened, commanding that she be well treated 'to the Lady's great annoyance' and that when Elizabeth's household was at Richmond, Mary refused to leave her chamber until Anne had left. Chapuys believed this softening was on the account of Henry's new love interest, although he was not sure: 'If it were not that the King is of amiable and cordial nature, and that the young lady his new mistress, who is quite devoted to the Princess, has already busied herself in her behalf, there might be some suspicion that the King's favors to the Princess were dissimulations, to conceal the guilt if any ill overtook the said Princess.'[8] And yet it was not a clear-cut case, as Chapuys was shrewd enough to acknowledge, understanding the tempestuous nature of the royal marriage:

> As to the King being dissatisfied with the Lady, it is true he sometimes shows it, but, as I have written before, they are lovers' quarrels, and not much weight is to be attached to them, unless the love of the King for the young lady of whom I wrote to you should grow warm and continue some time; of which it is impossible to form a judgment, considering the changeableness of this king. I have learned from the Master of the Horse that when the Lady began to complain of the said young lady, because she did not do either in word or deed the reverence she expected, the King went away from her very angry, complaining of her importunity. As to the instigation of this king against the relations of his said Lady, it does not appear otherwise. It is true that Rochford's wife was sent from Court for the reason that I have heretofore written, and the King has lately shown this favor to the said Rochford in some question he had with master Bryan. The Lady's sister was also banished from Court three months ago, but it was necessary to do so, for besides that she had been found guilty of misconduct, it would not have been becoming to see her at Court *enceinte*.[9]

As the main source of the information regarding this situation, Chapuys displays both shrewdness and credulity, knowing that when it came to personal matters, lovers' quarrels should not always be taken seriously, but also being a little too willing to accept gossip, later acknowledging a few occasions when he had been misled. Other evidence suggests that all was well between the king and queen, and that any arguments were mere ripples compared to the grander scheme of Henry's intentions. Whilst Chapuys paints a picture of their volatility, Henry was, in fact, pursuing legislation to further secure his marriage and command obedience to Anne from her subjects. As to her loss of French support, that October an 'instrument' was devised in the name of Francis I, by which he engaged to maintain the validity of Henry VIII's marriage with Anne Boleyn and the legitimacy of the princess Elizabeth, declaring that the late Pope Clement VII acknowledged to him at Marseilles by word of mouth that the dispensation of pope Julius was null, and the marriage with Catharine invalid.[10]

That November, Anne was with Henry at Hampton Court when she was granted the manor and park of Pyssowe in Hertfordshire, which had been in the Scrope family.[11] Her vice-chamberlain Edward Baynton was also rewarded, receiving custody of the manor of Sampford in Somerset, and the wardship and marriage of the late owner's heir.[12] Thomas Cromwell took a further step up the ladder, becoming Master of the Rolls.[13] Anne received approval from Henry's older sister Margaret, the former Queen of Scotland, who had been divorced and whose daughter, Lady Margaret Douglas, was a favourite in Anne's household. On 12 December, Margaret acknowledged a gift sent by Anne as being from her 'derrest cister' in a letter to Cromwell.[14] Anne and Henry appear to have passed a happy Christmas, according to John Husee, who delivered their New Years' gift from the Lisles, which was a cup engraved with the letters H and A on the top. He reported that a Lord of Misrule had been appointed and that the king and queen 'keep a great house'.[15] Anne sent a New Year's gift of a pair of gold beads with tassels, weighing 5oz to Lady Lisle in Calais.[16] However, the festivities may have been soured by a disagreement between George Boleyn and his cousin, Francis Bryan, over which the king sided with Bryan, although the details of this have not survived. It may not have been of significance.

In the middle of January, Anne appeared nervous, volatile, almost hysterical, at a feast given in honour of the Admiral of France. She behaved in an unqueenly manner, nearly causing a serious breach of courtesy with de Brion, and indiscreetly confessing her marital insecurities. The Admiral was seated beside Anne and then danced with her, during which she 'burst into a fit of uncontrollable laughter, without any occasion'. De Brion took offence, asking whether she was laughing at him. She explained her outburst was occasioned by the king telling her he was 'going to ask for the Admiral's secretary to amuse her, and that the King had met on the way a lady who made him forget the matter'.[17]

From this account of the exchange, Anne sounds like a woman on the edge, whose emotions were close to the surface. To confide such a matter in De Brion was an indiscretion, but honesty may have been Anne's only policy in order to avoid giving further offence. Her response to Henry's flirtation would imply this was not the first occasion he had acted in such a manner. Again, though, this is an image created at a remove, for the eyes of the Admiral and Anne's take on the situation could have been entirely different.

Anne apparently then quarrelled with her uncle, the Duke of Norfolk, and her former suitor Henry Percy, Earl of Northumberland. Percy's physician informed Chapuys that the Earl was upset by the 'oppressions and enormities now practised' in the realm, which he saw as weakening the country to the extent that it could be easy prey to invaders like the Emperor or the Turk. He was also critical of Anne's manner and tone, her 'arrogance and malice', having recently overheard an argument she had with Norfolk, during which she had 'spoken such shameful words... as one would not address to a dog', so that the Duke was 'compelled to quit the chamber'.[18] Anne may have lashed out against her uncle, speaking in anger, and her status meant he was unable to repond in kind. It might have been a moment of pressure, a disagreement or a sign of stress. Norfolk himself could have overstepped the line and provoked the comments – or else it might not have happened like that at all. Percy's words, reported by Chapuys, indicate that Anne had forgotten the respect that was due to the Duke, in terms of his status and their family connection. From her position at the forefront of the family, blazing a trail for the Boleyns and Howards, leading them to greater heights than ever before, Anne may have forgotten what she owed them by 1535. Having achieved the pinnacle of queenship, she overstepped boundaries of gender and family, if she spoke to Norfolk in such a way. The alienation of such a figure would constitute a serious misjudgement, leaving her open to criticism, even attack, that not even her queenly status would insulate her against. Below the king, Henry, power at court resided in the hands of Norfolk, Cromwell and Anne herself. Early in 1535, it suited the Duke to bite his tongue, as it was largely thanks to Anne that his daughter had been married to Henry's only son, Henry Fitzroy, but the incident suggests that Anne was beginning to overreach herself, that she was pushing too far, either through confidence or fear, and making powerful enemies of former friends.

It was the playwright Christopher Marlowe who re-introduced the literary character of the overreacher during the reign of Anne's daughter. Hindsight allows for the definition of Anne as a classic Marlovian overreacher, who stretches herself to transcend social boundaries, inexplicably linked with those of gender, pushes a little too far and falls, Icarus-like, because of a fatal flaw, or hamartia. Frequently, according to Marlowe, Shakespeare and their successsors, such characters have exceptional ability together with their ambition. Constrained by narrow cultural concepts of behaviour, which they attempt to overcome or redefine, they fail to recognise that their humanity and frailty undermine their efforts, leading to a tragic outcome. Anne's path to fame necessitated the transcending of boundaries of class and gender. Traditionally, queens were selected from a small gene pool of European royalty, with the notable exception of Henry's maternal grandmother, Elizabeth Woodville, whom Edward IV had married in secret, causing great controversy. Anne was certainly of the aristocracy, she was no 'commoner' as some have claimed, but there was a definitive barrier of blood around the royal circle which was jealously guarded to prevent it being diluted by marrying out. Royal blood went back centuries but just four generations before, the Boleyn family had been obscure country gentry. Anne had aspired to and won a place many of her contemporaries would have believed was not for her. It was a particular phenomenon of Henry's reign that low-born talents might rise to social heights as the result of hard work and ability. One need only consider the vitriol directed at Thomas Wolsey and Thomas Cromwell to see how much the Tudor upper classes resented outsiders, where the insults of choice always concerned their humble origins. They found that their success depended upon the king's favour which, once withdrawn, was a signal for the wolves to close in. A person out of their class, an upstart, an overreacher, was an uneasy thing to be at Henry's court. This does not mean Anne could not have made a good queen, but that she may have flourished under a less restrictive model of queenship, or else become more able to meet the codes over time.

Then there is the question of gender. Anne's intelligence, education, free spirit and her ideals when it came to marriage, meant that she was less willing to accept a traditionally female role, that of a subservient wife. Contemporary convention allowed a woman some degree of passionate licence so long as it was within a prescribed area; she might challenge and tease a man during courtship, and make a 'play' of ruling him before sating his passion. After the wedding service, she was expected to settle down to motherhood, to meekly accept the word and law of her husband, to be faithful, loyal, supportive and non-combative. It was for these reasons that the act of infidelity constituted petty treason, as it was a violation of the patriarchal bond, where the husband was 'king' and his wife the subject. Anne would have been aware of these conventions but, in many ways, Henry had misled her during their courtship. Theirs was a unique situation and he had led her to believe that their union was not bound by the usual rules. As a couple, they had taken an extraordinary degree of licence by rejecting the pope, and simply by being together. It was a defiant, original, rule-breaking relationship, redefining certain aspects of marriage and who might determine those rules. It explored the boundaries of control and the movement of power between spouses. Henry's letters make it clear that in 1527 it was a love match, that he was devoted and his love was exclusive: it was Anne's belief that their marriage would continue in that vein rather than revert to gender convention. She was intelligent and outspoken, passionate and prepared to speak out when the occasion demanded. When she did not like Henry's behaviour, she did not keep quiet, but commented on it, sometimes in public, even upbraiding him. This was not what a wife was supposed to do, or what Henry had expected from her. Her behaviour challenged the expected gender roles and resulted in some courtiers and ambassadors commenting on her ability to manipulate, and annoy, the king. In some instances, she caused Henry embarrassment. Women who defied male authority, whether that of the courts, of the church, or their husbands, were typically attacked along gender lines. If the perceived area of transgression was related to their femininity, even tenuously, this became for male and female critics the appropriate target. Misbehaving women might be described as masculine, or in possession of masculine traits, or have their 'good fame' or sexual conduct attacked, being called whores, temptresses, adulteresses, harlots or sexually voracious, regardless of the reality of their conduct. 'Unfeminine' behaviour justified all female-oriented slanders.

The concept of Anne as a proto-Marlovian overreacher implies that Anne herself was the driving force of her own career, carving the rungs of her own ladder in her desire to reach the throne. This may be an uncomfortable interpretation of Anne's character, which some may find unpalatable. It may seem shameful, even unladylike, but this response is a hang-over from patriarchal concepts of femininity. If Anne was truly ambitious, driving the course of her own destiny, modern interpretations should not be reluctant to acknowledge this. After all, it is a reading compatible with the ambition of her male Boleyn relatives and a measure of just how successful she was at achieving her goal.

Yet Anne did not reach her position alone. At the start of the courtship, according to the evidence of Henry's surviving letters, she was reluctant to be wooed by him, only acquiescing when he made an offer of marriage. Again, interpretations of her later actions are determined by the way her timidity in 1527 is read. Was she holding out for a crown, or did she hold off an ardent king before glimpsing with a shock the heights to which his passion might raise her? Henry was clearly of the conviction that he had 'made' Anne, and it is true that he had been the one to choose her, to promote and serve her and her family, through offices, gifts, favours and rewards. Yet Anne had earned these accolades with her own person. The question returns us to the conundrum of who was leading whom; who was the driving force in the relationship, and the extent of Anne's ambition. It is clear that from the moment she accepted Henry's proposal in 1527, queenship became a goal for Anne. How actively she pursued it is another matter. She did complain to him about the years of waiting, as her fertility dwindled, but this does not equate to driving ambition.

So, what did drive Anne? Was it the desire to be at Henry's side; was she as much in love with him as he was with her? Was it the wish to be well-married, to which all Tudor women aspired? In the marital game, the king was the ultimate, unexpected prize, to which none dared aspire. Was it the desire for wealth, or riches? Or else the urge to achieve, to push herself as high as she might go? To prove to her family that she could take the Boleyns a step further than any of the men had ever managed to reach? Or was it simply the desire to be queen, like the culmination of a fairy-tale, in which little girls throughout time have indulged? It is possible that Anne was driven by a deeper force, connected with her profound faith and the religious reforms that her marriage was initiating. Just as the Catholic Catherine considered that it was her mission to save Henry's damned soul, Anne may have seen herself as having been chosen to lead Henry along the correct religious path and to save the nation by presenting England with an heir. George Wyatt reported that Anne reacted to a prophecy against her life with the words, 'Yet for the hope I have that the realm may be happy by my issue, I am resolved to have him (Henry) whatsoever might become of me.' On 24 June 1533, the Venetian Ambassador, Carlo Capelli, met Anne, who assured him 'she knew that God had inspired his Majesty to marry her, and that he could have found a greater personage than herself, but not one more anxious and ready to demonstrate her love towards the Signory'.[19]

Did Anne have a sense of duty, a calling, a mission from God, in which her personal life was subservient to the role she might play in rescuing her country? There is little evidence for this, but it is not necessarily an emotion or state of mind that she would have committed to paper, or made public beyond what has been stated. It was a relationship between her and God. She must have been aware of the timing of her rise. A few years earlier, or a few years later, she would not have captured Henry's desire. The failure of five out of six of Catherine's pregnancies was essential to Anne's rise. Being at the right place at the right time could have seemed like divine providence.

Probably all these elements played a part in stirring and driving Anne's desire to be queen. The journey took her beyond the position she had expected to inhabit and challenged concepts of class and gender at court which, coupled with Henry's emotional volatility and established prerogatives, made for an explosive mix.

PART SEVEN

THUNDER
AROUND
THE THRONE

THIRTY-ONE

Change and Continuity, January–June 1535

A religious revolution was underway in England. At the end of January 1535, Friar George Browne preached a sermon indicative of the direction in which Henry was about to lead the English church. Before his consecration as Archbishop of Dublin, an appointment which Henry made independently of the pope, Browne was an Augustinian friar who had been employed by Henry to administer the Oath of Succession in the religious establishments of London and the South-East. His sermon that Sunday urged all bishops to burn papal bulls sent them from Rome and replace them with ones from the king, their new spiritual leader. Failure to do so would incur 'very severe punishment' and prevent them from discharging their clerical duties, as the pope was the idol of Rome and a 'limb of the devil'. The scandalised Chapuys believed Browne's language was so 'abominable' that 'it must have been prompted by the King or by Cromwell', whose right-hand man the ambassador thought Browne had become.[1] Centuries of adherence to Rome, of monastic order and Catholic practices, were to be swept away in the coming months.

The majority of religious establishments had sworn the oath, often under duress, but sworn it nevertheless. According to Cromwell's instructions, the inhabitants of each institution had been gathered in their chapter houses and examined separately, before being asked to submit to Henry as Supreme Head of the Church of England, and to reject the pope. The monks and nuns vowed to preach the word of God 'sincerely and simply, according to the meaning of the Holy Scriptures and Catholic doctors', to commend the king, Queen Anne and her child and the Archbishop of Canterbury to the people. Then they were requested to reveal their 'gold, silver and other moveable goods' to the inspectors and to deliver an inventory of this wealth.[2] The first oaths had been sworn in May and June 1534, with one, two or even three monasteries capitulating each day: Dartford Priory in Kent, St Andrew's in Rochester, the convent of Stoneley, Lincolnshire and St Bartholomew's Hospital, West Smithfield, London, were the first to surrender, followed by Elsing at Cripplegate, St Mary at Bishopsgate and then the London hospital attached to the church where Geoffrey Boleyn's Mercers had worshipped. The master at the time, Laurence Gopferler, and six others, signed the declaration at St Thomas of Acon on 23 June, 1534,[3] overlooked by the tomb of former mayor Henry Frowik. Through the month of July 1534, a further 37 establishments signed the oath, with dozens more following suit through the rest of that year.[4] The English diplomat in Spain, John Mason, recorded that there was little news from England except that the country had 'thrown off the Pope' and every man now swears 'in favour of the King and Queen'. He recorded that Sir Thomas More, former Lord Chancellor and John Fisher, Bishop of Rochester, had been committed to the Tower for refusing to swear the oath, and mused 'what will be (the) end of this tragedy, God knows. This may well be called a tragedy which began with a marriage.'[5]

In January 1535 Cromwell began to lay the groundwork for a national monastic inspection, recruiting Richard Layton, Thomas Legh, John Ap Rice and John Tregonwell as his agents, along with numerous members of the local gentry, clergymen, sheriffs and bishops, to examine church books and accounts, the morals and character of the inhabitants, their practices and adherence to religious rules, the value of their properties and lands, visitors to the place and the wealth they owned.[6] From January to the end of May, this information was compiled in a report entitled *Valor Ecclesiasticus*, which put a framework in place for Henry to act against the monasteries. That February, the Reformation Parliament, which had been sitting in different sessions since 1529, passed the Suppression of Religious Houses Act. The intention was to end the 'manifest sin, vicious, carnal and abominable living' that was 'daily used and committed among the little and small abbeys, priories and other religious houses' where the congregation numbered less than twelve people. Many of the abbots and priors, abbesses and prioresses were said to 'spoil, destroy, consume and utterly waste' their properties and the church's ornaments 'to the high displeasure of Almighty God... and to the great infamy of the king's highness and the realm'.[7] Despite their wide field of reference, the investigators' criticisms focused largely on two points: the idolatrous worship of relics and images and the sexual immorality of the monks and nuns.

A number of the Carthusian monks from the Charterhouse and Sion, and the Observant Friars of Richmond and Greenwich were prepared to embrace martyrdom rather than swear allegiance to Henry over the pope. Norfolk, Cromwell, and Thomas, Lord Audeley, who had taken over More's role as Lord Chancellor, sat in judgement upon them, and on May 4, three prominent Carthusians were hung, drawn and quartered at Tyburn for their disobedience. John Houghton, Prior of Charterhouse, John Lawrence Prior of Beauvale and Augustine Webber, Prior of Axholme, along with a Benedictine monk, Richard Reynolds, suffered the full traitor's penalty for their views. More Carthusians followed. Reputedly, Reynolds had also spread slanders, stating that 'the lady Dowager (Catherine) was the true queen', that Henry could not be head of the Church, that Henry 'had meddling (sic) with the Queen's mother', that the king was the 'Mouldwarp' of prophecy, and 'the pope would be in England before midsummer'.[8] A high-born audience assembled to witness the end of such outspoken traitors:

> It is altogether a new thing that the dukes of Richmond and Norfolk, the earl of Wiltshire, his son, and other lords and courtiers, were present at the said execution, quite near the sufferers. People say that the King himself would have liked to see the butchery; which is very probable, seeing that nearly all the Court, even those of the Privy Chamber, were there—his principal chamberlain, Norris, bringing with him 40 horses.[9]

On 19 June, three more monks from the Charterhouse were killed in the same way, and again, four members of Anne's family were present to witness the event: Thomas and George Boleyn, the Duke of Norfolk and his son-in-law, who was also Anne's stepson, the sixteen-year-old Henry Fitzroy. What Anne thought of this went unrecorded. Sometimes it is difficult for modern readers to reconcile such appalling suffering with the Christian faith, but in the sixteenth century, death by martyrdom was a way of cleansing the heretical soul. The application of the ultimate, horrible sanction is indicative of Henry's absolute stance on this question, of his complete inability to accept differences of opinion on a subject he felt to be of the utmost urgency. It was a function of his absolute monarchy. Any refusals could indicate a weakness in his position, and he was not a man to tolerate being undermined. At least 18 Carthusian monks died for their beliefs between 1535 and 1540, either in this barbaric fashion or in prison.

In May, Thomas More and John Fisher, both already confined to the Tower, were told that they had six weeks to consider their response to the Act of Supremacy, to which they had previously refused to swear. Their responses were that they were both 'ready to suffer what martyrdom pleased the King' and their opinions would not change.[10] Chapuys saw this as the next step in the growth of Henry's savagery and cast Anne as the temptress, arrogant and controlling, urging him on to greater cruelties. There is no evidence for such a view of Anne:

It is to be feared that if the King is getting so inured to cruelty he will use it towards the Queen and Princess, at least in secret; to which the concubine will urge him with all her power, who has lately several times blamed the said King, saying it was a shame to him and all the realm that they were not punished as traitresses according to the statutes. The said concubine is more haughty than ever, and ventures to tell the King that he is more bound to her than man can be to woman, for she extricated him from a state of sin; and moreover, that he came out of it the richest Prince that ever was in England, and that without her he would not have reformed the Church, to his own great profit and that of all the people.[11]

In 1534, Henry's old adversary Pope Clement had died and been replaced by Paul III. The following May, hearing of John Fisher's imprisonment, the new pope elevated Fisher to the cardinalcy of San Vitale, hoping that the appointment would encourage Henry to treat the prisoner more leniently. Instead, the news enraged the king, who would not allow Fisher's traditional red hat into the country, saying he would send the man's head to Rome for it instead. The pope asked several parties to intercede on Fisher's behalf, including Francis I and his ambassador, Jean du Bellay, but events in England moved swiftly. On 17 June, Fisher was condemned in Westminster Hall, before a jury that contained Cromwell and Thomas Boleyn. He was executed at Tower Hill on 22 June, after the sentence of hanging, drawing and quartering was commuted to beheading with a sword. Thomas More was executed in the same location on 6 July. George Boleyn was one of those who directly profited from his death, receiving his confiscated manor of Southe, in Kent.[12]

The news of these two deaths sent shockwaves across Europe. Pope Paul was determined to carry out the threat of excommunication that Clement had made to Henry, writing to the Emperor's brother, Ferdinand of Hungary, to rally support for his 'intention to deprive Henry VIII of his kingdom', which sounds as if England was on the verge of being invaded.[13] The executions also drove Francis into the arms of the Emperor, who was horrified by Henry's decision, an opportunity which Paul did not neglect to exploit:

Expecting to hear from day to day of the liberation of John (Fisher) Cardinal of Rochester, having recommended him most earnestly to

Francis, has been astounded by the announcement of his execution by king Henry. Doubts not but that Francis is sorely grieved, seeing that his intercession would appear to have hastened the cardinal's death. Deplores his loss to the Church, and especially the degrading mode of death inflicted on him. Regrets still more the cause of his death, defending, not the rights of a particular church, as St. Thomas of Canterbury, but the truth of the universal Church. Henry has thus even exceeded his ancestors in wickedness. Not content with disregarding the censures of Clement VII, with the notorious adultery, which gives rise to scandal in the Church, with the sacrilegious slaughter of so many clerks and religious men, with heresy and schism, and the withdrawal of his kingdom from the universal Church, and from obedience to the Roman Church, to which it is tributary, he commanded publicly to be executed a man who was elevated to the cardinalate because of his learning and holiness, after endeavouring to get him to recant and to deny the truth, which he would not do; and hastened his death on hearing of his creation as cardinal, thus committing the crime of lese-majesty, and incurring the usual penalties, especially that of privation.[14]

In England too, treasonable words continued to be spoken against the marriage, with Anne being cast as the corrupting influence. The tightening of the law in the Treason Act of 1534, hard on the heels of the Act of Supremacy, meant that far more cases were being reported, from idle gossip, neighbour to neighbour, up to speculation about the fate of Henry's and Anne's souls. Archbishop Cranmer sent to Cromwell a priest who had 'bid a vengeance on the king' and a woman who had said that 'since this new queen was made there was never so much pilling and polling in this realm'.[15] In another case, a Suffolk spinster named Margaret Chanseler, had declared that 'the Queen had one child by the King, which was dead-born, and she prayed she might never have another'. Presumably, this was referring to the miscarriage or stillbirth Anne had experienced in the summer of 1534, although the secrecy of that event might suggest that Margaret was misinformed about the birth and survival of Elizabeth. She went on to seal her fate with the accusation that 'the Queen was a... goggle-eyed whore', and stated that the King 'ought not to marry within the realm' and that Catherine was the righteous queen, before pleading drunkenness and possession by an evil spirit.[16] Her deposition was made before the Abbot of Bury, and ended up with Cromwell, to whom hundreds of cases were sent.[17] The stricter laws meant that examples were being made of individuals who transgressed, in order to deter others from speaking out. This certainly marked a cultural change, as it was now punishable by death to attack the king's marriage to Anne in speech or writing, and an offence incurring fines or imprisonment to slander her person, character or reputation. Cases that might have formerly been dismissed as foolish, idle or harmless gossip – as Hall recorded, 'the common people daily murmured and spoke their follish fantasies',[18] were now treated with greater severity, and it was remarked that 'the king will hang a man for a word speaking nowdays' and 'it is now no novelty among us to see men slain, hung, quartered or beheaded, some for trifling expressions, which were explained or interpreted as having been spoken against the king'.[19]

Anne's Vice-Chamberlain, Sir Edward Baynton, had been given the task of sifting through and recording the possessions which Catherine of Aragon had left behind at Baynard's Castle. Out of dozens of items from the former queen's wardrobe and closet, from hangings in her bedroom and personal objects like chess pieces and slippers, a number were forwarded to Anne for her use. These included a horn cup with a cover, decorated with antique work, with feet and knob of ivory, two stools of red and green velvet and two of ivory, one set within the other, a case of a dozen wooden trenchers and a coffer covered in crimson velvet with four tills. Henry took his former wife's embroidered cloth depicting the baptism of Christ in gold and her red and white ivory chessmen.[20] Along with the crown jewels Anne had worn to Calais and the Spanish christening gown she had coveted, and Catherine's former furniture, palaces, staff and routines, the transfer of such items indicated a change at the top, but they were also valuable as signs of the continuity of monarchy. Royal items passed from one pair of hands to the next, just as the crown itself did.

While most of the country, even in the most far-flung places, would have heard word of Catherine's replacement by Anne, for the majority, who would never see royalty in the flesh, it was an abstract concept. They replaced Catherine's name with Anne's in their prayers, even perhaps regretted the loss of Catherine as an enduring symbol of majesty and motherhood, but the substitution of one woman for another had little real impact in a personal sense. The queen was the woman at the king's side, wearing the jewels. It was a more general sense of monarchy that prevailed across the country, equating to stability and continuity of peace and good rule, or good lordship. Those who spoke up against Anne rarely knew her, but attacked her as either a symbol of change or a gender aberration; a woman behaving badly. She and Henry might have predicted the handful of comments calling her a whore; these mattered far less than the good opinions of those in her close-knit circle at court, where her reputation, her 'good-fame' was a critical element in Henry's eyes.

In the spring of 1535, Anne's peace was undermined again. The new French ambassador Palamedes Gontier found her to be on edge, anxious to secure his country's support, as if it was essential to her survival. She complained of the delay in Henry receiving communications from the Admiral, de Biron, before whom she had laughed the previous December. These delays, she admitted, 'had caused her husband many doubts', perhaps as a result of her former awkward exchange with de Biron, of which Henry is certain to have heard, from the same court gossips who informed Chapuys. Anne implored Gontier to ask the Admiral to 'apply some remedy, and act towards the King so that she may not be ruined and lost'. She saw herself 'very near that and in more grief and trouble than before her marriage' and asked Gontier to beg de Biron to 'consider her affairs, of which she could not speak as fully as she wished, on account of her fears, and the eyes which were looking at her, her husband's and the lords' present'. She added that she 'could not write, nor see him again, nor stay longer'.[21] This is an astonishing account of the ambassador's meeting with Anne, about which he had no reason to lie. It reads more like situations that Catherine described herself to be in, during 1530 and 1531, conscious of the eyes and ears of the court, feeling she was caught on a knife edge. The desperate tone, the appeals to France as being her last chance, are also reminiscent of Wolsey, just before his fall. Anne left Gontier's company because of 'the king going to the next room, where the dance was beginning'. The ambassador's conclusion was that 'she is not at her ease on account of the doubts and suspicions of the king'.[22] Exactly what Henry suspected his wife of, is not clear.

Gontier's report might indicate an occasion when Anne's flirtatious words first caused trouble in her household. Much has been made of an argument that she had with Henry Norris days before her arrest, in which she overstepped the line and suggested that he wished to marry her after the king's death. With some justification, this has been considered the catalyst for her arrest at a time when her enemies were seeking just such an opportunity. That those words were crucially mis-timed is clear from the fact that she made a statement in similar vein, over a year before that incident in April 1536. This first transgression might have made waves, but it was not sufficient to topple Anne, because she was otherwise secure. If Anne was on edge in late February 1535, it may be that she had aroused Henry's suspicion, but weathered the storm.

Following her arrest, Anne admitted to Mrs Coffin that she had teased Weston 'because he did love her kinswoman Mrs Shelton, and that she said he loved not his wife'. To this, he 'made answer that he loved one in her house better than them both'. When Anne asked who this person was, Weston replied, 'It is yourself.' Such a statement was just acceptable within the bounds of the courtly love tradition; it had been offered by Weston himself, rather than sought by Anne, and was an acknowledgement of his devotion to her as his 'Lady' and queen. Yet perhaps Henry heard of it, and did not like it. It is possible that he heard it from the very lips of the other woman involved, the Mrs Shelton Weston was neglecting.

Around the same time as Gontier's meeting with the queen, Chapuys recorded that Henry had begun a new flirtation. The 'young lady who was lately in the King's favour is so no longer,' he wrote. She had been replaced by 'a cousin german of the concubine, daughter of the present gouvernante of the Princess'.[23] This was the same daughter of Lady Shelton to whom Anne was referring as being the object of Francis Weston's affections, known as 'Madge', a traditional abbreviation of 'Margaret', although historians have disagreed over whether this was Margaret Shelton or her sister Mary. Margaret appears to have been the elder of the daughters, who entered Anne's household in February 1535, and is reputed to have become Henry's mistress for around six months. Whether this was a full-scale physical affair or another courtly dalliance, a new lady for the king to serve, is not clear. Anne is far less likely to have tolerated the former. Mary, perhaps as much as a decade younger, was a contributor to the Devonshire Manuscript, a compilation of poems written or copied out by those in the queen's household. It has been suggested that Anne herself promoted Henry's liaison with 'Madge' as a way to divert her husband's attention away from his former love interest, but Anne appears to have taken a zero-tolerance approach to infidelity, citing the strength of her feelings for Henry as the reason why she could not acquiesce in this matter, as Catherine had done. None of Henry's flirtations of 1535 posed any serious danger to Anne's position. It would take a combination of other factors before any rival could have the opportunity to depose her.

Anne was still exercising her influence as queen on behalf of those she wished to help. Patronage and 'good ladyship' were considered an important facet of her position, as an approachable face, able to secure advancement or ease disputes. Sometimes this was done in tandem with Cromwell, with whom she and her family appeared to still have a good working relationship, with questions relating to domestic and political matters passing between them. In early 1535, Anne clearly considered Cromwell to be Henry's righthand man, and thus, also at her disposal. She referred cases of slander to him and, that spring, wrote to Cromwell to help conclude some business on behalf of her receiver, George Taylor, and the king's dyer, John Baptist.[24] She extended her patronage to promising scholars and graduates, overseeing their studies and employing a number in her household. In May 1534, she wrote to the Abbot of York, who had promised to support the studies of a John Aylmer at Cambridge, but had summomed him home and charged him with 'certain offices, to the great disturbance of his studies'. She requested that he be allowed to return to the university, 'with sufficient maintenance to pursue his studies'.[25]

By Easter, when Anne was at Richmond, around nine months had passed since the mysterious end of her second pregnancy but she had not conceived again. Chapuys reported that she believed this was due to the continuing existence of Catherine and Mary, as if their lives inhibited hers in some supernatural way. He wrote that she had used subterfuge in an attempt to remove them; she had 'suborned a person to say that he has had a revelation from God that she cannot conceive while the said two ladies are alive' and constantly spoke of them as 'rebels and traitresses deserving death'. The ambassador did not doubt that Anne had mentioned this to Henry and had 'lately sent the man to Cromwell'.[26] Whatever the truth of this tale, or indeed the existence of the 'person', Anne surely was concerned by the absence of any new pregnancy, especially given that she had conceived again so swiftly after the birth of Elizabeth. A letter from Sir William Kingston to Lord Lisle, included in the State Letters and Papers for June 1535, refers to the queen having a 'goodly belly', but this is surely a mistake. There are no other surviving references to a pregnancy, especially an advanced one, in the summer of that year. However, it was in June the previous year that Anne had been reaching the end of her second, ill-fated pregnancy, so it would appear this is a case of a misdated letter, rather than a third conception.

In early April 1535, Anne fled to Hampton Court, on account of an outbreak of measles affecting her gentlewomen[27] but Henry was not with her, travelling to a number of locations before planning to join her a week later. Chapuys reports another unusual story at this time which, had Anne known of it, may have caused her alarm. Reputedly, the ambassador had a conversation with Henry about the possibility of him returning to Catherine, a topic which can only have raised by Chapuys as Henry had no intention of returning to his former wife, in the full knowledge that she had passed through the menopause in 1524–5 and would give him no more children. Chapuys did his best, pressing the former queen's case, but to no avail:

> Moreover, that if he took back the Queen, this kingdom would give him as much as he could ask, and he should be the more induced to do so because it is probable he would sooner have male issue from the Queen than from this woman, as I am informed by physicians and others,—this being one of the principal points alleged by the King

in favour of his second marriage, that the Queen was not capable of bearing children, being already past 48. I mentioned to him some ladies even of this country who had had children at 51. He said that her mother was 52 when she conceived her; and thereupon said a thousand good things of the Queen, cursing, nevertheless, those who had ever made the marriage which had been the cause of innumerable troubles, and made the King spend three millions of gold.[28]

In early June, Chapuys reported the first indication that Cromwell and Anne may not be as close as the queen believed:

Cromwell told me that if the King's lady knew the freedom with which we conversed together she would procure some trouble, and that only three days ago they had had words together, and that she had said she would like to see his head cut off, but he had such confidence in the King, his master, that he thought she could do nothing to him. I suspect he invented this to raise the value of his goods; for I told him all the world regarded him as her right hand, although I am informed on good authority that the said lady does not cease night or day to procure the disgrace of the duke of Norfolk, whether it be because he has spoken too freely of her or because Cromwell, desiring to lower the great ones, wishes to commence with him.[29]

Anne's alleged comment here, that she would have Cromwell's head cut off, does not sound completely implausible, if uttered in anger. She had previously made similar comments, not least to Sir Henry Guildford, which Henry had instructed him to ignore as women's talk, and may also have insulted her uncle. It is possible that Cromwell and Anne quarrelled, or else Anne vented her frustration upon her husband's servant, but there is nothing else to suggest it was serious, or that lasting damage was done. There is also the possibility that the wily Cromwell was leading Chapuys astray, playing a double game in order to make the ambassador believe he was sympathetic to his cause. Equally, in the light of the overtures he made to Mary and his desire for an Imperial alliance in the spring of 1536, the canny servant may have been hedging his bets, seeking to ensure his own survival. As the summer progress of 1535 approached, there was scant evidence of marital bliss, but the union was still viable and, over the coming weeks, the indications were that Henry and Anne were growing closer. Soon, they would be on much firmer ground.

THIRTY-TWO

Being Merry, June–September 1535

The watchword for Henry and Anne in the summer of 1535 appears to have been 'merry'. They were 'merry' at Windsor on 16 June, according to Sir John Dudley,[1] 'merry' again in the words of Thomas Culpeper, writing to Lady Lisle on 24 June[2] and still full of 'mirth' and 'good cheer' by the time they reached Wolf Hall, the Wiltshire home of the Seymour family, in early September.[3] Aiming to travel as far west as Bristol, they enjoyed the hospitality of friends and courtiers, took advantage of the local hunting and hawking, while Henry occasionally paused to deal with issues arising with France, or Ireland, or the impending closure of the monasteries. It does appear that, in spite of a number of external pressures, the marriage was a happy one during the second part of 1535 and that Anne had everything to look forward to.

Shortly before they left, Henry settled payments owing to Lord Windsor, the Keeper of the Great Wardrobe. These included the bills of his tailor John Malte, his skinner Thomas Addington, his silk-woman Lettice Worsop, his hosier William Crofton, the cordwainers Henry Cornelys and Henry Johnstone, and to William Sporyar for making robes, doublets and 'stuff' for the king. Sporyar was also rewarded for delivering 'satin etc' to the queen and for making gowns and coats for the king's fool, William Somers, and his new page, Thomas Culpeper.[4] Then aged around twenty-one, the young Culpeper is better known to history for his indiscreet behaviour with Henry's fifth wife, but he was already at court in 1535, possibly in the service of Viscount Lisle, although his elder brother was in the household of Cromwell. They might have been advanced through their connection to Anne, as distant cousins on the Howard side. He would quickly become a favourite with Henry and witness the dramatic events of the following year.

As one new courtier arrived, another departed. Concerned about his faltering relations with France, Henry dispatched George Boleyn, along with Norfolk and Sir William Fitzwilliam, on a mission to conclude the proposed marriage between Princess Elizabeth and the Duke of Angoulême. The mood towards Francis was hostile, though, before his departure, with Chapuys reporting how George had spent 'a long time' conversing with his sister and reputedly, 'both then and several times since she has been in a bad humour'. If Chapuys is to be believed, Anne had turned against the country where she had spent so much of her youth, uttering 'a thousand shameful words of the King of France and generally of the whole nation'.[5] George crossed the Channel with his sister's words ringing in his ears, which perhaps coloured his approach to the negotiations. Henry's terms were that Francis maintain the 'second marriage of the king of England with his present queen Anne as legitimate and immutable, and the issue therefrom legitimate and capable of inheriting England, and the daughter of the first marriage to be illegitimate'.[6] He also wished that the little Duke, Charles, who was then aged thirteen, should be sent to reside in England before the wedding. This was not an unreasonable request, and common practice among European royalty, although it was usually the prospective bride who was dispatched to the foreign realm. In this case, though, it was Elizabeth who was set to inherit her country and the Duke would become her consort. Henry had previously sent his illegitimate son, Henry Fitzroy, to reside at Francis's court for around a year following the Calais visit of 1532, so the request was nothing out of the ordinary. However, the changing religious climate in England made the situation far more volatile than it had been just four years before, and Henry's decision to execute More and Fisher did little to promote his cause with Francis. Remaining at Calais, George did not see Francis, but negotiated instead with 'the Admiral', probably de Brion again, who flatly refused to let the boy come to England.

The Bishop of Faenza was not impressed by the efforts of George Boleyn, who stayed for eight days but, 'as far as could be seen, did nothing'. The bishop believed it was 'only from his relation to the Queen that he is employed, for the King has very few to trust in'. He reported that 'all business passes through the hands of people who depend on the new Queen, and must therefore be settled according to her purpose'.[7] After de Brion refused to 'declare in any way against the Church, or in favour of the king's second wife', the ambassadors 'separated very ill satisfied'. Francis declared his reason to be 'respect to the Holy See' whereas Henry was 'a most bitter enemy of the Church, and so firm in his opinion that he intends to die in it, and tries to have this kingdom for company'. Faenza also reported that the Duke of Norfolk stated he would 'sooner die than see any change as regards the King or the new Queen', which the Bishop put down to his own ambition as, 'being one of the greatest men in the kingdom', he hoped to marry Elizabeth to one of his sons, or 'if disorder ensued, to get the rule into his own hands'.[8] At the start of July, Francis came out decisively against England, and made a personal attack upon Anne:

> Francis also spoke three days ago of the new queen of England, how little virtuously she has always lived and now lives, and how she and her brother and adherents suspect the duke of Norfolk of wishing to make his son King, and marry him to the King's legitimate daughter, though they are near relations. It seems to him there can be little friendship between the two kingdoms… Francis has spoken of it like a Christian and a virtuous prince, expressing his great grief, and that he knows that the King is given up to perdition, and no good can be expected of him, so that he sees clearly he cannot have friendship with him, since he sets himself in this way against the honor of God and the Church.[9]

Oblivious to the harsh words Francis had used to repay hers, Anne set off on progress with Henry. They left the very next day after the Bishop's last letter and, by 8 July, had arrived at Reading Abbey in Berkshire, twenty miles East of Windsor. There, they were the guests of Abbot Hugh Farringdon, who had hosted Henry and Anne back in 1532. He would later become a royal chaplain, sending the king gifts while he was hunting nearby and receiving a New Year's gift in 1532 of a white leather purse containin £20. Farringdon would jump through all Henry's religious hoops in the coming years, until 1539, when he was accused of assisting rebels in the north and suffered a traitor's death. He was a close friend of the king's illegitimate half-uncle, Viscount Lisle, who would also fall foul of Henry's suspicious nature two years after the Abbot's death.

By 12 July, Henry and Anne had moved on to Ewelme, in Oxfordshire, one of the homes of the Duke of Suffolk, Charles Brandon, who was then aged around fifty. Two-and-a-half months after the death of his wife, Henry's sister Mary, former Queen of France, Brandon had married his son's fiancée, the thirteen-year-old Catherine Willoughby, daughter of one of Catherine of Aragon's Spanish waiting women. By the time that Henry and Anne visited, the new duchess was seven months pregnant with her first child, but it is not clear whether she was in residence at the time. During Henry and Anne's two-day visit, business continued and ties of loyalty were reaffirmed amongst their inner circle. Thomas Boleyn wrote to Cromwell from Hever on 13 July, thanking him for his kindness in forwarding a bill of complaint made against the Boleyns by a Leonard Spencer of Norwich. Boleyn told Cromwell that such acts would bind his loyalty 'as long as I live'.[10] On the same day, William, Lord Sandys, Henry's Lord Chamberlain, wrote to Cromwell from the Vyne, from where he had been planning to ride to meet Henry in the coming days:

> Please to remember that whereas I have advertised you of the state of myself and my wife during the last week, I have been attacked anew with the sweat. I am grieved I cannot wait upon the King to execute his office. I beg therefore you will excuse me. As the King will shortly repair to East Hampstead, I dare not come near him unless I am signified of his pleasure. My son's wife is also very sick, on whose account I have sent this bearer, Master Augustine, to whom, as I hear, you have been special good master. And whereas he should have waited upon you on Sunday last, he is prevented by the above-mentioned reason. I trust you will not be displeased at his absence. He is worthy to serve the King.[11]

The sweating sickness was rife that summer, preventing Sandys from fulfilling his duties, and would later necessitate a change to the planned itinerary of the progress. On 14 July, Henry and Anne left Ewelme, riding twelve miles east to Abingdon Abbey, in Oxfordshire. In recent years, there had been tension between Cromwell and Abbot Thomas Pentecost, or Rowland, with the Abbot resisting the minister's attempts to secure positions for his protegés within the establishment. Early in 1535, Cromwell had written again to Rowland, requesting a date that the Abbey accounts might be viewed, following a dispute with the steward there, and the Abbot's response that he 'was bound by his religion to attend daily to the service of God' betrays his resentment at the interference. Eventually, Rowland suggested 14 June 1535, asking that all four of Cromwell's commissioners be spared to conduct the investigation so that it would be 'settled before the King and Cromwell leave'.[12] It cannot have made for an easy atmosphere when Henry and Anne arrived just weeks later. They remained at the abbey for two days, before heading twenty miles north-west to the Old Palace of Langley in Oxfordshire. The king's auditors arrived a month later.[13]

Not to be confused with King's Langley in Hertfordshire, the Old Palace stood on the edge of the village of Shipton-under-Wychwood, and may have once been owned by King John. It had been in the Neville family, before passing to the crown on the death of George, brother of Edward IV, in 1478. Later recorded as a royal hunting lodge, then being replaced by a farmhouse, it was convenient for hunting in the forest of Wychwood. It was at the Old Palace that Anne wrote two letters to Cromwell which demonstrate that they still had a mutually benefical and supportive working relationship. First, she appealed to him on behalf of a friend of Robert Powre, whom she had sent to serve Cromwell, asking for a Lincolnshire abbacy, and secondly, for a ward of hers, where her tone is far more familiar and warm:

Master Secretery, I pray you despatche with speede this matter, for myn honneur lies muche on ytt, and wat should the Kynges attornney do with Poyns hoblygassion, sens I have the chyld be the Kynges grace gyfte, but onlly to troble hym hereafter, whyche be no means I woll suffer, and thus far you as well as I wold ye dyd. Your lovyng mistress Anne the Quene.[14]

This letter gives a unique insight too, as it is almost possible to hear Anne's voice, with her French accent, in the word 'obligation', which she writes phonetically as 'hoblygassion'. Anne was trusting Cromwell to deal with an issue regarding an obligation towards the child, named Poyns, with which she did not want to trouble Henry. This may well have been one of the Poyntz children, as the family frequently spell their own name in this manner in correspondence of 1535; the young courtier Nicholas Poyntz had a large family. The eldest son, born in 1528, also named Nicholas, was perhaps the child Anne referred to. Norfolk and George Boleyn were also writing to Cromwell as a useful enabler of their inner circle of reformed thinkers, from Langley on 19 July, hoping he would intercept Luther's colleague Philip Melanchthon on his journey to France and persuade him to come to England, 'considering the conformity of his doctrines here, and the good reception he will meet with'.[15] This is a measure of the mutual trust between Cromwell and the Boleyn-Howard faction, who considered him serviceable, but it is not tantamount to genuine friendship. This was, essentially, due to Cromwell's class, and his position as a functional figure at court, a facilitator. Primarily, he was the king's servant, and the Boleyn-Howard faction had the king's ear, therefore it was also his job to serve their needs.

Between 21 and 26 July, Henry and Anne were at Sudeley Castle, the state rooms of which had been rebuilt by Richard III in the 1480s, but had passed to Henry's great uncle, Jasper Tudor, after the Yorkist defeat at Bosworth. The house had been neglected for a while before the royal progress of 1535, and some of it may not have been habitable, causing the rest of the court to be lodged at Winchecombe Abbey, a mile away. This may have afforded the king and queen a brief respite, and comparative quiet, in their five days there. On 26 July, they headed twelve miles west to Tewkesbury Abbey in Gloucestershire, where Henry's grandfather had secured the decisive victory over the Lancastrians in 1471, regaining control of the crown. Four days were spent in the seclusion of the small abbey, under the hospitality of Abbot John Wakeman. Along with its other properties, the Abbey was assessed by Cromwell's investigators in 1535 as being worth £1,598 10s 3d, out of which 144 servants were sustained, as was a Master of the Spices, on a salary of £47 13d 11s. When it was dissolved in 1540, there were 36 or 37 resident friars listed.[16]

On the last day of July, Anne and Henry rode ten miles to the south and made a ceremonial entrance into the city of Gloucester. They were welcomed by the Mayor, aldermen and other city dignitaries, led by the current incumbent, John Falconer, a wealthy capper in the top twelve tax payers of the city, who employed 'a great number of people in the spinning and knitting of caps' and who left £40 on his death in 1545 for the use of the poor workers in the parish.[17] Here was another self-made man, who had risen through the commercial ranks, paralleling the Boleyn origins, just as Geoffrey had started out as a hatter and reached the heights of mayoralty. The royal party stayed for three days at Gloucester Abbey, amid the peaceful fan-vaulted cloisters, close to the shrine of Edward II, with its delicately carved canopy and alabaster image of the king, probably in the lodgings of Abbot William Parker, who had been in the post since 1514. Dedicated to St Peter, the Abbey also contained a thirteenth century Lady Chapel, popular with pilgrims and long associated as an intercessor for female health and fertility. Whether Anne visited the chapel is not recorded. If she did, would it have been reverently, in prayer, or in the spirit of observation and cynicism? In 1534, the Act of Supremacy had been signed by the Abbot and thirty-five monks and its yearly income was assessed at slightly under that of Tewkesbury, at £1,400 4s 3d. The Abbey would be dissolved on 2 January 1540, and the remaining site incorporated into what is now the Cathedral. Whilst enjoying the hospitality of the Abbot, Henry hunted in nearby Coberley and Miserden, and also paid a visit to Painswick, the manor house of Sir William Kingston, Keeper of the Tower. It was during their stay in the area that Cromwell's visitors were scrutinising the vices and assets of Bath Abbey.

On 6 August, Cromwell's outspoken and irreverent agent, Richard Layton, who had just been involved in the examinations of Fisher and More, reported his findings in his unmistakeable style:

We have visited Bath. Found the prior a very virtuous man, but his monks more corrupt than any others in vices with both sexes; some of them having 10 women, some 8; the house well repaired, but £400 in debt. At Farley, cell to Lewes, the prior had only 8 whores, the rest of the monks fewer. The place is a very stews, and unnatural crimes are both there and at Lewes; especially the subprior, as appears by the confession of a fair

young monk, a priest late sent from Lewes. I have matter sufficient to bring
the prior of Lewes into great danger, si vera sint quœ narrantur [roughly,
'which would be true if the event is']. I send you vincula S. Petri, which
women put about them at the time of their delivery. It is counted a great
relic, because St. Peter is supposed to be the patron of the church. It is a
very mockery and a great abuse that the prior should carry it on Lammas
day in a basin of silver in procession, and every monk kiss it after the
Gospel with great solemnity, though they have no writing to show how
they came by it. I send you also a great comb called Mary Magdalene's
comb, and St. Dorothy's, and St. Margaret's combs. They cannot tell how
they came by them... I send you a book of our Lady's miracles, well able
to match the Canterbury tales, which I found in the library.[18]

Leaving Gloucester Abbey on 6 August, Henry and Anne spent one night at
one of the Abbey's cells at Leonard Stanley, valued at £106 17s that year. In
a village barely sustaining a few households, it would be dissolved in 1538.
From there, they passed on to Berkeley Castle, more of a manor house
than a castle, built from the local Cotwolds pink and yellow stone, where
the rooms in which they stayed are reputedly still part of the current 'great
suite'. They remained at Berkeley for six days before riding south west
along the Severn Estuary to Thornbury Castle, the residence of Sir William
Paulet. Then aged around fifty, Paulet was Master of the King's Wards and
Comptroller of the Household. Later in life he would be given the Earldom
of Wiltshire, after it fell vacant upon the death of Thomas Boleyn. The
castle had been built in 1511 by Edward Stafford, Duke of Buckingham,
almost as a folly, crenelated but never intended as a defensible building.
Incomplete on the Duke's execution in 1521, it had passed into the hands
of the crown, but was rarely used by Henry. From there, the royal party
had planned to travel the short distance to the city of Bristol but, before
their departure, news arrived that illness had broken out there, so instead,
Henry received a delegation of Bristolians on 20 August bringing gifts and
greetings. Less welcome words came from the nearby town of Bridgwater,
where an Irish hooper named David Leonard, had said 'God save King
Henry and Queen Catherine his wedded wife, and Anne at his pleasure, for
whom all England shall rue'. The 'accursed' slanderer had been sent to gaol
'to wait the King's pleasure'.[19]

It was at this time, at their closest to Bristol, that Henry's fool, or jester,
fell foul of the king. The degree of licence allowed to fools apparently did
not extend to speaking openly on the topic of Catherine and Anne, as
Chapuys related. It is interesting that the fool, who may or may not have
been William Somers, sought refuge with the Grand Esquire, Nicholas
Carew, clearly no friend to Anne by this point:

He the other day nearly murdered his own fool, a simple and innocent man, because he happened to speak well in his presence of the Queen and Princess, and called the concubine 'ribaude'(ribald) and her daughter 'bastard'. He has now been banished from Court, and has gone to the Grand Esquire, who has sheltered and hidden him.[20]

On 23 July, Henry and Anne arrived at Acton Court in Gloucestershire, six miles from Thornbury. It was owned by the Poyntz family, and their host for the next two days was Nicholas and his wife Joan, perhaps the parents of the child Nicholas, in whom Anne was taking an interest. The house was newly finished after a nine-month building programme in anticipation of the royal visit, with a new East wing added specially for the use of Henry and Anne. The luxurious rooms had large windows, in-built garderobes and newly-painted friezes and were connected to the main, moated house by a covered walkway. Recent archaeological works have uncovered fragments of contemporary Italian majolica ware and Venetian glass, representing the finest table ware, which may have been bought especially for the occasion. Henry was certainly appreciative of the efforts made by his host, knighting Nicholas Poyntz during the visit.

On 25 August, Henry and Anne thanked the Poyntz family and rode six miles to the east, to Little Sodbury Manor, home to Nicholas' uncle and aunt, Sir John and Lady Anne Walshe. The Walshes had employed William Tyndale in the early 1520s, before he had fled abroad and, in 1535, on the very day that Henry arrived at Little Sodbury, Nicholas's uncle, Thomas, wrote to his brother John from Antwerp. It is not clear why he was then resident in Antwerp, although it was likely on business, as he attended the Easter trade market, but as a religious reformer, he had been sheltering Tyndale for nine months and was convinced there was no man better. Now though, Tyndale had been betrayed during Poyntz's absence, arrested, sent to Vilvoorde Castle and was likely to be sentenced to death:

I write to you for a great matter concerning the King. Though I am here inhabyting, yet my natural love to the country I was born in, and the oath and obedience which every true subject is bound by the law of God to have to his Prince, compel me to write what I perceive may be prejudicial to the King... It was said here that the King had granted letters in favor of one Wm. Tyndall, who is in prison, and like to suffer death unless the King help him. It is thought now that the letters have been stopped. He lodged with me three quarters of a year, and was taken out of my house by a sergeant-of-arms...

As Tyndale has lived in my house three quarters of a year, I know that the King has no truer-hearted subject living, for he knows he is bound by the law of God to obey his Prince. He would not do contrary to be lord of the world, however the King is informed...

The death of this man would be a great hindrance to the Gospel, and one of the highest pleasures to the enemies of it. If the King would send for this man, so that he might dispute with them at large the articles which they lay to him, it might be so opened to the Court and the Council that they would be at another point with the bishop of Rome in a short space. I think he will shortly be condemned, for there are two Englishmen at Loven who have applied it sore, and have taken great pains to translate into Latin what may make against him, so that the clergy may understand and condemn him...

The knowledge that I have of this man causes me to write as my conscience binds me. The King would have of him as high a treasure as of any man living, that has been of no greater reputation. I therefore desire you to have this matter solicited to his Grace, for in my conscience there be not many perfecter men this day living.[21]

The letter was addressed to John Poyntz at his home in North Ockendon, Essex, and did not reach its destination until 20 September, when John forwarded it to Cromwell.[22] Little could be done for Tyndale, despite the efforts of Henry and Cromwell. The reformer was executed at the beginning of October 1536.

On 27 August, the court arrived at Bromham House in Wiltshire, home of Anne's Vice-Chamberlain, Edward Baynton, and his wife Elizabeth. It was one of their longest rides, covering twenty-two miles. The house was extensive, large enough to take in 700 guests around three sides of a huge quadrangle. Since inheriting the property from his father in 1516, Baynton had increased it significantly, to the tune of £15,000, using stone taken from the nearby ruined Devizes Castle and another manor at Corsham. In 1536, he would acquire Stanley Abbey after its dissolution, demolish it and use the stone to create the Spye Arch gatehouse at Bromham, although other stories relate that this was funded by Catherine of Aragon. Henry and Anne stayed at Bromham for a week and it was during this time that Pope Paul III passed the sentence of excommunication against the king, although it would not reach Henry yet.[23] Cromwell did though, catching up with the court, sending out dispatches from the house on 31 August.

The next stop on the royal itinerary was Wolf Hall in Wiltshire, where the party arrived on 3 September 1535. The original house was demolished in 1569, but it was likely to have been red brick and timber-framed, set around a courtyard with a tower and chapel. Some of its stained glass may have been reset in the parish church of nearby St Mary's at Great Bedwyn. Wolf Hall was the backdrop to a significant turning point in Henry and Anne's marriage, as they were welcomed by the Seymour family, whose daughter Jane would become Henry's wife ten months later. Without the advantage off hindsight, the royal visitors of 1535 simply enjoyed the hospitality of their hosts for a week, possibly staying additional days even though their intended schedule would have seen them departing after four. The Seymours had weathered the unpleasant scandal arising from an affair between Sir John Seymour and his daughter-in-law, Catherine Filliol. Catherine had married John's eldest son Edward in around 1527 and bore him two sons, but when the relationship was discovered, and doubt was cast upon their paternity, the marriage appears to have been over. Catherine may have retired to a convent, as one source hints, but she had died by early 1535, when Edward married again. By the time of the royal arrival, Sir John had apparently lost his wits and would die the following year, while Edward had married the formidable Anne Stanhope. Sir John's wife, Margery Wentworth, may have been known to Anne, as she was her mother's cousin and featured, in her youth, in the same Skelton poem as Elizabeth, the *Garland of Laurel*, in which she was lauded for her beauty. After marrying Sir John in 1494, Margaret had borne ten children, six of whom survived infancy.

Henry and Anne were greeted by members of the Seymour family but, tantalisingly, it is not clear exactly which ones. Sir Edward and his new wife are likely to have been present, and perhaps Edward's unmarried brother Thomas, although their other brother Henry, the then Keeper of Taunton Castle, may not have been. Jane Seymour, then aged around twenty-seven and unmarried, is likely to have been at the parental home along with her sister Elizabeth, who had been widowed the year before and had two small children. The third sister, Dorothy, may also have been present, but it is unclear exactly when her marriage took place. Thus, Jane was one among a host of hosts, a spinster of advanced age according to the times, and quite the opposite of the queen in her demure, quiet ways.

Sir Thomas Audeley wrote to Cromwell from Colchester on 9 September, thanking him for his 'good news' about the 'mirth and good health of the King and Queen'.[24] The next day, the royal entourage moved on again. The significance of their visit to Wolf Hall could not have been imagined. A French visitor, writing to Marguerite of Angoulême, now Queen of Navarre, described seeing the king and queen that September. Anne reputedly sent her recommendations and expressed pleasure to hear of Marguerite's recovered health. Her greatest wish, she added 'next to having a son, is to see you again'.[25] The result of all their summertime merriment was that Anne had, in fact, conceived again, and this time she was carrying a boy.

THIRTY-THREE

Progress and Reform, September–December 1535

Through the early autumn, Henry and Anne continued their progress, heading south and west between fields ripening with crops. They spent a night or two with Thomas and Mary Lisle at their home of Thruxton in Hampshire, before riding down to Hurstborne Priors, owned by the Priory of St Swithin and finally arriving in Winchester on 12 or 13 September. The city on the western end of the South Downs had an association with the Tudors that predated Henry. It was the location his father had chosen for the birth of his first son, Arthur, Catherine of Aragon's first husband, destined to be king until his untimely death at the age of fifteen in 1502. It was dominated by the longest Gothic cathedral in Europe, which then still had the status of a priory, alongside the deanery where Arthur had arrived and the Pilgrim's Hall, where pilgrims rested after completing, or before commencing, their long journeys. Winchester Castle contained a medieval version of the legendary King Arthur's round table, which Henry himself had ordered to be painted afresh in 1522, but it appears that he and Anne stayed at the Bishop's Palace of Wolvesey Castle nearby, until 18 September.

They had escaped the sweat that had gripped Bristol and London that summer, but the illness was still breaking out in pockets across the countryside. On 13 September, Thomas Audeley wrote to Cromwell that he 'dared not go back to his house at Brittons, as a woman had died there'. He would have 'borrowed the Queen's house at Havering, but knew not how his suit would be taken'.[1] Cromwell passed this request on to Anne, who did lend him her property of Havering-atte-Bowe in Essex, whilst the sweat made his home unsafe. On 27 September he wrote to thank Cromwell for 'moving the Queen for her house' and asked him to thank Anne on his behalf.[2] On the last day of their visit to Winchester, Henry and Anne attended a service of consecration in the

Cathedral, during which the reformers Hugh Latimer, Edward Foxe and John Hilsey were invested as bishops. Anne's principal chaplain, Latimer, became Bishop of Worcester, Foxe as King's almoner and author of a treatise in defence of the royal supremacy, became Bishop of Hereford, and Hilsey, a protegé of Cromwell's and commissioner investigating the monasteries, took John Fisher's position of Bishop of Rochester. The proceedings were overseen by Thomas Cranmer and put a new wave of forward-thinking clerics in key positions, something of which Anne must have approved.

After the ceremony, Henry and Anne rode ten miles south, around the edge of the Downs, to the Palace at Bishop's Waltham. The residence of the incumbent of Winchester, currently Stephen Gardiner, the palace was one of the most luxurious of its kind, representing a position that brought considerable wealth. After much development in the late fifteenth and early sixteenth century, the palace was at its height, and reconstructions suggest a moated rectangular complex with apartments, great hall, church, cloisters, service range and inner courtyard. Gardiner was absent on an embassy to France. It was during his stay in the palace that Henry wrote further instructions for him to negotiate a friendship and begin to organise the mutual invasion of Italy.[3] On Monday 20 September, Anne's Receiver-General, George Taylor, wrote to Lady Lisle thanking her for sending gifts including a bow to Anne, which she 'accepted... very well and sends thanks'. Taylor commented that 'she favours Lady Lisle very well'. He finished by noting Henry and Anne's closeness, 'my lady will go with the King all this progress' but that there was 'no news here but after the old fashion'.[4] Towards the end of September, the Michaelmas accounts were settled, with George Taylor recording Anne's annual income of £6,381 8s 9d from her lands and the payments required to her staff in fees and rewards, and for offerings, expenses, stables and wardrobes, being just over £6,348.[5] After eight days in the palace, Henry and Anne returned to Winchester, where there was more important business to be done.

As Chapuys reported, 'the King having arrived at Winchester... (he) caused an inventory to be made of the treasures of the church, from which he took certain fine rich unicorns' horns, and a large silver cross adorned with rich jewels. He has also taken from the Bishop certain mills, to give them to the community in order to gain favour. Cromwell, wherever the King goes, goes round about visiting the abbeys, making inventories of their goods and revenues.'[6] Perhaps it was an attempt to placate the king's chief minister that led Henry Brooke, Prior of St Swithin's Monastery in the city, to grant Cromwell and his son Gregory 'an annuity of £10 out of the manors of Hurstbourne and Crundall'.[7] Such small acts could not prevent the wholescale acquisition of monastic wealth that Cromwell and his agents were undertaking. During their second stay at Wolvesey, Cromwell received a report from Richard Layton, who was then investigating establishments in Sussex:

> On Friday night I came to an abbey called Durforde, in Sussex. It might better be called Dirtford, the poorest abbey I have seen, as this bearer, the abbot, can tell you, far in debt and in great decay. This young man, for his time, has done well, and I have licensed him to repair to you for the liberty of himself and his brethren, as I could not meddle. A priory of nuns and another of canons close together, near Chichester, being of their poverty unable to lodge us.[8]

Layton's colleague, Thomas Legh, was visiting Merton Priory in Surrey, where he dismissed two canons outright and asked for Cromwell's permission to eject eight more. He had found them practising 'voluntary pollutions' with women and boys, and that they were in possession of various relics, such as the arm bone of St Blasius and an image of St Faith, reputed to cure cases of illness.[9] When Merton Priory was dissolved in 1538, the masonry was used in the construction of Henry's new palace of Nonsuch.

Henry and Anne arrived in Southampton on 1 October, either making their way to the castle on the sea defences or to the town house of royal favourite Sir Richard Lyster and his wife Isabel. Appointed Chief Baron of the Exchequer in 1529, and having ridden in Anne's coronation procession, Lyster owned considerable land and properties in the area, including the house in Bugle Street, which was staffed by eight servants. The next day, Sir Richard Graynfeld reflected on the visit so far that the king and queen were merry and went hawking daily and that they had liked Winchester 'and that quarter and praise it much'.[10] A few days later they travelled down the coast to nearby Portsmouth, perhaps ignoring the road in favour of one of Henry's ships, sailing in the *Harry Grace Dieu*, as one account suggests.[11] They spent the night of 4 October in the royal apartments at Portchester Castle, overlooking the harbour at Portsmouth.[12]

Anne cannot have been oblivious to the findings of Cromwell and his investigators as more news about the monasteries trickled in. Since the examinations had begun at the start of August, a picture of immoraility and decadence was emerging: exactly the scenario that the king was looking to find. Sometimes, the inpectors laid it on a bit thick. It is impossible now to know whether the Prior of Shelbrede was keeping seven women and if his monks really had four or five each, as Richard

Layton wrote to Cromwell on the day the king arrived in Portsmouth.[13] Yet there was an expectation of condemnation, as the royal objective had been absorbed by the inspectors, placing the monasteries in opposition to the crown. Through the second half of 1535, this was increasingly being understood across the country. As a John Whalley warned Cromwell: 'the monks of Canterbury are afraid, and they of Christchurch will "make their hands", as it is said. It is the richest house in jewels, plate, and money in England: knows a person who can show Cromwell's visitors, when they come, where secret treasure is kept.'[14] The imminent reform of the establishment was expected, with petitioners approaching Cromwell in anticipation of the spoils. A William Kemp had been informed that the offices would be 'given to secular men' and requested one for his brother, a poor man living in Canterbury.[15]

While the monks quaked at the imminent arrival of Richard Layton, Henry and Anne continued, still 'merrily'. John Vesey, Bishop of Exeter, reported on 6 October that he had been 'with the King on Friday last,' and that 'he, the Queen and all other nobles of the court were in good health and merry', and thanked Sir Thomas Arundel for sending venison, wine and other gifts.[16] His sentiment was echoed by Sir Anthony Windsor three days later, who wrote that 'the king and queen were very merry in Hampshire'.[17] Their light spirits were not dampened by reports that 'a great troop of citizens' wives and others' had cheered Princess Mary on her departure from Greenwich, 'weeping and crying that she was Princess, notwithstanding all that had been done'.[18] Nor are the accounts compatible with the comment of the Bishop of Tarbes that October, that Henry's love for Anne 'diminishes every day because he has new amours'.[19]

From Portsmouth, the long train of courtiers and staff followed the king and Anne as they doubled back and headed west again, to Salisbury. Awaiting them at Church House on 9 October was John Tuchet, Baron Audley, who had served Henry in France back in 1513. It was from there that Sir William Paulet wrote to Cromwell confirming the king had made the decision that Princess Elizabeth was to be weaned 'with all diligence' and that Langley Palace was to be prepared for her.[20] On 10 October, Henry and Anne were at Clarendon Park, on the other side of Salisbury, a former palace that was now used as a hunting lodge, where they stayed for five days. From there, they went east to the Vyne, now that Lord Sandys had recovered from the sweat, enjoying the familiar house and park they had visited in 1531. After they left, Sandys wrote to Cromwell, who had not been with them, 'the King and Queen came to my poor house on Friday the 15th of this month, and continued there till Tuesday. I expected to have seen you, which would have been a great comfort to me and my poor wife'.[21] Sandys would have been pleased to hear Sir Francis Bryan report that 'the king's grace is merry'.[22]

While Anne was at the Vyne, Richard Layton was seventy miles to the south east inspecting Lewes Priory and Battle Abbey:

> At Lewes I found corruption of both kinds, and, what is worse, treason, for the subprior has confessed to me treason in his preaching. I have caused him to subscribe his name to it, and submit himself to the King's mercy. I made him confess that the prior knew of it, and I have declared the prior to be perjured, per hæc verba [by these words]. At Battle I found the abbot and his convent, except two or three, guilty of unnatural crimes and traitors. I have also commanded him to be at the Court. He is... the arrantest churl that ever I see. The black sort of devilish monks, I am sorry to know, are past amendment.[23]

The next stage of the royal progress was hosted by Sir William Paulet, Comptroller of the household since 1532, at his new home of Basing House, in Hampshire. Only begun in 1531, Basing stood on top of the old Norman castle that had occupied the site, but developed into a Tudor palace worthy of a king. Henry and Anne passed two days there, before travelling ten miles east to Bramshill House, the home of Henry Daubeney. Built in the 1350s, the house was built around a courtyard measuring 100 by 80 feet and surrounded by a 2,500-acre park. Daubeney was only two years younger than the king, had fought for him at the Battle of the Spurs in 1513, was present at the Field of Cloth of Gold, and again at Calais in 1532. He had married, as his second wife, Anne's cousin, Katherine Howard, daughter of the Duke of Norfolk, but the marriage was unhappy and by 1535, he was seeking a divorce. From Bramshill, Henry and Anne moved on to Easthampstead, arriving on 22 October. On the same day, Richard Layton was at Folkestone and then Langdon Abbey, near West Langdon, in Kent, where he composed one of his most controversial reports:

> On Friday, 22 October, I rode back to take an inventory of Fowlstone and thence went to Langden, where I sent Bartlett, your servant, with my servants to circumspect the abbey and keep all starting-holes. I went alone to the abbot's lodging joining upon the fields and wood even like a cony clapper full of starting-holes, and was a good space knocking at the door. I found a short pole axe and dashed the door in pieces, and went about the house, with the pole axe, for the abbot is a 'dangerous desperate knave, and hardy'. Finally the abbot's whore, alias his gentlewoman, 'bestirred her stumps towards her starting-holes', where Bartlett took

'the tender damoisel.' After examination, sent her to Dover to the mayor to set in some cage or prison for eight days.[24]

His reputation preceding him, Layton arrived at Christchurch, Canterbury, the following day, and was lucky to escape with his life:

This Saturday I came to Christchurch, Canterbury, where one of my servants called me up suddenly, else I had been burnt in my bed. The great dining chamber, called the King's lodging, where the bishop of Winchester lay before I came, took fire by some firebrand or snuff of a candle setting the rushes on fire. My servants were nearly choked in their beds. After I had found a back door I called up the house, and sent to the town for help; but before water came the great lodging was past recovery. Only three chambers were burnt, called the new or the King's lodging. The gable ends of the house, made of strong brick, kept the fire from the houses adjoining. As soon as I had set men to quench the fire, I went into the church, and set four monks with bandogs to keep the shrine, and put the sexton in the vestry to keep the jewels, appointing monks in every quarter of the church with candles. I sent also for the abbot of St. Augustine's to be in readiness to take down the shrine, and send the jewels into St Augustine's. If I had not taken this order, harm would have been done. Such bedding as was cast into the cloister was embezzled by poor folks, who came rather to spoil than to help.

The prior of Dover and his monks are as bad as others. Sodomites there is none, for they have no lack of women. The abbot of Langden is worse than all the rest, the drunkenest knave living. His canons are as bad as he, without a spark of virtue. The abbot made his chaplain take a woman and brought her up to his own chamber, and made his chaplain's bed in the inner chamber, and made him go to bed with her. The house is in utter decay, and will shortly tumble down. You must depose him at once, and take an inventory of the goods. I have pronounced him perjured, reserving the punishment to you. Langden is three miles from Dover.[25]

It is not specified anywhere that Anne read these reports. Returning to Windsor at the end of October, she may have been briefed by Cromwell, or even heard tales from Layton himself, but given her relationship with Henry and her strong reformist views, it it difficult not to believe that the couple discussed the accounts of clerical misdemeanours. Gossip and rumours spread further afield as the commissioners continued to report, even though none received quite as warm a reception as Layton had that night in the prior's lodgings at Canterbury.

In Europe, the confiscation of clerical wealth, relics and other objects of veneration was considered a scandal.[26] As Dr Ortiz wrote to the Empress, England was getting 'more and more disorderly, revealed by a 'miracle' recorded at the Charterhouse, whereby the dead rose and showed 'the glorious crown of martyrdom obtained by the Cardinal of Rochester'.[27] Of course, Ortiz was clear as to what, or who, was the source all of this wanton destruction: 'Cromwell, who procures everything that Anne wishes, has forbidden these revelations to be published.'[28]

Although she may not have considered herself as much the driving force behind these changes as Dr Ortiz speculated, Anne was witnessing a moment of seismic cultural change in England. She was all in favour of reform, of a closer, more personal relationship with God, as is evidenced by her reading material and her patterns of patronage. In 1535, she acquired a copy of Miles Coverdale's translation of the English Bible, which had been dedicated to 'the most victorious Prynce and our most gracious sovereign Lorde, Kynge Henry the eight (and) your dearest just wife and most virtuous Pryncesse, Quene Anne'. The reformer William Marshall dedicated to her his work on the relief of the poor. It may have been Anne who enabled him to gain his printer's licence for further works of 1535 that would have been to her tastes, such as *The Defence of Peace*, an anti-papal tract, and the controversial *Pictures and Images*, which Audeley felt went too far, but Cromwell approved. However, it is not clear just how comfortable Anne was with some of the extremes of censure displayed by figures like Layton. Religious change in England was inevitable, as it gradually swept across Europe under the influence of thinkers like Luther, Calvin and Zwingli, but the pace of change in the English church was swifter than elsewhere and perhaps more dramatic as a consequence. It was a top-down phenomenon, whereas in other countries, reform tended to arrive slowly, percolating from below to alter the beliefs of individual rulers one by one, often meeting with considerable resistance, even persecution. The first phase of the English reformation was concertinaed into the early 1530s as a result of Henry's marital difficulties, of which Anne was the symbol, even the catalyst, but not the cause.

There had been 850 religious houses in England and Wales when Henry had come to the throne in 1509, but by 1535, 563 were left, with approximately 7,000 monks and 2,000 nuns, employing around 35,000 lay brethren and servants engaged in manual work. Some of the smaller establishments had already been targeted by Wolsey, and the majority of the closures were not effected until after March 1536, but Anne was intelligent enough to see the ideological pitfalls of Henry's new acquisitions. Citing the theft of the church of England from previous monarchs, he had vowed in 1533 to reclaim the wealth that clergymen had stolen from the crown, stripping the altars and centuries-old shrines and directing cartloads of silver, plate and jewels to the royal coffers.

Anne objected. And just as Catherine of Aragon had refused to be silenced when she feared for Henry's mortal soul, Anne spoke up too. The account of William Latimer was written early during the reign of Elizabeth, but he had first-hand experience of Anne, having served as her chaplain as a young man and was probably a relative of Hugh. In *A Briefe Treatise or Chronickill of the most Vertuous Lady Anne Bulleyne late quene of England*, Latimer states that Anne asked him to preach before Henry in an attempt to persuade him not to channel confiscated monastic money into the treasury but to use it for education and charity. Wary of accusing the king directly, she found a subtler route by focusing on the influence of his chief minister. Cromwell was accused before the Council of greed, compared with Old Testament figures and, for the first time, this placed him in ideological opposition to the queen. Both thought they were serving Henry: Anne by steering him back on the right path to salvation and Cromwell by enacting his wishes. The end seemed to be the same, but the two were not compatible. If Cromwell saw this as a personal threat, potentially undermining his position of trust with the king, he did not reveal his hand yet.

It is not possible to say that Anne foresaw the impact of the monastic closures; that would be a judgement overly influenced by hindsight, and Anne was not a visionary. She was hardly the 'cause and principal nurse' of all heresy in England, as Chapuys would have it. She died before the majority of the closures were implemented and the full effects of the Reformation felt, but her objections in 1535 suggested she was independent of thought and had her own, different views, about the route this should take. For all Henry's protestations of conscience, his Reformation was a personal one, bound up in notions of kingship and nationhood, bringing him back powers that he felt had been stripped from his ancestors. Anne's Reformation was more outward looking, perhaps closer to a clear ideology with the purpose of humanist and social reform.

The Reformation in England, in its first phase under Henry, and then under his son, Edward VI, brought complete change to the fabric of the country, in methods of worship, patterns of patronage, landownership, the culture of towns and villages, customs and practices. Communities suffered from the loss of services offered by open houses, such as the distribution of alms and medical care, the hospitals sheltering the sick and the travellers, the niches that were found for the infirm and others who didn't fit the social boxes. An entire infrastructure of social welfare was swept away. Monks, friars and nuns were offered a pension if they complied with the closures in the late 1530s, but thousands of monastic servants found themselves out of work. The monasteries were also repositories of medical knowledge, for the use of herbs and remedies, often shared in the wider monastic community by correspondence. They housed libraries and centres of learning, acting as repositories of manuscripts containing works of art and literature, the loss of which closed avenues of education and careers. The dissolution created a cultural shift in focus for the community, with the former hierarchies of bishops, abbots and monks being replaced by secular rulers, often an absentee aristocrat or wealthy merchant who purchased large swathes of monastic land. Setting the question of religious reform aside, the English Reformation under Henry VIII may have begun as a search for intellectual honesty and human freedom but it ended by looking like an elitist move that rewarded the rich and created want and beggary. It is impossible to know what influence Anne would have had over this process, had she not been sent to her death in 1536. Perhaps the same events would have unfolded regardless, but her early impulse towards the redistribution of wealth among the poor, and to educate, certainly addressed some of the questions that Henry and Cromwell failed to answer.

That November, hostile sources paint pen portraits of the two most influential figures at court besides the king, who were about to collide. In answer to an inquiry from a secretary, Chapuys related what was known about Cromwell's background and power:

Cromwell is the son of a poor farrier, who lived in a little village a league and a half from here, and is buried in the parish graveyard. His uncle, father of the cousin whom he has already made rich, was cook (*cousinier*) of the late archbishop of Canterbury. Cromwell was ill-behaved when young, and after an imprisonment was forced to leave the country. He went to Flanders, Rome, and elsewhere in Italy. When he returned he married the daughter of a shearman, and served in his house; he then became a solicitor. The cardinal of York, seeing his vigilance and diligence, his ability and promptitude, both in evil and good, took him into his service, and employed him principally in demolishing five or six good monasteries. At the cardinal's fall no one behaved better to him than Cromwell. After the cardinal's death Wallop attacked him with insults and threats, and for protection he procured an audience of the King, and promised to make him the richest king that ever was in England. The King immediately retained him on his Council but told no one for four months. Now he stands above every one but the Lady, and every one considers he has more credit with his master than Wolsey had.[29]

The next day, Dr Ortiz described Anne's reactions to her step-daughter Mary, characterising the queen as malicious and absolute:

> The Princess with only three women is in the same house as the daughter of the Wench (Anne), under the charge of the Wench's aunt. Formerly the Ambassador was allowed to send to her two days a week, but now this leave has been taken away. When she asked to be allowed to live with her mother she was refused, because it would make her more obstinate in disobeying the statutes, which was not safe in consequence of the penalty imposed by them. The King told his mistress that while he lived, the Princess should not marry. She has told the King several times that it is the Princess who causes war, and that it will be necessary to treat her as the cardinal of Rochester has been treated. She has often said of the Princess 'She is my death and I am hers; so I will take care that she shall not laugh at me after my death.'[30]

Yet if Anne was speculating about who would bring about her death in late 1535, she was looking in the wrong place. As the year drew to a close, she and Henry seemed to have exhausted their supply of mirth.

THIRTY-FOUR

The Last Spring, January–April 1536

As Henry and Anne were spending the Christmas of 1535 at Eltham Palace, news arrived at court that Catherine of Aragon was seriously ill. Shut away at Kimbolton Castle in Cambridgeshire, her health deteriorating rapidly, the former queen lingered over the festive period and rallied briefly before breathing her last on 7 January. She was fifty, and probably suffering from some form of cancer. Chapuys, who had visited her during her final days, and been sent away with reassurances about her recovery, described the reaction at court:

> You could not conceive the joy that the King and those who favor this concubinage have shown at the death of the good Queen, especially the earl of Wiltshire and his son, who said it was a pity the Princess did not keep company with her. The King, on the Saturday he heard the news, exclaimed 'God be praised that we are free from all suspicion of war'; and that the time had come that he would manage the French better than he had done hitherto, because they would do now whatever he wanted from a fear lest he should ally himself again with your Majesty, seeing that the cause which disturbed your friendship was gone.
>
> On the following day, Sunday, the King was clad all over in yellow, from top to toe, except the white feather he had in his bonnet, and the Little Bastard was conducted to mass with trumpets and other great triumphs. After dinner the King entered the room in which the ladies danced, and there did several things like one transported with joy. At last he sent for his Little Bastard, and carrying her in his arms he showed her first to one and then to another. He has done the like on other days since, and has run some courses at Greenwich.[1]

As callous as Henry's actions and the words of the Boleyns appear here, the ambassador was always going to present them in such a light, in the literal wake of Catherine's death. Yellow was the traditional colour of mourning in Spain, so their choice may not have been as disrespectful as it appears. There may well have been relief, even celebrations, as an outlet for release, just as Sir Thomas had commissioned a play after Wolsey's fall, a vision of the cardinal's entry into hell. The realpolitik of the Tudor court encouraged such fulcrums: individuals, families and factions rose as their enemies fell. Personal and dynastic survival was concomitant upon the misfortunes of others and Henry's methods of distancing himself from fallen favourites allowed for a process of dehumanisation to take place. Catherine, not glimpsed at court since the summer of 1531, had been stripped of her individuality, and thus any sympathy for her position, except among her inner circle. Time, distance and her stubbornness had reduced her to a symbol, an obstacle to Henry's will that had now been removed. Cruel as it sounds, the Tudor court was full of similar examples. It is anchronistic to seek post-Romantic concepts of the self at the Tudor court, which upheld a more general sense of the aristocratic or royal figure as a representative of a particular lineage and the embodiment of abstract qualities. Thus, Catherine had been defined by her status as queen, widow, Catholic, wife, mother, Spaniard, and now martyr: what she had represented still mattered, but allegiance among her supporters made a smooth transition to her daughter.

Anne was aware of the regrouping around Mary, but chose to extend the hand of friendship on 21 January. Genuine sympathy for Mary's loss might have provoked the message she sent through her aunt, Anne Shelton, that Anne would be the 'best friend to her in the world and be like another mother' to her. If Mary set aside her obstinacy, Anne promised that she might have anything she asked, and if she came to court, she would be exempt from holding the tail of Anne's gown. Anne Shelton was said to have delivered this message 'with hot tears' and implored her charge to 'consider these matters'.[2] Equally, this may have been a politically shrewd act on Anne's part, a recognition that her opponents would be more concentrated by their grief, and were now backing a far more dangerous figure, a young woman of almost twenty, an adult with an hereditary claim to the throne. With her own daughter, Elizabeth, not yet three, Anne must have hoped to reconcile potential conflict between the two, with the intention of securing Elizabeth's succession. Perhaps Anne considered that Mary's youth, and her recent loss, might dispose her to compromise, as part of a longer-term strategy to obtain her step-daughter's obedience.

Enclosed in the letter Chapuys sent to Emperor Charles was what purported to be a copy of that which Anne had sent to her aunt. It is subject to a range of potential problems, but still worth including as expressive of Anne's sentiments, or the sentiments which Mary received. The letter phrases Anne's gesture as an act of charity in line with the 'Word of God', and interprets Mary's former resistance as loyalty to her mother, an obedience she no longer owed.

> Mrs. Shelton, my pleasure is that you do not further move the lady Mary to be towards the King's Grace otherwise than it pleases herself. What I have done has been more for charity than for anything the King or I care what road she takes, or whether she will change her purpose, for if I have a son, as I hope shortly, I know what will happen to her; and therefore, considering the Word of God, to do good to one's enemy, I wished to warn her before hand, because I have daily experience that the King's wisdom is such as not to esteem her repentance of her rudeness and unnatural obstinacy when she has no choice. By the law of God and of the King, she ought clearly to acknowledge her error and evil conscience if her blind affection had not so blinded her eyes that she will see nothing but what pleases herself. Mrs. Shelton, I beg you not to think to do me any pleasure by turning her from any of her wilful courses, because she could not do me [good] or evil; and do your duty about her according to the King's command, as I am assured you do.[3]

Whether or not this is a true composition, and the details do sound convincing, it is written from a position of strength. Anne was confident that she was soon to bear a son and that she was beyond the reach of any harm that Mary or her party might intend her. The letter distances Anne from self-interest in the matter, presenting the purest motives, urging Mrs Shelton to action out of her duty to the king. The tone is not consistent with Chapuys' contemporaneous report that Anne frequently wept in the period immediately following Catherine's death, in the realisation that a significant obstacle had been removed should Henry choose to set her aside. But then, Anne discovered Jane Seymour sitting on Henry's knee and, although Henry told her 'peace be, sweetheart and all will be well with thee', Anne became hysterical. Worse still, on 24 January, Henry was thrown from his horse whilst taking part in a tournament at Greenwich. Dressed in full armour, he was pinned under his horse and lay unconscious for two hours, whilst rumours flew around the court that his injuries were fatal. The news was broken to Anne by her uncle Norfolk, in a way that she later described as having been rather abrupt. Although Henry recovered, this incident gave Anne a shock and raised the question of the succession. Had Henry died that January, statesmen and courtiers would have had to decide whether to back the adult Mary, the 'legitimate' two-year-old Elizabeth, or wait until the birth of Anne's child in the hope that it would prove male. It would have created a succession crisis, and the council understood just how volatile that situation would have been.

On 28 January, Chapuys reported that 'some days ago' he had been informed from various quarters that 'notwithstanding the joy shown by the concubine at the news of the good Queen's death, for which she had given a handsome present to the messenger, she frequently wept, fearing that they might do with her as with the Good Queen'.[4] His source, which was Henry Courtenay, Marquis of Exeter and his wife Gertrude Blount, had been informed by 'one of the principal persons at court' that Henry had 'said to someone in great confidence, and as it were in confession, that he had made this marriage, seduced by witchcraft and for this reason he considered it null'. According to Exeter, Henry believed that the lack of male issue was evidence that the marriage was invalid, so 'he might take another wife, which he gave to understand that he had some wish to do'.[5] Witchcraft itself was not an indictable offence until 1542, or a capital offence until 1563, but the thought that Henry was seeking to replace her would have unsettled Anne. Yet this letter was composed on the morning of 29 January 1536, when Anne was still pregnant. After she and Henry had been happy during the latter half of 1535, and anticipating the arrival of a son, it is unlikely that Anne was feeling insecure during most of January 1536. What happened later that day, though, would shake the foundations of her new-found confidence.

On 29 January, Catherine of Aragon was laid to rest in Peterborough Catherdral with the honours due to a dowager Princess of Wales. Later that same day, Anne lost the child she was carrying, at around fifteen weeks, which had the appearance of being male. According to Chapuys, this had caused Henry 'great distress' and he was keen to speculate as to the cause. He cited Anne as wishing to 'lay the blame on the Duke of Norfolk, whom she hates, saying he frightened her by bringing the news of the fall the king had', but disagreed with this theory, saying it was 'well known that is not the cause, for it was told her in a way that she should not be alarmed or attach much importance to it'. Court speculation suggested it was 'owing to her own incapacity to bear children' or due to 'fear that the King would treat her like the late queen', especially in the light of his recent interest in Jane Seymour. The rumours extended to Elizabeth's nursery, where Anne Shelton and her daughters and niece, were concerned that if Elizabeth knew of the loss, they 'would not for the world that she knew the rest', which Chapuys interpreted to mean 'that there was some fear the King might take another wife'.[6] Likewise, Dr Ortiz repeated rumours that reached the continent that 'La Ana fears now that the King will leave her to make another marriage'.[7]

The hostile account of Nicholas Sander comments that the foetus was 'a shapeless mass of flesh' and has given rise to speculation among later historians that the child was somehow deformed and the stigma of this caused Henry to reject Anne. The arrival of a misshapen child was considered by many at the time to be indicative of sexual immorality in the parent, so this may have been taken to imply that this was not Henry's child. But Sander was only born in 1530; he didn't see the foetus, any more than Chapuys did, and his colours had already been decidedly declared against Anne. The arrival of two pieces of news together – Henry's fall and the miscarriage – prompted some commentators to identify a connection between them which may have been spurious, such as the Bishop of Faenza, who wrote to the Prothonotary Ambrogio that 'the king of England has had a fall from his horse, and was thought to be dead for two hours. His lady miscarried in consequence'.[8]

The one account of Anne's bravery in the face of such a disappointment also comes from the pen of the Imperial ambassador, who had been 'credibly informed', perhaps again by Gertrude Blount, that Anne 'consoled her maids who wept, telling them it was for the best, because she would be the sooner with child again and that the son she bore would not be doubtful like this one, which had been conceived during the life of the Queen'. Chapuys could not resist the inference that by this statement, Anne acknowledged that a doubt existed over the legitimacy of her daughter, Elizabeth.[9] Predictably, Chapuys' letter had more to say on the matter, including his knowledge of a lengthy estrangement between Henry and Anne, his cruel comments to her and his abandonment of her at Greenwich:

I learn from several persons of this Court that for more than three months this King has not spoken ten times to the Concubine, and that when she miscarried he scarcely said anything to her, except that he saw clearly that God did not wish to give him male children; and in leaving her he told her, as if for spite, that he would speak to her after she was 'releuize'. The said Concubine attributed the misfortune to two causes: first, the King's fall; and, secondly, that the love she bore him was far greater than that of the late Queen, so that her heart broke when she saw that he loved others. At which remark the King was much grieved, and has shown his feeling by the fact that during these festive days he is here, and has left the other at Greenwich, when formerly he could not leave her for an hour.[10]

Henry did leave Anne behind at Greenwich on 4 February, when he travelled to York Place, now Whitehall, where he kept Shrovetide. Yet this need not have been sinister. In keeping with custom and medical advice of the time, Anne was still lying-in after the miscarriage, a process which might last up to a month, before her formal return to society and her ceremony of churching. There is no record of Anne undertaking that Catholic ritual of cleansing, by which the veiled woman carried a taper to the church door and was blessed before offering up her child's chrisom cloth in payment. It was associated with the old ways, and would undergo reform after Anne's death; she may have gone through a service of that nature in the third week of February, giving thanks for her survival and offering prayers for a swift new conception. Clearly, Anne was not in any fit state to travel on 4 February, but nor did Henry choose to stay at Greenwich with her. This may have been due to his need to attend the final session of the Reformation Parliament; yet from Whitehall, he sent presents and messages to Jane Seymour, before summoning Anne to his side on 24 February.

In spite of her personal suffering, Anne was still considered a figure of mercy and intercession, especially by women and charities. At the end of January, she received a petition from Dame Anne Skeffington, the widow of Sir William, Lord Deputy of Ireland, who had died on the last day of December 1535. The widow felt that she and her children had been 'clearly undone by her husband's service' and asked the queen to support a petition she was sending to Cromwell, who, she hoped, would petition the king.[11] It may be that Anne's personal situation prevented her from acting to assist Lady Skeffington, who was still writing to complain of bad treatment by the king after Anne's death. At the end of February, Anne received letters from the Vice-Chancellor and University of Cambridge, thanking her for 'her gentle and loving acceptance' of their letters delivered to her on the progress to the west country, and her 'promotion of their petition to the King for the remission of tenths and first-fruits due to him from the University', which charge would 'greatly diminish the number of scholars in every college'.[12]

Throughout March, there were intermittent signs of royal favour being invested in the Seymour family, although this was not yet at the cost of the Boleyns. An official inventory drawn up on 3 March of all grants made to Thomas and George Boleyn is difficult to interpret. It was probably too early for Henry to have been considering depriving them of positions, as he would add to them at the end of the month, and it may have simply been routine. Of greater concern for Anne, though, was Henry's decision to evict Cromwell from his rooms at Greenwich, so that Edward Seymour and his wife could move into them. This certainly was sinister, as a private corridor gave them access to the king's chamber, in a move that was reminiscent of Henry moving Anne into position in 1528, whilst under the same roof as Catherine. Chapuys reported that 'the new amours' of Henry and Jane continued, 'to the intense rage of the concubine',[13] stoked by Edward Seymour's admittance to the Privy Council on 18 March. Yet, all was still to play for, as the granting to Thomas and George Boleyn of the lease of manors in Rayleigh, Eastwood, Thundersley and other places in Essex, indicated. Henry's closest companion, Henry Norris, was also still in favour, receiving the grant of the manor of Minster Lovell in Oxfordshire.[14]

It was Chaucer who wrote that April brought the contrast of rain after drought and stirred in people a sort of wanderlust that made them seek out adventures; and of course it was T. S. Eliot who described it as 'the cruellest month... mixing / Memory and desire'. As April 1536 arrived, with the signs of spring firmly established in the palace gardens and the surrounding countryside, so began Anne's final month of liberty. From the start, forces were gathering against her, although this was not yet a concerted effort and did not yet have the backing of the king or Cromwell. On 1 April, Gertrude Blount, Marchioness of Exeter, sent Chapuys a note asking him to back Jane Seymour, to which he readily agreed. The letter that he wrote the Emperor that day illustrates the way that Jane was being 'coached' to replace Anne by seeking marriage, by rejecting the king's gifts and influencing his thinking when it came to the popular attitude to his union with Anne:

> The King being lately in this town, and the young lady, Mrs. Semel (Seymour), whom he serves, at Greenwich, he sent her a purse full of sovereigns, and with it a letter, and that the young lady, after kissing the letter, returned it unopened to the messenger, and throwing herself on her knees before him, begged the said messenger that he would pray the King on her part to consider that she was a gentlewoman of good and honorable parents, without reproach, and that she had no greater riches in the world than her honor, which she would not injure for a thousand deaths, and that if he wished to make her some present in money she begged it might be when God enabled her to make some honorable match.[15]

The said Marchioness has sent to me to say that by this the King's love and desire towards the said lady was wonderfully increased, and that he had said she had behaved most virtuously... the same young lady, who has been well taught for the most part by those intimate with the King, who hate the concubine, that she must by no means comply with the King's wishes except by way of marriage; in which she is quite firm. She is also advised to tell the King boldly how his marriage is detested by the people, and none consider it lawful; and on the occasion when she shall bring forward the subject, there ought to be present none but titled persons, who will say the same if the King put them upon their oath of fealty. And the said Marchioness would like that I or some one else, on the part of your Majesty, should assist in the matter; and certainly it appears to me that if it succeed, it will be a great thing both for the security of the Princess and to remedy the heresies here, of which the Concubine is the cause and principal nurse, and also to pluck the King from such an abominable and more than incestuous marriage. The Princess would be very happy, even if she were excluded from her inheritance by male issue. I will consult with them again today, and on learning her opinion will consider the expedient to be taken, so that if no good be done, I may at least not do any harm.[16]

Given the nature of court life, with its intrigues, rumour and counter-rumours, it is likely that Anne had some awareness that Henry's relationship with Jane had changed. If nothing else, the move of the Seymours into Greenwich would have given her pause for thought but, when she acted, it was not through faction and intrigue, but through the medium of her faith, to appeal to her husband's conscience. Anne had a tradition of employing chaplains who made provoking sermons, stirring thoughts of reform. Hugh Latimer was well-known for giving powerful performances questioning papal supremacy, absolution, purgatory and the worship of icons and saints.[17] Now she used religion as a vehicle to try and bring her husband back to her.

On 2 April, Anne's almoner, John Skip, delivered a sermon on the text 'Which among you accuses me of Sin?' which urged Henry to resist evil councillors. Depicting the king as the Old Testament Ahasuerus, King of Persia, Skip cast Cromwell as Haman, his wicked minister, and suggesting that 'a good woman' (Anne) was Queen Esther, who warned that her husband 'lost his true nobility towards the end of his life by sensual and carnal appetite in the taking of many wives and concubines'.[18] Skip also drew on the stories of Solomon's son Rehoboam, who was lazy and covetous and refused to deliver his people from their yoke, and others where evil ministers led good kings astray. This was tantamount to Anne publicly scolding Henry for infidelity and taking bad advice, and in this, Anne went too far.

Henry and Cromwell were both angered at the sermon and if Cromwell had not yet seen himself in opposition to the queen, this would have marked the turning point. Skip was arrested and interrogated for 'preaching seditious doctrines' and slanders. When asked to what end he had intended the example of Solomon, he admitted he had intended 'to touch the king's grace with the said similitude' and with the story of Rehoboam, he stated, damningly, that if he had not intended it to warn the council, then the sermon was not fit for its audience. He was critical of royal councillors who made 'renovations or alterations in civil matters that have been instituted for the common wealth by good men'.[19] This would appear to be Skip – and Anne – attempting to draw Henry back towards a more moderate approach to the monasteries.

Anne had previously intervened in the elections for Wilton Priory and may now have attempted to prevent the dissolution of Catesby Priory in Northamptonshire.[20] When the commissioners made their report, finding the priory gave no cause for criticism, Anne was already in the Tower, so her connection with it pre-empted the investigation, suggesting that she knew and could vouch for the place or the prioress, Joyce Berkeley, personally. As was reported on 12 May:

> We found the house in very perfect order, the prioress a wise, discreet, and religious woman, with nine devout nuns under her, as good as we have ever seen. The house stands where it is a great relief to the poor, as we hear by divers trustworthy reports. If any religious house is to stand, none is more meet for the King's charity and pity than Catesby. We have not found any such elsewhere.[21]

It is conceivable that, whilst approving of reforms and closures that were being proposed for institutions that were found to be corrupt, Anne objected to the blanket approach that Henry and Cromwell were pursuing, which appeared to promise a wide-reaching, indiscriminate dissolution. Anne may have wanted something more specific, tailored to merit and performance. Her reputation as a reformer was pushed by John Foxe and William Latimer, keen to claim her as an instrument of change, and rehabilitate her reputation during the reign of her daughter. Many historians have followed this line, with Maria Dowling claiming Anne as a 'fervent and committed evangelical' and Eric Ives calling her an 'active promoter of the Gospel' who played a 'major part in pushing Henry into asserting his headship of the church'; but perhaps this goes too far.

Anne was certainly pious and committed to charity, distributing clothing whilst on progress, giving out weekly alms, washing the feet of poor women and as mentioned previously, was the dedicatee of William Marshall's 1535 study of poor relief in Flanders.[22] It can also be asserted that she was devoted to ideological reform, reading Fish and Tyndale, which she shared with Henry, promoting forward-thinking clerics, making loans to Hugh Latimer and Nicholas Shaxton. According to the reminiscences of an eighty-year-old woman named Rose, Anne asked Mercer William Lok to bring her the Gospels, Epistles and Psalms translated into French.[23] Perhaps, in early 1536, her religious vision was diverging from that of Henry and Cromwell, and she took a more moderate approach towards monastic dissolution. Her championing of Catesby Priory suggests she was seeking a house-by-house solution. Contrary to Chapuys' allegation that Anne was a great Lutheran, it was Henry who sent Edward Foxe, Bishop of Hereford, to meet Luther in Wittenburg that spring, and appointed a group of Bishops to refine what would become the Ten Articles of June 1536. While history had judged that it was Anne who pushed Henry to religious extremes, even she may have had reservations by that May, of the direction of the new Supreme Head of the Church of England. Her request for the sacraments in the Tower, her stoic acceptance of death and desire for prayers for her soul whilst on the scaffold, suggest a more moderate stance.

In 1536, Joyce Berkeley of Catesby Priory felt herself forced to resort to bribery, offering Cromwell 100 marks to buy a gelding, and 2,000 marks to Henry for the purchase of the Priory. Yet this did not prevent them from suppressing the establishment at the end of 1536. Anne may also have received an appeal on behalf of the Benedictine Priory of Nun Monkton in Yorkshire, run by a Prioress Joan, who hoped for the queen's intercession in her favour.[24] The closure took place in the same year. Anne's well-known reformist convictions, coupled with her genuine piety and instances of past patronage, encouraged some to see her as a figure of mercy. As the full extent of Henry's intentions was sinking in across the country, she may have been considered in these two cases at least to offer an opportunity for leniency, or even simply fair treatment. Did Anne question Henry's intentions, and speak up in favour of houses that already provided examples of godly living? If so, it was surely a move too far away from Henry's agenda, and from the work of Cromwell, whose mission was to filfil the king's will.

That Anne saw her queenship as a conduit for divine work was apparent when she performed the tradition of washing the feet of beggars on Maundy Thursday, 13 April. To question Henry's will on divine matters could be construed by the king as Anne offering an alternative interpretation of God's intentions, when Henry was now Supreme Head of the English Church, and had the final say.

THIRTY-FIVE

The Net Closes, April–May 1536

Referring to Anne as 'the Concubine', the 'Putain' and 'the Lady', it is in the voice of Eustace Chapuys, Ambassador to the Imperial court, that we hear of the events of Anne's final year. A diligent observer, Chapuys was cast on the opposing side to Anne by birth and employment, and his disparagement of her was the inevitable outcome of his support of Catherine of Aragon, whom he considered to be a saintly figure. Aged forty-six at the time of Anne's arrest, Chapuys was a canon of Geneva and doctor of canon and civil law, a humanist who had corresponded with More and Erasmus and, frequently, a man of compassion and sympathy. His reputation for slandering Anne is not entirely deserved, as the comparably more poisonous vitriol of other sources like Sander and Harpsfield shows. Having arrived in England after Anne's ascendancy, he had been an observer of court life since August 1529, but it was not until Tuesday 18 April 1536 that he first set eyes upon Anne Boleyn.

Having been denied an audience with the king on Easter Sunday, Chapuys was invited to court and enthusiastically greeted at the gates of Greenwich Palace by George Boleyn and other lords. The diplomatic tide was turning, and Anne's family understood the need for Henry to make an alliance with Emperor Charles, now that his aunt Catherine was no longer a consideration. Chapuys had recently called on Cromwell at home, 'a very fine house which the king has presented him with, fully furnished' and, hearing that his 'indignation at French behaviour had lately increased', promptly offered him letters from the Emperor which he 'kissed and received most reverently'.[1] Cromwell confided in the ambassador that the entire council had turned against France, but could not openly declare it, as Henry 'still clings to their King';[2] perhaps, also to the pro-French Anne. On 18 April, George openly expressed his desire for friendship with the Emperor, praised Chapuys for the role he was playing in it, and even tried to engage the ambassador in Lutheran debate. He was then invited by Cromwell to attend Anne, which could have been a breakthrough in international relations, but Chapuys was unwilling:

> Before the King went out to mass Cromwell came to me on his part to ask if I would not go and visit and kiss the Concubine, which would be doing a pleasure to this King; nevertheless, he left it to me. I told him that for a long time my will had been slave to that of the King, and that to serve him it was enough to command me; but that I thought, for several reasons, which I would tell the King another time, such a visit would not be advisable, and I begged Cromwell to excuse it, and dissuade the said visit in order not to spoil matters.[3]

However, Chapuys then went to attend chapel and the circumstances made it impossible for him to avoid acknowledging Anne. The gesture upset Mary and her circle, but not to have bowed to the anointed queen of England would have provoked a diplomatic breach perilous to the survival of the new alliance.

> I was conducted to the Chapel by lord Rochefort, the concubine's brother, and when the offering came a great many people flocked round the King, out of curiosity, and wishing no doubt to know what sort of a mien the concubine and I should put on; yet I must say that she was affable and, courteous enough on the occasion, for on my being placed behind the door by which she entered the chapel, she turned round to return the reverence which I made her when she passed.[4]

Chapuys was invited to dine with the King and the rest of the company, 'at the concubine's lodging' but he elected instead to dine in the Presence Chamber with George Boleyn and 'all the principal men of the Court'. Anne was clearly disappointed at missing the opportunity to flaunt her newly-found Imperial affiliatons before the ambassador:

> I am told the concubine asked the King why I did not enter there as the other ambassadors did, and the King replied that it was not without good reason. Nevertheless, I am told by one who heard her, the said concubine after dinner said that it was a great shame in the king of France to treat his uncle, the duke of Savoy, as he did, and to make war against Milan so as to break the enterprise against the Turks; and that it really seemed that the king of France, weary of his life on account of his illnesses, wished by war to put an end to his days.[5]

One theory about Anne's fall places her in opposition to Cromwell, who was advocating the alliance with Charles and a potential Anglo-Imperial marriage for one of Henry's daughters. Yet Anne's enthusiasm for the scheme exposes the flaws in this idea, nor does it justify the extent of the attack upon her circle. Having been a Francophile all her life, it is plausible that Cromwell and others suspected her motives, but Anne was shrewd enough to play the political game on behalf of her daughter and hope to steal the marital prize away from Mary.

As late as 20 April, Anne's position still appeared to be secure. Her trip to Calais with Henry, scheduled for 4 May, was still being spoken of as firmly etched in the diary. George Boleyn had written to Lord Lisle three days earlier to confirm that 'the King intends to be at Dover within this fortnight' and asking for assistance for his servant 'to such things as he shall need for my provision'.[6] The trip was referred to again as a certainty on 25 April, just days before the intended date of departure, with plans for Anne's reception in the town by Lady Lisle, and again on 28 April. As an outward symbol of marital harmony, the Calais trip projected the message that any tension in the royal household was of a temporary nature and that the business of kingship, queenship and international diplomacy would continue as normal. Yet there was one ominous development, suggestive of activity behind the scenes.

On 20 April, Cromwell claimed illness and withdrew from court, heading to his home of Great Place, by St Dunstans in Stepney Green, and a day later Chapuys reported that he had taken to his bed. It may be that Cromwell was genuinely unwell but, as he asserted to Chapuys in June, he had in any case retreated in order to prepare evidence against Anne, acting upon Henry's instructions. He returned on 23 April, perhaps with a strategy, perhaps with new information, and approached the king along with Thomas Wriothesley, in whom he appears to have confided. Eye-witness Scottish Alexander Aless observed that the king was 'furious' but quickly 'dissembled his wrath'.[7]

The nature of Anne's opposition has long divided historians, with some envisioning a well-orchestrated campaign that united her enemies and had been planned for months, while others see a less cohesive force of dissent that responded to the king's withdrawal of favour in the week or two before Anne's arrest. By 23 April, when Henry could barely conceal his fury, there were already a number of significant individuals who were actively hoping to see Anne's disgrace. The hostility of the Catholic, or Marian faction, was no secret and included Henry Courtenay, Marquis of Exeter and his wife Gertrude, who had been feeding Chapuys information, and who enlisted him to their cause early in the month, along with the remnant of Catherine's old household and friends, including the Pole family, the rising Seymours, Sir Thomas Elyot and others. Either Anne had alienated her former friends, or they had chosen to stand against her for reasons best known to them; her cousin Nicholas Carew was another Imperial informant who sheltered Jane Seymour during Henry's courtship of her and her other cousin, Sir Francis Bryan, was reputedly tutoring Jane in the best ways to gain Henry's hand in marriage. In April, Bryan wrote to Sir John and Lady Seymour, to inform them that their daughter would soon be 'well-bestowed in marriage', leaving no doubt about his allegiances or intentions. There was also the formidable Duke of Norfolk, to whom Anne had spoken harshly, who was prepared to detach his destiny from hers, so long as he suffered no loss of position as a result. Yet this group does not appear to have had a sense of itself as a movement with intent, until the start of April, when Gertrude Courtenay approached Chapuys.

Then there is the question of Cromwell's floating loyalties. Until early in 1536, he had worked with Anne, accommodating at least one outburst she made against him, but seeing his service of her as synonymous with the will of the king. In February and March, Chapuys observed that Cromwell was making overtures of friendship towards Mary and her friends, in accordance with his move towards an Imperial agenda. He had formerly been at odds with this group but, if his intention was to destroy the Boleyn faction, he now needed to solicit their support. What still causes debate, though, is whether this attack was initiated by the King or by Cromwell, who required Anne's destruction and brought about a coup, or else he read Henry's intentions and presented his monarch with the solution to his desires. Whichever of them instigated the action, Cromwell would not have been confident of success unless he had already secured the king's full support, or anticipated doing so. To take a chance by acting against Anne independently was too great a risk and may have ended with Cromwell on the scaffold instead. The minister's motivation was to serve the king; everything he did, he did with Henry's permission, either tacit or overt. It was Henry who prompted Cromwell's investigations around 20 April. Whatever Cromwell presented him with, three days later, was almost enough to seal Anne's fate, but not enough.

As recently as 14 April, Henry had granted Sir Thomas Boleyn rights to the town and lands of King's Lynn, but nine days later, at the annual service of the Order of the Garter, the vacant seat went not to George Boleyn, but to Nicholas Carew.[8] This was to the 'great disappointment of Rochford, who was seeking for it,' but was interpreted by Chapuys as a sign that 'the Concubine has not had sufficient influence to get it for her brother'.[9] It was also Chapuys who pointed out the significance, given Carew's involvement with the Seymour cause:

> In fact, it will not be Carew's fault if the aforesaid concubine, though a cousin of his, is not overthrown one of these days, for I hear that he is daily conspiring against her, and trying to persuade Miss Seymour and her friends to accomplish her ruin. Indeed, only four days ago the said Carew and certain gentlemen of the King's chamber sent word to the Princess to take courage, for very shortly her rival would be dismissed, the King being so tired of the said concubine that he could not bear her any longer.[10]

The following day, 24 April, Henry signed a commission presented by Cromwell to investigate 'unknown treasonable conspiracies' although, according to hostile witness Geoffrey Pole, he had already sought advice from Bishop Stokesley regarding a divorce from Anne. Even more ominously, Sir Thomas Audeley, Lord Chancellor, set up two special commissions for the oyer and terminer courts, which constituted a clear order to the men concerned to toe the line of the king's business. They would be in place, ready to serve, when the allegations broke. Many of those who were summoned had recently hosted Anne in their homes, and included Cromwell, Norfolk, Suffolk, William Lord Sandys, Sir William Fitzwilliam, Sir William Paulet and Sir Richard Lyster. Interestingly though, Sir Thomas Boleyn was also summoned, suggesting that a clear decision had been made before the attack upon Anne, that he would not be tarnished by his children's guilt. Chapuys reported that the council were sitting every day at Greenwich, from early in the morning until nine or ten at night. Anne can hardly have failed to sense that some important business was afoot.

On 25 April, the penultimate reference was made to the Calais trip going ahead. Henry's letters to the English ambassadors in France and Rome used the forumla 'the likelihood and appearance that God will send us heirs male (by) our most dear and entirely beloved wife, the queen' but this may have been used to maintain the appearance of normality, as Henry continued to do at court, in chapel, over dinner. As he was used to the rules of performance, of literal masking for entertainment, and the metaphorical masking of emotions, he played the role of king as usual, but not well enough to create a false sense of security for Anne. It was around 26 April, that Anne sought out her chaplain Matthew Parker and begged him to ensure that Elizabeth was looked after if anything happened to her. Two days later, mother and daughter were at Greenwich, where Anne made the final payments for silver and gold fringe and buttons, a saddle for the king, two leading reins with great buttons and long tassels for Elizabeth and a cap of taffeta with a cowl of damask gold.

A letter written on 28 April, by a Thomas Warley to Lord Lisle, assumes that plans for the Calais visit were still in place, although this might represent a pretence of normality until such time as the king was ready to strike. Warley expected that Henry and Anne would sleep at Rochester in a week's time, Tuesday 4 May, and had been informed by Margery Horsman, that Anne wished to be met by Lady Lisle at Dover.[11] This was cutting things very fine, as the Lisles would be making preparations for the visit and planning their imminent trip across the Channel and back. The next day, 29 April, Chapuys reported that Cromwell had been in continual meetings for four days with Richard Sampson, Dean of the Chapel and an expert in canon law, who had once been Thomas Boleyn's co-ambassador. There were also meetings taking place in the Privy Chamber in support of Mary, between Francis Bryan, Henry's companion Sir Anthony Browne and Sir Thomas Cheney, whom Anne had helped to preferment. Bryan's visit to Henry Parker, Lord Morley, the father of George Boleyn's wife Jane, at home at Great Hallinbury in Essex, must have been intended to ensure support in that quarter. Did Parker see that he had to abandon his son-in-law in order to survive, and did he instruct his daughter to do likewise? Jane Boleyn's public repudiation of her husband has confused historians ever since, but she was likely to have been acting as a dutiful Tudor daughter and following instructions. It may have been significant that, for the first time in ages, Henry Parker appears in the list of grants made by Henry in April, along with his son. Morley was granted the site of the late monastery of Augustine Canons at Latton in Essex, which had recently been confiscated while Henry junior was given a place at court, as page of the chamber, with a pension of £6 13s 4d. This may imply that deals were being done and Cromwell was gathering allies, in advance of his strike.[12] On 29 April, the Privy Council received formal notification of proceedings taking place against Anne and, the next day, Cromwell presented his final conclusions to Henry.

On around 30 April, the strain on Henry and Anne's marriage was witnessed. Alexander Aless saw the couple arguing through a window. As he later told Elizabeth, Anne was holding her daughter in her arms, appearing to be begging Henry:

> Never shall I forget the sorrow which I felt when I saw the most serene queen, your most religious mother, carrying you, still a baby, in her arms and entreating the most serene king your father, in Greenwich Palace, from the open window of which he was looking into the courtyard, when she brought you to him. I did not perfectly understand what

had been going on, but the faces and gestures of the speakers plainly showed that the king was angry, although he could conceal his anger wonderfully well. Yet from the protracted conference of the council (for whom the crowd was waiting until it was quite dark, expecting that they would return to London), it was most obvious to everyone that some deep and difficult question was being discussed.[13]

On Sunday, 30 April, Anne had an indiscreet conversation with Henry Norris, which sealed both their fates. Norris had been widowed in 1531, and although he had made overtures towards Anne's cousin, Madge Shelton, the pair had not yet arranged their wedding. Questioning Norris as to why he was being so tardy, Anne would not accept his non-committal answers regarding the courtship and took the convention of courtly love too far, crossing the line between safe verbal play and the suggestion of treason. Perhaps she was angry with Norris, or she was overwhelmed by the tension of recent weeks; perhaps she feared her close friend was becoming distant, or was siding against her, and wished to provoke a declaration of loyalty from him. It may be that she had heard rumours that Henry was seeking to set her aside, or gossip that she was seeking out a new husband, and tried to parody that in a way that fell flat when she told Henry Norris, 'You look for dead men's shoes, for if ought came to the king but good, you would look to have me.' This was an unwise comment. Even during happier times, it would have been difficult for Anne to brush aside but, in the current climate of suspicion and whispers, it was a disaster. The unwitting Norris was horrified and stammered that if he had any such thought, 'he would his head were off'.[14] Yet Anne did not stop, replying that she could undo him if she wished, which led to further arguments between them, before witnesses. Norris was so unsettled by the incident that he hurried to find Anne's almoner, John Skip, to take an oath that the queen was 'a good woman', perhaps on her instructions.[15] That news of the argument was widespread is clear from the fact that it was known independently by Kingston, who wrote to Cromwell, and by Edward Baynton at Greenwich, who referred to 'the communication that was last between the queen and Master Norris'. It was a deeply misjudged comment, made at a critical time, which can only have stemmed from Anne being under extreme pressure.

Anne did not know it, but the first of a series of arrests also took place that day, among those who would accompany her to her death. Mark Smeaton, a musician in his early twenties, had been a member of Wolsey's boy choir, before joining Henry's Chapel Royal, where Anne had noticed his ability and transferred him to her household. Alleged to be the son of a carpenter, he had become Groom of the Privy Chamber in 1532, and this social rise created tension between him and certain members of the court. Thomas Percy, brother of Anne's former love, could not understand how he was in possession of so much money, Thomas Wyatt commented on his social climbing and others disliked his tone and forward manner. Even Anne once had chastised him as an 'inferior person' for speaking to her too familiarly. He was on the outside of her household, never admitted to the inner circle because of his position and class; like Cromwell, he was a functionary at court, rather than an intimate. His arrest was probably prompted by a conversation he had with Anne in late April, when she commented upon his melancholy, and he replied that he must be content only with a single look from her. Smeaton was removed to Cromwell's house at Stepney and questioned. He may also have been tortured, as George Constantine and the Spanish Chronicle relate, with a knotted rope tightened about his head, forcing him into making a confession of adultery with the queen. He was sent to the Tower at around six the next day. Thus at a stroke Anne was defined as an upstart, of deviant sexuality, who sought corrupt pleasures with a man far beneath her class.

Through Monday, 1 May, while Smeaton was being questioned, the flags and tents were being erected at Greenwich for the traditional May Day tournament. George Boleyn was the leading challenger, riding into the lists with his colours fluttering, showing his 'skill in breaking lances' against Henry Norris, the leader of the defenders.[16] When Norris' horse refused to co-operate, and would not enter the lists, the King offered to lend him his. Either by accident or design, all Anne's co-accused were also riding that day – Thomas Wyatt, Francis Weston and William Brereton – save for her musician Mark Smeaton of course, whose class would have debarred him from competing anyway. Lancelot de Carles related that Henry appeared to be in a good mood, being friendly to all, giving them the touch of his hand in a last staged show-piece of patronage before their imminent ruin. Anne watched from her platform and 'often conveyed sweet looks to encourage the combatants who knew nothing of their danger'.[17] The hostile Nicholas Sander described how Norris picked up Anne's handkerchief and wiped his face with it, which prompted Henry to leave. However, no other source contains this detail and it seems too Othelloesque in the light of Norris' recent argument with Anne, and his demonstrated concern not to appear to have overstepped boundaries. Other sources suggest that, towards the end of the jousting, Henry received a message and left. Hall related that men 'mused' about his sudden departure, but 'most chiefly the queen'.[18] According to George Constantine, the king rode away with Henry Norris, questioning him about his relationship with Anne all the way from Greenwich to Westminster. He promised Norris a pardon if he confessed all, but Norris, who must have been reliving the argument he had with Anne just days before, repeated that he had nothing to confess. This was expanded upon by Gilbert Burnet, a seventeenth-century Bishop of Salisbury, who extrapolated from Norris's words 'that in his conscience he thought her innocent of these things laid to her charge; but whether she was or not, he would not accuse her of anything; and he would die a thousand times, rather than ruin an innocent person'.[19]

Anne was left abandoned at Greenwich, without explanation. She must have spent the evening and night of 1 May wondering what was happening, perhaps feeling anxious. She was still a queen and was treated as such, as she dined, said her prayers and prepared for bed. The following day, 2 May, she was summoned to appear before the King's Council at Greenwich. Perhaps she thought she would see Henry and receive some sort of explanation, or have an opportinuty to plead her case with him. If she did, she was soon to realise her mistake: it was an act of deliberate policy that she would never see her husband again. Having taken Anne under his protection in 1526, Henry withdrew that protection on 1 May 1536. She was now alone, a vulnerable target, open to attack. That morning, Norris was arrested, Rochford was taken after eating his dinner at Whitehall, reaching the Tower at around two, and Weston and Brereton soon followed.

Anne found herself before a panel of three. She may initially have been relieved to see that the little deputation was headed by her uncle, the Duke of Norfolk, along with Sir William Paulet, at whose home of Basing she had stayed the previous October, and William Fitzwilliam, Treasurer of the Household, who had travelled with them, and with whom she must have been familiar. All three men had been part of her or the king's household, in close proximity to the queen. She must have considered them to be her supporters in the past. This illusion was rapidly dispelled. Norfolk informed Anne that she stood accused of adultery and incest, the investigation into her conduct had already pointed the finger of suspicion at Smeaton and Norris, and a third man, who was unnamed at that stage. With the withdrawal of Henry's support, the tone of the interview indicated a change in attitudes towards Anne. According to Cavendish, Anne herself described their approach as 'ill-treatment' and that Fitwilliam was openly rude. Norfolk shook his head and said 'tut, tut, tut' and only Paulet was 'a very gentleman'.[20] She was conveyed downriver to the Tower, accompanied by Norfolk and two others, whom Wriothesley names as Cromwell and Thomas Audeley, while Chapuys states it was William, Baron Sandys of the Vyne, and John de Vere, Earl of Oxford. In a strange inversion of her coronation procession three years earlier, she was met in the same location, the Byward Tower, again by Sir William Kingston, who conducted her to the same rooms she had occupied on the former occasion. Anne is alleged to have noted the irony, saying that she was 'received with greater ceremony last time (she) was there'. Anne was finding it difficult to accept what was happening, suggesting to Kingston that Henry was putting her through a test, and that if anyone were to accuse her, they could produce no witnesses.[21]

Kingston described her arrival to Cromwell, during which she appears to have alternated between tears and laughter:

On my lord of Norfolk and the King's Council departing from the Tower, I went before the Queen into her lodging. She said unto me, 'Mr. Kingston, shall I go into a dungeon?' I said, 'No, Madam. You shall go into the lodging you lay in at your coronation.' 'It is too good for me, she said; Jesu have mercy on me;' and kneeled down, weeping a good pace, and in the same sorrow fell into a great laughing, as she has done many times since. She desyred me to move the Kynges hynes that she might have the sacarment in the closet by her chamber, that she might pray for mercy, for 'I am as clear from the company of man as for sin as I am clear from you, and am the Kynges trew wedded wyf'. And then she said, 'Mr. Kynston, do you know wherefor I am here?' and I sayd, Nay. And then she asked me, 'When saw you the Kynge?' and I sayd I saw hym not syns I saw him in the Tilt Yarde. 'And then, Mr. K., I pray you to telle me wher my Lord, my father, is?' And I told hyr I saw hym afore dyner in the Court. 'O, where is my sweet brother?' I sayd I left hym at York Place; and so I dyd. 'I hear say,' said she, 'that I should be accused with three men; and I can say no more but nay, withowt I should oppen my body'. And therewith opened her gown. 'O, Norris, hast thow accused me? Thow are in the Towre with me, and thou and I shall die together; and, Marke, thou art here too. O, my mother, thou wilt die with sorrow; and muche lamented my lady of Worceter, for because that her child did not stire in hyre body.' And my wyfe sayd, 'what shuld be the cause?' And she said, 'for the sorow she toke for me'. And then she sayd, 'Mr. Kyngston, shall I die without justice'? And I sayd, 'the poorest subject the Kyng hath, hath justice.' And therewith she laughed.[22]

The initial reaction to Anne's arrest was disbelief, especially among those who knew her well. On Wednesday 3 May, Anne's Vice-Chamberlain, Edward Baynton, wrote to Fitzwilliam of 'much communication', all confirming that 'no man will confess anything against her... only Mark of any actual thing'. Baynton could not 'believe but the other two (Norris and Rochford) be as fully culpable as ever was he' and reported that the queen 'standeth stiffly in her opinion' because she had faith in the two men. He also ventured that 'if it should no farther appear... it should much touch the king's honour', meaning that it the case could not be proved, it would be harmful to Henry. Of course, Henry would not permit himself to be harmed, so, it followed that the case would have to be proven.[23] Nor could Anne's close friend, Archbishop Cranmer, accept what was being alleged against her, and although he bravely expressed his doubts to Henry, he was politic enough to realise that he owed obedience to the king, whose word trumped every other loyalty:

If the reports of the Queen be true, they are only to her dishonor, not yours. I am clean amazed, for I had never better opinion of woman; but I think your Highness would not have gone so far if she had not been culpable. I was most bound to her of all creatures living, and therefore beg that I may, with your Grace's favor, wish and pray that she may declare herself innocent. Yet if she be found guilty, I repute him not a faithful subject who would not wish her punished without mercy. 'And as I loved her not a little for the love which I judged her to bear towards God and His Gospel, so if she be proved culpable there is not one that loveth God and His Gospel that ever will favor her, but must hate her above all other; and the more they favor the Gospel the more they will hate her, for then there was never creature in our time that so much slandered the Gospel; and God hath sent her this punishment for that she feignedly hath professed his Gospel in her mouth and not in heart and deed.' And though she have so offended, yet God has shown His goodness towards your Grace and never offended you. 'But your Grace, I am sure, knowledgeth that you have offended Him.' I trust, therefore, you will bear no less zeal to the Gospel than you did before, as your favor to the Gospel was not led by affection to her... Since writing, my lords Chancellor, Oxford, Sussex, and my Lord Chamberlain of your Grace's house, sent for me to come to the Star Chamber, and there declared to me such things as you wished to make me privy to. For this I am much bounden to your Grace. They will report our conference. I am sorry such faults can be proved against the Queen as they report.[24]

There was predictable gloating among the Imperial supporters at these dramatic developments. Chapuys was keen to claim credit with the Emperor for the vanishingly small role he had played in Anne's fall, employing 'several means to promote the matter, both with Cromwell and others... which has come to pass much better than anybody could have believed, to the great disgrace of the Concubine'.[25] Chapuys commented that Henry was seeking an annulment on the grounds of a precontract between Anne and Henry Percy and, indeed, Percy did submit a statement to the effect that no such precontract existed, but this would have involved Henry making a tacit admission that his first marriage had been valid. However, as Chapuys recognised, the discovery of the adultery rendered this unnecessary,[26] but he was mistaken in the report that Norris had been arrested for keeping silent regarding her relations with Smeaton. Another Imperial source stated that it was George Boleyn who had concealed essential information about his sister's infidelity.[27]

As was the case with the Tudor court, as soon as the wealthy fell from power, those below them sought what they had lost – positions, lands and possessions. Just as Anne and her family had benefited materially from the falls of Wolsey and Catherine, her disgrace and those of her co-accused released assets and triggered requests that would lead to social advancement. It was as early as 2 May, the day of her arrest, that a Richard Staverton wrote to Cromwell, observing that 'various offenders have been committed to the Tower' including Norris, 'who has various rooms in the parts about me near Windsor,' for which Staverton hoped Cromwell would keep him 'in remembrance... as I have fourteen children'.[28] Likewise an inventory of Norris' goods was undertaken on 3 May, from his residences at Kew and Greenwich.[29] Such acts did not bode well for his survival.

THIRTY-SIX

Bloody Days, May 1536

'These bloody days have broken my heart,' wrote Sir Thomas Wyatt, looking back at the events of May 1536, from which he narrowly escaped with his own life. Much remains mysterious about the circumstances of Anne's arrest, from the choices of individuals to the motivation that underpinned the process, which may never be satisfactorily answered. Not least of these are the reasons that propelled five very different men out of their daily existence, into a scandal the likes of which they could never have imagined, so that their names were spoken across Europe, in awe and disbelief. George Boleyn, Henry Norris, Francis Weston, Nicholas Brereton and Mark Smeaton were selected for different reasons to share Anne's fate, but the queen was of course the common factor. Essentially, they were members of Anne's inner circle, and if Anne's guilt as an adultress was to be convincing, she had to have slept with somebody. The more lovers she reputedly had, the more corrupt and debased she appeared, and the easier she would be to convict. Each engaged with her in a different way, determined by their relationship and class, their function at court and the duration of their connection with her. As each awaited trial, they must have revisited their recent interactions with the queen, replayed conversations and gestures, wondering whether friends or foes had spoken against them. Perhaps they understood from the start that, once again, they were the supporting acts to the queen, except the court masques had been exchanged for a far more deadly game.

Almost everything that is known of Anne's final weeks comes from the reports written for Cromwell by Sir William Kingston, which were gleaned from interviews, observation and snippets passed on by her female attendants. She was under intense, constant scrutiny, which suggests that Henry hoped she would reveal more incriminating evidence whilst under duress, to supplement what Cromwell had already gathered against her. Anne was not pleased with the choice of women who were sent to wait upon her: her aunts, Anne Shelton and Lady Elizabeth

Boleyn, Margaret Coffin, Mrs Stonor and Mary, Lady Kingston, all of whom she professed to have never held in affection. She commented that it was 'much unkindness in the King to put such about me as I never loved,' and when Kingston reassured her that she was served by 'honest and good women', she wished she might have 'had of my own privy chamber which I favour most'.[1] The first three were commanded to have 'no communication with her' unless Lady Kingston was present, which served as a further constraint, regardless of their own wishes. Elizabeth Boleyn and Margaret Coffin were Anne's bedfellows, lying on her pallet with her at night, with the Kingstons stationed at the door, perhaps with Anne Shelton and Mrs Stonor nearby. An ambiguous comment made by Kingston about Mrs Coffin could suggest that she may have tried to protect Anne, or that she was diligent in passing information on. The statement 'I have every thynge told me by Mestrys Cofyn that she thinkes met for you',[2] may mean that Margaret was passing on everything that was 'meet', or fitting, for Cromwell to know, or that she was only passing on that which was fitting, and judging other comments not to be suitable for other ears.

It has been suggested that these women were spies, maliciously guarding Anne and seeking out evidence, the vipers in her bosom, who wished her harm. That might be true, although there is nothing to suggest they had served her with anything less than diligence during her reign, with her aunts trusted with the care of Elizabeth and Mary. Their appointment may also have been a conscious choice, as Anne believed, for 'the Kyng knew what he dyd when he put such two abowt her as my lady Boleyn and Mestres Cofyn; for they could tell her now thynge of my Lord her father, nor nothynge ellys'.[3] So they were chosen for their ignorance of the situation, or their neutrality. With the nature of Anne's arrest, when men like her former allies Norfolk, Cromwell and Kingston suddenly became her persecutors, it would be understandable for Anne to question the motives and loyalties of all those around her. It is just as likely, if not more so, that her waiting women were equally uncertain, confused and afraid about what was happening. When Anne commented that she had wished to be with those she favoured, not those she had never loved, she may have meant that they were not her close personal friends, and that she longed for her intimate companions, to whom she could open her mind freely. Of them all, Elizabeth Boleyn may have spoken most sternly to Anne, and upbraided her for her behaviour, saying ambigiously that 'suche desyre as you have had to such tales has brought you to this'. These women should not necessarily be cast as villains, but as individuals also in fear of their own reputations and lives: perhaps they feared they may share her fate if they did not cooperate.

Cromwell does appear to have accompanied Anne to the Tower, as Wriothesley stated, or at least to have been present there on the day of her arrival, 2 May, as Kingston informed him about Anne's behaviour 'after your departing'. That evening, Lady Kingston and Margaret Coffin passed on the news that Anne had 'been very merry' and had eaten a 'great dinner' before calling for supper.[4] She asked for Kingston, wondering where he had been all day, still expecting to be entertained like a queen. When he arrived, and told her he had been with other prisoners, she complained about the poor treatment she had received at the hands of her uncle Norfolk and Fitwilliam. As she commented that the king was testing her, she 'did light with all and was very merry'. She wished she had her bishops present, certain that they would petition Henry on her behalf, and she was confident that 'the most part of England prays for me'. If she were to die, she predicted, Kingston would see the 'greatest punishment for me' that England had experienced in the last seven years, and she was sure of her place in Heaven for she had 'done many good deeds in my days'.[5] Anne had also requested to receive the sacrament in her closet and wished for the presence of her almoner, John Skip. Her mood, according to Kingston, was volatile, as 'one hour she is determined to die and the next hour much contrary to that'.[6]

In the hours after her arrival, as Anne was wondering what had prompted her arrest, and that of the five men, she revealed to Mrs Coffin the recent conversation she had had with Norris, and the previous one, with Weston. Margaret dutifully passed these on. Kingston was keen to update Cromwell, adding different sections to his letters as more information emerged:

> Sir, since the makynge of thys letter the Quene spake of Weston, saying that she had spoke to hym bycause he did love hyr kynswoman Mrs. Shelton (Madge), and sayd he loved not hys wyf, and he made ansere to hyr again that he loved one in hyr howse better then them bothe. And the Queen said, Who is that? It is yourself. And then she defyed hym, as she said to me.[7]

Anne went on to speak about Mark Smeaton, upon which Mrs Stonor told her he was the 'worst cherished' of any of the male prisoners, as he wore irons, due to his status, 'because he was no gentleman'. Baffled by his inclusion, Anne commented that Mark had only been in her chamber once, at Winchester, during the summer progress of 1535, when she had been lodged above the king and had summoned him to play on the virginals. Since then, she had only spoken to him once, which had been on the Saturday before May Day, when she found him standing before the round window in her presence chamber, and asked him the cause of his melancholy. This had given rise to her comment that he was an 'inferior' person and his response that he must be content with a single look.[8]

On 3 May, Anne's Vice-Chamberlain, Edward Baynton, attempted to stand up for his mistress, writing to Lord Fitzwilliam of his recent reflections upon Anne's conversation with Norris, and the strange behaviour of 'Margery', probably Margery Horsman, who had not given away any information about Anne, but had been the queen's 'great friend'. Some of the letter is missing, but Baynton appears to be offering to volunteer his thoughts upon the issue that no one would speak against Anne, and his disbelief in the guilt of George Boleyn and Norris. Alternatively, he may have been willing to make an open confession of his suspicions, in order to ally himself to Cromwell's cause, and escape any accusation in such a climate of distrust:

> I think much of the communication which took place on the last occasion between the Queen and Master Norres. Mr. Almoner [told] me that I might speak with Mr. Secretary and you, and more plainly express my opinion in case they have confessed 'like wrct... all things as they should do than my n... at a point'. I have mused much at the conduct of Mrs. Margery, who hath used herself strangely toward me of late, being her friend as I have been. There has been great friendship of late between the Queen and her. I will gladly wait upon you. Greenwich.[9]

A letter survives dated 6 May, which was reputedly written by Anne to Henry, 'from my doleful prison in the Tower'. The script is clearly an Elizabethan hand, although that may simply be a copy of an original, as it was common practice to preserve documents in such a way. In fact, an Elizabethan attempt to preserve the original, under the reign of Anne's daughter, only adds to the credibility of the source. Whatever the letter's provenance, it is worth including, as Anne's possible final words to her husband:

> Your Grace's displeasure and my imprisonment are things so strange unto me as what to write or what to excuse I am altogether ignorant. Whereas you sent unto me, willing me to confess a truth and so to obtain your favour, by such an one whom you know to be my ancient professed enemy, I no sooner received this message by him than I rightly conceived your meaning; and if, as you say, confessing a truth indeed may procure my safety, I shall with all willingness and

duty perform your command. But do not imagine that your poor wife will ever confess a fault which she never even imagined. Never had prince a more dutiful wife than you have in Anne Boleyn, 'with which name and place I could willingly have contented myself if God and your Grace's pleasure had so been pleased.' Nor did I ever so far forget myself in my exaltation but that I always looked for such an alteration as now; my preferment being only grounded on your Grace's fancy. You chose me from a low estate, and I beg you not to let an unworthy stain of disloyalty blot me and the infant Princess your daughter. Let me have a lawful trial, and let not my enemies be my judges. Let it be an open trial, I fear no open shames, and you will see my innocency cleared or my guilt openly proved; in which case you are at liberty both to punish me as an unfaithful wife, and to follow your affection, already settled on that party for whose sake I am now as I am, 'whose name I could somewhile since have pointed unto, your Grace being not ignorant of my suspicion therein'. But if you have already determined that my death and an infamous slander will bring you the enjoyment of your desired happiness, then I pray God he will pardon your great sin, and my enemies, the instruments thereof. My innocence will be known at the Day of Judgment. My last request is that I alone may bear the burden of your displeasure, and not those poor gentlemen, who, I understand, are likewise imprisoned for my sake. 'If ever I have found favor in your sight, if ever the name of Anne Boleyn has been pleasing in your ears, let me obtain this request, and so I will leave to trouble your Grace any further.'[10]

Other reports from Kingston to Cromwell from the same day, 5 May, were partially burned during the fire at the Cotton Library at Ashburnham House in 1731, but the surviving fragments suggest that Anne was still fluctuating between different moods, resisting or defying her ladies and predicting that there would be rain until she was released. Such a comment reminds us that for all her advanced, reformist views, Anne was a woman of the sixteenth century and, if she had considered herself crowned by the will of God, then her imprisonment was contrary to his wishes. In an era of predictions, perhaps she feared that such a comment would provoke the King's conscience, or perhaps it came from fear and desperation.

On 7 May, hearing of the news relating to his old Kent neighbours, Sir Henry Wyatt wrote from Allingham Castle to his son Thomas, uring him to act on behalf of the King. Sir Henry considered himself 'unfortunate' that he was unable to ride and 'do his duty to the King in this dangerous time that his Grace has suffered by false traitors'.

He urged Thomas to wait on the King 'night and day' and that 'the false traitors... be punished according to justice to the example of others'.[11] The following day, 8 May, Thomas Wyatt was arrested and sent to the Tower, along with Sir Richard Page, a gentleman of the Privy Chamber who had sided with Anne against Wolsey. Both were questioned on charges of adultery with the queen.

It was disturbing for many that the net still seemed to be open for new victims as late as 8 May. It may have been that Henry was recalling an incident that appears in the hostile Spanish Chronicle, suggesting that Wyatt had pursued Anne, even to the point of quarrelling with Henry over her, as far back as the late 1520s. This may have triggered his arrest:

> Wyatt was entertaining Anne one day as she did needlework and he playfully grabbed a jewel hanging from her pocket and decided to keep it as a trophy, wearing it around his neck. When the King and Wyatt were playing bowls one day, they argued over a shot. Wyatt declared that it was his, but the King declared 'Wyatt, I tell thee it is mine' as he pointed to the wood with the finger on which he wore Anne's ring. Wyatt saw the ring and replied 'If it may like your majesty to give me leave to measure it, I hope it will be mine' and he took the jewel from around his neck and began to measure the cast with the ribbon. This angered the King who broke up the game and then demanded an explanation from Anne Boleyn, who assured him that Wyatt had stolen the jewel from her and that it was no love token.[12]

In addition, Sir Francis Bryan was summoned to court to be questioned about Anne, but he seems to have been in no real danger, and was never sent to the Tower. It may have been for show, or else he was being eliminated from the enquiry, or helping provide evidence to convict his cousin. Having been informed of his son's arrest by Cromwell, but also apparently reassured about his safety, Sir Henry Wyatt wrote on 11 May, thanking him for the 'comfortable articles therein touching his son Thomas and himself' and asking 'when it shall be the King's pleasure to deliver him'.[13] Wyatt and Page would also be released after Anne's death. When Anne's chaplain, William Latimer, arrived back in the country having visited Flanders, he was detained, questioned and searched at Sandwich, before being permitted to continue his journey.

On 9 May, Henry summoned a grand jury at Westminster, to assemble the following day, and Cromwell was called to his side, to 'treat of matters relating to the surety of his person, his honour and the tranquility of the realm'. They met at Westminster on 10 May, before the commissioned judges Sir John Baldwin, Sir Richard Lisle, Sir John

Porte, Sir John Spelman, Sir Walter Luke, Sir Anthony Fitzherbert and Sir William Shelley, with a jury of sixteen men, seven esquires and nine gentlemen, headed by Thomas More's son-in-law Giles Heron. The others had been assembled by the London sheriffs, local men who were previously unassociated with Anne, but drawn from the city: Roger More, Richard Awnsham or Anselm, Thomas Billington, Gregory Lovell, John Worsop or Wesley, William Blackwall, William Goddard, John Willford, William Berd, Henry Hubblythorn, William Hungyng, Robert Wales, John England, Henry Lodesman and John Avery.[14] The jury gave their verdict that there was sufficient evidence for the case against Anne, George, Norris, Weston, Brereton and Smeaton to proceed to trial. A second jury, meeting at Deptford in Kent the following day, reached a similar conclusion.[15] The Constables of the Tower were instructed to 'bring up the bodies' of Weston, Norris, Brereton and Smeaton and it was also probably on this occasion that Henry summoned an executioner from France, a man who reputedly was the best swordsman in St Omer. His identity is unknown. Anne's fate had already been sealed before the first trials began.

The charges were that:

…whereas queen Anne has been the wife of Henry VIII. for three years and more, she, despising her marriage, and entertaining malice against the King, and following daily her frail and carnal lust, did falsely and traitorously procure by base conversations and kisses, touchings, gifts, and other infamous incitations, divers of the King's daily and familiar servants to be her adulterers and concubines, so that several of the King's servants yielded to her vile provocations; viz., on 6th Oct. 25 Hen. VIII., at Westminster, and divers days before and after, she procured, by sweet words, kisses, touches, and otherwise, Hen. Noreys, of Westminster, gentle man of the privy chamber, to violate her, by reason whereof he did so at Westminster on the 12th Oct. 25 Hen. VIII.; and they had illicit intercourse at various other times, both before and after, sometimes by his procurement, and sometimes by that of the Queen. Also the Queen, 2 Nov. 27 Hen. VIII. and several times before and after, at Westminster, procured and incited her own natural brother, Geo. Boleyn, lord Rocheford, gentleman of the privy chamber, to violate her, alluring him with her tongue in the said George's mouth, and the said George's tongue in hers, and also with kisses, presents, and jewels; whereby he, despising the commands of God, and all human laws, 5 Nov. 27 Hen. VIII., violated and carnally knew the said Queen, his own sister, at Westminster; which he also did on divers other days before and after at the same place, sometimes by his own procurement and sometimes by the Queen's. Also the Queen, 3 Dec. 25 Hen. VIII., and divers days before and after, at Westminster, procured one Will. Bryerton, late of Westminster, gentleman of the privy chamber, to violate her, whereby he did so on 8 Dec. 25 Hen. VIII., at Hampton Court, in the parish of Lytel Hampton, and on several other days before and after, sometimes by his own procurement and sometimes by the Queen's. Also the Queen, 8 May 26 Hen. VIII., and at other times before and since, procured Sir Fras. Weston, of Westminster, gentleman of the privy chamber, &c., whereby he did so on the 20 May, &c. Also the Queen, 12 April 26 Hen. VIII., and divers days before and since, at Westminster, procured Mark Smeton, groom of the privy chamber, to violate her, whereby he did so at Westminster, 26 April 27 Hen. VIII

Moreover, the said lord Rocheford, Norreys, Bryerton, Weston, and Smeton, being thus inflamed with carnal love of the Queen, and having become very jealous of each other, gave her secret gifts and pledges while carrying on this illicit intercourse; and the Queen, on her part, could not endure any of them to converse with any other woman, without showing great displeasure; and on the 27 Nov. 27 Hen. VIII., and other days before and after, at Westminster, she gave them great gifts to encourage them in their crimes. And further the said Queen and these other traitors, 31 Oct. 27 Hen. VIII., at Westminster, conspired the death and destruction of the King, the Queen often saying she would marry one of them as soon as the King died, and affirming that she would never love the King in her heart. And the King having a short time since become aware of the said abominable crimes and treasons against himself, took such inward displeasure and heaviness, especially from his said Queen's malice and adultery, that certain harms and perils have befallen his royal body.

And thus the said Queen and the other traitors aforesaid have committed their treasons in contempt of the Crown, and of the issue and heirs of the said King and Queen.[16]

With the relevant dates extracted, a picture emerges of Anne's reputed adultery, which the research of Eric Ives and others has definitively exposed as being largely a fiction. Only six of the dates appear plausible, whilst on thirteen occasions, the court was not at the location specified. On some of these dates, Anne was at an advanced stage of pregnancy, or had just emerged from her lying-in after delivering Elizabeth. Barely a month after first giving birth, Anne was alleged to have 'procured' Sir Henry Norris to 'violate' her at Westminster on 6 October, 1533. She had given birth at Greenwich on 7 September, so may not even have gone through the churching process yet, while Henry had signed warrants to the Great Wardrobe at Greenwich on 7 October, remaining with Anne during her uninterrupted residence. She was alleged to have slept with Norris again at Westminster on 12 October and on 12 and 19 November at Greenwich, but on the latter date, Chapuys indicates that the court was investigating the case of Elizabeth Barton at Westminster.[17] Yet somehow, the insatiable Anne found time for Sir William Brereton between these encounters, sleeping with him at Greenwich on 16 and 27 November and on 3 and 8 December at Hampton Court, even though the court was at Greenwich on the last date and, although Brereton's movements for November are unknown, Ives states that he had a cast-iron alibi for December.[18]

Anne would have been five, or even six months pregnant when she was reputed to have 'procured' Mark Smeaton to sleep with her on 12 April 1534 at Westminster, and her condition even more advanced when intercourse was alleged with Weston on 8 and 20 May, also at Westminster. Henry's own letters reveal that he was at Greenwich on 18 May[19] and Sir Francis Byran commented that the king was not removing until Whitsun, at the end of the month. Anne would have been approaching her due date, looking to soon enter her second confinement, when she apparently slept with Weston at Greenwich on 6 and 20 June, 1534 but she was actually at Hampton Court from 3–26 June that summer. The charges stated that ten months elapsed before Anne erred again, being 'violated' by Smeaton at Westminster, even though Henry himself had signed a letter to Cromwell from Greenwich on that very day, 26 April, 1535. On 13 May, when Anne 'allured' Smeaton into bed again, she was indeed at Greenwich, as alleged, composing a letter to the Abbot of York[20] but seven days later, when she was alleged to have done it again, she was at Richmond. Smeaton's whereabouts during this time is unclear, but he was with Anne during the summer progress, when she invited him into her chamber at Winchester, above that of the King, in order to play her the virginals. Yet this opportunity was not taken by Anne – or by Cromwell.

Anne was reputed to have plotted Henry's death immediately after her return to Windsor in October 1535, after their 'merry' summer holiday was over. Anne would have been almost two months pregnant when she 'procured' her brother George to sleep with her on 2 and 5 November, before giving gifts to her lovers at Westminster on 27 November, the latter hardly a treasonable offence, although she was actually at Windsor Castle. On 22 and 29 December, she reputedly slept with her brother again at Eltham Palace, in spite of contemporary medical advice which strongly warned against sex during pregnancy, and Anne would have certainly taken no risks when it came to the survival of this third child.

Finally, she was accused of plotting the king's death with her lovers on 8 January 1536, at Greenwich, when she was around three months pregnant, and she was actually resident at Eltham Palace in the wake of the Christmas season. Leading historians Eric Ives, G.W. Bernard and Alison Weir, who have studied Anne's movements and the allegations in detail, have concluded that they were composed in haste, and are absurd. The charges were also on dubious legal ground, as intercourse with a consenting queen was not an act of treason, and the term used during the men's trials was that of violation, not rape. The only legal aspect to the case was that Henry's life was in danger, as a result of their reputed plotting against him. Bernard has also, in the interests of fairness, entertained the possibility of Anne's guilt, her weakening under duress, but the majority of scholarship, and evidence, stands against this.

On 12 May, Henry Norris and William Brereton, both in their early fifties, and Francis Weston and Mark Smeaton, in their early to mid-twenties, were brought out of confinement by the Constable of the Tower in order to face the jury at Westminster. Before them was ranged a panel of their peers including Norfolk, Suffolk, Cromwell and Thomas Boleyn, along with Exeter, Northumberland, Fitzwilliam and a number of religious conservatives and supporters of Cromwell and his allies, who were not predisposed to challenge the wishes of the king. As John Husee related to Lord Lisle, the four men were 'arraigned and are judged to be drawn, hanged and quartered'.[21] He reported speculation that some said Weston would escape, while others believed 'none shall die but the Queen and her brother, others that Wyatt and Mr Page are as likely to suffer'.[22] Norris, Weston and Brereton pleaded not guilty whilst Mark Smeaton pleaded guilty to 'violation and carnal knowledge of the Queen', or as Chapuys put it, that 'he had been three times with the said putain and concubine'.[23] Yet even the ambassador reported that they 'were condemned upon presumption and certain indications, without valid proof or confession'.[24] Nevertheless, all four were condemned to death.

The charges were so colourful as to play into the deepest male fears regarding female misbehaviour, and perhaps we look in the wrong place, with too modern a perspective, when we consider how the dates and places do not match up. Cromwell didn't need to create a watertight case, or to research all those critical details that a twenty-first century court would subject to forensic analysis and deconstruction. What he needed to do, as he was well aware, was to arouse in the minds of Tudor men, their ultimate horror: that of the adulterous wife, who threatened their lineage and made them into a figure of public mockery. Contemporary cases of adultery and divorce at Henry's court illustrated just how emasculating this could be, in the cases of Thomas Wyatt,

Edward Seymour, William Parr and others. Cromwell's case rested upon the emotions and deep-seated taboos of Tudor domestic life, not facts. Ultimately, it was Cromwell's word against Anne's and he exploited his reputation as the King's chief minister, and the fact that he enjoyed Henry's full support, to cast Anne as the stereotypical wanton woman, a horror that his peers were swift to recognise and, shuddering, to accept. John Husee was convinced by the 'evidence' and his reaction includes the familiar dichotomy of women as saints ('good women') or sinners:

I think verily, if all the books and chronicles were totally revolved, and to the uttermost persecuted and tried, which against women hath been penned, contrived, and written since Adam and Eve, those same were, I think, verily nothing in comparison of that which hath been done and committed by Anne the Queen; which, though I presume be not all thing as it is now rumoured, yet that which hath been by her confessed, and other offenders with her by her own alluring, procurement, and instigation, is so abominable and detestable that I am ashamed that any good woman should give ear thereunto. I pray God give her grace to repent while she now liveth. I think not the contrary but she and all they shall suffer.[25]

Cromwell confirmed, on 13 May, that Anne was indeed this cultural aberration, from whom the minister had saved the imperilled king. The following day, her marriage, that defining aspect of the very identity of a Tudor woman, was pronounced invalid. She had lured Henry into her bed under false pretences, and proved herself to be not the woman who resisted his lust for six years, but a rampant sexual temptress. Just as Anne had bewitched and emasculated Henry, now she had conformed to type as the corrupting Eve:

The Queen's incontinent living was so rank and common that the ladies of her privy chamber could not conceal it. It came to the ears of some of the Council, who told his Majesty, although with great fear, as the case enforced. Certain persons of the privy chamber and others of her side were examined, and the matter appeared so evident that, besides that crime, there brake out a certain conspiracy of the King's death, which extended so far that all we that had the examination of it quaked at the danger his Grace was in, and on our knees gave God laud and praise that he had preserved him so long from it.[26]

On 15 May 1536, George and Anne Boleyn both stood trial, within the Tower. First, Anne was conducted by Sir William Kingston into the

King's Hall, where a crowd of around 2,000 had gathered.[27] Anne had dressed with a sense of the theatrical, in a gown of black velvet with a dramatic red damask petticoat, a cap perched on top of her head, sporting a black and white feather. De Carles reported her composed demeanour, walking forward 'in fearful beauty and seemed unmoved as a stock, not as one who had to defend her cause, but with the bearing of one coming to great honour'.[28]

On a great platform, Norfolk sat under the cloth of estate, holding the white rod of office, with his son, the Earl of Surrey at his feet, flanked by Lord Chancellor Audeley and Brandon, Duke of Suffolk. Looking around, Anne would have seen other familiar faces on the jury, not least that of her old flame Henry Percy, as well as men who had served within her household who had benefited from her patronage, and her own father. Alexander Aless, a close friend of Cromwell, wrote that Thomas Boleyn was included in the trial 'in order that his daughter might be the more confounded, and that her grief might be the deeper. Yet she stood undismayed, nor did she ever exhibit any token of impatience, or grief, or cowardice.'[29] When the charges were read against her, she did not reply, but her face betrayed her feelings, 'but no one before her would have thought her guilty'.[30]

Thomas Wriothesley, who was undoubtedly present, recorded the charges read by Sir Christopher Hales, that Anne,

> ...despising her marriage, and entertaining malice against the king, and following daily her frail and carnal lust, did falsely and traitorously procure by base conversations and kisses, touchings, gifts and other infamous incitations, divers of the king's daily and familiar servants to be her adulterers... so that several of the king's servants yielded to her vile provocations... She procured by sweet words, kisses, touches and otherwise Henry Norris to violate her... procured and incited her own natural brother George Boleyn, Lord Rochford, to violate her, alluring him with her tongue in the said George's mouth, and the said George's tongue in hers... he violated and carnally knew the said Queen, his own sister Anne saying she never loved the king in her heart and would marry one of them once he was dead.[31]

Chapuys' version does not differ hugely, although he was not present, but it includes the significant details that Anne had ridiculed Henry as a man, adding to the sense that she had emasculated the King. She was also alleged to have disdained his poetry and mocked his sexual prowess, and in this, Chapuys may have come close to uncovering the truth behind Henry's motivation. For all his professed naivety, the ambassador had an instinctive understanding of the dynamic between the couple, and the complexities of their connection. Again, it was about the gender dynamic between a man and a woman. Henry's passionate feelings turned from love to loathing, because he believed that Anne held him in contempt. She wounded his male pride, and thus, his sense of majesty, and pride was a quality that Henry had in excess:

> What she was principally charged with was having cohabited with her brother and other accomplices; that there was a promise between her and Norris to marry after the King's death, which it thus appeared they hoped for; and that she had received and given to Norris certain medals, which might be interpreted to mean that she had poisoned the late Queen and intrigued to do the same to the Princess. These things she totally denied, and gave to each a plausible answer. Yet she confessed she had given money to Weston, as she had often done to other young gentlemen. She was also charged, and her brother likewise, with having laughed at the King and his dress, and that she showed in various ways she did not love the King but was tired of him.[32]

One of the more unusual pieces of evidence used in the trial was a letter Anne had written before her marriage, to her friend Bridget Wingfield, which reputedly exposed her bad behaviour. Bridget had died in 1534, so was conveniently unable to refute any claims against her, or to disprove the allegation that she 'shared the same tendencies' as the queen. This was an essential piece of framing on the part of the prosecution, in order to make an otherwise innocuous letter appear to conceal a dark secret. Yet Bridget's 'indiscreet trouble' might have been many things, from a female illness or condition related to pregnancy, or something relating to the third marriage she was contemplating at the time, where her choice of husband may have displeased Anne:

> I pray you as you love me, to give credence to my servant this bearer, touching your removing and any thing else that he shall tell you on my behalf; for I will desire you to do nothing but that shall be for your wealth. And, madam, though at all time I have not showed the love that I bear you as much as it was in deed, yet now I trust that you shall well prove that I loved you a great deal more than I fair for. And assuredly, next mine own mother I know no woman alive that I love better, and at length, with God's grace, you shall prove that it is unfeigned. And I trust you do know me for such a one that I will write nothing to comfort you in your trouble but I will abide by it as long as I live. And therefore I pray you leave your indiscreet trouble, both for displeasing

of God and also for displeasing of me, that doth love you so entirely. And trusting in God that you will thus do, I make an end. With the ill hand of Your own assured friend during my life,
Anne Rochford [33]

In spite of all this, Anne acquitted herself so well that observers felt the case against her simply could not stand. One anonymous account suggests that Anne's responses to the charges were certainly good enough to secure her freedom: Anne 'having an excellent quick wit, and being a ready speaker, did so answer to all objections that, had the peers given their verdict according to the expectation of the assembly, she had been acquitted. But they, wholly applying themselves to the King's humour, pronounced her guilty.'[34] Her uncle Norfolk, as Lord High Steward of England, condemned her to death, either by being burned or beheaded. When the inevitable guilty verdict was read out in court, Henry Percy collapsed and had to be helped from the room, although this may have been more due to mortal illness than emotional turmoil. In a twist of cruel irony, Anne was condemned under the same statute of 1534 that had been created to protect her and her daughter. Tudor law had decided that she was the 'onchaste wife, the spotted queen, causer of all (Henry's) strife', as she was described in a poem by George Cavendish.[35] She had transgressed as a woman, emasculating her husband by capturing his slavish devotion, and then daring to disagree with him, criticise him and, worst of all, laugh at him. Because her crimes were those of gender, she needed to be destroyed by equally gendered tools: she needed to be destroyed as a woman. Thus, the case against her was designed to trample upon the most precious commodity of an aristocratic lady, or queen: her good name.

George's trial also exposed this element of the charges. Although he was a man, he too had threatened the King's masculinity, perhaps by his charisma and charm, but largely in his closeness to Anne, as the person in whom she had confided, and who had shared her amusement at Henry's inadequacies. George daringly read out to the court the note he had been instructed to keep secret. In it, Anne and Jane Boleyn had allegedly discussed the King's inability in the bedroom, with the queen claiming he lacked 'vertu' and 'puissance', or ability and power, or strength. When passed to him, George 'immediately declared the matter, in great contempt of Cromwell and some others, saying he would not in this point arouse any suspicion which might prejudice the king's issue'.[36] Although George did not confirm the account, reading the charge was an act of rebellion that counted against him, as did the report that he had spread rumours that Princess Elizabeth had been fathered by Henry

Norris. There is no evidence to suggest whence this titbit sprang, but Boleyn would not have been so foolish as to cast doubt on his niece's claim. He was charged with having once spent too long with Anne and 'with certain other little follies'.[37] Witness Lancelot de Carles wrote that 'one never saw a man respond better' and judged that George was eloquent and knowledgeable.[38]

Perhaps it was the inclusion of Jane Boleyn's name in the scandalous note touching the King's sexual performance that led Jane to fear for her own life. Whatever her motivation, she testified against her husband, claiming a relationship between George and Anne, as one anonymous Portuguese account related, 'that person who, more out of envy and jealousy than out of love towards the king, did betray this accursed secret, and together with it the names of those who had joined in the evil doings of the unchaste queen'.[39] George Wyatt later commented on Jane's action, but framed it with her gender in a way similar to that by which Anne was condemned, as the ultimate wicked woman: 'in this principal matter (of incest) between the queen and her brother, there was brought forth, indeed, witness, his wicked wife, accuser of her own husband, even to the seeking of his blood.'[40] Jane provided the only evidence for incest. Despite onlookers betting ten to one that George would be acquitted,[41] he had offended the king and was too close to Anne, so he was sentenced along with the rest. As Chapuys related, 'her brother, after his condemnation, said that since he must die, he would no longer maintain his innocence, but confessed that he had deserved death. He only begged the King that his debts, which he recounted, might be paid out of his goods.' This was a conventional final request for the time, springing from the acceptance of death, the sense of personal unworthiness and the settling of debts: all were considered, in contemporary literature, to be essential in smoothing the passage to Heaven. Yet even after this, Anne clung to hope. Returned to the Tower to await her fate, she suggested at dinner on 16 May to Kingston that she would retire to a nunnery and was 'in hope of life'. Presumably George was also fighting for his life, as Kingston delivered his petition to the king the same day.[42] They hoped in vain.

On 17 May 1536, George Boleyn, Henry Norris, Francis Weston, William Brereton and Mark Smeaton were led out in turn to the site of the scaffold on Tower Hill. Chapuys said Anne was made to watch them from a window in the Tower, to 'aggravate her grief'.[43] First to die due to his rank, George's final speech contained the admission that he was a wretched sinner, and deserved death, a formula consistent with his religious beliefs, rather than indicative of any actual wrongdoing, and warned the crowd to 'trust not in the vanity of the world and especially in the flattering of the court'. He openly confessed that he had not been devout enough or put his reading into practice as much as he should, which is not the same as Chapuys' report that he had repented of his 'Lutheranism':

> I have one thing for to say to you, men do come and say that I have been a setter forth of the word of God, and one that have favoured the Gospel of Christ; and because I would not that God's word should be slandered by me, I say unto you all, that if I had followed God's word in deed as I did read it and set it forth to my power, I had not come to this. I did read the Gospel of Christ, but I did not follow it; if I had, I had been a live man among you: therefore I pray you, masters all, for God's sake stick to the truth and follow it, for one good follower is worth three readers, as God knoweth.[44]

After George came Norris, retracting a confession he had been deceived into making by Thomas Wriothesley, Earl of Southampton. His servant, George Constantine, who had sent him messages of support through his imprisonment, related that he said very little else. Francis Weston was next, despite the efforts of his family and the Bishop of Tarbes to intervene. He took to the scaffold and said, 'I thought to have lived in abomination yet these twenty or thirty years and then to have made amends. I thought little it would have come to this.' While some have interpreted the use of 'abominations' as an admission of guilt, even of homosexuality, with which it was sometimes then considered a synonym, it is far more likely that Weston was referring to simpler pleasures, such as his comparative youth, and his anticipation of having lived at least as long as Norris or Brereton. Following him, William Brereton, like George, declared that 'I have deserved to die if it were a thousand deaths, but the cause wherefore I die, judge not'. Smeaton was last, repeating the formula, asking the crowd to pray for him as he had deserved death. Just as Anne woud state 'I do not intend to reason my cause', none of them argued for their innocence, because it was not the place to do so. They believed that the manner of their deaths, in making a good, accepting end without bitterness or regret, was as significant as living a good life when it came to achieving salvation.

Anne believed that she was to die the following morning, 18 May, so she summoned her almoner, John Skip, to sit up with her in prayer. His loyalty, like that of Hugh Latimer, Matthew Parker, and evidenced in Cranmer's veiled attempt to defend her, illustrates a crucial, often overlooked point about Anne's reputed guilt. It is of considerable significance that the majority of Anne's secular household turned against her while those serving her in a religious capacity did not. Those men who knew her intimate feelings, who had heard her confession and secrets, her religious convictions, were not in doubt about her innocence. Those who served her in a secular capacity, rising under the structure of patronage at the Tudor court, were quick to shift their allegiance once it was clear that Anne was about to fall. Many of them abandoned her to ride the next wave, finding employment in the household of Jane Seymour. Yet Anne did not die on 18 May, because the swordsman from St Omer had not yet reached London. He arrived later that day.

On the night of 18 May, which was her last, Anne made her final confession. Chapuys heard the contents of it second hand: 'the lady who had charge of her has sent to tell me in great secresy that the Concubine, before and after receiving the sacrament, affirmed to her, on the damnation of her soul, that she had never been unfaithful to the King.'[45] These were words between Anne and God alone; anticipating imminently meeting her maker, Anne would not have played with the destiny of her soul, or been so arrogant as to attempt deception. She sent for Kingston to witness her words, who diligently reported her final hours to Cromwell, and the way she received the host. She said to him, 'Mr Kingston, I hear say I shall not die before noon, and I am very sorry therefore, for I thought to be dead by this time and past my pain.' He told her that it would not hurt, that it was so 'subtle' or cleverly done. Anne replied, 'I heard say the executioner was very good and I have a little neck', and put her hand about it, laughing heartily. Kingston related that he had seen many men and women executed, and they had all 'been in great sorrow' but to his knowledge, 'this lady has much joy and pleasure in death'.[46] According to contemporary advice, Anne had reconciled herself with her impending end by virtue of the strength of her faith.

At dawn on 19 May, Anne heard Mass and dressed herself in a French gable hood and a gown of black or dark grey damask trimmed with ermine, over a red kirtle. The Constable of the Tower led her on the short walk to the scaffold on Tower Green, where she mounted the steps and looked down at the crowd. A document in the Vienna archive records that she 'looked very frequently behind her' and was 'much exhausted and amazed',[47] while another account in the Archives of Brussels relates that she was led, 'feeble and half-stupefied' looking back at her ladies.[48] A couple of versions exist of her final speech, subtly different due to translation, but the overall effect was traditional and dignified:

Good Christian people, I have not come here to preach a sermon; I have come here to die. For according to the law and by the law I am judged to die, and therefore I will speak nothing against it. I am come hither to accuse no man, nor to speak of that whereof I am accused and condemned to die, but I pray God save the King and send him long to reign over you, for a gentler nor a more merciful prince was there never, and to me he was ever a good, a gentle, and sovereign lord. And if any person will meddle of my cause, I require them to judge the best. And thus I take my leave of the world and of you all, and I heartily desire you all to pray for me.[49]

Before an audience that included Cromwell, Audeley, Suffolk, Henry Fitzroy and 'a great number of the king's subjects'[50] the Queen of England removed her cloak and coif and tucked her hair under a cap. Then she knelt in the straw, one of her ladies bound her eyes and the executioner removed her head with one stroke of the sword. When her head fell, it was covered by a white cloth and carried, along with her body, into the chapel of St Peter ad Vincula, where it was laid to rest. It was an unprecedented moment in national history: never before had a queen been executed.

The reactions to Anne's death were varied but predictable. Although she had not enjoyed the same popularity as Catherine among the people, it was less about personal dislike than rejection of the role she had played as the former queen's replacement. The manner of her sudden death, though, the nature of her convictions and the unprecedented brutality of her end, did prompt some confusion and sympathy. George Cavendish related there was 'much muttering' about her death and even Chapuys, who could not resist commenting that 'everybody rejoices at the execution of the putain,' admitted that 'there are some who murmur at the mode of procedure against her and the others, and people speak variously of the King'.[51] John Husee described Anne's death as 'bold' and that Anne's receiver general George Taylor, and the servants of George Boleyn were 'at liberty to serve where they please'.[52] Mary, Queen of Hungary, saw Anne's death as the removal of an obstacle to international relations, hoping 'the English will not do much against us now, as we are free from his lady,' but recorded that 'people think he invented this device to get rid of her'. Mary also made a wider point about Henry's actions setting a precedent: 'when he is tired of this one (Jane Seymour) he will find some occasion of getting rid of her. I think wives will hardly be well contented if such customs become general. Although I have no desire to put myself in this danger, yet being of the feminine gender I will pray with the others that God may keep us from it.'[53]

The rumours spread around Europe in different versions. The Venetian Harvel drew out the class aspect of the relationship, commenting that it was 'great infamy to that woman to have betrayed that noble prince in such a manner, who had exalted her so high and put himself to peril, not without perturbation of all the world, for her cause'.[54] Still, he referred to the event as a tragedy, as did Philip Melanchthon, the friend of Luther, whom Henry had hoped to entice to England.[55] The Viennese archives list a version of events referring to Anne as the 'unjustly called' queen, and that her death was a fulfilment of the prophecy of Merlin, in which a queen of England would burn. Others recalled the dun cow prophecy, that 'when the cow rideth the bull, then, priest, beware thy skull', with the dun cow as a symbol of royalty[56] being mastered by the bull of Bulleyne, to the detriment of the church.

The Spanish Chronicle, composed by a Spanish merchant living in London before 1552, gave an inevitably inaccurate and hostile account of Anne's story. It stated that the devil drove Anne to adultery, and contained the story that Anne hid Smeaton in a closet, aided by an old woman, who brought him out when Anne called for marmalade. Norris and Brereton were jealous as they had been supplanted by Smeaton, and Smeaton was tortured, with a rope of knots about his head, tightened by a cudgel. *The Chronicle* also put words into the mouth of Anne, who, in a great rage, said 'I have never wronged the king, but I know well that he is tired of me, as he was before of the good Lady Catherine... It has all been done... because the king has fallen in love, as I know, with Jane Seymour, and does not know how to get rid of me... and any confession that has been made is false.'[57]

On the same day as Anne's execution, barely before her body was cold, Archbishop Cranmer issued a dispensation for Henry to marry Jane Seymour, without the publication of banns, even though they were related twice, in the third degree of affinity.[58] The following day, Jane, who had been lodged with Nicholas Carew, 'came secretly by river this morning to the King's lodging' and was betrothed to Henry by nine o'clock. As Chapuys reported, Henry had hoped to keep this secret until the end of the month, 'but everybody begins already to murmur by suspicion, and several affirm that long before the death of the other there was some arrangement'.[59] He had heard that immediately upon hearing the news of Anne's death, Henry entered his barge and went to Jane, who was waiting a mile away. Even Chapuys was forced to admit that if this was true, 'it sounds ill in the ears of the people, who will certainly be displeased'.[60] With his new-found freedom, Henry was 'going about banqueting with ladies, sometimes remaining after midnight, and returning by the river'. He supped that week 'with several ladies' in the house of the Bishop of Carlisle 'and showed an extravagant joy' before producing his own work on the subject. As Chapuys relates, 'he had before composed a tragedy, which he carried with him; and, so saying, the King drew from his bosom a little book written in his own hand, but the Bishop did not read the contents. It may have been certain ballads that the King has composed, at which the *putain* and her brother laughed as foolish things, which was objected to them as a great crime.'[61]

On 30 May, a William Marche arrived in London, from Calais, about the business of Lord Lisle, and the gossip in the streets was still fresh enough for him to be able to write that 'this day, the King is known to be married unto one Mrs Jane Seymour', before moving on to other news.[62] Anne had been dead for eleven days when the funeral baked meats 'did coldly furnish forth the marriage tables', and Jane Seymour adorned herself in the royal clothes and jewels, slept in her bed, owned her possessions, used her furniture and occupied her place at Henry's side, just as Anne had Catherine's.

Whichever way it is looked at, the burning question of why Anne had to die returns to one answer. And that answer is Henry. There was undoubtedly love in the marriage, deep attraction and volatile passion, combined with mutual interest and a particular set of religious and political circumstances that had propelled Anne into Henry's orbit. At the start, he was fascinated with her, obsessed and devoted, scarcely able to leave her side. She may have considered that she had a mission, perhaps divinely appointed, to produce a male heir for England, or influence his faith. This did not translate well to marriage, in which certain behaviours were expected, or queenship, where they were required. It was a turbulent, rather than an unhappy marriage, with cycles of difficulty followed by periods of happiness.

Retha Warnicke argues that Anne a victim of sexual prejudice.[63] There was, unquestionably a gender and class element to Anne's fall, but this only became an issue after Henry had withdrawn his support of her, and it was more a question of gender boundaries and masculine identity. Anne had stretched herself beyond the dictates of what a woman of her class might aspire to and this made her an easy target, with highly visible areas of vulnerability in a male-dominated court. Nor could Anne be simply put aside, divorced or sent to one of the nunneries that Henry was on the brink of dissolving. He would have been forced to admit that he had been wrong about Anne, after having moved mountains to be with her. The intense male pride of an absolute Tudor monarch could not allow him to be ridiculed on the European stage as having made such a serious error of judgement, so the blame for their failure had to be shifted onto Anne's shoulders.

Then there is the question of sex. At some point in 1536, Henry hinted to Chapuys that Anne had been 'corrupted' in France. Alison Weir presents a theory[64] that Anne experienced some degree of sexual intimacy, but not full copulation, at the court of Francis I, and this realisation proved a crucial turning point for Henry, cooling his ardour. Also, Anne had secured Henry, in his opinion, upon the basis of promises she had failed to deliver. She had not given him the son he had hoped for and her miscarriages were starting to look dangerously like the pattern he had followed with Catherine, only this time he was in his mid-forties, and not getting any younger. If Anne's indiscreet comments about Henry's clothes and poetry or, worse still, his sexual performance, had been reported to the king in late April 1536, the criticism of his masculine identity may have been sufficient to turn him against her, coming after years of his courtly deference.

Ultimately Anne's death occurred because Henry wanted it to. If the early 1530s had revealed nothing else, it was that Henry, capricious, mercurial, volatile and narcissistic, had achieved a number of extraordinary, unprecedented feats in order to satisfy his will. He had set Catherine aside, defied and broken with the pope, taken a second wife of his own choosing, beheaded those who would not support him, made gossip against him a treasonable offence and begun the process of taking for himself the wealth of a centuries-old national monastic network. Such a man got what he wanted. If he wanted to be rid of Anne, he would be rid of Anne. Where historians have often disagreed, is just who instigated and pursued the attack upon Anne. Some see it as Henry's policy, while others favour the notion of a coup, managed by Cromwell, working in conjunction with the Catholic or Marian faction, or a more serendipitous collision of all Anne's enemies at a time when she was vulnerable. The latter readings, though, underestimate the king. On some level, Henry made the decision to be rid of Anne and he asked Cromwell to achieve it for him. Cromwell simply continued to do his job, of providing the king with what he desired. Cromwell later claimed credit for Anne's fall, in secret communications with Chapuys, but this was after it had been successful and he was seeking Imperial support. But Cromwell hadn't played the king, he had served him.

Anne was vulnerable because she broached expectations of class and gender, stirring up deeply felt convictions about how women should relate to men, especially to their husbands. Just like Wolsey and, indeed all those whom Henry favoured then rejected – Buckingham in 1521, Catherine, Wolsey, Fisher, More and, in 1540, Cromwell – her death was the result of Henry's choice, his caprice. Ultimately, they all died because he wanted them to. Anne's death, all their deaths, return us to what Eric Ives calls the paradox of Tudor history: the psychology of Henry VIII.[65]

APPENDIX

Anne's Bills and Debts

The Queen's Reckoning:

12 Dec 1535.:—40 yds. garnish of Venice gold for a nightgown, at 4*s*.

To Blase, her 'brotherer', ½ lb. Venice silver, 24*s*.

Stuff delivered to Floide, yeoman of her wardrobe, Stywarde her saddler, and Jervice, servant to Mr. Everest.

18 Jan. 1536:—Boat-hire from Greenwich to London and back to take measure of caps for my lady Princess, and again to fetch the Princess's purple satin cap to mend it.

23 Jan.:—25 yds. of cadace fringe, morrey color, delivered to Skutte, her tailor, for a gown for her Grace's woman fool, and a green satin cap for her. A purple satin cap, laid with a rich caul of gold, the work being roundelles of damask gold, made for my lady Princess.

19 Feb.:—Tassels of fine Florence gold to Hen. Cryche, clerk of the Wardrobe.

20 Feb.:—'A pair of pyrwykes' for my lady Princess, delivered to my lady mistress.

28 Feb.:—A button of silk and gold, delivered to Mrs. Coffyn.

10 March:—2¼ yds. crimson satin, at 15*s*., an ell of 'tuke' and crimson fringe for the Princess's cradle head.

13 March:—Crimson fringe for a chair, to Grene, her coffer-maker. 2 fine pieces of 'nydle rybande' to roll her Grace's hair withal.

17 March:—6 'forfruntes' wrought with laid work, delivered to Mrs. Margery.

20 March:—A white satin cap laid with a rich caul of gold for the Princess, 4*l*., and another of crimson satin, 3*l*. 13*s*. 4*d*. 2 rich tassels of Florence gold for your Grace's beads, 10*s*.; a pound of starch, 4*d*.

20 April:—To Floide and Thos. Chapell, a fringe of Venice gold and silver for the little bed. To Baven, the bed-maker, fringe for the great bed. Green riband to garnish a pair of clavichords. Green fringe 'to perform the green chair'.

27 April:—Venice gold fringe and silk and gold points for a saddle for my lady Margaret. 2 round buttons of silk and gold for the bridle.

28 April:—Silver and gold fringe, black silk fringe, and gold and silver buttons for a saddle for your Grace. 2 leading reins with great buttons and long tassels. Red fringe to mend the harness of the Queen's mules. A cap of taffeta covered with a caul of damask gold for the Princess, 4 mks. And many other items.

Total, 68*l*. 4*s*. 1½*d*.[1]

Debts owinge by the late queen Anne at the time of her death:

The wardrobe of robes.

Mercers:—To Wm. Lok, Ambros Barker, Thos. Abraham, Hen. Brayne, Wm. Pecoke, Ric. Gresshame, and Symonds Low, 218*l*. 2*s*. 8½*d*.

Drapers: Chr. Campyon, John Middleton, Wm. Hewtson, Rowe, and Ph. Herderman, 27*l*. 5*s*. 0¾*d*.

Tailors:—John Malte and Scutte, 34*l*. 9*s*. 8*d*.

Embroiderers: — Gilliame, Wm. Ibgrave, and Stephen Umble, 55*l*. 1*s*. 6*d*.

John Aware, clothier, 11*l*. 11*s*. 4*d*. Lawrence Carewe, fustian maker, 28*s*. Mrs. Curtes, Mrs. Kelinge, and Mrs. Phillips, silkwomen, 7*l*. 12*s*. 10*d*. Sharpe, pinner, 21*s*. 4*d*. Thos. Fretton, groom of the wardrobe of robes, 110*s*. Robt. Everest, yeoman of the wardrobe of robes, 119*s*. 4*d*. Wm. Greene, coffer maker, 60*s*. 4*d*. Ric. Sylkokes, gold wire drawer, 38*l*. Thos. Adington, for furs, 29*l*. 19*s*. 2*d*. Thos. Hardy, hosier, 22*s*. Baptiste, dyer, 34*l*. 16*s*. 6*d*. Arnolde, shoemaker, 42*s*. 6*d*. Costs of the Maundy, 27 Hen. VIII., 31*l*. 3*s*. 9½*d*. Total, 508*l*. 5*s*. 11¾*d*.

Wardrobe of beds:

William Lok and Symson, mercers, 30*l*. 0*s*. 11½*d*. Stephen Umble, embroiderer, 26*l*. 9*s*. 4*d*. Dormer, linendraper, 6*l*. 4*s*. 8*d*. Bawen and Chapell, bed-makers, 9*l*. 14*s*. 4*d*. Rypley, joiner, 39*s*. Bayne, ironmonger, 72*s*. 8*d*. Roman, the King's farrier, and Cornelys Smyth, 6*l*. 8*s*. 2*d*. Greene, coffer-maker, 104*s*. 2*d*. Mrs. Vaughanne, silkwoman, 68*l*. 4*s*. 1½*d*. Cloth of gold, 7*l*. 20*d*. Androw, paynter, 29*s*. 4*d*. Total, 166*l*. 8*s*. 5*d*.

The stable:

Pecoke, mercer, 11*l*. 12*s*. Wm. Hewtson, draper, 14*l*. 6*s*. Gilliame and Stephen Umble, embroiderers, 20*l*. 6*s*. 4*d*. Edw. Stewerd, saddler, 21*l*. 4*s*. 10*d*. The farrier, 105*s*. 4*d*. Oats, &c. by the account of Denys Coppes, avener and clerk of the stable, ended 31 March 27 Hen. VIII., 59*l*. 6*s*. 0¾*d*. Wages of the avener and yeoman of the Queen's horses, 24*l*. 17*s*. 3*d*. Total, 156*l*. 17*s*. 9¾*d*.

Thos. Alsoppe, apothecary, 41*l*. 9*s*. 10*d*. Nic. Thorne, of Bristow, for 49 lb. of slevyd silk of Granatho, at 25*s*., delivered in accordance with a letter of her hand, dated Westminster, 14 Dec., 61*l*. 5*s*.

Total debts, 934*l*. 7*s*. 0½*d*.[2]

Notes

Part One: Ambitious and Capable Men

One: The Boleyn Origins 1420–63

1. Warnicke, Retha *The Rise and Fall of Anne Boleyn* Cambridge University Press 1989
2. Blomefeld, Francis and Parkin, Charles *An essay towards a Topographical History of the county of Norfolk.* W Miller 1807
3. Dyer, Christopher *Standards of Living in the Later Middle Ages* Cambridge University Press 1989
4. Meadows.P (ed) *A Source Book of London history from the Earliest Times to 1800*, London: G. Bell and Sons, Ltd, 1914; pp. 44-45
5. Sharpe, Reginald R *Calendar of Letter-Books from the City of London: K*, HMSO London 1911
6. Sutton, Anne F *The Mercery of London: Trade, Goods and People, 1130-1578*
7. Sharpe, Letter-Book K
8. Jefferson, Lisa *The Medieval Account Books of the Mercers of London* Routledge 2016
9. Sutton
10. Jefferson
11. Ladd, R *Antimercantilism in Late Medieval English Literature* Springer 2010
12. Sharpe, Letter-Book K
13. Gairdner, James (ed) *The Paston Letters* Chatto and Windus 1904
14. Sutton
15. https://en.wikipedia.org/wiki/List_of_Lord_Mayors_of_London
16. Jefferson
17. Ibid

18. Ibid
19. Ibid
20. Jefferson
21. Blomefeld
22. *Calendar of Patent Rolls 1461-7* HMSO, London 1897
23. Castor, Helen *Blood and Roses* Faber and Faber, 2005
24. Nichols, Nicholas Harris *Testament Vetusta* Volume I Nichols and Son, London 1826
25. Gurney, Daniel *The Record of the House of Gournay* Thew and Son, King's Lynn, 1858
26. Weir, Alison *Mary Boleyn: The Great and Infamous Whore* Jonathan Cape 2011
27. Sharpe, Reginald R *Calendar of Letter-Books from the City of London*: L, HMSO London 1912
28. Testament Vetusta Vol I
29. Sharpe, Letter-Book L

Two: From Commerce to Court 1463–1505

1. Calendar of Fine Rolls Henry VI Volume 19 1452-61 HMSO 1911
2. *Calendar of Patent Rolls* Edward IV Volume 1 1461-7 HMSO, London 1897
3. *Testament Vetusta*
4. Ibid
5. p17
6. Lyte, Maxwell H C (ed) 'Deeds: C.1901 - C.2000', in *A Descriptive Catalogue of Ancient Deeds: Volume 2*, (London, 1894), pp. 461-471.
7. *Calendar of Patent Rolls* Edward IV, Edward V, Richard III 1476-85 HMSO, London 1901
8. Ibid
9. Ibid
10. Ibid
11. Ibid
12. Gairdner, James (ed) *Letters and Papers Illustrative of the Reigns of Richard III and Henry VII*, Volume 1 Longman, Green, Longman and Roberts, London 1861
13. http://www.exclassics.com/skelton/skel061.htm
14. Gairdner, *Letters and Papers*
15. Cunningham, Sean *Prince Arthur: The Tudor King who Never Was*. Amberley 2016
16. May 1503; *Calendar of State Letters and Papers Henry VII 1485-1509* (ed G.A.Bergenroth) Longman, Green, Longman and Roberts, London 1862
17. *Testament Vetusta*

Three: Anne's world 1501–6

1. Henry VI, Edward IV twice, Edward V, Richard III
2. A consensus taken from a range of sources, see bibliography
3. Sneyd, Charlotte Augusta *A Relation, or Rather, A True Account, of the Island of England* John Bowyer Nichols and Son, London 1847
4. Ibid
5. Ibid
6. https://www.manuscripts.co.uk/stock/24353.HTM
7. http://www.christies.com/lotfinder/Lot/burghley-william-cecil-1st-baron-1521-1598-letter-5578664-details.aspx
8. https://www.the-saleroom.com/en-gb/auction-catalogues/spink/catalogue-id-srspi10091/lot-e89d2421-f6be-45c3-943a-a632011f86ea
9. Clifford, Henry *The Life of Jane Dormer, Duchess of Feria* London, Burns and Oates 1878
10. Ibid
11. Warnicke
12. Paget, Hugh "The Youth of Anne Boleyn" *Historical Research* Volume 54, Issue 130, November 1981, p162-170
13. Ives, Eric *Anne Boleyn* Blackwell, 1986
14. Sander, Nicholas and Lewis, David (ed) *Rise and Growth of the Anglican Schism* Burns and Oates, London 1877
15. Herbert, Edward, Lord Herbert of Cherbury *Life and Reign of King Henry VIII* M Clark 1683
16. Ibid
17. Fraser, Antonia *The Six Wives of Henry VIII* Weidenfeld and Nicolson, 1996
18. Ives
19. Loades, David *The Boleyns: The Rise and Fall of a Tudor Family* Amberley 2012
20. Weir *Mary Boleyn*
21. Lingard, John *A Vindication of Certain Passages in the Fourth and Fifth Volumes of the History of England.* J.Mawman, London 1826.
22. *State Letters and Papers of Henry VIII Volume 1 1509-1514* (ed. J.S.Brewer) HMSO 1920
23. Froude, James Anthony *History of England* Longmans, Green and Co 1893
24. Warnicke

Four: Change, 1501–9

1. Loades
2. Ibid
3. Various *The Land we Live in: A Pictorial and Literary Sketch Book of the British Empire.* Volume 3, Charles Knight, London 1847

4. Ibid
5. Ibid
6. Nash, Joseph *The Mansions of England in the Olden Time,* Volume II Henry Sotheran and Company 1870
7. Ibid
8. SLP Henry VIII Vol 1 f125
9. SLP Henry VIII Vol 1 101
10. Erasmus, Desiderius, *Epistles from Erasmus: From his Earliest Letters to his Fifty-First Year* (ed) Nichols, Francis Morgan, Longman, Green and Co, 1901
11. Fox, Julia *Sister Queens* Weidenfeld and Nicolson 2011
12. Hall, Edward *Hall's Chronicle of England* (ed. Grafton, Richard) J.Johnson et al, London 1809
13. SLP Henry VIII Vol 1 82
14. Shaw, William Arthur *The Knights of England: A Complete Record from the Earliest Time to the Present Day...* Volume I Genealogical Publishing Com 1971
15. SLP Henry VIII Vol 1 82
16. Hall
17. Ibid
18. Ibid
19. SLP Henry VIII Vol 1 92

Five: A Courtier's Daughter 1510–13

1. Hall
2. Ibid
3. SLP Henry VIII Vol 1 Account of the Revels
4. SLP Henry VIII Vol 1 698
5. Hall
6. Hall
7. SLP Henry VIII Vol 1 Grants 19 Feb 1511
8. Grants 26 Feb 1512
9. SLP Henry VIII Vol 1 1196
10. Grants May 1512 27
11. SLP Henry VIII Vol 1 1213
12. SLP Henry VIII Vol 1241
13. SLP Henry VIII Vol 1 1252
14. SLP Henry VIII Vol 11338
15. SLP Henry VIII Vol 1 1430
16. SLP Henry VIII Vol 1 1476
17. SLP Henry VIII Vol 1 Grants December 1512 39

Part Two: European Polish

Six: Burgundian Splendour 1513–14

1. Russell, Gareth Confessions of a Ci-Devant 6 April 2010 http://garethrussellcidevant.blogspot.co.uk/2010/04/age-of-anne-boleyn.html
2. Picker, Martin (ed) *The Chanson Albums of Marguerite of Austria* University of California Press, 1965
3. Weir, Alison *Mary Boleyn: The Great and Infamous Whore* Jonathan Cape 2011
4. Picker
5. Ibid
6. Ibid
7. Ives
8. Ives
9. Ibid
10. *Chronique métrique de Chastellain et de Molinet: avec des notices sur ces auteurs et des remarques sur le texte corrigé.* J.M.Lacrosse, Brussels 1836
11. SLP Henry VIII Vol 1 1241
12. SLP Henry VIII Vol 1 1252
13. Tremlett, Giles *Catherine of Aragon: Henry's Spanish Queen* Faber and Faber 2010
14. Ibid
15. Tremayne, Eleanor E The First Governess of the Netherlands, Margaret of Austria. Methuen 1908
16. *Chronique*
17. Tremayne
18. Ibid
19. Picker
20. Hall
21. SLP Milan 13 Sept 1522
22. Hall
23. Ibid
24. Ibid
25. Tremayne
26. Warnicke
27. SLP Henry VIII Vol 1 3147
28. SLP Henry VIII Vol 1 3171
29. Hodgkin
30. Warnicke
31. Norton, Elizabeth *Anne Boleyn: In her own Words and the Words of Those who Knew Her.* Amberley 2011
32. Sergeant, Philip W *The Life of Anne Boleyn* Hutchinson and Co, London. 1923

Seven: Among the Valois 1514–15

1. SLP Henry VIII Vol 1 3348
2. Warnicke
3. Denny, Joanna *Anne Boleyn: A New Life of England's Tragic Queen* Piatkus 2004
4. Holinshed, Raphael *Chronicles of England, Scotland and Ireland in Six Volumes* J.Johnson London 1807
5. Knecht, R.J *Francis I* Cambridge University Press 1982
6. Weir, Alison *Mary Boleyn. The Great and Infamous Whore* Jonathan Cape 2011
7. Denny
8. Weir
9. Knecht
10. Weir
11. Norton
12. Ibid
13. Ibid
14. Licence, A *The Six Wives and Many Mistresses of Henry VIII* Amberley 2014
15. Knecht
16. Hall
17. Knecht
18. Brown, Cynthia J *The Queen's Library; Image-Making at the Court of Queen Anne of Brittany 1477-1514*. University of Pennsylvania Press, 2011.
19. Durant, Will *The Reformation* Simon and Schuster, 1957

Eight: French Renaissance 1515–19

1. Brown
2. Ibid
3. Ibid
4. Ibid
5. Princess Michael of Kent, *The Serpent and the Moon: Two Rivals for the Love of a Renaissance* King Simon and Schuster 2004
6. Norton
7. Knecht
8. Ibid
9. Henry VIII SLP Vol 2 1273
10. Henry VIII SLP Vol 2 1656

Nine: An Anglo-French Woman 1519–20

1. SLP Henry VIII Vol 2 1573
2. SLP Henry VIII Vol 2 3346
3. SLP Henry VIII Vol 2 3489

 4. SLP Henry VIII Vol 2 3756
 5. SLP Henry VIII Vol 2 3783
 6. SLP Henry VIII Vol 2 4481
 7. SLP Henry VIII Vol 2 4469
 8. SLP Henry VIII Vol 2 4481
 9. SLP Henry VIII Vol 2 4491
10. SLP Henry VIII Vol 3 9
11. SLP Henry VIII Vol 3 70
12. SLP Henry VIII Vol 3 121
13. SLP Henry VIII Vol 3 125
14. SLP Henry VIII Vol 3 122
15. SLP Henry VIII Vol 3 142
16. SLP Henry VIII Vol 3 145
17. SLP Henry VIII Vol 3 161
18. SLP Henry VIII Vol 3 Book of Payments
19. SLP Henry VIII Vol 3 189
20. Ibid
21. SLP Henry VIII Vol 3 170
22. SLP Henry VIII Vol 3 289
23. SLP Henry VIII Vol 3 223
24. Ibid
25. SLP Henry VIII Vol 3 122
26. SLP Henry VIII Vol 3 447
27. SLP Henry VIII Vol 3 Preface
28. SLP Henry VIII Vol 3 629
29. SLP Henry VIII Vol 3 454
30. Ibid
31. SLP Henry VIII Vol 3 549
32. SLP Henry VIII Vol 3 468
33. SLP Henry VIII Vol 3 549
34. SLP Henry VIII Vol 3 662
35. SLP Henry VIII Vol 3 663
36. Ibid

Ten: Gold 1520–21

 1. SLP Henry VIII Vol 3 702
 2. SLP Henry VIII Vol 3 673
 3. SLP Henry VIII Vol 3 677
 4. SLP Henry VIII Vol 3 698
 5. SLP Henry VIII Vol 3 698
 6. SLP Henry VIII Vol 3 681
 7. SLP Henry VIII Vol 3 725

8. SLP Henry VIII Vol 3 702
9. SLP Henry VIII Vol 3 729
10. SLP Henry VIII Vol 3 797
11. SLP Henry VIII Vol 3 806
12. SLP Henry VIII Vol 3 808
13. SLP Henry VIII Vol 3 835
14. SLP Henry VIII Vol 3 869
15. Hall
16. SLP Henry VIII Vol 3 870
17. Ibid
18. Ibid
19. Hall
20. SLP Henry VIII Vol 3 869
21. Ibid
22. SLP Henry VIII Vol 3 870
23. SLP Henry VIII Vol 3 896
24. SLP Henry VIII Vol 3 870
25. SLP Henry VIII Vol 3 750
26. SLP Henry VIII Vol 3 870
27. SLP Henry VIII Vol 3 869
28. Ibid
29. Ibid
30. Ibid
31. Ibid
32. Hall
33. SLP Henry VIII Vol 3 870
34. Hall
35. Ibid
36. Ibid
37. Ibid
38. Ibid
39. Ibid
40. Ibid
41. SLP Henry VIII Vol 3 870
42. Ibid
43. Ibid
44. SLP Henry VIII Vol 3 1004
45. SLP Henry VIII Vol 3 1011
46. Norton
47. SLP Henry VIII Vol 3 893
48. 934
49. SLP Henry VIII Vol 3 987

50. SLP Henry VIII Vol 3 1167

51. SLP Henry VIII Vol 3 1303, 1331

52. SLP Henry VIII Vol 3 1308

53. SLP Henry VIII Vol 3 1344

54. Ibid

55. SLP Henry VIII Vol 3 1361

56. SLP Henry VIII Vol 3 1382

57. SLP Henry VIII Vol 3 1385

58. SLP Henry VIII Vol 3 1521

59. SLP Henry VIII Vol 3 1538

60. SLP Henry VIII Vol 3 1547

61. SLP Henry VIII Vol 3 1693, 1694

62. SLP Henry VIII Vol 3 1696

63. SLP Henry VIII Vol 3 1751

64. SLP Henry VIII Vol 3 1816

65. SLP Henry VIII Vol 3 1995

66. CSP Venice Vol 3 413

67. SLP Henry VIII Vol 3 1994

68. SLP Henry VIII Vol 3 2012

Part Three: 1522–6

Eleven: Perseverance 1522

1. Hall

2. Ibid

3. Ibid

4. Ibid

5. Ibid

6. Ibid

7. Ibid

8. SLP Henry VIII Vol 3 Grants in April 1522, 24, 29.

9. Starkey, David *Six Wives of Henry VIII* Vintage 2004

10. SLP Henry VIII Vol 3 2288

11. SLP Henry VIII Vol 4 463

12. Ibid

13. SLP Henry VIII Vol 4 420

14. SLP Henry VIII Vol 3 2305

15. Ibid

16. Ibid

17. Ibid

18. SLP Henry VIII Vol 4 466

19. SLP Henry VIII Vol 4 467

20. SLP Henry VIII Vol 4 479
21. CSP Spain Vol 2 463
22. Ibid
23. Hall
24. SLP Henry VIII Vol 4 507
25. Ibid

Twelve: First Love 1522–4

1. Ives
2. Cavendish
3. Ibid
4. Ibid
5. Ibid
6. Ibid
7. Ibid
8. SLP Henry VIII Vol 3 2481
9. SLP Henry VIII Vol 3 2567
10. SLP Henry VIII Vol 3 2750
11. SLP Henry VIII Vol 3 2764
12. SLP Henry VIII Vol 3 2773
13. SLP Henry VIII Vol 3 2878
14. SLP Henry VIII Vol 3 2908
15. SLP Henry VIII Vol 3 3153
16. SLP Henry VIII Vol 3 3376
17. Cavendish
18. Ibid
19. Ibid
20. Norton
21. Cavendish
22. Ibid
23. Ibid
24. Ibid
25. Ibid
26. Ibid
27. Ibid
28. SLP Henry VIII Vol 3 3937
29. Ibid
30. Norton

Thirteen: Hever 1524–25

1. SLP Henry VIII Vol 3 3504
2. SLP Henry VIII Vol 4 Grants in July 1524

3. SLP Henry VIII Vol 4 Grants in November 1524
4. SLP Henry VIII Vol 4 Grants in April 1525
5. Hall
6. Weir
7. Cavendish
8. SLP Henry VIII Vol 4 1198
9. DNB
10. SLP Henry VIII Vol 4 1266
11. SLP Henry VIII Vol 4 1305
12. Ibid
13. SLP Henry VIII Vol 4 1266
14. SLP Henry VIII Vol 4 1600
15. Ibid
16. SLP Henry VIII Vol 4 1431
17. Ibid
18. Ridgway, Claire and Cherry, Clare *George Boleyn* MadeGlobal 2014
19. SLP Henry VIII Vol 4 Eltham Ordinances
20. Ibid
21. Hall

Fourteen: Return to Court 1526

1. Norton
2. Ibid
3. Ibid
4. Ibid
5. Grueninger, Natalie and Morris, Sarah *In the Footsteps of Anne Boleyn* Amberley 2013
6. Norton
7. Ives
8. Shulman, Nicola *Graven with Diamonds: The Many Lives of Thomas Wyatt* Short Books 2012
9. Cavendish
10. Norton
11. Ibid
12. Ibid
13. Norton
14. Hall

Fifteen: The King's Secret 1527

1. Hall
2. SLP Henry VIII Vol 4 2773
3. SLP Henry VIII Vol 4 3104

4. Ibid
5. Ibid
6. Ibid
7. Denny
8. CSP Venice Vol 4 105
9. Ibid
10. Ibid
11. SLP Henry VIII Vol 4 3564
12. SLP Henry VIII Vol 3124
13. CSP Venice Vol 4 112
14. Hall
15. SLP Henry VIII Vol 4 3253
16. SLP Henry VIII Vol 4 3267
17. SLP Henry VIII Vol 4 3251
18. Ibid
19. Ibid
20. SLP Henry VIII Vol 4 3311
21. Ibid
22. SLP Henry VIII Vol 4 3312
23. SLP Henry VIII Vol 4 3611
24. Ibid
25. SLP Henry VIII Vol 4 3313
26. SLP Henry VIII Vol 4 3644
27. Ibid

Part Four: Anne's Ascendancy

Sixteen: Love Letters 1527

1. Weir
2. Luce
3. Ibid
4. Norton
5. Luce
6. Ibid
7. Ibid
8. Ibid
9. SLP Henry VIII Vol 4 3360
10. SLP Henry VIII Vol 4 3318

Seventeen: Turning Point 1527–8

1. Cavendish
2. SLP Henry VIII Vol 4 3509

3. SLP Henry VIII Vol 4 3619
4. SLP Henry VIII Vol 4 3564
5. SLP Henry VIII Vol 4 3575
6. SLP Henry VIII Vol 4 3638
7. SLP Henry VIII Vol 4 3643
8. SLP Henry VIII Vol 4 3694
9. SLP Henry VIII Vol 4 3644
10. Ibid
11. SLP Henry VIII Vol 4 3693
12. SLP Henry VIII Vol 4 3715
13. Ibid
14. Cavendish
15. Luce
16. SLP Henry VIII Vol 4 3686
17. Hall
18. Ibid
19. Ibid
20. SLP Henry VIII Vol 4 2857
21. Durant
22. Ibid
23. SLP Henry VIII Vol 4 3132
24. Hall
25. SLP Henry VIII Vol 4 4106
26. Doernberg, Edwin Henry VIII and Luther: An Account of their Personal Relations Stanford University Press, 1961
27. Ibid
28. Ibid
29. Ibid
30. Rex, Richard *Henry VIII and the English Reformation* Palgrave Macmillan 2006
31. Doernberg.

Eighteen: Anne and Wolsey 1528

1. SLP Henry VIII Vol 4 3913
2. Ibid
3. Ibid
4. Ibid
5. SLP Henry VIII Vol 4 4005
6. Ibid
7. SLP Henry VIII Vol 4 4081
8. Ibid
9. SLP Henry VIII Vol 4 4251

10. Ibid
11. Ibid
12. Ibid
13. SLP Henry VIII Vol 4 4360
14. SLP Henry VIII Vol 4 4391
15. Ibid
16. Ibid
17. Luce
18. SLP Henry VIII Vol 4 4409
19. Ibid
20. Luce
21. Ibid
22. SLP Henry VIII Vol 4 4409
23. SLP Henry VIII Vol 4 4428
24. SLP Henry VIII Vol 4 4429
25. SLP Henry VIII Vol 4 4439
26. SLP Henry VIII Vol 4 4440
27. Ibid
28. SLP Henry VIII Vol 5 Miscellaneous 1531
29. Luce
30. SLP Henry VIII Vol 4 4542
31. SLP Henry VIII Vol 4 4197
32. Luce

Nineteen: The Ideal Woman 1528

1. Castiglione, B *Book of the Courtier* 1528
2. Ibid
3. Ibid
4. Ibid
5. Ibid
6. Ibid
7. Ibid
8. SLP Henry VIII Vol 4 Appendix 2 256
9. SLP Henry VIII Vol 4 4267
10. Luce
11. Ibid
12. SLP Henry VIII Vol 4 4538
13. SLP Henry VIII Vol 4 Grants in November 1528 15, SLP Henry VIII Vol 4 5248
14. Watson, Foster (ed) *Tudor School-Boy Life: The Dialogues of Juan Luis Vives* J.M.Dent, London 1908
15. Luce

16. Luce
17. SLP Henry VIII Vol 4 4649

Twenty: Anne the Heretic, 1528–9

1. SLP Henry VIII Vol 4 3438
2. SLP Henry VIII Vol 4 4038
3. SLP Henry VIII Vol 4 4175
4. Ibid
5. Ibid
6. Ibid
7. SLP Henry VIII Vol 4 4218
8. Ibid
9. Ibid
10. SLP Henry VIII Vol 4 4260
11. SLP Henry VIII Vol 4 4282
12. Ibid
13. SLP Henry VIII Vol 4 5416
14. Ibid
15. Warnicke
16. Nichols
17. SLP Henry VIII Vol 4 3345
18. SLP Henry VIII Vol 4, Appendix 2 147
19. Ibid
20. Warnicke
21. SLP Henry VIII Vol 4 5607

Part Five: The King's Great Matter

Twenty-One: Campeggio and the Legatine Court 1529

1. SLP Henry VIII Vol 4 4535
2. Ibid
3. SLP Henry VIII Vol 4 4656
4. SLP Henry VIII Vol 4 4789
5. Luce
6. SLP Henry VIII Vol 4 4795
7. SLP Henry VIII Vol 4 Appendix 2 206
8. Luce
9. Grueninger
10. SLP Henry VIII Vol 4 5014
11. SLP Henry VIII Vol 4 5038
12. SLP Henry VIII Vol 4 4897
13. SLP Henry VIII Vol 4 5016

14. SLP Henry VIII Vol 4 4779
15. SLP Henry VIII Vol 4 4779
16. Norton
17. Ibid
18. Kelly, H A *The Matrimonial Trials of Henry VIII* Wipf and Stock 2004
19. SLP Henry VIII Vol 4 5657
20. Hall
21. Ibid
22. Norton
23. Ibid
24. Ibid
25. SLP Henry VIII Vol 4 5702
26. Ibid
27. SLP Henry VIII Vol 4 5255
28. SLP Henry VIII Vol 4 5815
29. SLP Henry VIII Vol 4 5906

Twenty-Two: Wolsey's Fall 1529

1. Norton
2. Lysons, Daniel *The Environs of London, Volume 2: Middlesex.* T Cadell and W Davies, London 1795
3. SLP Henry VIII Vol 4 5869
4. SLP Henry VIII Vol 4 5875
5. SLP Henry VIII Vol 4 5864
6. SLP Henry VIII Vol 4 5925
7. Norton
8. Ibid
9. Ibid
10. Ibid
11. Ibid
12. SLP Henry VIII Vol 4 5965
13. SLP Henry VIII Vol 4 5966
14. SLP Henry VIII Vol 4 6011
15. SLP Henry VIII Vol 4 6019
16. SLP Henry VIII Vol 4 6025
17. SLP Henry VIII Vol 4 6026
18. Ibid
19. Ibid
20. Nichols, Nicholas Harris *The Privy Purse Expenses of King Henry VIII 1529-1532* W.Pickering 1827
21. Ibid
22. CSP Spain 1529 Nov 30

23. Ibid
24. SLP Henry VIII Vol 4 6075
25. Ibid
26. SLP Henry VIII Vol 4 6076
27. SLP Henry VIII Vol 4 6151
28. Ibid
29. Ibid
30. SLP Henry VIII Vol 4 6199
31. SLP Henry VIII Vol 4 5996
32. SLP Henry VIII Vol 4 6073
33. SLP Henry VIII Vol 4 6083
34. CSP Spain Volume 4 232
35. SLP Henry VIII Vol 4 6115
36. SLP Henry VIII Vol 4 6163
37. SLP Henry VIII Vol 4 6111
38. SLP Henry VIII Vol 4 6142
39. SLP Henry VIII Vol 4 6290
40. SLP Henry VIII Vol 4 6307
41. SLP Henry VIII Vol 4 6355
42. SLP Henry VIII Vol 4 6393
43. SLP Henry VIII Vol 4 6090

Twenty-Three: Days Spent waiting 1530

1. SLP Henry VIII Vol 4 6285
2. SLP Henry VIII Vol 4 6279
3. SLP Henry VIII Vol 4 6393
4. SLP Henry VIII Vol 4 6513
5. SLP Henry VIII Vol 4 6320
6. Nichols, Privy Purse
7. Ibid
8. Ibid
9. Ibid
10. Ibid
11. Ibid
12. SLP Henry VIII Vol 4 6411
13. Nichols
14. CSP Spain Volume 4 354
15. Ibid
16. Nichols
17. Ibid
18. Ibid
19. Ibid

20. SLP Henry VIII Vol 4 6516
21. SLP Henry VIII Vol 4 6554
22. SLP Henry VIII Vol 4 6574
23. SLP Henry VIII Vol 4 6459
24. SLP Henry VIII Vol 4 6461
25. SLP Henry VIII Vol 4 6491
26. SLP Henry VIII Vol 4 6550
27. SLP Henry VIII Vol 4 6505
28. SLP Henry VIII Vol 4 6518
29. Nichols
30. Ibid
31. Ibid
32. Ibid
33. Ibid
34. SLP Henry VIII Vol 4 6627
35. Nichol
36. SLP Henry VIII Vol 4 6738
37. Ibid
38. Ibid
39. Norton
40. SLP Henry VIII Vol 4 6738
41. Ibid
42. CSP Spain Volume 4 509
43. Vergil, Polydore *Anglia Historia* 1555
44. CSP Spain Volume4 257
45. Guth, J.Delloyd and McKenna, John W. *Tudor Rule and Revolution: Essays for G.R.Elton and his American Friends.* Cambridge University Press, 2008
46. *CSP Spain* Volume 4, Part 1, 522
47. *CSP Spain* Vol 4, 1, 525
48. *CSP Spain,* Vol 4, 1 584
49. *CSP Spain* 4, 2, 584a

Twenty-Four: Stalemate 1531

1. SLP Henry VIII Vol 4 6772
2. Nichols, Privy Purse
3. Hall
4. SLP Henry VIII Vol 5 24
5. Ibid
6. SLP Henry VIII Vol 5 27
7. SLP Henry VIII Vol 5 31
8. SLP Henry VIII Vol 5 30
9. SLP Henry VIII Vol 5 45

10. Ibid
11. Ibid
12. SLP Henry VIII Vol 5 61
13. SLP Henry VIII Vol 5 64
14. Ibid
15. Ibid
16. SLP Henry VIII Vol 5 70
17. Ibid
18. SLP Henry VIII Vol 5 112
19. Ibid
20. SLP Henry VIII Vol 5 120
21. SLP Henry VIII Vol 5 1531 Miscellaneous
22. Ibid
23. SLP Henry VIII Vol 5 6183
24. Guth
25. SLP Henry VIII Vol 5 171
26. Ibid
27. SLP Henry VIII Vol 5 176
28. Hall
29. Nichols, Privy Purse
30. Ibid
31. Ibid
32. Ibid
33. Ibid
34. Ibid
35. SLP Henry VIII Vol 5 682
36. Nichols
37. Ibid
38. SLP Venice Vol 4 682
39. Nichols
40. SLP Venice Vol 4 694
41. Ibid
42. CSP Venice Vol 4 701
43. Ibid
44. Hall
45. SLP Henry VIII Vol 5 628

Twenty-Five: Life with Henry 1531–2

1. SLP Venice Vol 4 694
2. Ibid
3. Nichols

4. SLP Henry VIII Vol 5 682
5. Ibid
6. Ibid
7. Leland, John *Antiquarii de Rebus Collectanea* Thomas Hearne 1776
8. Nichols
9. Ibid
10. Ibid
11. Ibid
12. Leland
13. Nichols
14. SLP Henry VIII Vol 5 375
15. XXXX
16. SLP Venice 682
17. Nichols
18. Ibid
19. Hall
20. SLP Henry VIII Vol 5 Grants in October 1531
21. Nichols
22. Ibid
23. SLP Henry VIII Vol 5 488
24. Nichols
25. SLP Henry VIII Vol 5 531
26. Nichols
27. Hall
28. SLP Henry VIII Vol 5 563
29. SLP Henry VIII Vol 5 695
30. Ibid
31. SLP Henry VIII Vol 5 746
32. Nichols
33. Ibid
34. Ibid
35. Ibid
36. SLP Henry VIII Vol 5 216
37. Ibid
38. Friedmann, P *Anne Boleyn* Amberley 2010
39. Froude, James Anthony *History of England* Longmans, Green and Co 1893
40. Nichols
41. Ibid
42. SLP Henry VIII Vol 5 216
43. SLP Henry VIII Vol 5 1313
44. Nichols

45. Ibid
46. SLP Henry VIII Vol 5 Grants in June 1532
47. SLP Henry VIII Vol 5 1165
48. SLP Henry VIII Vol 5 1202
49. Ibid
50. SLP Henry VIII Vol 5 Grants in July 1532

Part Six: Anne Triumphant

Twenty-Six: The Return to France 1532

1. SLP Henry VIII Vol 5 1127
2. Ibid
3. SLP Henry VIII Vol 5 1187
4. Ibid
5. SLP Henry VIII Vol 5 1232
6. SLP Henry VIII Vol 5 1239
7. SLP Henry VIII Vol 5 1335
8. SLP Henry VIII Vol 5 1376
9. SLP Henry VIII Vol 5 1256
10. SLP Henry VIII Vol 5 1274
11. Ibid
12. SLP Henry VIII Vol 5 1292
13. SLP Henry VIII Vol 5 1316
14. SLP Henry VIII Vol 5 1377
15. Norton
16. Hall
17. Nichol
18. Norton
19. Hall
20. Ibid
21. Ibid
22. Nichols
23. Hall
24. Norton
25. Hall
26. Nichols
27. Ibid
28. Ibid
29. Ibid
30. SLP Henry VIII Vol 5 1685
31. Ibid
32. SLP Henry VIII Vol 5 1449

Twenty-Seven: Queen at Last 1533

1. CSP Spain Vol 4 Part 2 1047
2. Ibid 1048
3. Ibid 1053
4. Ibid 1055
5. Ibid
6. Ibid
7. Ibid 1057
8. Ibid 1058
9. Ibid
10. Ibid
11. Ibid
12. Ibid 1077
13. Ibid 1062
14. Ibid
15. Ibid
16. SLP Henry VIII Vol 5 878
17. CSP Venice 870
18. Ibid 872
19. Ibid 873
20. Ibid 886
21. Ibid
22. SLP Henry VIII Volume 6 525
23. CSP Venice 889
24. Hall
25. SLP Henry VIII Volume 6 563
26. Hall
27. SLP Henry VIII Volume 6 601
28. SLP Henry VIII Volume 6 563
29. SLP Henry VIII Volume 6 601
30. Ibid
31. Ibid
32. SLP Henry VIII Volume 6 912
33. Ibid
34. SLP Henry VIII Volume 6 561
35. Ibid
36. SLP Henry VIII Volume 6 601
37. Herbert, W *History of the Worshipful Company of Ironmongers of London* J and C Adlard, 1837
38. Hunt, Alice *The Drama of Coronation: Medieval Ceremony in Early Modern England* Cambridge University Press 2008
39. Ibid

40. Ibid
41. Hunt, Hall
42. Hall
43. Ibid
44. Ibid
45. SLP Henry VIII Volume 6 653
46. SLP Henry VIII Volume 6 585
47. Ibid
48. SLP Henry VIII Volume 6 613, 631
49. SLP Henry VIII Volume 6 582
50. Ibid
51. Hall
52. SLP Henry VIII Volume 6 912
53. SLP Henry VIII Volume 6 601
54. SLP Henry VIII Volume 6 582
55. SLP Henry VIII Volume 6 634
56. SLP Henry VIII Volume 6 657

Twenty-Eight: Elizabeth 1533

1. SLP Henry VIII Volume 6 613
2. Ibid
3. SLP Henry VIII Volume 6 692
4. SLP Henry VIII Volume 6 602
5. SLP Henry VIII Volume 6 1446
6. Warnicke
7. Ives
8. SLP Henry VIII Volume 6 670
9. Ives
10. SLP Henry VIII Volume 6 720
11. SLP Henry VIII Volume 6 733
12. SLP Henry VIII Volume 6 923
13. Ibid
14. SLP Henry VIII Volume 6 760
15. SLP Henry VIII Volume 6 805
16. SLP Henry VIII Volume 6 879
17. SLP Henry VIII Volume 6 918
18. SLP Henry VIII Volume 6 807
19. SLP Henry VIII Volume 6 918
20. SLP Henry VIII Volume 6 941
21. SLP Henry VIII Volume 6 953
22. SLP Henry VIII Volume 6 1018

23. SLP Henry VIII Volume 6 738
24. SLP Henry VIII Volume 6 1047
25. SLP Henry VIII Volume 6 998
26. Denny
27. SLP Henry VIII Volume 6 1069
28. SLP Henry VIII Volume 6 1070
29. SLP Henry VIII Volume 6 1054
30. CSP Spain Vol 4 Part 2 1117
31. SLP Henry VIII Volume 6 1069
32. SLP Henry VIII Volume 6 1528
33. SLP Henry VIII Volume 6 1112
34. SLP Henry VIII Volume 6 1111 SLP Henry VIII Volume 6

Twenty-Nine: Disappointment 1534

1. SLP Henry VIII Volume 6 1392
2. SLP Henry VIII Volume 7 3
3. Ibid
4. SLP Henry VIII Volume 7 121
5. SLP Henry VIII Volume 7 171
6. SLP Henry VIII Volume 7 214
7. Porter, Linda *Mary Tudor: The First Queen* Portrait 2007
8. Hall
9. SLP Henry VIII Volume 7 24
10. SLP Henry VIII Volume 7 9
11. SLP Henry VIII Volume 7 21
12. SLP Henry VIII Volume 7 96
13. SLP Henry VIII Volume 6 1445
14. SLP Henry VIII Volume 7 114
15. SLP Henry VIII Volume 7 126
16. SLP Henry VIII Volume 7 232
17. SLP Henry VIII Volume 7 25
18. SLP Henry VIII Volume 6 1466
19. SLP Henry VIII Volume 6 1468
20. SLP Henry VIII Volume 6 1599
21. SLP Henry VIII Volume 7 171
22. Ibid
23. Bindoff, S.T *Tudor England* Penguin 1950
24. SLP Henry VIII Volume 7 296
25. Ibid
26. Ibid
27. SLP Henry VIII Volume 7 373

28. SLP Henry VIII Volume 7 690
29. Tanner, J.R *Tudor Constitutional Documents* Cambridge University Press, 1922
30. Ibid
31. Ibid
32. SLP Henry VIII Volume 7 386
33. SLP Henry VIII Volume 7 424
34. SLP Henry VIII Volume 7 469
35. SLP Henry VIII Volume 7 780
36. SLP Henry VIII Volume 6 1668
37. *https://lucychurchill.wordpress.com/2012/05/14/the-moost-happi-portrait-of-anne-boleyn-a-rec/*
38. SLP Henry VIII Volume 7 559
39. SLP Henry VIII Volume 7 530
40. SLP Henry VIII Volume 7 556
41. SLP Henry VIII Volume 7 555
42. SLP Henry VIII Volume 7 613
43. SLP Henry VIII Volume 7 654
44. SLP Henry VIII Volume 7 664
45. SLP Henry VIII Volume 7 682
46. SLP Henry VIII Volume 7 823
47. SLP Henry VIII Volume 7 840
48. SLP Henry VIII Volume 7 871
49. SLP Henry VIII Volume 7 958
50. 1081
51. 964
52. 989
53. 1013
54. 1193
55. Norton
56. SLP Henry VIII Volume 7 1174
57. SLP Henry VIII Volume 7 1257
58. Ibid

Thirty: Marriage as Battle 1534–5

1. SLP Henry VIII Volume 7 1193
2. SLP Henry VIII Volume 7 1554
3. SLP Henry VIII Volume 7 1655
4. SLP Henry VIII Volume 7 1427
5. SLP Henry VIII Volume 7 1482
6. SLP Henry VIII Volume 7 1369
7. SLP Henry VIII Volume 7 1279
8. SLP Henry VIII Volume 7 1297

9. SLP Henry VIII Volume 7 1554
10. SLP Henry VIII Volume 7 1348
11. SLP Henry VIII Volume 7 1498
12. SLP Henry VIII Volume 7 Grants in November 1534 40
13. SLP Henry VIII Volume 7 Grants in November 3
14. SLP Henry VIII Volume 7 529
15. SLP Henry VIII Volume 7 1581
16. SLP Henry VIII Volume 8 46
17. SLP Henry VIII Volume 7 48
18. SLP Henry VIII Volume 8 1
19. SLP Henry VIII Volume 7 924

Part Seven: Thunder around the Throne

Thirty-One: Change and Continuity, January–June 1535

1. SLP Henry VIII Volume 8 121
2. SLP Henry VIII Volume 8 590
3. SLP Henry VIII Volume 8 921
4. SLP Henry VIII Volume 8 1024
5. SLP Henry VIII Volume 8 945
6. SLP Henry VIII Volume 8 76
7. Ibid
8. SLP Henry VIII Volume 8 565
9. SLP Henry VIII Volume 8 666
10. Ibid
11. Ibid
12. SLP Henry VIII Volume 8 Grants in April 1535
13. SLP Henry VIII Volume 8 1116
14. SLP Henry VIII Volume 8 1117
15. SLP Henry VIII Volume 8 838
16. SLP Henry VIII Volume 9 196
17. Cressy, David *Dangerous Talk: Scandalous, Seditious and Treasonable Speech in Pre-Modern England* Oxford University Press 2010
18. Hall
19. Cressy
20. SLP Henry VIII Volume 9 209
21. SLP Henry VIII Volume 9 174
22. Ibid
23. SLP Henry VIII Volume 9 263
24. SLP Henry VIII Volume 9 358
25. SLP Henry VIII Volume 9 209
26. SLP Henry VIII Volume 9 431

27. SLP Henry VIII Volume 9 516
28. SLP Henry VIII Volume 9 750
29. SLP Henry VIII Volume 9 826

Thirty-Two: Being Merry, June-September 1535

1. SLP Henry VIII Volume 9 882
2. SLP Henry VIII Volume 9 928
3. SLP Henry VIII Volume 9 310
4. SLP Henry VIII Volume 8 937
5. SLP Henry VIII Volume 8 826
6. SLP Henry VIII Volume 9 340
7. SLP Henry VIII Volume 8 909
8. Ibid
9. SLP Henry VIII Volume 8 985
10. SLP Henry VIII Volume 8 1031
11. SLP Henry VIII Volume 8 1034
12. SLP Henry VIII Volume 8 824
13. SLP Henry VIII Volume 9 156
14. SLP Henry VIII Volume 8 1956
15. SLP Henry VIII Volume 8 1062
16. Page, William (ed) Victoria County History, Gloucestershire, Volume 2, London 1907
17. Ibid
18. SLP Henry VIII Volume 9 42
19. SLP Henry VIII Volume 9 136
20. CSP Spain Vol 5 Part 1, 184
21. SLP Henry VIII Volume 9 182
22. SLP Henry VIII Volume 9 405
23. SLP Henry VIII Volume 9 207
24. SLP Henry VIII Volume 9 310
25. SLP Henry VIII Volume 9 378

Thirty-Three: Progress and Reform, September – December 1535

1. SLP Henry VIII Volume 9 358
2. SLP Henry VIII Volume 9 450
3. SLP Henry VIII Volume 9 443
4. SLP Henry VIII Volume 9 402
5. SLP Henry VIII Volume 9 477
6. SLP Henry VIII Volume 9 434
7. SLP Henry VIII Volume 9 438
8. SLP Henry VIII Volume 9 444

9. SLP Henry VIII Volume 9 472
10. SLP Henry VIII Volume 9 525
11. SLP Henry VIII Volume 9 467
12. SLP Henry VIII Volume 9 525
13. SLP Henry VIII Volume 9 533
14. SLP Henry VIII Volume 9 534
15. SLP Henry VIII Volume 9 633
16. SLP Henry VIII Volume 9 555
17. SLP Henry VIII Volume 9 571
18. SLP Henry VIII Volume 9 566
19. Weir, *Lady in the Tower*
20. SLP Henry VIII Volume 9 568
21. SLP Henry VIII Volume 9 663
22. SLP Henry VIII Volume 9 639
23. SLP Henry VIII Volume 9 632
24. SLP Henry VIII Volume 9 668
25. SLP Henry VIII Volume 9 669
26. SLP Henry VIII Volume 9 681
27. Ibid
28. Ibid
29. SLP Henry VIII Volume 9 862
30. 873

Thirty-Four: The Last Spring, January–April 1536

1. SLP Henry VIII Volume 10 141
2. SLP Henry VIII Volume 10 141
3. SLP Henry VIII Volume 10 308
4. SLP Henry VIII Volume 10 199
5. Ibid
6. SLP Henry VIII Volume 10 282
7. SLP Henry VIII Volume 10 427
8. SLP Henry VIII Volume 10 294
9. SLP Henry VIII Volume 10 352
10. SLP Henry VIII Volume 10 351
11. SLP Henry VIII Volume 10 185, 186
12. SLP Henry VIII Volume 10 345
13. SLP Henry VIII Volume 10 495
14. SLP Henry VIII Volume 10 Grants in April 3, 27
15. SLP Henry VIII Volume 10 601
16. Ibid
17. SLP Henry VIII Volume 10 346

18. SLP Henry VIII Volume 10 615
19. Bernard, G.W Anne Boleyn's Religion "The Historical Journal" Cambridge University Press Vol 36 No 1, 1993 p1-20
20. Weir
21. SLP Henry VIII Volume 9 858
22. Bernard
23. Ibid
24. Weir

Thirty-Five: The Net Closes, April-May 1536

1. CSP Spain Volume 5 Part 2 43a
2. Ibid
3. SLP Henry VIII Volume 10 699
4. CSP Spain Volume 5 Part 2 43a
5. SLP Henry VIII Volume 10 699
6. SLP Henry VIII Volume 10 675
7. Norton
8. SLP Henry VIII Volume 10 715
9. SLP Henry VIII Volume 10 752
10. CSP Spain Volume 5 Part 2 47
11. SLP Henry VIII Volume 10 748
12. SLP Henry VIII Volume 10 Grants in April 6, 14
13. CSP Foreign Elizabeth Volume 1 1303
14. Ives, Eric *The Fall of Anne Boleyn Reconsidered* "The English Historical Review" Vol 107, No 427, July 1992 p651-664
15. Ibid
16. Ibid
17. Hall
18. Ibid
19. Burnet, Gilbert *The History of the Reformation of the Church of England*, Clarendon Press, Oxford, 1816
20. Norton
21. Ibid
22. Bernard, G.W Anne Boleyn's Religion "The Historical Journal" Cambridge University Press Vol 36 No 1, 1993 p1-20 793
23. Norton
24. SLP Henry VIII Volume 10 792
25. SLP Henry VIII Volume 10 782
26. Ibid
27. SLP Henry VIII Volume 10 784
28. SLP Henry VIII Volume 10 791
29. SLP Henry VIII Volume 10 794

Thirty-Six: Bloody Days, May 1536

1. SLP Henry VIII Volume 10 797
2. SLP Henry VIII Volume 10 793
3. SLP Henry VIII Volume 10 798
4. SLP Henry VIII Volume 10 797
5. Ibid
6. Ibid
7. SLP Henry VIII Volume 10 793
8. SLP Henry VIII Volume 10 798
9. SLP Henry VIII Volume 10 799
10. Norton
11. SLP Henry VIII Volume 10 891
12. Norton
13. SLP Henry VIII Volume 10 840
14. SLP Henry VIII Volume 10 876, Turner
15. SLP Henry VIII Volume 10 876
16. Ibid
17. SLP Henry VIII Volume 10 1445
18. Ives, Eric 'The Fall of Anne Boleyn Reconsidered' *The English Historical Review* Vol 107, No 427, July 1992 p651-664
19. SLP Henry VIII Volume 10 684
20. SLP Henry VIII Volume 10 710
21. SLP Henry VIII Volume 10 855
22. SLP Henry VIII Volume 10 865
23. SLP Henry VIII Volume 10 908
24. Ibid
25. SLP Henry VIII Volume 10 866
26. SLP Henry VIII Volume 10 873
27. SLP Henry VIII Volume 10 908
28. Norton
29. Ibid
30. Ibid
31. Ibid
32. SLP Henry VIII Volume 10 908
33. SLP Henry VIII Volume 12 Part 2 74,75
34. Norton
35. Ibid
36. SLP Henry VIII Volume 10 908
37. Ibid
38. Norton
39. Ibid
40. Ibid

41. SLP Henry VIII Volume 10 908

42. SLP Henry VIII Volume 10 890

43. SLP Henry VIII Volume 10 908

44. Norton

45. SLP Henry VIII Volume 10 908

46. SLP Henry VIII Volume 10 910

47. Norton

48. Ibid

49. Ibid

50. SLP Henry VIII Volume 10 908

51. Ibid

52. SLP Henry VIII Volume 10 920

53. SLP Henry VIII Volume 10 965

54. SLP Henry VIII Volume 10 970

55. SLP Henry VIII Volume 10 990

56. The Dun Cow was associated with the house of Warwick.

57. Norton

58. SLP Henry VIII Volume 10 915

59. SLP Henry VIII Volume 10 926

60. 926

61. SLP Henry VIII Volume 10 908

62. SLP Henry VIII Volume 10 993

63. Warnicke

64. Weir

65. Ives

Appendix: Anne's Bills and Debts.

1. SLP Henry VIII Volume 10 913

2. SLP Henry VIII Volume 10 914

Bibliography

The Love Letters of Henry VIII and Anne Boleyn John W. Luce and Company, Updike, The MerryMount Press, Boston 1906

Benson, Pamela Joseph *Invention of the Renaissance Woman* Penn State Press 2010

Bernard, G.W. *Anne Boleyn: Fatal Attractions.* Yale University Press, 2010

Bindoff, S.T. *Tudor England* Penguin 1950

Blomefeld, Francis and Parkin, Charles *An essay towards a Topographical History of the county of Norfolk* W. Miller 1807

Brown, Cynthia J. *The Queen's Library; Image-Making at the Court of Queen Anne of Brittany 1477-1514* University of Pennsylvania Press, 2011.

Bruce, Marie Louise *Anne Boleyn* William Collins 1972

Calendar of Fine Rolls Henry VI Volume 19 1452-61 HMSO 1911

Calendar of Patent Rolls Edward IV 1461-7 HMSO London 1897

Calendar of Patent Rolls Edward IV, Edward V, Richard III 1476-85 HMSO London 1901

Calendar of State Letters and Papers Henry VII 1485-1509 (ed G.A.Bergenroth) Longman, Green, Longman and Roberts, London 1862

Calendar of State Papers Spain Volumes 1–5 Bergenroth, G.A, Mattingly, Garrett, Gayangos, Pascual de, 1865/1947

Calendar of State Papers Venice Volumes 1 and 2 Rawdon Brown, London 1864

Castor, Helen *Blood and Roses* Faber and Faber, 2005

Cavendish, George *The Life and Death of Cardinal Wolsey* Houghton, Mifflin and Co 1905

Chapman, Lissa *Anne Boleyn in London* Pen and Sword 2017

Chronique métrique de Chastellain et de Molinet: avec des notices sur ces auteurs et des remarques sur le texte corrigé J. M. Lacrosse, Brussels 1836

Clifford, Henry *The Life of Jane Dormer, Duchess of Feria* London, Burns and Oates 1878

Cunningham, Sean *Prince Arthur: The Tudor King who Never Was* Amberley 2016

Denny, Joanna *Anne Boleyn: A New Life of England's Tragic Queen* Piatkus 2004

Dixon, William Hepworth *History of Two Queens, Catherine of Aragon and Anne Boleyn*, Volume II. B Tauchnitz 1873

Doernberg, Edwin *Henry VIII and Luther: An Account of their Personal Relations* Stanford University Press 1961

Durant, Will *The Reformation* Simon and Schuster 1957

Dyer, Christopher *Standards of Living in the Later Middle Ages* Cambridge University Press 1989

Erasmus, Desiderius *Epistles from Erasmus: From his Earliest Letters to his Fifty-First Year* (ed) Nichols, Francis Morgan, Longman, Green and Co 1901

Erickson, Carolly *Great Harry: The Extravagant Life of Henry VIII* Robson Books 1998

Fox, Julia *Sister Queens* Weidenfeld and Nicolson 2011

Fraser, Antonia *The Six Wives of Henry VIII* Weidenfeld and Nicolson, 1996

Friedmann, P *Anne Boleyn* Amberley 2010

Froude, James Anthony *History of England* Longmans, Green and Co 1893

Gairdner, James (ed) *Letters and Papers Illustrative of the Reigns of Richard III and Henry VII,* Volume 1 Longman, Green, Longman and Roberts, London 1861

Gairdner, James (ed) *The Paston Letters* Chatto and Windus 1904

Grueninger, Natalie and Morris, Sarah *In the Footsteps of Anne Boleyn* Amberley 2013

Gunn, Stephen, Grummit, David and Cools, Hans *War, State and Society in England and the Netherlands 1477–1559* Oxford University Press, 2007

Gurney, Daniel *The Record of the House of Gournay* Thew and Son, King's Lynn 1858

Hall, Edward *Hall's Chronicle of England* (ed. Grafton, Richard) J.Johnson et al, London 1809

Harpsfield, Nicholas *A Treatise on the Pretended Divorce between Henry VIII and Catherine of Aragon* Camden 1878

Herbert, Edward, Lord Herbert of Cherbury *Life and Reign of King Henry VIII* M. Clark 1683

The Manuscripts of J. Eliot Hodgkin, Fifteenth Report, Appendix, Part II

Holinshed, Raphael *Chronicles of England, Scotland and Ireland in Six Volumes* J. Johnson London 1807

Ives, Eric *Anne Boleyn* Blackwell 1986

Jefferson, Lisa *The Medieval Account Books of the Mercers of London* Routledge 2016

Kelly, H. A. *The Matrimonial Trials of Henry VIII* Wipf and Stock 2004

Kent, Princess Michael of *The Serpent and the Moon: Two Rivals for the Love of a Renaissance King* Simon and Schuster 2004

Knecht, R. J. *Francis I* Cambridge University Press 1982

Ladd, R. *Antimercantilism in Late Medieval English Literature* Springer 2010

Leland, John *Antiquarii de Rebus Collectanea* Thomas Hearne 1776

Lingard, John *A History of England* O'Shea 1800

Lingard, John *A Vindication of Certain Passages in the Fourth and Fifth Volumes of the History of England* J. Mawman, London 1826.

Loades, David *The Boleyns: The Rise and Fall of a Tudor Family* Amberley 2012

Lyte, Maxwell H C (ed) 'Deeds: C.1901–C.2000', in *A Descriptive Catalogue of Ancient Deeds: Volume 2*, (London, 1894) pp. 461-471

Mattingly, Garrett *Catherine of Aragon* Jonathan Cape 1942

Matusiak, John *Henry VIII: The Life and Rule of England's Nero* The History Press 2013

Meadows, P. (ed.) *A Source Book of London history from the Earliest Times to 1800* London: G. Bell and Sons, Ltd 1914

Michelant, Henri Victor *Inventaire des Vaisselles, joyaux, tapisseries, peintures, livres et manuscripts de Marguerite d'Autriche* F. Hayez, Brussels 1870

Mortimer, Ian *The Time Traveller's Guide to Medieval England* Vintage 2009

Nash, Joseph *The Mansions of England in the Olden Time*, Volume II Henry Sotheran and Company 1870

Nichols, Nicholas Harris *Testament Vetusta* Volume I, Nichols and Son, London 1826

Nichols, Nicholas Harris *The Privy Purse Expenses of King Henry VIII 1529-1532* W. Pickering 1827

Norton, Elizabeth *Anne Boleyn: Henry VIII's Obsession* Amberley 2008

Norton, Elizabeth *Anne Boleyn: In her own Words and the Words of Those who Knew Her* Amberley 2011

Norton, Elizabeth *The Boleyn Women* Amberley 2013

Paget, Hugh 'The Youth of Anne Boleyn' *Historical Research* Volume 54, Issue 130, November 1981, pp162-170

Picker, Martin (ed) *The Chanson Albums of Marguerite of Austria* University of California Press 1965

Reid, Jonathan *King's Sister; Marguerite of Navarre and her Evangelical Network* BRILL 2009

Rex, Richard *Henry VIII and the English Reformation* Palgrave Macmillan 2006

Ridgway, Claire *The Anne Boleyn Collection II: Anne Boleyn and the Boleyn Family* MadeGlobal 2015

Ridgway, Claire and Cherry, Clare *George Boleyn* MadeGlobal 2014

Sander, Nicholas and Lewis, David (ed) *Rise and Growth of the Anglican Schism* Burns and Oates, London 1877

Sergeant, Philip W *The Life of Anne Boleyn* Hutchinson and Co, London 1923

Sharpe, Reginald R. *Calendar of Letter-Books from the City of London*: K, HMSO London 1911

Sharpe, Reginald R *Calendar of Letter-Books from the City of London*: L, HMSO London 1912

Shaw, William Arthur *The Knights of England: A Complete Record from the Earliest Time to the Present Day...* Volume I Genealogical Publishing Com 1971

Shulman, Nicola *Graven with Diamonds: The Many Lives of Thomas Wyatt* Short Books 2012

Sneyd, Charlotte Augusta *A Relation, or Rather, A True Account, of the Island of England* John Bowyer Nichols and Son, London 1847

Starkey, David *Six Wives of Henry VIII* Vintage 2004

State Letters and Papers of Henry VIII Volume 1 1509-1514 (ed. J. S. Brewer) HMSO 1920

Sutton, Anne F. *The Mercery of London: Trade, Goods and People, 1130-1578* Routledge 2005

Stow, John *A Survay of London* 1598

Tremayne, Eleanor E. *The First Governess of the Netherlands, Margaret of Austria* Methuen 1908

Tremlett, Giles *Catherine of Aragon: Henry's Spanish Queen* Faber and Faber 2010

Urban, Sylvanus (ed) *Gentlemen's Magazine and Historical Chronicle for the Year 1865* Volume 2, July-December. Volume 219 John Henry and James Parker, London 1865

Various *The Land we Live in: A Pictorial and Literary Sketch Book of the British Empire*. Volume 3, Charles Knight, London 1847

Vergil, Polydore *Anglia Historia* 1555

Warnicke, Retha *The Rise and Fall of Anne Boleyn* Cambridge University Press 1989

Watson, Foster (ed) *Tudor School-Boy Life: The Dialogues of Juan Luis Vives* J. M. Dent, London 1908

Weever, John *Antient Funeral Monuments of Great-Britain, Ireland and the Islands Adjacent*. (1631) W. Tooke, London 1767

Weir, Alison *Mary Boleyn: The Great and Infamous Whore* Jonathan Cape 2011

Weir, Alison *The Lady in the Tower* Jonathan Cape 2009

Weir, Alison *The Six Wives of Henry VIII* New Grove 1991

Wilkinson, Josephine *Mary Boleyn: The True Story of Henry VIII's Favourite Mistress* Amberley 2009

Wilkinson, Josephine *The Early Loves of Anne Boleyn* Amberley 2009

Williams, Patrick *Katharine of Aragon* Amberley 2013

Wilson, Derek *The English Reformation* Robinson 2012

List of Illustrations

21. Sir Nicholas Carew. From *Drawings of Holbein* by A. L. Baldry (G. Newnes, 1906)

22. Sir Henry Guildford, Master of the Horse and Comptroller of Henry's household. From *Drawings of Holbein* by A. L. Baldry (G. Newnes, 1906)

23, 24. Henry VIII, a manuscript illustration from the British Library's copy of 'The Penitential and other Psalms'. (Courtesy of the British Museum)

25. Henry VIII, depicted in 1618 or 1628. (Courtesy of the Yale Centre for British Art)

26. Henry VIII's field armour. (Courtesy of the Metropolitan Museum of Art)

27. Sir Thomas Wyatt. From *Drawings of Holbein* by A. L. Baldry (G. Newnes, 1906)

28. Henry and Anne at Wolsey's home, York Place. (Courtesy of the Library of Congress)

29. William Warham, Archbishop of Canterbury. From *Drawings of Holbein* by A. L. Baldry (G. Newnes, 1906)

30. John Fisher, Bishop of Rochester. From *Drawings of Holbein* by A. L. Baldry (G. Newnes, 1906)

31. Sir Thomas More. From *Drawings of Holbein* by A. L. Baldry (G. Newnes, 1906)

32. Thomas Cranmer, Archbishop of Canterbury. (Courtesy of the Library of Congress)

33. Hampton Court. (Courtesy of Charlie Dave under Creative Commons 2.0)

34. Silver testoon of Henry VIII. (Courtesy of the Metropolitan Museum of Art)

35. William Somers, Henry's court jester. (Courtesy of the Yale Center for British Art)

36. Waltham Abbey. (Author's collection)

37. The doom painting at Waltham Abbey. (Author's collection)

38. Tewkesbury Abbey, Gloucestershire. (Author's collection)

39. Thornbury Castle, Gloucestershire. (Courtesy of gibborn_134 under Creative Commons 2.0)

40. Thomas Cromwell. (Courtesy of the Rijksmuseum)

41. Tower of London. (Courtesy of David Martin under Creative Commons 2.0)

42. Elizabeth I. (Courtesy of the Rijksmuseum)

43. Anne's execution. From Cassell's *Illustrated History of England* (1895)

Acknowledgements

Thank you so much to my editors at Amberley, Jonathan Jackson and Shaun Barrington, for their hard work on this book, to Hazel and Philip for their work in promoting this book, the designers and others. I have been particularly blessed to have some wonderful friends: thank you especially to Anne Marie Bouchard and Sharon Bennett Connolly for keeping me sane during the writing of this book, but there have been others. Also to my godmother 'Lady' Susan Priestley, for her kindness and support. Thanks also to all my family, to my husband Tom and my sons Rufus and Robin, to Paul Fairbrass, Sue and John Hunt, and Pascale Rose. Most of all, it is for my mother for her invaluable proof-reading skills and for my father for his enthusiasm and open mind: this is the result of the books they read me, the museums they took me to as a child and the love and imagination with which they encouraged me.

Index